Dynamic Social Psychology

Consulting Editor: PETER I. ROSE *Smith College*

Dynamic Social Psychology

Toward Appreciation and Replication

DWIGHT G. DEAN

Iowa State University

RANDOM HOUSE, NEW YORK

To
Ruth
and our sons
Philip *and* Robert

Preface

It has been my intention to bring together the thoughts and research of scientists in the field of social psychology. Since permissions were obtained from authors as well as publishers, I trust that no one's work has been unfairly reflected upon. Criticism is, of course, a normal procedure in the business of scientific investigation; and each author, if he is successful, stimulates others to build upon his work—and in doing so, make it obsolete. It should be noted that the writings were selected from many different sources, published at different times and for different purposes by different authors. Authors may not, therefore, have the chance to defend themselves when their writings are juxtaposed with the works of others.

The product represented by this collection of readings grew out of classes in which traditional lectures, tests, and term papers were abandoned in favor of a free and constant interplay of the work and thoughts of one author with another. While any instructor will conduct a course according to his own philosophy, values, and purposes, it may be of interest to know the different approaches which have proved useful. I found it productive to assign to my students a short paper relating to each topic-chapter, with the suggested method of attack being one of the following:

1. A paper giving the student's own definition of the concept, hopefully with the inclusion of operational procedures.
2. A paper suggesting ways in which a thorough understanding of a particular concept and its exploitation might be profitable in some career (say, how a school superintendent might understand the community and his students better through a knowledge of the literature on social class, or what a foreign investor needs to know of the culture in which his business operates).
3. A paper further elaborating a concept under study, making use of the annotated bibliography at the end of each chapter.
4. A paper relating the topic under consideration to another one in the series (such as the relationship between alienation and authoritarianism; alienation and conformity; or values and social class).
5. A paper relating the current topic to another field entirely, such as "Authoritarianism and Attitudes Concerning International Relations."
6. A paper proposing and outlining a research project, such as one might later do in what some schools call "honors" or "directed study" projects, in which a particular concept will be a critical variable or of central concern.

The instructor may wish for the sake of variety to utilize different approaches for different topics. It is hoped that while reading these selections the student will come to find that theory and research can be enjoyable and can become all-engrossing. Like any skill which presupposes conscientious and continued practice for achievement, learning and research are maximal when there is active collaboration with the material.

Dwight G. Dean
Ames, Iowa

Acknowledgments

Intellectual debts can only be acknowledged, never repaid. So many scholars and friends whom I can never thank adequately have contributed ideas and encouragement at various stages of my development. Dr. Murray Leiffer of Garrett Seminary first whetted my appetite for sociology. Dr. Melvin Seeman, now of the University of California, Los Angeles, was a most dynamic teacher whose method of approach is reflected in the organization of this volume. Dr. Raymond Sletto of Ohio State University first encouraged me to write; Dr. Peter I. Rose of Smith College, Random House Consulting Editor, has read the manuscript and suggested numerous improvements, and Miss Dorothy Grosvenor, Random House editor, has gone over the manuscript, line by line.

The authors and publishers of the articles herein reprinted have graciously given their consent, for which specific acknowledgment is given at appropriate places.* The American Psychological Association has permitted brief quotations from about 175 abstracts appearing in *Psychological Abstracts;* and *Sociological Abstracts* has granted permission to quote about 125 abstracts in bibliographical notes at the end of each chapter. Citations are indicated by *PA* and *SA*, respectively, with the reference number indicated for those who wish to read further.

* Institutional identification of the authors pertains to the time when the article was originally published.

Contents

Dynamic Social Psychology

Introduction

Systematic inquiry into any subject matter is limited by existing capacities to measure with some precision the critical variables in the area. Social Psychology has been no exception.[1]

—NEWCOMB, TURNER, and CONVERSE

Behavioral scientists frequently urge that the major concepts of our several disciplines be subjected to continuous efforts toward clarification and rigor. While such clarification is often advocated, it has, with notable exceptions, been less frequently demonstrated by the preparation of articles or monographs devoted to the task of bringing together the issues, controversies, and consensuses with respect to a principal concept.[2]

—DEFLEUR and WESTIE

A science is known by the concepts it keeps. Chemistry did not develop extensively as long as it was thought that the elements of the earth were composed of fire, earth, water, and phlogiston. The social-psychological concepts that serve as chapter headings for this collection have proven productive in the investigations of social psychologists, even though any or perhaps all of them may eventually prove to be about as crude as the early conceptualization of matter. It is to be expected that conceptualizations cannot remain static, but must undergo refinement, respecification, de-

---

[1] Newcomb, T. M., Turner, R. A. and Converse, P. E. *Social psychology*. New York: Holt, Rinehart and Winston, 1965, 496. Quotation used by permission.

[2] DeFleur, M. L. and Westie, F. R. Attitude as a scientific concept. *Social Forces*, 1963, 42 (1), 17. Quotation used by permission.

limitation with the increase in knowledge. Indeed, it may be that an increase in knowledge *results* from refinement, respecification, and delimitation of concepts.

This work evolved from wrestling with the problem of definition and measurement of several of the variables which are commonly utilized by social psychologists. Some of the topics considered here—such as the *self-concept, culture, attitudes,* the *small group, values,* and *social class* —have proved to be invaluable assets. Others—such as *inner* or *other-directed* personality types, *authoritarianism, conformity,* and *role*—are of relatively recent vintage. All share the need for sharpening and honing; all are community property of psychologists and sociologists.

The term "social psychology" itself originated in 1908, when William McDougall [3] in England and Edward Ross [4] in the United States each published a book by that title. Since the former was a psychologist and the latter a sociologist, the field is the result of dual paternity. Yet the overlapping interests represented by the two fields made a speciality inevitable. The nature of subject matter in many fields, for that matter, defies the convenient departmental classification of universities, as may be witnessed by reference to such disciplines as astrophysics, biochemistry, and geoacoustics.

Cross-fertilization often improves the product, though the unity of social psychology is perhaps more evidenced by the title than by shared research and teaching. Robert Roth [5] has indicated that courses in social psychology taught by psychology and sociology departments differ in content, approaches, and texts chosen, with little overlap. Nevertheless there is a considerable amount of interaction, as may be illustrated by Cantril's study of collective behavior [6] (a traditional topic of sociology) or the investigation of aspirations (motivation being a subject usually reserved for psychology) by Dynes, Clarke, and Dinitz. [7] It is in the hope of stimulating further collaboration and cross-fertilization that this collection of readings is presented. The attempt has been made to center the book on topics of shared concern and to avoid those which have been substantially the province of one discipline or the other. Thus there is no material on such common psychological concepts as *motivation, cognition,* or *perception* on the one hand, nor such central sociological constructs as *bureaucracy, social control,* or the *community,* on the other hand.

With the plethora of literature today, it has become impossible to treat

[3] MacDougall, W. *Introduction to social psychology.* London: Methuen, 1908.

[4] Ross, E. A. *Social psychology.* New York: Macmillan, 1908.

[5] Roth, R. H. A survey of the undergraduate course in social psychology. *J. Soc. Psychol.* 1963, *61* (1), 49–55.

[6] Cantril, H. *Invasion from Mars.* Princeton: Princeton University Press, 1940.

[7] Dynes, R. R., Clarke, A. C., and Dinitz, S. Levels of occupational aspiration: some aspects of family experience as a variable. *Amer. Soc. Rev.* 1956, *21* (2), 212–215.

subjects exhaustively. Each of the topics considered here has been the subject of books and course offerings. The purpose of this book, however, is not to present an extended analysis of certain topics, but to offer an opportunity for the student to become somewhat familiar with a number of the basic, shared concepts and perspectives of psychology and sociology. Consequently, a survey of the field or a systematic history of its development has been avoided—these can readily be obtained in any one of a number of the excellent treatises available. Rather, a few selected topics of provocative if not controversial nature are presented in the hope of inducing the student to wrestle diligently with concept formulation, precise definition, scale construction, and at least rudimentary social research.

It may be noted that, for the most part, selections are of recent vintage; for the purpose of this collection is to bring together a compendium of the "cutting edge" of thought in the field. As Kurt Lewin is reported to have said, it is not necessary if one wishes to measure the speed of a ball down an incline to inquire how the ball came to be at the top of the incline. Exhausting the history of conceptual development is not necessarily the most fruitful approach to understanding a concept nor to inspiring research, though sound investigation is of course not conducted in isolation.

In addition to selecting stimulating articles which are of interdisciplinary interest, we have tried to select works which represent themes of general and abiding interest. Though as earlier indicated, both "old" and "new" topics are included, all are characterized by a need for more precise specification and measurement, and some have been challenged as to their right to exist at all (such as the concepts of *attitude* and *alienation*). They have, however, excited the interests of social scientists as both independent and dependent variables.

Care has been taken to provide a variety of experimental designs and research techniques. Like the bulk of research in social science, the majority of the articles are of the *cross-sectional* or simultaneous type. Within this group may be found examples using Semantic Differential (selection 3, Schwartz and Tangri), Likert scales (selection 6, Peterson; selection 8, Rhyne; selection 11, Lefcourt and Ladwig; selection 12, Simpson and Miller; selection 34, Pettigrew); polls (selection 14, Newcomb); interview (selection 15, Fendrich; selection 27, Campbell and Pettigrew; selection 32, Freeman *et al.*) and case study (selection 38, Shellow and Roemer; selection 39, Lieberson and Silverman).

Fewer selections employ a successional design. Of those "looking backward" and approaching the ex-post-facto type, one might list selection 4 (Dornbusch and Hickman) and selection 25 by Greenstein (both of which employ the *content analysis* technique). Though none is clearly "before-after" in the classical sense, some do involve a time span (selection 14, Newcomb; selection 18, Blake and Mouton; and selection 31, Pryer *et al.*).

The format for this collection was originally conceived in a framework of four articles for each concept:

1. An article defining or introducing the concept in a general way.
2. A selection reporting research stimulated by or in some direct way making use of the concept.
3. An article indicating some practical utility, some applied aspect, some evidence of "the difference it makes," so that a greater appreciation of the concept might result.
4. Finally, a selection criticizing or attempting to refine or respecify the concept in such a way as to furnish a take-off for further research.

Because of space limitations it has not been possible to maintain this scheme. Consequently, many articles illustrating the importance or "the difference it makes" have necessarily been relegated to the annotated bibliography, where the interested individual may pursue the matter on his own. It has been further necessary at times to have the author or the editor rather than an introductory article define the concept.

Chapter One

The Self-concept

The study of personality, the central interest of psychology, is also a matter of concern to many sociologists. Difficult to define, defiant of measurement, and incredibly complex, the topic of personality nevertheless has been and is continuing to be a subject of viable theoretical and research development; so much so that a bibliography of thousands of items could readily be garnered.

One way to delimit our study and yet to grasp a significant aspect of the study of personality is to turn to a concept that is at once relatively ancient yet the subject of renewed interest recently. In the early years of social psychology, Charles Horton Cooley discussed what is perhaps the most critically important aspect of personality: the concept which one has of himself. Writing in 1902, Cooley developed the idea of the "looking-glass self." This may be described best in his own words:

> A self-idea of this sort seems to have three principle elements: the imagination of our appearance to the other person; the imagination of his judgment of that appearance; and some sort of self-feeling, such as pride or mortification.[1]

A more elaborate formulation of the development of the self-concept was offered by George Herbert Mead somewhat later:

> The self is something which has a development; it is not initially there at birth, but arises in the process of social experience and activity, that is, develops in the given individual as a result of his relations to that process as a whole and to other individuals within that process.[2]

The self, he wrote, can be an object as well as a subject. For:

> The individual experiences himself as such, not directly, but only indirectly, from the particular standpoints of other individual members of the

[1] Cooley, C. H. Human nature and the social order. New York: Scribner, 1902. 152.
[2] Mead, G. H. Mind, self and society. Chicago: University of Chicago Press, 1934. 135.

same social group, or from the generalized standpoint of the social group as a whole to which he belongs. . . . For he enters his own experience as a self or individual, not directly or immediately, not by becoming a subject to himself, but only in so far as he first becomes an object to himself just as other individuals are objects to him or in his experience.[3]

While a perfunctory nod has customarily been given to the views of these two scholars in most sociology textbooks and pertinent articles in psychology, little concrete research was generated from their works until recent years. The articles which follow are indicative of a renewed vigor which the concept has and the promise of a more systematic exploitation of the concept in the future.

John M. Shlien, in the first selection in this chapter, gives a rather thorough explication of the theoretical and practical importance of the concept and indicates areas for future research. Next, to turn the lens from the macroscopic to the microscopic, an article by Martin L. Maehr, Josef Mensing, and Samuel Nafzger reports a study concerning how "significant others" (in this case, a confederate posing as a physical education expert) can influence the self-concept high school boys have of their physical skills. Finally, a study by Michael Schwartz and Sandra S. Tangri is presented to demonstrate what is to be the central thrust of this work: the building upon previous research to define, refine, extend and project present research, exploit it for replication, and point the way to further refinement and research in the future.

[3] Mead, *op. cit.*, 138.

1

The Self-Concept in Relation to Behavior: Theoretical and Empirical Research

JOHN M. SHLIEN
Department of Psychology,
University of Chicago

INTRODUCTION

In the past dozen years, the field of psychology has undergone a fascinating change in focus. The concept of the "self" is once again prominent. This resurgence of the self, evidenced in many ways, is accounted for by a variety of other main currents in the changing climate of opinion in the field of psychology and the culture at large.

When Carl Rogers gave his presidential address to the American Psychological Association in 1947 (77), he said, "The self has come back into psychology." Two years later, the presidential address by Ernest Hilgard made a plea for the "study of the self as indispensable to a complete understanding of defense mechanisms of the Freudian ego" (51). The last dozen years have seen a heeding to this plea and to Rogers' observation, to the tune of over a thousand published papers and researches having to do with the subject of the self.

If the self has come back (and it certainly has) where has it been, and why the return? The concept of the self has been in the shadows, as it were. "Ego psychology" pre-empted the attention of the clinical fellows almost up to the time of Hilgard's address. More than that, the experimental energies in the profession were mainly taken up with learning theory and its demonstrations in various complex sub-human (for the most part) experiments in learning and conditioning. When animals are the chief subject material, as they were during the so-called "era of the rat," there is not much likelihood of "self-theory" arising or being countenanced. Further, stimulus-response theory, the main basis of most learning experiments in the period preceding the resurgence of self-theory, appears to be antithetical to self-theory. This has always been in evidence, in every phase of the cycle. No one had written more profoundly or con-

Reprinted from *Religious Education* (July–August, 1962) 57, 4 (Research Supplement) S111–127, by permission of the author and the publisher, The Religious Education Association, New York City.

vincingly (no one has yet) of the self than the great American psychologist William James (56). Yet his work passed into the shadows when
Watsonian behaviorism was in full swing, and it was another self-theorist,
George H. Mead (69), who took up the battle against stimulus-response
learning theory and perhaps started the new phase of the cycle. Self-theorists are most likely to be aligned with Gestalt theories of learning if they
take a position on learning at all (8). In some instances, self-theorists
lean in the direction of "one-trial learning" theory, rather than long drawn
out reinforcement procedures, "goal-gradient" theories, and the like. To
put it very simply, self-theorists do not believe that the organism is wholly
subject to the conditions of and conditioning by the environment. They
believe that the organism (human) has a special capacity (which makes
it human, and without which it is less than human) to develop a *self*,
which is self-conscious and self-evaluating, and which therefore chooses,
acts upon its environment, has much responsibility because it has volition.
To the extent that self-theorists depend upon stimulus-response learning
theory at all, they at least modify it to read "stimulus-*meaning*-response"
theory, with the self as an intermediary supplying the meaning or interpretation to a given stimulus. This supply of meanings is one main sense
in which self-theory is linked to phenomenology, of course. Nor are self-
theorists alone in this supposedly philosophical position. It is considered
simply the intelligent view. H. Kluver, one of the greatest living psychologists, speaking of his work with monkeys, incidentally, says, "Whether or
not behavior takes this or that direction is, generally speaking, dependent
on whether or not this or that *phenomenal* property exists. The fact that
something appears phenomenally as 'red,' 'larger than,' etc., cannot be
deduced from the properties of the atom but only from studies of reacting
organisms" (59).

Why has interest in the self-concept revived? Partly because learning
theory no longer casts such a big shadow. Partly because of the development of new techniques for conceiving, in operational, measurable terms,
the description of the self and its interactions. Partly because more psychologists are turning to the clinical area as prestige and money factors
shift the rewards from one area to another. Partly because a good idea
and a basic human quality cannot be denied attention indefinitely. Partly
because psychology has been the most controversial and least productive
of the natural sciences, and the pressures from within and without dictate
that we find our true subject matter, at least. Other influences come from
the cultural attitudes which change the political and economic climate in
which personality theory develops. There is presently movement away

from scarcity economics, where men must compete for inadequate supplies at a subsistence level, and where basic survival is an issue in terms of
food, clothing, shelter. There is instead a movement toward an economics
of abundance. Whatever problems this brings in the way of leisure, un-
accustomed affluence, etc., it means that *emergency* drives are diminished,

and other possibilities and psychological potentialities are enhanced. We see Maslow now distinguishing between "deficiency motives" and "growth motives"—the former clearly appropriate to conditions of scarcity, the latter to those of abundance (67). More recently, White has revisited the whole field of motivation and promotes the idea of "competence" (curiosity, stimulus hunger, desire and capacity for new experience) as a motive to supplant the older concept of "drive" (97). This is very much in keeping with the idea of "self-realization" as a motive. Finally, there is an ideological current which one finds in the art and the intellectual speculation of the culture which leads directly to a heightened concern about or interest in the nature and meaning of the self; this current is one of special interest to this conference. Some of the most lucid statements of it are found in fiction. As Kirilov puts it in Dostoevsky's *The Possessed*, "If there is no God, then I am God." Tillich details some undercurrents of present day attitudes:

> For God as subject makes me into an object which is nothing more than an object. He deprives me of all my subjectivity because he is all powerful and all knowing. I revolt and try to make *him* into an object, but the revolt fails and I become desperate. God appears as the invincible tyrant, the being in contrast with whom all other beings are without freedom and subjectivity. He is equated with the recent tyrants who with the help of terror try to transform everything into a mere object, a thing among things, a cog in the machine they control. He becomes the model of everything against which Existentialism revolted. This is the God Nietzsche said had to be killed because nobody can tolerate being made into a mere object of absolute knowledge and absolute control (96).

In Baumer's recent *Religion and the Rise of Scepticism*, the death of God is traced through many phases to the "age of longing" in which the chief characteristic is that man becomes his own question mark (9). Psychology operates in this cultural context. Many Gods and many beliefs have been challenged, if not destroyed, by war and nearly total disillusionment. When and while the greatest remaining mystery and/or the most known and knowable subject is ourselves, it is understandable that psychology will turn to a study of "the self."

Problems in Research

Much of such study will be phrased as "research." What is that? Let it be, for us, a word to stand primarily for thinking, for thinking of ways to test that thinking, and for ways of interpreting the outcomes of that testing. Too much prestige is attached to the use of technical tools and to measurement of often trivial data for the sake of measurement (38). Empirical findings are inherently of no more worth than theories; "nothing is so practical as a good theory"; and the greatest lack at present is theoretical research. As it stands in the field of personality, for almost every empirical finding there exists another finding which at least weakens the first, if it does not actually contradict it, and opposite interpretations are sometimes drawn from the same evidence. Research should be seen as a scientific approach to *understanding*. It does not need to seek for "prediction and control." Politicians do that. Understanding is the only true goal of research, and it cannot come about through the empty use of technique or formal statistics. Research on the self-concept suffers from all the disabilities of the usual research procedures, plus some special ones of its own. One of these is the definition of the subject.

Definitions and Related Concepts

What is the "self" or "self-concept"? Is it inferred, or can it be directly experienced? Is it objective or subjective? Can it be known only through the self-reports of the knower? How can the self-report be validated? How can the known be its own knower? (It can; that is the very capacity of self-consciousness.) Is the self a social product, or is society the consequence of interacting selves? Is there one self or are there many? Is the self stable over time? Consistent over situations? The most crucial review problem arising from these and similar questions is this: not all researchers conceive of the self in the same way, therefore do not refer to the same entity when they use the word "self"; not even all researchers who use essentially similar definitions use the same operational representations or instruments; as a consequence, most studies of "self-concept and behavior" are not directly comparable.

The search for "a psychic agent which regulates, guides and controls man's behavior" has been conducted throughout the history of man, and certainly throughout the more recent history of science. At one time, the soul was considered such an agent. In the early days of scientific psychology, the soul and also all "mentalistic" concepts of agentry were sternly banished. Modern self-theory, Hall and Lindzey point out, is not a return to the older views under a new name. "The self is not a metaphysical or religious concept; it is a concept that falls within the domain of a scientific psychology. Self-theory represents a serious attempt to account for certain phenomena and to conceptualize one's observations of certain aspects of behavior" (47). The self, though often spoken of as a "doer" is now conceived of as a *process* or a *group of processes*.

William James opened up the field (56). He did not come to conclusions (for the most part) which left researchable hypotheses. His "material self" is like the "organism" referred to by others to follow. The organism has more central and intimate parts, and holds these most dear. One can easily have one's hair cut, unless it is an essential part of one's self, but loss of toes, limbs, facial or genital parts, etc., may be unbearable psychologically. James extends the material self to include more distant properties, such as family, home, products of one's labor—all to the degree with which one has invested one's self in them. James' "social self" is a type of role one plays and for which one receives recognition. This is the precursor of role theory in psychology. James believes that one *"has as many social selves as there are individuals who recognize him* and carry an image of him in their mind." This self is assigned by others, and "lived up to" by the individual if he so desires. James' "Spiritual self" is a cognitive division—the "thinker." It is a "reflective process," the master-builder, and the "self of selves." It is "intermediary between ideas and overt acts." This is a definition which crops up again and again in current views.

Cooley, a sociologist of early fame, developed a simpler constellation of ideas called "the looking glass self" which introduced in a more obvious way the social-psychology frame of reference. This self has "three principal parts" (processes, we would say): (1) "the imagination of our appearance to the other person; (2) the imagination of his judgment of that appearance, and (3) some sort of self-feeling, such as pride or mortification" (29). Cooley's self is clearly an "other-directed" concept. As early social-psychology goes, his ideas were improved upon by George H. Mead in *Mind, Self and Society* a theory and set of observations to be used later (69). Symonds listed four aspects of the self: (1) how a person perceives himself, (2) what he thinks of himself, (3) how he values himself, and (4) how he attempts through various actions to enhance or defend himself (92). To Cooley's ideas, this adds at least the patterns or manners of behavior used in relation to self-perceptions. Symonds, like Hilgard, is skeptical about the validity of the individual's conscious self-report of his image of himself. Both believe that projective material, clinical interviews and external observations are the more accurate methods, since one's conscious self picture can be distorted by unconscious factors (to say nothing of conscious defenses). Of course the unconscious factors in the observers can distort, too, but it is perfectly true that if one is to attach validity to self-descriptions, one makes the assumption that the describer truly knows himself and is willing as well as able to reveal what he knows. One subscribes to this assumption at some peril. On the other hand, there is no greater justification for the assumption that an outsider can see more clearly and tell more truly than can the insider. All research on the self fastens (perhaps founders) on one or the other of these rocks, or tries to steer in between. (This latter course is an endless journey since the channel is forever hedged on both sides.)

There are many other conceptions of the self, but this review is not intended to be exhaustive or exhausting. A sampler is to be found in Hall and Lindzey (47), and Wylie (99), to name two recent works. An outstanding and highly influential piece of work from a radically phenomenological point of view is that of Snygg and Combs. They believe that "all behavior, without exception, is completely determined by and pertinent to the phenomenal field of the behaving organism" (87, 88). The phenomenal field is that part of one's total perceptions which are at the moment in awareness. There are levels of awareness which range from the more to the less conscious, but no *unconscious* is postulated. This is essentially the position taken by Carl Rogers and most of the researchers who have worked with him, or upon whom he has drawn. The self-theory of this orientation has been the most developed and elaborated, and has promoted the largest body of research and practice related to behavior change.

To Rogers, the self is an organized, consistent, conceptual Gestalt composed of perceptions of the *characteristics* of the "I" or "me", and the perceptions of the *relationships* of the "I" or "me" to others and to various aspects of life, together with the *values* attached to these perceptions. The self-concept is a person's view of himself. The self-*structure* is a person viewed from an *external* frame of reference.

The self is composed of perceptions, but is *also* a perceiver, or a lens through which perceptions are filtered. It sees, it sees itself, and because of the ways in which it sees itself, it sees beyond itself in peculiar ways, "distorted" or "realistic" as the case may be. Raimy thought of the self-concept as a *map*, which each person consults in order to take stock of himself and his position. According to the map, one may advance or retreat, for there are feelings one has in regard to the topography of one's terrain. These feelings are most grossly categorized as approving, disapproving, or ambivalent. In one of the earliest studies, Raimy found that verbatim transcripts from therapy cases could be reliably classified when self-referents were grouped in one of the three categories mentioned above. Successful cases shifted toward a self-approving balance. Unsuccessful cases did not (75). This study is one which used the raw clinical data, with few inferences and no "instrumentation," and it set off a score of subsequent studies which tend to verify the findings and the method. Perhaps the largest fraction of self-concept studies are in the field of therapy. This does not limit their general implications; it largely reflects the fact that therapy provides a laboratory situation dedicated to the study of behavior change, and by its nature, therapy focuses on the individual and his private perceptions. Self-theory has lent itself very well to the organization of these data from therapy.

Theory of Self-Concept and Behavior

In a study of client-centered therapy, Shlien has summarized some of the Rogerian propositions as they are hypothesized to operate in the ordering and change of behavior (85). These fundamentals state:

1. Each person is unique. No one else can ever completely know his experience. Since each person's neurological capacities and life history combine in unique ways, the closest approach to another's experience is to see it through his own eyes, in so far as possible. Some of his experience is consciously symbolized. Some is at lower levels of awareness, where it has a lesser influence, perhaps a less controllable influence, on behavior.

2. Behavior is a consequence of perception. The organism reacts to reality as it is perceived and defined *by that organism*. The "objective evidence" of the thermometer not withstanding, he who thinks the room hot opens the window; who thinks it cold closes the same window. Who sees a light red, stops; sees the same light green, goes; sees an object as delicious, eats it; the same object as refuse, avoids it or sickens from it. Whatever "it" may be—by consensus, physical measurement, or philosophical proof, the way in which "it" is perceived will determine behavior toward it.

3. From this, it follows that if one wants to promote a stable change in behavior, one must change the *perception* of the one who is behaving. (Unstable changes can be forced from outside, but enduring alterations motivated by internal shifts depend on new perceptions.)

4. The perception of threat is always followed by defense. Defense may take many forms—aggression, withdrawal, submission, etc.—but it is the general and categorical response to danger.

5. Perception is narrowed and rigidified by threat. (Experimentally, the phenomenon of "tunnel vision" can be evoked by threat.) Narrowed and rigidified perception blocks change in behavior. Threat, therefore, does not permanently change behavior. It only arouses defenses. Attacking the defense system is likely to complicate it, causing more of the psychological economy to be devoted to defense, still further restricting perception and inhibiting change.

6. Of the whole perceptual field, a portion becomes differentiated as the self. *This is the self-concept.* The self-concept has dimensions, and the dimensions have values. Thus the self-concept may be one of weakness or strength, for instance. Lovable—hateful, lucky—unlucky, worthy or contemptible, are other examples of dimensions which influence behavior. They influence behavior because the interpretation of the self leads to a reactive interpretation of the external object. For instance, if one feels strong, a boulder is a weapon to push into the treads of an armored tank; if weak, the same boulder is a refuge to hide behind. If one feels sick and helpless, the nurse is a creature of mercy, appealed to for comfort. The same nurse may be seen as a temptress, to be sexually pursued, if the patient sees himself as well and sturdy. All experience is evaluated as friendly or dangerous, interesting or boring, possible or impossible, etc. depending *not* upon the nature of the experience so much as upon the *self-concept of the experiencer.*

In short, the self-concept stands between the stimulus and the response. Luckily, the self-concept is itself a perception. Since perceptions can change, the self-concept can change; the stimulus then can be perceived in a new way and responded to differently. This makes psychotherapy, and education, possible. How much change in self-perception is necessary to influence what new responses to the environment? This has never been tested, and since the human reaction is fluid and growing, it may not be possible to seize a static state for long enough to make such a test. We do know, from laboratory experiments by Sherif, Asch, and others, that changed self-perceptions seem to influence immediately the task at hand. Persons who are ridiculed, and who allow the ridicule to affect their self-concepts, then tend to make judgments (about length, size, position, etc. of ambiguous objects) which conform to external social standards. Those who are praised, or whose self-concept is secure and positive, tend to maintain their estimates in the face of outside pressures. Similar interpretations can be made of some of the early Postman-Bruner studies on the influence of "need" upon perception. Children from lower socio-economic groups tend to over-estimate the size of a coin. Presumably this is because their need is greater than the need of children from more affluent homes. But beneath the sociological indices is the self-concept. The rich person who *sees* himself as poor will behave as if he *were* poor, all the weighty objectivity of a million dollars in the bank notwithstanding. Of the many examples possible, one comes from O'Neill's biographical play *Long Day's Journey Into Night*, in which his father is depicted as miserly. He turns out tiny light bulbs to save current, marks the level on the whisky bottle, skimps on medical care for his wife and children, all in spite of the fact that he has become a rich and "propertied" man. Why? Because, he explains, he has never gotten over his early experience of starvation in a fatherless Irish immigrant home, of working as a youth ten hours a day for fifty cents, etc. To others, he has changed into a successful actor and wealthy landowner. To himself, he still feels insecure, weak, dependent, precarious, unconfident. This may sound as if a large constellation of experience is involved, all needing to be altered in present perceptions. On this point, Rogers makes the following observation from clinical experience: "We were not dealing with an entity of slow accretion, of step by step learning, of thousands of unidirectional learnings." (He is speaking of the reversals of self-perception one often sees in therapy, and here one can see the opposition to simple stimulus-response theory as an explanation.) "These might all be involved, but the product was clearly a Gestalt, a configuration in which the alteration of one minor pattern could completely alter the whole pattern. One was forcibly reminded of the textbook illustration of a Gestalt, the double picture of an old hag and a young woman. Looked at with one mind set, the picture is clearly that of an ugly old hag. The slightest change, and the whole becomes a portrait of an attractive girl. So with our clients" (79).

Some Implications for Education and Character Study

Lecky elaborates this view with a point in regard to education. He says, "The greatest handicap to constructive action in education is the well entrenched dogma that learning is the direct result of teaching, a mechanical reaction to the school environment instead of a purposive achievement" (61). (Another anti-stimulus-response precinct heard from.) Lecky argues that *self-consistency* is a basic characteristic of the personality. It is more than a characteristic; it is a motive. It gives direction. When "a student shows resistance toward a certain type of material, this means that it would be inconsistent for him to learn it." The intelligent student who cannot learn to spell (or the psychologist who cannot learn to dance, or the historian who does not "have a mathematical mind") is reacting on the basis of a concept of himself. He does not perceive himself as capable in this area. This turns out to be a "self-fulfilling prophecy" because it has a controlling effect, so that it justifies this and further anticipation of the same sort. The "definition of the situation," we see once again, depends on the "definition of the self." We tend to mistake or underrate the effect of self-consistency as a motive because we do not approve of some of its consequences, very much as we resent "stubbornness" and admire "conviction." But Lecky points out that one does not learn to spell for the same reason that one refuses to be a thief: it is inconsistent with one's self-concept. Thus, an apparent deficiency can be due to the same motive underlying a proficiency we respect, such as moral behavior!

Two interesting points stem from Lecky's thought. One has to do with the theory of self-consistency, the other with the problem of moral behavior. Rogers drew upon Lecky to state as one of his propositions about personality: "Most of the ways which are adopted by the organism are those which are consistent with the concept of the self" (76). (It is worth a note in passing to point out that the physical "organism" is often subordinate to the interest of the self. Men endure hunger, pain, deprivation to the point of death, in order to keep secrets, protect comrades, advance causes. Why? Because the maintenance of the self-concept—as a faithful believer, for instance—is often a more powerful motive than physical survival.) Cartwright tested a part of Rogers' hypothesis, using memory for nonsense syllables invented by the subject as opposed to syllables given from an external list, and using items of clothing, other objects, and personal effects which could be identified by the subject as "me" or "not me." When subjects were asked to recall the syllables and items, he found evidence that "stimuli which are consistent with the self-structure are better recalled than stimuli which are inconsistent with the self-structure" (24).

A famous study by Hartshorne and May is one of the few appropriate researches on morality (48). They began looking for psychological entities or personality traits such as "honesty." It was found that school children would cheat on one examination in one time or place, but not another. The researchers felt forced to the conclusion that an individual's honesty or dishonesty is not a general characteristic but that "the consistency with which he is honest or dishonest is a function of the situation in which he is placed. . . . We interpret these facts to mean that the consistency of the individual is a function of the situation." According to this, they formulated the so-called "doctrine of specificity." This makes every act a function of the situation, in a stimulus-response model, and denies self-consistency or even self-concept as a factor. Lecky argues that the self-concept directs the interpretation of each situation, and selects that part of it which is to motivate behavior. For instance, he finds "two-thirds of these children admitting that they cheated in order to do well on the test." The children *"subjectively"* give the explanation that supports self-consistency theory; they always want to "look good," "stand high." *"Objectively,"* they cheated sometimes, not other times, supporting the "doctrine of specificity." (The kinds of answers one gets depends on where one looks.) We cannot expect children to be all or none creatures, wholly criminal or saint. The self is never so fully formed, nor resistance to external pressures so intense as all that. But another enlightening research on this subject comes from the work of Dymond (37). Clients before therapy were asked to describe themselves "as you are," and then again "as you are in relation to three significant others" (father, boss, friend, etc.). The performance was repeated after therapy had ended, and the better adjusted clients now showed higher average intercorrelations of the self and self-in-other-situations than at pretherapy. This suggests that *greater self-consistency is present when the person is better adjusted.* He is then "more himself," less a function of the situation. When we look again at the experiments of Hartshorne and May in this light, it seems that the "doctrine of specificity" may apply best to the psychologically weaker person, and that as psychological health increases, the possibility of "honesty as a matter of principle" (or morality in a general and dependable sense) becomes greater.

Some Technical Considerations

The self-report or self-description has already been noted in researches mentioned thus far, and it has also been stated that the development of new techniques greatly affected the history of research in self-theory. The prime example of this is the "Q-technique" as described by Stephenson in a work largely designed for clinical applications (89). This technique has been widely used and misused. Some of the main criticisms were discussed by Mowrer (71). The more technical aspects are not appropriate to this paper, but it should be said that the technique is basically designed to be subjected to factor analysis, using a correlation matrix of self-reports given by one person over many times or situations (as opposed to many people over one time or situation). It is a remarkably flexible tool and can be used in a variety of ways. The subject "sorts" (places) a "Q-deck" (a number of cards on which are printed descriptive statements) in a distribution (usually forced-normal) according to how much the descriptive statement is *like* or *unlike* himself. Strictly speaking, these descriptive statements should be taken from the subject himself, as uniquely significant to him.

More often, the technique is modified, so that one population of items is used for a number of different people, allowing for comparison between persons. The "social desirability factor" then becomes a problem, since most sets of items will contain some culturally approved array of traits which may influence sorting to some extent (32). This Q-deck is, then, an inventory of statements placed according to their value to the sorter. Various instructions may be given to the sorter, such as: "describe yourself as you are," "as you would ideally like to be," "as you are in relation to x person or situation," "as you were in the past," "as you will be in the future," as you are seen through the eyes of y," "as you ought to be," or "describe the average person," etc. Each distribution of the deck can be correlated with any other. From these are derived various "scores." The correlation between "self" and "ideal" provides the self-ideal correlation widely used as an index of self-esteem (21). A correlation between "self" and "self in various situations" gives an index of self-consistency (37). Correlations between "self" of person A and of person B gives an index of their similarity, which may be used in studies of "identification," etc. (65). Correlations between groups of people may be analyzed to show what subgroups exist in terms of factors (20). Correlations between one person and himself over time show the change occurring and the factors involved. The sort may be used in an uncorrelated way, simply as an adjustment scale according to the placement of items (36). Nor is it necessary to use the Q-sort deck alone. Various inventories or check lists have been used similarly (19) (13). The Q-sort may consist of adjectives (scared, willful, etc.) or more descriptive statements ("I am intelligent," "I fear the worst") or highly idiosyncratic and personal descriptions ("My mother-in-law is the person I feel most strongly about." "Rain always depresses me"). The value of the Q-deck depends much on the wisdom of its construction, but the virtue of the technique lies in its forced normal distribution, which allows for easy and justifiable correlation and a factorable matrix of correlations.

Some Applications: The Self and Ideal

It is estimated that over 2,000 "Q-studies" have been made since 1950. One of the most widely quoted is that by Butler and Haigh (21). They used the self-ideal correlation as a measure of status on a variable named self-esteem, on the grounds that the greater the discrepancy between what one is and what one wants to be, the more discomfort and less confidence one feels. Shlien has shown that this interpretation of self-esteem is justifiably derived from William James' ratio:

$$\text{"Self-Esteem} = \frac{\text{Success}}{\text{Pretention}}\text{"}$$

and Kurt Lewin's ratio of "level of aspiration" to "level of achievement," as well as from the theory of Karen Horney and others (84). He has also presented evidence that the self-ideal ratio may be measured abstractly, without reference to particular concrete statements, and that the abstract measure is more highly related to idiosyncratic items than to culturally common ones. Butler and Haigh administered the self-ideal instructions to pretherapy clients, then at post-therapy and follow-up periods found a significantly increased level of self-esteem, on the average. Matched normal control groups were, on the average, higher than therapy cases, but did not change over time without therapy. Other control cases who applied for therapy and were tested before and after a three month waiting period were at a lower level of adjustment than the normals and did not change, as a group, over time without therapy. The increase in self-esteem after successful therapy was considerable, and highly significant statistically. Most of the change was in the self-concept, which tended to move toward the ideal. The ideal had a large "common cultural" factor, and was relatively stable, though it often moves "downward" toward the self-description to some extent. Changes in self-esteem have been found to be related to other measures of change such as the TAT, therapist ratings, client ratings, judgments by friends, and other adjustment scores. This result was generally confirmed in a study by Shlien, where therapy was deliberately brief, and again in a study by Shlien, Mosak and Driekurs when Adlerian therapy was studied (84). It should be noted that the self-ideal correlation fares moderately well as a measure of adjustment in cross validation studies, though not when the outer limits of a supposedly linear relationship are tested. Low S-I correlations do represent poor adjustment, and the middle and upper middle ranges of S-I correlations seem well related to other measures of adjustment, but the extremely high correlations reported between self and ideal are suspect, and generally invalid. Chodorkoff (27, 28) made one of the best of many studies which show that very high S-I correlations are probably defensive self-reports made by the most maladjusted subjects. This finding has been confirmed in relation to the Rorschach, TAT, MMPI, and clinical observations, all of which report a curvilinear rather than straight line relationship (15) (14) (23).

Self-acceptance

It is often hypothesized that greater self-acceptance (as measured by congruence between self and wanted self or "I am" and "I wish I were") will lead to greater acceptance of others. Fromm and Rogers so theorized, for instance. Berger (10, 11) found this to be so, using self and other "acceptance scales." Rosenman, using ratings of interviews with therapy clients, found "increased positive actions toward self and others, increased positive evaluation of self, but decreased positive evaluations of others" (80). Sheerer rated acceptance of self and others on a reliable five-point scale for therapy cases, and found a "marked and regular increase in self-acceptance" from beginning to end of therapy, but an uneven, though similar increase of acceptance and respect for others (82). Stock also analyzed interview material and found a significant correlation between the way one feels about himself and about others (90). Some of these changes take place due to other kinds of growth experience than therapy, of course (74, 101, 40, 41). Taylor (93) showed that self-ideal correlations increased for "normal" subjects repeatedly given Q-sorts. Positive attitudes toward self and others develop in the same direction, but to a lesser degree than for those subjects experiencing therapy.

Estimations of Self-Concepts

Judgments about others are generally questionable, and stereotypes often predict as well as do calculated estimations. There is some evidence, however, that the sensitivity of the judge is a crucial factor. Kell (58) asked experienced counselors, students in training to be counselors, and a group of chemists, to listen to a recorded interview and sort the Q-deck as they would predict the client would sort for herself. Counselors were the most accurate, students much less so, and chemists quite inaccurate. Dymond (35) obtained from ten counselors a Q-sort predicting how their clients would describe themselves after therapy. From a composite stereotype thus established, a prediction was made for each client. The counselor's prediction of the client's actual Q-sort was better than the stereotype 90% of the time. Such findings are important, since much work on self-concept depends upon correlative studies of someone's perception of someone else. It is not always true that stereotypes predict more accurately than deliberate appraisals; more skillful appraisers can understand and describe themselves and/or another person quite well.

Changes in Self and Behavior

Changes in behavior following after apparent changes in self-concept are the most prevalent attempts at linkage of the two variables. The order of these attempts probably stems from the fact that so many researches in self-concept change took place in relation to psychotherapy. Some of the best experiments, however, attempt to look at this linkage "backwards." Manipulated changes in behavior are observed for their apparent effect on the self-concept. Most of these changes have to do with the effects of success or failure, often induced and sometimes "faked." The tasks range over a variety of puzzles, games, "tests of intelligence," indices of accuracy of judgment, of emotional stability, of social effectiveness, etc. Dittes (34) arranged for the subjects to receive evaluations which were derogatory from other members of the group. He found, as expected, that the threat of lowered esteem caused behavior which seemed designed to restore feelings of self-esteem—in this case quick and impulsive efforts to obtain closure on ambiguous tasks. Dittes also found that the subjects with high self-esteem needed favorable evaluation from the group less than did subjects who had lower self-esteem. Levanway (62) told subjects that their task behavior indicated serious emotional conflict. He found that after threat of such devaluation, subjects reacted with more favorable ratings of self, others, and pictures of persons than before the devaluating experience. This might be interpreted as contradictory to other typical findings in similar experiments. Howard and Berkowitz (54) caused subjects to think they had failed on an intelligence test. They found that subjects who had high levels of aspiration were more likely to question the observer's low opinion of their performance. Festinger, Torrey, and Willerman (39) found that the more a person valued a group, the more he appreciated their good evaluation of him, and the more he depreciated their poor evaluation of him. Stotland and Zander, and Stotland, et al. (91) tested the hypothesis that self-esteem was too general a quality to be affected by single specific experimentally induced success and failure. Their results were inconclusive. Diggory and Magaziner (33) attacked much the same problem, and concluded that the specific success or failure influenced global self-esteem only if the task was seen as related to a capacity the person judged to be significant to his goal achievement. Miller and Worchel (70), and Solley and Stagner (86) studied low and high self-esteem groups in relation to stress and failure situations. Their findings, with those of thirteen others, were appraised by Wylie (99) who concluded that people will, "under certain conditions, change their self-evaluations after experimentally induced success and failure." This conclusion is hedged with several reservations, however, even in this area of best designed and most easily controllable studies in self-concept changes.

Other Variable and Self Studies

The self-concept has been studied in relation to gross variables such as sex, and social class. Berger (11) found women more acceptant of others than are men. McKee and Sherriffs (83) find both male and female college students looking more favorably at the male stereotype. Lynn (64) believes that male characteristics are more favorably regarded progressively as children grow from pre-adolescence to adulthood. Several studies find expected typical differences between "male" and "female" characteristics, such as adventurousness, resourcefulness, maturity, etc. Sarbin and Rosenberg (81) find that women exceeded men in checking such adjectives as feminine (!) emotional, affectionate. Many of these studies are simply actuarial statements which qualify as "research" because of style rather than content. This does not mean that their findings are completely without significance, but they are more limited than the majority of researches in this field which are themselves mainly correlational exercises seldom approaching the goal of testing "if-then hypotheses" showing sequences of cause and effect.

Identity and Self in Process

Studies of age and changes in self-concept should give some clues to developmental sequence in the formation of selves and ideals. Ames (7) made observations from one month to four years and shows that a growing sense of self can be demonstrated through analysis of verbalizations from self to others. Havighurst, Robinson and Dorr (49) studied essays, written by children of differing ages, to discover the ideals after which children try to fashion themselves. The children tend to move outward from the family circle as they grow older. Those from six to eight typically idealize parents or other family members. From eight to sixteen, glamorous persons are chosen: then visible attractive adults, and finally, composite imaginary persons.

The parent-child relation has been studied more than has any other of the four categories in the Havighurst, et al. report. Helper (50) found a tendency for children's ideals to resemble more closely parents' ideals than a stereotype or composite. An expected similarity of boys' ideals with fathers, and girls' ideals with mothers was in evidence. Boys in higher socio-economic levels show more emulation of fathers' ideals, and there is more stability of the ideal concept for boys in upper class status, and also for children of both sexes where both parents have similar ideal concepts. Lazowich (60) found lower manifest anxiety (Taylor scores) in children who showed greater similarity of self-concept with parents' self-concept. Manis (66), using the MMPI, found high and low "adjustment scores" associated with high and low perceptions of the esteem which college students felt their parents granted them. Over all, the researches on self-concept indicate that parents are important to children in the formation of these concepts, but why, or how important in what ways is not made more clear by research evidence than it has been by speculation. Peer groups and friendships also have a powerful effect on self and ideal concept formation, and the researches in this area tend to be more congruent, less contradictory to each other. There is more similarity, for both self and ideal, among persons chosen sociometrically as friends than among those not chosen, according to the Q-sort and MMPI (42) (63). Thompson and Nishimura (94) find the average intercorrelation between one's own ideal and the description of a friend to be higher than one's own self-ideal correlation! McKenna, et al. (65) could not replicate this, but found correlations of equal magnitude for self-ideal and friend-ideal. Thompson and Nishimura strengthened their findings by showing that the correlation between ideal and description of a non-friend is near zero. In all, it is rather plain one's perceptions of self and of ideals are related to the apparent ideals of those one chooses to be close to whether it be parents, teachers, or friends. Again, the order of consequence is not clear. Probably influence runs in both directions, and a single cause-effect relation is a spurious assumption for human interaction studies.

The Genesis and Destruction of the Self

The best ideas we have on the development of the self do not yet come from empirical research but from theoretical research. G. H. Mead made clinical and social observations of humans in various stages of growth, and his cogent ideas on the genesis of the self have been the basis for most of the work since, whether directly acknowledged or not (69). Mead believes that the self is a social product. Man is not born with a self; it grows out of and thrives upon social interaction; in isolation it would wither and die. A child begins social life by responding in imitation, using its natural capacities, such as smiling and laughing. (Behaviors such as these do not develop in isolation.) It comes to the point of pretending, in its play, to be other objects and persons—a horse, truck, policeman, a mommy, a giant. Gradually, through this type of play experience (role playing) he differentiates a role of his own. He begins to "draw the map" of himself. As he learns to take the role of the other, he learns also to (1) estimate and *anticipate how the other feels*, and to (2) *learn a language*. These two learnings make him human, give him the social and intellectual tools necessary for possession of a "mind" (besides a brain), and a "self" (beyond the physical organism). When we interact as selves, we take each other's roles to some extent. The lecturer speaks to his audience, gauging how he sounds to them by putting himself in their place, and is guided by it. The mother punishing her child feels some of the pain she inflicts, and limits herself because of it. The lover who excites his companion comprehends the excitement by participating in it, and is further aroused by it. That is what we call empathy. It means that what we do to others we do at the same time to ourselves. This means that the self is social, and that humans respond to each other in human ways because they know how it feels to be human. The cognitive part of this act is the communication via symbols, i.e., language. Language contains what Mead calls "significant symbols." The significant symbol is one which is *reflexive*, in that it arouses in both the speaker and the hearer the same feelings. When you speak, you know what you mean, you know what your words should sound like to the other, you know how he is likely to react because you empathically anticipate his reaction and share it. The self is established through social, empathic communication, and it is maintained as long as the communication, or memory of it, remains. Since the communication is always to another, and the empathy is for another, the active self *always requires and presupposes another*, even though it be only in a generalized or abstract sense: "society at large," "what will they think," one's "reference group" or "the unknown person who will read this paper," etc. This "other" finally becomes one-half of an *autonomous duality within one's own consciousness,* and it enables us to live in our human way through that consciousness even during periods of isolation.

That is how the self develops, theoretically. The other end of the problem is how it deteriorates or ends. It ends with the end of consciousness in physical death once the nervous system disintegrates sufficiently, but it sometimes deteriorates or ends while the body still lives. Then a person is "not himself" or "loses his mind." This process has been studied in observations of psychotic stress using Mead's theory as a frame of reference (85). The self undertakes to defend itself from knowledge of acts inconsistent with the self-concept. Such experiences are denied or distorted, when possible, to avoid feelings of guilt and shame. The self, in effect, will lie in its own defense. The lie is an act peculiarly human, learned in early years while the self is in formation. Lying is a conscious act of deliberate concealment of a known truth, usually a response to shame or to fear of punishment. A more complicated form of this defense is *self-deception,* which is a response to guilt rather than simple shame. While the effort is to deceive the *other* person, social communication is still maintained, and the self is intact. The lie may be immoral, it may be socially corrosive, but it is not necessarily self-destructive. The person who lies also has sure contact with the truth (since that is what he is trying to conceal) and is therefore "in contact with reality." *Self*-deception is another matter. There one tries to lie to one's self, which turns out to be either impossible or to lead to *self-negation,* as Sartre calls it.

Mead explained that mind (and self) is formed of two parts of a process of communication—the communicator and the communicatee, each of whom shares the other's role to some extent. The autonomous self contains these two parts within it—the known and the knower, or the speaker and the listener. "Knowing" is actually believing (for no one "knows" anything), and to believe, one must also have the capacity to doubt. Skepticism, in ourselves and in the other, is what we pit ourselves against, but it also assures us of something being there, and gives meaning to belief. When, out of defensiveness against guilt, the self attempts self-deception, it will either: fail, because the deceiver cannot hide from himself his own intention to deceive, or—succeed and thus destroy or negate the fundamental duality of the self. That duality is a differentiation between self and other which gives "boundaries to the map"—it is also, within one person, the differentiation between the self and the internalized other, or the believer and the doubter. Once this essential differentiation is lost, the person cannot even know the one thing he still is—a being in a state of self-deception. When this is the case, he suffers loss of self, with consequent isolation and its further ill effects. This idea of the loss of self is based on a theory of cognitive malfunction, rather than, for instance, excess emotional stress. It explains the mechanism by which self is destroyed in the same terms in which it was created, and gives a rather literal psychological meaning to "the wages of sin is death." It is not sin which is killing, but the defense against guilt in the service of that guiding principle, the self.

SUMMARY AND RESEARCH PERSPECTIVES

In the present state of psychological thinking, self-theory has a prominent place. The self is considered a dynamic process which makes a powerful difference in behavior via its intermediary influence upon perception.

Talents and abilities being widely distributed, it is often the self-concept which makes the difference between successful or failing performance, since one's self-concept can either encourage or incapacitate. The person who says "I can't swim" is simply crippled by a negative self-concept, since in fact anyone who can walk can learn to swim. The influence of the self-concept on behavior has wide implication for education, mental health, character study and development.

Much of what we think about the self—its formation, change, deterioration, and recovery—is buttressed by research. Upon critical examination, however, the quality of most of this research is not overpowering. It leaves much to be desired in the way of clarity and certainty, and has often been more concerned with method than with problem. Though we have considerable information about the self, and the self is often related to the "ideal" as a point of comparison, relatively little is known about the ideal, and *its* sources, modes of change, and influence upon behavior. It is not even clear that the "ideal" is of the same order as the self, though they are often compared. The more positive self-concept may free one's capacity to take a course of action. But, unless the capacity is its own and only motive (a distinct possibility in the theory of "self-realization" or "competence"), what makes one *want* to do difficult but possible things—swim, stand up for an unpopular position, etc.? Probably it is one's ideals. Though self-theory would generally fit the idea that "a man's reach must exceed his grasp," psychologists studying the self have studied the grasp, which seems more within their empirical province, rather than the reach.

Ideals, as sets of values which lead to action, seem to be culturally given, but obviously, they are or have been at some point *invented*, perhaps more often than we are led to think by models of imitation and identification theory most common to psychology. This is the point at which the theologian or the social scientist concerned with values and religious problems may have a special interest, and a special access to the data, being concerned with critical problems of life, death, doubt, belief, faith and morality. He is in a position to complement the psychologists' study of the self, and make an immense contribution thereby. Far from being intimidated by what self-theory has produced, he can take heart in knowing that the best research, and perhaps in the most crucial areas, has yet to be done.

How to go about this? Technical advice is easily come by. The most important single point he can draw from the knowledge obtained by self-concept studies thus far is to take for his own the attitude, "I can think."

References

1. Adler, G. Notes regarding the dynamics of the self. *Brit. J. Med. Psychol.*, 1951, 24, 97–106.
2. Aidman, T. Changes in self-perception as related to changes in perception of one's environment. *Amer. Psychologist*, 1948, 3, 286.
3. Allport, F. H. Self-evaluation: a problem in personal development. *Ment. Hyg.*, 1927, 570–583.
4. Allport, G. W. *Personality: a Psychological Interpretation*. N. Y.: Holt, 1937.
5. ————. The ego in contemporary psychology. *Psychol. Rev.*, 1943, 50, 451–478.
6. Ames, E. An experimental study of self in psychology. *Psychol. Monogr.*, 1926, 35, No. 165.
7. Ames, Louise B. The sense of self of nursery school children as manifested by their verbal behavior. *J. genet. Psychol.*, 1952, 81, 193–232.
8. Angyal, A. *Foundations for a Science of Personality*. New York: Commonwealth Fund, 1941.
9. Baumer, F. *Religion and the Rise of Scepticism*. New York: Harcourt Brace, 1961.
10. Berger, E. M. Relationships among acceptance of self, acceptance of others and MMPI scores. *J. counsel. Psychol.*, 1955, 2, 279–284.
11. ————. The relation between expressed acceptance of self and expressed acceptance of others. *J. abnorm. soc. Psychol.*, 1953, 47, 778–782.
12. Bertocci, P. A. The psychological self, the ego and personality. *Psychol. Rev.*, 1945, 52, 91–99.
13. Bills, R. E. Acceptance of self as measured by interviews and the index of adjustment and values. *J. consult. Psychol.*, 1954, 18, 36–38.
14. ————. Rorschach characteristics of persons scoring high and low in acceptance of self. *J. consult. Psychol.*, 1953, 17, 36–38.
15. Block, J. and Thomas, H. Is satisfaction with self a measure of adjustment? *J. abnorm. soc. Psychol.*, 1955, 51, 254–259.
16. Bonthius, R. H. *Christian Paths of Self-acceptance*. New York: Kings Crown Press, 1948.
17. Brownfain, J. J. Stability of the self-concept as a dimension of personality. *J. abnorm. soc. Psychol.*, 1952, 47, 597–606.
18. Bugental, F. J. Further studies in self-perception. *American Psychologist*, 1950, 5, 464.
19. Bugental, J. F. and Zelen, G. Investigations into the self-concept. I. The W-A-Y technique. *J. Person.*, 1950, 18, 483–498.
20. Butler, J. M. Factorial studies of client-centered psychotherapy. *Counseling Center Discussion Papers*, Chicago, VII, 9, 1956.
21. ————, and Haigh, G. V. Changes in the relation between self-concepts and ideal-concepts. In C. R. Rogers and Rosalind F. Dymond (eds.), *Psy-*

chotherapy and Personality Change. Chicago: Univer. of Chicago Press, 1954.

22. Calkins, M. W. The self in scientific psychology. *Amer. J. Psychol.*, 1915, 26, 495–524.

23. Calvin, A. D. and Holtzman, W. H. Adjustment and discrepancy between self-concept and inferred self. *J. consult. Psychol.*, 1953, 17, 39–44.

24. Cartwright, D. G. Self-consistency as a factor affecting immediate recall. *J. abnorm. soc. Psychol.*, 1956, 52, 212–218.

25. Cattell, R. B. On the disuse and misuse of P, Q, and O techniques in clinical psychology. *J. clin. Psychol.*, 1951, 7, 203.

26. Chein, I. The awareness of self and the structure of the ego. *Psychol. Rev.*, 1944, 51, 304–314.

27. Chodorkoff, B. Adjustment and the discrepancy between perceived and ideal self. *J. Clin. Psychol.*, 1954, 10, 266–268.

28. ———. Self-perception, perceptual defense, and adjustment. *J. abnorm. soc. Psychol.*, 1954, 49, 508–512.

29. Cooley, C. *Human Nature and the Social Order.* New York, 1902.

30. Cowen, E. The negative self concept as a personality measure. *J. consult. Psychol.*, 1954, 18, 138–142.

31. Cowen, E. L., Heilizer, F., and Axelrod, H. S. Self-concept conflict indicators and learning. *J. abnorm. soc. Psychol.*, 1955, 51, 242–245.

32. ———, and Tongas, R. N. The social desirability of trait descriptive terms: applications to a self-concept inventory. *J. consult. Psychol.*, 1959, 23, 361–365.

33. Diggory, J. and Magaziner, D. E. Self-evaluation as a function of instrumentally relevant capacities. *Bull. de l'Ass. int. de Psychol., appl.*, 1959, 8, 2–19.

34. Dittes, J. E. Effect of changes in self-esteem upon impulsiveness and deliberation in making judgments. *J. abnorm. soc. Psychol.*, 1959, 58, 348–356 (also 1959, 59, 77–82).

35. Dymond, R. Can clinicians predict individual behavior? *J. Pers.*, 1953, 22, 151–161.

36. Dymond, R. F. Adjustment changes over therapy from self-sorts. In C. R. Rogers and R. F. Dymond (eds.) *Psychotherapy and personality change.* Chicago: Univer. of Chicago Press, 1954, 76–84.

37. Dymond, R. (Cartwright). Effects of psychotherapy on self-consistency. *J. counsel. Psychol.*, 1957, 4, 1.

38. *Education for Research in Psychology.* Amer. Psychologist, 1959, 14, 4.

39. Festinger, L., Torrey, J. & Willerman, B. Self-evaluation as a function of attraction to the group. *Hum. Relat.*, 1954, 7, 161–174.

40. Fey, W. F. Acceptance of self and others, and its relation to therapy readiness. *J. clin. Psychol.*, 1954, 10, 269–271.

41. ———. Acceptance by others and its relation to acceptance of self and others: a re-evaluation. *J. abnorm. soc. Psychol.*, 1955, 50, 274–276.

42. Fiedler, F., et al. Unconscious attitudes as correlates of sociometric choice in a social group. *J. abnorm. soc. Psychol.*, 1952, 47, 790–791.

43. Gamble, E. A. A defense of psychology as a science of selves. *Psychol. Bull.*, 1915, 12, 197.

44. Gardner, J. W. A quantitative study of the sources of self-esteem. *Psychol. Bull.*, 1940, 37, 504.

45. Ghiselli, E. E. The forced-choice technique in self description. *Personnel Psychol.*, 1954, 7, 201–208.

46. Gordon, T. and Cartwright, D. The effect of psychotherapy upon certain attitudes toward others. In C. R. Rogers and Rosalind F. Dymond (eds.). *Psychotherapy and Personality Change: Co-ordinated Studies in the Client-centered Approach.* Chicago: Univer. of Chicago Press, 1954, 167–195.

47. Hall, C. and Lindzey, G. *Theories of Personality.* New York, John Wiley, 1957.

48. Hartshorne, H. and May, M. *Studies in the Nature of Character.* Vols. I, II, III. New York: Macmillan, 1930.

49. Havighurst, R. J., Robinson, M. Z. and Dorr, M. The development of the ideal self in childhood and adolescence. *J. educ. Res.*, 1946, 40, 241–257.

50. Helper, M. M. Learning theory and the self-concept. *J. abnorm. soc. Psychol.*, 1955, 51, 184–194.

51. Hilgard, E. R. Human motives and the concept of the self. *Amer. Psychologist*, 1949, 4, 374–382. Reprinted in H. Brand (ed.). *The Study of Personality.* New York: Wiley, 1954, 347–361.

52. Hillson, J. W. and Worchel, P. Self concept and defensive behavior in the maladjusted. *J. consult. Psychol.*, 1957, 21, 83–88.

53. Hogan, R. A. A theory of threat and defense. *J. consult. Psychol.*, 1952, 16, 417–425.

54. Howard, R. C. and Berkowitz, L. Reaction to the evaluators of one's performance. *J. Pers.*, 1958, 26, 494–507.

55. Jackson, D. N. and Bloomberg, R. Anxiety: unitas or multiplex? *J. consult. Psychol.*, 1958, 22, 225–227.

56. James, W. *Principles of Psychology.* New York: Dover, 1950.

57. Kenny, D. T. The influence of social desirability on discrepancy measures between real self and ideal self. *J. consult. Psychol.*, 1956, 20, 315–318.

58. Kell, B. An experimental study of ability to predict the self-concept of the individual. Unpublished doctoral dissertation, Univer. of Chicago.

59. Klüver, H. *Behavior Mechanisms in Monkeys.* Chicago: Univer. of Chicago Press, 1933.

60. Lazowick, L. M. On the nature of identification. *J. abnorm. soc. Psychol.*, 1955, 175–183.

61. Lecky, P. *Self-consistency: a Theory of Personality.* New York: Island Press, 1945.

62. Levanway, R. Effect of stress on expressed attitudes toward self and others. *J. abnorm. soc. Psychol.*, 1955, 50, 225–226.

63. Lundy, R., et al. Self acceptance and descriptions of sociometric choices. *J. abnorm. soc. Psychol.*, 1955, 51, 260–262.

64. Lynn, D. B. A note on sex differences in the development of masculine and feminine identification. *Psychol. Rev.*, 1959, 66, 126–136.

65. McKenna, H. V. and Hofstaetter, P. R. The concepts of the ideal self and the friend. *J. Pers.*, 1956, 24, 262–271.

66. Manis, M., Personal adjustment, assumed similarity to parents, and inferred parental evaluations of the self. *J. consult. Psychol.*, 1958, 22, 481–485.

67. Maslow, A. H. *Motivation and Personality.* New York: Harper, 1954.

68. ———. Self-actualizing people: a study of psychological health. *Person.*, 1950, Symposium No. 1, 11–34.

69. Mead, G. H. *Mind, Self and Society.* Chicago: Univer. of Chicago Press, 1934.

70. Miller, K. and Worchel, P. The effects of need achievement and self-ideal discrepancy on performance under stress. *J. Pers.* 1956, 25, 176–190.

71. Mowrer, O. H. "Q Technique"—description, history and critique. In

O. H. Mowrer (Ed.). *Psychotherapy: Theory and Research*. New York: Ronald Press, 1953, 316–375 (b).

72. Murphy, G. *Personality*. New York: Harper, 1947.

73. Nunnaly, J. C. An investigation of some propositions of self-conception: the case of Miss Gun. *J. abnorm. soc. Psychol.*, 1955, 50, 87–92.

74. Phillips, E. L. Attitudes towards self and others: a brief questionnaire report. *J. consult. Psychol.*, 1951, 15, 79–81.

75. Raimy, V. C. Self reference in counseling interviews. *J. consult. Psychol.*, 1948, 12, 153–163.

76. Rogers, C. R. *Client-centered Therapy: Its Current Practice, Implications, and Theory*. Boston: Houghton, 1951.

77. ———. Some observations on the organization of personality. *Amer. Psychologist*, 1947, 2, 358–368.

78. ———, and Dymond, Rosalind F. (eds.). *Psychotherapy and Personality Change; Co-ordinated Studies in the Client-centered Approach*. Chicago: Univer. of Chicago Press, 1954.

79. ———. A theory of therapy, personality and interpersonal relationships. *Counseling Center Discussion Papers*, 1956. (Also in Koch, S. (ed.). *Psychology: A Study of a Science*. III, 1961.)

80. Rosenman, S. Changes in the representations of self, other and interrelationship in therapy. *J. counsel. Psychol.*, 1955, 2, 271–277.

81. Sarbin, T. R. and Rosenberg, B. G. Contributions to role-taking theory: IV. A method for obtaining a qualitative estimate of the self. *J. soc. Psychol.*, 1955, 42, 71–81.

82. Sheerer, E. Analysis of the relationship between acceptance of and respect for self and acceptance of and respect for others. *J. consult. Psychol.*, 1949, 13, 169–175.

83. Sherriff, A. C. and McKee, J. Qualitative aspects of beliefs about men and women. *J. Pers.*, 1957, 25, 251–264.

84. Shlien, J. M. Toward what level of abstraction in criteria? In Strupp, H. and Lubrosky (eds.). *Second Research Conference in Psychotherapy*. Amer. Psychol. Assoc., 1961. (In press)

85. Shlien, J. A client-centered approach to schizophrenia: first approximation. In A. Burton (ed.). *Psychotherapy of the Psychoses*. New York: Basic Books, 1961.

86. Solley, C. M. and Stagner, R. Effects of magnitude of temporal barriers, type of goal, and perception of self. *J. exp. Psychol.*, 1956, 51, 62–70.

87. Snygg, D. The need for a phenomenological system in psychology. *Psychol. Rev.*, 1941, 48, 404–424.

88. ———, and Combs, A. W. *Individual Behavior*. New York: Harper, 1949.

89. Stephenson, W. *The Study of Behavior*. Chicago: Univer. of Chicago Press, 1953.

90. Stock, Dorothy. An investigation into the interrelations between self-concept and feelings directed toward other persons and groups. *J. consult. Psychol.*, 1949, 13, 176–180.

91. Stotland, E. and Zander, A. Effects of public and private failure upon self-evaluation. *J. abnorm. soc. Psychol.*, 1958, 56, 223–229.

92. Symonds, P. M. *The Ego and the Self*. New York: Appleton-Century-Crofts, 1951.

93. Taylor, D. M. Changes in the self concept without psychotherapy. *J. consult. Psychol.*, 1955, 19, 205–209.

94. Thompson, W. R. and Nishimura, R. Some determinants of friendship. *J. Pers.*, 1952, 20, 305–314.
95. Thorne, R. B. The effects of experimentally induced failure on self-evaluation. Unpublished doctoral dissertation, Columbia Univer., 1954.
96. Tillich, P. *The Courage to Be.* New Haven: Yale Univer. Press, 1952.
97. White, R. Motivation reconsidered: the concept of competence. *Psychol. Review.* V. 66, 1959, 297–333.
98. Wolberg, L. R. The problem of self-esteem in psychotherapy. *N. Y. State J. Med.*, 1943, 43, 1415–1419.
99. Wylie, R. *The Self-concept.* Univer. of Nebraska Press, 1961.
100. Zimmer, H. Self-acceptance and its relation to conflict. *J. consult. Psychol.*, 1954, 18, 447–449.
101. Zuckerman, M., Baer, M. and Monashkin, I. Acceptance of self, parents and people in patients and normals. *J. clin. Psychol.*, 1956, 12, 327–332.

2

Concept of Self and the Reaction of Others*

MARTIN L. MAEHR,
JOSEF MENSING, and
SAMUEL NAFZGER
Concordia Senior College

It is generally assumed that the concept of self develops as a result of and in response to the reaction of *significant others*. In several studies this hypothesis has been tested by examining the relationship between various concepts of self and the view that others have toward the individual.[1] Few studies have treated these variables experimentally. A notable exception is to be found in a study by Videbeck,[2] where social reaction was controlled and the predicted changes in self-regard were observed. Since the Videbeck study virtually stands alone, it is appropriate to re-test the hypothesis under the same or under systematically varied conditions. This is the burden of the research reported here.

Following Videbeck, three specific predictions were made. (1) If a *significant other* reacts approvingly toward some attribute of the subject, then the subject's concept of that attribute will increase; conversely, if a *significant other* reacts disapprovingly toward some attribute of the subject, then the subject's concept of that attribute will decrease. (2) Approval and disapproval treatments will produce different absolute amounts of change. (3) There will be a gradient of effect from specifically approved or disapproved attributes to "related" and "unrelated" attributes.

Although these hypotheses are functionally equivalent to those tested by Videbeck, the two studies differ in one important respect. Whereas

Reprinted from *Sociometry*, 25, 4 (December 1962), 353–357, by permission of the authors and The American Sociological Association.

* W. R. Baller, A. P. Bates, R. E. Stake, R. Videbeck, and H. I. Haas have been especially helpful to the senior author in his continuing research in self theory. This help is reflected in the present study and deserves acknowledgment.

[1] Malcolm M. Helper, "Learning Theory and the Self Concept," *Journal of Abnormal and Social Psychology*, 51 (September, 1955), pp. 184–194; Malcolm M. Helper, "Parental Evaluations of Children and Children's Self-Evaluations," *Journal of Abnormal and Social Psychology*, 56 (March, 1958), pp. 190–194; Melvin M. Manis, "Social Interaction and the Self Concept," *Journal of Abnormal and Social Psychology*, 51 (November, 1955), pp. 362–370.

[2] Richard Videbeck, "Self-Conception and the Reaction of Others," *Sociometry*, 22 (December, 1960), pp. 351–359.

Videbeck tested these hypotheses with college speech students, the present study concerns itself with body concepts of adolescent boys.

METHOD

Subjects. Thirty-one members of a high school physical education class served as subjects. Subjects were male and ranged in age from 14 to 16 years. The experiment was described as a "physical development test," an explanation they seemed to accept.

Measuring Instrument. The measuring instrument consisted of 30 items which required the subject to rate himself on a nine point scale (ranging from "extremely adequate" to "extremely inadequate") in regard to body coordination and agility (the *criticized items*), athletic skill (the *related items*), and physical fitness in general (the *unrelated items*). The *criticized items* corresponded directly to the evaluations to be given by the *significant others*. The instrument approximated the one used by Videbeck in every respect, except in regard to the class of self-attributes considered.

The Experiment. The experiment consisted of four phases. Phase one was the pre-test phase. All subjects were administered the self-rating test in order to obtain a measure of their self-regard previous to the introduction of the independent variable. The remaining three phases of the experiment took place consecutively in the course of a sixty minute time period. In the second phase the subject was introduced to one of six "experts" in physical development. The "expert" then asked the subject to perform several rather simple physical tasks, such as dribbling a basketball, walking a straight line, and a sequence of calisthenics. After he had completed these tasks the "expert" responded with approval or disapproval. The approval and disapproval statements were standardized and were read and/or repeated from memory by the "experts." The formal differences between the two statements were kept to a minimum. The same wording and phraseology were used in both statements, except in those cases where obvious changes had to be made in order to convey the desired approving or disapproving tone. The experts randomly approved or disapproved of subjects without concern for actual performance. Thirteen subjects received the approval treatment and 18 received the disapproval treatment.[3]

Phase four was the post-test phase. After the subjects had performed and been approved or disapproved they were sent to another area of the building where they were re-administered the self-rating test. In order to maximize the potential for free expression the test administrator did not

---

[3] It was planned that 18 subjects would receive approval and 18 disapproval. Unfortunately, five subjects who were approved failed to participate in each of the four experimental phases.

TABLE 1

Mean Self-Ratings Before and After Introduction of Approval and Disapproval Treatments

Type of Items	Before		After		Difference	t	Significance (one-tailed-test)
	$\overline{X}$	S.D.	$\overline{X}$	S.D.			
Approval Group (N = 13)							
Criticized items	6.57	0.88	7.20	1.28	0.63	2.72	<.01
Related items	6.18	1.37	6.60	1.31	0.42	1.94	<.05
Unrelated items	6.31	1.05	6.63	1.02	0.32	1.56	>.05
Disapproval Group (N = 18)							
Criticized items	6.79	0.92	5.92	1.15	−0.87	4.17	<.0005
Related items	6.45	1.56	6.18	1.54	−0.27	3.48	<.005
Unrelated items	6.44	0.90	6.34	1.09	−0.10	0.64	>.05

participate in the judging and care was taken to dissociate him from this activity as much as possible.

RESULTS

Hypothesis 1: Direction of Change. The first hypothesis is acceptable (Table 1). The approval group significantly increased in their ratings of self on the criticized items following the experimental treatment. The disapproval group showed a corresponding decrease.

Hypothesis 2: Absolute Amount of Change. The second hypothesis is not acceptable. It is apparent from Table 2 that the treatments did not bring about significantly different amounts of absolute change.

Hypothesis 3: Spread of Effect. Hypothesis 3 is acceptable. As Figure 1 indicates there is a diminishing spread of effect from the *criticized items* through the *related items* to the *unrelated items*. The rate of decrease is greater in the case of disapproval treatment than in the case of approval treatment.

TABLE 2

Differences in Absolute Change Subsequent to Approval and Disapproval Treatment

Type of Items	Approval Treatment (N = 13)		Disapproval Treatment (N = 18)		t	Significance (one-tailed-test)
	$\overline{X}$	S.D.	$\overline{X}$	S.D.		
Criticized items	0.63	0.80	−0.87	0.87	0.79	>.05
Related items	0.42	0.42	−0.27	0.58	0.84	>.05
Unrelated items	0.32	0.70	−0.10	0.42	0.84	>.05

SUMMARY AND CONCLUSIONS

The results of the present study, with one exception, were in accord with those obtained by Videbeck.[4] (1) In both studies the disapproving

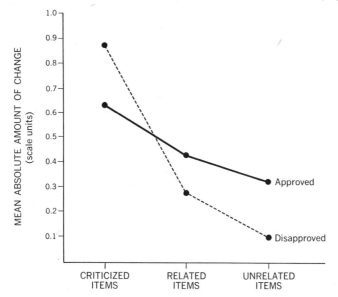

FIGURE 2-1

Spread of Effect through the Three Types of Items

reaction of the *significant other* resulted in a significant decrease in self-regard in the case of those attributes referred to directly. (2) In the present study approval also brought about a significant amount of change in a positive direction. There was a similar trend in Videbeck's study but the changes were not statistically significant. (3) In both studies there was a diminishing spread of effect to related areas of self-regard not directly approved or disapproved. (4) The findings of the present study contradicted those of Videbeck at one major point. Disapproval did not bring about a significantly greater amount of absolute change than approval.

On the basis of these findings two areas for future research are especially indicated. The first area concerns the question of whether or not such changes as were observed could in fact be considered analogous to the changes which take place as the self is formed. The second suggestion for future research concerns the role of individual differences in responding to the opinion of a *significant other*. Data on such subject characteristics as affiliation needs, ego-involvement, and acceptance of the "significant other" were gathered in connection with the experiment reported here, but findings will be reported later.

[4] *Op. cit.*

3

A Note on Self-Concept as an Insulator Against Delinquency

MICHAEL SCHWARTZ
Indiana University

SANDRA S. TANGRI
University of Michigan

Much theory and research on juvenile delinquency is focused on self-concept or self-esteem. Cohen, for example, has argued that the delinquent gang permits working-class boys to recoup self-esteem lost through defeat in middle-class institutions.[1] Reckless and his associates have been major contributors to this line of research and appear to have demonstrated that the quality of self-concept may be an excellent predictor of delinquency. Reckless' research seems to lend some credence to Cohen's formulation, since it indicates that poor self-concepts leave boys vulnerable to delinquency. Of course, this work does not indicate whether or not a poor self-concept is the product of defeat in school or other middle-class institutions.

The work of Reckless is interesting from several other points of view. It attacks the question of delinquency from a social-psychological as opposed to either a psychoanalytic or social structural perspective. That is, Reckless views a delinquent or "pre-delinquent" as trying to resolve his problems in terms of his own "personal equation." Individual behavior is viewed as a function of the articulation of society and self, and the question of delinquency becomes a research problem in socialization processes. This approach also appears to explain both delinquency and *non*-delinquency with a single set of variables. That is, self-concept or self-evaluation potentially accounts for the non-delinquent boy in a high delinquency area as well as for the delinquent boy in the same area.

The research of Reckless and his associates has been reprinted in a number of books of readings, and it is our impression that school administrators, probation officers and others in direct contact with youth are aware of it and try to act in terms of it. Nevertheless, the work seems to have some problems, examination of which will open some important research doors.

Reprinted from *American Sociological Review*, 30, 6 (December 1965), 922–926, by permission of the publisher and the authors.

[1] Albert K. Cohen, *Delinquent Boys: The Culture of the Gang*, Glencoe, Ill.: The Free Press, 1956.

Essentially, the Reckless studies have four parts. The first is a study of 125 white boys in the sixth grade in schools in the highest delinquency area of Columbus, O.[2] These are "good" boys, having been nominated by their teachers as unlikely ever to experience police or juvenile court contacts. Each was administered the delinquency proneness (De) scale and the social responsibility scale (Re) from Gough's California Personality Inventory (CPI), and a questionnaire on occupational preference (the data from which do not appear among the results). Each was asked about his concept of himself, his family, and his interpersonal relations. The boys' mothers were interviewed also.

The results obtained for the "good" boys were: (1) low scores on the De scale and high scores on the Re scale; (2) "self-evaluations which were law-abiding and obedient;" and (3) very favorable perceptions of family interaction and lack of resentment of close family (maternal) supervision. (4) Their families were maritally, residentially and economically stable. The authors concluded that "insulation against delinquency is an ongoing process reflecting internalization of non-delinquent values and conformity to the expectations of significant others."

This study alone is difficult to assess because it lacked a control or comparison group. But a follow-up study of these "good" boys four years later provides an interesting comparison.[3] Of the original group of 125 good boys, now age 16, 103 were located, and 99 were still in school. Teachers nominated 95 of the 99 boys as "good" boys again. The boys and their mothers were again interviewed and the boys again completed the De and Re scales. The boys' responses on the tests were consistent with their earlier performance; again they reported favorable family interaction patterns; and only four of the renominated "good" boys had had any police contact. Apparently these boys were insulated against delinquency over a four year period.

A similar longitudinal study was conducted with a group of 101 "bad" boys, that is, boys who were nominated by their teachers as likely to have police and juvenile court contacts. Of these 101 "bad" 12 year-old boys, 24 were already on record for previous offenses. Again, the boys and their mothers were interviewed, and the boys were administered the De and Re scales. The results were as follows. The "bad" boy scores

were significantly higher on the De and lower on the Re scales than those made by the "good boys" of the first study. Indeed, this mean delinquency vulnerability score was higher than that achieved by any of the non-delinquents and non-disciplinary sample subjects treated in other studies. Simi-

[2] Walter C. Reckless, Simon Dinitz and Ellen Murray, "Self Concept As An Insulator Against Delinquency," *American Sociological Review*, 21 (1956), pp. 744–746.

[3] Frank R. Scarpitti, Ellen Murray, Simon Dinitz and Walter C. Reckless, "The 'Good' Boys In A High Delinquency Area: Four Years Later," *American Sociological Review*, 25 (1960), pp. 555–558.

larly, the mean social responsibility score was lower than those recorded in other studies for all but prisoners, delinquents and school disciplinary cases. These scores seem to validate the judgments of the teachers in selecting these boys as ones who would get into future difficulties with the law.

Not only do these scales appear to differentiate between the potentially delinquent and non-delinquent, but even more importantly they were found to discriminate within the sample of nominated delinquents between those boys who had and those who had not experienced previous court contact.[4]

The follow-up study of the "bad" boys succeeded in locating 70 boys, now 16 years of age.[5] Twenty-seven (39 per cent) had had serious and frequent police and court contacts. The "bad" boys' mean scores on the De and Re scales had not changed and were still worse than the good boys' scores. The "bad" boys, then, seem to be more vulnerable to delinquency, and on the basis of the scale scores and the interview data, Reckless and his associates conclude that the discriminating factor is quality of "self-concept." The "bad" boys see themselves as likely to get into trouble in the future; their mothers and teachers agree. The "good" boys see themselves as unlikely to get into trouble; their mothers and teachers agree.

Our research is not a replication of this work, although it was stimulated by several important problems in the Reckless studies. First, Reckless assumes that mothers and teachers are significant others and that the boys incorporate mothers' and teachers' evaluations into their own self-concepts. Now, a delinquent may know at the cognitive level that others such as mother and teacher evaluate him negatively. But does he incorporate those perceived evaluations into his own concept of self? A "bad" boy who sees himself as likely to get into trouble may do so less as a consequence of poor self-concept than as an accurate prediction of future events based on prior experience. Reckless does not distinguish between an individual's knowledge of others' expectations as matters of fact and those that become part of his self evaluation. His treatment of self-concept is most unclear.

The primary problem raised by Reckless' treatment of self has to do with the kinds of conclusions one can draw about the self from any collection of questionnaire or interview responses. Since almost anything a person says may have some bearing on the self, one must extract from the statement *that aspect* or implication relevant to self. Otherwise, everything is "self," and the value of the term is lost. An indiscriminate collation of items from the CPI and questions asked of mother, sons, and teachers, all

[4] Simon Dinitz, Walter C. Reckless and Barbara Kay, "A Self Gradient Among Potential Delinquents," *Journal of Criminal Law, Criminology and Police Science*, 49 (1958), p. 231.

[5] Simon Dinitz, Frank R. Scarpitti, and Walter C. Reckless, "Delinquency Vulnerability: A Cross Group and Longitudinal Analysis," *American Sociological Review*, 27 (1962), pp. 515–517.

treated as self-concept, does not produce a meaningful definition of the term.

Finally, this research is missing a theoretical link. *Why* should poor self-concept leave the individual vulnerable to delinquency? One could argue, for example, that a poor self-concept ought to produce behavior conforming to the demands of significant others like mother or teacher. Or does a poor self-concept lead to a rejection of the rejectors and the attribution of significance to others who prove more rewarding (say, delinquent peers)? Does poor self-concept leave one vulnerable to delinquency only where delinquent alternatives to conformity are available? If so, does this mean that an upper middle-class boy with a poor self-concept and restricted opportunity for delinquency is apt to be a conflicted neurotic? Reckless has forced these and other significant questions upon us, and therein lies his greatest contribution.

THE PRESENT STUDY

These comments on previous work in no way demonstrate that self-concept does *not* differentiate nominated "good" boys from nominated "bad" boys. Our concern here was to devise measurement procedures suitable for determining the extent to which such a distinction does obtain between the two groups. Furthermore, we wished to investigate the extent to which varying self-concepts are a function of the consistency of self-definitions given to the boys by significant others, as those definitions are perceived by the boys themselves, and to determine, as far as possible, who the significant others really are. Another objective was to distinguish between a boy's judgments of the way others see him as a fact from his judgments in terms of self-evaluation. In other words, does a boy say that "My mother doesn't think I'm very nice, but it doesn't really matter what she thinks anyway" (his perception of the facts of the matter), or does he say, "My mother doesn't think I'm very nice, so I guess I'm not" (thus incorporating an evaluation perceived as given by a significant other).

In short, we began by asking whether a group of nominated "good boys" and a group of nominated "bad boys" can be distinguished in terms of quality of self-concept. Second, we asked about the relation between the self-concepts of good and bad boys and the perceived evaluations that others make of the boys. And finally, we asked which "others" seem to be perceived in terms of evaluation and which are less significant.

DATA

In the spring of 1964, sixth-grade teachers, and the principal and assistant principal in a single inner-city, all-Negro school in the highest delinquency area of Detroit were asked to nominate "good" and "bad" sixth-grade boys, i.e., to designate which boys they felt would never have police or court contacts and which boys they felt sure would have such contacts.

All 101 sixth graders were given a ten-scale Semantic Differential form to fill out. The polarities were: good-bad, useful-useless, superior-inferior, smart-stupid, square-cool, tough-soft, selfish-unselfish, friendly-unfriendly, kind-cruel, and important-unimportant. Seven of these pairs have high factor loadings on the evaluation factor Osgood found in his work;[6] the smart-stupid and tough-soft pairs are similar to ones Osgood used; and "cool-square" comes from the local argot. The phrases to be rated on these polarities were, "I Am," "My Friends Think I Am," "My Mother Thinks I Am," and "My Teachers Think I Am." Instructions were given orally by the authors, and they put several examples on the classroom blackboard with the concepts "Apple" and "My Shirt." Interestingly, these Negro students seemed to have vastly less difficulty with the instrument than middle-class white adolescents and adults have. Practically no subject failed to complete the instrument in its entirety, while in the senior author's experience college students have much more difficulty. Perhaps this is because sixth graders are cognitively less complex than college students.

The Semantic Differential forms of the boys nominated as "good" and "bad" (N's are 27 and 24, respectively) were separated and scored. (Since every boy was nominated as either "good" or "bad," the total of 51 includes all of the sixth-grade boys. The girls' data were not included in this analysis.) The scoring procedure took two forms. The self-concept score was taken from the ratings of the "I am" page. A score of one is given to a check mark on the space nearest the positive pole, such as

$$\text{good:}\sqrt{}:\ :\ :\ :\ :\ :\text{bad,}$$

and a score of seven is given to a check mark nearest the negative pole, such as

$$\text{good:}\ :\ :\ :\ :\ :\sqrt{}:\text{bad.}$$

The scales are thus scored from one to seven and the range of possible scores over ten scales is ten to 70.

The second scoring procedure was the computation of Di^2 scores. We wished to know not only whether the "good" boys have better self-concepts, but also the extent to which good self-concept goes with consistency of perceived feedback. To determine the consistency of perceived feedback the individual receives from significant others, we matched the scores for "My Friends Think I Am" and "My Mother Thinks I Am," for example, on a scale-by-scale basis. If a boy thinks his friends would give him a 2 on the good-bad scale, and his mother would give him a 5, then his $Di^2 = (2-5)^2$ or 9. Summing the Di^2 scores over all ten scales yields a discrepancy

[6] Charles E. Osgood, George J. Suci, Percy Tannenbaum, *The Measurement of Meaning*, Urbana: University of Illinois Press, 1957.

score, and this score was obtained for each combination of significant others.

RESULTS AND DISCUSSION

The mean self-concept score for the "good" boys was 23.48 while the mean self-concept score for the "bad" boys was 27.29 (the smaller the score, the more positive the self-concept). These data support the Reckless, *et al.*, notion that two such nominated groups do have different qualities of self-concept, although our data are based on a measure of self less ambiguous than the measures used by Reckless.

Differences between what "My Friends Think I Am" and what "My Mother Thinks I Am" were smaller for the "good" boys than for the "bad" boys: the mean ΣDi^2 score for the "good" boys was 34.51, while the mean ΣDi^2 score for the "bad" boys was 62.38. Similarly, comparing what "My Friends Think I Am" with what "My Teachers Think I Am"

TABLE 1

Self-Concept and Discrepancy Scores for 27 "Good" and 24 "Bad" Boys

	Range		Mean		Standard Deviation			
	Good	*Bad*	*Good*	*Bad*	*Good*	*Bad*	*t*	*P*
I am	12–37	16–42	23.48	27.29	6.14	6.45	2.12	<.05
My friends think I am	16–45	10–58	26.44	32.83	10.21	11.87	2.03	<.05
My mother thinks I am	10–40	10–60	23.44	30.04	8.33	10.75	2.42	<.05
My teachers think I am	10–45	16–64	26.85	36.16	7.46	10.95	3.50	<.001
Σdi^2 Friends vs. Mother	1–105	11–360	34.51	62.38	28.33	68.18	2.02	<.05
Σdi^2 Friends vs. Teachers	3–124	5–164	22.19	49.79	7.69	12.49	3.02	<.01

produced a mean ΣDi^2 score of 22.19 for "good" and 49.79 for "bad" boys. These data are summarized in Table 1, and may be considered support for a dissonance hypothesis of poor self-concept. The greater perceived inconsistency among reference groups manifested by the "bad" boys may also be taken as a measure of the quality of socialization, thus tending to support the Reckless studies' De-scale data, assuming that the De scale does represent quality of socialization.

The next question is whether mother's, friends' and teachers' evaluations of the boys, as the boys perceive them, are related to the boys' own evaluations of themselves. Correlations among the total scores for "I am," "My mother thinks I am," "My friends think I am," and "My teachers think I am" are shown in Table 2.

TABLE 2

Correlations Between Self-Concept and Perceived Mother's, Friends' and Teachers' Concepts

	"Good" Boys			"Bad" Boys		
	I am	Friends Think I am	Mother Thinks I am	I am	Friends Think I am	Mother Thinks I am
Friends	.27	. .	. .	.28	. .	. .
Mother	.18	.60*	. .	.67†	.54*	. .
Teachers	.42*	.68*	.32	.22	.61*	.41*

* Significant at .05 level.
† Significant at .001 level.

These intercorrelations vary greatly, and they are not easy to interpret. For example, the correlations between "I am" and "My friends think I am" for both "good" and "bad" boys are not significantly different from zero. Yet the relevant literature on this age group indicates an enormous dependency on peers for approval and self-definition. Perhaps what we observe in adolescent gangs or cliques is not dependency in an identification sense, but rather role-playing behavior, and the reflected images are accepted as fact and not as evaluations to be incorporated into the self-concept. Forced to re-examine our assumption that peers are truly *significant* others, we infer that peer dependency develops at a later age. Our boys were only 12 years old, and might not yet have developed a high level of dependency.

The differences between groups in the correlations between "I am" and "My mother thinks I am" proved very interesting. Although no significant correlation exists for the "good" boys, a very strong one does exist for the "bad" boys, accounting for about 45 per cent of the variance. This result was not anticipated. A plausible, though *post facto* explanation is that a close relation between self-concept and perception of mother's concept implies that mother remains very significant over a protracted time period, especially during the time when more masculine identifications are "normally" formed. Failure to give up mother obviously restricts the possibility that others might become significant in the boy's environment, which in turn restricts the possibility that others can control the boy's behavior by reflecting either negative or positive self-images. Note that the correlation between self-image and perceived teacher's image for "bad" boys is not different from zero, whereas for "good" boys, it is the largest and only significant correlation, much larger than the minor correlation with mother's image. Perhaps, then, defining self as "good" or "bad" is largely a function of the individual's own attribution of significance to others in varying situations. Among the directions indicated for further research, testing hypotheses concerning mother's control of independence training is an example.

An alternative interpretation is as follows. If it is true that peer evaluations are not, at this age, incorporated into a self-image, and therefore render little or no psychological support, and if a boy's teachers reject him (as is clearly the case when a teacher nominates the boy as "bad"), then where can a "bad" boy turn for support? At this age, it seems to be toward mother. Perhaps defeat in the broader environment, i.e., the school, forces the boy back to the family group. It is not that his mother fails to "let go," but rather that the son seeks to retain a relationship that a clinician would insist he ought to have given up. Even though mother seems to define him (as he perceives it) less favorably than the good boy thinks his mother defines him, she represents the primary source of self-definition, and her limited knowledge of his behavior on the streets leaves the "bad" boy relatively more free, in the psychological sense, to engage in delinquent behavior.

Whether the primary factor is the mother's failure to encourage her son's independence or the teacher's rejection, which forces the boy to rely on his mother, the results are similar, and the senior author's observations (as research director for a government-sponsored delinquency control project) support our interpretation of these data. A certain amount of latent homosexuality was evident among some of the older "bad" boys; sex, sex talk, and heterosexual encounters in general often seemed characterized by aggression more than by affection. Others have discussed the Negro matriarchy in terms of its potential for encouraging homosexuality among young men, but these data indicate an additional factor—that a Negro boy risks being driven back into a relationship to which he has no alternatives, if he is to find support for his conception of self.

The Reckless, et al., studies have not tapped these complex aspects of self. Here, we have made the distinction between fact and evaluation (or cognitive vs. cathectic modes) somewhat clearer. The high correlations between what these boys perceive as their friends' opinions of them and what they perceive as their mothers' and teachers' opinions, together with the lower correlations with their own conceptions (Table 2), suggest that a boy attributes to these others elements of his "self" definition that he finds irrelevant for his own evaluation of himself. Some aspects of what others say about one are relevant to one's own self-definition and other aspects are not. Reckless, however, treats all such perceptions as self. Moreover, some of the "others" whom the investigator may deem "significant" for the individual are clearly not significant at all—at least not enough to make the reflected self-definitions acceptable.

Our data have several implications, which we shall simply list in conclusion. First, self-concept, while still a vague and inadequately developed notion, is a much more complex phenomenon than the usual rhetoric of symbolic interaction would indicate. Second, the so-called "self-component" in vulnerability to delinquency may yet prove to be an extremely important road to follow for prediction and control. Finally, any solutions to the sociological problems of delinquency must, inevitably, incorporate social-psychological concepts. The cognitive structure that intervenes between delinquency and opportunity is a function of unique socialization experiences wherein lie an individual's reasons for choosing a deviant response to blocked opportunities. For those who wish to understand these reasons, self-concept research seems to provide fruitful directions.

For Further Reading

BOOKS

Berkowitz, L. *The development of motives and values in the child.* New York: Basic Books, 1964.

A review of the literature concerning the development of achievement motivation in the child.

Cohen, Y. (Ed.). *Social structure and personality: a casebook.* New York: Holt, Rinehart and Winston, 1961.

Readings on the relationship between socialization and social structure in nonliterate societies.

Crow, L. D. and A. *Child development and adjustment: a study of child psychology.* New York: Macmillan, 1962.

An introductory text; views the individual as dynamic and purposeful.

Hyman, H. *Political socialization.* Glencoe, Illinois: The Free Press, 1957.

Relates childhood socialization to the degree and direction of adult political involvement, with especial regard to conservative-liberal and authoritarian-democratic tendencies.

Jersild, A. T. *Child psychology.* Englewood Cliffs, N. J.: Prentice-Hall, 1960.

Revision of a widely-used text; emphasizes "ego" psychology.

Kardiner, A. and Preble, E. *They studied man.* New York: New American Library, Mentor, 1963.

The first portion reviews the contributions of Darwin, Spencer, Tyler, Frazer, Durkheim, Boas, Malinowski, Kroeber, Benedict, and Freud to the study of culture. The second part elaborates the contribution of anthropology to adaptational psychodynamics (the successful fulfillment of man's needs).

Mussen, P., Conger, J. and Kagan, J. *Child development and personality,* New York: Harper and Row, 1963.

Revision of a 1956 text; stresses learning theory.

Pearce, J. and Newton, S. *The conditions of human growth.* New York: Citadel, 1963.

Presents a theory of personality development based on the approach of Harry Stack Sullivan.

Rose, A. M. (Ed.). *Human behavior and social processes: an interactionist approach.* Boston: Houghton Mifflin, 1962.

This reader includes papers from outstanding contributors who, writing in regard to different kinds of social situations, deal with the theme of the continuous nature of socialization.

Smelser, N. J. and Smelser, W. T. (Eds.). *Personality and social systems.* New York: John Wiley and Sons, 1963.

Nearly 60 articles, many of which treat the social system as the independent variable and personality, and some in which the relationship is treated as the reverse.

Stoodley, B. H. (Ed.). *Society and self: a reader in social psychology.* New York: The Free Press, 1962.

A reader which stresses social structure, rather than the individual.

Wylie, R. C. *The self concept: critical survey of pertinent research literature.* Lincoln, Nebraska: Nebraska University Press, 1960.

A rigorous discussion of research and theory relating to the self-concept.

ARTICLES

Backman, C. W., *et al.* Resistance to change in the self-concept as a function of consensus among significant others. *Sociometry*, 1963, 26 (1), 102–111. PA 38, 2544.

The greater the number of significant other persons who are perceived to define an aspect of self congruently, the greater the resistance to change.

Bloom, K. L., Age and the self concept. *Amer. J. Psychiat.* 1961, *118* (6), 534–538. PA 36, 4FI34B.

Age does not seem to affect the self-concept a great deal.

Chambliss, W. J. The negative self. *Sociol. inquiry*, 1964, *34* (1), 108–112. SA 13, B6719.

The assumption that there are persons who possess negative self-conceptions may be totally wrong.

Clinard, M. B. and Fannin, L. F. Differences in the conception of self as a male among lower and middle class delinquents. *Social probl.*, 1965, *13* (2), 205–214. SA 14, C1690.

Self-conceptions were similar, but lower-class boys did conceive of themselves as being tougher, more fearless, powerful, fierce and dangerous.

Cottle, T. J. Self concept, ego ideal and the response to action. *Sociol. soc. res.*, 1965, *50* (1), 78–88. PA 40, 1541.

When there is discrepancy between the self-concept and action, evaluation anxiety ensues.

Dinitz, S., *et al.* Integration and conflict in self-other conceptions as factors in mental illness. *Sociometry*, 1959, *22* (1), 44–55. SA 9, 9765.

It is not the self–other discrepancies that are the important problem in mental illness but rather the patient's inability to perceive others realistically.

Ferullo, R. J. The self-concept in communication. *J. Communication*, 1963, *13* (2), 77–86. PA 38, 5987.

Better public speakers reveal a higher degree of self-acceptance, emotional control, and personality integration than the poorer speakers.

Fisher, S. Power orientation and concept of self-height in men: preliminary note. *Percep. Mot. Skills*, 1964, *18* (3), 732. PA 39, 4781.

Hypothesis (supported) that the man concerned with proving his superiority would have an exaggerated idea of his "bigness."

Haller, A. O. and Wolff, C. E. Personality orientations of farm, village and urban boys. *Rural Sociol.*, 1962, 27 (3), 275–293. PA 37, 2989.

There are personality differences related to rural or urban residence.

Horowitz, F. D. "The relationship of anxiety, self concept, and sociometric status among fourth, fifth and sixth grade children," *J. abnorm. soc. Psychol.*, 1962, 65 (3), 212–214. SA 11, A7716.

More anxious children tend to hold poorer self-concepts than do less anxious ones.

Lowe, C. M. *The self-concept: fact or artifact. Psychol. Bull.*, 1961, 58 (4), 325–336. PA 36, 3HJ25L.

Questions the validity of the self-concept.

Maccoby, E. E. The choice of variables in the study of socialization. *Sociometry*, 1961, 24 (3), 357–371. PA 37, 1008.

The different social sciences have not yet integrated a theory of socialization.

Murphy, V. Anxiety: common ground for psychology and sociology. *Amer. Catholic sociol. Rev.*, 1960, 21 (3), 213–220.

Subjects having the highest discrepancies between their ideal performance level and actual performance levels exhibited the greatest anxiety.

Perkins, H. V., Factors influencing change in children's self-concepts. *Child Develpm.*, 1958, 29, 221–230. PA 35, 3263.

Increasing congruency was observed in the self-ideal self of 251 fourth and sixth grade children (Q Sort Technique).

Phillips, A. S. Self concepts in children. *Educ. Res.*, 1964, 6 (2), 104–109. PA 38, 8081.

A review of theory and research in the self-concept, written especially for teachers.

Quarantelli, E. L. and Cooper, J. Self-conceptions and others: a further test of the Meadian hypotheses. *Sociol. Quart.*, 1966, 7 (3), 281–297. SA 15, C 4072.

Supports six of seven hypotheses generated from Mead's conception; findings stress the importance of the actor's perception of others (as contrasted to the actual behavior of others) in the formation of the self.

Reese, H. W. Relationships between self-acceptance and sociometric choice. *J. abnorm. soc. Psychol.*, 1961, 62 (2), 472–474. PA 36, 4FF72R.

The sociometric measures were not related to the discrepancy between ideal-self and self-concept scores.

Rooney, J. F. Group processes among skid row winos: a re-evaluation of the undersocialization hypothesis. *Quart. J. Stud. Alc.*, 1961, 22 (3), 444–460. SA 12, B 0719.

Doubt is cast on the validity of personality theories that characterize Skid Row excessive drinkers as "under-socialized" and unable to share in interpersonal experiences.

Rose, A. M. Incomplete socialization. *Sociol. soc. res.*, 1960, 44 (4), 244–250. SA 11, A4152.

Individualism occurs in societies where adults achieve a high degree of socialization; education, the church, mass media and voluntary associations are of limited value in encouraging socialization.

Rosen, B. C. Socialization and achievement motivation in Brazil. *Amer. sociol. Rev.*, 1962, 27 (5), 612–624. PA 37, 4827.

Brazilian mothers were less likely to train their sons in self-reliance, autonomy and achievement than were American mothers.

Rosengren, W. R. The self in the emotionally disturbed. *Amer. J. Sociol.*, 1961, 66 (5), 454–462. PA 36, 4HJ54R.

Changes in one function of the self tend to be associated with changes in other functions.

Scarpitti, F. R., *et al.* The "good" boy in a high delinquency area: four years later. *Amer. sociol. Rev.*, 1960, 25 (4), 555–558. PA 35, 2020.

Of original sample of 125, 103 were located four years later; once a favorable self-image has been developed it is as difficult to alter as a delinquent self-image.

Seeman, M. and Evans, J. W. Apprenticeship and attitude change. *Amer. J. Sociol.*, 1962, 67 (4), 365–378. PA 36, 5GD65S.

This study is concerned with the socialization of the physician during his internship.

Sewell, W. H. Some recent developments in socialization theory and research. *Ann. Amer. Acad. polit. soc. Sci.*, 1963, 349, 163–181. SA 12, A9932.

A review of theory and research in socialization.

Silverman, I. Self-esteem and differential responsiveness to success and failure. *J. abnorm. soc. Psychol.*, 1964, 69, (1), 115–119. SA 14, B8331.

Hypothesis (supported) that high self-esteem persons are generally more responsive to success experience than to failure, while lows show the opposite effects.

Smith, G. M. Six measures of self-concept discrepancy and instability: their interrelations, reliability, and relations to other personality measures. *J. consult. Psychol.*, 1958, 22 (2), 101–112. PA 35, 3443.

All six measures were found to be positively correlated with each other (discrepancy between Self and Ideal Self; discrepancy between Self and Social Self; discrepancy between Social Self and Ideal Self; instability of Self, Ideal Self, and Social Self).

Spitzer, S. P., *et al.* The self concept: test equivalence and perceived validity. *Sociol. Quart.*, 1966, 7 (3), 265–280. SA 15, C 4078.

Kuhn's 20 Statement Test, Bill's Index of Attitudes and Values, Fiedler's Semantic Differential Technique, and Gough's Adjective Check List cannot be considered equivalent.

Tippett, J. S. and Silber, E. Self-image stability: the problem of validation. *Psychol. Rep.*, 1965, 17 (1), 323–329. PA 40, 1579.

Discusses the problem of validation and suggests that the self-image may not be a unitary trait but it may contain specific components.

Williams, A. F. Self-concepts of college problem drinkers. *Quart. J. Stud. Alc.*, 1965, 26 (4), 586–594. SA 14, C 1486.

The hypothesis that problem drinking is associated with negative self-evaluation was supported.

Yinger, J. M. Research implications of a field view of personality. *Amer. J. Sociol.*, 1963, 68 (5), 580–592. PA 38, 2655.

Developing an adequate theory of personality and research procedures competent to test and extend it is one of the most challenging tasks faced by social science today.

One entire issue of *The Sociological Quarterly*, 1963, 7 (3), was devoted to "self and related issues."

Chapter Two

Inner and Other-directed Personality

In David Riesman's *The Lonely Crowd* [1] three types of personality orientation are delineated: *tradition-*, *inner-* and *other-directed*. Riesman and his collaborators related them to periods of history correlated with demographic factors. While Heberle[2] and others have justifiably criticized the supposed connections between population growth or decline and personality types, interest in the proposed typology itself has continued unabated.

The major focus of attention has been on the *inner- and other-directed* aspects of personality, since Riesman's *tradition-directed* character is portrayed as having been most prevalent in the preindustrial age. Riesman equates the traditional society to such familiar terms as "folk society," *gemeinschaft*, and so on, though he is careful to point out that even the most other-directed peoples are not devoid of tradition. The point is that with a short life expectancy, society provides pat answers; "little energy," he says, "is directed toward finding new solutions of the age-old problems, let us say, of agricultural technique or 'medicine,' the problems to which people are acculturated." [3] The *tradition-directed* character hardly thinks of himself as an individual, but rather as being in a network of family, group, or tribe.

The *inner-directed* personality type emerged with the Renaissance and Reformation: the greater choices provided with greater mobility, the development of technology, and expansion in the production of goods and people evoke a character type that can "manage to live socially without strict and self-evident tradition-direction." [4] This period of history witnessed the splintering of traditions. With the loosening of primary group ties, individuals needed a "gyroscope" to maintain a delicate balance be-

---

[1] Riesman, D., Glazer, N., and Denney, R. *The lonely crowd.* New Haven: Yale University Press, 1950. Esp. pp. 4–26. Pagination varies with different editions.

[2] Heberle, R. A note on Riesman's "The Lonely Crowd." *Amer. J. Sociol.*, 1956, 62 (1), 34–36.

[3] ———, *op. cit.*, p. 11. This and the following descriptions are paraphrased from Riesman.

[4] ———, *op. cit.*, p. 15.

tween the demands of life goals (such as money, power, fame, or goodness) and the buffetings of the external environment.[5]

With the accumulation of sufficient capital to provide not only for basic needs but for abundance, the problems of man increasingly involved other people rather than the material environment. Riesman suggests that especially in the upper classes and the "new" middle classes of the metropolitan areas, the *other-directed* personality has recently emerged. Now, increased sensitivity toward others is the rule and a "radar" type personality is rewarded. Though it is important who the "others" are, the process of paying close attention to others remains unaltered throughout life. "The tradition-directed person," he writes, "takes his signals from others, but they come in a cultural monotone; he needs no complex receiving equipment to pick them up. The other-directed person must be able to receive signals from far and near; the sources are many, the changes rapid. What can be internalized, then, is not a code of behavior but the elaborate equipment needed to attend to such messages and occasionally to participate in their circulation." [6]

As so often happens in provocative and imaginative writings, it was many years before anyone succeeded in empirically establishing whether indeed there was any such personality types as Riesman described. The typology has hardly been investigated and those studies which have been made are confined to the United States. Perhaps the first empirical work is represented by Dornbusch and Hickman, who report their investigation of the relationship of supposedly different personality types to changes in commercial advertising in the United States from the 1890s to the 1950s. Their use of content analysis to provide an indirect test of Riesman's hypothesized change from inner- to other-directed personality character may furnish an inspiration for the student to contrive other imaginative and indirect tests related to this and the other topics which follow.

The second article, that by Kassarjian, reports the first published account of an attempt to deliberately construct a scale to measure the incidence of these social character types. (This scale is incorporated in the selection.) In the Peterson selection, a much more sophisticated handling of scales to measure inner-other direction is reported.

[5] Heberle, R., *op. cit.*, p. 16.
[6] ———, *op. cit.*, p. 26.

4

Other-Directedness in Consumer-Goods Advertising: A Test of Riesman's Historical Theory*

SANFORD M. DORNBUSCH
Stanford University

LAUREN C. HICKMAN
University of Chicago Law School

Some of the most influential and scientifically significant theories in the social sciences are often difficult to formulate in terms amenable to empirical testing. Sewell notes the necessity for reformulation of the theory in order to derive testable hypotheses.[1] In this paper an attempt will be made to formulate and test the historical trend toward other-directedness in American life posited in the work of David Riesman.[2]

Although there are empirical studies applying Riesman's conceptual scheme to contemporary American society,[3] the authors know of no research on the historical aspects of his work. He assumes, with considerable illustrative material, a general trend in recent years away from a character

Reprinted from *Social Forces*, 38, 2 (December 1959), 99–102, by permission of the authors and The University of North Carolina Press.

* This research was done under the auspices of the Laboratory of Social Relations of Harvard University. We are indebted to the following persons who were consulted at various stages of the project: David Riesman, Florence Kluckhohn, Clyde Kluckhohn, and Samuel A. Stouffer.

[1] Wm. H. Sewell, "Some Observations on Theory Testing," *Rural Sociology*, XXI (March 1956), 1–12. An earlier paper by one of the present authors used a similar approach. See S. Frank Miyamoto and Sanford M. Dornbusch, "A Test of Interactionist Hypotheses of Self-Conception," *The American Journal of Sociology*, LXI (March 1956), 399–403.

[2] David Riesman, Nathan Glazer, and Reuel Denney, *The Lonely Crowd* (New Haven, Conn.: Yale University Press, 1950).

[3] Elaine Graham Bell, Inner-Directed and Other-Directed Attitudes (Unpublished Ph.D. dissertation, Yale University, 1955); E. G. Guba and J. W. Getzels, The Construction of an Other-Directedness Instrument, with Some Preliminary Data on Validity, paper read before the American Psychological Association, Sept., 1954; Michael S. Olmsted, "Character and Social Role," *The American Journal of Sociology*, LXIII (July 1957), 49–57.

structure based on internalized goals towards a social character emphasizing throughout life the guiding reactions of others. Since we cannot query the dead, it is obviously necessary to use an indirect set of data which can be assumed to bear some relationship to the hypothesized shift.

THE UNIVERSE UNDER ANALYSIS

A basic assumption of this research is the belief that a shift in the verbal themes of consumer-goods advertising is likely to reflect a corresponding change in the values of the audience for that advertising. Riesman himself makes more than twenty separate references to such advertising. The advertising in one magazine with a long period of uninterrupted publication was selected for analysis. All issues of the *Ladies' Home Journal* from 1890 to 1956 constituted the universe to be sampled. This magazine was chosen because it is essentially middle class in its orientation[4] and is directed solely at women. More than most journals, there appears to be stability in the type of readers, but it is obviously impossible to control the influence of changes in readership upon the themes to be analyzed. In our opinion, the findings reported below are of such magnitude that it is unlikely they are in any large measure a product of this uncontrolled variable.

THE SAMPLE

There were a total of 816 issues of the *Ladies' Home Journal* during this 67-year period. The sample of issues to be analyzed was drawn in the following manner. Each issue was assigned a number. By means of a table of random numbers, one issue from each year was selected for possible inclusion. The order in which the issues were to be analyzed was also assigned through a table of random numbers. Limitations of time and money permitted the analysis of issues from only 41 years.[5] This is a five percent sample of the total population.

It is important to note that the random assignment of the order in which these magazines were to be read effectively prevents changes in the perspective of the content analysts from producing shifts in the amount of other-directedness found in advertising. The trends noted below are not a function of changing standards of content-analysis procedure.

---

[4] Riesman claims that it is the middle-class character which is in transition.

[5] In the order of coding, the sample included one issue from each of the following years: 1926, 1920, 1902, 1908, 1922, 1917, 1953, 1950, 1914, 1899, 1932, 1939, 1954, 1903, 1952, 1909, 1890, 1897, 1907, 1936, 1931, 1940, 1894, 1910, 1929, 1927, 1912, 1943, 1924, 1915, 1895, 1891, 1944, 1893, 1921, 1941, 1900, 1896, 1951, 1923, 1946.

INDICES OF OTHER-DIRECTEDNESS

No indices of inner-directedness are employed in this study. Rather, the proportion of advertisements with some form of other-directed appeal is the basic measure. The hypothesis is that the proportion of other-directed advertisements will increase through time. The single advertisement is accordingly the basic context unit. No relationship was found between other-directed appeals and size of advertisement, so no bias is introduced by using this unit for the entire time period.

Six indices of other-directedness were used. They fall logically into two types: endorsements by persons or groups, and claims that use of a product is related to satisfactions in interpersonal relations.

Endorsements:

1. Testimonials ("Billie Burke wears Minerva Sweaters.")
2. Collective Endorsements ("Housewives like the Singer Sewing Machine.")
3. Quantitative Endorsements ("25 million men use Star blades.")

Interpersonal Satisfactions:

4. Positive Interpersonal ("He'll like you better if you use Revlon.")
5. Negative Interpersonal ("Her perspiration drove her friends away. She should have used Mum.")
6. Both Positive and Negative Interpersonal ("Jim lost his girl because poor breakfast foods gave him no pep. After eating Wheaties, he's won her back.")

These indices obviously bear only an indirect relationship to other-directedness as perceived by Riesman. They do have the advantage, however, of being sufficiently explicit to permit intersubjective reliability among coders. Indices 4, 5, and 6 are mutually exclusive, but more than one appeal per advertisement may be recorded among indices 1, 2, and 3. When combined into groups of indices, advertisements are simply viewed as containing an other-directed appeal or having no such appeal, thus eliminating any possible bias due to the coding of several appeals in a single advertisment.

RELIABILITY

Table 1 shows the number of advertisements with other-directed appeals which were found by two independent coders analyzing two issues randomly selected from the earlier period (up to 1921) and the more re-

TABLE 1

Comparison of Frequencies Recorded by Two Coders Analyzing the Same Issues of the Ladies'
Home Journal, October 1895, and July 1951

	1895		1951	
	Coder A	Coder B	Coder A	Coder B
Endorsements				
Any type of endorsement.......	9	10	24	27
Testimonial...............	2	3	9	9
Collective.................	7	7	14	14
Quantitative..............	2	2	7	10
Interpersonal				
Any type of interpersonal satis-				
faction...................	0	0	1	1

cent half of the sample.[6] The high level of reliability of coding for the
different types of endorsements is obvious. Unfortunately, these two issues
do not contain a sufficient number of advertisements with interpersonal
appeals to test the reliability of such coding. Two additional issues, those
of May 1926, and January 1936, were used for a separate study of the
reliability of coding. These issues are the two which contain the largest
number of references to interpersonal consequences of product use, according to the scores of the individual who coded all issues. A third person
scored these issues, and a different measure of reliability was employed.
Instead of comparing the frequencies for each issue, a reliability coefficient
was computed for the percentage of agreement between coders on specific
advertisements where either scorer found some other-directed appeal. The
level of agreement was very high. For the three endorsement indices, the
reliability coefficients were .95, .89, and .89. For the interpersonal appeals
combined, reliability was .80, based on 10 cases. There were not sufficient
cases to provide reliability measures for the three specific types of interpersonal effects of product use.

These are extremely high reliabilities, reflecting the explicit character
of the indices of other-directedness employed in this research. The reliability coefficients would be even higher if one considered the large
number of agreements with respect to the lack of other-directed devices
in most advertisements. The ads where other-directedness was at issue
were only a minority of all advertisements; thus these high coefficients of
reliability state the minimum level of agreement between the pairs of
readers.

[6] We are indebted to Caroline Roberts for her assistance in the reliability checks.

SUMMARY OF FINDINGS

The null hypothesis to be tested states, for each index and combination of indices, that the proportion of other-directed advertisements is the same in issues published up to 1921 and in issues appearing after that date. The year 1921 is the midpoint of our sample, therefore representing the best arbitrary cutting point. The chi square test, a nonparametric measure, is then used as the basic statistical tool. Eight separate analyses were undertaken: one for each of the six indices, one for the use of any endorsement device, and one for the use of any interpersonal appeal.

The results of this statistical analysis can be briefly stated. In each of the eight tests, the null hypothesis is rejected at the .001 level. To the extent that the indices formulated here reflect the position of Riesman, the results of these statistical tests lend empirical support to his approach. When one compares the advertising of consumer goods in the period 1890 to 1921 with the themes of more recent advertisements, there has obviously been a marked change in orientation closely related to the sphere of other-directedness.

A somewhat different statistical approach is even more indicative of the magnitude of the shift towards other-directed appeals. Each issue is scored as either above or below the median of the sample for each of two measures, the use of any endorsement technique or any mention of interpersonal satisfactions. Dividing the issues into an older group, up to 1921, and a more recent set, the identical results appear for each of the two measures. Of the 21 oldest issues, 19 are below the median in other-directedness. Of the 20 more recent issues, 18 are above the median in other-directedness. The null hypothesis of no shift in other-directedness through time can again be rejected at the .001 level. Even more definitive, the 19 earliest issues are the 19 lowest in the use of the endorsement technique. For the interpersonal approach, there is only one advertisement using such an appeal in the first 19 issues in the sample.

There is one aspect of the findings which was not an object of our study design. As can be observed in Table 2, all indices except Index 1, the use of testimonials, show a sharp decline in other-directed themes from 1940 to 1956. No tests of statistical significance are appropriate here, since the choice of cutting point arose from inspection of the data. It is possible, however, to give one additional piece of evidence that indicates a decline in other-directedness since 1940, as measured by these indices. The peak of other-directed appeals is found for each of the six indices, respectively, in 1932, 1932, 1926, 1936, 1936, and 1936. This is certainly contradictory to the expectations of a continual increase in other-directedness in recent years.

TABLE 2

Proportion of Other-Directed Advertisements in the Ladies' Home Journal by Six Indices

| | | ENDORSEMENTS | | | |
Decade	Number of Advertisements	Index 1 (testi-monials)	Index 2 (collec-tive)	Index 3 (quanti-tative)	Indices 1, 2, 3 (any endorsement)
1890–1899	1697	.0283	.0301	.0159	.0660
1900–1909	1296	.0262	.0502	.0262	.0965
1910–1919	1138	.0158	.0475	.0404	.0975
1920–1929	1569	.0656	.1173	.0969	.2390
1930–1939	502	.0677	.1235	.0916	.2151
1940–1949	1088	.0708	.0588	.0662	.1728
1950–1956	1102	.0662	.0635	.0699	.1570

| | | INTERPERSONAL SATISFACTION | | | |
Decade	Number of Advertisements	Index 4 (positive)	Index 5 (negative)	Index 6 (positive and negative)	Indices 4, 5, 6 (any interpersonal appeal)
1890–1899	1697	0	0	0	0
1900–1909	1296	.0008	0	0	.0008
1910–1919	1138	0	0	0	0
1920–1929	1569	.0057	.0038	0	.0096
1930–1939	502	.0179	.0100	.0100	.0378
1940–1949	1088	.0074	.0028	.0046	.0147
1950–1956	1102	.0027	.0018	.0018	.0064

DISCUSSION

We have found a dramatic shift in advertising themes in the *Ladies' Home Journal,* beginning about 1920. The direction of change is harmonious with the general orientation of Riesman and his associates, thus lending some empirical support to their position. It should be emphasized that the field of consumer-goods advertising is far removed from the central core of American values, and our findings should not be generalized beyond this consumption area. For ourselves, we must confess that our initial skepticism about the usefulness of Riesman's approach has been replaced by the view that it is testable, important, and has some predictive power.

The decline in other-directedness after 1940 which is indicated by our measures cannot be appropriately evaluated in the light of this first set of data. One view assumes the reality of the peak in the 1920's and 1930's, associating it with (a) the breakdown of fixed standards when the depression overthrew faith in the American economic system, and (b) the rise of feminism after World War I and woman's corresponding search for new values. A different interpretation relates the decline to increased subtlety of advertisers. Our measures are based on explicit statements by advertisers, partly because of our concern that reliability be high. Riesman comments, "Even though the social-class level of readers of the *Ladies' Home Journal* may not have risen, I would suspect that the educational level has risen considerably. . . . The ads and the articles, if not always the fiction, have gained in sophistication as the readership has gained in education and cosmopolitanism. . . . Is there more use now of polite implication rather than direct premise or direct threat?" [7] By this interpretation, the recent decline is a function of research technique rather than changes in the level of other-directedness in advertising. Only further research using different indices can answer this question.

[7] Personal communications, April 9 and April 11, 1957.

5

A Study of Riesman's Theory of Social Character*

WALTRAUD MARGGRAFF
KASSARJIAN
University of California, Los Angeles

David Riesman in his book *The Lonely Crowd* [1] forwarded an impressive theory of social character, which has had a great impact upon the social sciences. His terminology and concepts have become deeply embedded in the literature of the social scientist as well as that of the layman. Although Riesman, in his second volume,[2] presented extensive descriptive material based upon interviews, the work lacks the scientific rigor needed to support a new theory. Therefore, the three social character types proposed by Riesman—*tradition-directed, inner-directed,* and *other-directed*—still remained hypothetical. No other major attempts have been reported to transform them into scientific realities.

The theory asserts that, in general, human beings can be grouped into three major types of social character, each society or culture manifesting predominantly one or the other type according to the particular phase of population growth it finds itself in at a given time. The label attached to each one of the types already gives some indication as to what is meant. *Tradition-directed* people are oriented in the traditional ways of their forefathers; *inner-directed* people turn to their own inner values and standards for guidance in their behavior, while *other-directed* persons depend upon the people around them to give direction to their actions. The setting in present-day United States no longer supports tradition-directed people, but is a transitional state in which both inner- and other-directed people and many who combine features of both can be found. The problem to be investigated then is whether it is empirically possible to place individuals in the United States along a continuum from inner-

Reprinted from *Sociometry*, 25, 3 (September 1962), 213–230, by permission of the author and The American Sociological Association.

* This report is based upon a dissertation in social psychology submitted in partial fulfillment of the requirements for the degree of Doctor of Philosophy at the University of California, Los Angeles. The writer wishes to express her appreciation for the advice and suggestions from the late Professor Franklin Fearing.

[1] David Riesman, *The Lonely Crowd*, New Haven: Yale University Press, 1950.

[2] David Riesman, *Faces in the Crowd*, New Haven: Yale University Press, 1952.

to other-directedness after a reasonably reliable and valid instrument has been devised.

In spite of the wide interest in systematic theories of social processes and social behavior, research employing or testing Riesman's social character types is extremely scarce. Bourricaud,[3] Heberle,[4] Merrill,[5] and Brodbeck, Nogee, and DiMascio[6] discuss and criticize theoretical aspects of Riesman's formulations. Riesman himself in subsequent writings[7] gives no additional research data. Guba and Getzels,[8] Olmsted,[9] and Brodbeck, Nogee, and DiMascio[10] attempted to study only one or the other aspect of inner-other-directedness as it may be related to some outside factor.

An actual study directed at tapping inner-other-directedness as a whole was conducted by Graham[11] but is unpublished, and only meager published information is available for consideration at this time.[12] Graham employed the long paragraph method requiring open-end replies, which in turn had to be scored as to the degree of inner- or other-directedness displayed by the subject. No details of the scoring method nor data on the validity of the measure are available. Because of its unwieldiness, the writer does not consider Graham's long paragraph method a desirable approach to the development of an inner-other-directedness instrument. It also poses the additional problem of scoring open-ended responses consistently.

PROBLEM

Transposing a descriptive account of a new theory into an instrument to measure it validly and reliably is a rather complex task. A precise defi-

[3] François Bourricaud, "Quelques Remarques sur le Concept de 'Caractère National'," *Cahiers Internationaux de Sociologie*, 12 (1952), pp. 150–168.

[4] Rudolf Heberle, "A Note on Riesman's *The Lonely Crowd*," *American Journal of Sociology*, 62 (July, 1956), pp. 34–36.

[5] Francis Merrill, "Social Character and Social Problems," *Social Problems*, 3 (July, 1955), pp. 7–12.

[6] Arthur J. Brodbeck, Philip Nogee, and Albert DiMascio, "Two Kinds of Conformity: A Study of the Riesman Typology Applied to Standards of Parental Discipline," *Journal of Psychology*, 41 (July, 1956), pp. 23–45.

[7] David Riesman, *Individualism Reconsidered*, Glencoe, Ill.: Free Press, 1954.

[8] E. G. Guba and J. W. Getzels, "The Construction of an Other-directed Instrument with some Preliminary Data on Validity," *American Psychologist*, 9 (September, 1954), pp. 385–386.

[9] Michael S. Olmsted, "Character and Social Role," *American Journal of Sociology*, 63 (July, 1957), pp. 49–57.

[10] Brodbeck *et al.*, *op. cit.*, pp. 23–45.

[11] Elaine Graham, *Inner-directed and Other-directed Attitudes*, unpublished doctoral dissertation, Yale University, 1955.

[12] Carl I. Hovland and Irving L. Janis, editors, *Yale Studies in Communication, II: Personality and Persuasibility*, New Haven: Yale University Press, 1959.

nition of inner- and other-directedness would at best only be a condensation of Riesman's book into a paragraph. To this date there is no one outside criterion with which we can compare "social character," as Riesman chose to term the variable. There is no one equivalent in actual behavior which we can substitute for it. Inner-other-directedness is a composite of a number of factors, into which it can eventually be broken down. However, Riesman makes it quite clear that the term does not include all social behavior. He states: " 'Social character' is that part of 'character' which is shared among significant social groups and which, as most contemporary social scientists define it, is the product of the experience of these groups." [13] The link between this part of character and society ensures the necessary conformity from the individuals who compose it. In a particular society a mode of conformity is instilled in the child and usually stays with him through life.

An alternate way of describing "social character" was suggested by Riesman in the term, "mode of conformity" to the culture and society in which the individual participates. It is not a question of whether he conforms or not, or a degree of conformity, but of what he conforms to and in what manner.

"Social conformity" is used here in a special sense. At first glance one might call an other-directed person a "conformist," as compared with the "individualistic" inner-directed person. However, such a classification will not hold up under close scrutiny, at least not without further qualifying the term "conformity." To the layman the word conformity means compliance with established norms. In Merton's[14] words, social conformity usually denotes "conformity to the norms and expectations current in the individual's own membership group." No doubt, an other-directed person tries to go along with the group to gain its approval and acceptance. His behavior depends almost exclusively upon the expectations and influences of his peers. But the inner-directed individual may be just as much a conformist, if not more so. Riesman points out that he conforms for different reasons and in a different manner. He conforms almost rigidly to the established standards and values associated with his position and status in society, as he has learned them. He may also conform in a more definite group situation or even under group pressure, especially in order to get a certain task done. His drive for success and accomplishment may make him conform, rather than the need for approval which the other-directed individual must meet.

Rather than to employ existing terms and concepts to assess inner-other-directedness, the best way of ensuring adherence to Riesman's meaning is to borrow directly from his descriptions when developing a measuring

[13] David Riesman, *The Lonely Crowd*, Abridged and rev. ed., Garden City, N. Y.: Doubleday, 1956, p. 15.

[14] Robert K. Merton, *Social Theory and Social Structure*, Rev. ed., Glencoe, Ill.: The Free Press, 1957 (with Alice S. Rossi), pp. 225–386.

instrument. This is the approach used in the present study, whose main purpose it is to show that a measurable variable of inner-other-directedness actually does exist in the American society. Such a variable can be conceived of as a continuum and measured by means of a rating scale. The variable should not be identical with "social conformity" as measured by the California F-Scale. Furthermore, the variable is distinct from social extroversion-introversion, as measured by the SI-Scale of the MMPI. In an Asch-like experiment on conformity, a difference in performance between inner- and other-directed persons may show up.

METHOD

Since inner-other-directedness can best be conceived of as a continuum, the development of the inner-other-directedness instrument (*I-O* Scale) was along the lines of a five-point rating scale on each of a series of items. The items were made up from descriptive material furnished by Riesman in his book.[15] Generally, the items were confined to areas covered by Riesman, and the actual content was often taken from descriptions given to depict a typical situation in which inner- and other-directed people would be clearly distinguishable.

In a preliminary study it was found that a forced-choice type of item worded in the first person singular was superior for the purpose of this study to either the type of forced-choice item stated in paragraph form in the third person singular or the error-choice method suggested by Hammond.[16] Subjects were quite willing and capable of giving valid answers to the direct kind of question, both by their general response and the absence of gross indecision in making responses. Generally, the first type of forced-choice item had better internal consistency when compared with the total score and a better spread in the individual answers to any particular item than was found for the other types of questions. Only those items were retained which subjects repeatedly answered over all the possible five points and which proved to be of statistically significant (.05 level of confidence) internal consistency as determined by item analysis. Individual item reliability was checked by the test-retest method and evaluated by means of tetrachoric correlations coefficients. The results showed correlations ranging from .32 to .94, with only one item below .40; 24 items correlated .70 or higher. In a Chi-square analysis of the dichotomized data of the item reliability study, all but two of the items proved to be reliable at the .05 level of confidence. The two items were, however, retained because of their excellent internal consistency, wide

---

[15] David Riesman, *op. cit.*, 1956.

[16] K. R. Hammond, "Measuring Attitudes by Error-choice: an Indirect Method," *Journal of Abnormal and Social Psychology*, 43 (January, 1948), pp. 38–48.

spread, and good face validity. The final I-O instrument as used in the study consists of 36 items each of which is scorable along a five-point continuum from other- to inner-directedness.

The possible range of total scores for any one subject is from 0 (complete other-direction) to 144 (complete inner-direction), with 72 being considered the dividing point between inner- and other-directedness. For any particular item -2 is assigned to a strong other-directed answer, $+2$ to an all-out inner-directed reply, while 0 means that the subject was not able to make a decision, thus falling between inner- and other-directedness. In order to avoid negative total scores a constant of 72 is added to the sum of the individual item scores.

SUBJECTS

A sample of college students was used for the development of an I-O Scale. College students make suitable subjects for studies of this type because among them one may hope to encounter both social character types. There should be the outreaching, socially active person who experiences college as a social opportunity, and the rather self-contained student who is mainly concerned with the intellectual opportunities offered. Thus, in the course of all the preliminary and pilot studies, as well as part of the final study, undergraduate students at UCLA served as subjects. The validation studies were carried out with both graduate and undergraduate students, while a public opinion survey utilized a stratified sample of the Los Angeles population to investigate the general distribution of inner-other-directedness.

RESULTS AND DISCUSSION

The final and critical test of the I-O Scale was given to a sample of 150 undergraduate students enrolled in introductory classes in psychology. The students were asked to fill out the 36-item scale according to instructions given at the beginning of the questionnaire. The results obtained indicated a range of 87 points out of a possible 144, from 22 to 109, with a mean score of 72.20 and a standard deviation of 16.93. The median was 69.5. The obtained mean is for all practical purposes identical with the theoretical mean of 72 and the scores distribute themselves normally, as concluded from an insignificant Chi-square $(P > .30)$ obtained in a comparison of the distribution with a normal frequency distribution.

Samples of graduate students $(N = 96)$ obtained an overall mean score of 86.97 with a standard deviation of 17.85. An F-test showed the two variances not to be different beyond chance expectations $(P > .05)$, but the mean difference of 14.77 indicated a true difference $(t = 6.450,$

df = 244). Thus graduate students on the whole fall appreciably more toward inner-directedness on the *I-O* Scale than do undergraduate students. The differences between the two groups could be explained by any or all of the following three factors: (a) students become more inner-directed as they continue in school through prolonged and intensified association with books and research; (b) undergraduates, being younger, reflect the trend toward more and more other-directedness; (c) only the more inner-directed students continue into graduate school.

Reliability. The test-retest method on a sample of 52 undergraduate students over a four-week interval yielded a reliability coefficient of .85.

Validity: Differences between Pre-selected Groups. One of the means of establishing validity of an instrument is by predicting how pre-determined groups of individuals would score when the instrument is administered to them. As Riesman clearly pointed out, it is very difficult to isolate groups of people who can be expected *a priori* to be of inner-directed or other-directed social character. Not only are there relatively few people who are so definitely inner- or other-directed as to be easily pointed out, but there are also no one or two variables common to all inner- or all other-directed individuals which would facilitate locating aggregates of people of one or the other social character type. Any such group of people would only exhibit a trend toward a certain type, rather than consist of only other-directed or only inner-directed individuals.

Groups of graduate students majoring in certain fields were utilized for validation purposes. The selection of a particular area for graduate study and the choice of a definite profession should be indicative of a person's social character type. Many factors determine a person's choice of job and field of work, but due to the long training required and the intellectual processes involved in carrying out the job, social character may play the greatest role in the professional field. The groups of graduate students were chosen from a population of several thousand graduate students at the University of California. In order to make the groups as clear-cut as possible, only students majoring in fields which were considered clearly indicative of either inner- or other-directedness were included. The inner-directed sample was randomly drawn from students majoring in any of the natural sciences, philosophy, physical anthropology, or archaeology. The other-directed sample consisted of randomly chosen graduate students in the School of Education, in social welfare, political science, and various areas of business administration. One hundred copies of the *I-O* Scale were mailed out to each group of subjects, of which roughly 50 percent were returned. Since the attrition was almost equally great for both groups, no bias is expected to have entered at this point. The mean for the other-directed group (N = 46) was 79.4, with a standard deviation of 13.15; the mean for the inner-directed group (N = 50) was 93.9, standard deviation, 15.85. The variances of the two groups did not differ more than could be expected by chance (F-test, P > .05); hence a t-test was made to compare the difference between the means. The $t = 4.983$ at 94 degrees of freedom is significant at the .001 level of confidence. It was therefore concluded that the two groups represented truly different segments on the inner-other-directed continuum.

Validity: Relationship with Outside Criterion. A comparison between scores on the *I-O* Scale and reports on actual aspects of behavior which are also believed to reflect the social character of the subjects constitutes a second phase of validation for the scale. Riesman maintained that inner- and other-directed persons would tend to behave differently in various areas of their life space such as hobbies, sports, social life, etc. By measuring these behavioral characteristics of the sample, inner-other-directed behavior would be tapped on an objective basis, thus furnishing validating criteria for the actual *I-O* Scale.

For this purpose a questionnaire was developed and administered simultaneously with the *I-O* Scale and perfected in the pilot studies. In its final form this questionnaire yields ten measures of behavior. Each measure is scorable by the experimenter along a five-point scale from complete other-directedness (1 point) to complete inner-directedness (5 points). The areas included in the questionnaire were: hobbies, sports, use of free time, frequency of attendance at parties and social engagements, size of party preferred, last three books read, membership in organizations and clubs, aspirations in life, things not aspired to, and three most valued "personality aspects."

Scoring criteria were developed from Riesman's writings. For example, hobbies and leisure time interests could range from exclusive participation in group activities and spending considerable time at them, to all free time devoted to exclusively solitary activities. In the area of sports, a subject listing a variety of team sports would be scored other-directed, while the inner-directed individual is expected to engage in only individual sports like skiing, horseback riding, etc. A person attending a social event less than once a month would be scored definitely inner-directed; somebody participating in such events twice or more often a week received 1 point as an other-directed individual. In this manner similar criteria were developed for all the areas.[17]

A mean score for every subject on the questionnaire was computed by adding the individual ratings and dividing by the number of items contributing to the sum. Thus an individual could obtain a score anywhere from 1.00 to 5.00, with 3.00 being the midpoint. The Pearson r's computed between the scores on the *I-O* Scale and the mean scores for the behavior questionnaire are recorded in Table 1. Correlations of the magnitude obtained are considered to manifest satisfactory validity.

It can be concluded that the two methods of testing the validity of the newly developed *I-O* Scale have given positive results and have there-

[17] Waltraud M. Kassarjian, *A Study of Riesman's Theory of Social Character*, unpublished doctoral dissertation, University of California, Los Angeles, 1960, pp. 126–129.

fore indicated the instrument to be a valid as well as a reliable measure of inner- and other-directedness as described by David Riesman.

Correlation of I-O Scale with Other Measurements. As a means of attempting to establish inner-other-directedness as a distinctive psycholog-

TABLE 1

I-O Scale Compared with Reported Behavior

			Behavior Scale		
Sample	*N*	*r*	*Range*	*Mean*	*S.D.*
Undergraduates	150	.64	1.80–4.15	3.06	.511
Inner-directed graduates	48	.55	2.90–4.80	3.81	.428
Other-directed graduates	45	.53	2.40–4.60	3.27	.443
Both graduate samples	93	.64	—	—	—
Both undergraduates and graduates	243	.69	—	—	—

ical variable and apart from personality characteristics resembling the social character types, the F-Scale of the California Authoritarian Personality Study and the SI-Scale of the MMPI were administered to a sample of 52 students in conjunction with the *I-O* Scale. It was found that the *I-O* Scale does not measure the same factors tapped by the F-Scale (Pearson r—.005) and the correlation of .17 between the SI-Scale and the *I-O* Scale was too small to be of either statistical or practical significance.

In order to determine the relationship of inner-other-directedness with social conformity as it has been discussed earlier and is generally studied in laboratory experiments, a group method for Asch's experiments on dependence and independence of judgment under group pressure was devised [18] and tested for rendering results comparable to those obtained by Asch.[19] The Pearson r between the conformity scores and the *I-O* Scale for 80 subjects was .00. A scattergram made from the data also rules out the possibility of a curvilinear relationship. A comparison of the means of the *I-O* Scale scores for the two extreme groups (25 per cent each) on the conformity experiment resulted in a mean difference of 1.20, which yielded a t = .304, which is insignificant.

Apparently a different aspect of social conformity was tapped by Centers and Horowitz[20] in their study on susceptibility to social influence by inner- and other-directed individuals as determined by means of the *I-O*

[18] Waltraud M. Kassarjian and Harold H. Kassarjian, "Conformity of Judgment in a Group Situation," *Psychological Reports,* 10 (April, 1962), pp. 491–494.

[19] Soloman E. Asch, "Studies of Independence and Conformity: I. A Minority of One Against a Unanimous Majority," *Psychological Monographs,* 70 (1956), No. 9.

[20] Richard Centers and Miriam Horowitz, "Inner- and Other-directedness and Conformity: A Differential in Susceptibility to Social Influence," *Journal of Social Psychology,* in press.

TABLE 2

Comparison of Inner- and Other-Directed Subjects

| | UNDERGRADUATES | | | | GRADUATES | | | |
| | | | Probability | | | | Probability | |
Variables	Inner	Other	Over-all	Indiv.	Inner	Other	Over-all	Indiv.
Sex:			>.20				>.20	
Males	37	32			38	35		
Females	40	41			10	13		
Age:			.20				.10	
18 and under	42	50			—	—		
19–21	25	16			—	—		
22 and over	10	6			—	—		
20–24	—	—			10	16		
25–29	—	—			26	14		
30–34	—	—			8	11		
35 and over	—	—			4	7		
Marital Status:			>.20				>.20	
Single	68	66			19	18		
Married	7	7			28[a]	25		
Divorced	2	—			—	4		
Race:			.20				>.20	
White	68	66			46	45		
Oriental	5	6			—	2		
Indian	1	—			—	1		
Other	1	1			1	—		
Religion:			.10				.20	
Protestant	35	21			20	25		
Catholic	5	10			6	4		
Jewish	26	35			4	9		
Other	2	4			1	2		
None	9	3			17	8		
Home Town:			.20				.05	
<25,000	8	3			9	3		.10
25,000–200,000	5	10			4	9		.20
>200,000	60	56			33	35		>.20
Self-support:			>.20				>.20	
<25%	46	46			6	5		
25%–75%	17	18			7	4		
>75%	13	8			31	32		
No answer	—	—			4	7		

[a] Categories in brackets combined for X^2 analysis.

Scale. Centers and Horowitz successfully tried to influence responses to the items of the California F-Scale by supplying fictitious answers of "well-known and important people." The results indicated that other-directed people gave in more often to the outside influence.

TABLE 2—(Continued)

| Variables | UNDERGRADUATES | | | | GRADUATES | | | |
| | | | Probability | | | | Probability | |
	Inner	Other	Over-all	Indiv.	Inner	Other	Over-all	Indiv.
Major:			.05				.01	
Natural Sciences	20	9		.001	28	13		.001
Social Sciences	11	13		>.20	10	11		>.20
Education	13	18		.05	5	17		.001
Business	6	12		.20	1	5		
Arts	5	3		>.20	—	—		>.20
Humanities	15	5		.02	4	2		
Medicine	4	9		.20	—	—		
No answer	3	4		>.20	—	—		
Occupation Prep. for:			.05				.05	
Natural Sciences	18	7		.05	26	13		.01
Social Sciences	4	7		>.20	7	11		>.20
Education	28	25		>.20	8	18		.05
Business	6	12		.20	1	5		
Arts	5	1			—	—		
Humanities	1	—		>.20	2	1		>.20
Medicine	5	9			1	—		
Law	3	6		.10	1	—		
No answer	7	6		>.20				
Father's Occupation:			.20				>.20	
Professional	10	16			8	4		
White Collar	28	33			13	11		
Skilled	14	8			4	8		
Unskilled	5	8			3	5		
Other	8	3			5	1		
Farmer	1	1			1	1		
No answer	11	4			14	18		
Class:			>.20				>.20	
Freshman	48	52			—	—		
Sophomore	19	14			—	—		
Junior	7	4			—	—		
Senior	3	2			—	—		
<2 yrs. Graduate	—	—			11	12		
>2 yrs. Graduate	—	—			11	5		
No answer	—	—			26	31		

Personal Data of Inner- and Other-directed Subjects. In order to de-lineate some of the correlates of inner- and other-directedness, personal data were collected on the subjects. The results of an analysis of these data, with the median used as the dividing point between inner- and other-directedness, are presented in Table 2. In every case where the overall Chi-square was significant at or beyond the .05 level, individual Chi-squares were computed, comparing each category of a variable with the rest of the group. The majority of the variables did not yield sufficiently different results for inner- and other-directed individuals for statistical significance. Thus, neither sex, age, marital status, race, religion, degree of self-support, father's occupation, nor year in college seems to be a factor covarying with inner-other-directedness. It should be pointed out, however, that on the variables "race" and "marital status" subjects fall almost exclusively into one or two categories, respectively, so that no conclusions can properly be drawn. The significant results in major and future occupation are as expected and fit in with Riesman's theory. The differences in home town of the subjects are not as clear-cut as hypothesized, probably because the students sampled in this study are drawn predominantly from the Los Angeles metropolitan area. The undergraduate sample shows a tendency, although insignificant, that persons coming from towns of less than 25,000 population tend toward inner-direction. In the graduate sample the difference becomes more pronounced, to the point of yielding a .05 significance: persons from small towns (less than 25,000) are mainly inner-directed, while subjects from towns larger than that tend toward other-direction. A sample from an area more diverse with regard to size of towns may yield more definite results.

In general the differences on these personal variables between inner- and other-directed groups are greater among undergraduate students than among graduate students. Possibly the graduates are already a highly homogeneous group, considerably more inner-directed as measured by the *I-O* Scale than the undergraduates.

Inner-Other-Directedness among the General Population. In light of the limitations of studies based entirely on college populations inner-other-directedness was also studied in a sample of non-college adults in Greater Los Angeles. The *I-O* Scale was converted by Centers[21] in such a way as to make it amenable to public opinion surveying.[22] Since there was not time in such a survey to administer the full scale, 25 of the most discriminating and efficient items of the original scale were used.

Judging from the means of the samples, the general population seems to be slightly more inner-directed than the undergraduate college students tested. The age factor alone could account for the difference, since younger people tend to be more other-directed, while the older generation (not represented in the college sample) is still to a greater degree inner-directed.

Following the 25 items on inner-other-directedness, the interviewers also collected some personal information with regard to age, sex, education, race, religion, place of origin, socio-economic status, social class identification, political preference and occupation. Detailed analyses of the data

[21] Cf. Richard Centers, "An Examination of the Riesman Social Character Typology: A Metropolitan Survey," *Sociometry*, 25 (September 1962), pp. 231–240.

[22] For this portion of the study Professor Richard Centers graciously allowed the writer to process data collected by him.

collected in this manner were carried out by Centers using primarily a correlational method on the entire sample, and by the author[23] in a comparison of the 25 per cent most inner-directed and the 25 per cent most other-directed cases utilizing Chi-squares.

An interpretation of the author's findings showed the results on the abovementioned variables to be mainly in accord with Riesman's theory except with respect to place of origin and occupation.

The analysis of the occupational information was carried out in two distinct ways. First, the occupations listed were grouped into the customary categories from "professional" to "unskilled labor," without significant results. Second, from several listings of occupations 80 jobs were selected which appeared to have some obvious inner- or other-directed characteristics. Five judges, all of whom were very familiar with Riesman's writings, were asked to categorize these 80 occupations according to whether they required inner- or other-directed qualities in the persons holding them. Thereafter each subject could be classified as holding an inner-directed, an other-directed, or an unclassifiable job. When this breakdown was applied to the two extreme inner- and other-directed groups a 2×3 Chi-square did not show any significant differences.

In collecting data on place of origin the interviewers were instructed to obtain the name of the state in which the respondent was born, if outside the Los Angeles area, rather than size of hometown. Thus, only cases which clearly gave the city of birth as a metropolitan area or named a foreign country could be utilized in the author's analysis. The data grouped into "foreign born," "metropolitan," and "other" yielded an overall significant Chi-square. The foreign born subjects are significantly more inner-directed, as can be expected on the basis of Riesman's theory. Metropolitan-born individuals should be more other-directed, and this was the case, but not significantly so. If the information on all the subjects in the sample had been available, the picture might have been a clearer one.

SUMMARY AND CONCLUSIONS

It was the object of this study to provide an empirical test of David Riesman's theory of inner-other-directedness. In order to determine the existence of his social character types experimentally an instrument based on Riesman's descriptions was constructed, consisting of 36 individual items, each of which may be answered along a five-point scale. The scale, termed the *I-O* Scale, was tested on samples of undergraduate students. The critical sample showed a spread of scores over the greater part of the continuum from inner-directedness to other-directedness. The mean for all practical purposes coincided with the theoretical mean of the scale

[23] Waltraud M. Kassarjian, *op. cit.*, pp. 75–91.

and the median was not significantly different. The distribution was essentially normal.

By means of the test-retest method satisfactory reliability of the scale was established. The problem of validity was approached by two different methods. First, an outside criterion was obtained by means of reports on actual social behavior of the subjects. This method yielded an acceptable validity coefficient. Second, validity was tested by comparing pre-selected groups of individuals on their *I-O* Scale scores. For this purpose two groups of graduate students were selected on the basis of the major area of their studies, classified *a priori* as typically other-directed or inner-directed. Mean differences between the two groups on the *I-O* Scale proved to be significant beyond the .001 level of significance.

The *I-O* Scale was further found not to be related with the F-Scale of the California Authoritarian Personality Study nor with the SI-Scale of the MMPI. It was also ascertained that the variable being measured by the *I-O* Scale does not correlate with social conformity as demonstrated in an Aschlike laboratory experiment on dependence and independence of judgment under social pressure. The latter finding is contrary to the general expectation that other-directedness and conformity should covary.

In an additional phase of the study it was determined that the variable of inner-other-directedness extends beyond the original college sample to the general population in Greater Los Angeles by use of a modified form of the scale. Not all of the expected correlations between personal data and *I-O* Scale in the sample of the general population were confirmed.

It is concluded that inner-other-directedness exists as a relatively independent variable and can be measured reliably and validly by means of the present *I-O* Scale. The study provides substantial empirical confirmation of Riesman's theoretically proposed continuum of inner-other-directedness.

I-O SOCIAL PREFERENCE SCALE[*]

Directions: A number of controversial statements or questions with two alternative answers are given below. Answer every item as it applies to you. Indicate your preference by writing appropriate figures in the boxes to the right of each question. Some of the alternatives may appear equally attractive or unattractive to you. Nevertheless, please make a real attempt to choose the alternative that is *relatively more* acceptable to you.

If you definitely agree with alternative (a) and disagree   a   b
with (b), write 2 in the first box and leave the second blank: (2)   ( )

---

[*] First and fourth columns are scored as inner-directed; second and third columns are scored as other-directed.

If you definitely agree with (b) and disagree with (a), a   b
write 2 in the second box leaving the first blank: ( )   (2)

                                                      a   b
If you have a slight preference for (a) over (b), write: (1)   ( )

                                                      a   b
If you have a slight preference for (b) over (a), write: ( )   (1)

Do not write any combination of numbers except one of the four given. Never write more than one figure in for any one question. There are no right or wrong answers to this questionnaire. Do not spend too much time on any one item. And please do not leave out any of the questions unless you find it really impossible to make a decision.

1. With regard to partying, I feel   a   b
   a. the more the merrier (25 or more people present); ( )   ( )
   b. it is nicest to be in a small group of intimate friends (6 or 8 people at most).

2. If I had more time   a   b
   a. I would spend more evenings at home doing the ( )   ( )
   things I'd like to do;
   b. I would more often go out with my friends.

3. If I were trained as an electrical engineer and liked my work very much and would be offered a promotion into an administrative position, I would   a   b
   a. accept it because it means an advancement in ( )   ( )
   pay which I need quite badly;
   b. turn it down because it would no longer give me an opportunity to do the work I like and am trained for even though I desperately need more money.

4. I believe that   a   b
   a. it is difficult to draw a line between work and ( )   ( )
   play and therefore one should not even try it;
   b. one is better off keeping work and social actvities separated.

5. I would rather join   a   b
   a. a political or social club or organization;   ( )   ( )
   b. an organization dedicated to literary, scientific or other academic subject matter.

6. I would be more eager to accept a person as a group leader who   a   b
   a. is outstanding in those activities which are impor- ( )   ( )
   tant to the group;

b. is about average in the performance of the group
activities but has an especially pleasing personality.

7. I like to read books about
   a. people like you and me;
   b. great people or adventurers.

a   b   ( )   ( )

8. For physical exercise or as a sport I would prefer
   a. softball, basketball, volleyball, or similar team
      sport;
   b. skiing, hiking, horsebackriding, bicycling, or simi-
      lar individual sport.

9. With regard to a job, I would enjoy more
   a. one in which one can show his skill or knowledge;
   b. one in which one gets in contact with many dif-
      ferent people.

10. I believe
    a. being able to make friends is a great accomplish-
       ment in and of itself;
    b. one should be concerned more about one's achieve-
       ments rather than with making friends.

11. It is more desirable
    a. to be popular and well-liked by everybody;
    b. to become famous in the field of one's choice or
       for a particular deed.

12. With regard to clothing
    a. I would feel conspicuous if I were not dressed the
       way most of my friends are dressed;
    b. I like to wear clothes which stress my individuality
       and which not everybody else is wearing.

13. On the subject of social living
    a. a person should set up his own standards and then
       live up to them;
    b. one should be careful to live up to the prevailing
       standards of the culture.

14. I would consider it more embarrassing
    a. to be caught loafing on a job for which I get paid;
    b. losing my temper when a number of people are
       around of whom I think a lot.

15. I respect the person most who
    a. is considerate of others and concerned that they
       think well of him;
    b. lives up to his ideals and principles.

16. A child who has had intellectual difficulties in some
    grade in school
                                                      a   b

   a. should repeat the grade to be able to get more out ( ) ( )
    of the next higher grade;
    b. should be kept with his age group though he has
    some intellectual difficulties.

17. In my free time   a   b

   a. I'd like to read an interesting book at home; ( ) ( )
    b. I'd rather be with a group of my friends.

18. I have   a   b

   a. a great many friends who are, however, not very in- ( ) ( )
    timate friends;
    b. few but rather intimate friends.

19. When doing something, I am most concerned with a   b

   a. "what's in it for me" and how long it will last; ( ) ( )
    b. what impression others get of me for doing it.

20. As leisure-time activity I would rather choose   a   b

   a. woodcarving, painting, stamp collecting, photogra- ( ) ( )
    phy, or a similar activity;
    b. bridge or other card game, or discussion groups.

21. I consider a person most successful when   a   b

   a. he can live up to his own standards and ideals; ( ) ( )
    b. he can get along with even the most difficult
    people.

22. One of the main things a child should be taught is a   b

   a. cooperation;   ( ) ( )
    b. self-discipline.

23. As far as I am concerned   a   b

   a. I am only happy when I have people around me; ( ) ( )
    b. I am perfectly happy when I am left alone.

24. On a free evening   a   b

   a. I like to go and see a nice movie;   ( ) ( )
    b. I would try to have a television party at my (or a
    friend's) house.

25. The persons whom I admire most are those who a   b

   a. are very outstanding in their achievements; ( ) ( )
    b. have a very pleasant personality.

26. I consider myself to be   a   b

   a. quite idealistic and to some extent a "dreamer"; ( ) ( )
    b. quite realistic and living for the present only.

27. In bringing up children, the parents should   a   b
    a. look more at what is done by other families with ( )   ( )
       children;
    b. stick to their own ideas on how they want their
       children brought up regardless of what others do.

28. To me it is very important   a   b
    a. what one is and does regardless of what others   ( )   ( )
       think;
    b. what my friends think of me.

29. I prefer listening to a person who   a   b
    a. knows his subject matter real well but is not very ( )   ( )
       skilled in presenting it interestingly;
    b. knows his subject matter not as well but has an in-
       teresting way of discussing it.

30. As far as I am concerned   a   b
    a. I see real advantages to keeping a diary and would ( )   ( )
       like to keep one myself;
    b. I'd rather discuss my experiences with friends than
       keep a diary.

31. Schools should   a   b
    a. teach children to take their place in society;   ( )   ( )
    b. be concerned more with teaching subject matter.

32. It is desirable   a   b
    a. that one shares the opinions others hold on a par- ( )   ( )
       ticular matter;
    b. that one strongly holds onto his opinions even
       though they may be radically different from those
       of others.

33. For me it is more important to   a   b
    a. keep my dignity (not make a fool of myself) even ( )   ( )
       though I may not always be considered a good
       sport;
    b. be a good sport even though I would lose my dig-
       nity (make a fool of myself) by doing it.

34. When in a strange city or a foreign country I should
    have no great difficulty because   a   b
    a. I am interested in new things and can live under ( )   ( )
       almost any conditions;
    b. people are the same everywhere and I can get
       along with them.

35. I believe in coffee breaks and social activities for em-
    ployees because   a   b

    a. it gives people a chance to get to know each other ( )   ( )
       and enjoy work more;
    b. people work more efficiently when they do not
       work for too long a stretch at a time and can look
       forward to special events.

36. The greatest influence upon children should be   a   b
    a. from their own age group and from educational ( )   ( )
       sources outside the family since they can be more
       objective in evaluating the child's needs;
    b. from the immediate family who should know the
       child best.

6

Dimensions of Social Character: An Empirical Exploration of the Riesman Typology*

RICHARD A. PETERSON
University of Wisconsin

In the fourteen years since the publication of The Lonely Crowd,[1] the work, together with several of the terms coined in it, has received wide popular acclaim[2] and considerable critical comment.[3] A number of empirical studies of social character based on the Riesman typology have been made; but as Centers has recently noted, "to date, almost no empirical and quantitative evidence that Riesman's conceptualization is in accord with social reality has been presented [and what research has been done] . . . affords us no indication of the incidence of each type in any representative cross-section of the population." [4] The Centers study, based on "a cross-section sample of 1,077 adults in the Los Angeles metropolitan area," found scores covering almost the entire possible range, while the distribu-

Reprinted from Sociometry (June 1964), 27, 2, 194–207, by permission of the author and The American Sociological Association.

* An earlier version of the paper was presented to the Midwest Sociological Association, Milwaukee, Wisconsin, April 19, 1963. The author is indebted to Edgar F. Borgatta and the Wisconsin "Junior Jury" for valuable comments and criticisms of an earlier draft of the paper, and to Ann Wallace for her assistance in preparing the data. Financial support of the Research Committee of the Graduate School of the University of Wisconsin and the Russell Sage Foundation of New York is gratefully acknowledged.

[1] David Riesman, The Lonely Crowd, New Haven: Yale University Press, 1950.

[2] Riesman, together with two human figures representing his character types, appeared on the cover of a leading national magazine in 1954. See Time, 64 (September 27, 1954), pp. 22–25.

[3] The most thorough critique of Riesman's character typology is to be found in the set of essays collected by Seymour Martin Lipset and Leo Lowenthal, editors, Culture and Social Character: The Work of David Riesman Reviewed, New York: Free Press, 1961. For Riesman's most complete reply to his critics, see David Riesman, "The Lonely Crowd: A Reconsideration in 1960," in Lipset and Lowenthal, editors, ibid., pp. 419–458.

[4] Richard Centers, "An Examination of the Riesman Social Character Typology: A Metropolitan Survey," Sociometry, 25 (September, 1962), pp. 231–240. A similar observation has been made for cross-cultural analysis by Robert Gutman and Dennis H. Wrong, "David Riesman's Typology of Character," in Lipset and Lowenthal, editors, op. cit., pp. 295–315.

tion of scores approximated a normal curve.[5] In effect, this study, together with a number of others, suggests that the types are in accord with social reality and can be linked to demographic, social, and psychological variables.[6]

All of these empirical investigations of Riesman's typology of social character assume, at least implicitly, that inner-direction and other-direction form a single dimension.[7] This study takes as problematic the assumption of unidimensionality.

PROBLEM

In *The Lonely Crowd* Riesman typically refers to the character types in historical sequence (tradition-direction→ inner-direction→ other-direction) in such a way that at any point in time all three are present in some degree. In the second book on social character, *Faces in the Crowd*,[8] Riesman uses several formulations, but tends to place the types in developmental sequence, somewhat like rings of an onion. Thus, in effect, tradition-direction is truly primitive; inner-direction is tradition-direction with an outer layer of inner-direction; and other-direction is tradition-direction and inner-direction modified or contained by an outer cover of other-direc-

---

[5] Centers, *op. cit.*, p. 235.

[6] *Ibid.*, pp. 239–240. Empirical studies of the Riesman typology include Arthur J. Brodbeck, Philip Nogee, and Albert DiMascio, "Two Kinds of Conformity: A Study of the Riesman Typology Applied to Standards of Parental Discipline," *Journal of Psychology*, 41 (January, 1956), pp. 23–45; Richard Centers and Miriam Horowitz, "Social Character and Conformity: A Differential in Susceptibility to Social Influence," *Journal of Social Psychology*, 60 (July, 1963), pp. 343–349; Mary Jane Cramer, "Levels of Aspiration and Other-direction," unpublished Ph.D. dissertation, Ohio State University, 1958; Herbert W. Gross, "The Relationship Between Insecurity, Self-acceptance, Other direction, and Conformity Under Conditions of Differential Social Pressure," unpublished Ph.D. dissertation, University of Buffalo, 1959; Egon G. Guba and Jacob W. Getzels, "The Construction of an Other-directed Instrument With Some Preliminary Data on Validity," *American Psychologist*, 9 (September, 1954), pp. 385–386; Waltraud M. Kassarjian, "A Study of Riesman's Theory of Social Character," *Sociometry*, 25 (September, 1962), pp. 213–230; Harriet Linton and Elaine Graham, "Personality Correlates of Persuasibility," in Carl I. Hovland and Irving L. Janis, editors, *Personality and Persuasibility*, New Haven: Yale University Press, 1959, pp. 69–101; Michael S. Olmsted, "Character and Social Role," *American Journal of Sociology*, 63 (July, 1957), pp. 49–57; Matilda W. Riley, John W. Riley, and Mary E. Moore, "Adolescent Values and the Riesman Typology: An Empirical Analysis," in Lipset and Lowenthal, editors, *op. cit.*, pp. 370–388; and Elaine Graham Sofer, "Inner-direction, Other-direction, and Autonomy: A Study of College Students," in Lipset and Lowenthal, editors, *ibid.*, pp. 316–348.

[7] Kassarjian, for example, states explicitly that "inner-other-directedness can best be conceived of as a continuum." Kassarjian, *op. cit.*, p. 216. Sofer constructed her items as forced choices for the expressed reason that this would avoid the possibility of inner-other-direction not being a single dimension (Sofer, *op. cit.*, p. 317).

[8] David Riesman, *Faces in the Crowd*, New Haven: Yale University Press, 1952.

tion. Riesman asserts that in America today tradition-direction has been so completely supplanted or emasculated that it is not distinguishable as an important element in social character in any but the most socially isolated sections of the country. In effect then, all we must consider are the two later, or outer, types, inner-direction and other-direction.

As stated above, the research literature using the typology assumes that statements tapping attitudes, values, or beliefs can be constructed so that one answer indicates an inner-directed response, while the other indicates an other-directed response. For example, the first item in the Kassarjian I-O Scale reads as follows:

With regard to partying, I feel
   a. the more the merrier (25 or more people present);
   b. it is nicest to be in a small group of intimate friends (6 or 8 people at most).[9]

The choice of alternative "a" is scored as an other-directed response, while the choice of alternative "b" is scored as an inner-directed response. Using a number of such items, it is possible to place persons along a single scale, running from "always responded other-directed" to "always responded inner-directed."

Summation of the responses to a number of items requires the *assumption* that the relationship between inner- and other-direction is that of a unidimensional scale. However, there are a number of other possibilities. First, the response to any one item may be unrelated to the response to any of the other items. Such a result would imply that Riesman's notions of social character have no empirical referent. Enough empirical research which finds his concepts fruitful has been published to make this result highly unlikely. Second, inner- and other-direction may not be poles of *one* dimension, but rather may form two relatively independent dimensions. In this case, there would be four character types: inner direction, other direction, both, and neither.[10]

A third possibility is that the items might cluster in such a way as to form a *number* of independent dimensions, some, none, or all of which are related to the Riesman typology. A "related" dimension would be one in which inner- and other-directed responses do not fall on the same end of the scale, but the scale consists of only a limited range of items drawn from the domain of inner-other-direction. An "unrelated" dimension would be one in which both inner- and other-directed responses fall at both ends of the scale.

In summary, the study has been undertaken to explore the dimensional

---

[9] Kassarjian, *op. cit.*, p. 226.

[10] The "onion-ring" hypothesis would fit this case. All normal adults should fall into two cells: the cell "highly inner-directed only" and the cell "both inner-directed and other-directed." Riley, Riley, and Moore, *op. cit.*, found that their sample of 2,500 New Jersey pre-teenagers fell predominantly in two of four cells. However, they were "other-directed only" and "inner-directed and other-directed."

structure of a number of items generated to measure all facets of Riesman's social character typology.

PROCEDURES

The Instrument. The research instrument consisted of a cover page of instructions followed by 68 simple declarative statements to which respondents were asked to respond along a seven-point Likert-type agree-disagree continuum. The final page of the instrument consisted of eleven demographic questions. The social character items, with a few exceptions to be noted below, were made up directly from the descriptive material in Riesman's two books on social character.[11] Only a minority of the items were made up by the author for this study. Forty-seven of the items were adapted from Kassarjian,[12] eight from Gross,[13] and four from an unpublished study which Kathleen Archibald and the author made for Alvin Gouldner in 1958. Four items were taken from Bales' *value profile*,[14] and four items were generated by the author from the Miller and Swanson study of socialization.[15] These last eight items, while not derived explicitly from Riesman texts, were considered to be suggestive of his conception. In consequence of drawing items from a number of different sources, it is less likely that any one interpretation of Riesman has entered into the formulation of items, and thus the results are more likely to be representative of Riesman's published ideas than would be the case if all the items had been made up by one person.[16] Finally, it should be noted that *none* of the items has been drawn from the standard measures of authoritarianism, extroversion-introversion, anomie, and the like.

Sample. The research instrument was administered to 547 undergraduates taking introductory sociology courses during the fall terms of 1962–1963. This selection of subjects was more justifiable on the grounds of convenience than representativeness. However, students at the University of Wisconsin comprise a fairly broad cross-section of young people from Wisconsin, with gross under-representation only at extreme ends of the scales of intelligence and family wealth. Moreover, close to one-half of all students take an introductory sociology course; thus, it seems fair to say that the respondents do *not* represent one, esoteric segment of society, except

[11] Riesman, *op. cit.*, 1950 and 1952.

[12] Kassarjian, *op. cit.*

[13] Gross, *op. cit.*

[14] Robert F. Bales and Arthur S. Couch, *The Value Profile Form F.*, unpublished, n.d.

[15] Daniel R. Miller and Guy E. Swanson, *The Changing American Parent*, New York: Wiley, 1958.

[16] Many of the empirical distinctions Riesman makes relate not to differences in *behavior*, but differences in motivation. Such subtleties are only very imperfectly reflected in the questionnaire items.

of course in age.[17] The questionnaires of eight respondents were eliminated from further analysis on the basis of their having responded to a "blind-check" question which was placed 64th among the set of 68 items.[18]

The Instrument of Analysis. The product-moment correlations among the 67 statement-items were obtained, and 23 items were eliminated from further analysis because they did not have correlations of greater than $\pm .20$ with at least two other items.[19] The correlations among the 44 remaining items were then submitted to factor analysis. First, eight principal axis factors were extracted.[20] Then, the eight principal axis factors were rotated to simple structure by the orthogonal varimax criterion.[21]

RESULTS: THE DIMENSIONS EXPLICATED

Before looking at the rotated factors, a number of logically prior questions can be asked about the dimensional structure of the array of items generated to tap inner- and other-direction. To begin with, do the items belong to a relevantly coherent domain of content? As noted above, 23 items were excluded because they were not sufficiently correlated with the other items in the array. Nineteen of these were drawn from the Kassarjian study, and the other four were from the eight items included from the works of Bales and Miller and Swanson because the author thought they might be linked to inner- or other-direction. All of the items from the Gross study and the Archibald and Peterson study plus 28 of those from the Kassarjian study met the minimum criterion of being correlated more highly than $+.20$ with two other variables. The amount of item variance accounted for by the first eight principal axis factors ranged from a low of 13.2 per cent to a high of 60.7 per cent, with a mean of 41.1 per cent and a median of 43.4 per cent. Thus the 44 items do not comprise a *highly* integrated domain of content,[22] but this degree of "item saturation" is comparable with the results of other factor analytic studies of attitudes and value statements.[23]

[17] Over one-half of the respondents were 18 or 19 years of age.

[18] For a description of the technique of "blind-checking" used, see Richard A. Peterson, "A Technique for the Detection of Blind Checking in Questionnaire Research," *Educational and Psychological Research,* 21 (Summer, 1961), pp. 361–362.

[19] This rate of attrition is not low, but it is typical. Sofer used only 28 of 98 items (Sofer, *op. cit.,* p. 322). Kassarjian used only 25 of 36 items, even after these had been pretested (Kassarjian, *op. cit.,* p. 224).

[20] The decision to extract eight factors was made arbitrarily prior to the factor analysis.

[21] The varimax criterion was proposed by Henry F. Kaiser, "The Varimax Criterion for Analysis Rotation in Factor Analysis," *Psychometrica,* 23 (September, 1958), pp. 187–200.

[22] In the case of this result as in all others, reference is made to the data of this study alone, unless explicitly stated otherwise.

[23] Edgar F. Borgatta has noted in personal communication with the author that the

The next question which might be asked concerns the *singularity* of the domain. To the extent that items are related at all, are they related in such a way as to form one general factor; and if so, does this factor range from inner-direction on one pole to other-direction on the other? To answer this question, one needs to examine the proportion of variance explained by the first principal axis factor. If there is one single, general dimension, then the first factor will account for a major proportion of the explained variance. In fact, the first factor accounts for less than one quarter (22.8 per cent) of the variance explained by the first eight principal axis factors. The second factor accounts for 18.8 per cent, the third factor 13.9 per cent, the fourth factor 10.3 per cent, etc. Certainly, the results of this study reported so far suggest that there is no *single* inner-other dimension. Rather, there appear to be a number of dimensions, all, some, or none of which may be related to Riesman's characterizations.

From examination of the rotated factors, it appears that there are a *number* of dimensions related to inner- and other-direction. Overall support for this observation is supplied by the fact that no item preclassified as inner-directed appears with the same sign as an other-directed item loaded above +.40, on any of the eight factors.[24] In other words, when items defined *a priori* as related to inner-direction and other-direction have high loadings on the same factor, they appear with opposite signs.

The items with loadings greater than +.50 are given below in Table 1, grouped by factor. The four items with positive loadings on factor 1 had to do with a need for affiliation, and the one negative item, 47, together with item 38, suggests that the other pole of the dimension has to do with achievement, somewhat in the sense suggested by McClelland.[25] In a sense, factor 1 might be thought of as the "Carnegie" factor, ranging from Dale to Andrew.[26]

The items with high loadings on the second factor suggest the tough-minded, rugged individualist, reminiscent of the "independent" in the Asch conformity situation.[27] A concern for principle seems to characterize the items with high loadings in this second factor. In the case of factor 3, there is again a focus on achievement; however, it is not so individualistic. Rather, there is a singular focus on accomplishing the *task*, and the factor

---

only conditions in which item-saturations are notably higher is when values directly related to religious teaching are tapped.

[24] Only four such "cross-overs" appear loaded above ±30, and three of these are on the last three factors, which are least clearly related to Riesman's conception of social character.

[25] David C. McClelland *et al.*, *The Achievement Motive*, New York: Appleton-Century-Crofts, 1953; and McClelland, *The Achieving Society*, New York: Van Nostrand, 1961.

[26] The author is indebted to Alair Townsend for this suggestion.

[27] Solomon E. Asch, "Studies of Independence and Conformity: I. A Minority of One Against a Unanimous Majority," *Psychological Monographs*, 416 (1956).

TABLE 1

Items Defining the Eight Factors

Item Number	Factor Loading	Item
		FACTOR 1: AFFILIATION-ACHIEVEMENT
35	+.647	The most valuable talent a person can have is the ability to get along with others.
47	−.605	One should be concerned more about one's achievements than about making friends.
43	+.604	I believe that being able to make friends is a great accomplishment in and of itself.
46	+.597	The persons I admire most are those who have pleasing personalities.
38	+.512	It is more desirable to be popular and well-liked by everybody than to become famous in the field of one's choice.
		FACTOR 2: PRINCIPLE
57	−.634	One should hold on to his opinions even though they may be radically different from those of others.
62	−.606	You should always stand up for what *you* think is right.
22	−.567	To me it is very important what one *is* and *does* regardless of what others think.
11	−.501	I have more respect for the person who lives up to his ideals and principles regardless of what others think than for the person whose prime consideration is to be considerate of others and be well thought of.
		FACTOR 3: TASK FOCUS
36	−.556	What matters is what one can accomplish.
24	−.503	I dislike anyone who is loud and noisy.
18	−.502	I dislike anyone who doesn't take work seriously.
		FACTOR 4: EXTERNAL CONFORMITY-INDIVIDUALITY
32	+.711	I would feel conspicuous if I were not dressed the way most of my friends are dressed.
3	+.634	It is all right to be an individual but I wouldn't want to be very different from those around me
34	−.600	I like to wear clothes which stress my individuality and are not those which everybody else is wearing.
		FACTOR 5: EXTROVERSION-INTROVERSION
53	+.700	I'd rather be with a group of friends in my free time than to read an interesting book.
25	−.693	As leisure-time activity I would rather choose something you do alone such as painting or photography rather than something you do with people such as play cards or talk.
42	−.585	I am perfectly happy when I am left alone.
2	+.525	If I had more time, I'd rather spend more evenings out with my friends than staying at home doing things I enjoy.

TABLE 1—(Continued)

Item Number	Factor Loading	Item
	FACTOR 6: SELF-OTHER SOURCES OF SOCIALIZATION PATTERNS	
17	+.682	In bringing up children, parents should look at what other parents do with their children.
52	−.627	In bringing up children, parents should stick to their own ideas about how they want their children brought up regardless of what others do.
	FACTOR 7. PRAGMATISM	
34	−.693	Since there are no values which can be eternal, the only real values are those which meet the needs of the given moment.
27	−.553	The solution to almost any human problem should be based on the situation at the time, not on some general moral rule.
	FACTOR 8: STRUGGLE	
10	−.716	I like situations which are demanding.
21	−.677	I like situations which I have to struggle to master.
40	−.568	I am interested in new things and can live under almost any conditions.

suggests the "task leader" in the Bales studies of *ad hoc* group formation.[28]

The items with high loadings on factor 4 contrast individuality with conformity. Two of the items have to do with clothing, but the presence of item 3 on the factor indicates that it has to do with external conformity and external individuality more generally.[29] The concern with *externals* is at least as easily related to the tradition-directed shame at being "found out" as with the inner-directed anxiety to "fit in." Thus, we may have here an example of the transformation of historically earlier forms in the context of later forms of social character.

Three of the four items high on factor 5 deal explicitly with leisure. All of the items high on this factor contrast activity in groups with individual activity. This differentiation most clearly follows the distinction between

[28] The clearest view of different types of leaders in the Bales small-group situation is seen in Philip E. Slater, "Role Differentiation in Small Groups," *American Sociological Review*, 20 (June, 1955), pp. 300–310.

[29] Several authors have shown that there is a great difference between expressed, external conformity and more deeply committed conformity. See Halla Beloff, "Two Forms of Social Conformity: Acquiescence and Conventionality," *Journal of Abnormal and Social Psychology*, 56 (January, 1958), pp. 99–104; Martin L. Hoffman, "Some Psychodynamic Factors in Compulsive Conformity," *Journal of Abnormal and Social Psychology*, 48 (April, 1953), pp. 383–394; and Martin L. Hoffman, "Conformity as a Defense Mechanism and a Form of Resistance to Genuine Group Influence," *Journal of Personality*, 75 (May, 1957), pp. 412–414.

extroversion and introversion given by Carl Jung,[30] but without the neurotic overtones that these terms are given in much of the more recent empirical study of introversion-extroversion.[31]

Each of the factors discussed to this point has dealt with an aspect of inner-direction or other-direction or has contrasted one with the other. The same is not true of the remaining three factors, which, incidentally, account for relatively less variance than the five factors discussed so far. The top two items on factor 6 contrast inner-directed with other-directed sources of socialization patterns. However, two "inner-directed" socialization items have factor loadings of +.352 and +.305 respectively on the "other-directed" end of the factor. Thus, the dimension seems to have more to do with socialization *per se* than with inner- versus other-directed patterns of socialization.

Factor 7 is represented by two items expressing a pragmatic world view. All three of the Bales value profile items have loadings on this factor greater than ±.30, and only one other item (with a loading of +.479) has a loading greater than that magnitude. Thus, the dimension appears to be unrelated to Riesman's formulation. The three items defining factor 8 have to do with struggle of Faustian proportions. Each item was defined *a priori* as inner-directed. However, as Parsons and White[32] and Dahrendorf [33] have suggested, the degree of struggle and activism has not changed between inner- and other-direction so much as the goals of that struggle.[34] In the absence of items *differentiating* competition for material as over against social rewards, the poles of this factor cannot be defined as related to inner- or other-direction.

The purpose of this section has not been to present these factors as the definitive set of inner-other-direction-related dimensions. Rather, it has been first, to show that inner- to other-direction does not form a single, general factor, and second, to suggest some of the dimensional components of Riesman's formulation.

[30] Carl G. Jung, *Psychological Types*, New York: Harcourt, 1933.

[31] See for example Hans Jurgen Eysenck, *Dimensions of Personality*, London: Routledge and Kegan Paul, 1947.

[32] Talcott Parsons and Winston White, "The Link Between Character and Society," in Lipset and Lowenthal, editors, *op. cit.*, pp. 89–135.

[33] Ralf Dahrendorf, "Democracy Without Liberty: An Essay on the Politics of Other-directed Man," in Lipset and Lowenthal, editors, *op. cit.*, pp. 175–206.

[34] The conclusions of the Brodbeck *et al.*, study lend empirical support to the Parsons-Dahrendorf formulation. Clyde Kluckhohn, "Have There Been Discernible Shifts in American Values During the Past Generation? in Elting Elmore Morrison, editor, *The American Style: Essays in Value and Performance*, New York: Harper, 1958, and Seymour Martin Lipset, "A Changing American Character?" in Lipset and Lowenthal, editors, *op. cit.*, pp. 136–174, press this argument further to assert that the United States has been other-directed, at least since the time of the founding of the Republic.

RESULTS: DIMENSIONS AND
DEMOGRAPHIC VARIABLES

It is possible to *test* the assertion made above that the first five factors are related to the Riesman social character types. Riesman makes a number of assertions about the social concomitants of each of the character types. For example, other-directeds should be most pronounced among young, well-to-do, urban professionals. If our five factors are related to inner-direction and other-direction, then, to cite just one example, persons scoring near the other-direction end of each factor should come from families of higher socio-economic status (SES) than persons scoring near the inner-direction end of the factor.

The 539 respondents were given a score on each of the five dimensions by summing their responses to each of the items with loadings on the factor greater than +.50 in such a way that a low score indicated an other-while a high score indicated an inner-directed response. These five sets of dimension scores were then divided into octile ranges and the dimension scores cross-tabulated with each of the eleven demographic variables about which we had data from the questionnaire. In this way, 55 tables were generated, each showing the relationship between a factor and a demographic variable. From visual inspection, it was quite apparent that there was no clear trend of any sort relating the two sorts of data—the one characterological, the other social structural—with each other.[35]

Several interpretations of this lack of a relationship might be advanced. First, the link between social character and social structure posited by Riesman may not hold. This alternative seems unlikely in the light of the positive findings of other studies.[36] Another interpretation of our results is that Riesman is right, but our measures have not correctly operationalized his conceptions of social character types. This conclusion seems likely. In other words, *none* of the five dimensions is related to inner-other-direction; or rather, inner- and other-direction are not dimensions in anything approaching the factor analytic meaning of this term.

Rather than inner- and other-direction being viewed as *dimensions*, they may be conceived of as two discrete cells in a *property-space*[37] defined by a number of dimensions.[38] The available data could be used to

[35] In certain instances there was some variability. However, the nature of the sample does not justify minute tests of significance. Looking at the overall trend, it is fair to state that no difference stands up for any dimension across all demographic variables or for any demographic variable across all factors.

[36] A number of studies report significant findings. For findings relating to demographic variables, see especially Kassarjian, *op. cit.*, and Centers, *op. cit.*

[37] For an illustration of the concept of "property-space," see Allan H. Barton, "The Concept of Property-Space in Social Research," in Paul F. Lazarsfeld and Morris Rosenberg, editors, *The Language of Social Research*, New York: Free Press, pp. 40–53.

[38] This conception of inner- and other-direction is suggested by Gutman and Wrong, *op. cit.*, and by Riley, Riley, and Moore, *op. cit.*, Sofer, *op. cit.*, p. 342 ff., refers to

test, at least provisionally, the fruitfulness of this conception of Riesman's typology. By combining the scores of individuals on the five dimensions which seem to be related to the Riesman typology (factors 1 through 5), it is possible to assign a single summary score to each individual. If, as suggested here, inner- and other-direction correspond with two of the cells in the property space defined by the five factors, then the individuals scoring at the extremes on the combined score fall into the inner- and other-direction cells and should differ from each other on a number of demographic variables in the ways suggested by Riesman. In the section which follows, the ten per cent of the respondents at each extreme on the summary score were compared with each other on every one of the demographic variables available in the questionnaire. It is not always easy to infer from *The Lonely Crowd* what demographic correlates of characterological differences should be expected; therefore, the emphasis in the discussion which follows is placed on the total set of comparisons and not on the comparisons separately.[39]

The data on father's socio-economic status (SES) conform to Riesman's prediction. Inner-directeds are more common among those low in SES, and other-directeds are more common among those high in SES.[40] When specific occupations of respondents' fathers are noted, the children of professionals tend to be other-directed more often than others. This tendency is less marked for the free professionals than among technicians and engineers; children of managers, as distinct from owners, tend to be other-directed more often, while children of unskilled blue-collar workers tend more often to be inner-directed. The only occupational group to violate the prediction derivable from Riesman is the skilled blue-collar; their children were predominantly other-directed. No differences were found between inner-directed and other-directed groups in entrepreneurial versus bureaucratic source of family income.

Riesman characterizes the other-directeds as highly mobile; however, no difference was found between the two groups in the number of homes in which they had lived over their lives. However, in line with Riesman's predictions, other-directeds more often than inner-directeds came from large urban centers and towns growing rapidly during the period 1940–1960. In addition, inner-directeds were somewhat more likely to have traveled a great distance to attend the University.

Respondents from Catholic families tended to be more inner-directed, those from Jewish families equally divided, and Protestants to be predominantly other-directed (although there is considerable variability between the various Protestant groups). Those coming from families professing no

---

subscales of inner- and other-direction. However, the discussion focuses on correlates of these sub-scales and does not enumerate the items which comprise the scales themselves.

[39] A complete set of tables is available from the author upon request.

[40] There were no differences between the two samples as to sex or age of respondents. Thus, the findings cannot be attributed to variation in these variables.

religion were the most predominantly inner-directed. There are a number of indications that patterns more clearly separating the two groups could be constructed. For example, Catholic males more often were inner-directed and females more often other-directed, but the opposite was true in the case of Jews.

Data reported so far referred to gross differences in socialization environment. Data were also gathered on several variables representing recent choices made by the respondents. These include academic major and college residence. Majors with over-representation in inner-direction included the natural sciences, humanities, and social work (there were no engineers in the 10 per cent samples); those preparing for service occupations (except social work) and commerce students were over-represented among the other-directeds; psychology majors were over-represented among the inner-directeds, but other social science majors were under-represented at *both* extremes of social character. The data on college residence fits Riesman's conception nicely. Other-directeds more often live among their peers in the large, college-owned dormitories, while inner-directeds are more often found in the privately owned, and often status specific, "independent houses," private homes, and apartments.[41]

While sex and age were not confounding explanatory variables, data collected on the final item of the questionnaire suggest one possible source of variance in the results other than the social character of the respondent. To the question asking whether respondents had read David Riesman's *The Lonely Crowd* or William H. Whyte's *The Organization Man*,[42] nine inner-directeds and six other-directeds said "yes" to the latter, but more significantly, nine inner-directeds and only two other-directeds said "yes" to having read the Riesman book. Whether readers of the book become more inner-directed (at least at the level of ideology)[43] or inner-directeds read more books cannot be ascertained from our data, but this question of selective sensitivity of the variables being tested is a subject deserving of investigation.[44]

[41] Kassarjian, *op. cit.*, p. 223, reports data on many of these same variables, and the findings of the two studies are quite parallel in that variations in recent choices made by the respondents are more highly related to inner-other-directed character types than are the more gross differences in socialization environment. A study currently in process under the author's direction relates inner- and other-directed character types to peer versus parent socialization environments in much greater detail than reported in any studies published heretofore.

[42] William H. Whyte, Jr., *The Organization Man*, New York: Simon and Schuster, 1956.

[43] This possibility has been suggested by Eric Larrabee, "David Riesman and His Readers," in Lipset and Lowenthal, editors, *op. cit.*, pp. 404–418.

[44] For example, it would be interesting to learn whether readers of Riesman's book thought that our items were related to the character types, as well as how they conceive of themselves. The only data using inner-other *self*-conception does not compare these with data on character types evaluated by the investigator. See Olmsted, *op. cit.*

The data outlined above, while not showing all of the expected relationships between social character and demographic variables, add weight to the suggestion that inner- and other-direction might profitably be conceptualized not as poles of a single dimension but rather as two cells among many in a multidimensional property space.

SUMMARY

Most of the work published heretofore has assumed that inner-direction and other-direction form poles of a single dimension. This investigation was undertaken to explore empirically the dimensional structure of the social character typology presented by David Riesman. The factor analytic manipulation of items generated to tap inner-direction and other-direction suggests that these conceptions are not ends of a *unidimensional* scale. Rather, the data of the study suggest that they are *cells* in a relatively complex property-space definable in terms of relatively familiar concepts such as extroversion-introversion, external conformity-independence, and the like. Because of lack of correlation of these dimensions with demographic variables which Riesman asserts are correlates of inner-direction and other-direction, it is asserted that no *one* of the dimensions in itself can be used to represent the character types. When dimension scores are combined in the way suggested by the property-space model, however, the two groups of individuals representing the inner-direction and other-direction cells do show a number of the demographic characteristics attributed to them by Riesman. This finding lends added weight to the suggestion that inner-direction and other-direction are cells of a property-space rather than poles of a single dimension.

For Further Reading

BOOKS

Lipset, S. M. and Lowenthal, L. (Eds.). *Culture and social character.* Glencoe, Illinois: The Free Press, 1961.

A compilation of essays evaluating Riesman's *The lonely crowd.*

Riesman, D. in collaboration with Denney, R., and Glazer, N. *The lonely crowd: A study of changing American character.* New Haven: Yale University Press, 1950. [See especially pp. 5–25. In the paperback edition (Doubleday-Anchor) see especially pp. 23–43.]

In this work, Riesman presented what has since become his famous personality types: Tradition-directed, Inner-directed, and Other-directed. He related these types to various stages of the demographic process. Also available in paperback by Doubleday-Anchor.

ARTICLES

Adler, K. Art films and eggheads. *Studies in Public Communication*, 1959, 2 7–15. SA 10, A3961.

Hypothesis (not supported) that Riesman's inner-directed type would be the regular patron of art theatres, while the other-directed type would be the casual patron.

Centers, R. Social character and conformity: a differential in susceptibility to social influence. *J. soc. Psychol.*, 1963, 60 (2), 343–349. PA 38, 4191.

Hypothesis (supported) that other-directed persons are more susceptible to social influence.

Centers, R. and L. Social character types and beliefs about childrearing. *Child Developm.*, 1963, 34 (1), 69–79. PA 38, 5798.

Hypothesis (sustained) that other-directed types would foster dependency in their children and favor permissive childrearing.

Gaier, E. L. and White, W. F. Modes of conformity and career selection of rural and urban high school seniors. *J. soc. Psychol.*, 1965, 67 (2), 379–391.

Rural subjects appeared to follow the old-fashioned virtues (that is, more inner-directed), while urban youth were more other-directed.

Heberle, R. A note on Riesman's "The Lonely Crowd." *Amer. J. Sociol.*, 1956, 62 (1), 34–36. SA 3, 4235.

Relates Riesman's categories to Weber's traditional, value-rational, and purposive-rational social orientation; suggests that geographical and vertical mobility may be more related to changing character structure than is the population curve.

Kallen, D. J. Inner direction, other direction, and social integration setting. *Hum. Relat.*, 1963, 16 (1), 75–87. PA 38, 2477.

The shift from inner- to other-direction was found more often in a bureaucratic than in the entrepreneurial setting; more often among boys than among girls.

Kassarjian, H. H. and Waltraud, M. Occupational interests, social values and social character, *J. counsel. Psychol.*, 1965, *12* (1), 48–54. PA 39, 10055.

Inner- and other-directed personalities exhibited different occupational interests and different values (on the Allport-Vernon-Lindzey Study of Values scale).

Littunen, Y. and Gaier, E. L. Occupational values and morals of conformity. *J. soc. Psychol.*, 1960, *51* (1), 123–133. PA 36, 3GE23L.

Hypothesis that "capitalistic values" (individualism and self-initiative) would be related to inner direction was not sustained on a sample of 271 Finnish students.

Oppenheimer, F. M. Lament for unbought grace: The novels of John P. Marquand. *Antioch Review*, 1958, *18* (1), 41–61. SA 8, 7560.

Nine novels are analyzed for their treatment of the managerial elite; later ones present alternative value patterns to *The Late George Apley*—the solid, inner-directed man.

Riley, M., and J. Adolescent values and the Riesman typology: an empirical analysis. Chapter 16 in S. M. Lipset and L. Lowenthal (eds.), *Culture and social character*. New York: The Free Press, 1961. 370–386. SA 10, A2252.

A study of 2500 middle-class New Jersey high school students; other-directed tendency of the peer group is only one role of the adolescent.

Rogers, M. A plea for the study of autonomy. *Sociometry*, 1955, *18* (4), 497–500. SA 5, 3397.

Most research has been on the "other-directed"; often laboratory groups.

Williams, W. Inner-directedness and other-directedness in new perspective. *Sociol. Quart.*, 1964, *5* (3), 193–220. SA 13, B 4920.

Women applying for a job with a corporation scored significantly higher on other-directedness than did women already employed.

Wrong, D. H., Riesman and the age of sociology. *Commentary*, 1956, *21* (4), 331–338. SA 5, 2891.

A thoughtful critique.

Zeleznik, C. Inner-and-other directedness of the American abroad. *Phylon*, 1958, *19* (3), 258–267. SA 10, A1226.

The traditional-directed individual is not found abroad except under duress.

Chapter Three

Authoritarianism

If the major criterion for significant contribution to the scientific community is the number of research projects which a book stimulates, then surely *The Authoritarian Personality*,[1] published in 1950, would rank high in twentieth-century social science literature. Part of the fascination with the topic is undoubtedly related to the recent history of our world, especially the events of World War II; part of the interest can be explained as endemic in a democratic society. Roger Brown[2] has observed that, "*The Authoritarian Personality* had the greatest possible relevance to the social issues of its day." Yet after allowance is made for these cultural factors, there is an enduring theoretical interest in the typology presented by T. W. Adorno and his colleagues.

The *authoritarian personality* syndrome may be described as follows:

1. There is a rigid adherence to conventional, middle-class values.
2. There is a tendency toward submission to, and the uncritical acceptance of, the moral authorities of the in-group.
3. There is a tendency to reject and punish people who violate conventional values.
4. There is opposition to the subjective, the imaginative, the tender-minded side of life.
5. There is a belief in fatalism.
6. There is a tendency toward accepting conventional stereotypes.
7. There is a tendency to identify with power figures.
8. There is generalized hostility in the personality.
9. There is projection of unconscious emotional impulses and exaggerated concern with sexual "goings-on." [3]

---

[1] Adorno, T. W., Frenkel-Brunswik, E., Levinson, D. J., and Sanford, R. N. *The authoritarian personality*. New York: Harper and Brothers, 1950.

[2] Brown, R. *Social psychology*. New York: Free Press, 1965, p. 478. For an excellent discussion of the development of the authoritarianism concept and scales, and a review of the critiques, see pp. 477–544.

[3] This synopsis made from Adorno *et al.*, *op. cit.*, pp. 228 ff.

The scale which Adorno and his colleagues developed to measure authoritarianism (specifically, the "F" or Fascist scale) has been utilized in a multiplicity of settings. From the almost innumerable articles available, three have been selected which seem most productive of critical analysis. In the first, Edwin Barker reports that since the original study was solely concerned with authoritarianism in extreme conservatives or "rightists," the F scale is biased in that it measures rightist authoritarianism, not authoritarianism in general. He found Rokeach's Dogmatism scale[4] more adequate for measuring authoritarianism as a general personality characteristic, although the rightists in his university sample were still more likely to be dogmatic than the leftists. With this correction, Barker argues that the concept has proved viable and fruitful.

In the second selection, Rhyne presents an argument for a sociological interpretation of prejudice as superior to the interpretation of prejudice in terms of the authoritarian personality (which he rather sweepingly characterizes as the psychological approach, overlooking the fact that there are several other psychological interpretations of the prejudiced personality). His forceful confrontation of two theories is instructive and suggestive of an approach that might well have much wider application.

Finally, Berkowitz and Wolkon review the predominant criticisms of the authoritarianism scale: that much of the variation in authoritarianism scores and hence many of the correlations between it and other variables is due primarily to acquiescence in the respondents—i. e., the tendency to say "yes" to items. They present a method of overcoming this problem— the forced choice format of scales. This article then is of use not only for updating the concept of authoritarianism, but also for the contribution which these men and their predecessors have made to scale construction in general.

[4] Rokeach, M. *The open and closed mind.* New York: Basic Books, 1960.

7

Authoritarianism of the Political Right, Center, and Left

EDWIN N. BARKER

After the California studies of the late 1940's (Adorno, *et al.*, 1950) the belief became widespread that a personality syndrome called authoritarianism had been isolated and that it could be measured by the F scale. The California group initially studied anti-Semitism and ethnocentrism. After considerable work on these subjects they decided to construct a scale which would measure prejudice without appearing to have this aim. Specifically, they wanted a scale which would correlate highly with their scales for anti-Semitism and ethnocentrism. In addition, in line with their evolving theory of underlying personality characteristics of the anti-Semitic and ethnocentric individual, they hoped that the new scale would yield a valid estimate of general antidemocratic tendencies at the personality level. The F scale resulted.

The appearance of *The Authoritarian Personality* in 1950 stimulated a tremendous amount of further research and discussion. The authors were quite open in admitting that they emphasized the study of pre-fascist tendencies primarily and general authoritarianism only secondarily. However, many researchers have used the F scale as though it were a measure of general authoritarianism rather than rightist authoritarianism—seemingly forgetting one of the original purposes of the scale (as an indirect measure of anti-Semitism). Two studies are reported here which attempt to clarify the relations between authoritarianism and the F (Fascism) scale, between authoritarianism and political militancy and political "extremeness."

THE NEW YORK STUDY[1]

In 1957, data were gathered from 160 graduate students in the New York City area. The large majority of the sample were in their second year

Reprinted from *Journal of Social Issues*, 19, 2 (April 1963), 63–74, by permission of the author and the publisher.

[1] Based upon Barker, E. N. Authoritarianism of the political right, center, and left. Unpublished Ph.D. dissertation, Teachers College, Columbia University, 1958. The advisor for the study was Laurence F. Shaffer. The author is grateful to him for his help.

of graduate work in psychology or education. The following instruments were administered: The California Politico-Economic Conservatism Scale (PEC) was used to group the subjects as politically leftish, rightish, or middle of the road (Adorno, *et al.*, 1950, pg. 163). High scores on the 15 item scale signify acceptance of rightist ideology. A second measure used to form experimental groups was Rokeach's Dogmatism Scale, Form E (Rokeach, 1960). There is some evidence that it is closer to the concept of general authoritarianism than the F scale. The Dogmatism scale, unlike F, is not obviously related to political ideology. With the Dogmatism scale and PEC it was possible to group the subjects by political position and by level of dogmatism. The groups could then be compared as to F scale scores and scores on measures of authoritarian qualities. Form 60A of the F scale was used—a thirty-item form first published by Gough (1951).

The criteria for authoritarianism were selected in accordance with several conditions. Scales were selected which appeared to measure variables accepted as central to the authoritarian syndrome. No scale was considered unless it was known to have a significant relationship with the F scale. An attempt was made to choose measures which were free from bias to the Right or Left. The following measures of authoritarian qualities were administered: The Stereotype Test, constructed by Siegel (1954) to measure tendencies toward over-simplification and over-generalization with respect to groups of people. The Test for Tolerance-Intolerance of Cognitive Ambiguity (TICA), constructed by Siegel (1954) to measure the need to structure even when inappropriate. The sentence completion test for Anti-Intraception constructed by Hanfman and Getzels (1953) and modified by Dorris, Levinson, and Hanfman (1954) to measure the tendency to deny the self-relevance of one's own completions. The sentence completion test of Attitude to Authority, constructed by Mishler (1953) to measure the extent to which authority figures and demands are submitted to or rejected. The Opinionation Scale, constructed by Rokeach (1960) to measure the tendency toward intolerance and rejection of persons holding different beliefs. The scale is scored for Left Opinionation and Right Opinionation as well as for Total Opinionation. The Toughminded Scale was also included. It had been described by Eysenck (1955) as being essentially a measure of general authoritarianism.

The scale for Censorship Tendency was constructed for this study. The scale consists of names of well-known public figures associated with the political left and right and a list of organizations easily identified by their titles as being leftist or rightist. The subjects were instructed to indicate any of the persons listed whose tape recorded speeches they thought would be unwise for presentation on the radio and to indicate any of the organizations whose leaders should not be allowed to appear on television. The scale is scored for Left Censorship (censoring rightists) and Right Censoring (censoring leftists) as well as for Total Censorship.

The hypotheses of the study were as follows:

1. The F scale is biased toward authoritarianism of the right.
2. Authoritarians of the political right, center, and left are similar on measures of general authoritarianism.
3. Authoritarians of the political right and left differ in the manner in which they express their authoritarian qualities, i.e., in the "direction" or content of their authoritarianism.

RESULTS

An intercorrelation matrix was computed for the ten instruments. It was evident from the matrix that Eysenck's Toughminded Scale had no relationship with authoritarianism within this sample. The only significant correlation between Toughmindedness and the other nine scales was with PEC (−.33 indicating a negative relation between toughmindedness and conservatism). The results are at variance with Eysenck's findings. In a personal communication in 1958, Eysenck offered the hypothesis that the results may be accounted for by the difference in intelligence and education between these subjects and his. At any rate, the Toughminded Scale is clearly unrelated to the other scales and it is not included in the following analysis.

The matrix of correlations between the eight measures of authoritarianism is composed of 28 correlation coefficients. Sixteen of those coefficients are positive and significant beyond the .01 level. Even when correlations between all positively stated and similarly constructed questionnaires are ignored, 12 of the correlations are significant. The theory of an authoritarian syndrome is supported—the authoritarian measures do cluster.

After correlational analyses, the questionnaires were divided into six groups. The abbreviations in parentheses will be used to signify the experimental groups: Thirty dogmatic rightists, above the mean on Dogmatism and PEC (DR); twenty dogmatic middle of the roaders, above the mean on Dogmatism and within the semi-interquartile range on PEC (DM); thirty dogmatic leftists, above the mean on Dogmatism and below the mean on PEC (DL); thirty nondogmatic rightists, below the mean on Dogmatism and above the mean on PEC (NDR); twenty nondogmatic middle of the roaders, below the mean on Dogmatism and within the semi-interquartile range on PEC (NDM); thirty nondogmatic leftists, below the mean on Dogmatism and below the mean on PEC (NDL).

As for the hypotheses, the first one was that the F scale is biased toward authoritarianism of the right. The F scale had the following correlations: with PEC, .41 (significant beyond the .001 level); with Right Censorship and Right Opinionation, .57 and .55 (significant beyond the .001 level); and with Left Censorship and Left Opinionation .15 and −.22 (not significant). In addition, if the F scale is biased, one would expect the dogmatic leftists to score much lower on the F scale than the dogmatic rightists. The respective mean F scores were 97 and 120 (*t* test significant beyond the .001 level). It is clear that the F scale measures rightist authoritarianism quite well but does not discriminate left authoritarianism.

The second hypothesis was that authoritarians of whatever political position would obtain similar scores on the authoritarian criteria. Table 1

TABLE 1

Group Means on Authoritarian Criteria

| | Mean of Group | | | | | |
Scale	DR	DM	DL	NDR	NDM	NDL
Intolerance of						
Ambiguity	14.9	15.3	14.2	13.1	10.5	11.1
Anti-intraception	12.3	10.6	11.6	9.6	9.5	11.3
Censorship	12.3	9.9	13.9	9.3	10.5	8.7
Stereotype	9.1	9.5	7.6	6.1	4.1	3.6
Opinionation	146.6	158.8	151.1	133.2	123.3	120.2
Submissiveness	17.5	14.8	14.6	15.5	13.1	12.8

presents the means of the six groups. Except for the case of Submission (Attitude to Authority) there were no significant differences between the means of DR, DM, and DL on the authoritarian criteria. Submission was included in the analysis although it did not meet the expectation that it would be unrelated to PEC. Submission and PEC correlated .40 which is significant beyond the .001 level. On Submission, DR has a significantly higher mean than DL (.01 level). The second hypothesis is supported by five of the six predictions—the dogmatists of the left, center, and right are similar in their high scores on the authoritarian criteria. In addition, when all dogmatists are combined and all nondogmatists are combined and the means on the authoritarian criteria are compared, the dogmatists receive higher scores in each case. See Table 2.

TABLE 2

Means and Standard Deviations of Dogmatists and Nondogmatists on Authoritarian Criteria

| | Dogmatists | | Nondogmatists | | | |
Scale	*Mean*	*SD*	*Mean*	*SD*	*t*	*Significance of Difference*
Intolerance of						
Ambiguity	14.7	6.4	11.7	8.0	2.59	.01
Anti-intraception	11.6	5.7	10.2	6.3	1.50	.07
Censorship	12.7	8.0	9.4	7.8	2.61	.01
Stereotype	8.6	7.4	4.7	5.9	3.62	.001
Opinionation	151.3	20.6	129.6	26.0	5.80	.001
Submissiveness	15.7	4.4	13.8	4.1	2.76	.01

The third hypothesis was that authoritarians of the left and right would differ in the manner in which they express their authoritarian qualities. We have already seen that they differed on the conservatively slanted items of the F scale. In addition, t tests of mean differences on the subscales of the Censorship and Opinionation scales revealed the following: The dogmatic leftists had significantly higher scores than the dogmatic rightists on Left Censorship (.01 level) and Left Opinionation (.001 level). The dogmatic rightists had significantly higher scores than the dogmatic leftists on Right Censorship (.03 level) and Right Opinionation (.001 level). Thus, while the authoritarians of the left and right are *similar* in being high an Opinionation and Censorship Tendency, they are *different* in the direction of their censoring and opinionation.

Unfortunately, most studies of authoritarianism, including the one reported above, have correlated paper and pencil tests with other paper and pencil tests. While such studies are useful, it is desirable to bring our concepts to a test in "real life" whenever possible—to find suitable criterion groups, to test our predictive ability for example with types of political action or lack of it. In 1963 at The Ohio State University, such an opportunity presented itself.

THE OHIO STUDY

Columbus, Ohio, is commonly known as a rather conservative city politically. In the recent past it has generally voted Republican, in the last election overwhelmingly supporting a Governor running on a "balance the budget" platform. On the other hand, the Ohio State University has numbers of outspoken liberals as well as conservatives on the faculty. Thus, the University and the city are prone to a great deal of political controversy. In the months preceding this study, several controversies were prominent, the most intense one concerning the University's rules for allowing outside speakers on the campus. Within the past year the administration had refused to allow several speakers to appear on the campus to speak against the House Un-American Activities Committee. These actions touched off a great deal of political activity on the part of both faculty and students.

A student organization I will call The Leftists, numbering about 30 juniors and seniors, was quite active in the controversy, inviting more speakers to test the administration's position, putting out a daily mimeographed newsletter, picketing the administration building, even attempting to hire a plane to fly over the commencement exercises dragging a banner saying "Free Speech Now." Another student organization I will call The Rightists, numbering about 30 juniors and seniors, was not quite as active in this particular controversy. However, the group was quite active on other issues, inviting conservative speakers to forums and publishing regular ads in the school newspaper extolling the virtues of free enterprise, with cartoons depicting Good Capitalism, Evil Communism, and Sneaky Socialism.

Data were gathered from 26 of the Rightists and 29 of the Leftists. The instruments were administered individually by an undergraduate who knew the members of the groups and could reassure them concerning the anonymity of their responses. For a comparison group of non-organized juniors and seniors, data were gathered from 61 other students. The following instruments were administered to all groups: The PEC, the F scale, the Dogmatism scale, a revised and shortened form of the Censorship scale, and a political self-labelling scale, scored as follows: "Extreme Leftist" (1); "Socialist" (2); "Liberal Democrat" (3); "Democrat" (4); "Republican" (5); "Conservative Republican" (6); "States Rights" (7); "Extreme Rightist" (8).

The hypotheses of the study were as follows:

1. There is a strong relationship between the F scale and political ideology.
2. There is no relationship between authoritarianism (Dogmatism and Censorship) and political ideology.
3. There is no relationship between authoritarianism and extremity of political position.
4. There is no relationship between authoritarianism and degree of political activity (organized vs. non-organized students).

RESULTS

Table 3 presents the means of the three groups on the scales as well as the significance of the differences between the means.

The organized Rightists had an item mean on PEC of 5.5. On the

TABLE 3

Ohio State University Means

Scales	Organized Rightists		Non-organized Students		Organized Leftists
Conservatism (PEC)	82.7	(.0001)*	62.4	(.0001)*	39.9
F Scale	107.5	(.001)	89.4	(.001)	64.3
Dogmatism	150.9	(.02)	139.2	(N.S.)	135.8
Left Censorship	2.17	(N.S.)	2.12	(N.S.)	1.00
Right Censorship	5.21	(.01)	2.68	(.001)	0.12
Total Censorship	7.38	(N.S.)	4.84	(.01)	1.12
Political Self-Label	6.12	(.001)	4.32	(.001)	2.23

* The numbers in parentheses give the level of significance of the *t* tests computed between adjacent group means. Differences between Rightists and Leftists on Dogmatism reached the .01 level; on Left Censorship, not significant; and on Total Censorship, .001 level.

political self-labelling scale they primarily labelled themselves "Conservative Republican," and secondarily as "Extreme Rightist." The non-organized comparison group of students had an item mean on PEC of 4.4 and labelled themselves primarily as "Republican" or "Democrat." The organized Leftists had a PEC item mean of 2.6. They primarily labelled themselves "Socialist," and secondarily as "Liberal Democrat." The differentiation between the groups is striking. There is very little overlap between the groups on both PEC and the self-labelling scale. The PEC scale has a possible range of item means from 1.0 to 7.0. If we call subjects who have item means between 3.1 and 4.9, "moderates," and subjects scoring outside that range, political "extremists," we find the following: The organized Rightists and Leftists are 71 per cent extremists and 29 per cent moderates, while the non-organized students are 92 per cent moderates and only 8 per cent extremists!

This picture is even more pronounced on the self-labelling scale. The student political organizations seem to be composed mainly of students with highly crystallized and polarized political attitudes while the comparison group of students is strikingly low on deviants from the absolute center of the political scales. The comparison group of non-organized students was drawn from classes in the Education College. Their PEC mean (62.4) is comparable to those reported in other studies of college students, however their standard deviation (3.08) is smaller than any the author could find in the literature. It is known that PEC means vary according to college major and occupation. The present finding raises the question as to whether standard deviations vary in a similar manner. The finding may mean that Education students are an unusually homogeneous and politically moderate population. On the other hand, it may mean that students who have given no overt sign of political commitment by participating in political action are so uninformed that they answer political attitude scales inconsistently thereby receiving "middle of the road" scores. If the latter is so, studies (such as the New York Study reported above) which have used unselected college students for determining the correlates of political attitudes have less meaning than has been attributed to them. Before we make statements about correlates of being a "liberal" or a "conservative," we need to ascertain whether we actually have any such people in our sample.

The first hypothesis stated that the F scale is strongly related to political ideology. Table 3 indicates that the Rightists have a very significantly higher mean on the F scale than the Leftists. The Spearman rank order coefficient was computed for the F scale and PEC scores of the 61 non-organized students. R equalled .50 which is significant beyond the .01 level. In addition, if the F scale is biased toward conservatism, one would expect authoritarians of the right to score significantly higher on the F scale than authoritarians of the left. Those Rightist and Leftist subjects who scored above 150 on Dogmatism were compared as to their F scale means. The dogmatic Rightists had a mean F scale score of 114 while the dogmatic Leftists had a mean of 82. The difference is significant beyond the .001 level. It is clear that the F scale is measuring rightist authoritarianism—not general authoritarianism.

The second hypothesis stated that there is no relationship between general authoritarianism and political ideology. The findings in the New York Study appeared to justify using Dogmatism and Censorship as indices of general authoritarianism. Spearman rank order coefficients were computed for Dogmatism and PEC scores on the non-organized students. R equalled .07, not significant censorship, and PEC were also not significantly related. However, Table 3 indicates that the Rightists received significantly higher Dogmatism scores than the other two groups. In addition, on Total Censorship the Leftists received significantly lower scores than the other two groups. Thus, the second hypothesis is not supported. Although the differences are not as great as on the F scale, the Rightists do have significantly higher scores on general authoritarianism. How does one explain the contradiction between these findings and those of the New York Study? Or the contradiction between the insignificant R's of the unorganized students in this study and the significant differences between the groups?

It appears that when one is dealing with subjects who range only from mildly conservative to mildly liberal, one will find no apparent relation between authoritarianism and conservatism. However, when the range is extended—when one has some *committed* conservatives and Leftists in the sample, the differences in general authoritarianism begin to show. On Dogmatism for example, extreme Leftists, moderate Leftists, and moderate Rightists have approximately the same means. However, the Dogmatism mean of the extreme Rightists goes up considerably. Similarly, when moderate Leftists and moderate Rightists are compared on the scale for Censorship Tendency there is little difference. However, when extreme Rightists and Leftists are added, the difference becomes significant—primarily because the committed Rightists and Leftists censor Rightists about equally, while only the committed Rightists censor Leftists (Table 3). General authoritarianism is more associated with Rightist ideology than with Leftist ideology, although not as significantly as in "pre-fascist tendency" (F scale).

The third hypothesis was that there is no relationship between authoritarianism and extremity of political position. Some writers (Alexander, 1951; Bonnard, 1954; Drake, 1955; Taylor, 1960) have postulated an identity of the extremists of the left and right, implying the rigid, intolerant, authoritarian attitudes would be more common among "radicals" of whatever political persuasion. The New York Study had shown no evidence in support of such an hypothesis. All of the Ohio State subjects who scored between 46 and 74 on PEC were combined to test this hypothesis. There were 72 of these "moderates." The remaining 44 subjects were combined as the "extremists." The two groups were compared as to mean scores on all scales. There were *no* significant differences. The third hypothesis is supported. No relationship was found between authoritarianism *or* pre-fascist tendency and "political extremity" *per se*.

It is often implied in the press and popular literature that rigid, intolerant, authoritarian attitudes will be found more often among politically active, militant, committed persons than among less militant, presumably less emotionally involved and therefore more "rational" persons. The fourth hypothesis was that there is no relationship between authoritarianism and degree of political activity (organized vs. non-organized students). The Rightists and the Leftists in this study appear to merit the adjectives "active, militant, and committed," e.g., manning picket lines, planning elaborate programs to publicize their beliefs, turning out political handbills, fund raising, and lobbying both in the university and beyond. To test this hypothesis the combined Rightists and Leftists were compared to the non-organized students on all scales. There were no significant differences on any of the measures. The hypothesis is supported.

It has been established that in this study the political Right not only has many more high F's than the Left, as was expected, but also the Right has more general authoritarians as measured by Dogmatism. For a final analysis, the dogmatists and nondogmatists in each political organization were compared. Taking a score of 150 as the cutting point on the Dogmatism scale, dogmatists comprised 17 per cent of the Leftists, 28 per cent of the non-organized students and 53 per cent of the Rightists. Due to the small numbers of subjects in this analysis, the following statements must be taken as suggestive only. The dogmatic Rightists do not differ from the nondogmatic Rightists in the "extremeness" of their political position. The dogmatic Rightists censor more Leftists than the nondogmatic Rightists, and are higher on the F scale, especially those items indicating authoritarian aggression, tendency toward projectivity, and emphasis on power and toughness.

The dogmatic Leftists do not differ from the nondogmatic Leftists in the "extremeness" of their political position. The dogmatic Leftists censor more Rightists than the nondogmatic Leftists, and are higher on the F scale, especially those items indicating authoritarian aggression, projectivity, and power and toughness (like the dogmatic Rightists).

The dogmatic Rightists score higher on the F scale than the dogmatic Leftists. On Censorship, an intriguing result was found here as well as in the New York study: Dogmatic Leftists censor only Rightists, while dogmatic Rightists censor both Leftists and Rightists, thus receiving a total Censorship score.

DISCUSSION

Work in the area of the authoritarian personality has been going on now for about 15 years. Taking into account the material presented in

Christie & Jahoda (1954), in the review of the F scale literature (Titus & Hollander, 1957), the work of Rokeach, and the studies reported here, let us consider what we have learned. The first thing we can say with confidence is that the concept of an authoritarian syndrome has proven to be viable and fruitful. The expected clustering of variables does occur across groups, across time, and across geographical areas. Despite the deserved criticism of the details of the original California study, their major concept has been confirmed. Let us examine seven broad questions as to what we have come to know about the concept. We will consider the questions in a descending order of certainty, i.e., about the first questions we have a great deal of evidence and relatively sure answers. About the later questions we know less and our answers must be more tentative.

1. What is the relation of general authoritarianism to the F scale? It appears to be clear now that the F scale measures rightist authoritarianism (implicit pre fascist tendencies) primarily, general authoritarianism somewhat, and leftist authoritarianism not at all.

2. What is the relation of general authoritarianism to the liberal-conservative continuum? Before answering this question a word needs to be said about the concept of a unitary left-right dimension. Despite the logically valid criticisms of the concept of such a continuum, the fact remains that such a continuum exists in the minds of the general public and they generally (with the exception of the highly sophisticated) place themselves on such a continuum quite easily and with certainty. As long as this is so, the dimension "exists," and not only *can* be used as a variable, but *should* be used as a variable. Now, to the question. It appears to be established that there is somewhat greater compatibility between authoritarian traits and rightist ideology than between authoritarianism and leftist ideology. However, the correlation of authoritarianism and conservatism is not nearly so strong as was thought immediately after the California studies when the only measure available was the F scale. We now can state with confidence that it is quite possible to discriminate authoritarians at any point on the political continuum.

3. What is the relation of general authoritarianism to extremity of political position? The evidence appears to be that there is no relation. One can find authoritarians equally among "moderates" and "radicals." However, this question needs to be checked with samples with more extreme political positions than we have yet studied.

4. What is the relation of general authoritarianism to degree of political militancy? The evidence so far is that there is no relationship. It looks as though one can find equal numbers of authoritarians among political "passives" and "actives." However, more study is needed on possible differences in authoritarianism between different kinds of militancy.

5. What similarities and differences are there between authoritarians of the right and left? They are similar in that both groups score relatively

highly on all measures of authoritarian traits. They are different in several ways that we know of: First, the rightist authoritarians are a bit *more* authoritarian than the leftist authoritarians, and they compose a larger proportion of their political group. While the two groups are alike in being relatively intolerant of, and punitive toward, their perceived enemies, they differ, of course, in who they see as their enemies. The *direction* of their intolerance and authoritarian aggression is different. Also, the authoritarian leftists appear to be more selective in their intolerance, e.g., they tend to censor only rightists. The rightists, on the other hand, tend to be less discriminating, e.g., they censor other rightists as well as leftists. In addition, the authoritarian rightists appear to be more submissive to authority, or at least to the usual authority symbols in our society, than the authoritarian leftists.

6. What differences are there between leftist authoritarians and leftist non-authoritarians? There is very little evidence on this question. There is some indication that the authoritarian leftists are more intolerant and show more authoritarian aggression toward ideological opponents than the non-authoritarian leftists, e.g., tending to censor rightists whereas the non-authoritarian leftists do not.

7. What differences are there between rightist authoritarians and rightist non-authoritarians? As above, there is very little evidence on this question. It appears that the authoritarian rightists may be more motivated by generalized hostility than the non-authoritarian rightists, e.g., authoritarian rightists tend to censor more leftists *and* more rightists than the non-authoritarian rightists. These last two questions deserve far more study.

References

Adorno, T. W., Frenkel-Brunswik, Else, Levinson, D. J., and Sanford, R. N. *The authoritarian personality.* New York: Harpers, 1950.

Alexander, F. *Our age of unreason.* (Rev. Ed.), Philadelphia: Lippincott, 1951.

Bonnard, A. On political creed and character. *Psychoanalysis*, 1954, 2 (4), 55–58.

Christie, R., and Jahoda, Marie (Eds.) *Studies in the scope and method of "the authoritarian personality."* Glencoe, Ill.: Free Press, 1954.

Dorris, R. J., Levinson, D. J., and Hanfman, Eugenia. Authoritarian personality studied by a new variation of the sentence completion technique. *J. abnorm. soc. Psychol.*, 1954, 49, 99–108.

Drake, D. A psychoanalytic interpretation of social ideology. *Amer. Imago*, 1955, 12, 193–196.

Eysenck, H. J. *The psychology of politics.* New York: Praeger, 1955.

Gough, H. G. Studies of social intolerance: I. *J. soc. Psychol.*, 1951, 33, 237–246.

Hanfman, Eugenia, and Getzels, J. W. Studies of the sentence completion test. *J. proj. Tech.*, 1953, 17, 280–294.

Mishler, E. G. Personality characteristics and the resolution of role conflicts. *Publ. Opin. Quart.*, 1953, 17, 115–135.

Rokeach, M. *The open and closed mind.* New York: Basic Books, 1960.

Siegel, S. Certain determinants and correlates of authoritarianism. *Genet. Psychol. Monogr.*, 1954, 49, 187–230.

Taylor, I. A. Similarities in the structure of extreme social attitudes. *Psychol. Monogr.*, 1960, 74 (2).

Titus, H. E., and Hollander, E. P. The California F scale in psychological research: 1950–1955. *Psychol. Bull.*, 1957, 54, 47–64.

8

Racial Prejudice and Personality Scales: An Alternative Approach

EDWIN HOFFMAN RHYNE

College of William and Mary

Few issues in the field of social psychology, or in sociology, are more vexing than the relative importance of social and psychic factors in the formation of attitudes. The issue, it is true, seldom arises when the problem deals with variable attitudes among separate and distinct cultures. On the other hand, when the problem deals with variations among individuals from the same culture the issue almost invariably intrudes itself. The field of study then becomes an arena of battle between psychic drive and cultural norm, personality need and social expectation. Here and there one may see a clear victor emerging, but the more frequent vista of thrust and counter-thrust has inspired the conclusion that there can be no single victor. Rather, it is inferred, there should be no battle at all, and any differences of opinion should and could be settled by conversations between colleagues.

It is not the purpose of this paper to elaborate the "compromise" position. Rather than viewing the conflict as an out-worn luxury, this paper enters the field as a combatant. It is our argument that the conflict is too deep and fundamental to admit of any compromises which leave untouched the essential claims of each position. Because the conflict is so fundamental, we must either choose one alternative and reject the other or we must reject both. We cannot incorporate into one conception two positions which are mutually contradictory.

The thesis will be developed by the analysis of a specific problem. In this framework data from a questionnaire designed explicitly for this purpose will be the basis of a re-examination of the "Authoritarian Personality" explanation of individual variations in racial and ethnic prejudices. More explicitly, it is the specific thesis of this paper that a considerably more efficient explanation of racial and ethnic prejudice can be designed than the authoritarian explanation, either in its original 1950 version[1] or in its later more tempered form.[2]

Reprinted from *Social Forces*, 41, 1 (October 1962), 44–53, by permission of the author and The University of North Carolina Press.

[1] T. W. Adorno, Else Frenkel-Brunswik, Daniel J. Levinson, and R. Nevitt Sanford *The Authoritarian Personality* (New York: Harper and Brothers, 1950.)

[2] Gordon W. Allport, *The Nature of Prejudice* (Cambridge, Massachusetts: Addison-

Of necessity, the bulk of the paper will be devoted to the data bearing on the specific question of racial and ethnic prejudice. Besides its justification in its own right, the concentration on prejudice will be the vehicle for pointing up the more general issue.

WHICH THEORY OF PREJUDICE?

Since its publication in 1950, *The Authoritarian Personality* has been reviewed, rewarded, and reviled. A decade later the consensus among social psychologists appears to be that some measure of its thesis can be accepted even though some of the more extreme versions of the original have been rejected. Subsequent research may have stressed cultural and social variations,[3] or suggested other psychological or quasi-psychological factors as alternatives to authoritarianism,[4] but the value of personality factors as an explanation of prejudice has remained.

Instead of following the consensus view with its emphasis on social and psychological factors,[5] this paper will seek to determine if a more purely sociologistic approach can explain certain relationships more efficiently than either the original, almost purely psychologistic, theory or the later consensus view. It is our thesis that this can be done, even for the

---

Wesley Publishing Company, Inc., 1954): Arnold Rose, "Intergroup Relations vs. Prejudice: Pertinent Theory for the Study of Social Change," *Social Problems*, IV (October 1956), 173–176; Thomas F. Pettigrew, "Personality and Sociocultural Factors in Intergroup Attitudes: A Cross-National Comparison," *Conflict Resolution*, II (March 1958), 29-42; George E. Simpson and J. Milton Yinger, *Racial and Cultural Minorities* (New York: Harper and Brothers, Revised Edition, 1958); James G. Martin and Frank R. Westie, "The Tolerant Personality," *American Sociological Review*, 24 (August 1959), pp. 521–528; Thomas F. Pettigrew, "Regional Differences in Anti-Negro Prejudice," *Journal of Abnormal and Social Psychology*, 59 (July 1959), pp. 28–36; and Harry C. Triandis and Leigh Minturn Triandis, "Race, Social Class, Religion, and Nationality as Determinants of Social Distance," *Journal of Abnormal and Social Psychology*, 61 (July 1960), pp. 110–118.

[3] E. T. Prothro, "Ethnocentrism and Anti-Negro Attitudes in the Deep South," *Journal of Abnormal and Social Psychology*, 47 (January 1952), pp. 105–108; H. H. Hyman and Paul Sheatsley, "Attitudes Toward Desegregation," *Scientific American*, CXCV (December 1956), 35–39; Thomas F. Pettigrew, *op. cit.* (1958); and Thomas F. Pettigrew, *op. cit.* (1959).

[4] Walter C. Kaufman, "Status, Authoritarianism, and Anti-Semitism," *American Journal of Sociology*, LXII (January 1957), 370–382; A. H. Roberts and Milton Rokeach, "Anomie, Authoritarianism, and Prejudice: A Replication," *American Journal of Sociology*, LXI (January 1956), 355–358; Milton Rokeach, "Generalized Mental Rigidity as a Factor in Ethnocentrism," *Journal of Abnormal and Social Psychology*, 43 (July 1948), pp. 259–278; Patrick L. Sullivan and Joseph Adelson, "Ethnocentrism and Misanthropy," *Journal of Abnormal and Social Psychology*, 49 (April 1954), pp. 246–250; and Leo Srole, "Social Integration and Certain Corollaries: An Exploratory Study," *American Sociological Review*, 21 (December 1956), pp. 709–716.

[5] Although the importance of social factors *and* personality has been stressed in re-

frequently observed correlations between racial prejudice and scores on the California F-scale, by a systematic extension of the general notions applicable to socialization. If such an explanation is possible, then we shall find that there is no need to assume that certain specific psychic traits or needs underlie certain specific social attitudes.[6]

The Authoritarian Theory

We can paraphrase this theory thus: (1) The F-scale[7] is a true measure of important personality differences. (2) These personality differences have their origins in early family life. (3) Different personality types respond differently when exposed to ideas, pro and con, about racial and ethnic groups different from ego's own in-group.

The most crucial, logically, of these points is the last, for it includes the claim that particular psychic characteristics predispose one to prejudice[8] because of a peculiar "fit" between personality and idea. To speak analogically, those high in F are sponges who soak up quantities of water when prejudice rains and those low are ducks from whose backs water is shed (except, perhaps, when the rain is never-ending).

To say that the last point is the most crucial is to deny neither the importance of the other two nor their distinctiveness. The third point underlines the contention that F and prejudice are held together not by cultural concomitance nor by any "idea logic" but by psychodynamics.

---

search by scholars other than those who participated in the original California Study, the essential point in this view has also been stated by one of the original four. Frenkel-Brunswik has stated: "This does not mean that we attempted an explanation of the origin of ethnocentrism or of fascism in general on the basis of, say, the number of immature individuals in a given country or society." And further: "We have always stressed that the validity of our results is limited to relatively stable circumstances in which there is a choice between alternative ideologies with not too much suggestion or pressure exerted in either of the two directions . . ." Else Frenkel-Brunswik, "Further Explorations by a Contributor to 'The Authoritarian Personality,'" in Richard Christie and Marie Jahoda (Editors), *Studies in the Scope and Method of "The Authoritarian Personality"* (Glencoe, Illinois: The Free Press, 1954), pp. 227–228.

[6] It must be made absolutely clear that, in using what is called a sociologistic approach, we are *not* implying that what the person brings to the social situation is inconsequential. Nothing could be more inaccurate. What is accurate is to say that a sociologistic outlook questions whether the *social* attitudes a person brings to a situation are explicable *primarily as functions of psychic traits or needs*. To accept this latter position is ultimately to explain even the situation on psychologistic grounds; for the situation is, among other things, the expression of social attitudes by one or more alters, each of whom, if the psychic argument is correct, accepts the social attitude for non-social reasons.

[7] Hereafter, authoritarianism will also be referred to as the F-scale, F-scores, or just as F.

[8] For the sake of brevity the word prejudice will be used as a synonym for "racial prejudice." There is no attempt to deal with any generalized prejudice that would equate any or all hostile prejudgments under the same rubric.

The first two points are of great moment to the authoritarian theory, for they distinguish it from alternative explanations such as frustration, anomie, or mental rigidity, but, so long as the third point remains, the substitution of other psychologistic factors for authoritarianism still contrasts with a non-personality approach.

In summary, prejudice is to be regarded as a manifestation of a deeper psychic set; therefore, ideologies "regarding *each* social area *must* be regarded as a facet of the total person and an expression of more central ('subideological') psychological dispositions." [9] Because of his conventionality, authoritarian submission and aggression, anti-intraception, superstitious bent, "toughness," projectivity and exaggerated concern for sex,[10] the authoritarian finds it more "economic" to his psychodynamics to make hostile, stereotyped distinctions between himself and members of out-groups. We find variations in prejudice, therefore, because some of us are "sponges" and some are "ducks."

An Alternative Explanation

The starting point of this approach is the already noted observation that only cultural differences can explain, for instance, the greater anti-Negroism of southerners compared to northerners. The usual explanation is that the normal constraints of the culture bring into being more anti-Negroism among southerners than among northerners. Need we, however, limit cultural factors only to differences between region? Since we can not presume that each southerner experiences the same cultural constraints, it follows that variations on social attitudes may be a function of these variations within a culture. For some, the concatenation of family and friends, schoolbooks and arguments, accidents and recurrences, points toward prejudice; for others the concatenation is more neutral, and for some it must surely be anti-prejudicial. If we are willing to assume that within a culture each person is not given an equally uninstructed choice on prejudice, variations in cultural constraints can be as explanatory as certain personality constellations.

Since the emphasis on cultural differences by Allport, Pettigrew, Rose, and Simpson and Yinger leaves, in varying degrees for each author, an important role for personality, the term "cultural theory" is potentially misleading. To circumvent this possibility and to underline the similarity of the present argument with Sutherland's position in criminology, the term *differential learning approach* has been chosen.[11] This approach

---

[9] T. W. Adorno *et al.*, *op. cit.*, p. 207. Italics added.

[10] These are the F-scale clusters which characterize the authoritarian. *Ibid.*, pp. 224–241.

[11] Edwin H. Sutherland, *Principles of Criminology*, Fifth Edition, Revised by

makes the assumption that, even within cultures, the way in which each person is exposed to an idea or behavioral pattern involves a different combination of constraint and persuasion. Out of these differentials arise the differentials in prejudice.

With reference to the authoritarianism-prejudice correlation we can state the essential steps of the differential learning approach: (1) The F-scale does not differentiate fundamental personality structures but rather defines variations in socially derived and socially defined ideas.[12] (2) Variations on the F-scale are related to variations in exposure[13] to the ideas contained in the scales. (3) variations in racial prejudice are related to similar variations in exposure. (4) The correlation of these individual variations results from their concomitance in one's cultural experiences. It follows from (2) and (3) that since each set of ideas is separably "learnable," any concomitance from the viewpoint of individual psychology probably is fortuitous rather than causal, or, if causal, has to do with the logical similarity in the ideas.

In this view, prejudice is not an attitude one changes with ease, but it assumes that prejudice, like any other strongly held attitude, has an important niche in the personality. As such, prejudice is integrally related to other aspects of personality in any given case. But the approach emphatically contests the notion that a distinctive personality type (or types, or processes) is causally responsible for variations in prejudice, for it is the presumed connection between a *specific* personality type and a *specific* social attitude which is crucial in the authoritarian theory.

The differential learning approach makes the *explicit* assumption that there is no need to detail the exact process of acquiring prejudice. To grant the need for such a special theory is to deny the fundamental importance of the differential learning approach, for the direct implication of the approach is that the acquisition of prejudice is not different from the

---

Donald R. Cressey (Chicago: J. B. Lippincott Company, 1955). Cf. especially Chapter 4. The point of view expressed by this alternative is given subtle expression by Olive Westbrooke Quinn in "The Transmission of Racial Attitudes Among White Southerners," *Social Forces*, 33 (October 1954), pp. 41–47.

[12] This interpretation is congruent with findings that F is related to such clear indications of cultural diversity as social class, education, income, and sex. The criticisms voiced by Hyman and Sheatsley (Cf. Richard Christie and Marie Jahoda (Editors), *op. cit.*, pp. 70–106) about the reliability of the California study's scoring of interview data and the interpretations, based on them lend further circumstantial support that the supposed personality differences measured by the F-scale may not be such. See also Santo F. Camilleri, "A Factor Analysis of the F-scale," *Social Forces*, 37 (May 1959), pp. 316–323.

[13] For brevity's sake the single word "exposure" will be used to refer to the patterning of constraint and persuasion in which each person meets culturally derived ideas. It should not be construed in any simple mechanical fashion such as differing time-lengths of exposure.

acquisition of other social attitudes. The detailing, thus, can be found in the psychology of learning and the sociology of socialization. To continue to require a special theory would be sensible if, *and only if*, (1) prejudice is a special type of social attitude, (2) all attitudes are special types, or (3) attitudes are expressions of psychic phenomena.

The last possibility is contrary to the differential learning approach on its face and the other possibilities imply still other unwise assumptions. For instance, if all attitudes are special then we need a separate theory of socialization for every conceivable social attitude, including the predilection of many Americans for chocolate ice cream atop a cone, with no general theory of socialization possible. As for the first of these possibilities, any special qualities that have been ascribed to prejudice are likely to be the result of concern with prejudice as a practical social problem.

In summary, the differential learning approach looks to differential involvements within a culture for the principal explanation of individual variations in degree of prejudice. It explicitly contests the notion that these same individual variations are chiefly a function of specified psychic needs and processes. It obviously makes no claim as an explanation of why there are racial and ethnic prejudices within the culture in the first place, but, if we can accept the word of Else Frenkel-Brunswik[14] stated after the publication of *The Authoritarian Personality*, neither does the "authoritarianism" explanation. The explanation of the general existence of these prejudices is of much greater moment than the more limited topic investigated herein, but its treatment is much beyond our immediate scope. One need only note that one implication of the differential learning approach would be to shift our chief interest in prejudices to the structural situations in which they emerge and to which they apply, thus redirecting the essentially individualistic bias which is the necessary implication of any psychologistic theory such as "authoritarianism."

SAMPLES AND TECHNIQUES

All data are from a sample of 351 freshmen in an all-white college, Jews, persons over 21, and non-dormitory residents being excluded. Only freshmen were selected to reduce the effect of the college environment. A final total of 325 usable returns was obtained.

The questionnaire consisted of three parts: a) general information, b) 34 Likert-type statements drawn mainly from the California "Authoritarianism" study, and c) social distance scales on several out-groups. The main purpose of the first part was to make regional assignments of respondents. Although a three-fold system (South-Border-North) would have been desirable, statistical exigencies necessitated the dichotomy of

[14] Else Frenkel-Brunswik, *loc. cit.*

North and South.[15] The dichotomy resulted in 161 Southerners (60 boys and 101 girls) and 164 Northerners (81 boys and 83 girls).

Twenty-three statements in the second part of the questionnaire were taken from *The Authoritarian Personality*; the remaining 11 statements are from other studies and their results are not reported in this paper. Space limitations dictated a random selection of 15 statements from the original F-scale.[16] The Jewish and Negro subscales of the final version of the E-scale (Ethnocentrism) suggested by Levinson were the sources of statements of these two minorities.[17] A complete selection of these statements was not made because of the supposition that more than one dimension of prejudice was present. Those eight statements, four toward Jews and four toward Negroes, which were most clearly stereotypes expressing negative cognitions of the out-groups were used.

The other measurement of racial prejudice—derived from the last part of the questionnaire—was of the familiar Bogardus-type social distance scale, designed for collegiate circumstances. The eight relationships ranged from "Close kinship by marriage" to "Speaking acquaintance outside of home." Scalograms based on the Cornell Technique were constructed from the responses toward three out-groups, Jews, Negroes and Puerto Ricans. Coefficients of reproducibility ranged from 93.6% to 98.1%, and, as was to be expected, more social distance was expressed toward Negroes and less toward Jews.

"COGNITIVE" PREJUDICE

A high correlation between authoritarianism (as measured by the F-scale) and "cognitive" prejudice (as measured by scales of stereotypical statements) is fundamental to the authoritarian thesis. Whether the stereotypes be anti-Negro (AN) or anti-Semite (AS) is inconsequential, for both prejudices are seen as functions of the psychic ways of individuals. Any failure to find these correlations would be a serious questioning of the thesis, or at least the whole methodological apparatus through which the thesis has been elaborated.

Correlations between authoritarianism (F) and either anti-Negroism (AN) or anti-Semitism (AS) are not crucial to the differential learning approach, for the associations between F and cognitive prejudice are seen

---

[15] In like manner for contingency analysis it would have been desirable to use three categories (Low-Medium-High) for the scale scores, but the familiar difficulty of too few cases for accurate determination of theoretical frequencies made it impossible. For several tests of association reported below, it was possible to use trichotomies for scale scores and regional assignment. The results were in all cases consistent with the tests herein reported.

[16] T. W. Adorno, *et al.*, *op. cit.*, pp. 255–257.

[17] *Ibid.*, p. 142.

as functions of the coherence of these ideas in the culture. Again, why there is the coherence between these ideas—perhaps because of their logical similarities as opposed to any supposed psychological similarity—is not pertinent at the moment. What is pertinent is that if they do cohere in the culture one would expect different individuals to reflect the association in their own beliefs. As a further prediction of the differential learning approach, one would expect an association between AN and regional classification of the individual, the classification being taken as one clear evidence of cultural variability. There is no reason to expect an association of similar magnitude between AS and region.

Statistical tests of association confirm the expectations of each theory. As can be seen from Tables 1 and 2, each of the three associations, as

TABLE 1

Phi's for Authoritarianism and Cognitive Prejudice Controlled for Sex and Region in 2 × 2 Tables

| | PHI'S FOR AN | | |
	Males	Females	All
Southerners	.22	.31*	.30‡
Northerners	.35†	.18	.28‡
All	.31‡	.26‡	.30‡

| | PHI'S FOR AS | | |
	Males	Females	All
Southerners	.24	.24*	.25†
Northerners	.37‡	.30†	.36‡
All	.31‡	.27‡	30‡

* P < .05.
† P < .01.
‡ P < .001.

measured by *phi's*, expected to be significant are beyond the .001 level of confidence and the association that was not positively predicted—the AS-region association—is not statistically significant. These results are confirmed in 3 × 3 tables and by zero-order correlations. The coefficient of correlation (r) for F and AN is .38; the coefficient for F and AS is .46; and for AN and AS the coefficient is .61, all correlations being positive.[18]

Further inspection of Tables 1 and 2 indicate that the three associa-

[18] The correlations between F and each of the two prejudice scales are lower than those generally reported. The decline may be a function of the shortness of the prejudice scales or of the homogeneity of the sample; however, it is also obvious that neither of these possibilities evidently had much effect on the AN-AS correlation, which is not far from the most frequent findings.

TABLE 2

Phi's for Region and Cognitive Racial Prejudice Controlled for Sex and Authoritarianism in 2 × 2 Tables

	PHI'S FOR AN		
	Males	*Females*	*All*
F, High Half	.25*	.37‡	.28‡
F, Low Half	.37†	.24*	.28‡
All	.31‡	.30‡	.28‡
	PHI'S FOR AS		
	Males	*Females*	*All*
F, High Half	−.08	.11	.00
F, Low Half	.05	.18	.11
All	.00	.16*	.07

* P < .05.
† P < .01.
‡ P < .001.

tions maintain themselves when controlled for sex and either region (as in Table 1) or F (as in Table 2). Although the *phi's* for the cross-classifications are not equal (For example, in Table 1 the *phi* on the F-AN association for southern males is .22 and for northern males it is .35), the variations are what one normally expects to find because of sampling fluctuations. Since the minimum expectations of each thesis have been met, there is no basis on the data so far presented to make any choice as to the preferable explanation.

SOCIAL DISTANCE TOWARD OUT-GROUPS

According to the authoritarian thesis, we should expect no major change in the F-prejudice association when a different facet of prejudice is tapped. If the authoritarian person is negative toward an out-group, he should be as willing to discriminate against out-group members as he is to use stereotypes about them.

Since we have no previous estimates of the cultural coherence of F with a measure of social distance, we have no way of predicting from the differential learning approach the strength of the F-social distance association. We should, however, expect a continued association between region and prejudice toward the Negro even with a shift in the dimension of prejudice measured.

The associations of region and F with social distance toward Negroes (Negro SD) and social distance toward Jews (Jewish SD) are presented in Tables 3 and 4. The most striking thing about these associations is that

TABLE 3

Phi's for Authoritarianism and Social Distance Controlled for Sex and Region in 2 × 2 Tables

	FOR NEGRO SD		
	Males	Females	All
Southerners	.00	.11	.05
Northerners	.22*	.03	.12
All	.14	.09	.10

	FOR JEWISH SD		
	Males	Females	All
Southerners	.14	.08	.10
Northerners	.29†	.18	.25†
All	.22†	.13	.18†

* P < .05.
† P < .01.

the two measures of racial prejudice behave differently from the cognitive measurements. F shows a significant relation for the whole sample only with Jewish SD but lower than that with AS, and with the Negro SD the association falls just short of the .05 level of significance. On the other hand the associations between region and social distance show increases over the similar associations based on AN and AS.

The different behavior of the two measures might result from differentials in social conformity. In an area like the South with its tradition

TABLE 4

Phi's for Region and Social Distance Controlled for Sex and Authoritarianism in 2 × 2 Tables

	FOR NEGRO SD		
	Males	Females	All
F, High Half	.15	.45‡	.31‡
F, Low Half	.36†	.37‡	.38‡
All	.25‡	.41‡	.35‡

	FOR JEWISH SD		
	Males	Females	All
F, High Half	−.07	.20	.06
F, Low Half	.09	.33†	.21†
All	.00*	.26‡	.14*

* P < .05.
† P < .01.
‡ P < .001.

of open discriminatory practices, deviations in social distance attitudes would be subject to more immediate sanctions than cognitive attitudes. This supposition, however, can hardly account for the decrease in association of F with Negro SD without doing some violence to the authoritarian theory. Since the authoritarian person is conceived as one who dislikes out-groups for internal psychic reasons, as one who willingly conforms, it would appear that he would be quite willing verbally to establish his superiority to out-groups.

On the other hand, there is at least one way in which the small associations between F and social distance may not be damaging to the theory. It may be that the regional differences on social distance are so strong as to obscure the association between F and social distance. Perhaps if we look only at an *intraregional* subsample the expected relation may be found, for the authoritarian theory presumes that the individual variations are occurring *within a single culture.* Table 3 indicates, however, that the lack of association is not a function of inter-regional differences. For both Negro SD and Jewish SD the same pattern is found in the controlled subsamples as in the total sample. When analogous controls (Table 4) are placed on the association between Negro SD and region, we find, with one exception, the continuation of the original association. Only in the case of males high on F do we find a sharp decline.[19]

RACIAL PREJUDICE DIRECTED TOWARD TWO OR MORE OUT-GROUPS

A final problem deals with the tendency of people who are prejudiced toward one outgroup to be prejudiced toward another. The major qualification to this tendency that has been noted in previous research is that the prejudice toward one out-group may be more severe than it is toward others. These findings are confirmed here. In 2 × 2 tables, *phi* for AN and AS is .50 and for Negro SD and Jewish SD it is .48 (for both, P < .001). On the social distance scales we find only eight persons who have a scale type showing more prejudice toward the Jew than the Negro and 244 who exhibit more prejudice toward the Negro.

Regardless of any over-all differences in two or more racial prejudices, when persons are ranked on two scales the problem remains: Why do people who are relatively high on one scale tend to be relatively high on

[19] Although the decline of the F-prejudice association when moving from cognitive prejudice to social distance was not predictable from the differential learning theory, neither was it unpredictable. Like the four statements of the AN scale most of the F-scales deal with one's conception of the world rather than what one should be doing in the world. Therefore, we might expect two similar scales (F & AN) to be in closer agreement than a cognitive scale (F) and one supposedly measuring what one feels should be done.

another scale? The authoritarian theory points to the personality of the prejudiced person to account for this: Authoritarians have fundamentally different personalities from nonauthoritarians; the authoritarian will tend to retain all prejudices and the nonauthoritarian will tend to reject the same prejudices; therefore, a person high in prejudice toward one out-group tends to be high in prejudice toward another.

In terms of the data available to this study, two important hypotheses can be derived from this argument. (1) If AN (or AS) is controlled for, then the association between F and AS (or AN) should remain high although at a slightly lower level. This hypothesis is to be expected because of the independent association of F with both AN and AS and because each is considered as a function of F. Since neither association is perfect, at any given level of either AN or AS, we would expect variations in the other cognitive prejudice and in F. These variations should be associated positively, for even at the same level of one cognitive prejudice the more authoritarian person should "take" more readily to another cognitive prejudice.[20]

(2) A second hypothesis states: if F is controlled for, the association between AN and AS should decrease radically. The authors of *The Authoritarian Personality* suggest that for an authoritarian person a decrease in prejudice toward one out-group should normally lead to an increase in prejudice toward another.[21] This is perhaps too extreme, but if F is to be taken as an important cause of the AN-AS correlation, there must be a very substantial reduction when F is controlled for. If the associations remain high, then AN and AS hang together for some other reason.

According to differential learning the association among different racial prejudices is seen as a result of their coherence in the culture. This view leads to the following hypothesis: if F is controlled for, the association between AN and AS will remain at approximately the same or slightly lower level. Since the association between F and cognitive prejudice is not viewed as causal, there is no reason to expect any important change in the association of AN and AS at similar levels of F. If the fundamental cause of any prejudice is proper exposure to it and if different prejudices cohere in the culture, to hold constant for a fortuitous factor should be of little consequence.

A second hypothesis derivable from the differential learning theory is that the association between region and AN should maintain itself when AS is controlled for. If different regions can be taken as indicators of dif-

[20] Logically, there seems to be no reason not to except the same thing for social distance measures of prejudice; however, this test is not presented because of the originally low correlations of F with Negro SD and Jewish SD.

[21] They state, "if we should succeed in diverting hostility from one minority group we should be prevented from taking satisfaction by the knowledge that the hostility will now very probably be directed against some other group." T. W. Adorno, *et al.*, *op. cit.*, p. 973.

ferential exposure to a single racial prejudice, then the greater exposure in one region should lead to greater prejudice.

The results of controlling for the several factors discussed above are presented in Tables 5 through 8. The two hypotheses derivable from the

TABLE 5

Phi's for Authoritarianism and Anti-Negroism Controlled for Region and Anti-Semitism in 2 × 2 Tables

	AS, Low Half	AS, High Half	All
Southerners	.28*	.09	.30‡
Northerners	.08	.20	.28‡
All	.20*	.13	.30‡

* P < .05.
† P < .01.
‡ P < .001.

TABLE 6

Phi's for Authoritarianism and Anti-Semitism Controlled for Region and Anti-Negroism in 2 × 2 Tables

	AN, Low Half	AN, High Half	All
Southerners	.19	.07	.25†
Northerners	.24*	.30*	.36‡
All	.23†	.15	.30‡

* P < .05.
† P < .01.
‡ P < .001.

TABLE 7

Phi's for Anti-Negroism and Anti-Semitism Controlled for Region and Authoritarianism in 2 × 2 Tables

	F, Low Half	F, High Half	All
Southerners	.57‡	.43‡	.53‡
Northerners	.36‡	.46‡	.51‡
All	.48‡	.43‡	.50‡

‡ P < .001.

authoritarian theory are not sustained. Although some association is to be found between F and AN and between F and AS when the other prejudice is controlled for, the "partial" associations are much lower than the "total" associations. Contrariwise, the association between AN and AS remains much above the vanishing point when F is controlled for. These results,

TABLE 8

Phi's for Region and Anti-Negroism Controlled for Authoritarianism and Anti-Semitism in 2 × 2 Tables

	AS, Low Half	AS, High Half	All
F, High Half	.34†	.29†	.28‡
F, Low Half	.16	.40†	.27‡
All	.25†	.32‡	.28‡

† P < .01.
‡ P < .001.

thus, invert the expectations. The associations that were expected to remain near the same levels decrease; the association that was expected to decline substantially is very close to the original level.[22]

In contrast, both hypotheses derivable from the differential learning approach are essentially substantiated. When the controls are made, the hypothetical expectations of continued associations between AN and AS and between Region and AN are confirmed. When these latter tests are replicated using social distance measures in place of cognitive measures, the same results are obtained. Furthermore, no matter what pair of controls is used (F, AS, sex, father's education, religion) the independent association of Region with AN continues, as do the associations between AN and AS and between Negro SD and Jewish SD.

CONCLUSIONS

The major conclusion warranted by our findings is that several important hypotheses derivable from the authoritarian explanation of prejudice have not been confirmed, and that, consequently, doubt has been cast on the theory itself. When authoritarianism is compared with social distance, associations are found, but at a level lower than expected. When certain controls, as indicated by the theory itself, are placed on the original associations we find a pattern directly opposite to predictions. With particular reference to the latter findings it seems proper to conclude that when hypotheses *logically inherent in a theory are not confirmed* then the theory must be reconsidered.

On the other hand, the hypotheses derivable from the differential learn-

[22] Controls for the F-AN, F-AS, and AN-AS correlations can also be obtained by application of partial r's. The results are similar to those already presented. The partial r for F-AN when AS is partialed out is $+.13$ ($r_{12} = +.38$). The partial r for F-AS with AN partialed out is $+.32$ ($r_{13} = +.47$). Finally, the partial r for AN-AS with F partialed out is $+.53$ ($r_{23} = +.61$). It must be remembered, though, that partial r's for three inter-correlated variables will usually decline more for the smaller total r's than for the larger total r's. On the other hand, from the purely theoretical standpoint of authoritarianism the above pattern should not occur.

ing approach have been sustained with one possible exception (The exception being the failure to anticipate the association between region and social distance expressed toward the Jew). This pattern by no means "proves" the differential learning theory, but it does present the latter as more accurate in predicting our findings than the authoritarian theory. In no case are our findings definitely at variance with it as was the case several times for the authoritarian theory.[23]

The conclusion favorable to the differential learning approach must be tempered by several cautions. The first and most obvious is the nature of the sample. It is small, unrepresentative, and in a situation where a specific cultural *milieu* probably inhibits a full expression of attitudes. A second caution is the nature of the scales. Some are so short as to raise serious questions concerning the appropriateness of treating responses as falling on a continuum. However, this stricture applies in varying degrees to most other studies, even in part to *The Authoritarian Personality*.[24] Thirdly, it might be argued that to treat supposedly continuous data in terms of contingency tables is to do violence to the underlying distributions. This is of course true. If nothing else, the dichotomization of the scales "threw away" data. On the other hand, wherever possible quantitative techniques were used and they confirmed the results of contingency analysis. And if the dichotomization of the F-distribution "lost" data, it must be remembered that the regional classification can not be considered as a true "either-or" measurement of the cultural experiences of each person.

Even with the cautions—and it must be underscored that these same difficulties are shared by most research in this field—the conclusion seems clear: A consistently sociologistic approach has been more efficient in accounting for the variations in the data than a psychologistic approach. Wherever the psychologistic approach did account for the variations, the sociologistic approach was equally applicable with the added virtue that it could account for some variations beyond the range of the former and still other variations which ran counter to the expectations of the authoritarian theory.

The cautions place limitations on just how far the conclusion can be extrapolated beyond the present data. It is a commonplace observation, but a very true one, that such a limited study can not demonstrate an explanation for a specific problem, to say nothing of the general psycho-

---

[23] Other findings which support the conclusion but which are not reported in full include the following: (1) Non-southern Catholics show a significant *increase* in F over non-southern Protestants and a *decrease*, though not statistically significant, in AN (southerners were excluded because only four Catholics were from that region). (2) Persons from Connecticut, New York, New Jersey, and Pennsylvania exhibit slightly more social distance toward Puerto Ricans than Negroes; persons from all other sections show considerably more distance toward Negroes. (3) F is negatively associated with parents' education (at just the .05 level), with no significant association between education and prejudice.

[24] Cf. the five-item E-scale (Form 40). T. W. Adorno *et al.*, *op. cit.*, p. 128.

logistic-sociologistic issue. On the other hand, the failure of other studies seriously to consider any alternative to their chosen psychologistic explanations also should raise a major question-mark. When, for instance, in the nearly one thousand pages of *The Authoritarian Personality* there is no sustained willingness even to entertain the thought that other explanations might fit the data, the limitation of theoretical blinders is perhaps even more important than small size of sample or incompleteness of data. If such theoretical limitations were to be considered of lesser importance, then it would seem that scientific "victory" is being awarded to superiority of numbers rather than to cogency of explanation.

If this paper has succeeded in throwing serious doubts on the authoritarian answer to the question of individual variations in prejudice, its immediate purpose will have been attained. If it has succeeded in showing that a consistently sociologistic approach to the study of attitudes has not received the attention it merits, the more general and the more fundamental goal will have also been accomplished.

9

A Forced Choice Form of the F Scale—Free of Acquiescent Response Set*

NORMAN H. BERKOWITZ

Boston University

GEORGE H. WOLKON

Mental Health Rehabilitation and Research, Inc., Cleveland

It has been a number of years since the original study of the authoritarian personality was published. And it is now approximately seven years since serious attention was first turned to problems inherent in the measure of authoritarianism, and still the major problem remains. The difficulty stems from the fact that all items in the instrument are positively phrased. This results in a high score for persons who simply have a tendency to agree. Thus persons differing in amount of acquiescent response set might obtain different scores, perhaps masking or accentuating real attitudes about the content of the items. Today, few dispute the fact that the measurement of authoritarianism is confounded with acquiescent response set. To eliminate such confounding various investigators have constructed series of parallel items, all negatively phrased (F—). Examples of F— items may be found in Bass,[1] Jackson and Messick,[2] Chapman and Campbell,[3] and Christie, Havel and Seidenberg.[4]

Many researchers have observed that persons often agree both with the original, positively phrased items (F+) and their negatively phrased counterparts. Such observations strengthened the conviction that the F+

Reprinted from *Sociometry*, 27, 1 (March 1964), 54–63, by permission of the authors and The American Sociological Association.

* This research was partially supported by PHS research grant GN 5858 (C3) from the Division of Nursing, Public Health Service, and was conducted at the Human Relations Center of Boston University.

[1] Bernard M. Bass, "Authoritarianism or Acquiescence," *Journal of Abnormal and Social Psychology*, 51 (November, 1955), pp. 616–623.

[2] Douglas N. Jackson and Samuel J. Messick, "A Note on 'Ethnocentrism' and Acquiescent Response Sets," *Journal of Abnormal and Social Psychology*, 54 (January, 1957), pp. 132–134.

[3] Loren J. Chapman and Donald T. Campbell, "Response Set in the F Scale," *Journal of Abnormal and Social Psychology*, 54 (January, 1957), pp. 129–132.

[4] Richard Christie, Joan Havel, and Bernard Seidenberg, "Is the F Scale Irreversible?", *Journal of Abnormal and Social Psychology*, 56 (March, 1958), pp. 143–159.

scale measures more than the acceptance of item contents. It also turned attention to the investigation of acquiescent response set as a personality characteristic, interesting and worthy of study in its own right. However, for those still interested in authoritarianism, the problem of measurement remains.

In the interests of methodological rigor, investigators now frequently use F+ and F− scales in combination. The *counterbalanced* scale, as it is called, yields a single score for each subject. The counterbalancing procedure requires at least two assumptions. First, the items must be equivalent with regard to the content of the underlying attitude dimension. Second, each type of item, F− and F+, must be equally susceptible to the effects of response set; the inflation of scores on F+ items must be compensated for by a concomitant reduction on the F− items. Since those studying response set as a personality characteristic have identified a naysayer as well as a yeasayer, it must also be assumed that the same situation prevails for those with a tendency to disagree. Their scores should be deflated by about the same amount on the F+ as they are inflated on the F− items.[5] The correlation between these two types of items is an empirical measure of the adequacy of the assumptions in combination.

Table 1 contains data from several studies compiled by Chapman and Bock,[6] along with Mogar's data,[7] plus data collected by the present writers in a study of 89 nurses employed in Outpatient Departments (OPD). These correlations, representative of those in the literature, based on several different sets of reversals, clearly indicate that F+ and F− do not measure the same thing. Whether the inadequacy is due to lack of equivalence with respect to content, or to the inconsistency with which they deflate the scores of various respondents, cannot be determined. In addition it should be noted that the reliabilities of the F− items are lower than those of F+. Thus, not only are the reversals not highly related to the originals, but they are less internally consistent as well. Furthermore, the correlations do not approach their reliabilities. In addition to these data, item by item comparison of originals and reversals demonstrate the noncomparability of items in the forms which comprise the full counterbalanced scale.[8]

---

[5] It may also have to be assumed that the two parts of the counterbalanced scale are equivalent with respect to internal consistency. Otherwise the correlation between this measure and other variables may be primarily a function of the more reliable half, thereby negating the counterbalancing effort.

[6] Loren J. Chapman and R. Darrell Bock, "Components of Variance Due to Acquiescence and Content in the F Scale Measure of Authoritarianism," *Psychological Bulletin*, 55 (September, 1958), pp. 328–333.

[7] Robert E. Mogar, "Three Versions of the F Scale and Performance on the Semantic Differential," *Journal of Abnormal and Social Psychology*, 60 (March, 1960), pp. 262–265.

[8] Edward B. Klein, "Stylistic Components of Response as Related to Attitude Change," unpublished doctoral dissertation, Columbia University, 1960; Leonard

TABLE 1

Some Obtained Reliabilities of the F Scale[1]

| | Studies Reported by Chapman and Bock | | | | | | | | Mogar | | OPD Study |
	a[2]	b[2]	c[2]	d	e[3]	f	g	h	i[5]	j[5]	k[3]
Reliabilities											
F+	.69	.53	.71	.52	—	—	.60	.69[4]	.67	—	.71
F−	.41	.41	.42	.43	.77	—	.42	—	.61	.59	.40
Correlation of F+ and F−	.17	−.01	.29	.05	−.35	.17	.19	.25	.18	−.14	−.16

[1] Chapman and Campbell's reversals used in columns a, b, and c; Christie's reversals used in columns d, f, g, and k; Jackson and Messick's reversals used in columns e and j; Bass' reversals used in column i; Levitt's reversals used in column h.
[2] Kuder-Richardson "Formula 20" reliabilities.
[3] Corrected split half reliabilities (Spearman-Brown).
[4] Correlation with other positive items.
[5] Retest reliability.

Several papers have shown that the F+ is a better predictor than are either the reversals alone or the counterbalanced scale. For example Mogar has shown that the F+ predicted to his criterion (use of extremes on the semantic differential) better than did either Jackson and Messick's or Bass' reversals. Chapman and Campbell [9] report that when the F− is compared to ethnocentrism and intelligence scores, lower correlations are obtained than when these comparisons are made using the F+. Our own data with nurses show that although F+ correlated only −.22 with the tendency to integrate competing expectations in paper and pencil conflict situations, the F− and counterbalanced forms evidenced still poorer relationships, each correlating only −.14 with such responses.[10] Although some (e.g., Chapman and Campbell [11]) may attribute the lower correlations obtained using the counterbalanced scale to the neutralization of agreement response set (which itself might be correlated with the criterion variable, producing spuriously high correlations between F+ and the criterion), there may be a more parsimonious explanation. Since the negative items have lower reliabilities than originals, they should exhibit lower relationships with other variables. In addition, a counterbalanced scale not only becomes somewhat less reliable by the inclusion of the reversed items, but also may be composed of two separable factors. Because there is only a low correlation between the two parts of the total combined scale, such a measure might well be expected to exhibit lower correlations with other variables. Therefore rather than indicating success in the elimination of response set, these data may represent the inadequacy of such attempts.

The investigator is therefore forced to choose between a counterbalanced form which has been shown to be inadequate by virtue of unreliability and perhaps multi-dimensionality, and the F+, which similarly is composed of at least two dimensions, one of them a tendency to agree to the items. The two-dimensionality is especially unfortunate, since it lessens the opportunity to discover the characteristics of the authoritarian through an examination of the contents of the items with which he agrees.

Solomon and Edward B. Klein, "A Comparison of Response Tendencies in Normal and Schizophrenic Samples." Paper read at annual meetings of Eastern Psychological Association, Philadelphia (April, 1961).

[9] Loren J. Chapman and Donald T. Cambell, "The Effect of Acquiescence Response Set Upon Relationships Among the F Scale, Ethnocentrism, and Intelligence," Sociometry, 22 (June, 1959), pp. 153–161.

[10] The only data which have come to our attention contradicting the results of these studies are those reported by Small and Campbell [Donald O. Small and Donald T. Campbell, "The Effect of Acquiescence Response Set upon the Relationship of the F Scale and Conformity," Sociometry, 23 (March, 1960), pp. 69–71]. In an experiment predicting to conformity they found the lowest correlation (.17) with F+ and higher ones with F− (.26) and the counterbalanced scale (.27). But due to the stated unreliability of their criterion variable it is difficult to interpret the inconsistency of their results with those presented above.

[11] Chapman and Campbell, 1959, op. cit., 129–132.

THE FORCED-CHOICE FORM

In short, the attempts to eliminate response set as a factor in the F scale have been of questionable success, in spite of the fact that several different sets of reversals have been constructed. The difficulty may not reside in the items themselves, but in the procedure. With this possibility in mind we have attempted to use an alternative approach, namely, the forced-choice method. In this format each F+ statement is paired with its negatively phrased counterpart. The respondent is instructed to select one statement of the pair and indicate the extent to which he agrees with it relative to the other item. The response categories can be varied to suit the purposes of the investigator, but here six categories were used, comparable to those employed in the original study of authoritarianism. The negative half of the pair can, of course, either be constructed anew, or items already available may be used. We chose the latter course. A sample item from the forced-choice form illustrates the general procedure.

A. *Astrology will never explain anything.*
B. *Some day it will probably be shown that astrology can explain a lot of things.*

___ I agree a great deal more with A than B.
___ I agree somewhat more with A than B.
___ I agree slightly more with A than B.
___ I agree slightly more with B than A.
___ I agree somewhat more with B than A.
___ I agree a great deal more with B than A.

The items were scored 1 to 7 with 4 representing the absent midpoint. In this form the problem of agreement response set disappears, since *all* answer categories involve agreement. That which differentiates high and low authoritarians is the half of the pair with which they agree. Although such a procedure eliminates the possibility of acquiescence as a factor, there is no guarantee that a test composed of such items measures authoritarianism in any acceptable fashion. To determine the adequacy of the procedure the following study was conducted.

METHOD

Twenty-five items which appear in the original F scale and also in both Bass' and Christie's sets of negatively phrased items were selected. These 75 items, 25 originals and two sets of reversals, arranged in random order, comprise Form I. From the items in Form I, two forced-choice scales were constructed. Form II (FCC) used the original item paired with Christie's reversals; each pair constituted an item. The items appeared in random order. Form III (FCB) was exactly the same as the previous one, except that Bass' reversals were coupled with the original F statement. Items appeared in exactly the same order used in Form II. In each forced-choice form (FC), for 13 randomly chosen items, the original statement from the F scale preceded its reversal, while in the other 12 items, the reversal came first. The original F+ statements appeared first in the same items of each FC form. In short, the *only* difference between the two forms used was in the set of reversed items employed in the pairing.

Subjects. The tests were administered to two major groups.[12] The first, a sample of 153 Junior College students (JC sample), were given the tests in three different orders.

Condition 1 (N = 51): Form II (FCC) followed by Form I
Condition 2 (N = 54): Form I followed by Form III (FCB)
Condition 3 (N = 48): Form III (FCB) followed by Form I,
              followed by Form II (FCC)

These orders were used since in only one class was there sufficient time to collect data using all the forms.

The second sample, composed of 135 students attending the summer school of the College of Liberal Arts of Boston University (LA), completed the tests in four different conditions.

Condition 1 (N = 25): Form I followed by Form II (FCC)
Condition 2 (N = 23): Form I followed by Form III (FCB)
Condition 3 (N = 43): Form II (FCC) followed by Form I
Condition 4 (N = 44): Form III (FCB) followed by Form I

It should be noted that one change was made in Form I of this administration. The total number of items was reduced from 75 to 50 by eliminating the Bass reversals. There were no other changes. The two FC forms remained exactly the same.

Procedure. The questionnaires were administered in class. The forms were distributed one at a time. The form to be administered second was presented only after the previous form had been completed and collected. Subjects wrote their names on their booklets and were aware they could be identified. They were assured, however, that neither individual answers nor scores would be shown to instructors or administrators of their school.

---

[12] The authors are indebted to Kenneth Wolkon and Alan Leiman at Worcester Junior College and Leon Brenner, Phyllis Oram, Bernard Phillips, and Paul Rhudick at Boston University for making class time available.

RESULTS

Reliability. In order to permit examination of the reliabilities of the various forms, the data were combined across conditions. Although some condition differences emerged in some analyses, conditions did not differ in any consistent fashion, and it therefore seems justifiable to combine them. Different analyses will have different sample sizes because of the nature of the study design; i.e., not all conditions included all forms. The largest sample possible, however, is presented for each analysis.

TABLE 2

Reliabilities* of Scales

Scale	JC Sample		LA Sample	
	Reliability	*N*	*Reliability*	*N*
F+	.68	153	.79	135
CF−	.60	153	.66	135
BF−	.53	153	Not collected	—
FCC	.59	99	.69	68
FCB	.41	102	.71	67

* Hoyt procedure.

From these data it may be seen that one form has no particular advantage over the others with respect to internal consistency. In the JC sample the FCB form (using Bass reversals) has a reliability somewhat lower than the other forms, but the finding is not replicated in the LA sample. The reliabilities of tests composed only of reversals are considerably higher here than in previous studies (see Table 1). This may well be a consequence of the length of the tests. For here we have used a 25 item form for each set of reversals, while many studies use fewer items, usually ranging from 10 to 15. In our data, however, the FC forms exhibit levels of reliability comparable to the reversals, although they fall somewhat short of that obtained for the original F scale.

Validity. As a measure of validity, scores yielded by the various forms were compared with those obtained using the original F scale. It will be noted that tests composed only of reversals have somewhat higher correlations with the F+ items than have previously been reported (see Table 1). Once again this finding is probably due to the increased length of the tests, which in turn increases reliability and thereby increases their correlations with the F scores. However, in spite of the higher correlations between the F+ and F−, validity coefficients fall considerably short of those obtained using either of the forced-choice forms. Furthermore, the correlations between F+ and F− are considerably lower than their reliabilities.

Another important point emerged from the data. The FC forms by and large correlated well with both the scores obtained from the F+ and F− items, although the latter did not correlate well with one another. In the JC sample the Bass reversals (BF−) correlated only .34 with F scale scores; while the FCB correlated .42 with the BF− and .69 with the F+ items. The data necessary for these same comparisons in the LA sample

TABLE 3

Validity* of Alternate Measures of Authoritarianism

	JC Sample		LA Sample	
Scale	*Validity*	*N*	*Validity*	*N*
CF−	.33	153	.48	135
BF−	.34	153	Not collected	—
FCC	.74	99	.84	68
FCB	.69	102	.83	67

* Correlation with F+.

were not collected. In the JC sample Christie's reversals (CF−) correlated only .33 with the F+ items. However the FCC form correlated .68 with the CF− alone and .74 with the original F+ items. In the LA sample much the same situation prevails. The CF− alone correlates .48 with the F+ items, while the FCC correlates .72 with the former and .84 with the latter. Thus the forced-choice form predicts well to both a measure confounded with agreement response set and another confounded with disagreement response set. This seems to suggest that the FC format is relatively insensitive to each of these opposing response tendencies.

It is of course possible that the rather high correlation of each FC form with its corresponding F− scale and with the original F+ is attributable to the fact that the items of the latter two together comprise the FC forms. However, we have only attempted to construct a form which measures the same thing as does the original instrument, while circumventing the problem of yeasaying and naysaying. So although we may understand the correlations in terms of item overlap, this interpretation in no way negates their importance as indicating some success in the construction of an alternative measure of authoritarianism, free of acquiescence response set.

Relationship between F Scores and Intelligence. As was previously mentioned, the correlation of F scores with intelligence has on occasion been regarded as evidence that response set is prevalent in the original F items. This argument suggests that those who are less intelligent, have less knowledge and a less committed position on the contents covered by the items, and are therefore more apt to be influenced by response set, score higher on the F scale. The lower correlations using the counterbalanced forms, as compared to those obtained using the original F scale, were regarded as supporting this contention, and by implication, as supporting the claim that counterbalancing eliminated such response tendencies. In this study we were fortunate to have intelligence scores made available to us for the JC sample.[13]

TABLE 4

Correlations between I.Q. and Various Measures of Authoritarianism

Scale	N	r
F+	120	−.42*
CF−	120	−.27*
BF−	120	−.20†
FCC	76	−.42*
FCB	81	−.22†

* P < .01.
† P ≤ .05.

The intelligence scores used in these correlations were obtained from the Ohio State Test, Form 21. These data support previous findings of lower correlations obtained using F− items only. However, the more reliable of the two FC forms yields exactly the same correlation with intelligence as does the F scale itself. The lower correlation using the FCB form is probably a function of its lower reliability for this sample (see Table 2), a factor which could easily account for its lower correlation with intelligence. However even with a forced-choice measure which eliminates acquiescence, authoritarianism and intelligence are negatively related.[14]

A Short Form of the FCC Test. On the basis of the item-total score correlations, in combination with correlations between items and the total scores on the F+ scale, 12 items were selected from the FCC form using data from the JC sample only. The items were selected from this form because it exhibited a somewhat higher reliability in the JC sample. The validation of the short form was conducted upon the LA sample. Its reliability was found to be .58, using the Hoyt procedure, and the correlation with the original F+ scores was .77. Such a form might be acceptable to those who wish to employ fewer items in their measurement procedures.[15]

[13] The authors are grateful to Dean George Douglas of Worcester Junior College for making the I.Q. scores available.

[14] In this connection it might be noted that the JC sample had higher scores on each measure of authoritarianism than did the LA sample (for each measure P < .01). Although I.Q. scores for the latter sample are not available, it seems reasonable to assume higher scores for students attending a regular four year institution. If this assumption is correct the differences in authoritarianism obtained for the two samples lend further support for the negative relationship.

[15] The specific items used in the short form and in all other forms are available upon request.

RESPONSE SET IN THE FC FORM

The data presented in this paper suggest that a forced choice format has some potential for the elimination of agreement response set from the F scale. Apart from the empirical support the procedure receives here, it also has the advantage of avoiding the inclusion of items to eliminate response set which are themselves susceptible to the opposite tendency. This eliminates the necessity for making highly questionable assumptions concerning the neutralizing effects of parts of the counterbalanced form.

Although the forced choice format seems to eliminate acquiescent response set, it may be subject to another type. The reader will recall from the methods section that F+ items were placed before their reversals in half the items and after them in the other half, because of the possibility that order might have some effect. The data indicate that it may. In the JC sample the correlation between those items in which the F+ preceded and followed the F− was only .26 for the FCC and .24 for the FCB. These do not compare particularly well with the correlations between the F− and F+ items. However since these correlations in the FC forms are based on only half the number of items, a better basis of comparison may be found below.[16] Fortunately, these correlations for the FC forms increase considerably in the LA sample, to .41 for the FCC and .54 for the FCB. However, in spite of this increase in association, at least some doubt is cast on the freedom of this format from some sort of response set.

To determine whether scores based on the items in which F+ preceded or followed the F− were differently related to scores on the original F scale, separate analyses were performed.

The data in Table 5 suggest that if there is response set in the FC form, it does not cause the items to exhibit a differential association with F+ scores. Regardless of the position of the F+ items in the forced choice pair, the association with scores obtained on the original F+ scale is essentially the same.

DISCUSSION

In previous work, when counterbalanced scales were constructed, two parts were combined despite their low correlation. Since one half of such a form is the criterion itself, doubt is cast on the validity of the other. Another problem, apart from validity, is that such a combination must produce a non-unidimensional scale. The correlations between the two halves of the FC forms suggest that they too may be subject to the latter

[16] So that the reader may compare directly the correlation between the two parts of the FC forms with those between the two parts of the counter-balanced forms (in Table 3), the following correlations, corrected for length of test are presented. In JC sample: .41 for FCC and .39 for FCB; in LA sample: .58 for FCC and .70 for FCB.

TABLE 5

Validity* of Scores Based on Forced Choice Items in which F+ Statements Precede and Follow F—

Form	Position of F+ in Item Pair	JC Sample	LA Sample
FCC	F+ precede F—	.62	.64
	F+ follow F—	.55	.76
FCB	F+ precede F—	.52	.78
	F+ follow F—	.56	.67
Short form	F+ precede F—	Not analyzed†	.62
	F+ follow F—	Not analyzed†	.67

* Correlation with F+.

† The items for the short form were selected using data from the JC sample. The validation was performed on the LA sample, and therefore scores necessary to perform these correlations were available only for the latter sample.

difficulty, and raises the prospect of substituting a positional response set for acquiescence. It is not yet possible to assess this difficulty. Such an examination will involve a determination of the extent to which the two halves are differentially associated with other variables. So far all that is known is that they correlated equally with the original F scale. These comparisons must be extended to other variables including overt behavioral responses.

Further Considerations. Since the reversals employed in the FC items are those which have been shown to have low correlations with the F+, some doubt is introduced with regard to the meaning of the response to the FC items. The problem is that each FC item is a composite of two items which are themselves not highly associated. But the low correlation between F+ and F— may be attributed to several factors, each of which results in a different evaluation of the FC form.

The first explanation is that the reversals are different in meaning from the original F+ items. If this be the case, each item of the FC form can be considered non-unidimensional. The responses of the subjects might under such circumstances be attributable to some other element, e.g., social desirability.[17] There remains however, the possibility that the meanings of the F— items change *in the presence* of their opposite F+. The F— items may be adequate reversals within the new format, although the originals and their reversals convey different contents when they appear in separate scales. If such is the case, items in the FC could be considered unidimensional.

[17] However, this extraneous factor would also have to be present in both F+ and F— scales since FC correlates highly with each. Considering the low correlations generally obtained between F+ and F— such an explanation is considered unlikely although by no means impossible.

The lack of association between F+ and F− may also be attributed to the failure of acquiescent response set to deflate scores correspondingly on negatively worded items, as it inflates them on positively phrased items. (The opposite difficulty for negative response set is of course also involved here.) Thus the low correlation may simply be a function of the differential effects of response sets on positive and negative items. If such an explanation is accepted, the composite FC items may be viewed as unidimensional, and by eliminating yeasaying and naysaying would be expected to reveal high correlations with each of the other scales. Given such an assumption, the lack of association between F+ and F− has little bearing on the unidimensionality of the FC items.

A final consideration of more general concern involves the selection of an appropriate measure of validity for any new measure of authoritarianism. Once it is assumed that the F+ scores themselves are not completely valid, demonstrating their association with scores derived from new measures does not firmly establish the latter's validity. The fact that a better index is not yet available does not alter the logical problem, and claims of validity must be tempered by the recognition of the difficulty. Attempts must be made to predict to behaviors, linked by theory to authoritarianism, so as to clarify the question of validity for any particular scale. Given the number of questions raised in this discussion it is clear that although the Forced Choice format seems to have potential for the solution of certain measurement problems, the overall superiority of any form has yet to be demonstrated. Research is currently in progress aimed at the examination of many of the issues presented in this paper.

.   .   .

AUTHORITARIANISM SCALE[*]

Directions: Below are listed a number of statements which reflect attitudes commonly held today. Check whether you agree with the first or the second statement in each pair, and how strongly you agree with one or the other. (There are no "right" or "wrong" answers.)[1]

Reprinted by permission.

[*] This forced-choice modification was presented by Richard Christie, Joan Havel and Bernard Seidenberg, in "Is the F Scale Irreversible?" *Journal of Abnormal and Social Psychology,* 56 (March 1958), 143–159. Reprinted by permission of Dr. Richard Christie.

[1] The scoring, indicated here on each item, would be omitted when administering the scale to a sample group. Note that a non-response would be scored as "4." The higher the total score, the more authoritarian the respondent.[†]

[†] Scores would be omitted when administering test.

Example:

A. *Everything is relative and there just aren't any definite rules to live by.*

B. *There is an ultimate moral order and one can find the right thing to do if he wishes.*

____ A3 I agree a great deal more with A than B.

____ A2 I agree somewhat more with A than B.

____ A1 I agree slightly more with A than B.

____ B1 I agree slightly more with B than A.

____ B2 I agree somewhat more with B than A.

____ B3 I agree a great deal more with B than A.

Please place a check mark in the blank following each set of items which will represent the direction and intensity of your feelings.

1. A. It is highly unlikely that astrology will ever be able to explain anything.
   B. Some day it will probably be shown that astrology can explain a lot of things.
   (1) A3 (2) A2 (3) A1 (4) (5) B1 (6) B2 (7) B3

2. A. If it weren't for the rebellious ideas of youth there would be less progress in the world.
   B. Young people sometimes get rebellious ideas, but as they grow up they ought to get over them and settle down.
   (1) A3 (2) A2 (3) A1 (4) (5) B1 (6) B2 (7) B3

3. A. It would be a good thing if people spent more time thinking and talking about ideas just for the fun of it.
   B. If people would talk less and work more, everybody would be better off.
   (1) A3 (2) A2 (3) A1 (4) (5) B1 (6) B2 (7) B3

*4. A. Nowadays more and more people are prying into matters that should remain personal and private.
   B. There are times when it is necessary to probe into even the most personal and private matters.
   (7) A3 (6) A2 (5) A1 (4) (3) B1 (2) B2 (1) B3

*5. A. What a youth needs most is strict discipline, rugged determination, and the will to work and fight for family and country.
   B. In the long run it is better for our country if young people are allowed a great deal of personal freedom and are not strictly disciplined.
   (7) A3 (6) A2 (5) A1 (4) (3) B1 (2) B2 (1) B3

*6. A. The businessman and the manufacturer are much more important to society than the artist and the professor.
   B. The artist and the professor are probably more important to society than the businessman.
   (7) A3 (6) A2 (5) A1 (4) (3) B1 (2) B2 (1) B3

*7. A. Obedience and respect for authority are the most important virtues children should learn.
  B. One of the most important things children should learn is when to disobey authorities.
  (7) A3 (6) A2 (5) A1   (4)   (3) B1 (2) B2 (1) B3

8. A. Most honest people admit to themselves that they have sometimes hated their parents.
  B. There is hardly anything lower than a person who does not feel great love, gratitude, and respect for his parents.
  (1) A3 (2) A2 (3) A1   (4)   (5) B1 (6) B2 (7) B3

*9. A. The wild sex life of the old Greeks and Romans was tame compared to some of the goings-on in this country, even in places where people might least expect it.
  B. In spite of what you read about the wild sex life of people in important places, the real story is about the same in any group of people.
  (7) A3 (6) A2 (5) A1   (4)   (3) B1 (2) B2 (1) B3

10. A. It's nobody's business if someone is a homosexual as long as he doesn't harm other people.
  B. Homosexuals are hardly better than criminals and ought to be severely punished.
  (1) A3 (2) A2 (3) A1   (4)   (5) B1 (6) B2 (7) B3

11. A. When a person has a problem or worry, it is best to face it and try to think it through, even if it is so upsetting that it keeps him from concentrating on other things.
  B. When a person has a problem or worry, it is best for him not to think about it, but to keep busy with more cheerful things.
  (1) A3 (2) A2 (3) A1   (4)   (5) B1 (6) B2 (7) B3

*12. A. Every person should have complete faith in some supernatural power whose decisions he obeys without question.
  B. It's all right for people to raise questions about even the most sacred matters.
  (7) A3 (6) A2 (5) A1   (4)   (3) B1 (2) B2 (1) B3

For Further Reading

BOOKS

Adorno, T. W., Frenkel-Brunswik, E., Levinson, D. J., and Sanford, R. N. *The authoritarian personality.* New York: Harper and Brothers, 1950.

Reports the original research which eventuated in the concept of The Authoritarian Personality.

Rokeach, M. *The open and the closed mind.* New York: Basic Books, 1960.

An excellent presentation of theory and research into belief systems and the nature of the open and the closed mind. The Dogmatism scale is included.

ARTICLES

Anderson, R. C. Learning in discussions: a résumé of the authoritarian-democratic studies. *Harvard Educational Rev.,* 1959, 29 (3), 201–215. SA 10, A 1697.

The evidence fails to demonstrate that either authoritarian or democratic leadership is consistently associated with higher productivity.

Bendig, A. W. A further factor analysis of the California F scale. *J. psychol. Stud.,* 1960, 11 (6), 248–252. PA 35, 6472.

Authoritarianism is not a unitary syndrome but a cluster of at least three correlated sub-traits.

Byrne, D. Authoritarianism and response to attitude similarity—dissimilarity. *J. soc. Psychol.,* 1965, 66 (2), 251–256. PA 39, 1492.

Authoritarianism has no significant effect on response to attitude dissimilarity.

DeSoto, C. *et al.* Social perception and self-perception of high and low authoritarians. *J. soc. Psychol.,* 1960, 52 (1), 149–155. PA 35, 6333.

High authoritarians, rating pictures of strangers, exhibited general fear, suspicion and moralistic condemnation of the strangers.

Deutsch, M. Trustworthiness, and the F scale, *J. abnorm. soc. Psychol.,* 1960, 61 (1), 138–140. PA 35, 2107.

In a game situation, authoritarians tended to be suspicious and untrustworthy as compared to nonauthoritarians.

Dustin, D. Attitudes toward political candidates. *Psychol. Rep.,* 1965, 16 (3), 1212. PA 39, 14938.

The more authoritarian respondents were less accurate in predicting Johnson's percent of the vote in the 1964 elections.

Kates, S. L. First-impression formation and authoritarianism. *Hum. Relat.* 1959, 12 (3), 277–286. PA 35, 828.

High authoritarians were not as accurate in perceiving others as were low-authoritarians.

Kelman, H. C., and Barclay, J. The F scale as a measure of breadth of perspective. *J. abnorm. soc. Psychol.*, 1963, 67 (6), 608–615. SA 13, B 6728.

Scores on the F-scale are related to the breadth of a person's perspective, or range of tolerance.

King, P. T., and Ross, D. R. Test transparency as related to test response. *Personnel Guid. J.*, 1965, 43 (7), 669–673. PA 39, 12292.

Scores on the California Test of Personality differed when instructions were given to 10th-graders to pretend to be "happy" and to pretend to be in "a bad frame of mind."

Klein, E. B. A factor analysis of the F and Reversed F scales in three regional samples. *J. soc. Psychol.*, 1965, 65 (1), 127–134. PA 39, 12293.

Christie's reversals of the F-scale is really an independent scale, not simply a reversal.

Lipsitz, L. A working-class authoritarianism: a re-evaluation. *Amer. Sociol. Rev.*, 1965, 30 (1), 103–109. SA 13, B 6730.

The greater authoritarianism of the working class is largely a product of lower education.

Mandel, J. Esoteric theories and erroneous statistics in studies of prejudice. *Social Forces*, 1963, 42 (3), 237–241. SA 12, B0174.

Questions whether Rhyne (see selection no. 8) used the appropriate statistical procedures in analyzing his data, and argues that the differential learning and authoritarian hypotheses are not mutually exclusive. Rejoinder by Rhyne.

McCarthy, J., and Johnson, R. C. Interpretation to the "City Hall Riots" as a function of dogmatism. *Psychol. Rep.*, 1962, 11 (1), 243–245. PA 37, 4867.

Students who were low on Rokeach's Dogmatism scale tended to accept the student account of the disturbance, while subjects high in Dogmatism were more likely to accept the police version.

Melikian, L. H. Authoritarianism and its correlates in the Egyptian culture and in the United States. *J. soc. Issues*, 1959, 15 (3), 58–68. PA 36, 1GB58M.

While low authoritarianism is related to better personal adjustment in the United States, the opposite is true of Egypt—where authoritarianism is more characteristic of the culture.

Photiadis, J. D., and Bigger, J. Religiosity, education, and ethnic distance, *Amer. j. Sociol.*, 1962, 67 (6), 666–672. PA 37, 6584.

Of several variables tested (religious orthodoxy, anomie, status concern, withdrawal or antisocial tendencies) only authoritarianism related positively to ethnic distance.

———— and Johnston, A. L. Orthodoxy, church participation, and authoritarianism. *Amer. j. Sociol.*, 1963, 69 (3), 244–248. PA 38, 8203.

Authoritarian and prejudiced persons tend either to retain or to become strong orthodox believers, but persons who are authoritarian and orthodox become more tolerant through church participation.

Plant, W. T., *et al.* Some personality differences between dogmatic and non-dogmatic groups. *J. soc. Psychol.*, 1965, 67 (1), 67–75. PA 39, 15370.

Dogmatic versus nondogmatic men and/or women (Rokeach scale) differ on all five California Psychological Inventories; dogmatic individuals are more impulsive, defensive, and stereotyped in their thinking.

Rokeach, M. Authority, authoritarianism, and conformity. *Conformity and Deviation*, edited by I. A. Berg and B. M. Bass. New York: Harper and Brothers, 1961. Pp. 230–257. PA 36, 4GE3OR.

Questions several assumptions in the literature on authoritarianism; for example the reliance on authority versus the reliance on reason.

Rudin, S. A. The relationship between rational and irrational authoritarianism. *J. Psychol.*, 1961, 52 (1), 179–183. PA 36, 2GD79R.

There is no correlation between the tendency to accept irrational authority and the tendency to accept rational authority.

Siegman, A. W. A cross-cultural investigation of the relationship between religiosity, ethnic prejudice and authoritarianism. *Psychol. Rep.*, 1962, 11 (2), 419–424, PA 37, 7936.

In a United States sample, religiosity was not correlated with authoritarianism; in an Israeli sample, authoritarianism correlated with certain religious beliefs but not with religious observance.

Steiner, I. D., and Johnson, H. H. Authoritarianism and conformity, *Sociometry*, 1963, 26 (1), 21–34. SA 11, A 6401.

Suggests that outside the laboratory, the "peer group" usually does not present unanimity, and hence the authoritarian may be a nonconformist.

Stewart, D., and Hoult, T. A social-psychological theory of the authoritarian personality. *Amer. j. Sociol.*, 1959, 65 (3), 274–279. SA 8, 6925.

The psychoanalytic theory of authoritarianism is inadequate because it pertains to selected authoritarians only; numerous studies indicate that authoritarians manifest inadequacies in role-taking and role-playing.

Strickland, L. H., and Janicki, W. P. An alternative form of a forced choice "F" scale. *Psychol. Rep.*, 1965, 16 (3), 933–940. PA 39, 15202.

Presents data concerning the relative merits of a forced-choice form of the "F" scale versus a "counterbalanced" form.

Taylor, I. A., Similarities in the structure of extreme social attitudes. *Psychol. Monogr.*, 1960, 74 (2), Whole No. 489. PA 35, 3346.

Intense "Liberalism" or "Conservatism" both have basic personality similarities (F scale and others).

Troldahl, V. C., and Powell, F. A. A short-form dogmatism scale for use in field studies. *Social Forces*, 1965, 44 (2), 211–214. SA 14, CO957.

Presents data on 10, 15, and 20-item forms of the Rokeach Dogmatism scale (as opposed to the original 40-item one).

Vaughan, G. M., and White, K. D. Conformity and authoritarianism re-examined. *J. Personality soc. Psychol.*, 1966, 3 (3), 363–366. SA 15, C3467.

Consistently high conformers score higher on a forced-choice version of the F Scale than do consistently low conformers.

Weitman, M. More than one kind of authoritarian. *J. Personality*, 1962, 30 (2), 193–208. PA 38, 8300.

Pro-authoritarians, Antiauthoritarians, and Nonauthoritarians differ in acquiescence response set, prejudice, and ability to cope with cognitive tasks.

Williams, C. D. Authoritarianism and student reaction to airplane hijacking. *J. soc. Psychol.*, 1963, 60 (2), 289–291. PA 38, 4186.

High authoritarians were more likely to approve a senator's proposal to use military force to recover a commercial plane that had been hijacked.

Williams, J. A., Jr. Regional differences in authoritarianism. *Social Forces*, 1966, 45 (2), 273–277. SA 15, C4795.

There is a greater percent of white southerners having authoritarian attitudes than persons from other regions of the United States.

Chapter Four

Alienation

Though the theoretical foundations of the concept of *alienation* may be traced to Hegel and Marx, it is only in the last decade or two that there has been a lively theoretical and research interest in the topic. In 1953 Robert Nisbet commented:[1]

> At the present time, in all the social sciences the various synonyms of alienation have a foremost place in studies of human relations. Investigations of the "unattached," the "marginal," the "obsessive," the "normless," and the "isolated" individual all testify to the central place occupied by the hypothesis of alienation in contemporary social science . . . It has become nearly as prevalent as the doctrine of enlightened self-interest was two generations ago. It is more than a hypothesis; it is a perspective.

There is evidence that the perspective of which Nisbet spoke has become prevalent among laymen also. The subject of *alienation*—often in corrupted and almost unrecognizable form—appears as a topic of campus symposia, in the daily press, and in mass circulation magazines. Even among social scientists, the word has many connotations and as might be expected, there are some who so despair of ever attaining precise meaning and measurement that they would eliminate the word from the scientific vocabulary entirely.[2 and 3]

An analytical discussion by Melvin Seeman,[4] in which he delineated five subtypes of *alienation* as *powerlessness, meaninglessness, normlessness, isolation,* and *self-estrangement,* may be viewed as a watershed in the development and explication of this concept. The first subtype, he noted, derives from the work of Marx: "The worker is alienated to the extent

[1] Nisbet, R. A. The quest for community. New York: Oxford University Press, 1953, p. 15.

[2] Feuer, L. What is alienation? The career of a concept. *New Politics,* 1962, 1 (3), 116–134.

[3] Kaufman, A. S. On Alienation. *Inquiry,* 1965, 8 (2), 141–165.

[4] Seeman, M. On the meaning of alienation. *Amer. Sociol. Rev.,* 1959, 24 (6), 783–791.

that the prerogative and means of decision are expropriated by the ruling entrepreneurs."[5] By extension, individuals in most occupations and professions are subject to the same inability to control decisions and events which influence their lives—indeed, citizens generally have little influence over the policy-making which may involve fateful decisions regarding inflation–depression measures or the possibility of war, limited or otherwise.

In a second major usage of the alienation concept, which Seeman labels *meaninglessness*, the individual is seen as being unclear as to what he ought to believe, as perceiving the world as unintelligible or nearly so.

A third variant *normlessness* is developed from Durkheim's discussion of *anomie*. In this tradition, the reference is to the loss of commonly-held standards of belief and behavior; the absence of values that give purpose or direction to life.

The fourth idea involved is that of *social isolation*, of apartness, of separation from the group and its standards.

Finally, Seeman identified a type which he called *self-estrangement*. He observed the use of the term by Fromm in *The Sane Society* as denoting "a mode of experience in which the person experiences himself as an alien" and to Mills' characterization of the salesgirl and others in the industrial society whose personality becomes the instrument of an alien purpose; personality comes to have extrinsic value rather than intrinsic.[6]

Dwight G. Dean, working under the direction of Seeman, attempted to construct scales to measure the five variants of alienation.[7] It developed, however, that both meaninglessness and self-estrangement could be viewed as so closely related to powerlessness that they might be subsumed under that rubric.[*] The items from Srole's scale[8] were included in 139 items submitted to experts as a part of the validation procedure; the five items were scattered among the three categories of powerlessness, normlessness and social isolation, rather than consistently being assigned to one or another. (At the time this work was completed, Nettler's contribution[9] had not yet been published.) The first selection elaborates the connotations of the terms powerlessness, normlessness, and social isolation, and describes the construction of the appropriate scales.

The fruitfulness of the alienation concept may be represented by a study of Herbert M. Lefcourt and Gordon W. Ladwig. They were in-

---

[5] Seeman, M., *op. cit.*, 784.

[6] ———, *op. cit.*, 789.

[7] Dean, D. G. Alienation: its meaning and measurement. *Amer. Sociol. Rev.* 1961, 26 (5), 753–759.

[*] Whether or not this was justified, it is noteworthy that no one since has attempted to construct scales to measure these two constructs.

[8] Srole, L. Social integration and certain corollaries: an exploratory study. *Amer. Sociol. Rev.*, 1956, 21 (6), 709–716.

[9] Nettler, G. A measure of alienation. *Amer. Sociol. Rev.*, 1957, 22 (6), 670–677.

terested in exploring the variables behind the fact that blacks tend to score lower than whites on intelligence tests. They hypothesized that many a Negro has come to feel that he has little personal control over the rewards for his behavior, and may be characterized "as a person who has a low expectancy that he can control his reinforcements." [10] In their investigation, black prisoners were found to have a significantly greater sense of powerlessness and normlessness than did the white prisoners; and both black and white prisoners scored significantly higher on these scales than did a sample from the general population.

The third selection by Richard L. Simpson and H. Max Miller utilizes Srole's scale of *anomia* (which is similar to but not identical with normlessness) to study the relationship of social class and anomia. "The anomic individual," they note, "as identified by Srole's five questions, feels that community leaders are indifferent to his needs, that the social order is essentially unpredictable, that he and people like him are retrogressing from the goals they have reached, that he cannot count on anyone for support, and that life itself is meaningless." [11] Inspection of these five aspects will illustrate why this scale could not be fitted by Dean's judges into the *powerlessness-normlessness-isolation* categories, but were randomly distributed or not accepted at all (see Selection No. 10).

Finally, a short selection by J. L. Simmons gives the results of a study specifically designed to test the interrelationships of Dean's *powerlessness*, *normlessness*, and *social isolation* scales, Srole's *anomie* scale, a *misanthropy* scale constructed by Rosenberg, and scales Simmons developed to measure *low self-esteem*, *life-dissatisfaction*, and *attitude uncertainty*. It is regrettable that Nettler's *estrangement from society* scale was not included.

All of these selections represent attempts to wed theory and research into meaningful and creative activity. They avoid either an uncritical acceptance of the construct (prevalent among the lay public and all too be the case with the philosophers Lewis Feuer and Arnold S. Kaufman).[12] The selections illustrate that with the concept of alienation, like most concepts in this collection, there is need both for consensual definition and operational measurement.

[10] Lefcourt, H. M. and Ladwig, G. W. The American Negro: A problem in expectancies. *J. Personality soc. Psychol.*, 1965, 1 (4), 377–380.

[11] Simpson, R. L. and Miller, H. M. "social status and anomia," *Social Problems*, 1963, 10 (3), 257.

[12] See footnotes 2 and 3 above.

10

Alienation: Its Meaning and Measurement*

DWIGHT G. DEAN
Denison University

DELINEATION OF THE CONCEPT

The concept of Alienation, rooted deeply in sociological tradition, has recently enjoyed a new popularity. Theorists have suggested numerous possible correlates of Alienation, such as Apathy,[1] Authoritarianism,[2] Conformity,[3] Cynicism,[4] Hoboism,[5] Political Apathy,[6] Political Hyperactivity,[7] or Personalization in Politics,[8] Prejudice,[9] Privatization,[10] Psychosis,[11] Regression[12] and Suicide.[13] Only recently have scientists attempted to develop

Reprinted from *American Sociological Review*, 26, 5 (October 1961), 753–759, by permission of The American Sociological Association.

*Grateful acknowledgment is made for the encouragement and guidance of Melvin Seeman, University of California, Los Angeles and to Raymond Sletto and Christen Jonassen of The Ohio State University. This is a revised version of a paper read before The Ohio Academy of Science, Antioch College, Yellow Springs, Ohio, April 22, 1960.

[1] Kenneth Keniston, "Alienation and the Decline of Utopia," *The American Scholar*, 29 (Spring, 1960), p. 164; Eric Kahler, *The Tower and the Abyss*, New York: Braziller, 1957.

[2] Theodor W. Adorno, *et al.*, *The Authoritarian Personality*, New York: Harper and Brothers, 1950, p. 618.

[3] Erich Fromm, *Escape from Freedom*, New York: Harper and Brothers, 1958, p. 185; Keniston, *op. cit.*, p. 169.

[4] Robert Merton, *Mass Persuasion*, New York: Harper and Brothers, 1947, p. 143.

[5] Morton Grodzins, *The Loyal and the Disloyal*, Chicago: University of Chicago Press, 1956.

[6] Morris Rosenberg, "The Meaning of Politics in Mass Society," *Public Opinion Quarterly*, 15 (Spring, 1951), pp. 5–15.

[7] David Riesman and Nathan Glazer, "Criteria for Political Apathy," in *Studies in Leadership*, edited by Alvin Ward Gouldner, New York: Harper and Brothers, 1950, pp. 505–559.

[8] Adorno, *op. cit.*, p. 618.

[9] *Ibid.*

[10] Ernst Kris and Nathan Leites, "Trends in Twentieth Century Propaganda," in *Reader in Public Opinion and Communication*, edited by Bernard Berelson and Morris Janowitz, Glencoe, Ill.: The Free Press, 1950, p. 283.

[11] E. Gartly Jaco, "The Social Isolation Hypothesis and Schizophrenia," *American Sociological Review*, 19 (October, 1954), pp. 567–577.

[12] Sebastian DeGrazia, *The Political Community: A Study of Anomie*, Chicago: University of Chicago Press, 1948, esp. pp. 8–20 and 115–122.

[13] See, for example, E. H. Powell, "Occupation, Status, and Suicide: Toward a

scales to measure this phenomenon.[14] Numerous references to Alienation (or to similar concepts variously labeled) are, frequently, implicit rather than explicit. Sometimes the same writer includes several nuances of meaning. Seeman[15] has brought order out of this chaos with his fivefold classification: Powerlessness, Meaninglessness, Normlessness, Isolation and Self-Estrangement.

The first element, *Powerlessness*, was suggested long ago by Hegel [16] and by Marx[17] in their discussions of the worker's "separation" from effective control over his economic destiny; of his helplessness; of his being used for purposes other than his own. Weber[18] argued that the worker was only one case of the phenomena; for in the industrial society, the scientist, the civil servant, the professor is likewise "separated" from control over his work.

Parenthetically, the feeling of helplessness may have other sources besides the economic order of which Hegel, Marx, and Weber wrote. DeGrazia,[19] for example, has argued that the child's gradual awakening to the limitations of his parents sends him in search of a "ruler" who is "in charge of affairs," and who is favorably disposed toward the individual.

A succinct description of this element is provided by Kris and Leites:[20]

> Individuals in the mass societies of the twentieth century are to an ever-increasing extent involved in public affairs; it becomes increasingly difficult to ignore them. But "ordinary" individuals have ever less the feeling that they can *understand* or *influence* the very events upon which their life and happiness is known to depend.

What we consider the second component, *Normlessness*, is derived from Durkheim's concept of *anomie*. For, as Durkheim observed, sudden

---

Redefinition of Anomie," *American Sociological Review*, 23 (April, 1958), pp. 131–139.

[14] See, for example, Allan H. Roberts and Milton Rokeach, "Anomie, Authoritarianism, and Prejudice: A Replication," *American Journal of Sociology*, 61 (January, 1956), pp. 355–358; Gwynn Nettler, "A Measure of Alienation," *American Sociological Review*, 22 (December, 1957), pp. 670–677; and Leo Srole, "Social Integration and Certain Corollaries: An Exploratory Study," *American Sociological Review*, 21 (December, 1956), pp. 709–716.

[15] Melvin Seeman, "On the Meaning of Alienation," *American Sociological Review*, 24 (December, 1959), pp. 783–791.

[16] Cited in Herbert Marcuse, *Reason and Revolution*, New York: Oxford University Press, 1941, p. 34.

[17] Marcuse, *op. cit.*, p. 273.

[18] Hans H. Gerth and C. Wright Mills, *From Weber: Essays in Sociology*, New York: Oxford University Press, 1946, p. 50.

[19] DeGrazia, *op. cit.*, pp. 8–20 and pp. 115–122.

[20] Ernst Kris and Nathan Leites, *op. cit.*, p. 283. Italics are authors'.

economic losses or gains result in situations where previous scales cannot remain unchanged, the "calibration is turned . . . topsy-turvy . . . yet no new graduation can be quickly improvised." [21] DeGrazia,[22] in searching for clues to Durkheim's meaning, has noted:

> The specific words and phrases in French that Durkheim repeatedly used—*un perpétuel état de mécontentement, tourments, déceptions ré-pétées, inutilité, désorientée, inquiétude douloureuse, malaise, stérilité, intolérable, désenchantement, douloureux*—help us create the composite picture of anomie as it affects the individual. It becomes apparent that anomie as Durkheim conceived it in the subjective sense had three characteristics: a painful uneasiness or anxiety, a feeling of separation from group standards, a feeling of pointlessness or that no certain goals exist.

A perusal of the literature indicates that at least two rather distinct subtypes of *Normlessness* may be differentiated. The first subtype, *Purposelessness*, has been noted by MacIver,[23] who has described *anomy* as "the absence of values that might give purpose or direction to life, the loss of intrinsic and socialized values, the insecurity of the hopelessly disoriented."

An illustration of the obverse—i.e., a group whose activities bear striking testimony to the efficacy of purpose—would be the physicians among the Polish Jews in the Ghetto during the uprising against the Nazis. When defeat became obvious, these men countered utter hopelessness and resignation by carrying on medical research on their starving compatriots until the very end.[24] Bettelheim[25] has described his own reaction to the loss of standards that characterized the Nazi concentration camp in which he was imprisoned. He attributes his survival as a sane being to the fact that he had determined ahead of time that he would preserve his personality by forcing his experiences to yield insights into behavior under extreme conditions. His orientation to research furnished a "norm" which held him steady while community and civil life all around him disintegrated. Wolff [26] has utilized somewhat the same terms in explaining differential morbidity and mortality among American prisoners of war in Japan: "[man] is capable of enduring incredible burdens and taking cruel punish-

---

[21] Translation by DeGrazia, *op. cit.*, p. 3.

[22] *Ibid.*

[23] Robert M. MacIver, *The Ramparts We Guard*, New York: The Macmillan Company, 1950, pp. 84–87.

[24] Martin Gumpert, "The Physicians of Warsaw," *The American Scholar*, 18 (Summer, 1949), pp. 285–290. Reprinted in Joseph B. Gittler, *Social Dynamics*, New York: McGraw-Hill Book Company, 1952, pp. 15–21.

[25] Bruno Bettelheim, "Individual and Mass Behavior in Extreme Situations," *Journal of Abnormal and Social Psychology*, 38 (October, 1943), pp. 417–452.

[26] Harold G. Wolff, "A Scientific Report on What Hope Does for Man," *Saturday Review*, 40 (January 5, 1957), p. 45.

ment when he has self-esteem, hope, purpose, and belief in his fellows."

[The second subtype of *Normlessness* may be considered as *Conflict of Norms.*] DeGrazia[27] has described at some length the contemporary conflict between the "Cooperative" and the "Competitive" Directives, and between the "Activist" and the "Quietist" Directives. Karen Horney,[28] in similar vein, has described the difficulties of a person who incorporates in his personality conflicting norms such as the standards of Christianity versus the success imperative, the stimulation toward a constantly-higher material standard of living versus the practical denial of a high standard for many people, and the alleged freedom of the individual versus the factual limitations on his behavior. Ruesch[29] and Petersen[30] have described the same idea in their discussions of social mobility. The studies so far undertaken[31] have, it seems to us, not adequately considered the possibility that *Normlessness* may have several facets.

A third component, *Social Isolation*, may also be traced to Durkheim's conception of *anomie*, which included "a feeling of separation from the group or of isolation from group standards." [32] Jaco,[33] writing on "The Social Isolation Hypothesis," has shown that residential areas with the highest schizophrenic rates are those characterized by anonymity, spatial mobility, a smaller percentage of voting, low social participation, greater unemployment, fewer memberships in lodges and fraternal organizations, more job turnover, fewer visits with friends, etc. Halmos[34] related social mobility to psychoneurosis and schizophrenia. Kohn and Clausen[35] found a relationship between social isolation (rejection by one's peers) and mental disease.

[27] DeGrazia, *op. cit., Chapter* III, "Conflict Between Belief Systems," pp. 47–72.

[28] Karen Horney, "Culture and Neurosis," in *Sociological Analysis*, edited by Logan Wilson and William L. Kolb, New York: Harcourt, Brace and Company, 1949, pp. 248–251.

[29] Jurgen Ruesch, "Social Technique, Social Status, and Social Change in Illness," in *Personality in Nature, Society, and Culture*, edited by Clyde Kluckhohn and Henry A. Murray, New York: Alfred A. Knopf, 1950, p. 125.

[30] William Petersen, "Is America Still the Land of Opportunity?" *Commentary*, 16 (November, 1953), pp. 477–486.

[31] We did not use Srole's scale of *anomie* for two reasons: (a) one of his five items related to the political realm, which was the dependent variable in our study (see footnote 38, below) and (b) our conception of *anomie* seems to have a different meaning. See T. C. Keedy and M. J. Vincent, "Anomie and Religious Orthodoxy," *Sociology and Social Research*, 43 (September–October, 1958), pp. 34–37; Wendell Bell, "Anomie, Social Isolation and the Class Structure," *Sociometry*, 20 (June, 1957), pp. 105–116; Dorothy L. Meier and Wendell Bell, "Anomia and the Achievement of Life Goals," *American Sociological Review*, 24 (April, 1959), pp. 189–202.

[32] DeGrazia, *op. cit.*, p. 3.

[33] Jaco, *op. cit.*, pp. 567–577.

[34] Paul Halmos, *Solitude and Privacy*, London: Routledge and Kegan Paul, 1951.

[35] Melvin L. Kohn and John A. Clausen, "Social Isolation and Schizophrenia," *American Sociological Review*, 20 (June, 1955), pp. 265–273.

THE DEVELOPMENT OF SCALES

In order to determine what empirical relationships, if any, existed between the several components of *Alienation,* it was necessary to construct scales to measure each. A total of 139 items presumably measuring Alienation (which had been gleaned from the literature, over 70 interviews, or specially constructed) were typed on 3 × 5 cards. Seven experts (instructors and assistants in the Department of Sociology at The Ohio State University) were requested to judge each statement as to its applicability or nonapplicability, first, to the component of *Powerlessness* (using a one-page description as the criterion). When this part of the task was finished, each expert received a second set of cards to judge, again, each of the 139 items as to whether each item specifically and only referred to *Normlessness;* then, finally, a third set of cards was presented for judging of items as they might relate to *Social Isolation.*[36] For retention of an item, agreement on the part of at least five of the seven judges was required, with no judge placing the item in more than one category. Finally, the usual "DP" tests were applied.

Typical of the nine items in the final scale for *Powerlessness* were:[37]

There is little or nothing I can do towards preventing a major "shooting" war.

We are just so many cogs in the machinery of life.

Reliability of this sub-scale, tested by the "split-half" technique, was .78 (N = 384) when corrected by the Spearman-Brown prophecy formula.

Typical of the six items in the *Normlessness* scale, constructed simultaneously by the same method, were:

The end often justifies the means.

I often wonder what the meaning of life really is.

The reliability on this sub-scale, when corrected, was .73.

Typical of the nine items of the *Social Isolation* sub-scale were:

Sometimes I feel all alone in the world.

One can always find friends if he shows himself friendly.

The *Social Isolation* sub-scale had a "split-half" reliability of .84 when corrected for attenuation.

[36] This method adapted from John K. Hemphill and Charles M. Westie, "The Measurement of Group Dimensions," in *The Language of Social Research,* edited by Paul Lazarsfeld, *et al.,* Glencoe, Ill.: The Free Press, 1955, pp. 325ff.

[37] A mimeographed copy of the scales, with scoring instructions, follows at the end of this article.

The three sub-scales were combined to make up the *Alienation scale, which thus consisted of 24 items.* The items from each of the sub-scales were rotated in order to minimize the possibility of halo effect. The total *Alienation* scale had a reliability of .78 when corrected.

It seemed desirable to determine whether *Alienation* may be considered a general syndrome or whether the various components are somewhat discrete. The correlation coefficients between the sub-scales were, as shown in Table 1, considerably above the .01 level of significance. This suggests

TABLE 1

Inter-correlations Among the Alienation Scale Components (N = 384)

Components	Normlessness	Social Isolation	Alienation (total)
Powerlessness	.67	.54	.90
Normlessness		.41	.80
Social Isolation			.75

that it is quite feasible to consider the sub-scales as belonging to the same general concept. However, there appears to be enough independence among the sub-scales to warrant treating them as independent variables.

It seemed advisable to investigate the relationship of our scales measuring *Alienation* and Adorno's "Authoritarianism" scale. A low inter-correlation would lead one to believe that the scales we have developed do measure something other than Authoritarianism, and are not simply another way of scaling the same variable.

The correlation coefficients between the various components of *Alienation* and Adorno's "F" scale (for a college sample pretest of 73 respondents) were as follows:

Powerlessness and Authoritarianism   .37
Normlessness and Authoritarianism   .33
Social Isolation and Authoritarianism   .23
Alienation and Authoritarianism   .26

The first two correlation coefficients are significant at the .01 level of confidence; the latter two are significant at the .05 level of confidence.

Hypotheses. Our hypotheses were: (1) There is a *negative* correlation between social status (as measured by a modified version of the North-Hatt Occupational Prestige Scale, the amount of education attained, and income) and *Alienation* and its several components; (2) There is a *positive* correlation between advancing age and *Alienation* and its components; and (3) There is a *negative* correlation between rural background and *Alienation* and its components.

The Sample. The data were collected in Columbus, Ohio, as part of the writer's dissertation on *Alienation and Political Apathy*, a part of which is reported elsewhere.[38] Four of the nineteen wards in Columbus, Ohio, were selected on criteria related to voting incidence and socio-economic variables. Within these four wards, precincts were selected by random sampling; and, within the precincts, individuals were selected by random sampling. Of 1108 individuals who presumably received our questionnaire, 433 or 38.8 per cent responded. Of these 433, we were able to use 384 in our analysis.[39]

Findings. Table 2 indicates that while the hypotheses were in most instances sustained at statistically significant levels, the correlation coeffi-

TABLE 2

Correlation Coefficients Between Alienation and Five Background Factors ($N = 384$)

Components	Occupation	Education	Income	Age	Community
Powerlessness	−.20†	−.22†	−.26†	.14†	−.10*
Normlessness	−.21†	−.18†	−.14†	.13†	−.10*
Social Isolation	−.07	−.11*	−.13†	−.03	−.06
Alienation	−.19†	−.21†	−.23†	.12†	−.10*

* Significant at the .05 level of confidence.
† Significant at the .01 level of confidence.

cients are uniformly of such a low magnitude that it would not be feasible to predict the degree of *Alienation* from the score on any of the five social correlates measured:

It is of interest to note that, in general, with increased status in society, there is less of a feeling of *Alienation*. If we assume that older people in our culture have decreased status, the positive correlation that we found between age and *Alienation* would be expected. In this, our findings parallel Bell's work.[40]

Discussion. The generally low order of correlations raises a number of theoretical considerations. To the extent that we may assume the validity of the *Powerlessness, Normlessness* and *Social Isolation* sub-scales, we did not find *Alienation* correlated with social status, age or community background to any noticeable extent. If we reject the hypotheses of a negative correlation between these social background factors and *Alienation*, we ought to investigate further, since each of the sub-scales exhibited a normal curve of score distribution, with scores extending almost the

[38] Dwight G. Dean, "Alienation and Political Apathy," *Social Forces*, 38 (March, 1960), pp. 185–189.

[39] The merits of questionnaires versus interviews cannot be discussed here. We decided, on the basis of preliminary interviews, to use the questionnaire in the belief that respondents would more likely answer truthfully than when an interviewer was confronting them. See Claire Selltiz, *et al., Research Methods in Social Relations,* New York: Henry Holt and Company, 1959, pp. 240ff.

[40] Bell, *op. cit.,* pp. 105–116.

entire possible range. This would seem to indicate that these components and scales are not merely artifacts.

One explanation might be that *Alienation* is not a personality "trait," but a situation-relevant variable. It is plausible, for example, that an individual might have a high *Alienation-Powerlessness* score in regard to political activity, but a low one in regard to religion. For example, the "premillennialists" among Fundamentalists might be politically apathetic precisely because they believe that international crises cannot be solved by man, but that the world can only be "saved" by Divine intervention.

In regard to the *Alienation-Normlessness* component, it is interesting to note that Keedy,[41] using Srole's scale, found *anomie* related to religious orthodoxy among Protestants. Bell,[42] using the same scale but controlling for socio-economic status, found no correlation between *anomie* and being Protestant, Catholic, or Jewish; nor with frequency of attendance at church. It may be speculated that a *Normlessness* scale clearly differentiating the *Purposelessness* and *Conflict of Directives* sub-types might prove more fruitful.

Further investigations should be made in regard to the syndrome of *Alienation*. In this connection, it may be noted that Srole's scale could not be retained in our *Alienation* scales because his items failed to meet our judging and item analysis criteria. His *anomie* scale, however, correlated .31 with our *Normlessness* sub-scale on a college pretest sample of 73. The fact that Nettler's scale[43] also correlated with Srole's scale at about the same magnitude seems to indicate that "estrangement from society" may be empirically separable from the other components.

Finally, while most of the literature and our particular research have conceptualized *Alienation* as a phenomenon of Society, others,[44] have made the local community or associational activities the referent. Perhaps the individual's identification with, or *Alienation* from, Society, is experienced with reference to primary groups or voluntary associations.

It may very well be that *Alienation* is not a unitary phenomenon, but a syndrome. In this respect, Davids' conceptualization of eight components seems challenging.[45] In any case, certainly much more research is required before the *Alienation* concept can be empirically validated.

---

[41] Keedy, *op. cit.*, pp. 34–37.

[42] Bell, *op. cit.*, pp. 105–116.

[43] Gwynn Nettler, "A Measure of Alienation," *American Sociological Review*, 22 (December, 1957), pp. 670–677.

[44] John P. Clark, "Measuring Alienation Within A Social System," *American Sociological Review*, 24 (December, 1959), pp. 849–852; Wayne E. Thompson and John E. Horton, "Political Alienation as a Force in Political Action," *Social Forces*, 38 (March, 1960), pp. 190–195.

[45] Anthony Davids, "Alienation, Social Apperception, and Ego Structure," *Journal of Consulting Psychology*, 19 (February, 1955), pp. 21–27 and "Generality and Consistency of Relations Between the Alienation Syndrome and Cognitive Processes," *Journal of Abnormal and Social Psychology*, 51 (July, 1955), pp. 61–67.

THE ALIENATION SCALE*

Public Opinion Questionnaire

Below are some statements regarding public issues, with which some people agree and others disagree. Please give us your own opinion about these items, i.e., whether you agree or disagree with the items as they stand.

Please check in the appropriate blank, as follows:

      ___ A (Strongly Agree)
      ___ a (Agree)
      ___ U (Uncertain)
      ___ d (Disagree)
      ___ D (Strongly Disagree)

I 1. Sometimes I feel all alone in the world.
      (4) A (3) a (2) U (1) d (0) D*

P 2. I worry about the future facing today's children.
      (4) A __ a __ U __ d __ D

I 3. I don't get invited out by friends as often as I'd really like.
      (4) A __ a __ U __ d __ D

N 4. The end often justifies the means.
      (4) A __ a __ U __ d __ D

I 5. Most people today seldom feel lonely.
      (0) A (1) a (2) U (3) d (4) D*

P 6. Sometimes I have the feeling that other people are using me.
      (4) A __ a __ U __ d __ D

N 7. People's ideas change so much that I wonder if we'll ever have anything to depend on.
      (4) A __ a __ U __ d __ D

I 8. Real friends are as easy as ever to find.
      (0) A __ a __ U __ d __ D*

P 9. It is frightening to be responsible for the development of a little child.
      (4) A __ a __ U __ d __ D

N 10. Everything is relative, and there just aren't any definite rules to live by.
      (4) A __ a __ U __ d __ D

[Editor's note: to encourage replication, the *Alienation* scale, with scoring key, is herewith reproduced. The letter to the left of each item indicates whether it belongs to the Powerlessness, Normlessness or Isolation sub-scale. Obviously, scores would be omitted when administered.]

I   11. One can always find friends if he shows himself friendly.

           (0) A __ a __ U __ d __ D*

N   12. I often wonder what the meaning of life really is.

           (4) A __ a __ U __ d __ D

P   13. There is little or nothing I can do towards preventing a major "shooting" war.

           (4) A __ a __ U __ d __ D

I   14. The world in which we live is basically a friendly place.

           (0) A __ a __ U __ d __ D*

P   15. There are so many decisions that have to be made today that sometimes I could just "blow up."

           (4) A __ a __ U __ d __ D

N   16. The only thing one can be sure of today is that he can be sure of nothing.

           (4) A __ a __ U __ d __ D

I   17. There are few dependable ties between people any more.

           (4) A __ a __ U __ d __ D

P   18. There is little chance for promotion on the job unless a man gets a break.

           (4) A __ a __ U __ d __ D

N   19. With so many religions abroad, one doesn't really know which to believe.

           (4) A __ a __ U __ d __ D

P   20. We're so regimented today that there's not much room for choice even in personal matters.

           (4) A __ a __ U __ d __ D

P   21. We are just so many cogs in the machinery of life.

           (4) A __ a __ U __ d __ D

I   22. People are just naturally friendly and helpful.

           (0) A __ a __ U __ d __ D

P   23. The future looks very dismal.

           (4) A __ a __ U __ d __ D

I   24. I don't get to visit friends as often as I'd really like.

           (4) A __ a __ U __ d __ D

.   .   .

For comparative purposes, data from several samples are given below:

	(1)	(2)	(3)	(4)	(5)	(6)
POWERLESSNESS:						
Mean	13.65			12.73	10.90	
Standard Deviation	6.1					
NORMLESSNESS:						
Mean	7.62	8.63	3.77	7.63	3.55	see below
Standard Deviation	4.7	3.26	3.50			
SOCIAL ISOLATION:						
Mean	11.76			14.85	15.16	
Standard Deviation	4.6					
(TOTAL) ALIENATION:						
Mean	36.64			36.25	30.16	
Standard Deviation	13.5					

(1) Columbus, Ohio, N 384 (men), stratified sample, 1955.

(2) Protestant Liberal Arts College, N 135 (women), random sample, 1960.

(3) Catholic Women's College, N 121 (women), random sample, 1960.

(4) Protestant Liberal Arts College, N 75 (women), random sample, 1955.

(5) Catholic Women's College, N 65 (women), random sample, 1955. This and sample #3 are identical except for date.

(6) A State University, Midwest, Normlessness scores were: Catholics 12.84, S.D. 3.51; Protestants 14.40, S.D. 3.13. Questionnaires sent to a sample of 245, about 55% return.

11

The American Negro: A Problem in Expectancies[1]

HERBERT M. LEFCOURT
University of Waterloo, Ontario

GORDON W. LADWIG
*Veterans Administration Hospital,
Chillicothe, Ohio*

Recent reviews of research pertaining to Negro-white differences by Shuey (1958) and Dreger and Miller (1960) have noted the reliable finding that Negroes perform less adequately than whites on intelligence measures. This kind of data has resulted in such polemic arguments as that between Chein and Garrett (1962) which debates hereditarian versus environmentalist interpretations and conclusions. Recently, a body of research findings has been developing which emphasizes the situational and personality variables operative in Negroes which produce the apparent intellectual inferiority noted in intelligence testing.

Roen (1960) found Negroes' intelligence scores correlated with certain personality measures. He concluded that Negroes

> incorporate intellectually defeating personality traits that play a significant role in their ability to score on measures of intelligence [p. 150].

In a series of studies by Katz (Katz & Benjamin, 1960; Katz & Cohen, 1962; Katz & Greenbaum, 1963) Negro students were found to be anxious and unproductive in problem-solving situations especially when confronted with white partners.

The present research represents a further exploration of Negro-white differences on personality variables related to achievement behavior and its correlate, intelligence test performance. Rotter, Liverant, and Seeman (1962) have described an expectancy construct referred to as internal-external (I-E) control of reinforcements. Internal control refers to a

Reprinted from *Journal of Personality and Social Psychology*, 1, 4 (April 1965), 377–380, by permission of the authors and The American Psychological Association.

[1] This report is based partially on a doctoral dissertation submitted by the senior author to the Graduate School, Ohio State University, August 1963. The senior author wishes to express his appreciation to Alvin Scodel for his guidance in the course of the study. This research was supported in part by the United States Air Force, under Contract No. AF 49(638)–317 monitored by the Air Force Office of Scientific Research of the Air Research and Development Command.

generalized expectancy that reinforcements occur as a consequence of one's own actions and are thereby under personal control. External control refers to the belief that reinforcements are unrelated to one's own behaviors and therefore beyond personal control.

This variable may prove important in attempting to understand the problem of Negroes' intelligence test difficulty. Crandall, Katkovsky, and Preston (1962) have found that internal-control children show more intellectual interest and better intelligence test performance than external-control children. This suggests that a person perceiving his reinforcements as being externally controlled, is less likely to try and succeed. Rose (1956), in his condensation of Myrdal's *The American Dilemma*, noted that

> the ambition of Negro youth is cramped not only by . . . segregation and discrimination but also by the low expectation from both white and Negro society. . . . And if he is not extraordinary he will not expect it of himself and will not really put his shoulder to the wheel [p. 218].

The Negro may be characterized as a person who has a low expectancy that he can control his reinforcements. The first hypothesis in this study, then, is that Negroes will score higher on external control than a comparable group of whites, in tests designed to measure the I-E dimension. Second, in achievement tasks that demand self-evaluation Negroes will perform in a manner that can be described as reflecting a greater expectancy of external control.

METHOD

To test these hypotheses 60 Negro and 60 white inmates from two correctional institutions were used as subjects. There were no significant differences in social class, intelligence, age, or reason for incarceration between the two groups. For the most part the subjects were of lower class origin. Their intelligence levels were within the average range with beta IQs between 90 and 110 (Kellogg & Morton, 1935). The mean age was 21.6 years and the typical crime leading to incarceration was car theft.

Each subject was given the Rotter Level of Aspiration Board (LOA) using Rotter's (1942) standard instructions. In addition, the subject was instructed that he would earn a pack of cigarettes for each 50 points he had at the conclusion of the task. This was done to enlist cooperation and to encourage "realistic" goal setting.

Three indices of LOA performance which theoretically are related to the I-E dimension were employed: number of shifts, number of unusual shifts, and patterns. The number of shifts (changes in the subject's prediction of his next score) in the LOA relates to general stability and self-confidence. High frequencies of shifts characterize individuals who do not

use previous experience to establish consistent estimates of their performance. Unusual shifts (up after failure, down after success) likewise suggest
failure of the subject to establish reliable estimates of his skill. Unusual
shifts tend to indicate dependence on luck or magical, externally controlled factors. Of the LOA patterns described by Rotter (1945) Patterns
1 and 3 indicate a stable, ambitious, confident approach while the other
patterns generally indicate a failure-avoidant, defensive approach. In both
patterns there are an average number of shifts and generally an absence
of unusual shifts. In Pattern 1, D scores usually range from 0.0 to +3.0,
while in Pattern 3, the range is from +3 to +6.0. Patterns 1 and 3 demonstrate the task involvement and realistic self-appraisal characteristic of
internal controls. Previous research has demonstrated the relationship of
these latter two indices (unusual shifts and patterns) with the I-E dimension (Simmons, 1959).

After the LOA task the subjects were given the I-E scale of Rotter et
al. (1962) and Dean's (1961) Powerlessness and Normlessness scales.
The former was developed in the framework of Social Learning Theory
(Rotter, 1954) to assess the I-E control variable. The test consists of 23
forced-choice items with 6 filler items. Illustrative items are as follows:

I more strongly believe that:

    6. a. Without the right breaks one cannot be an effective leader.
       b. Capable people who fail to become leaders have not taken ad-
         vantage of their opportunities.
    9. a. I have often found that what is going to happen will happen.
       b. Trusting to fate has never turned out as well for me as making
         a decision to take a definite course of action.
  17. a. As far as world affairs are concerned, most of us are the victims
        of forces we can neither understand nor control.
      b. By taking an active part in political and social affairs the people
        can control world events.
  23. a. Sometimes I can't understand how teachers arrive at the grades
        they give.
      b. There is a direct connection between how hard I study and the
        grades I get.

Dean's scales were constructed to measure two of the five variables
that Seeman (1959) has defined as components of alienation. Powerlessness, like external control, refers to an individual's expectancy that he cannot control his fate. Normlessness refers to the high expectancy that socially unapproved behaviors are required in order to achieve given goals.
The Powerlessness measure consists of nine Likert scale items. Illustrative
items are as follows:

There is little or nothing I can do towards preventing a major "shoot-
    ing" war.

We're so regimented today that there's not much room for choice even in personal matters.

Typical of the six Likert scale items in the Normlessness measure were:

Everything is relative, and there just aren't any definite rules to live by. The only thing one can be sure of today is that he can be sure of nothing.

The predictions are that Negroes will score higher on external control and claim greater powerlessness and normlessness than whites. In the LOA task it is predicted that Negroes will shift more, make more unusual shifts, and will produce fewer Patterns 1 and 3 than whites.

RESULTS

As indicated in Table 1, all predicted differences in Level of Aspiration Board performance were obtained. Negroes shifted more frequently and

TABLE 1

Level of Aspiration Board Results

	Negroes	Whites	t
Number of shifts			
M	9.08	7.00	
SD	5.02	3.57	2.60*
Proportion of subjects making one or more unusual shifts	.72	.48	2.68†
Proportion of subjects making two or more unusual shifts	.52	.22	3.41‡
Proportions of subjects showing Patterns 1 and 3	.25	.53	3.14‡

NOTE. All tests are two-tailed based on samples of 60 in each group.

*$p = .02$.

†$p = .01$.

‡$p = .001$.

made more unusual shifts than whites. In a comparison of the overall patterns of performance, significantly fewer Negroes showed Patterns 1 and 3, the patterns indicative of internal control.

In the comparison of number of shifts Negroes were more variable than whites (t between standard deviations $= 2.57$, $p < .02$). However, since the Ns were equal a parametric test of differences between the means was justified (Boneau, 1960).

Subjects making no unusual shifts were compared with those making one or more unusual shifts. A second comparison of those making zero to one, versus those making two or more unusual shifts, was also made to minimize the possibility that subjects were included in the "unusual-shift" group who made an occasional unusual shift for justifiable reasons, i.e., when a previous failure was just short of the stated goal.

Table 2 indicates that Negroes scored significantly higher on the three

TABLE 2

Comparisons on Scale Measures

Measure	Negroes	Whites	t
I-E			
M	8.97	7.87	2.00*
SD	2.97	3.03	
Powerlessness			
M	17.30	14.63	2.89†
SD	5.02	4.98	
Normlessness			
M	12.60	9.37	3.49‡
SD	4.40	4.53	

NOTE. All tests are two-tailed based on samples of 60 in each group.
* $p = .05$.
† $p = .01$.
‡ $p = .001$.

attitude measures related to the I-E control dimension. Since the largest difference between Negroes and whites was obtained on the Normlessness scale it might be plausible to suggest that Negroes are even more dubious about the avenues open to them than about their own adequacy to achieve.

A third comparison was undertaken between the Negro and white inmate samples and norms reported by Dean which were based on a stratified sample of 384 male subjects drawn from the Columbus, Ohio, area. It was expected that reformatory inmates, in general, would score higher on powerlessness and normlessness than a non-institutionalized population, and that Negroes, in particular, would be more markedly deviant from such norms.

As Table 3 indicates, Negro inmates' scores are considerably higher in an external-control direction than Dean's normative group. A similar comparison with white inmates showed no significant difference from the norm group in powerlessness ($t = .71$, ns) although on normlessness white inmates also scored higher than Dean's norm group ($t = 2.48$, $p < .05$).

In brief, reformatory inmates seem to have higher expectancies than the general population that socially unapproved behaviors are required to achieve valued goals. Negro inmates appear even more pessimistic about socially acceptable means than white inmates. However, only Negro inmates appear radically different from the general population in regard to the powerlessness variable which is more directly related to the I-E control dimension than is normlessness.

TABLE 3

Comparison of Negro Inmates with Dean's Norms for the Powerlessness and Normlessness Scales

	Dean's Sample (N = 384)	Negro Inmates (N = 60)	t
Powerlessness			
M	13.65	17.30	4.35*
SD	6.1	5.0	
Normlessness			
M	7.62	12.60	7.73*
SD	4.7	4.4	

*$p = .001$.

DISCUSSION

Literature concerning the American Negro has often focused on their feelings of low self-esteem and pessimism. This investigation has been directed toward a study of these problems making use of the I-E control variable. Negroes have been found to have low expectancies for internal control of reinforcements both in attitude and behavior measures. Although research is required to clarify the development of the expectancy of external control, it would seem likely that segregation and discrimination facilitate the growth of an external orientation. They deny positive reinforcements to Negroes despite individual achievements, thus providing the kind of experience necessary for the development and maintenance of generalized expectancies of external control. As Rose has suggested, such expectancies should result in a minimum of effort to achieve and a lack of interest in achievement-related pursuits. Crandall's findings, noted previously, tend to support this thesis. In view of the findings in this study it may be hypothesized that Negroes' poorer performance on intelligence tests reflects a withdrawal from middle-class achievement goals. The externally oriented Negro may well see these goals as being unobtainable through his own efforts. It is possible that in the current Negro mass movement for civil rights, there will be greater opportunity for Negroes to witness concrete changes deriving from their social action. If so, the differences between Negroes and whites obtained in this study may not be as extreme in the not too distant future.

References

Boneau, C. A. The effects of violations of assumptions underlying the *t* test. *Psychological Bulletin*, 1960, 57, 49–64.

Chein, I., & Garrett, H. Rejoinder and surrejoinder. *Society for Psychological Study of Social Issues Newsletter*, May 1962.

Crandall, V. J., Katkovsky, W., & Preston, A. Motivational and ability determinants of young children's intellectual achievement behaviors. *Child Development*, 1962, 33, 643–661.

Dean, D. G. Alienation: Its meaning and measurement. *American Sociological Review*, 1961, 26, 753–758.

Dreger, R. M., & Miller, K. S. Comparative psychological studies of Negroes and whites in the United States. *Psychological Bulletin*, 1960, 57, 361–402.

Katz, I., & Benjamin, L. Effects of white authoritarianism in biracial work groups. *Journal of Abnormal and Social Psychology*, 1960, 61, 448–456.

———, & Cohen, M. The effects of training Negroes upon cooperative problem solving in biracial teams. *Journal of Abnormal and Social Psychology*, 1962, 64, 319–325.

———, & Greenbaum, C. Effects of anxiety, threat, and racial environment on task performance of Negro college students. *Journal of Abnormal and Social Psychology*, 1963, 66, 562–567.

Kellogg, C. E., & Morton, N. W. *Revised beta examination.* New York: Psychological Corporation, 1935.

Roen, S. R. Personality and Negro-white intelligence. *Journal of Abnormal and Social Psychology*, 1960, 61, 148–150.

Rose, A. *The Negro in America.* Boston: Beacon Press, 1956.

Rotter, J. B. Level of aspiration as a method of studying personality: II. Development and evaluation of a controlled method. *Journal of Experimental Psychology*, 1942, 31, 410–422.

———. Level of aspiration as a method of studying personality: IV. The analysis of patterns of response. *Journal of Social Psychology*, 1945, 21, 159–177.

———. *Social learning and clinical psychology.* New York: Prentice-Hall, 1954.

———, Liverant, S., & Seeman, M. Internal versus external control of reinforcement: A major variable in behavior theory. In N. Washburne (Ed.), *Decisions, values and groups.* Vol. 2. London: Pergamon Press, 1962.

Seeman, M. On the meaning of alienation. *American Sociological Review*, 1959, 24, 783–791.

Shuey, A. M. *The testing of Negro intelligence.* Lynchburg, Va.: J. P. Bell, 1958.

Simmons, W. L. Personality correlates of the James-Phares scale. Unpublished master's thesis, Ohio State University, 1959.

12

Social Status and
Anomía*

RICHARD L. SIMPSON and
H. MAX MILLER
University of North Carolina

Research has consistently shown that anomia, measured by Srole's scale, is more prevalent in the lower than in the higher social classes, but little research has dealt with variations in anomia within given status levels. This paper presents survey data bearing on three hypotheses which relate aspects of status to variations in anomia within status levels. The data fail to support the "status inconsistency" hypothesis that inconsistent statuses lead to anomia, or the "social failure" hypothesis that differential failure to achieve life goals explains variations in anomia within status levels. A third hypothesis, consistent with our own and earlier research findings, is tentatively advanced though it cannot be fully tested with the data at hand: the "attitudinal exposure" hypothesis, which asserts that among people currently at the same status level, those with more past exposure to the anomic attitudes of lower-status groups will be more anomic.

Research has consistently shown that anomia, as measured by Srole's well known scale, is more prevalent in the lower than in the higher social classes.[1] An examination of Srole's definition of anomia and the items in

Reprinted from *Social Problems*, 10, 3 (Winter 1963), 256–264, by permission of the authors and The Society for the Study of Social Problems.

* Revision of a paper presented at the Southern Sociological Society meetings, Miami Beach, April, 1961. The research reported herein was performed pursuant to a contract with the United States Office of Education, Department of Health, Education, and Welfare, and was also supported by the Ford Foundation through the Urban Studies Program, Institute for Research in Social Science, University of North Carolina. We are indebted to David R. Norsworthy for suggestions and for help in analysis, and to Ida Harper Simpson for a critical reading of the manuscript.

[1] Alan H. Roberts and Milton Rokeach, "Anomie, Authoritarianism, and Prejudice: A Replication," *American Journal of Sociology*, 61 (January, 1956), pp. 355–358; Leo Srole, "Anomie, Authoritarianism, and Prejudice," and Milton Rokeach, "Rejoinder," letters to the editor, *American Journal of Sociology*, 62 (July, 1956), pp. 63–67; Leo Srole, "Social Integration and Certain Corollaries," *American Sociological Review*, 21 (December, 1956), pp. 709–716; Wendell Bell, "Anomie, Social Isolation, and the Class Structure," *Sociometry*, 20 (June, 1957), pp. 105–116; Dorothy L. Meier and Wendell Bell, "Anomia and Differential Access to the Achievement of Life Goals," *American Sociological Review*, 24 (April, 1959), pp. 189–202; Melvin M. Tumin and Ray C. Collins, Jr., "Status, Mobility, and Anomie: A Study in Readiness for Desegrega-

his scale makes it clear why one would expect this to be so. He defines anomia as a "generalized, pervasive sense of . . . 'self-to-others alienation.' . . ."[2] The anomic individual, as identified by Srole's five questions, feels that community leaders are indifferent to his needs, that the social order is essentially unpredictable, that he and people like him are retrogressing from the goals they have reached, that he cannot count on anyone for support, and that life itself is meaningless.[3] One might reasonably expect these gloomy attitudes to be most common in the lower classes. Objectively, lower-class people have to struggle harder for smaller rewards than middle-class people. Their economic position is precarious and it is difficult for them to plan successfully and predictably for the success goals with which the surrounding culture bombards them.[4]

Hardship and frustration, however, are prevalent throughout the lower classes, yet not all lower-class people are equally anomic, and conversely, some people in the higher social classes score high in anomia. This paper asks: what aspects of class status are especially likely to produce varying degrees of anomia *within* class levels? What is it, for example, that makes some middle-class people anomic when most middle-class people are not anomic?

tion," *British Journal of Sociology*, 10 (September, 1959), pp. 253–267; Ephraim H. Mizruchi, "Social Structure and Anomia in a Small City," *American Sociological Review*, 25 (October, 1960), pp. 645–654; Edward L. McDill, "Anomie, Authoritarianism, Prejudice, and Socio-Economic Status: An Attempt at Clarification," *Social Forces*, 39 (March, 1961), pp. 239–245; Lewis M. Killian and Charles M. Grigg, "Urbanism, Race, and Anomia," *American Journal of Sociology*, 67 (May, 1962), pp. 661–665. Roberts and Rokeach feel that their data show only a negligible relationship of status (measured by income) to anomia, but Srole disagrees; their difference of opinion concerns only the strength of the relationship, not the direction. Killian and Grigg find the usual relationship between status and anomia among whites and urban Negroes; among rural Negroes they find almost no relationship.

[2] Srole, "Social Integration and Certain Corollaries," *op. cit.*, p. 711.

[3] This description is condensed and paraphrased from Srole's definition of the five components of his anomia scale in "Social Integration and Certain Corollaries," *op. cit.*, pp. 712–713.

[4] For discussions of success goals in the lower classes see Ely Chinoy, "The Tradition of Opportunity and the Aspirations of Automobile Workers," *American Journal of Sociology*, 57 (March, 1952), pp. 453–459; Robert H. Guest, "Work Careers and Aspirations of Automobile Workers," *American Sociological Review*, 19 (April, 1954), pp. 155–163; Robert K. Merton, "Social Structure and Anomie" and "Continuities in the Theory of Social Structure and Anomie," in *Social Theory and Social Structure*, rev. ed., Glencoe, Ill.: Free Press, 1957, pp. 131–194; Robert Dubin, "Deviant Behavior and Social Structure: Continuities in Social Theory," *American Sociological Review*, 24 (April, 1959), pp. 147–164; Richard A. Cloward, "Illegitimate Means, Anomie, and Deviant Behavior," *American Sociological Review*, 24 (April, 1959), pp. 164–176; Robert K. Merton, "Social Conformity, Deviation, and Opportunity-Structures: A Comment on the Contributions of Dubin and Cloward," *American Sociological Review*, 24 (April, 1959), pp. 177–189; Meier and Bell, *op. cit.*; Seymour Martin Lipset and Reinhard Bendix, *Social Mobility in Industrial Society*, Berkeley and Los Angeles: University of California Press, 1959, pp. 176–181; Ephraim H. Mizruchi, "Social Structure, Success Values and Structured Strain in a Small City," paper read at the annual meeting of the American Sociological Association, St. Louis, 1961.

We shall present data bearing on three alternative hypotheses which relate aspects of class status to differing degrees of anomia, to see if we can account for variations in anomia within class levels. The first two hypotheses described below are derived from the literature. Neither of them successfully accounts for the data, to be given later, on within-status differences in anomia, and the third is tentatively advanced as our own attempt to explain the differences.

Status Inconsistency. Lenski has found that people with status inconsistency—i.e., people who hold differing ranks by different stratification criteria, such as Negro physicians or uneducated rich men—tend to hold leftist political beliefs and to participate less than one would expect in voluntary associations.[5] He interprets their radicalism and their avoidance of social participation as reactions to "social experiences of an unpleasant or frustrating nature" due to their wish to be treated on the basis of their highest statuses and people's habit of treating them instead on the basis of their lowest statuses.[6] Lenski is not very precise in describing the psychological process which intervenes between these unpleasant experiences and their behavior outcomes—the leftist vote or social withdrawal—but he seems to be postulating a mental state closely akin to anomia. From Lenski's theory one might therefore predict that within a given status level as measured by a given status criterion, status inconsistency will be associated with high anomia. By this reasoning a person becomes anomic not because his status attributes are generally low, but because he has a mixture of high and low status attributes.

Social failure. In an alternative formulation Meier and Bell hypothesize that anomia results "when individuals lack access to means for achievement of life goals" because of their "position in the social structure. . . ."[7] In support of this view they report relationships of anomia to occupation, education, income, and subjective class identification, among other things. Their explanation may be called the "social failure" hypothesis: people become anomic because their low status represents an inability to achieve life goals. Our intention is not to question Meier and Bell's assertion that social failure explains between-status differences in anomia, but to see whether it can also explain within-status differences.

Attitudinal exposure. It will be shown later that neither the status in-

<hr>

[5] Gerhard Lenski, "Status Crystallization: A Non-Vertical Dimension of Social Status," *American Sociological Review*, 19 (August, 1954), pp. 405–413; Gerhard Lenski, "Social Participation and Status Crystallization," *American Sociological Review*, 21 (August, 1956), pp. 458–464. For findings contradictory to those in the first Lenski article, See William F. Kenkel, "The Relationship between Status Consistency and Politico-Economic Attitudes," *American Sociological Review*, 21 (June, 1956), pp. 365–368. For early treatments of the idea of status inconsistency, see Emile Benoit-Smullyan, "Status, Status Types, and Status Interrelationships," *American Sociological Review*, 9 (April, 1944), pp. 151–161; and Everett C. Hughes, "Dilemmas and Contradictions of Status," *American Journal of Sociology*, 50 (March, 1945), pp. 353–359.

[6] Lenski, "Status Crystallization," *op. cit.*, p. 412.

[7] Meier and Bell, *op. cit.*, p. 190.

consistency nor the social failure hypothesis satisfactorily explains the within-status anomia differences in our data. As a tentative alternative we shall propose the attitudinal exposure hypothesis. This will be described more fully later, but in brief it asserts that within a given social status level, anomia will be especially prevalent among people who have had the most exposure to the relatively more anomic atmosphere of lower-status groups.

In the remainder of the paper we present and discuss some survey data bearing on these hypotheses.

SOURCE OF DATA

The data are from a survey conducted in 1959 using a random block sample of white adult males in two southern cities. Three hundred eighty interviews were obtained, for a return rate of 70 percent of all eligible respondents living in the selected blocks. Of these, 366 were usable for the part of the study reported here. The refusal rate was below five percent and nearly all the missing interviews represent people in blocks where some interviewing had been done, who had not yet been reached when the time and money available for interviewing came to an end. Despite the random procedures that were used, the sample overrepresents white-collar workers and especially professionals and managers. This bias does not seem important for the present analysis, which examines relationships within status levels and does not attempt to describe the total population.[8]

Data used in this paper include the respondent's present job and the first "regular full-time job" he ever had, both classified by Hollingshead's seven-level index of occupational status;[9] the respondent's age and educa-

[8] For the major Census occupational groups, the 1960 Census percentages, for white males in the two cities combined, and our 1959 sample percentages respectively, are as follows: professional, technical, and kindred, 16.1, 23.0; farmers and farm managers, 4.7, 0.0; managers, officials, and proprietors except farm, 15.4, 23.3; clerical and kindred, 8.1, 8.8; sales, 11.8, 8.8; craftsmen, foremen, and kindred, 19.2, 13.7; operatives and kindred, 16.0, 15.6; private household workers, 0.1, 0.0; service except private household, 4.9, 3.8; farm laborers and foremen, 1.2, 0.0; laborers except farm and mine, 2.5, 3.0. These figures give a rough idea of the representativeness of our sample, but the sample bias is less than the figures suggest. The Census figures for the two cities cover their entire incorporated areas, including some semi-rural territory recently annexed, but our sample was drawn from areas sufficiently urbanized to appear on city block maps prepared by the cities' planning departments. Evidence that the Census figures refer to a wider territory is seen in the figures for farmers and farm workers. These comprised nearly six percent of the Census totals but were not represented by any worker in our block sample.

[9] The Hollingshead index of occupational status is described in August B. Hollingshead and Frederick C. Redlich, *Social Class and Mental Illness*, New York: Wiley, 1958, pp. 387–397; and in August B. Hollingshead, "Two Factor Index of Social Position," New Haven: Yale University, Department of Sociology, 1957 (mimeographed).

tional attainment; and the Srole anomia scale.[10] Anomia is scaled trichotomously and ranges from 0 (absence of anomia) to 10 (very high anomia).[11]

FINDINGS AND INTERPRETATION

Table 1 shows the median and range of anomia scores for respondents classified by occupational level and by educational attainment. As ex-

TABLE 1

Anomia by Occupation and by Education

	Anomia		
Status Variable	*Median*	*Range*	*(N)*
Occupational Status*			
1 (high)	2.85	0-8	(51)
2	3.80	0-6	(48)
3	3.95	0-8	(63)
4	4.75	0-10	(73)
5	5.93	0-10	(48)
6-7 (low)	6.86	2-10	(80)
Years of Education			
17 or more (postgraduate)	2.94	0-7	(42)
16 (college graduation)	3.71	0-8	(59)
13-15 (some college)	4.17	0-9	(50)
12 (high school graduation)	4.75	0-10	(79)
10-11 (some high school)	5.67	0-8	(37)
7-9	6.43	0-10	(69)
0-6	7.10	1-10	(26)

* Occupational status is classified by Hollingshead's index in which classes 1–4 are non-manual and 5–7 are manual.

pected, low-status men tended to be more anomic than high-status men; this relationship was consistent, with no reversals. However, the ranges indicate a considerable amount of variation in anomia within status levels and overlap between levels, and our next task is to examine this variation in the light of our hypotheses.

Status inconsistency. Our data allow two tests of this hypothesis. The first is to see whether men who were low in either occupation or educa-

[10] Srole, "Social Integration and Certain Corollaries," *op. cit.*

[11] Using the Cornell technique with dichotomous scaling and agreement vs. disagreement as the cutting point for each item, preliminary analysis of a subsample of 100 interviews indicated a coefficient of reproducibility of .94, but the minimum reproducibility was .82 and the scores were heavily clustered near the low end of the scale. We therefore decided to scale anomia trichotomously with arbitrarily chosen cutting points, since this gave a wider distribution. Our analysis employs the trichotomous anomia scale, which had a coefficient of reproducibility of .72 with minimum reproducibility .48.

tion but relatively higher in the other were more anomic than men who were equally low in both attributes.[12] Table 2, which cross-classifies respondents by occupation and education, shows that this was not the case. Instead, occupation and education were separately and cumulatively related to anomia. The rows in Table 2 are numbered for easy examination

TABLE 2

Anomia by Cross-Tabulation of Occupation and Education

	Anomia	
Occupation and Education*	*Median*	*(N)*
1. 1–2; 17 or more	3.00	(41)
2. 1–2; 13–16	3.31	(49)
3. 3–4; 13–16	4.11	(55)
4. 3–4; 12	4.31	(45)
5. 3–4; 0–11	5.30	(36)
6. 5; 12–16	6.00	(15)
7. 5; 0–11	6.25	(33)
8. 6–7; 12–16	6.37	(19)
9. 6–7; 0–11	7.00	(61)

* Some categories with N's below 15 are omitted. Some education categories used in Table 1 are combined to produce N's of 15 or more.

of the several relevant comparisons. The relation of occupation to anomia, with education controlled, can be seen by comparing rows 2 and 3; rows 3 and 4 combined, row 6, and row 8; and rows 5, 7, and 9. Again, in each instance, the lower the educational attainment, the greater was the anomia. The respondents who were highest in both occupation and education were the least anomic, and those who were at the bottom in both occupation and education were the most anomic.[13] Since these figures show greater anomia among men with consistently low status attributes than among men with mixed high and low attributes, they argue against the status inconsistency hypothesis.

The second test of the hypothesis involves a variable which we have

[12] Lenski ("Status Crystallization," *op cit.*) also used income and ethnicity in his measure of status consistency. We lack data on income and cannot use ethnicity since our sample was all white and almost all native Protestant.

[13] Other studies also suggest that the relationships of different status attributes to anomia are cumulative. Roberts and Rokeach, *op. cit.*, do not directly address this question but their findings show that when education is controlled, the relation of income to anomia is markedly reduced but does not disappear. Bell, *op. cit.*, differentiates between neighborhood and individual status, which he measures with a composite of variables, and his findings suggest that the two are cumulatively related to anomia. Meier and Bell, *op. cit.*, find that low individual status attributes have cumulative effects on anomia.

called "occupational success." Unusual occupational success or failure in comparison with age-mates of similar education is a form of status inconsistency. The successful man may be rejected by his occupational equals because he is younger or less educated than they, and the failure may be rejected by his age and educational equals because of his low occupational status. In Table 3 we have categorized respondents' occupational success by sorting them into seven educational groups and, within each of these, three age groups (34 and under, 35 to 44, 45 and over). Within each of these 21 groups matched in age and education, workers in the median Hollingshead occupational level were defined as "normals," those above this occupational level were defined as "successes," and those below, as "failures." In this way 109 men were classified as successes, 151 as normals, and 106 as failures. From the status inconsistency hypothesis one would predict relatively low anomia among the normals at a given occupational level and high anomia among the successes and failure. Table 3 fails to

TABLE 3

Anomia by Occupation and Occupational Success

	Anomia	
Occupation and Occupational Success	*Median*	*(N)*
1–2, success	3.86	(29)
1–2, normal	2.83	(56)
3–4, success	4.75	(68)
3–4, normal	4.50	(38)
3–4, failure	4.67	(27)
6–7, normal	8.00	(22)
6–7, failure	6.27	(55)

substantiate this prediction. In occupational levels 1 and 2 the successes were more anomic than the normals, but in levels 6 and 7 the normals were more anomic than the failures, and in levels 3 and 4 the three groups were almost identical and the relationship of anomia to occupational success was not consistent. (There were not enough failures in the top group, successes in the bottom group, or successes or failures in level 5 to analyze meaningfully.)[14]

[14] A comparable table was run with the initial classification by education (three levels) rather than by occupation. Among the college graduates and high school graduates the normals had somewhat the lowest anomia scores, but among the men who had not finished high school the normals had by far the highest anomia scores—a result which is at best ambiguous so far as the status inconsistency hypothesis is concerned and certainly does not support it. What is happening is that small *N*'s obscure differences between ostensibly equated groups, since with small *N*'s the matched groups have to be gross. Finely detailed tabulations show a tendency to high anomia among the groups lowest in either education or occupation within the gross groups

These results do not confirm the status inconsistency hypothesis, which thus is not supported by either of two tests.

Social failure. Our data permit two tests to see whether this hypothesis, which Meier and Bell advance to explain between-status differences in anomia, can also explain within-status differences. The first involves a second look at Table 3. From the social failure hypothesis one would predict high anomia among the failures and low anomia among the successes, with the normals intermediate.[15] The findings are the opposite of this in two of the three occupational categories where there are enough cases to make comparisons, the exception being in occupational levels 3 and 4, where men in the three success categories did not differ appreciably in anomia.

TABLE 4

Anomia by Present Occupation and Career Mobility, Among Men 30 and Older

	Anomia	
*Occupational Status and Career Mobility**	*Median*	*(N)*
1–2, upward	3.64	(54)
1–2, stationary	3.14	(33)
3–4, upward	4.23	(79)
3–4, stationary	4.88	(20)
5–6, upward	6.75	(45)
5–6, stationary	5.60	(39)

* Downward mobile workers are omitted because of small N's. Workers with current level 7 are omitted because by definition they could not have been upward mobile.

The second test of the social failure hypothesis concerns career mobility (Table 4), measured by comparing the occupational levels of the respondents' first and current jobs. (Any movement from one of Hollingshead's seven levels to another was defined as mobility. Men under 30 were

---

shown in our tables. When the groups shown in Table 3 are further divided by small educational distinctions, the differences within occupational levels turn out to be largely explainable by differences in educational attainment, which, as was shown in Table 2. was independently related to anomia with occupation controlled.

[15] Both of our tests of the social failure hypothesis assume that those who fail to achieve the usual degree of upward career mobility actually interpret their lack of mobility as failure. Indirect evidence that they are likely to do so is given in Richard L. Simpson, David R. Norsworthy, and H. Max Miller, "Occupational Mobility in the Urbanizing Piedmont of North Carolina," mimeographed report submitted to the Cooperative Research Branch, United States Office of Education, Department of Health, Education, and Welfare, by the Institute for Research in Social Science, University of North Carolina, Chapel Hill, 1960, pp. 133–135, which shows that the downward mobile tended to be the most dissatisfied and the upward mobile the most satisfied with their occupational situations, with the stationary intermediate. For other studies giving roughly similar findings see the works cited in footnote 4 by Chinoy, Guest, Meier and Bell, Lipset and Bendix, and Mizruchi.

eliminated from the analysis. Downward mobile workers were also eliminated from the sample since there were too few of these to analyze meaningfully.) From the social failure hypothesis one would predict higher anomia among the stationary, who had failed to move up during their careers, than among the upward mobile. The findings do not verify this prediction. There were enough cases for comparison of upward mobile and stationary workers in combined current-job categories 1–2, 3–4, and 5–6. In two of these three comparisons greater anomia was found among the upward mobile than among the stationary, contrary to the social failure hypothesis. (The only exception, again, involved men in occupational levels 3 and 4, the lower white-collar group.)[16]

Thus both tests argue against the social failure hypothesis as the explanation of within-status variation in anomia.

Attitudinal exposure. Since the data do not fit the status inconsistency or social failure hypothesis, we propose as a tentative alternative the attitudinal exposure hypothesis, which fits the data from all the studies we have cited and suggests some directions which research might profitably take. This hypothesis asserts that within a given social status level, the greatest degree of anomia will be found among people who have had the most exposure to life in lower-status groups, where the prevailing attitudes are more anomic.

Consider the various findings. In research by Srole, Roberts and Rokeach, McDill, Meier and Bell, Mizruchi, Tumin and Collins, and the present authors, the one relationship which is consistently found is between anomia and *any indication of low status in adult life, past or present*, no matter how status is measured.[17] Seen in this context, some of our negative findings concerning the status inconsistency and social failure hypotheses cease to be problematic. The finding of a generally positive relationship between occupational success and anomia (Table 3) seems to mean simply that within occupational levels, the less educated were apt

---

[16] Again, as in the case of Table 3 (see footnote 14), the differences within occupational levels as shown in Table 4 are explainable, when very fine breakdowns are used, by differences in educational attainment. When the initial classification is by education (college graduates vs. high school graduates vs. non-high school graduates) instead of by occupation the same relationships between mobility and anomia are found within each educational level as within the roughly corresponding occupational level shown in Table 4. Among the college graduates and those who had not finished high school, the upward mobile were anomic, and among the high school graduates, the stationary were more anomic. In tabulations including men under 30, the same relationships held.

[17] For references to these other studies, see footnote 1. We say "in adult life" because tables with intergenerational mobility as a variable—e.g., holding the worker's current occupation constant and varying the father's occupation—produced no marked or consistent anomia patterns. No such test gave either clear support or clear refutation to any of the three hypotheses considered in this paper. From our data we can only conclude that anomic or nonanomic attitudes are acquired in adult life, or at least no visible pattern fitting any of the three hypotheses stems from childhood status when current status is held constant.

to be more anomic. The finding that the upward mobile were generally more anomic than the occupationally stationary (Table 4) means that of any two men currently at the same status level, the one with the lower previous status was likely to be the more anomic. Table 5, which reworks

TABLE 5

Anomia by Present and First Occupation for Selected Categories of Workers

	Anomia	
Present and First Occupational Status*	*Median*	*(N)*
1, 1	2.40	(27)
1, 2–4	3.40	(21)
2, 2	3.33	(13)
2, 3–4	3.92	(27)
3, 4	3.25	(19)
3, 5–7	4.29	(33)
4, 4	4.89	(25)
4, 5–7	4.75	(42)
6, 6	6.25	(41)
6, 7	8.50	(18)

* Men under 30 are included but downward mobile men and categories with N smaller than 10 are omitted.

the Table 4 data using finer categories, gives a clearer picture. Arbitrarily designating 15 as the smallest N for which a median can be computed, Table 5 affords comparisons by first-job level for workers whose current jobs were in Hollingshead levels 1, 3, 4, and 6. In three of these four comparisons, the exception being current-job level 4, the men with the lower first jobs had higher anomia. If 10 instead of 15 is taken as the lowest acceptable N, the men with current jobs in level 2 add another case in which anomia is associated with low initial job level.

　　If low status, present or past, makes for anomia, how do we explain this and why do we call it an "attitudinal exposure" hypothesis? The reasoning is straightforward. (1) The Meier and Bell "social failure" hypothesis seems adequate to explain differences in anomia between (but not within) status levels. It is understandable if low-status people feel more anomic than high-status people. Their life-chances are inferior; as Meier and Bell put it, they have less opportunity to achieve life goals; in many situations they are accorded less respect and dignity. (2) With each low-status attribute, the likelihood increases that a person's social circle will include other people of low status. Whatever the attribute may be, low rank can prevent the person from associating as an equal with others whose status is high.[18] (3) Since low status and anomia go together for

[18] We lack data to demonstrate this for our sample, but it seems a safe assumption to make on the basis of the overwhelming evidence for it in previous research. For a

reason number one, this means that each low-status attribute increases the probability that one's associates are anomic. Therefore the social environment of a low-status person exposes him to an anomic climate of opinion. Attitudes formed in primary-group contexts and reinforced by the attitudes of one's associates may linger even after one's own status has changed for the better, hence the finding that the anomia scores of people who had experienced upward career mobility retained traces of the attitudinal climates of the low-status groups they had left behind.

The attitudinal exposure hypothesis is advanced tentatively. We lack the direct information on past and present social circles of our respondents which would be needed to give it a fully adequate test. It is, however, consistent with the findings of our study and earlier studies relating status level to anomia. It also fits Blau's more general analysis of the "acculturation effect," in which he finds that various attitudes of the socially mobile are intermediate between the typical attitudes of the classes they have left and the classes they have entered.[19]

ANOMIA SCALE *

.   .   .

The interviewer's introduction was:

"Now I'd like your opinions on a number of different things. I'm going to read you several statements. Some people agree with each statement; some people disagree. As I read each one, will you tell me whether you *more or less agree* with it, or *more or less disagree* with it?"

summary of several studies on the relation of social rank to interaction and attraction patterns, see Morton B. King, Jr., "Socioeconomic Status and Sociometric Choice," *Social Forces*, 39 (March, 1961), pp. 199–206. King presents data from George A. Lundberg and Margaret Lawsing, "The Sociography of Some Community Relations," *American Sociological Review*, 2 (June, 1937), pp. 318–335; Charles P. Loomis and J. Allan Beegle, *Rural Social Systems*, New York: Prentice-Hall, 1950, pp. 450–453, taken from Harvey J. Schweitzer, Jr., "The Rural Church and the Social Structure of Sebewa Township, Ionia County, Michigan," unpublished M.A. thesis, Michigan State College, 1947; August B. Hollingshead, *Elmtown's Youth*, New York: Wiley, 1949; and from unpublished portions of a study conducted by King in rural Mississippi. See also data in W. Lloyd Warner and Paul S. Lunt, *The Social Life of a Modern Community*, New Haven: Yale University Press, 1941, *passim*. For general discussions see Bernard Barber, *Social Stratification*, New York: Harcourt, Brace, 1957, p. 67; John F. Cuber and William F. Kenkel, *Social Stratification in the United States*, New York: Appleton-Century-Crofts, 1954, pp. 151–152; Joseph A. Kahl, *The American Class Structure*, New York: Rinehart, 1957, pp. 136–138; Kurt B. Mayer, *Class and Society*, Garden City, N. Y.: Doubleday, 1955, pp. 43–45; and Leonard Reissman, *Class in American Society*, Glencoe, Ill.: Free Press, 1959, pp. 177–183.

[19] Peter M. Blau, "Social Mobility and Interpersonal Relations," *American Sociological Review*, 21 (June, 1956), pp. 290–295.

* [Editor's note: to encourage replication, Srole's *anomia* scale is reproduced below.] Reprinted by permission of Dr. Leo Srole.

The respondent was given a score of one for each item to which the answer was an unqualified "more or less agree." "Agrees" that were further qualified were scored zero (as were, of course, the "disagree" items).

1. Most people in public office are not really interested in the problems of the average man.
2. These days, a person doesn't really know whom he can count on.
3. Nowadays, a person has to live pretty much for today and let tomorrow take care of itself.
4. In spite of what some people say, the situation of the average man is getting worse, not better.
5. It's hardly fair to bring a child into the world with the way things look for the future.

13

Some Intercorrelations Among "Alienation" Measures*

J. L. SIMMONS

University of California, Santa Barbara

This paper is a brief presentation of the matrix of correlations among eight measures of "personal disturbance." The variables—normlessness, powerlessness, social isolation, despair, misanthropy, low self-esteem, life dissatisfaction, and attitude uncertainty—have been frequently construed as facets or concomitants of "alienation." [1] Since these findings emerged as a byproduct of a larger study of liberalism and deviance, they will be concisely presented, without discussion of their theoretical relevance and implications, so that they may be available to other researchers and scholars working with alienation.

The normlessness, powerlessness and social isolation scales used were those developed by Dean;[2] the despair measure is Srole's Anomia scale;[3] the Misanthropy scale was developed by Rosenberg;[4] and the low self-esteem, life-dissatisfaction, and attitude uncertainty scales were developed by the author.[5]

The data consists of the responses of 391 students enrolled in sociology and anthropology courses at a major midwestern university. It should be emphasized that the present findings can only be regarded as suggestive,

Reprinted from *Social Forces*, 44, 3 (March 1966), 370–372, by permission of the author and The University of North Carolina Press.

* I am indebted to David Gold and George J. McCall for their critical suggestions.

[1] See, for example, Karl Marx, "Alienated Labor," Eric and Mary Josephson (trans.), in Eric and Mary Josephson, *Man Alone* (New York: Dell Publishing Co., 1962), pp. 93–105; Erich Fromm, *The Sane Society* (New York: Rinehart & Co., 1955); Melvin Seeman, "On the Meaning of Alienation," *American Sociological Review*, 24 (December 1959), pp. 783–791; Dwight Dean, "Alienation: Its Meaning and Measurement," *American Sociological Review*, 26 (October 1961), pp. 753–758.

[2] Dean, *op. cit.*

[3] Leo Srole, "Social Integration and Certain Corrollaries," *American Sociological Review*, 21 (December 1956), pp. 709–717.

[4] Morris Rosenberg, "Misanthropy and Political Ideology," *American Sociological Review*, 21 (December 1956), pp. 690–695.

[5] For a detailed discussion of these and the above five scales and presentation of their univariate distributions for the sample, c.f., Jerry Laird Simmons, "The Relationships Between Attitude Position, Alienation, and Personal Disturbance," Ph.D. dissertation, State University of Iowa, 1962, Appendix B.

because of two major weaknesses inherent in them. First, sample biases make the generalization of the findings hazardous. The respondents were entirely students who had elected to enroll in social science courses, so that they are not even representative of student bodies as a whole, let alone nonstudent populations. However, as Zetterberg points out, representativeness of sample is not crucial when the research concerns relationships between variables.[6]

Second, the validity or correspondence between the scales and the concepts they purport to measure is problematic, although the first five of them have been widely used. Therefore, the correlations presented here should probably not be employed without consideration of the literature on the development and use of the scales. Also the fact that some of the measures have Guttman scaled for some populations, does not necessarily mean that they would do so for others.

The hypothesis that these eight social-psychological disturbance measures are interrelated, generates a matrix of 28 specific predictions of a correlation between each possible pair of variables.

TABLE 1

*Correlations (r) Among the Disturbance Measures**

	Powerlessness	Social Isolation	Despair	Misanthropy	Low Self-esteem	Life Dissatisfaction	Attitude Uncertainty
Normlessness	.43	.33	.25	.20	.16	.33	.29
Powerlessness		.53	.35	.30	.22	.35	.21
Social Isolation			.23	.36	.28	.37	.21
Despair (Srole A. scale)				.35	.02	.10	.08
Misanthropy					.10	.19	.07
Low Self-esteem						.42	.30
Life-dissatisfaction							.35

* With an N of 391, an *r* of greater than .10 is significant at the .05 level and an *r* of greater than .13 is significant at the .01 level.

The actual matrix of observed correlations (Pearsonian *r*) among the measures is presented in Table 1. Examination of the table reveals that all 28 correlations are in the predicted direction and that 23 of them are significant at the .01 level. An overall appraisal of the table would seem to suggest that there is a modest but pervasive interrelationship among the eight variables. This suggests that there might exist a general personality pattern or syndrome running from "complacency" to "disturbance." How-

[6] Hans Zetterberg, *On Theory and Verification in Sociology* (rev. ed.; Totowa, New Jersey: Bedminster Press, 1963), pp. 54–55.

ever, it should also be noted that the scales still display a large measure of independent variation.

A possible alternative explanation of the correlations is that the empirical measures of the variables are contaminated by each other. The content of the specific questions may be so similar that the scales are distinct in name only. However, a careful examination of the scale items reveals that many of the scales with dissimilar content nevertheless have at least moderate correlations. For example, the misanthropy and the social isolation scales differ markedly in content yet show an r of .36. Therefore, although some contamination through overlap of content no doubt exists, it cannot entirely account for the pattern of associations found.

The highest correlation (.53) exists between powerlessness and social isolation. This might be taken to suggest the speculation that the two variables are but aspects of a more general subjective sense of a circumscribed opportunity structure.

The moderate correlations of life-dissatisfaction each with self-esteem (.42), social isolation (.37), powerlessness (.35), attitude uncertainty (.35), and normlessness (.33), would seem to lend empirical support to the classic proposition that it is difficult to lead a successful and satisfying life without integration into a web of values and interpersonal relationships.[7]

Other modest associations exist between normlessness and powerlessness (.43), powerlessness and despair (.35), despair and misanthropy (.35), and misanthropy and social isolation (.36).

Three additional remarks should be made concerning the present findings. First, an examination of the original bivariate contingency tables reveals that most of the associations are not entirely linear; there is a good deal of scatter along the lower and middle ranges of the variables which then funnels and often becomes curvilinear for the high portion of the ranges. Therefore *gamma* or *eta* would have been a more appropriate estimate of association. Future researchers will probably find the latter two statistics more useful when they have reason to expect skewed distributions and/or stepwise, funneling, or curvilinear types of associations. Both skewedness and non-linearity are frequent in studies of deviance, "social problems" and personality.

Second, the writer does not wish to assert or imply that given positions on the "disturbance" scales are "better" than other positions. Most of us would probably agree that a pervasive dissatisfaction with one's lot, or extreme feelings of despair, are states to be avoided, if possible. However, a bovine complacency may pose as many "social problems" as "disturbance" in many areas of modern life.

Finally, the direction of influence in the above relationships is probably two-way and it probably varies from respondent to respondent. For exam-

[7] Emile Durkheim, *Suicide* (Glencoe, Illinois: The Free Press, 1951), *passim.*

ple, social isolation may lead to a greater sense of powerlessness and the resultant apathy may then in turn produce greater social isolation. Going beyond the data, it might be speculated that a marked change in any one of these variables will tend to alter the individual's position on many of the other variables. A marked increase in disturbance on a particular scale might thus tend to generalize to increased disturbance on other scales, and conversely, a reduction on one scale might produce a generalized reduction in disturbance. This proposition, however, is only a speculation for future research.

For Further Reading

BOOKS

Blauner, R. *Alienation and freedom: the factory worker and his industry.* Chicago: University of Chicago Press, 1964.

This work attempts to establish the thesis that differing kinds of industrial environment produce differing degrees of alienation. Printing (high degree of worker control over job), textile (low worker control but high community integration), automobile (least control and community integration) and the automated chemical industry (new kind of control) are contrasted. Data from a 1947 *Fortune* survey.

Clinard, M. B. (Ed.). *Anomie and deviant behavior: A discussion and critique,* New York: The Free Press of Glencoe, 1964.

Deals with anomie and gang delinquency, mental disorder, drug addiction, alcoholism, and so forth. Contains an inventory of research on the correlates of anomie, anomia, and alienation.

Josephson, E. and M. (Eds.). *Man alone: alienation in modern society.* New York: Dell, 1962.

A collection of articles from Karl Marx to James Baldwin. Many perceptive studies, none of which define or measure the phenomena of alienation.

Kenniston, K. *The uncommitted: alienated youth in modern society.* New York: Harcourt, Brace & World, 1965.

About half of the book consists of case studies of a dozen "alienated" young people; the balance of the book discusses the alienating society.

Mizruchi, E. H. *Success and opportunity: a study of anomie.* New York: The Free Press, 1964.

An investigation of Merton's hypothesis (i.e., a discrepancy between the emphasis on material success and the failure to emphasize the means of attaining this goal). Uses Srole scale on a systematic sample of upstate New York.

Pappenheim, Franz. *The alienation of modern man.* New York: Monthly Review Press, 1959.

A well-written account of man's inadequate self-definition in a depersonalized society.

ARTICLES

Aiken, M., and Hage, J. Organizational alienation: a comparative analysis. *Amer. sociol. Review,* 1966, *31* (4), 497–507. SA 13, C3547.

Both alienation from work and alienation from expressive relations are found to be more prominent in highly centralized and highly formalized organizations.

Burchinal, L. G. Personality characteristics and sample bias. *J. appl. Psychol.,* 1960, *44* (3), 172–174. PA 35, 3426.

The more alienated and authoritarian are less likely to respond.

Clark, J. P. Measuring alienation within a social system. *Amer. sociol. Review,* 1959, 24 (6), 849–852. SA 8-6929.

Alienation in regard to an agricultural cooperative is negatively correlated with the member's satisfaction, participation, and knowledge of the organization.

Cloward, R. A. Illegitimate means, anomie, and deviant behavior. *Amer. sociol. Review,* 1959, 24 (6), 164–176. PA 35, 4773.

A theoretical discussion analyzing the relationship between social structure and deviant behavior through a combination of the theories of Durkheim and Merton.

Couch, C. J. Self-identification and alienation. *The sociol. Quart.,* 1966, 7 (3), 255–264. SA 15, C4057.

A modified version of the 20 Statements Test is proposed; may be a fruitful way of approaching alienation from and attachment to statuses occupied by the respondent.

Dean, D. G. Alienation and political apathy, *Social Forces,* 1960, 38 (3), 185–189. SA 10, A2416.

Alienation was not found to correlate with political apathy. It was suggested that alienation might be related to direction of voting.

————, and Reeves, J. A. Anomie: a comparison of a Catholic and a Protestant sample. *Sociometry,* 1962, 25 (2), 209–212. PA 37, 3006.

Testing Durkheim's hypothesis that Protestants exhibit a higher degree of anomie (normlessness) than Catholics, this study reports that in this sample of college women, there is a significantly greater degree of anomie among Protestants.

Erbe, W. Social involvement and political activity: a replication and elaboration. *Amer. sociol. Rev.,* 1964, 29 (2), 198–215. SA 12, B1818.

Alienation, socioeconomic status and organizational involvement are associated with political participation. Alienation, being correlated with the other two, drops out as a predictor when the other two factors are controlled.

Feuer, L. What Is alienation? The career of a concept. *New Politics,* 1962, 1 (3), 116–134.

Asserts that alienation is not a modern phenomenon and in addition is so multiform and widespread that it is useless as a scientific concept.

Gamson, W. A. The fluoridation dialogue: is it an ideological conflict? *Publ. Opinion Quart.,* 1961, 25 (2), 526–537. SA 11, A4335.

Proposes alienation (powerlessness) as an interpretation of opposition to fluoridation.

Gerson, W. M. Alienation in mass society: some causes and responses. *Sociol. soc. Res.,* 1965, 49 (2), 143–152, SA 13, B7790.

The technoindustrial revolution, the bureaucratic reorganization, consumption and leisure life, and disenchantment and the Freudian Ethic have contributed to the alienation of modern man. This author uses the term "alienation" in a much more limited sense than do most writers.

Hajda, J. Alienation and the integration of student intellectuals. *Amer. Sociol. Review,* 1961, 26 (5), 758–777. SA 9, A0966.

In this research, graduate students were classified as alienated intellectuals, integrated intellectuals, alienated nonintellectuals and integrated nonintellectuals. Variation of alienation is explained by the kind of ties the intellectual establishes with nonacademic people.

Hobart, C. W., and Warne, N. On sources of alienation. *J. Existent.*, 1964, 5 (18), 183–189. PA 39, 7514.

Attempts to outline the societal circumstances that cause feelings of powerlessness, meaninglessness, normlessness, isolation and self-estrangement. It describes how the anxiety potential may be virtually eliminated by certain characteristics of the social structure.

Horton, J. Dehumanization of anomie and alienation: a problem in the ideology of sociology. *Brit. J. Sociol.*, 1964, 15, 283–300. SA 13, B7571.

Alienation for Marx and Anomie for Durkheim were metaphors for a radical attack on the dominant institutions and values of industrial society. [Has there been] a transformation from the radical to the conformist definition and values under the guise of value-free sociology?

Horton, J. E. and Thompson, W. E. Powerlessness and political negativism: a study of defeated local referendums. *Amer. J. Sociol.*, 1962, 67 (2), 485–495. SA 10, A2425.

There is a consistent relationship between powerlessness and negative votes in those cases where a feeling of powerlessness took the form of alienation from certain symbols of power in the community.

Jaffee, L. D. Delinquency proneness and family anomie. *J. crim. Law, Criminol.*, 1963, 54 (2), 146–154. SA 12, B0624.

A study of the relationship between delinquency and anomie (translating Durkheim's conception into value confusion in the family).

Jarritt, W. H., and Haller, A. Situational and personal antecedents and incipient alienation: an exploratory study. *Genetic Psychol. Monogr.*, 1964, 69 (1), 151–191. PA 39, 1352.

Alienation (from home and school) accompanies a lack of success-producing resources.

Kaufman, A. S. On alienation. *Inquiry*, 1965, 8 (2), 141–165. SA 14, B9117.

Argues that alienation is a moral term; should be eliminated from the scientific vocabulary.

Levin, M. B., and Eden, M. Political strategy for the alienated voter. *Publ. Opinion Quart.*, 1962, 26 (1), 47–63. SA 11, A4804.

An article arguing that the way to win friends and influence elections is to appeal to the voters' sense of powerlessness by emphasizing the tyranny of the incumbents and the candidate's own powerlessness; and an appeal to the sense of meaninglessness by offering the voter information that he did not expect to receive; and other strategies.

Lowry, R. P. The functions of alienation in leadership. *Sociol. soc. Res.*, 1962, 46 (4), 426–435. PA 37, 3053.

While the writer uses a rather restricted definition of alienation, he is provocative in suggesting that alienation may have positive functions.

Manheim, E. Reaction to alienation. *Kansas J. Sociol.*, 1965, 1 (3), 108–111. SA 14, C0055.

Reaction to alienation can take forms of (1) fatalism; (2) withdrawal in protest; (3) revolutionary impulse; and (4) involvement in change.

McCloskey, H., and Schaar, J. H. Psychological dimensions of anomy. *Amer. sociol. Rev.*, 1965, 30 (1), 14–40. SA 13, B6731.

Anomic responses are powerfully governed by cognitive and personality factors (for example, hostility, anxiety, and so forth). Sense of normlessness results from impediments to interaction, communication and learning.

McDill, E. L. Anomie, authoritarianism, prejudice, and socioeconomic status: an attempt at clarification. *Social Forces*, 1961, 39 (3), 239–245. PA 36, 1GD39M.

Authoritarianism and anomie are equally important in accounting for intolerant attitudes toward minority groups; a common psychological dimension underlies all three scales.

————, and Ridley, J. C. Status, anomia, political alienation, and political participation. *Amer. J. Sociol.*, 1962, 68 (2), 205–213. SA 11, A4805.

Low social status, anomie, and political alienation . . . are significantly related to a negative vote and unfavorable attitude on the issue of metropolitan government in Nashville, Tennessee.

Miller, C. R., and Butler, E. W. Anomie and eunomia: a methodological evaluation of Srole's Anomia scale. *Amer. sociol. Review*, 1966, 31 (3), 400–405. SA 14, C2677.

Did not meet the criterion of a pure Guttman scale.

Mizruchi, E. Social structure and anomia in a small city. *Amer. sociol. Rev.*, 1960, 25 (5), 645–654. SA 8, 8593.

Significant associations (in a small city) are reported between Srole's anomia scale and social class, class identification, formal and informal social participation.

Neal, A. G., and Rettig, S. Dimensions of alienation among manual and non-manual workers. *Amer. sociol. Review*, 1963, 28 (4), 599–608. SA 12, A8312.

Developed powerlessness and normlessness scales by factor analysis; is independent of Srole's scale. None related to mobility.

Nettler, G. A measure of alienation. *Amer. sociol. Review*, 1957, 22 (6), 670–677. SA 7, 5292.

This article presents one of the earlier and now classical measures of alienation, which the writer designates as "estrangement from society."

Olsen, M. E. Alienation and public opinions. *Publ. Opinion Quart.*, 1965, 29 (2), 200–212. SA 14, C0260.

Estrangement from society was found to be inversely related to occupational status, education and income, with occupation being the dominant factor. Estrangement has considerable influence on other attitudes, including tolerance of racial integration, willingness to limit freedom of speech, and disapproval of United States participation in international organizations.

Pearlin, L. I. Alienation from work: a study of nursing personnel. *Amer. sociol. Rev.*, 1962, 27 (3), 314–326. SA 10, A3903.

Alienation (subjective powerlessness) more likely where there is greater positional disparity between superordinates and their subjects; and where personnel are working in isolation and without outside social ties to fellow workers.

Putney, S. A. and Middleton, R. Ethical relativism and anomia. *Amer. J. Sociol.*, 1967, 67 (4), 430–438. SA 1 A1736.

Ethical relativists do not appear to exhibit a greater degree of anomia than absolutists.

Rhodes, L. Anomia, aspiration and status. *Social Forces,* 1964, *42* (4), 434–440. SA 14, B8538.

Anomia is more closely related to occupational aspiration than to occupational level for a sample of adolescents.

———. Authoritarianism and Alienation: the F-scale and the Srole scale as predictors of prejudice. *Sociol. Quart.,* 1961, 2 (3), 193–202. SA 10, A2781.

The positive relationship is independent of two indexes of socioeconomic status, organizational participation, and religious preference. Perceived self-to-group alienation may lead to acceptance of authoritarianism.

Richardson, A. Attitudes to fluoridation in Perth, Western Australia. *Australian Dental J.,* 1963, *8* (6), 513–517. SA 14, B8538.

Significantly associated with "opposed" and "undecided" attitudes toward fluoridation: (1) over 40 years of age; (2) presence of children 12 years of age or over; (3) identification with a social class; (4) having a sense of social and political powerlessness.

Rose, A. Alienation and participation: a comparison of group leaders and the "Mass." *Amer. sociol. Rev.,* 1962, *27* (6), 834–838. PA 38, 2599.

Presidents of statewide organizations in Minnesota were different in degree, not kind, from the general population on the Srole scale. Differences may be due to greater social participation of the leaders.

———. Prejudice, anomie, and the authoritarian personality. *Sociol. soc. Res.,* 1966, *50* (2), 141–147. SA 14, C0951.

In the United States (Teamster's Union, Minneapolis), anomia has a stronger relationship to race prejudice than does authoritarian personality; in Italy, the low level of race prejudice is not matched by low levels of anomie or authoritarian personality.

Seeman, M. Alienation and social learning in a reformatory. *Amer. J. Sociol.,* 1963, *69* (3), 270–284, PA 38, 8211.

Hypothesis (confirmed) that inmates scoring low in powerlessness would better learn and retain parole information.

———. On the meaning of alienation. *Amer. sociol. Rev.,* 1959, *24* (6), 783–791. SA 8, 6922.

By now a definitive work, Seeman classified many references to alienation under the rubrics of powerlessness, meaninglessness, normlessness, (social) isolation, and self-estrangement.

Simmons, J. L. Liberalism, alienation, and personal disturbance. *Sociol. soc. Res.,* 1965, *49* (4), 456–464. SA 14, C0063.

Using a forced choice questionnaire and an availability sample, this study found that liberalism, alienation from society, and personal disturbance varied independently to a fairly large extent.

Srole, L. Social integration and certain corollaries: an exploratory study. *Amer. sociol. Rev.,* 1956, *21* (6), 709–716. SA 6, A3944.

Anomia is positively correlated with prejudice toward minorities. The author presents here perhaps the earliest and still most widely used scale for measuring alienation.

Struening, E. L., and Richardson, A. H. A factor analysis exploration of the alienation, anomie and authoritarianism domain. *Amer. sociol. Rev.*, 1965, 30 (5), 768–776. SA 14, C0064.

Presents eight factors, determined from factor analysis.

Templeton, F. Alienation and political participation: some research findings. *Publ. Opinion Quart.*, 1966, 30 (2), 249–261. SA 14, C2789.

Social status is negatively related to alienation; alienated voter tends to view his vote as a choice between the lesser of two evils.

Thompson, W. E., and Horton, J. E. Political alienation as a force in political action. *Social Forces*, 1960, 38 (3), 190–195. SA 10, A2435.

Political alienation is inversely related to socioeconomic status and leads to an attitude on a given issue which represents a protest against the existing power structure in the community.

Wassef, W. Y. The influence of religion, socioeconomic status and education on anomie. *Sociol. Quart.*, 1967, 8 (2), 233–238. SA 15, C8060.

A replication of the Dean-Reeves study (above) confirmed their finding of a higher *normlessness* score for Protestant than for Catholic college women.

Chapter Five

Attitudes

In an article dealing with the history and definition of the concept of *Attitude*, Melvin DeFleur and Frank Westie observed: "Perhaps no other concept from the behavioral sciences has been so widely used by theorists and researchers." [1] It certainly has as long a history as any of the constructs we use, yet we are still plagued by imprecise definitions and measurements.

As an orientation to our study of attitudes, we may well utilize the definition of Milton Rokeach: "An attitude is (1) a relatively enduring (2) organization of beliefs (3) around an object or situation (4) predisposing one to respond (5) in some preferential manner." [2] The "enduring" and "predisposing" aspects of the term are well illustrated in Theodore M. Newcomb's article. In this, he reports a follow-up study of his now-famous earlier Bennington college research, in which he investigates the concomitants of the persistence of political attitudes in his subjects over a 20-year period.

It is noteworthy that most definitions incorporate terms such as "predisposition" or "tendency." The implicit assumption has been that if one could adequately know the attitudes of individuals or groups, he could accurately predict their behavior. This assumption was called into question as long ago as 1934, when Richard LaPiere published his now-classical "Attitudes vs. Action" article.[3] In that paper he reported his experiences on a transcontinental auto trip with a Chinese couple. During this tour, the group was refused service in only one establishment out of 250 for dining and lodging; however, questionnaires sent to managers afterwards elicited a 95 percent negative response to the question of accommodations for a Chinese couple. Since his investigation, interest in the relationship between attitudes and overt behavior has continued unabated.

An excellent illustration of continuing concern is James M. Frendrich's

[1] DeFleur, M. and Westie, F. R. Attitude as a scientific concept. *Social Forces*, 1963, 42 (1), 17.

[2] Rokeach, M. The nature of attitudes. *International Encyclopedia of the Social Sciences*, vol. 1. 449–467. New York: The Macmillan Co. and The Free Press, 1968.

[3] LaPiere, R. T. Attitudes vs. actions. *Social Forces*, 1934, 13 (2), 230–237.

article, "A Study of the Association Among Verbal Attitudes, Commitment and Overt Behavior in Different Experimental Situations." His contention is that an attitude is situation-specific, rather than general. He includes his attitude scale and a commitment scale in the article.

The selections in this chapter have been chosen to illustrate the abiding interest in *attitudes*, the critical importance of precise definition, and the continuing potency of the concept as an instigator of research.

14

**Persistence and
Regression of
Changed Attitudes:
Long-Range Studies***

THEODORE M. NEWCOMB

I

One-half score and seven years ago, here in Philadelphia, I read a paper before this society. It was properly, which is to say polysyllabically, titled—something about autistic hostility—and its manuscript pages numbered just 28. Doubtless I would long since have forgotten about it had I not discovered, several years later, that another man had stolen my central idea, some five-score years before I was born. The name of the thief was William Blake, and a striking feature of *his* paper was that its total number of *words* was just 28. Let me quote them:

> *I was angry with my friend:
> I told my wrath, my wrath did end.
> I was angry with my foe:
> I told it not, my wrath did grow.*

Though I'm not sure that Blake would accept the phrasing, our common theme had to do with the change and persistence of attitudes. What I, at least, was trying to say was that one's attitudes toward another person are not likely to change if one so manipulates one's environment that one cannot add to or correct one's information about that person. Today I shall pursue a similar theme, though in a somewhat different direction.

One's attitude toward something is not only a resultant of one's previous traffic with one's environment but also a determinant of selective response to present and future environments. Viewed in the latter way, existing attitudes may determine one's selection among alternative environmental settings, and these in turn may serve to preserve or undermine the very attitudes that had been initially responsible for one's selection

Reprinted from *Journal of Social Issues*, 19, 4 (October 1963), 3–14, by permission of the author and The American Psychological Association.

* This paper, the Kurt Lewin Memorial Award Address (1962), was read before The American Psychological Association, in Philadelphia, Pa., September 2, 1963.

among the alternatives. Insofar as attitudes are self-preserving, such tendencies to select a supportive environment would, if empirically supported, provide an important explanation of their persistence. In its most general form, the hypothesis would run somewhat as follows: Existing attitudes are most likely to persist, other things equal, when one's environment provides most rewards for their behavioral expression. But this platitudinous proposition ("things persist when conditions are favorable to their persistence") is not very interesting, and is probably not even testable. A more interesting and more testable form of the proposition would take account of both change and persistence, both of attitudes and of environmental supportiveness. In particular, it would say something about a changed selection of environments following attitude change, about the ways in which the recently formed attitude is or is not reinforced by the new environment, and about the persistence of the attitude in both supportive and hostile environments. Such a proposition, in its simplest form, would run somewhat as follows: A recently changed attitude is likely to persist insofar as it leads to the selection of subsequent environments that provide reinforcements for the behavioral expression of the changed attitude.

Among the many possible forms of environmental reinforcements of behavioral expressions of attitudes, I shall consider a single class: behavior on the part of other people that one perceives as supportive of one's own attitudes. With few exceptions, such support comes from persons or groups toward whom one is positively attracted, according to the principles of what is perhaps most frequently known as balance theory (Cf. Heider, 1958; Brown, 1962; Newcomb, 1963). I am, in short, about to defend the limited proposition that a recently changed attitude is most likely to persist if one of its behavioral expressions is the selection of a social environment which one finds supportive of the changed attitude. This proposition differs from the one about autistic hostility primarily in that persistence of a recently acquired attitude depends upon continuing rather than cutting off sources of information about the attitude-object.

II

There are various ways in which such a proposition might be tested in the laboratory. But insofar as one is interested, as I have been, in long-range effects, one will make use of "natural" settings. I shall therefore cite a few findings from two of my own studies, mentioning only briefly the less immediately relevant one (1961), which involved the daily observation of two populations of 17 male students, all initial strangers to one another, who lived intimately together for four-month periods. The only attitudes of these subjects that showed much change, from first to last, were their attractions toward each other—attitudes which had not even existed, of course, before their initial encounters in this research setting. Expressions of interpersonal attraction during the first week or two were highly unstable. but after about the fifth week they showed only slow and slight changes (Cf. Newcomb, 1963).

Under the conditions of this research, imposed environments (in the form of arbitrarily assigned rooms, roommates, and floors) had no consistent effects beyond the first week or two in interpersonal preferences. That is, one could predict little or nothing about interpersonal attraction from the fact of being roommates or floormates. Self-selected interpersonal environment, however, was closely associated with interpersonal attraction. At all times later than the first week or two, pairs of subjects who were reported by others to belong to the same voluntary subgroups were almost invariably pairs whose members chose each other at very high levels of attraction. If this seems to be a commonplace observation (as indeed it is), let me remind you of my reason for reporting it; interpersonal environments are not only consequences of existing attraction but also sources of future attraction. It is an everyday phenomenon that, having developed differential attitudes toward one's several acquaintances, one manipulates one's interpersonal environment, insofar as one can, to correspond with one's interpersonal preferences. And insofar as one is successful, chances are that the preferences will be further reinforced. My data, showing stability both of preferences and of voluntarily associating subgroups following the first month or so, indicate that exactly this was occurring. The fact that it is an everyday occurrence enhances rather than negates the importance of the principle involved, namely, that a recently acquired attitude will persist insofar as it results in the selection of an environment that is supportive of that attitude.

III

I now turn to a totally different set of data, or rather to two sets of data from the same subjects, obtained over an interval of more than 20 years. The earlier responses were obtained between 1935 and 1939 at Bennington College (Newcomb, 1943); the later ones, obtained in 1960 and 1961, were from almost all of the subjects who had been studied for three or more consecutive years during the 1930's. To be specific, out of 141 former students in this category who in 1960 were alive, resident in continental United States, and not hopelessly invalided, 130 (scattered in 28 states) were interviewed, and 9 of the remaining 11 completed more or less parallel questionnaires. The interview dealt primarily with their present attitudes toward a wide range of public-affairs issues, with attitudes of their husbands and other contemporary associates, and with their histories and careers since leaving the College.

Before telling you some of the follow-up findings, I ought to report a few of the original ones. During each of four consecutive years (1935–1936 through 1938–1939), juniors and seniors were on the average markedly less conservative than freshmen in attitude toward many public issues of the day. Studies of the same individuals over three- and four-year intervals showed the same trend, which was not attributable to selective withdrawal from the College. Comparisons with other colleges showed almost no intercollege differences in freshmen attitudes, but much less conservatism at Bennington than at the other institutions on the part of seniors. Individual studies showed that at Bennington nonconservatism was rather closely associated with being respected by other students, with participation in college activities, and with personal involvement in the College as an institution. The relatively few malcontents were, with surprisingly few exceptions, those who held conservative attitudes toward public issues.

Given these initial findings, one of my concerns in planning the follow-up study was the following: Under what conditions would individuals who had become less conservative during their college years remain relatively nonconservative 20-odd years later, and under what conditions would they "regress" to relatively conservative positions? (As to the problem of comparing attitudes toward one set of issues in the 1930's with those toward quite different issues in the 1960's, I shall for present purposes note only that at both times we used indices of relative, not absolute standing: each subject is compared with the same set of peers.)

By way of noting the general pattern of persistence vs. regression on the part of the total population, I shall first compare one early with one later datum. In the 1940 presidential election, 51% of our interview sample who reported a preference for either major candidate chose the Democrat, F. D. Roosevelt, and 49% the Republican, W. Willkie. Twenty years later, the comparable figures were 60% for J. F. Kennedy and 40% for R. M. Nixon. No single election, of course, provides a very good test of what might be termed "general conservatism concerning public affairs," but at any rate this particular comparison does not suggest any conspicuous regression toward freshman conservatism. This conclusion is also supported by the following finding: In six consecutive presidential elections (1940 through 1960), an outright majority of our interviewees (51%) reported that they had preferred the Republican candidate either once or never, whereas only 27% of them had preferred that candidate as many as five times out of the six times.

The problem of regressive effects can also be approached by comparing relative conservatism on the part of the same individuals over the interval of 20-odd years. In terms of party or candidate preference in 1960, the degree of individual stability is startling. As shown in Table 1, individuals who were in the least conservative quartile of the total population, on graduating, preferred Kennedy by frequencies of 30 to 3, and those in the next quartile by 25 to 8; 83% of this half of the population preferred Kennedy 20 years later, while 37% of the initially more conservative half preferred Kennedy after 20 years. Political party preferences, and also an

TABLE 1

Presidential Preferences in 1960, According to Quartiles of PEP Scores on Leaving College in the Late 1930s

PEP Quartile	Nixon Preferred	Kennedy Preferred	Total
1 (least conservative)	3	30	33
2	8	25	33
3	18	13	31
4 (most conservative)	22	11	33
Total	51	79	130

index of general political conservatism, showed about the same relationship to political conservatism more than two decades earlier. These data provide no support for a prediction of general regression—either toward previous conservatism or in the statistical sense of regression toward the mean.

Other evidence concerning the general nonconservatism in this population in the early 1960's includes the following:

77% of them considered themselves "liberal" or "somewhat liberal," as compared with 17% who were "conservative" or "somewhat conservative";

76% "approved" or "strongly approved" of "Medicare" for the aged under Social Security;

61% "approved" or "strongly approved" of admitting Red China into the United Nations.

These and other data suggest that the population as a whole is now far less conservative than is to be expected in view of its demographic characteristics. Its socio-economic level may be judged from these facts: (1) 77% of the 117 respondents who were or had been married were judged by the interviewer to be at least "fairly well-to-do," with annual incomes of not less than $20,000; and (2) of 113 mothers in the population, 65% had sent at least one of their children to a private school. In religious background, about three-quarters of them were Protestants (more than half of whom were Episcopalian), and less than 10% were either Catholic or Jewish. According to information assembled for me by the Survey Research Center of the University of Michigan,[1] the proportion of Protestant women college graduates at the income level of this population who in 1960 expressed a preference for Kennedy over Nixon was less than 25—as compared with 60% of this alumnae population.

I shall now revert to my earlier theme: If this population is now less

---

[1] By my colleague Philip Converse, to whom I am most grateful.

conservative than one might expect, to what extent is this explainable in terms of its members' selection of post-college environments that were supportive of nonconservative attitudes? It proves to be very difficult to categorize total environments from this point of view, and so for the present I shall limit myself to a single aspect of post-college environments: husbands. I am making no assumptions here except that (1) husbands were indeed a part of their wives' environments; (2) wives had had something to do with selecting this part of their environments; and (3) husbands, as environmental objects, were capable of being either supportive or non-supportive of their wives' attitudes.

Nearly 80% of our respondents both had a husband and were able to report on his attitudes toward most of the issues with which we were concerned, during all or most of the past 20 years; one reason for placing a good deal of confidence in their reports is that they seem highly discriminating, as indicated by such responses as these: "I don't think I know how he'd feel on that particular issue," or "Now on *that* one he doesn't agree with me at all." Here are some summaries concerning all husbands whose wives were willing to attribute attitudes toward them (nearly all wives on most issues):

54% of the husbands in 1960 favored Kennedy over Nixon;
64% of them either "approved" or "strongly approved" of "Medicare" for the aged under Social Security;
57% of them either "approved" or "strongly approved" of admitting Red China into the United Nations.

And so it is almost as true of husbands as of wives that they are less conservative than is to be expected in view of their demographic characteristics: husbands' and wives' demographic characteristics are taken to be identical except for a very few couples differing in religious background, and their present attitudes are highly similar (90% of 1960 presidential preferences by pairs of spouses, for example, being reported as the same in 1960). It would hardly seem to be a matter of sheer chance that a set of men who are less conservative than is to be expected are married to a set of women of whom just the same thing is true. It seems necessary, therefore, to assume that attitudes toward public affairs had something to do with husbands' and wives' reciprocal selection of one another, or with post-marital influence upon one another, or with both. Here is one statistical support for this assumption: the correlation between wives' scores on an instrument labeled Political and Economic Progressivism, as of their graduating from college in the late 1930's, with the number of Republican candidates that their subsequent husbands voted for between 1940 and 1960 was .32; this does not account for much of the variance, but its p value is $< .0005$.

Another interesting finding has to do with the number of women in our interview sample whose husbands had attended Ivy League colleges; one would expect this proportion to be high, since so many of the women's fathers and brothers had attended these colleges. The actual frequency turned out to be just 50%. These Ivy League husbands' voting preferences in 1960, however, turned out to be much more like their wives' preferences than like their classmates' preferences: 52% of husbands whose wives were able to state a preference were for Kennedy—which is to say that they did not differ at all in voting preferences from all non-Ivy League husbands. This total set of facts can best be interpreted as follows: Our Bennington graduates of the late 1930's found their husbands in the kinds of places where their families expected them to be found, but they selected somewhat atypical members of these "proper" populations of eligibles; they tended not to have conservative attitudes that were then typical of these populations.

One evidence of this atypical selection is to be seen in the occupational distribution of these women's husbands. Only 38% of all husbands are classifiable as "in management or business," the remaining 62% representing for the most part a wide range of professions (especially college teaching, entertainment, and the arts) and public employment (especially in government). Husbands in these two general categories (management and business vs. all others) differed sharply in their voting preferences in 1960; of the 113 husbands whose wives attributed preferences to them, 26% of those in management and business preferred Kennedy, and 68% of all other husbands preferred Kennedy. In sum, these women's husbands had typically come from "the right" places but a majority of them did not have "the right" attitudes or occupational interests.

If, therefore, I were to select a single factor that contributed most to these women's maintenance of nonconservative attitudes between the late 1930's and early 1960's, I think it would be the fact of selecting husbands of generally nonconservative stripe who helped to maintain for them an environment that was supportive of their existing attributes.

IV

Now I shall turn from the total population of interviewees to some comparisons of subpopulations. The most crucial of these, from the point of view of my proposition about supportive environments, are to be found within the population of nonconservatives on leaving college in the late 1930's: What seems to be the differences between those who do and those who do not remain nonconservative in the early 1960's? Such comparisons will have to be impressionistic, since numbers of cases are small.

Among 22 individuals previously labeled as clearly nonconservative in their third or fourth year of attendance at the College, just half belong in the same category now. Only three of them are clearly conservative today, the remaining eight being classified as intermediate. Here are these wives' descriptions of their husbands' political positions over the years:

3 presently conservative wives: 3 Republican husbands (100%)
7 presently intermediate wives: 3 Republican husbands (42%)
8 presently nonconservative wives: 2 Republican husbands (25%)

Of the three presently conservative women, none mentions having engaged in activities related to political or other public issues; of the eight who are intermediate, six mention some activity of this kind, but they identify their activity only in such general terms as "liberal" or "Democratic Party"; of the 11 still nonconservative women, eight mention such activities, more than half of them specifying such "causes" or organizations as labor unions, civil liberties, the ADA, or the NAACP.

Each interviewee was also asked about the general orientation of "most of your friends" toward political and other public affairs. More than half (12) of the 22 women originally labeled as clearly nonconservative described their environment of friends as "liberal," in spite of the fact that most of them lived in suburbs or other geographical areas not generally renowned for liberalism. Interestingly enough, those who are now relatively conservative answered this question in just about the same way as did those who are still relatively nonconservative. The 16 women originally labeled as clearly conservative, on leaving college, answered this question somewhat differently; more than half of them (9) described their environment of friends as predominantly "conservative," but answers differed with the present attitudes of the respondents. That is, those who are now, in fact, relatively conservative with near-unanimity describe their friends as conservative, whereas those who are now relatively nonconservative consider a substantial proportion or even most of their friends to be "liberal." Thus only those who were quite conservative in the late 1930's and who still remain so see themselves surrounded by friends who are primarily conservative.

In sum, nearly all of the still nonconservative women mention either husbands or public activities (most commonly both) that have served to support and maintain previously nonconservative attitudes, while none of the three formerly nonconservative but presently conservative women mentions either husband or public activities which have served to maintain earlier attitudes.

What about attitude persistence on the part of those who, after three or four years in college, were still relatively conservative? Sixteen of those who were then labeled conservative were interviewed in the early 1960's, ten of them being categorized as still conservative and three as now nonconservative. Only one of the nonchangers reported having a husband who was a Democrat, and in this lone case he turned out to have voted for Nixon in 1960. Two of the three changers, on the other hand, report husbands who were Democrats and Kennedy voters in 1960. Only two of the persistent conservatives mentioned public activities presumably supportive of their attitudes (in behalf of the Republican Party, in both cases); eight of the ten described most of their friends either as conservative or as Republicans. The conditions that favor the persistence of conservatism over the 20-odd years are thus about the same as those that favor the persistence of nonconservatism: supportive environments in the form of husbands, local friends, and (for the nonconservatives but not the conservatives) in the form of associates in activities related to public issues.

There is a special sub-population of students who, as of graduating in the late 1930's, were candidates for regression; that is, they became much less conservative during their college years. Of these, about one-third (9 of 28) were among the most conservative half of the same population in the early 1960's, and may be regarded as regressors, in some degree at least. Eight of these potential regressors were, for various reasons, unable to report on husbands' preferences. Among the remaining 19 respondents, five were actual regressors, four of whom reported their husbands to be Republicans or "conservative Republicans." Among 14 actual nonregressors reporting, ten described their husbands as Democrats or "liberal Democrats," two referred to them as "Republicans who have been voting Democratic," and only two call their husbands Republicans. These are highly significant differences: the actual regressors can pretty well be differentiated from the nonregressors merely by knowing their husbands' present attitudes. By this procedure only 3 of 19, or 16% of all predictions would not have been correct.

This total set of data suggests that either regression and persistence of attitudes as of leaving college are, over the years, influenced by husbands' attitudes, or early post-college attitudes had something to do with the selection of husbands, or both. In either case, both regression and persistence are facilitated by the supportiveness of husbands.

V

If there is any very general principle that helps to account for this whole range of phenomena (both my 1946 and my 1963 versions), I believe that it is to be found in an extended version of "balance theory," as originally outlined by Heider (1946, 1958). Heider's formulations are formulated in individual and phenomenological terms; a balanced state is a strictly intrapersonal, psychological state. But it is also possible to conceptualize an objective, multi-person state of balance, referring to the actual relationships among different persons' attitudes, regardless of the persons' awareness of each other. Such a concept is psychologically useful not only because it describes an actual, existing situation—an environment of which each person is himself a part, as suggested by Asch (1952)—but also because it describes a relationship which, given reasonably full and accurate communication, comes to be accurately perceived. My own recent work on the acquaintance process has been interesting to me primarily because it inquires into the processes by which and the conditions under which *intra*personal states of balance come to correspond with *inter*personal ones. As outlined by Heider, and subsequently by many others (Cf. Brown *et al.*, 1962), the processes by which imbalanced states serve as goals toward the attainment of balanced ones include both internal, psychological changes and external modifications of the environment. Thus, one may achieve a balanced state with the important figures in one's social environment—whether by selecting those figures, by modifying one's own attitudes, or by influencing others' attitudes—and at the same time continue to perceive that environment accurately.

According to such an extended, *inter*personal concept of balance, an imbalanced state under conditions of continued interaction is likely to be an unstable one, simply because when it is discovered it arouses *intra*personal imbalance on the part of one or more of the interactors, and this state arouses forces toward change. Given marked attitude change on the part of one but not the other member of a dyad actually in balance with respect to that attitude, imbalance results. This was what typically happened to students at Bennington College vis-à-vis their parents, in the 1930's. A common way in which they attempted to reduce imbalance was by avoidance—not necessarily of parents but of the divisive issues as related to parents. As Heider might say, unit formation between issue and parents was broken up, and psychological imbalance thus reduced. Such a "solution" resembles autistic hostility in that it involves a marked restriction of communication.

But this solution, as many of my subjects testified, was not a particularly comfortable one. Hence, it would hardly be surprising if many of them, during early post-college years, were in search of environments that would provide less uncomfortable solutions—or, better yet, more positively rewarding ones. An ideal one, of course, would be a husband who was rewarding as a supporter of one's own attitudes as well as in other ways.

And so, vis-à-vis parents and fellow-students at first, and later vis-à-vis husbands (or perhaps working associates), forces toward balance were at work. Specifically, support from important people concerning important issues came to be the rule, and its absence the exception. Support sometimes came about by changing one's own attitudes toward those of needed supporters, or, more commonly, by selecting supporters for existing attitudes. The latter stratagem represented not merely an automatic tendency for attitudes to perpetuate themselves. More significantly, I believe, it represents an adaptation to a world that includes *both* persons and issues. Such a dual adaptation can be made, of course, by sacrificing one's stand on the issues (regression). But if the dual adaptation is to be made without this sacrifice, then an interpersonal world must be selected (or created) that is supportive—in which case we can say that the attitude has been expressed by finding a supportive environment.

According to my two themes (of 1946 and 1963) an existing attitude may be maintained by creating environments in which *either* new information can be avoided *or* in which other persons support one's own information. In either case, the fate of an attitude is mediated by the social environment in which the individual attempts to maintain or to restore balance regarding that same attitude. Insofar as that environment excludes disturbing information or provides reinforcing information, the attitude persists. And insofar as the selection or the acceptance of that environment is a consequence of holding the attitude, we have a steady-state, self-maintaining system.

References

Asch, S. E. *Social Psychology*. New York: Prentice-Hall, 1952.

Brown, R. Models of attitude change. In Brown, R., Galanter, E., Hess, E. H., & Mandler, G. *New Directions in Psychology*. New York: Holt, Rinehart & Winston, 1962.

Heider, F. Attitudes and cognitive organization. *J. Psychol.*, 1946, 21, 107–112.

——. *The Psychology of Interpersonal Relations*. New York: Wiley, 1958.

Newcomb, T. M. *Personality and Social Change*. New York: Holt, Rinehart & Winston, 1943.

——. Autistic hostility and social reality. *Human Relations*, 1947, 1, 69–86.

——. *The Acquaintance Process*. New York: Holt, Rinehart & Winston, 1961.

15

A Study of the Association Among Verbal Attitudes, Commitment and Overt Behavior in Different Experimental Situations*

JAMES M. FENDRICH

Florida State University

Studies examining racial attitudes and overt behavior have often reported inconsistency between the measure of verbal attitudes and overt behavior.[1] One explanation for the discrepancy is that characteristics of the overt situation, rather than attitudes, determine the action toward the attitude object.[2] Another way of interpreting the findings involves the recognition

Reprinted from *Social Forces*, 45, 3 (March 1967), 347–355, by permission of the author and The University of North Carolina Press.

* The author is indebted to Santo F. Camilleri and Archie O. Haller for their valuable advice and criticism in the designing and carrying out of this study. This investigation was supported by a Public Health Service predoctoral fellowship 1-F1-MH-28, 021-01 from NIMH.

[1] There are numerous articles on this topic: Douglas W. Bray, "The Prediction of Behavior From Two Attitude Scales," *Journal of Abnormal and Social Psychology*, 45 (1950), pp. 64–84; Wilber Brookover and John Holland, "An Inquiry Into the Meaning of Minority Group Attitude Expressions," *American Sociological Review*, 17 (April 1952), pp. 196–202; Lewis M. Killian, "The Adjustment of Southern White Migrants to Northern Urban Norms," *Social Forces*, 32 (October 1953), pp. 66–69; Bernard Kutner, Carol Wilkins and Penny Yarrow, "Verbal Attitudes and Overt Behavior Involving Racial Prejudice," *Journal of Abnormal and Social Psychology*, 47 (1952), pp. 649–652; Richard T. LaPiere, "Attitudes vs. Actions," *Social Forces*, 13 (December 1934), pp. 230–237; Lawrence S. Linn, "Verbal Attitudes and Overt Behavior: A Study of Racial Discrimination," *Social Forces*, 45 (1965), pp. 353–364; Milton Malof and Albert Lott, "Ethnocentrism and the Acceptance of Negro Support in a Group Situation," *Journal of Abnormal and Social Psychology*, 65 (October 1962), pp. 254–258; Gerhart H. Saenger and Emily Gilbert, "Customer Reactions to the Integration of Negro Sales Personnel," *Public Opinion Quarterly*, 4 (1950), pp. 57–76.

[2] Herbert Blumer, "Research on Race Relations in the United States of America," *International Social Science Journal*, 10 (1958), pp. 403–447; Melvin L. DeFleur and Frank A. Westie, "Attitude as a Scientific Concept," *Social Forces*, 42 (October 1963), pp. 17–31; Earl Raab and Seymour Martin Lipset, "The Prejudiced Society," *American Race Relations Today*, (ed.) Earl Raab (New York: Doubleday & Co., 1962), pp. 29–55; Dietrich C. Reitzes, "Institutional Structures and Race Relations," *Phylon* (Spring 1959), pp. 48–66; and Arnold M. Rose, "Intergroup Relations vs. Prejudice: Pertinent Theory for the Study of Social Change," *Social Problems*, 4 (1956), pp. 173–176.

that situational factors influence behavior in both measurement situations. When measuring verbal attitudes, the situational characteristics can be markedly different than characteristics in the overt situation. The disparity between the situational characteristics which influence respondents' role-playing in each setting may contribute to the inconsistency.

The present study examines the relationship between expressed racial attitudes and overt behavior, looking at characteristics of the research setting which influence the expression of attitudes and affect the consistency between verbal attitudes and overt behavior. The objectives are: (1) to manipulate the definition of the situation while measuring verbal attitudes in order to explore the extent to which different definitions of the situation influence the degree of association between verbal attitudes and overt behavior; and (2) to compare the relative power of verbal attitudes and commitment in predicting overt behavior.

The definition of the situation is used to refer to the respondent's subjective attempt to orient himself to the context in which he finds himself, ascertain his interest, and then proceed to cope with the circumstances.[3] The definition of the situation is a process whereby present stimuli and past experience are synthesized in some meaningful whole to facilitate interaction. When a situation has been defined "decisions can be made as to what behavior and objects can be appropriately woven into the interaction sequence and what cannot." [4] Role-playing is considered to be the overt manifestation of a set of perceived normative expectations resulting from defining the situation.[5] By altering the definition of the research setting, the role-playing involved in expressing attitudes was expected to vary. Verbal attitudes were considered to be the outward manifestation of two internal processes. One is the acquired behavioral dispositions toward a class of objects. The other is the definition of the situation. Both processes shape the expression of attitudes. Commitment was considered as the act of making perceived voluntary decisions to participate in a consistent pattern of action that involves some risk.[6] The perceived voluntary decisions refer

[3] Tamotsu Shibutani, *Society and Personality* (Englewood Cliffs, New Jersey: Prentice-Hall, 1961), pp. 41–42.

[4] Glenn M. Vernon, *Human Interaction* (New York: The Ronald Press, 1965), p. 154.

[5] Shibutani, *op. cit.*, pp. 46–50.

[6] This short definition was derived from Jack W. Brehm and Arthur Cohen, *Explorations in Cognitive Dissonance* (New York: John Wiley & Sons, 1962), pp. 8–9, 198, 217; Amitai Etzioni, *A Comparative Analysis of Complex Organizations* (New York: The Free Press of Glencoe, 1961), pp. 8–11; Kurt Lewin, "Frontiers in Group Dynamics," *Field Theory in Social Science*, (ed.) Dorwin Cartwright (New York: Doubleday & Co., 1965), pp. 227–235; Carl I. Hovland, Enid H. Campbell and Timothy Brock, "The Effects of 'Commitment' on Opinion Change Following Communication," *The Order of Presentation in Persuasion* (New Haven: Yale University Press, 1957), pp. 23–32; Harold B. Gerald, "Deviation, Conformity and Commitment," *Current Studies in Social Psychology*, (ed.) Ivan D. Steiner and Martin Fishbein (New York: Holt, Rinehart & Winston, 1965), pp. 263–276; Leon Festinger, *Conflict, Decision, and Dissonance* (Stanford: Stanford University Press, 1964), pp. 155–156.

to the choices between a limited set of possible alternatives that will affect subsequent behavior. The consistent activity involves a series of acts which are not easily reversible. The risk of commitment results from making decisions to engage in a particular pattern of overt behavior. Thus, the committed person by acting out his decisions exposes himself to the sanctioning of significant others. Overt behavior refers to observable acts directed toward the attitude object.

A number of authors have suggested the usual testing situation has unique characteristics which influence respondents' role-playing. Hyman states the inconsistency between verbal attitudes and overt behavior results from inconsistencies between the interpretations researchers put upon attitude measurements and the measurements' relation to behavior. In attempting to account for the lack of a one-to-one relationship between verbal attitudes and overt behavior, Hyman states that in the typical testing situation respondents are not subject to the normal coercive forces of everyday life. In contrast, outside the testing situation respondents are held to account for what they have said or how they have acted.[7] Cicourel and Back *et al.*, outline game theory models to explain behavior in the testing situation. They stress the researcher tries to create a testing situation that is considered a special kind of interpersonal system, very similar to play.[8] The behavior is separate in time and space, uncertain, unproductive, free and governed by rules of make-believe.[9] Linn has described the characteristics of role-playing when measuring racial attitudes of students. While attending a university which has a reputation for being more politically and racially liberal than many other institutions, there is a social and cultural norm held by most Ss to take a liberal position on racial integration. In the usual testing situation many Ss actively play, or attempt to play, their social role of the liberal college student; consequently, they express favorable attitudes toward Negroes.[10] Linn's description of active role-playing suggests that Ss in trying to cooperate, may bias the results of the attitude measure.

The association between verbal attitudes and overt behavior was not expected to be highly correlated in the usual research setting due to its play-like characteristics. In this type of setting it was assumed that subjects would define the situation as an attempt to find out how prejudiced they were toward Negroes. In actively trying to cooperate some subjects would try to demonstrate they were not prejudiced while others would cooperate

[7] Herbert H. Hyman, "Inconsistencies as a Problem of Attitude Measurement," *Journal of Social Issues*, 5 (1959), pp. 38–42.

[8] Aaron V. Cicourel, *Method and Measurement in Sociology* (New York: The Free Press of Glencoe, 1964), pp. 203–209; Kurt W. Back, Thomas C. Hood, and Mary L. Brehm, "The Subject Role in Small Group Experiments," *Social Forces*, 43 (December 1964), pp. 181–187.

[9] Back, Hood, and Brehm, *op. cit.*, p. 181.

[10] Linn, *op. cit.*, p. 359.

in revealing how they *felt* toward Negroes. In neither interpretation would they be revealing how they would *act* toward the attitude object.

Hyman states if the aim is to predict a given kind of behavior in a given social setting, tests should be designed to incorporate the fundamental aspects of the overt setting into the testing situation.[11] One of the most important characteristics of overt behavior is the sanctioning of significant others.[12] A commitment measure was designed to incorporate this fundamental aspect of the overt setting into the testing situation. Since committing one's self involves volunteering to engage in future acts that will be sanctioned by significant others, it was hypothesized the commitment would be significantly related to overt behavior.

Measurement of verbal attitudes does not normally tap commitment. Verbal attitudes are statements of preference that have no specific consequences for subsequent behavior. Definite decisions are not made to interact with the attitude object outside the testing situation. Therefore, attitudes can be expressed without consideration of the sanctioning of significant others. Thus, the relationship between commitment and overt behavior was expected to be greater than verbal attitudes and overt behavior.

If expressed commitment preceded verbal attitudes in the testing situation, the role-playing in the research setting was expected to change. Role-playing in the measurement of verbal attitudes would no longer retain its playlike characteristics, but would be played within a framework of previous commitment. When the attitude measurement immediately followed the measurement of commitment, verbal attitudes were expected to be consistent with the expressed level of commitment. Therefore, the relationship between verbal attitudes and overt behavior was expected to be greater in the research setting involving previous commitment to the attitude object. In summary, three hypotheses were tested:

1. *The greater the degree of favorable commitment, the greater the degree of overt behavior.*

2. *The degree of relationship between commitment and overt behavior will be greater than the relationship between verbal attitudes and overt behavior.*

3. *The greater the extent to which attitudes are expressed in a research setting involving previous commitment to the attitude object, the greater the relationship between verbal attitudes and overt behavior.*

[11] Hyman, *op. cit.*, p. 40.

[12] DeFleur and Westie, *op. cit.*, p. 672 and Linn, *op. cit.*, pp. 363–364 have indicated that the overt behavior toward members of minority groups is strongly influenced by significant others. As another part of this study it was found that perceived support from significant others was significantly related to attitude, commitment and overt behavior. See James M. Fendrich, "A Study of White Attitudes, Commitment and Overt Behavior Toward Members of a Minority Group," unpublished Ph.D. dissertation, Michigan State University, 1965.

EXPERIMENTAL METHODOLOGY

Research Design

The attitude and commitment data were gathered in face-to-face interviews. There were two experimental treatments. The two treatments were designed to create different definitions of the attitude measurement situation. Treatment A was similar to the usual testing situation. Students were asked to express their attitudes toward Negroes. They were not told they would later be asked to commit themselves to interaction with Negroes. In essence a playlike environment was created. In Treatment B, Ss were asked to commit themselves to interaction with Negroes before they responded to the attitude items. Commitment involved interacting with Negroes in the future, creating the risk of being sanctioned by significant others. The commitment scale was designed to reduce sharply the playlike conditions of the testing situation. After taking the risk of committing themselves, Ss were asked to respond to the attitude scale. In treatment B role-playing was expected to be consistent with commitment.

After responding to both the attitude and commitment questions, respondents were asked if they would be willing to attend a small group discussion with Negro and white members of a campus chapter of the "National Association For The Advancement of Colored People" (NAACP).[13] The discussions were planned for the week following the administration of the instruments. The expressed purpose of the discussions was to improve interracial understanding in the college community.

Sample

The interview data were gathered by sampling from the undergraduate population at a large "Big Ten" university. The university was not considered solely as an institution of higher learning; it was considered to be a community. Within this community Ss interact with people directly and indirectly involved with the academic institution. Sampling criteria were used to select those most likely to be participants in the university community. Freshmen were excluded because they were relatively new arrivals on campus and were not familiar with the prevalent attitudes and sanctions governing the patterns of interracial interaction. With the assistance of the university's Data Processing Center a small representative sample of 65 sophomores, juniors and seniors was drawn. From this sample Ss were selected if they were U.S. citizens, white, full-time students who lived on

---

[13] The NAACP was chosen for its saliency to the respondents. At the time the study was conducted, the NAACP was the only effective civil rights organization on campus. It held regular meetings and the group activities were frequently reported in the school daily. Membership in the organization varied from timid support to advocators of strong militancy.

campus or in the community surrounding the university. Foreign Ss were excluded because their familiarity with interracial activities in the United States was considered to be either limited or viewed from a different perspective. Students who lived outside the community and Ss who were not attending the university on a full-time basis were excluded because of their often minimal contact with other Ss outside of the classroom. Six Ss who did not complete all of the scales were excluded. The remaining 46 Ss were interviewed at their place of residence. Randomization procedures were used in order that each S would have the same probability of falling into either treatment.

Attitude Scale

The operational definitions consist of scales designed to measure three variables—verbal attitudes, commitment and overt behavior. A 32-item scale was developed to measure verbal attitudes toward Negro Ss.[14] A variety of campus experiences were included in the items, e.g., dating, student government, housing, athletics, academic abilities, militancy, etc. Thirteen items expressed a favorable attitude toward Negro Ss and 19 expressed an unfavorable attitude. To be consistent Ss had to both agree and disagree with items. All of the attitude scale items had a range of five possible responses—"strongly agree," "agree," "undecided," "disagree," and "strongly disagree." The estimated split-half reliability of the study was .91. Item-total score correlations indicated that the scale was internally consistent. Twenty-eight of the 32 items were significantly correlated with the total score. The remaining four approached significance. The following 32 items were used to construct the attitude scale:

1. I think there are Negroes qualified to be class presidents.
2. Negro students all look alike.
3. I think research would show that Negroes definitely get much poorer grades than white students.
4. I wouldn't want Negroes in positions of responsible student leadership on campus.
5. I wouldn't mind at all if I lived in an area that was integrated.
6. I find some Negroes attractive.
7. Negroes on campus want too much.
8. I would like to go on a double date with a Negro couple.
9. I would feel extremely uncomfortable dancing with a Negro student.
10. Negroes are better in sports because they come from more primitive backgrounds.

---

[14] It was felt that the class of social objects should be clearly specified and they should be similar to the object of the commitment and overt behavior.

11. Eating at the same table with a Negro wouldn't bother me.
12. It would be a good experience to get to know more Negroes on campus.
13. Negro students don't take care of their personal hygiene.
14. I'd hate to be seen walking across campus alone with a Negro.
15. Negroes should stick to themselves.
16. Any white student is better than a Negro student.
17. No one forgets so easily as a Negro student.
18. When given a chance Negroes can do just as well in school as anyone else.
19. I wouldn't want to see a Negro president of student government.
20. Only unprincipled students would go on an interracial date.
21. I would like to see Negroes get equal treatment in all areas of campus life.
22. Negroes want the same things out of life that I do.
23. The more Negroes come to this university the lower the standards get.
24. I wouldn't mind working with Negroes on some campus project.
25. I hate to see a white and Negro going steady together.
26. I would prefer sharing living quarters with any white rather than with a Negro student.
27. I think the only thing that Negroes can contribute to campus life is better athletics.
28. The only way that Negro students can obtain full equality on campus is through the help of white students.
29. The more Negro professors we get on campus the lower will be the quality of teaching.
30. The reason why Negroes want fraternities and sororities of their own is so they can stay by themselves.
31. I think there are Negroes on campus who will be more successful in the future than I will.
32. Some Negro students are smarter than I am.

Commitment Scale

A 10-item scale was developed to measure commitment.[15] Questions were designed to imply participation in interracial activities with Negro Ss. The interviewer stated the questions involved possible interaction with Negro Ss in the future. Following this introduction, Ss were asked if they would be willing to commit themselves to nine different forms of activities. If they committed themselves to any of the nine activities, they were then asked to give their phone number. This last item was included in the scale

[15] It was unrealistic to create a longer scale. The longer the scale, the more students would have become skeptical of the manifest function of the commitment items.

to reinforce the idea of being committed to future interaction. Care was taken to construct items that would appear realistic to the Ss. Items varied in the extent of personal involvement in the interracial activities. The following 10 items were used to construct the commitment scale:

1. Would you agree to go to coffee or lunch with a mixed racial group of students to talk about interracial problems on campus?
2. Would you agree to have a Negro as a roommate next year or next term?
3. Would you agree to spend a weekend at the home of a Negro attending the university if he or she invited you?
4. Would you agree to invite a Negro at the university to spend a weekend at your home?
5. Would you agree to participate in a small group discussion on the topic of white students' social relations with Negroes on campus?
6. Would you agree to attend a lecture or conference on the topic of white students' social relations with Negroes on campus?
7. Would you agree to protest against segregated housing in the city with Negro students?
8. Would you agree to attend a meeting of the Campus Chapter of the NAACP?
9. Would you, if asked, agree to contribute $1.00 to help finance the activities of a Negro action group, (SNCC) (NAACP) or (CORE)?
10. (If respondent says yes to any of the above items) Would you give your phone number?
    No. . . . .

The Ss were given three choices of responses to each of the ten items— "yes," "maybe," and "no." Since the primary interest was the degree of positive commitment, it was decided to score the "yes" responses as one and the remaining two responses as zero. The estimated split-half reliability was .82. Every item was significantly correlated to the total score.

Overt Behavior Scale

The overt behavior scale was developed to measure behavior congruent with verbal attitudes and commitment toward Negro Ss. After responding to the attitude and commitment scales, Ss were asked if they were willing to attend small group discussions with members of the NAACP that were scheduled in the near future. During the five-day period following the administration of the attitude and commitment scales, Ss were contacted to determine if they still definitely planned to attend the discussions. The NAACP representatives tried to obtain firm decisions and answer any questions. The Ss were given the opportunity to attend one of four discussions.[16] If the Ss declined, the representatives did not force the issue and noted either a refusal or acceptance to attend the discussions. At the small group discussions every S was asked to give his name in order that name-tags could be used to facilitate interaction. This information was used to associate Ss with their interview data. At the beginning of each meeting the researcher defined himself as a member of the NAACP and he introduced other members who had previously volunteered to take part in the discussions. At each session the campus history of the organization was presented, particular areas of discrimination on- and off-campus were cited, and future activities were brought to the students' attention. Afterwards Ss participated in lively and pointed conversation with the members of the NAACP. At the end of the discussions they were asked if they were willing to sign up to participate further in interracial activities. The activities involved a number of committees of the NAACP, e.g., publicity, program of research, entertainment, membership, direct action, housing, and the NAACP Newsletter. Besides these activities Ss were given the opportunity to help organize a talent show to raise money for projects in southern states, volunteer to work in Mississippi during the summer, or recruit students for summer work, take part in a civil rights program sponsored by student government, assist in a campus fund raising drive for students volunteering for summer projects and circulate a petition in the local community to obtain signatures of residents which would be used as evidence to support a "Fair Housing Ordinance" being considered by the City Council.

The overt behavior scale measures behavior outside of the research setting. The scale has four discrete points:

0 = Refusing invitation to attend small group discussions designed to improve race relations on campus.
1 = Accepting invitation to attend small group discussions designed to improve race relations on campus.
2 = Participating in small group discussions.
3 = Signing up for ongoing civil rights activities.

Inspection of the scale revealed very few inconsistencies. The time ordering of responses that increased in degree of involvement in interracial activities reduced the possibility of inconsistency. Using scalogram analysis procedures, resulted in a coefficient of reproducibility of .99.

Table 1 reports the scores of the Ss on the three scales. The Ss in both treatments had favorable attitudes toward Negro Ss. The commitment

[16] The scheduling of the small group discussions was designed to provide every student the opportunity to attend; however, the students independently selected the evening discussions. Some of the students brought friends who did not take part in the interviews.

TABLE 1

Scores on the Attitude, Commitment and Overt Behavior Scales, by Student

	Treatment A				Treatment B		
Student	Attitude	Commit-ment	Overt Behavior	Student	Attitude	Commit-ment	Overt Behavior
1	131	5	3	23	118	4	0
2	127	7	2	24	118	4	0
3	138	2	1	25	108	0	0
4	118	6	1	26	141	8	2
5	106	3	0	27	127	5	1
6	113	6	1	28	131	10	1
7	113	4	0	29	110	4	1
8	118	4	0	30	144	8	3
9	149	8	0	31	144	10	3
10	131	10	3	32	132	6	1
11	118	6	1	33	159	10	2
12	143	8	1	34	126	5	0
13	137	7	0	35	116	3	0
14	123	6	0	36	139	6	1
15	117	10	0	37	124	6	0
16	146	9	1	38	136	6	2
17	137	7	0	39	129	8	0
18	127	8	1	40	133	6	1
19	124	5	0	41	128	10	1
20	149	10	0	42	136	10	2
21	124	6	0	43	113	7	1
22	132	3	0	44	123	5	0
				45	111	7	1
				46	123	7	1

scores were widely dispersed and the overt behavior scores were more varied in Treatment B than Treatment A.

Statistical Treatment

In contrast to other studies on verbal attitudes and overt behavior, this study does not employ a theoretical model that posits there will be a linear one-to-one association between the independent and dependent variables. This type of model for testing hypotheses is artificially stringent. It was felt that a better theoretical and methodological approach would be to consider verbal attitudes and commitment as contributory causes of overt behavior, i.e., they are important independent variables but not the sole determinants of overt behavior. The most useful measures for testing the consistency hypothesis are measures reporting the "predictability" of the dependent variable from known values of the independent variable.

Since interest was primarily in the proportional-reduction-in-error variance of overt behavior from knowledge of attitude and commitment, a measure was chosen that meets Costner's criteria for proportional-reduction-in-error measures.[17] The overt behavior scale was an ordinal scale and the data were not normally distributed. Therefore, *gamma* was chosen as the measure of association. If the explained variance was $\geq.50$ the independent variable was considered a good predictor of overt behavior.

RESULTS

Test of Hypothesis 1

Table 2 reports the results of the measures of association by treatment. In Treatment A the attitude scale preceded the commitment scale. The order was reversed in Treatment B. Hypothesis 1 states that the level of

TABLE 2

Association Among Verbal Attitudes, Commitment and Overt Behavior, by Treatment

	Treatment A	Treatment B
	Attitude Measured Before Commitment	*Commitment Measured Before Attitude*
Relationship	gamma	gamma
Attitude-Commitment	.37*	.66†
Attitude-Overt Behavior	.12	.69†
Commitment-Overt Behavior	.18	.72†
	N = 22	N = 24

* P < .05.
† P < .01.

commitment is an effective predictor of overt behavior. In Treatment B the relationship between commitment is significant beyond the .01 confidence level. The level of commitment explains .72 of the variance of overt behavior scores. In Treatment B, Ss responded to the experimental design, engaging in acts of commitment that were consistent with their overt behavior.

In Treatment A the relationship was not significant at the .05 level of confidence. The level of commitment explains only .18 of the variance of overt behavior scores. The proportion of explained variance in Treatment A did not meet perceived expectations. It was felt that the threat of sanc-

[17] Herbert L. Costner, "Criteria for Measures of Association," *American Sociological Review*, 30 (June 1965), pp. 341–353. Computation of a confidence interval for *gamma* takes ties into account. The magnitude of *gamma* is not affected by ties, but a large proportion of ties affects sampling variability. For more information on *gamma*, see Leo A. Goodman and William H. Kruskal, "Measures of Association for Cross-Classification: III Approximate Sampling Theory," *Journal of the American Statistical Association*, 58 (1963), pp. 322–330.

tions from significant others would make acts of commitment consistent with overt behavior. Evidently there were two major types of social pressures operating in the interview situation. The first was to respond in a consistent manner to the interviewer. The second social pressure was to be consistent with the expectations of significant others outside of the testing situation. Recent research on cognitive dissonance theory has demonstrated the extent to which respondents strain to act consistently in a voluntary experimental situation.[18] This strain to act consistently was expected to be greater in Treatment B when measuring attitudes after commitment, but it was not expected to operate as strongly in Treatment A when measuring commitment after verbal attitudes. Thus, the strain to give consistent response patterns within the testing situation was underestimated in Treatment A. One conclusion that can be drawn is that commitment is a useful predictor of overt behavior if the research setting is not contaminated by previous acts unrelated to overt behavior with which the respondent is forced to be consistent.

Test of Hypothesis 2

Hypothesis 2 states commitment will be a better predictor of overt behavior than verbal attitudes. Since the pressure to be consistent with the first expression of either commitment or verbal attitudes strongly influenced the second expression, the measure of association between verbal attitudes and overt behavior in Treatment A and commitment and overt behavior in Treatment B were used to test the hypothesis. The research situations in which these two measures were obtained were comparable. Both measures were presented first in the respective treatments, and therefore, were unaffected by interaction with the second variable. In Treatment B the level of commitment explains .69 of the variance of overt behavior. In Treatment A the degree of favorable attitudes explains only .12 of the variance of overt behavior. Under comparable research conditions commitment is a much stronger predictor of overt behavior than verbal attitudes.

Test of Hypothesis 3

Hypothesis 3 states the greater the extent to which attitudes are expressed in a research setting involving previous commitment to the attitude object, the greater the relationship between verbal attitudes and overt behavior. In Treatment B verbal attitudes were expected to be consistent with commitment, and therefore, significantly related to overt behavior. Data from Treatments A and B support the hypothesis. The difference between $gamma_1$–$gamma_2$ was .57, i.e., verbal attitudes in Treatment B explained 57 percent more of the variance in overt behavior than verbal attitudes in

[18] Brehm and Cohen, *op. cit.*, p. 303.

Treatment A. This great a difference of *gammas* was considered to be significant. The results suggest the definitions of the research settings were markedly different, producing one set of responses that were consistent with overt behavior and one set of inconsistent responses.

DISCUSSION

The results of this study caution against simplistic explanations of either consistency or inconsistency between verbal attitudes and overt behavior. The expression of attitudes is not simply an expression of an orientation toward action with the attitude object, and thus, consistent with overt behavior. The definition of the measurement situation influences the way respondents express their attitudes. Previous research that explains the inconsistency between verbal attitudes and overt behavior as being due to different situational factors in the overt situation and the attitude measurement situation appears to be correct. The researchers, however, did not recognize the flexibility of the research setting. Verbal attitudes can be useful predictors of overt behavior, if the artificial play atmosphere of the testing situation is reduced. Hyman's suggestion that fundamental aspects of the overt setting should be incorporated in the testing situation, which is designed to predict behavior, is useful advice. In this study a measure of commitment to interaction with the attitude object did incorporate the fundamental aspects of overt behavior. When the expression of attitudes immediately followed the measured commitment, attitudes were consistent with overt behavior.

The findings of this study add to the growing body of literature on social behavior in the research process.[19] It is dangerous to assume that participants are willing, but docile subjects in social research, rather, they are active agents who define a social situation and play what they perceive to be the appropriate role. The results of this study suggest that recognition of the social psychology of the research process can contribute to designing experiments to collect reliable and valid predictors of overt behavior. Lacking this knowledge researchers may draw false conclusions from their findings.

In criticizing a recent article that tended to polarize conceptualizations of attitudes into "probability conceptions" and "latent process conceptions," Weissberg made a point that is well taken. The effects of attitudes in behavior should not be considered from a perspective of theoretical

[19] Cicourel, *op. cit.*, pp. 39–72; Back, Hood, and Brehm, *op. cit.*, pp. 181–187; M. T. Orne, "On the Social Psychology of the Psychological Experiment: With Particular Reference to Demand Characteristics and Their Implications," *American Psychologist*, 17 (1962), pp. 776–783; Robert Rosenthal, "On the Social Psychology of the Psychological Experiment," *American Scientist*, 51 (1963), pp. 268–283; and William H. Form, "On the Sociology of Social Research," *Rassegna di Sociologia* (September 1963), pp. 463–481.

monism. Verbal attitudes are, "simply one of the terms in the complex regression equation we use to predict behavior." [20] One possible way of solving this equation is to adopt a field theory orientation, considering behavior both in and outside an experimental environment as being a function of both personality and environmental factors. Such an approach prevents positing theories of contemporaneity or theories of predispositional determinism.

SUMMARY

The data for this study were gathered from 46 randomly selected college sophomores, juniors and seniors at a "Big Ten" university. The Ss were randomly distributed between two experimental treatments. Under Treatment A Ss were encouraged to define the research setting as the usual playlike experiment. In Treatment B Ss were encouraged to define the research setting as a situation where current acts would have consequences for future behavior. In Treatment A verbal attitudes toward Negroes were not found to be good predictors of the degree of involvement in a campus chapter of the NAACP. In contrast verbal attitudes in Treatment B were good predictors of the same overt behavior.

This study demonstrates the importance of the social psychology of the research process. The way respondents define a situation, and consequently, play the corresponding role, significantly affects the relationship between independent and dependent variables. *Verbal attitudes can be either consistent or inconsistent with overt behavior, depending upon the way respondents define the attitude measurement situation.* The results caution against simplistic interpretations of verbal attitudes relationship to overt behavior. As Hyman has stated the inconsistency between verbal attitudes and overt behavior frequently results from inconsistencies between the interpretations researchers put upon attitude measurements and the measurements' relationship to behavior, rather than from evidence of measures of association.

Data also suggest that measures of commitment may be better predictors of overt behavior than measures of attitude, if the measurement situation is not contaminated by role-playing unrelated to overt behavior with which respondents feel forced to be consistent. Unlike attitude measures, commitment incorporates in the measurement situation the fundamental aspect of overt behavior—the possible sanctioning of significant others. Since the measurement of commitment involves the reduction of the playlike atmosphere of the usual testing situation, it serves the function of providing a good predictor for overt behavior.

---

[20] Norman C. Weissberg, "On DeFleur and Westie's 'Attitude as a Scientific Concept,'" *Social Forces*, 43 (March 1965), p. 422.

For Further Reading

BOOKS

Cohen, A. R. *Attitude change and social influence.* New York: Basic Books, 1964.

A digest of the results of about 150 studies on social influence, most of them published in the last decade.

Fishbein, M. (Ed.) *Readings in attitude theory and measurement.* New York: Wiley, 1967.

Includes sections on historical foundations (articles by Allport, Thurstone, LaPiere, and others), standardized measurement techniques (Bogardus, Thurstone, Likert, Guttman), multidimensional techniques (such as Lazarsfeld's latent structure analysis), problems and prospects of attitude measurement, and attitude theory.

Sherif, C. W. and Sherif M. (Eds.). *Attitude, ego-involvement, and change* (New York: Wily, Inc., 1967).

The outgrowth of a symposium on "Attitude and Social Change" at Pennsylvania State University in 1966, this volume contains papers varying from laboratory experiments on attitude change to the measurement of social attitudes and mass communication.

——— and Nebergall, R. E. *Attitude and attitude change.* Philadelphia: W. B. Saunders, 1965.

A highly competent discussion of theory and research on attitude, attitude change, judgment and self-involvement.

ARTICLES

Alexander, C. N. Attitude as a scientific concept. *Social Forces,* 1966, *45* (2), 278–281. SA 15, C4768.

Some "inner state" conception of attitude is necessary if nonhistorical variables are to be used to predict behaviors in situations other than that of initial measurement, that is, if attitude is to be used as an independent variable.

Barclay, A., and Thumin, F. J. A modified semantic differential approach to attitudinal assessment. *J. of clin. Psychol.,* 1963,19 (3), 376–386. PA 39, 7574.

Students observed slides involving a student studying and having coffee, tea, or No-Doz beside him. Students observing the No-Doz slide presented more negative attitudes than the students in the other groups.

Cole, D. L., *et al.* Attitudes to Caryl Chessman as a function of his reprieve and execution. *J. soc. Psychol.,* 1962, *57* (2), 471–475. PA 37, 4849.

Following the execution, shifts in item endorsements were in the direction of justifying the execution.

Deutsch, M. The effect of motivational orientation upon trust and suspicion. *Human Relations*, 1960, *13* (2), 123–139. PA 35, 6334.

Cooperative orientation leads to trusting behavior, competitive orientation leads to suspicious and untrustworthy behavior.

Diab, L. N. Some limitations of existing scales in the measurement of social attitudes. *Psychol. Rep.*, 1965, *17* (2), 427–430. PA 40, 1499.

A critical analysis of attitude scales, with special reference to neutral attitudes.

Eysenck, H. J. Primary social attitudes: a comparison of attitude patterns in England, Germany and Sweden. *J. of abnorm. soc. Psychol.*, 1953, *48* (4), 563–568. SA 2, 251.

The structure of attitudes in these four countries is very similar, hence generalization of research findings beyond the immediate culture is justified.

Fishbein, M. An investigation of the relationships between beliefs about an object and the attitude toward that object. *Human Relations*, 1963, *16* (3), 233–240. SA 12, 9415.

A test of the hypothesis that an individual's attitude toward any object is a function of his beliefs about it.

Fishbein, M., and Raven, B. The AB scales—an operational definition of belief and attitude. *Hum. Relat.*, 1962, *15* (1), 35–44. SA 11, A5636.

Attitude is the evaluative dimension, belief is the probability dimension of a concept; there was no correlation between belief and attitude with respect to racial prejudice, extrasensory perception or atomic fallout.

Goldberg, P. A., and Stark, M. J. Johnson or Goldwater? Some personality and attitude correlates of political choice. *Psychol. Rep.*, 1965, *17* (2), 627–631. PA 40, 1501.

Goldwater supporters were more authoritarian, more religious, more orthodox in their religious views and generally more guarded and conservative; Johnson supporters were more maladjusted (Rotter Incomplete Sentences and MMPI). The possibility of confounding assessment of unconventionality and maladjustment was discussed.

Goldstein, M. J. The social desirability variable in attitude research. *J. of soc. Psychol.*, 1960, *52* (1), 103–108. PA 35, 6316.

Studies should control for social desirability; methods for doing this are presented.

Katz, D. The functional approach to the study of attitudes. *Publ. Opinion Quart.*, 1960, *24* (2), 163–204. PA 38, 830.

Reasons for holding or changing attitudes are viewed in the framework of functions they perform for the individual—adjustment, ego defense, value expression, and knowledge.

Krumholtz, J. D., and Varenhorst, B. Molders of Pupil Attitudes. *Personnel and Guidance Journal*, 1965, *43* (5), 443–446. PA 39, 9967.

Ninth-grade pupils agreed most with the statements when they were attributed to counselors (as opposed to parents or peers).

Lehmann, I. J., and Payne, I. K. An exploration of attitude and value changes of college freshmen. *Personnel Guid. J.*, 1963, *41* (5), 403–408. SA 12, A9101.

Measured value changes at beginning and end of freshman year. Academic instruction, courses, and so forth had virtually no impact; extracurricular activities some. Reinforcement of existing values, rather than modification, was found.

Mouton, J., *et al.* Influence of partially vested interests on judgment. *J. of abnorm. soc. Psychol.*, 1963, 66 (3), 276–278. PA 37, 7948.

A vested interest in an inferior position led to judgments different from those obtained from nonvested pairs.

Mueller, E. Ten years of consumer attitude surveys: their forecasting record. *J. Amer. Statistical Assoc.*, 1963, 58 (304), 899–917. SA 12, A8895.

Attitudes contribute significantly to our ability to account for fluctuations in durable goods spending.

Taylor, J. B. What do attitude scales measure: the problem of social desirability. *J. abnorm. soc. Psychol.*, 1961, 62 (2), 386–390. PA 36, 4GD86T.

Social desirability was found to influence scores on several kinds of questionnaires.

Tuddenham, R. C. Constancy of personal morale over a fifteen-year interval. *Child Developm.* 1962, 33 (3), 663–673. PA 37, 4879.

Attitudes were found relatively constant over a 15-year period; opinions (for example the fairness of the courts) were less constant.

Weatherley, D. Maternal response to childhood aggression and subsequent anti-semitism. *J. abnorm. soc. Psychol.*, 1963, 66 (2), 183–185. SA 12, B0567.

Relatively stern maternal discipline toward childhood aggressive behavior was associated with a relatively high level of anti-Semitism in 39 college women.

Chapter Six

The Small Group

One of the earliest, distinctive concepts of sociology was that of the group. So preoccupied has sociology been with this topic that some scholars have defined sociology as the study of the *group*. Marie Borgatta recently traced the developmental history of this field of interest.[1] The work of Hegel, Comte and Spencer, she points out, turned attention from the contribution of the individual members to the group to a consideration of the group as such. Gumplowicz felt that the groups most suited would survive in society. "Durkheim argued that the group possesses a reality of its own, which is distinguished from individual expressions and transcends any direct sum of them." Giddings, Toennies, and Simmel simply assumed that groups were real, and proceeded to study the functions of groups as such. Cooley's contribution is perhaps best known, because of his coining of the phrase "primary group," to describe the intimate, face-to-face relationship characterized by a "we" feeling.[2]

Evidence of continued concern may be found in the first article by David Horton Smith, in which he makes careful analysis of several dimensions of the concept.

The importance of using the group as a frame of reference is evidenced here by the research of Dean C. Barnlund, in which he reports that group judgment on a complex intellectual task was superior to the judgment of individuals working alone.

It is important to note, however, that sociologists do not interpret groups as unmixed blessings, any more than gravity may be interpreted as "good" or "bad."[3] One of the dysfunctions of membership in a group is illustrated in the work of Robert R. Blake and Jane S. Mouton, who show that even in an experimental setting loyalty to one's group inhibits the ability to judge objectively any solutions to problems other than that worked out by one's own group.

[1] Borgatta, M. L. The concept of the group: a brief consideration. *Sociol. and soc. res.* 1958, 43 (2), 83–89.

[2] Cooley, C. H. Social Organization. New York: Scribner, 1915, pp. 23–24.

[3] This expression is borrowed from "You Are Not Alone," Record Number 8 in *Ways of Mankind*, edited by Walter Goldschmidt; produced by the National Association of Educational Broadcasters.

16

A Parsimonious Definition of "Group": Toward Conceptual Clarity and Scientific Utility*

DAVID HORTON SMITH

University of Southern California

There has been a tremendous outpouring of research in the past two decades on the behavior of individuals in group settings, not only the kind provided by small informal groups but also those which are large and complex in their organization. Yet theories of group phenomena have not kept pace with this empirical explosion. This paper and related work in preparation may be viewed as small parts of the effort needed to provide a general theory of groups. Specifically, the necessary and sufficient conditions for the occurrence of "grouplike phenomena" will first be identified and then incorporated into a precise but general definition of the term "group."

A *group* is defined here as (1) *the largest set of two or more individuals who are jointly characterized by* (2) *a network of relevant communications,* (3) *a shared sense of collective identity,* and (4) *one or more shared goal dispositions with associated normative strength.* It shall be maintained that this definition simultaneously optimizes the evaluative criteria of parsimony, conceptual clarity, and scientific utility. Parsimony will be demonstrated by showing that the four elements of the foregoing definition are necessary and sufficient for the emergence of grouplike phenomena. Fewer elements will not suffice; more are not necessary. Conceptual clarity is to be accomplished through precise and operational specification of the nature of each such element. Scientific utility will be suggested (but left open for future judgment by others) by showing not only that the present definition comes very close to encompassing just those observable grouplike phenomena that are of most interest to the scientific student of groups but also that it excludes other, unwanted phenomena.

Reprinted from *Sociological Inquiry*, 37, 2 (Spring 1967), 141–167, by permission of the author.

* An earlier draft of this paper was read by and has benefited from the comments of the following colleagues: Richard Ames, Philip Bonacich, LaMar Empey, Joseph Feagin, William Hill, Malcolm Klein, Sanford Labovitz, Marijo Miller, Robert Priest, Clarence Schrag, and Herman Turk. Special thanks are due Herman Turk for his detailed comments on style as well as substantive matters, although he is not to be held responsible for any remaining deficiencies.

The plan of the paper involves (A) a brief discussion of the reality of groups, followed by (B) a short review of prior definitions of group. Then we shall return in greater depth and detail to (C) the definition of group used here, explaining the implications of each of the four elements included. A rather lengthy statement (D) of the external criterion of utility in defining group, as well as a discussion of the internal criteria of clarity and parsimony, will follow. After this will come (E) an evaluation of the present definition in terms of the criteria of utility, clarity, and parsimony, and then (F) a discussion of the definitional relevance of other analytical elements of group structure and functioning. Finally, (G) the discussion will be concluded by suggesting several important implications of the present definition for future research and theory.

A. ARE GROUPS REAL?

Throughout this paper we shall assume that groups are real. Many theorists and investigators hold to various kinds of nominalism. They argue that while people or members of groups are real, groups themselves are mere names for collections of persons, and, hence, that groups are not real. This nominalist position (as well as several related positions) was dealt with quite effectively over a decade ago by Horowitz and Perlmutter[1] and subsequently by Warriner.[2] Both of these articles reaffirmed the idea that groups are just as real as persons—and just as *unreal* in a sense. For both groups and persons are analytical concepts; they are both abstractions rather than concretely observable entities. The value of either concept lies in its utility for understanding and predicting observable events.

Given that groups are real but abstract, analytic entities, the need is redoubled for a precise analytical definition of the theoretical term "group" over what such need would be were this term to fall into the same category as the observational terms "chair" and "banana." This immediately leads one to ask what are the existing definitions of group; and which of these, if any, are sufficiently precise and adequate for conceptual and empirical developments in research on group phenomena?

[1] Milton W. Horowitz and Howard V. Perlmutter, "The Concept of the Social Group," *Journal of Social Psychology*, 37 (February, 1953), pp. 69–95.

[2] Charles K. Warriner, "Groups Are Real: A Reaffirmation," *American Sociological Review*, 21 (October, 1956), pp. 549–554.

B. PRIOR DEFINITIONS OF THE TERM "GROUP"

Many different definitions of the term "group" are to be found in the literature. These definitions stress varying combinations of the elements to be reviewed in the present paper and occasionally include other elements as well. Some define groups mainly in terms of interaction among two or more individuals,[3] others stress the notion of role differentiation,[4] and still others emphasize shared goals[5] or some other property. The present definition does not purport to be startlingly new in terms of the elements it employs. Moreover, the claim shall not be made that the four elements have never been used jointly before in suggesting definitions of group. Instead, the aim of the present paper will lie in calling attention to the parsimony and utility of the present definition, while attempting to improve its conceptual and operational precision.

More often than not, small group investigators, students of formal organization, and other scholars who deal with group phenomena either ignore the problem of defining a group entirely or else very quickly pass over it by quoting some well-known existing definition. Many would argue that a precise and generally accepted definition of the term "group" is not particularly pressing or important for the development of research on group phenomena.[6] This argument is probably true indeed for certain kinds of investigations. Still there are other types of group research and, especially, theory for which an adequate definition of "group" is essential. The study of *group formation* is a good example, for adequate distinctions among non-groups, near groups, and true groups depend upon a precise definition of "true groups" or, simply, of "groups."

When investigators and theorists *do* pay attention to the problem of group definition, a common flaw often mars their efforts. Namely, the terms employed tend either to be too broad or too narrow to be of maximum use. On the one hand, groups are often defined so that the term encompasses nearly any form of social interaction or social behavior, ignoring thereby the distinctive, emergent structural properties of groups. On the other hand, groups are often so defined as to include only the so-called "small groups." Defining groups in this restricted manner ignores some very important similarities between small informal groups and such

---

[3] Cf. George C. Homans, *The Human Group*, New York: Harcourt, Brace, 1950, pp. 1, 84.

[4] Cf. Scott A. Greer, *Social Organization*, New York: Random House, 1955, p. 18.

[5] Cf. Tamotsu Shibutani, *Society and Personality*, Englewood Cliffs, New Jersey: Prentice-Hall, 1961, p. 33 f.

[6] Marie L. Borgatta, "The Concept of the Group: A Brief Consideration," *Sociology and Social Research*, 43 (November–December, 1958), pp. 83–89. Here it is concluded that, "Any definition of the group is arbitrary, but the definition in any specific instance must be determined by its usefulness, with full awareness of the limitations involved."

other grouplike entities as formal organizations, "collective behavior," or national states.

A comprehensive and exhaustive reply to the question, how have groups been defined in the past, is beyond both the scope and interest of the present paper. Since the potential sources of such definitions number in the thousands, their review is impracticable for the present. More important, however, such review was felt to be unnecessary. The major definitions of group should be available in dictionaries of sociology and psychology, in commonly used social psychology textbooks, and in major monographs and articles concerned with group theory and research. Having examined some twenty-odd sources of this kind,[7] one is unlikely to have missed many of the really essential elements of group, as the concept is used currently. Moreover, the review performed before preparing this paper was meant to be illustrative rather than exhaustive. The intention was not to derive theory through summary or synthesis of common definitional parlance, but rather to elicit the major *elements* that have been used in defining group. The elements appearing most frequently were either included in the present definition of group or cited under "F. The Relevance

[7] *Dictionaries.* Horace B. English and Ava C. English, A *Comprehensive Dictionary of Psychological and Psychoanalytic Terms*, New York: Longmans, Green, 1958, p. 232; Henry P. Fairchild, *Dictionary of Sociology and Related Sciences*, Ames, Iowa: Littlefield, Adams and Co., 1957, p. 133.

Textbooks. Theodore Caplow, *Principles of Organization*, New York: Harcourt, Brace and World, 1964, p. 12; Scott A. Greer, *Social Organization*, New York: Random House, 1955, p. 18; Ernest T. Hiller, *Social Relations and Structures*, New York: Harper, 1947, p. 247; William W. Lambert and Wallace E. Lambert, *Social Psychology*, Englewood Cliffs, N.J.: Prentice-Hall, 1964, p. 87; Edward C. McDonagh and Thomas E. Lasswell, *Sociology: An Introduction*, Columbia, Mo.: Lucas Brothers, 1953, p. xv; Theodore M. Newcomb, Ralph H. Turner, and Philip E. Converse, *Social Psychology*, New York: Holt, Rinehart, and Winston, 1965; Muzafer Sherif and Carolyn W. Sherif, *An Outline of Social Psychology, Revised*, New York: Harpers, 1956, p. 144; Tamotsu Shibutani, *Society and Personality*, Englewood Cliffs, N.J.: Prentice-Hall, 1961, p. 33; Robin M. Williams, Jr. *American Society: A Sociological Interpretation*, New York: Knopf, 1959, p. 446f.

Research Articles, Monographs, or Summaries. Alan P. Bates and Nicholas Babchuk, "The Primary Group: A Reappraisal," *Sociological Quarterly* 2 (July, 1961), pp. 181–191; Frederick L. Bates, "A Conceptual Analysis of Group Structure," *Social Forces*, 36 (December, 1957), pp. 103–111; Emory S. Bogardus, "Group Behavior and Groupality," *Sociology and Social Research*, 38 (July–August 1954), pp. 401–403; Marie L. Borgatta, "The Concept of the Group: A Brief Consideration," *Sociology and Social Research*, 43 (November–December, 1959) pp. 83–89; A. Paul Hare, *Handbook of Small Group Research*, New York: Free Press of Glencoe, 1962, p. 10; George C. Homans, *The Human Group*, New York: Harcourt, Brace, 1950, pp. 1, 84; Robert K. Merton, *Social Theory and Social Structure, Revised*, Glencoe, Ill.: The Free Press, 1957, p. 285 f.; Michael S. Olmsted, *The Small Group*, New York: Random House, 1959, p. 21; Muzafer Sherif, "Sociocultural Influences in Small Group Research," *Sociology and Social Research*, 39 (September–October, 1954), pp. 1–10; Pablo Lucas Verdú, "Notas Para Una Sociologia de los Grupos Humanos," (Notes Toward a Sociology of Human Groups), *Review of International Sociology*, 13 (January–June 1955), pp. 15–41.

of Other Analytical Elements Not Used," one of the sections to follow.

C. THE PRESENT DEFINITION

1. *Group Size.* The first element of the present definition deems a group to be "the largest set of two or more individuals who are characterized by" the other elements of group definition. Here the term "individual" may refer to human beings, higher primates, or possibly other living organisms, but not to inanimate objects.[8] By the phrase "largest set" is meant that in its entirety a particular group includes *every* individual in space-time who satisfies the definitional criteria for membership in that group. Operationally, this first element of a group requires that individuals of various species be considered potential group members throughout the space-time continuum—past, present, and future. In certain research undertakings, however, one may wish to restrict his observations to the human species (or at most a few others), as well as to individuals who are most available in space-time—e.g., in the same planet, country, state, or city over some rather limited period close to the present. In such cases this definition has the investigator studying partial groups in most cases rather than complete groups.

2. *Communication Network.* The second element used here in defining a group is "a network of relevant communications." Such a network is present when (a) each member of a set of individuals has received at least one communication (message) relevant to the existence or purposes of a particular collective entity and (b) when each member of the set of individuals is "connected" with every other member of the set by some finite number of relevant communication links. If a particular individual has never received any such relevant communication, he is not and has not been a member of the group which constitutes the locus of that collective entity. Receipt of a relevant communication may be measured by (inferred from) content analysis of the various stimuli which affect any given individual over time, or more simply by asking the individual—provided that he happens to be a socialized human being and can be reached by the investigator's communications—if he has ever heard of or been asked to join such and such organization or group.

Note that no specific mention is made of the *time period* during which the communication must take place. This allows sets of individuals who are separated in time, even over generations or centuries, to be members of the same group. Similarly, no specification is made of the location of individuals nor of the *means of communication*—e.g., face-to-face com-

---

[8] This usage of the term "individual" makes it an interesting empirical question whether any non-human animals form groups.

munication is not required—; this allows individuals despite spatial separation to be members of the same group. Nor is it necessary that the communication be *two-way* for a group to exist; this again permits the existence of groups composed of members who are widely separated in space-time or who are reacting to a commonly perceived event or message without ever having had any opportunity for feedback communication to the source.[9]

Further, it should be noted that the relevant message received by members of the set of individuals need not have been sent by a member of the set. Hence, a group can even exist where the set had been stimulated entirely by an outside "organizer" or institutionalizing agency, or by some written, photographed, tape recorded, or otherwise preserved message. For example, a powerfully written religious tract may provide sufficient "relevant communication" to lead to the formation of a religious group which endures over time. This could occur despite denial of membership by the author of the tract and even though the individual members, following norms set forth in the tract, never come into direct communication with one another!

The "connectivity" criterion for "a network of relevant communications" uses the concept, "relevant communication link." A relevant communication link may be inferred from a relevant communication that has passed in at least one direction between two individuals or between an individual and some inanimate object which serves to store or transmit messages. The rather loose connectivity requirement of the present definition permits considering a set of individuals to constitute a group in spite of a long chain of relevant communication links between any given individual in the group and some other member who is distant from him in space-time.

The key to all this is, of course, the operational definition of "relevant communication." Relevant communication may be defined as an observable (inferable) flow of information into the sensory apparatus of an individual wherever such information refers to the existence, purposes, norms, or other important characteristics of a collective entity. This definition in turn requires "collective entity" to be defined. By collective entity is simply meant the abstract image of a group or of grouplike phenomena. As such, a collective entity is not a mystical concept. Operationally, the existence of relevant communication may be determined by examining first the content of communications received by individuals in a set. Any indications of the actual or potential existence of grouplike, supraindividual, collective entities should be noted. Then, for each such hypothetical collective entity or image of a group, the communications received by each member of the set should be judged by an objective observer in order to

[9] The sort of communication network required by the present definition has been termed an "arborescence." See Claude Flament, *Application of Graph Theory to Group Structure*, New York: Prentice-Hall, 1963.

determine whether any of the messages received by the member deal in important or significant ways with any such collective entity. If each member of the set can be shown to have received at least one message relevant to a given collective entity, then the criterion of relevant communication is operationally satisfied for that set of individuals and for that collective entity.

Thus, by way of summary, although there tends to be a great deal of two-way communication on a variety of themes among the members of most groups, a *defining* characteristic of groups is that every member received information at least once from a source external to himself which dealt with the main goal and the very existence of the group. Also, even though a small number of relevant communication links (often only one link) can be described which connect any given member with any other member, a *defining* characteristic of groups is that a finite number of links be identified between any given member and any other member.

3. *Shared Collective Identity.* A shared sense of collective identity, the third element of this definition of group, refers to the observable condition that each member of a set (a) believes himself to be a member of (or participant in) some specific collective entity, and (b) believes that there is at least one other individual in space-time who also views himself as a member of that same collective entity and who in turn believes in the existence of the other member(s). In general, each member of the set will tend to have such a sense of collective identity because of his perception that he and others have some important property in common and his perception that this common feature is recognized by others as both present and important. This commonly recognized feature often is a shared goal disposition, but a sense of collective identity may arise from other sources, such as propinquity in space-time or physical similarity. But whatever the basis, there is a belief in mutual membership, in unity, among the individuals of a set if they are designated as having a shared sense of collective identity. This condition may be inferred by observing the non-verbal behavior of the sets' members, but it is approached most meaningfully and efficiently through questions asked of every member— provided, of course, that the set is human.

Note that the shared sense of collective identity does *not* assume perfect enumerability of all members of the group by any given member of the group. Once again the group concept is permitted to encompass members who are distant from one another in space-time. It also includes "underground organizations" or "spy networks," which are groups despite having members who are mostly unaware of one another's identity. It should also be noted that the element, shared sense of collective identity, as defined, does not require that there *in fact* be any distinguishing trait or property of the members of the set beyond mutual belief in some sort of unity. Thus, from the scientist's standpoint, the members of a set may be under collective delusion regarding some trait but still be a group if the remaining definitional criteria are met. For example, a group might be formed of persons who all thought they were witches or all thought they were Christ.

The shared sense of collective identity is meant to be an essentially intellectual rather than emotional phenomenon, although emotions may also be involved to varying degrees. Thus, to say that each member of a set has a sense of collective identity means that each conceives of himself and others as members of a group, *not* necessarily that each or any member of the set is emotionally involved with the group's existence. Emotional commitment of a group member to the group's existence or actions is a variable, not a defining characteristic of the group.

4. *Shared Goal Dispositions.* The fourth element of the definition of group offered here refers to "one or more shared goal dispositions with associated normative strength." By "goal disposition" is meant the tendency to prefer or want some end-state or configuration of events. In stating that the members of a set "share" a certain goal disposition (or several of them) we mean that each member of the set believes in some sense that he has this disposition, that other members of the set have it also, and that there is reciprocal awareness of its shared character. Once again, it is not necessary for every member of the set to be aware of the existence and identity of every other member of the set for there to be a shared goal disposition, but yet there must be something more than merely similar goals. The awareness of others sharing one's own goal disposition(s) is crucial, even though it may not be too specific in some groups. In most groups, however, and especially in small groups and most formal organizations, the awareness of who shares one's own goals may be quite precise and explicit.

The remaining factor of importance is "associated normative strength." By this is meant some significant moral feeling, a sense of social duty, "oughtness," conscience, or internal obligation and compulsion which accompanies the shared goal dispositions of the members of a set. Normative strength can best be operationalized by asking questions or eliciting non-verbal responses from individuals regarding how each feels about a given shared goal disposition. The fourth and final requirement for the existence of a group is satisfied to the extent that each of the members of a set not only shares the same goal disposition but also feels some social or moral obligation to the other members of the set to help accomplish the goal in question. Thus, in order for a set of individuals to be a group in terms of the present definition, there must be at least one norm present, the norm of accomplishing the shared goal.

The content of the shared goal need not be specified in the definition of group. At the very minimum, any shared goal disposition with associated normative strength will refer to the preservation of a shared sense of collective identity over time. Achieving such continuity of identity will in turn entail a variety of actions of an instrumental sort. Many types of groups also have their specific instrumental goals whose accomplishment is normative for group members and which are shared as goal dispositions for all members. Still the present definition of group allows us to classify sets of individuals as groups who have no clear cut instrumental goals, rather tending towards casual, interpersonal, and socioemotional content. Here the main shared goal is simply mutual interaction. It should also be noted that the present definition of group does not *require* that shared, normatively supported goal dispositions be manifest in any overt behavior. It is possible for a group to exist whose members differ from non-members only in their covert mental and emotional processes. Such a group would be difficult to identify, to be sure, but might nevertheless be inferred to exist in terms of certain subtle evidence. The interesting point is that the present definition allows us to call such a set a group under certain conditions, whereas other definitions would exclude it.

D. THE CRITERIA FOR EVALUATING ANY DEFINITION OF "GROUP"

The External Criterion of Utility in Defining "Group." Definitions are not right or wrong, true or untrue, but rather they have varying degrees of utility for certain scientific purposes. Earlier definitions of group were rejected as either being too broad or too narrow in most cases. The case made for the present definition is that it approaches the ideal of scientific utility in terms of an observable external criterion. Specifically, the present definition is considered to be of maximum use, because its elements represent a "critical mass" in some real, empirical sense. Thus, one might refer to sharp increases in the probability that grouplike phenomena will occur once observable configurations of events satisfy our four definitional elements of a group.

Such sharp increase in the occurrence of grouplike phenomena may be referred to as a "discontinuity," at least figuratively, although in fact it is simply a rapid change in a continuous probability distribution over all observable configurations of events. In order to test the utility of this definition, it would be necessary to muster past research or undertake future research that will permit determination of whether grouplike phenomena are indeed markedly more common where all four elements of our definition are satisfied than where they are not. If grouplike phenomena occur almost equally often where these elements are not jointly present, the definition should either be replaced or modified to maximize the prediction of grouplike phenomena.

The crux of this argument rests on the definition of "grouplike phenomena." In one sense this phrase might be treated as a primitive term whose referent is intuitively obvious to all other social scientists. On the other hand, there exists an obligation to explicate the meaning of the term, not only to avoid misunderstanding but also so that it may be made operational. Grouplike phenomena are concerted, self-conscious and other-conscious thoughts, feelings, or actions, on the part of a set of individuals.

The presence of such concerted behavior may generally be assumed when by merely knowing that several individuals of a set form a group and by knowing the global nature of the group (its goals, norms, roles, etc.),[10] the total variance in behavior among members of the set may be predicted to some significant degree without having additional information at hand about each individual member of the set.

The more developed the group culture and the greater the corresponding breadth and specificity of group roles and norms, the greater will be the increment in predictability which results from knowing that a set of individuals forms or is part of a group. This is not simply recognition of the general fact that the more one knows about something, the better one can predict events or characteristics of that thing or situation. Rather, we are arguing that groups structure covert and usually overt behavior in a manner that makes such behavior more predictable than generally is the case for non-grouplike sets of individuals with equal numbers of members. This group structuring of individual behavior may be termed "supraindividual patterning of behavior."

If the entire set of individuals did not comprise a group but did contain one or more groups of smaller size within it, the increment in predictability would be less—other things being equal—than if the whole set formed a single group. Roughly speaking, the predictability increment which results from the constitution of a group by part of a set of individuals will be directly proportional to the percentage of members of the set who are members of that group. Nevertheless, there still remains, one would think, a rather sharp discontinuity in average predictability between sets of individuals who are members of the same group as contrasted with sets of merely similar (let alone dissimilar) individuals who are not members of the same group.

In addition to sharply increased predictability in the *current* behavior of group members compared to other sets, there will also be further increase in the predictability of the *future* behavior patterns. Thus the emergence of grouplike properties within a given set of individuals is pregnant with probability for the development of still further grouplike properties and phenomena. For example, once a set of individuals has become a group, the group tends to have a future of its own that is independent of the fate of single individuals within it. Similarly, individuals

[10] By "global nature of the group" is meant what the goals, norms, roles, interpersonal relations patterns, and the like are for the group, as determined by sampling the total group or by sampling the group's leaders (formal or informal). Thus, the global nature of the group may be determined *without* first studying each individual in the group and then summing these individual characteristics. If the latter were necessary, explanatory/predictive power would not be gained by use of the group concept. As it stands, however, such power *has been* gained.

who have become a group in terms of the minimal elements suggested here tend to engage in concerted action in order to accomplish their normatively strengthened and shared goal dispositions. Pursuit of these common goals tends to involve the development of normative strategies for goal implementation, role differentiation and functional interdependence, mutually satisfying social relations among group members, the formation of group representative roles and interaction with other groups, as well as a variety of other grouplike phenomena. Thus, the grouplike phenomena observable among a set of individuals at any given point in time are systematically and probabilistically related to future grouplike phenomena that may be observed within that same set. Grouplike phenomena generally are *sequences* of highly interrelated event configurations, not just isolated instances of heightened but highly temporary predictability.

Such heightened predictability, both present and future, is necessary but not sufficient for the recognition of emergent grouplike phenomena. Other factors are necessary in differentiating grouplike phenomena from predictable patterns that result from other causes. For instance, there may be highly predictable convergences in the behavior of several individuals that can principally be attributed to hereditary causes in conjunction with particular environmental stimuli (e.g., various kinds of instinctive behavior). Further, there may be highly predictable patterns of multiple individual behavior that can principally be attributed to physical causes in the environment of these individuals (e.g., sets of individuals caught in the same tornado vortex or in the same rushing floodwaters). Thus, the explication of "grouplike phenomena" may further be refined by stating that *emergent grouplike phenomena are complex events that not only manifest a predictable supraindividual patterning of the present and future behavior of multiple individuals but which also permit such increased predictability without primary dependence on sheer physiological-genetic causation or on the coercion of external environmental factors.*

This does not imply that physiological-genetic factors and/or environmental factors have no causal influence in emergent grouplike phenomena. Rather, it emphasizes that in grouplike phenomena there must be some significant causal influence attributable to factors other than those of a physiological-genetic or environmental nature. The physiological-genetic substrata of the individuals (whatever their species, age, or current condition) are still present and important, as are the influences of stimuli and conditions of the external environment, but these types of influences will not exhaustively explain the observed regularities in grouplike phenomena, either alone or in combination.

There is one final aspect to the explication of the nature of grouplike phenomena. Namely, that it is probably possible to find predictable supraindividual event configurations that meet the above criteria but that one would nevertheless not wish to include in the class of grouplike phenomena. That is, there are supraindividual patterns of non-hereditary, uncoerced behavior which should preferably not be attributed to the existence of a group. For example, there tends to be a good deal of supraindividual, patterned predictability for the set of all females, the set of all English- (or other language-) speaking individuals, the set of all persons of recent German extraction throughout the world, even the set of all red-heads in the United States. Yet one would hesitate to view these event configurations as though they were full-fledged grouplike phenomena. Instead, use can be made of the term, "social role phenomena," a broader class that includes grouplike phenomena as a subtype. Thus one could argue that the explication presented so far for the term "grouplike phenomena" is in fact a statement suitable for recognizing all "emergent social role phenomena."

It is the existence of normative expectations that permits the patterned predictability of all emergent social role phenomena. Such norms are associated with possession by individuals of one or another combination of properties having social importance. Such individuals represent an abstract social identity; they constitute a recognizable category of persons having importance for other persons. Roles may be viewed as the set of norms (normative expectations for behavior, both covert and overt) associated with a particular social identity. The heightened predictability of all English speakers, all females, and the like proceeds from the fact that any member of these descriptive categories has a recognizable social identity, thus having been taught and having learned one or more of the norms which comprise the role which is associated with his particular social identity.

But such norm learning and norm following, so basic to all social role phenomena, does not presume any shared self-consciousness among role incumbents, nor any shared sense of interconnected "fate" (outcomes of future events), nor any shared sense of concerted effort to achieve common goals. *Grouplike phenomena may therefore be distinguished from other social role phenomena by the presence of a self-conscious and other-conscious unity behind grouplike patterns that may be lacking in certain other types of role phenomena.* The distinction between grouplike phenomena and other, "non-grouplike" role phenomena cannot be made hard and fast. Rather, gradations may be observed from the extreme case of grouplike phenomena, where there is an intense sense of unity among the individuals involved, to the other extreme of non-grouplike or categorical social role phenomena (e.g., the case of red-heads in the United States), where although there may be supraindividual patterning of behavior in some sense ("quick tempers," for example), there is little or no sense of unity among role incumbents.

The attempt has been made to describe the kinds of observable configurations of events to which the term "group" should presumably be applied restrictively in order to maximize scientific utility. The essence of the explication has been to point to a certain kind of heightened supraindividual predictability in the behavior of multiple individuals. But in the end this heightened predictability was not sufficient in itself to denote or provide the empirical referent for the term "group." The idea of a self-conscious unity among the individuals who manifest this heightened predictability had to be added. Only in this way can one avoid having the term "group" refer to all manner of social role phenomena, including the phenomena of simple social categories or social identities. By thus explicating the term "grouplike phenomena," the term "group" may be applied in a manner that is consonant with past usage but also more precise.

The nature of grouplike phenomena having been explicated, there now exists an external, observable criterion for the utility of any definition of group. If the present discussion of grouplike phenomena is accepted by other social scientists as valid and useful, then one might ask whether the definition suggested for the term "group" specified the necessary and sufficient conditions for the emergence of grouplike phenomena. In this sense, the present definition of group need not be considered arbitrary, nor need be viewed as just another, perhaps fruitless attempt to improve the precision of previous definitions. Through advance knowledge of the kind of event configurations to which the term "group" is to refer, it is possible to escape the vicious circle wherein group often means what some particular social scientist wants it to mean.

The Internal Criteria of Parsimony and Precision in Defining "Group." The previous section elaborated on an important external criterion for the scientific utility of any definition of group. The present section will draw brief attention to two other important evaluative criteria, this time ones that are internal to any definition rather than external to it. "External" refers to the denotation or empirical referent of a definition, while "internal is concerned with the connotation or inherent logical structure and content of a definition.

A maximally valuable or useful definition should be parsimonious, including only as many elements as are necessary to denote the phenomena of interest and no more. In addition, a maximally useful definition should be precise and operational, providing clearcut rules for the application of certain of its component terms to observable events in the real world, and clearly defining all of its other component terms through use of the aforementioned sorts of observational terms as well as primitive (undefined) grammatical terms.

E. THE PRESENT DEFINITION IN TERMS OF THE THREE EVALUATIVE CRITERIA

Each of the four elements defining a "group" will be discussed in the light of the evaluative criteria suggested in the preceding section of the paper.

1. *Group Size.* Requiring two or more individuals is obviously necessary, for without at least two individuals there cannot be any emergent

grouplike phenomena, as these were described earlier; but there *can* be such phenomena with only two persons. While two is a minimum number of individuals who may be considered to form a group, one may expect a larger number of emergent grouplike phenomena with increasing size. Requiring that "group" refer to the *largest* set of individuals which satisfies the other conditions for a group is necessary if the term is to be sufficiently inclusive of a particular set of grouplike phenomena. This requirement was included in order to cope with the group boundary problem.

The term "group" (when unmodified) should be strictly applicable to *all* those individuals who satisfy the criteria for the existence of and membership in a particular group. The elements that define the existence of a group have been stated; therefore it only remains to note that a group member is an individual who is one of a set that satisfies the criteria for existence of a group. When membership is defined in this way, group boundaries are not set by physical locations in space-time. Individuals may themselves be considered to be group members only during those time periods when they satisfy the criteria for membership—i.e., when they recognize a shared sense of collective identity and shared goal dispositions with normative strength, after having received at least one relevant communication at some prior time and having been connected in an abstract sense by a finite number of communication links to all other members of the group. Thus individual group membership is timebound, even when the existence of the group is not.

A group may be said to exist as soon as two or more individuals have satisfied the criteria. One would think that it has died when there is no longer any living group member. But, although one can easily determine when a given group was "born" in most cases, it is interesting to note that one cannot ever be sure that a given group has "died" until *all* life ceases. The fact that there are no living members of a given group is *supporting* evidence for its death, but not *conclusive evidence;* since at any future time (as long as there are living organisms) one or more individuals may join. This insight is crucial in understanding the abstract, supraindividual, and spatio-temporally unbounded nature of groups and grouplike phenomena.

Thus, in its most inclusive sense, a group reaches throughout space-time to include all individuals who ever were members. Individuals cross the hypothetical "boundary" of the group when they become members of the group or cease to belong. At any given time, only a small proportion of the total membership of a group may be living or have member status. The individuals who are living members of a particular group at some point in time or during some period might best be termed "current group members," or collectively, a "current group." Thus a current group is a temporal cross-section and should not be confused with the group as a whole. This approach clearly points to the dynamic and continually changing nature of groups.

2. *Communication Network.* The presence of a network of relevant communications is an obvious necessity for the emergent grouplike phe-

nomena described earlier. Once physiological-hereditary factors and environmental coercion have been eliminated as primary causes for grouplike phenomena, only similar patterns of individual learning can account for the predictability of grouplike phenomena. Similar patterns of individual learning cannot be accounted for on any broad scale except through reference to some sort of similar relevant communications (e.g., norms) received by potential or actual group members. The probabilities are low indeed that any given set of individuals will manifest grouplike phenomena spontaneously unless each has learned through relevant communication that a group of some sort exists or might exist and that it has certain goals which have normative strength.

The criterion of relevancy is necessary because the individuals of a set may be receiving many kinds of communication from other individuals who are inside or outside the set. Unless intercommunication begins to take on some relevance to a collective entity and to the possibility of shared goals with normative strength within the set, grouplike phenomena are unlikely to emerge. Also, neither direct, nor face-to-face, nor two-way communications are necessary aspects of the communication network of a group, since grouplike phenomena can emerge from simpler networks. For example, many such phenomena are present in voluntary associations whose members are spread all over a city, a state, a nation, or the entire world. Most of the members may never come in face-to-face, direct, or even two-way contact with more than a few (if any) other members, and yet, members' behavior can manifest predictably patterned regularity owing to the existence of a group. The most extreme example might be that of a secret religious group or organization that attracted members by one-way communication through a written tract which enjoined anyone who became a group member to do good works in accord with the religion but without ever revealing his group membership to anyone. Such a situation would both fit the criteria of emergent grouplike phenomena as well as those of "groupness" but without entailing any of the excluded aspects of the communication system.

For similar reasons, only a loose connectivity criterion is needed to define a group. In most groups the number of relevant communication links required to "connect" one individual in the group to another individual in the group will tend to be small. In a very closely knit current group whose members are frequently involved in intense personal interaction, only one relevant communication link might be necessary to connect any two members. In order to refer to all grouplike phenomena, however, it seems advisable not to limit the term "group" to the latter situation, but rather to require only that a group permit *some* relevant linkage between any two members provided that enough links are used. The previous example of a secret religious group shows how grouplike phenomena may occur readily without any stricter connectivity requirement than that suggested in our definition.

3. *Shared Collective Identity*. A shared sense of collective identity or

unity is necessary to the definition, since it is an essential aspect of group-like phenomena as these have been explicated. The essential and emergent quality of grouplike phenomena as concerted, self-conscious and other-conscious feelings, thought, or behavior can occur and will occur with any degree of regularity among human beings only where there is a shared sense of unity among the individuals in a set. Concerted action, and by inference rudimentary concerted thought and feeling, exist in ant colonies and beehives; but one would hesitate to speak of group behavior or group-like phenomena here, since control by heredity seems clear. And occasionally there may be a sufficiently strong external stimulus or physical force in the environment of a set of individuals to cause them to behave in an apparently concerted manner without their awareness of a collective sense of unity.

Such situations (for instance, a simple panic) might be examples of collective behavior but not group behavior, although it is possible for the two to overlap in many other situations. Lacking the cohesive force of collective identity, the set of individuals would not manifest grouplike phenomena in the present, let alone the future.

4. *Shared Goal Dispositions.* The final requirement for grouplike phenomena is that there be one or more shared goal dispositions with associated normative strength. Given that a set of individuals are receiving relevant communications with regard to some potential collective entity and that they are beginning to have a sense of collective identity, grouplike phenomena will still not emerge unless there is also some shared goal disposition backed by normative support. Without this element, the set of individuals would still have no motivational unity, no instrumental unity, and hence would not engage in concerted behavior. There are a multitude of grouplike phenomena that can and will emerge only once a shared, normatively perceived goal disposition is present—role differentiation, patterned actions by members, development of group actions and group representatives, growth of norms to guide member actions in accomplishing group goals, and the like.

Short of shared goal dispositions, there is nothing that will provide for regularity in the behavior of a set of individuals once hereditary-physiological factors and sheer physical forces or stimuli from the external environment have been eliminated. Further, the emergence of grouplike phenomena and their persistence through time rests upon perception that the similar goal dispositions are shared, so that each member of the set believes that others exist somewhere in space-time who also hold the goal disposition and who also believe in turn in such sharing of goals. Along with this shared sense of collective goals goes some normative strength, a feeling of moral compulsion or social obligation to work together for the achievement of the shared goal disposition. Without the normative component, it is unlikely that grouplike phenomena will emerge with any great frequency or clarity nor that they will persist. This normative component provides a kind of cohesion among group members that goes beyond self-interest in achieving the shared goal disposition. From this, emergent grouplike phenomena will result.

F. THE RELEVANCE OF ANALYTIC ELEMENTS NOT USED

The four elements in the present definition of group have been shown to be *necessary* for the emergence of grouplike phenomena; it now remains to be considered whether these four elements are *sufficient* for the emergence of grouplike phenomena.

Sufficiency would mean parsimony. The relevance of several other analytic aspects of groups to the emergence of grouplike phenomena—hence, to the definition—must therefore be considered. These include (1) face-to-face interaction, (2) norms regarding means, (3) role differentiation, (4) action, (5) duration, (6) external perception of group identity or membership, (7) socioemotional patterns among group members, (8) mutual need satisfaction, and (9) intergroup relations and group representative roles.

1. *Face-to-Face Interaction.* Some scholars[11] argue that face-to-face communication is necessary for a group to exist, but in most cases these scholars would agree that such definitional requirement is most relevant for defining "small groups" rather than for defining groups in general as was done here. Communication has been shown to be an essential element in the emergence of grouplike phenomena. Whether it is face-to-face or mediated by others or by electro-mechanical means was shown not to be crucial, however.

2. *Norms Regarding Means.* It has been suggested by several scholars[12] that norms which order behavior among group members and towards outsiders or the external environment are necessary for a group to exist. The present definition accepts this argument in part but also rejects it to some degree. The necessity of at least one norm has been accepted when it came to the shared goal dispositions of the group. It may also be granted that in *most* cases some general norms guide communication and underlie the existence of a group and the emergence of grouplike phenomena. However, it is quite conceivable that a set of individuals with no common language or communication norms might form a group if circumstances were sufficiently demanding of group action for mutual preservation. Therefore, although general norms of communication and interaction do underlie most group formation and grouplike phenomena, and although such norms do tend to emerge once a group has formed, it is still true that

[11] See Bogardus, English, Homans, *loc. cit.*
[12] See Bates, Bogardus, Greer, Hare, Sherif and Sherif, *loc. cit.*

they are not necessary for the existence of grouplike phenomena and hence not necessary for defining "group."

Norms regarding other means, those which define ways of accomplishing group goals, are also not necessary for defining "group"; for grouplike phenomena can easily emerge before there are any clearcut and mutually accepted norms regarding means. Grouplike phenomena emerge as soon as a set of individuals have the characteristics stated in the present definition. The members will often pursue their shared goals in some trial-and-error fashion at first, unless or until norms regarding means are present. If the group is to endure over time, norms will tend to develop, no doubt, and guide group behavior in the attainment of group goals; but groups can certainly be formed without having such norms. An example would be a set of individuals trapped in an elevator for a short period. In most cases, they would become a group and engage in grouplike phenomena over a short period of time, having the shared goal of getting out of the elevator quickly. But they would most likely be experimenting with a variety of means in cooperating to get out rather than immediately developing a set of normative strategies. And once they had achieved success, the group would probably disband before the successful means had a chance to become binding upon the group members. Thus, if the time span of a group's existence is very short and its organization is casual rather than highly formal, few or no normative means will be present. The set of individuals forming the group will nonetheless manifest the emergent grouplike phenomena of concerted action, thought, or feeling simply as a product of their communication and mutually shared sense of unity and goals. The longer a group endures, however, other things being equal, the more likely it is to develop norms concerning means.

3. *Role Differentiation.* Related to the suggested requirement of norms regarding means is the requirement of role differentiation and functional interdependence in the accomplishment of tasks.[13] If a role is defined as a set of norms associated with individuals possessing a particular social identity, then all members of a group will have by definition at least the role of group member to enact. Moreover, if a group has just formed, the role of group member may be described as just having been "differentiated" from all other roles and activities of living organisms. But "role differentiation" customarily means differential task allocation. Viewed this way, role differentiation is clearly not necessary for defining a group because many kinds of grouplike phenomena may be identified that involve little or no differential task allocation. Insofar as a group is small or recently formed and insofar as the shared goal is simple, casual, expressive, or interpersonal (rather than complex, urgent, or instrumental), the differential allocation of tasks will tend to be rudimentary or nonexistent. And if role differen-

---

[13] See Bates, Bogardus, Greer, Hare, Lambert and Lambert, Merton, Sherif and Sherif, Shibutani, Verdú, Williams, *loc. cit.*

tiation is negligible, so also is functional interdependence. Hence, neither role differentiation nor functional interdependence is necessary for grouplike phenomena to occur.

4. *Action.* It has sometimes been suggested that action must be included in a definition of group. Grouplike phenomena certainly include the overt actions of individuals as well as their covert thoughts and feelings. But it is possible for grouplike phenomena to exist exclusively at the level of shared thought, feelings, and goal dispositions, either before group or individual action or even in a more enduring way. For instance, there might be a religious group whose outlook, goals, and norms were so otherworldly that group membership resulted in no group-relevant actions whatsoever, the entire emphasis being placed on covert prayer and communion with a spiritual being while continuing in one's normal everyday life. In such a case, one could infer the existence of a group and of group members by questioning individuals, if they were able and willing to reply, but not by observing their normal actions. Yet grouplike phenomena would be present, since group membership would be closely related with certain regularly recurring thoughts and feelings.

5. *Duration.* Bogardus[14] and Verdú[15] have suggested that a necessary characteristic of groups be that they endure in time. The enduring quality of groups may be granted as a tendency, but endurance through time is certainly not a defining element of a group. Empirically, one can point to many emergent grouplike phenomena that are present in sets of individuals who are in concerted, self-conscious and other-conscious action, thought, or feeling over a very brief span of time. The aforementioned elevator example is a case in point. If there were to be some minimum time requirement, it could be fairly short (somewhere between a few seconds and several minutes) and still yield grouplike phenomena. But adding a time requirement really contributes little to the identification of groups or grouplike phenomena; since grouplike phenomena will occur whenever a set of two or more individuals have a network of relevant communications, a shared sense of collective identity, and one or more shared goals with associated normative strength regardless of time.[16]

[14] See Bogardus, *loc. cit.*

[15] See Verdú, *loc. cit.*

[16] As implied earlier, groups can be found in the extreme case where some members have no overlapping life spans. If one is serious about the notion that "group" refers to a supraindividual theoretical construct, then such a situation should not be surprising or discomforting. A group is a concept or construct used to refer to patterns of observable behavior. Since time does not enter the definition of a group, one may use the group concept to refer to patterns of behavior over very long periods of time. Insofar as the total set of individuals comprising the group satisfy the definitional criteria of a group, it makes no difference where or when they are located. And if individuals widely separated in space and time do meet these criteria, then there should be no hesitation in calling them all members of the same group, even though at any given time most of the group's members may be dead!

6. *External Perception of Group Identity and Group Membership.*
Several scholars[17] have argued that groups must be seen by *non*-group
members as having a collective identity, unity, or common goal. But it
can easily be shown that this characteristic of groups is not necessary at
all, even though a sense of collective identity is necessary among the members themselves. For instance, consider a secret society or underground
movement of some sort. This set of individuals may have all of the essential group characteristics suggested in the present definition and may manifest all manner of highly developed grouplike phenomena without being
recognized by very many, if any, outsiders as a collectivity. Recognition as
a collective entity by outsiders is a usual characteristic of groups, especially of well developed, formalized, large, or more enduring groups. Yet
such recognition is clearly not necessary for a group to exist; rather it is
a variable characteristic of groups.

7. *Socioemotional Patterns.* A few scholars[18] have argued that a pattern of mutual social relations, of friendliness and tension release, of interpersonal attraction, of mutual sociometric choices, or of other types of
socioemotional relations is necessary as a definitional characteristic of
groups. Empirically one can find, however, many examples of grouplike
phenomena, especially over short periods, where the members of a set have
little or no positive attraction to one another or even exist in a state of
mutual hostility. In the well-known "prisoner's dilemma," for example,
people have a tendency to form groups and develop norms for their own
mutual benefit even though no love is lost among them. There are many
kinds of "conflict groups" and "least of all evils" groups of this kind. In
addition, many types of economic groups (partnerships, corporations, and
the like) are formed on the basis of relevant communication, shared sense
of unity, and shared goals, without the presence of strong interpersonal
ties among the members. And since grouplike phenomena can occur
among sets of individuals who are widely separated in space-time, there
is all the more reason to deny inclusion of close interpersonal relationships in the definition of a group. Thus, patterns of interpersonal attraction and sociometric choice are variable rather than defining characteristics of groups. This is not to deny that in many kinds of groups—especially in those which are small, expressive, or face-to-face—there is a high
level of interpersonal attraction and mutual positive feeling among the
group members and that these relationships provide important satisfactions for many of the members, but only to say that this need not be true
of all groups.

8. *Mutual Need Satisfaction.* The preceding discussion raises another
possibility to be considered here. It has been argued by some[19] that a

[17] See Borgatta, Caplow, English, Fairchild, Merton, Newcomb, Williams, *loc. cit.*
[18] See Bates and Babchuk, Hare, Williams, *loc. cit.*
[19] See English, Greer, Hiller, Shibutani, *loc. cit.*

defining characteristic of groups is the psychological interdependence (not task interdependence) and mutual need satisfaction they provide for their members. The sources of such need satisfaction might lie in relations with fellow members, in sheer group membership, in participating in the group's activities and its goal attainment, in the external goals that group membership makes attainable, or in any combination of these. But here again the *necessity* of mutual need satisfaction cannot be demonstrated, in spite of its frequent occurrence among sets of individuals manifesting emergent grouplike phenomena.

Just as one can point to empirical entities that clearly are groups while possessing very poor interpersonal attraction patterns, so can one also point to those that are groups in the sense of emergent grouplike phenomena while providing members with very little, if any, mutual need satisfaction. Certainly one would expect the entrance rate to be low for such groups and the exit rate to be high, but over some period of time the members could still manifest grouplike phenomena, justifying use of "group," even though the group's capacity for satisfying the needs of its members were negligible, inadequate, or declining.

An individual tends to join a group because he *thinks* membership in it will bring him some satisfaction, or at least minimize his dissatisfactions. He joins because of what he perceives the group's nature and activities to be.[20] Whether or not he is actually satisfied after he has joined is another question. The relative preponderance of satisfactions over dissatisfactions for each member will determine whether or not he remains in the group and actively participates. The greater the relative preponderance of dissatisfactions over satisfactions (both in numbers and in importance), the shorter the period from time of measurement that an individual will tend to remain in the group. Therefore, it is possible at any given point in time, and even quite likely if the set is large, to find sets of individuals manifesting grouplike phenomena despite minimal satisfactions or an unfavorable ratio of dissatisfactions to satisfactions.

9. *Intergroup Relations and Group Representative Roles.* One final element to be considered [21] as a defining characteristic of groups refers to the idea of intergroup relations and group representative roles. This requirement would state that a group is present only where there is some representative of a set who is seen as acting for the other members of the set. This representative may simply be acting as a leader in internal rela-

[20] Evidence for this assertion in the area of participation in formal voluntary organizations may be found in the author's "A Psychological Model of Individual Participation in Formal Voluntary Organizations: Application to Some Chilean Data," *American Journal of Sociology,* 72 (November, 1966), pp. 249–266. See also his unpublished paper titled, "A Sequential Specificity Model of Voluntary Role Selection," Department of Sociology and Anthropology, University of Southern California, 1967.

[21] Following the point of view, for instance, of Herman Turk and Myron J. Lefcowitz, "Towards a Theory of Representation Between Groups," *Social Forces,* 40 (May, 1962), pp. 337–341.

tions of the set of individuals (for example, sanctioning one member in the name of the whole set) or he may be acting for the whole set in dealing with the external environment, either physical or social. The importance of these sorts of grouplike phenomena cannot be denied, but the presence of such representative individuals or roles is not necessary for the emergence of grouplike phenomena. In most cases the development of representative roles comes *after* the emergence of a group and may be viewed as yet another aspect of the broader process of role differentiation. Many sorts of casual, informal groups could be pointed out that manifest grouplike phenomena without having any clearly representative role characteristics.

To summarize thus far, none of the criteria suggested by other writers need be added to the four included in the present definition in order for grouplike phenomena to occur. Thus the four elements are not only necessary, as demonstrated before, but they are also sufficient for defining a group in terms of the criteria employed here. This means that parsimony has been achieved in the present definition of group, at least for the purpose at hand. The definition is also quite precise, and it meets the stated criterion of scientific utility, that of predicting empirical grouplike phenomena. Another aspect of its utility lies in the promise for future theory and research, claimed for it in the subsequent section.

G. IMPLICATIONS OF THE PRESENT DEFINITION OF "GROUP"

As defined here, a group is a theoretical construct that may be used to help in understanding and predicting certain types of sense observations and configurations of events. The definition was intended to provide a capsule summary of past knowledge regarding grouplike phenomena while at the same time leading to prediction of future observations. It is maintained that the present definition applies in the vast majority of past situations in which emergent grouplike phenomena were observed. Moreover it is also maintained that emergent grouplike phenomena occurred in the vast majority of past situations in which the four definitional elements were present. These are empirical statements, since we have defined each of the four elements of groups independently of the nature of emergent grouplike phenomena and in empirical terms. Aid is sought in bringing more evidence to bear on these assertions, especially when it comes to the alleged "discontinuity" between the predictability of sets of individuals having the four definitional characteristics and sets of individuals lacking one or more of these characteristics.

Constituting only a part of a developing theory, the present definition of group should begin to supply a theoretical explanation for the emergence of grouplike phenomena. Such explanation has been given in rudimentary form by emphasizing the presence of a number of individuals, a network of relevant communications, a shared sense of collective identity, and one or more shared goal dispositions with associated normative strength. When viewed in combination with certain information about the external environment, the physiological nature of man, and his psychological nature, the mutual influences and patterning of these four elements of groups should lead to a fuller explanation of group phenomena in subsequent work. A suitable definition of the construct "group" is the cornerstone of such a general theory of groups—hence, the present attempt to provide such a definition.

"Groupness" as an Attribute and as a Location in a Multi-Dimensional Property Space. Throughout this paper groups and grouplike phenomena were discussed almost as if they were perfectly demarcatable from other phenomena and situations. This tendency reflected a heuristic device. However simple and precise the four essential elements of groups may seem, their long run value will lie in their service as crucial dimensions rather than as dichotomous attributes in defining groups. Typologies which cannot readily be decomposed into their dimensional elements are not particularly fruitful for science, if the past is any criterion. And yet typologies, such as the present one, that do in fact denote underlying property spaces can prove extremely useful, combining as they do the virtues of simple summary with empirical applicability.

And not only do the four definitional elements of a group yield dimensions, so also do the other analytic elements which were reviewed and discarded as candidates for inclusion in the definition. Thus it becomes an empirical question whether and to what extent groups are characterized by face-to-face interaction, by norms guiding group goal accomplishment, by endurance through time, by a collective identity perceived by outsiders, by role differentiation and functional interdependence in the accomplishment of tasks, by positive interpersonal choices among the members, by the provision of various sorts of satisfactions to the members, by overt action, by representative roles, or by other characteristics which have not even been considered here.[22] All of these characteristics may be seen as forming a property space of important elements of groups, so the general scientific problem to be faced is to explain movement through this property space in a systematic way.

The Study of Group Prevalence. Having a precise definition of groups

---

[22] For research and theory on the problem of group description, see such works as Edgar F. Borgotta and Leonard S. Cottrell, Jr., "On the Classification of Groups," *Sociometry*, 18 (December, 1955), pp. 665–678; John K. Hemphill and Charles M. Westie, "The Measurement of Group Dimensions," *Journal of Psychology*, 29 (January, 1950), pp. 325–342; Dwight Sanderson, "Group Description," *Social Forces*, 16 (March, 1938), pp. 309–319; James G. March and Herbert Simon, *Organizations*, New York: John Wiley and Sons, 1958; Allen Barton, *Organizational Measurement and its Bearing on the Study of College Environments*, New York: College Entrance Examination Board, 1961.

permits performance of certain kinds of much needed but hitherto difficult research. For instance, there has been relatively little systematic work done in the past in establishing prevalence rates and the determinants of such rates for all kinds of groups within various types of large social systems (cities, states, and nations, for example). Where such research has been done, it has generally taken one of two expedient but ultimately inadequate approaches. On the one hand, only formally organized groups (organizations) with proper names, clear leadership, and explicit membership criteria have been included in the survey.[23] On the other hand, the existence of groups has been inferred from mutual choice patterns in sociograms or from face-to-face interaction patterns.[24] Yet, if the present theoretical definition of groups is to be adopted, neither of these prior approaches is quite satisfactory—the first being too narrow, the second too broad.

With a precise and operational definition of the term "group" it may now be possible to examine all of the different combinations of individuals present in a given social system or systems in order to determine how many current groups are present and of whom they consist. Once knowing this, it will subsequently become possible to sample *groups* in studying group phenomena, rather than merely sampling persons (often group members) as we now tend to do. By making a few complete surveys of existing groups we shall be able to devise new sampling methods which are appropriate for groups rather than simply for individuals.

The Study of Group Formation or Incidence. A precise and operational definition of "group" is also vital to the much neglected problem of group formation or the rate of group formation within some population. Without such a definition one can scarcely begin to study the causes of group formation and the emergence of groups in their natural settings. The simple reason behind this is that one would be without a sufficiently systematic method of recognizing the existence of a group or of determining when a set of individuals has passed from non-group to group. A subsequent paper[25] will employ the present definition of groups to suggest a

---

[23] Data on the prevalence of formal work organizations (businesses, industrial firms, etc.) are cumulated by Standard and Poors, Inc. Certain data on the prevalence of formal voluntary organizations that are national in scope are to be found in the *Encyclopedia of Associations*, periodically published and prepared by the Gale Research Company of Detroit, Michigan. An explanatory survey of the prevalence of formal voluntary organizations in historical societies, in contemporary nations, in the states of the United States, and in the cities of Massachusetts is currently underway under the direction of the author at the Laboratory for Organizational Research, University of Southern California.

[24] For example, see James S. Coleman, *The Adolescent Society*, New York: The Free Press of Glencoe, 1961, Chap. 7; and John James, "The Distribution of Free-Forming Small Group Size," *American Sociological Review*, 18 (October, 1953), pp. 569–570.

[25] See the unpublished paper by the author titled "Group Formation: Steps Toward a Markov Model," Department of Sociology and Anthropology, University of Southern California, 1967.

Markov model for the explanation of group formation. There discussion will center around the paths which lead from various non-group states to the group state, the probabilities of movement along these paths, and the types of independent variables that determine movement along these paths for any given group.

The Study of Group Development, Growth, and Change. Another equally important line of inquiry suggested by the present definition of "group" is the explanation of group development and elaboration. Here interest focuses on the factors leading to change from a rudimentary group, which just barely fits the definition, to more complex and highly developed group structures and phenomena. Several scholars[26] have turned their attention to these phenomena in recent years, and yet a suitable theory that encompasses all kinds of groups and all lines of development remains little more than an aspiration. When such a general theory of group development does come, however, it must grow out of and utilize some such analytic definition of group as the present one.

Groups and General Social Theory. A final implication of the definition offered here lies in the broad context of sociological theory. The central concern of sociology and hence of sociological theory is with emergent social role phenomena and especially with grouplike phenomena as described on the foregoing pages. Nearly all of the major phenomena which tend to concern sociologists are directly related to emergent grouplike phenomena and hence related to groups as they have been defined here. Complex or formal organizations are groups; so-called "small groups" are groups in many cases (although sometimes they are only "small bunches" or sets of individuals); most societies are groups; social systems are generally groups; roles and norms, customs and laws, develop as a consequence of the existence of groups; so-called "collective behavior" is very frequently the behavior of groups, though not always; and so on for other social phenomena. Therefore, what has been called "group" here might be viewed as synonymous with such terms as "social system" or "association," which are taken to have the broadest theoretical meaning

[26] Investigations of the problem of group development in the recent past reported in Warren G. Bennie and Herbert A. Shepard, "A Theory of Group Development," *Human Relations*, 9 (November, 1956), pp. 415–437; Eugene Jacobson, "The Growth of Groups in a Voluntary Organization," *Journal of Social Issues*, 12 (Second Quarter, 1956), pp. 18–23; Donald W. Olmstead, "A Developmental Model of the Social Group," *The Sociological Quarterly*, 3 (July, 1962), pp. 195–207; Theodore M. Mills, *Group Transformation*, Englewood Cliffs, N.J.: Prentice-Hall, 1964; Margaret Phillips, *Small Social Groups in England*, London: Methuen and Co., 1965; George A. Theodorson, "Elements in the Progressive Development of Small Groups," *Social Forces*, 31 (May, 1953), pp. 311–320; John X. Tsouderos, "Organizational Change in Terms of a Series of Selected Variables," *American Sociological Review*, 20 (April, 1955), pp. 206–210; William H. Starbuck, "Organizational Growth and Development," in James G. March, editor, *Handbook of Organizations*, Chicago: Rand McNally, 1965, Chapter 11; David Horton Smith, "Group Development: Steps Toward a General Model," Unpublished Manuscript, Department of Sociology and Anthropology, University of Southern California, 1967.

and empirical significance in sociology. Further, the ideas of social role phenomena and of grouplike phenomena which have been explicated here provide an opportunity to define "sociology" in clear and precise analytical terms: Sociology is the scientific study of social role phenomena and especially of grouplike phenomena and their ramifications, including the relationships among different groups or roles.

More importantly, perhaps, the present definition of groups can be viewed as part of the groundwork for developing a general theory of groups or a general theory of social systems. It differs from certain well-known approaches—for example Parsons' general theory of action or Homans' exchange theory of social behavior—by *not* starting out with the social behavior of individuals ("actors") *qua* individuals, but rather focusing on the empirical fact of emergent grouplike phenomena and building a group construct suitable for denoting this empirical reality. Whether the present approach to general social theory will prove more fruitful in the long run than other approaches is an as yet unanswered but extremely important empirical question.

17

A Comparative Study of Individual, Majority, and Group Judgment

DEAN C. BARNLUND

San Francisco State College

The comparative quality of decisions made by groups and by individuals working alone has been tested under a wide variety of experimental conditions. In general, these studies indicate that group judgments are superior to individual judgments on certain types of intellectual problems (2, 6). Where experiments have employed groups composed of persons of different levels of ability, however, it is not clear whether the quality of the decisions is due to the greater influence of the more capable members of the group or is a specific consequence of group thinking itself. Do groups make better decisions because the less intelligent capitulate to the more intelligent members? Or are there psychological factors inherent in group interaction which produce the higher level of performance? When each group member possesses unique information or ideas it is not unreasonable to expect that interaction will increase the total amount of information and enlarge the perspective of the group as a whole. But what happens to the level of group judgments when interaction occurs among persons who are equally informed and talented?

The present investigation is concerned with how decisions made by individuals working alone compare with the pooling of individual judgments through majority vote and with decisions reached through the process of group discussion when: (*a*) the membership of the group is homogeneous with respect to ability to solve the assigned problem; (*b*) the task is complex, couched in prejudicial terms, and involves a range of possible solutions; and (*c*) individuals and groups are permitted the same length of time to complete their tasks. Finally, the study seeks to determine some of the factors that account for any differences observed in individual and group performance.

Reprinted from *Journal of Abnormal and Social Psychology*, 58, 1 (January 1959), 55–60, by permission of the author and The American Psychological Association.

METHOD

Subjects

The Ss used in this experiment were students enrolled in freshman courses in group discussion over a three-year period at Northwestern University. The members of eight classes were used, 174 students in all. Of these, 143 were assigned to experimental groups, and the remaining 31 served as control Ss.

Procedure

At the first meeting of the classes, Form A or Form B of the "Recognition of Valid Conclusions" test was administered. Form A and Form B were alternated as the first and final measures of problem-solving ability throughout the experiment to reduce any biasing effects growing out of differences in the two forms. Each student was given a copy of the test and an answer sheet and instructed to work out his solutions to the 30 problems individually. Ss were given the 50-minute period to complete the test items.

Each member of the class was then ranked according to the total number of items he answered correctly on the first form of the test. Eight or nine weeks later, before the end of the academic quarter, experimental groups were created. Four or five groups were formed in each of the classes used in the experiment. All students who received the same or similar scores on the first test were placed together so that homogeneous groups were created. Experimental groups were then given a single answer sheet and copies of the alternate form of the test and instructed to reach a group decision on each of the 30 problems. Experimental and control Ss were again given 50 minutes to finish the test. Members of the control classes repeated the test under the original conditions, solving items on the alternate forms of the test individually. A total of 29 experimental groups participated in the experiment.

The final 10 group sessions were tape recorded in their entirety. An analysis was made of each of the 30 decisions reached by the 10 groups to isolate the specific kinds of mistakes that contributed to the majority of group errors. Following all group tests, discussions were held with the experimental Ss concerning the factors they felt influenced their performance as members of the groups.

Problem

Many investigators of group phenomena have admitted difficulty in finding or constructing suitable instruments for testing the efficiency and accuracy of group decision-making. Problems, to be realistic, should be complicated enough so they cannot be solved by intuition. They should be sufficiently difficult to test the limits of individual and group thinking. Social problems normally can be solved in a variety of ways, and test problems should contain this same feature. The difference between a right and wrong decision, however, should be clear and demonstrable. If possible, problems should be presented so as to involve the total personality of the individual and permit his prejudices to influence his judgment as they do in a majority of everyday problem-solving experiences.

The instrument used in this experiment, the Bradley test of *Formal Validity in Problem Solving*, seemed particularly well adapted for this purpose (1). The first section of the test entitled, "Recognition of Valid Conclusions," proved long enough and sensitive enough to provide data on the experimental hypothesis. The 30 problems which make up the test consist of partially constructed arguments of varying degrees of difficulty. Two statements are given which are to be assumed to be materially true. The problem is to select the conclusion that follows most logically from the premises. The arguments cover a wide range of subjects and are phrased deliberately to complicate the decision for the reader; that is, statements involve atheists, Communists, Republicans, college professors, and other terms likely to prejudice judgment. An example of one of the problems is given below:

Some Communists are advocates of heavy taxes;
All advocates of heavy taxes are conservative Republicans;

Therefore:
    a. Some advocates of heavy taxes are not Communists
    b. Some Communists are conservative Republicans
    c. Some conservative Republicans are Communists
    d. Some Communists are advocates of heavy taxes
    e. None of these conclusions follows

The validity and reliability of the instrument has been established. The 30 problems on each of the two forms include the 19 valid moods of the syllogism along with the 11 most common fallacies. The test has been successful in discriminating among college students with different backgrounds in logic, mathematics, and problem solving. Intercorrelation of the two forms yields a raw score "r" of .85 (PE, .015) and a weighted "r" of .88 (PE, .012). Items have been carefully scaled in the final forms so that similar scores represent similar patterns of individual errors.

RESULTS

Measures of the relative effectiveness of individual, majority, and group judgments were obtained from scores made on the two forms of the "Recognition of Valid Conclusions" test.

The number of items answered correctly on the first form was used to set up homogeneous groups and to determine the level of ability represented by the average scores and "superior" scores of members of the experimental groups when working alone.[1] The relative accuracy of problem solving under conditions of majority rule was derived from an item analysis of the individual answers of each group member. This "mathematical majority" indicated how the groups would have scored if they had pooled their opinions by secret ballot. Of the total of 829 decisions made by the experimental groups, 22 were found to be deadlocks. These occurred whenever a group of four or six Ss divided their votes equally between right and wrong answers. The results of splitting these decisions evenly and from crediting all of them to the advantage of the majority are recorded in Table 1 under "Deadlocks divided" and "Deadlocks cred-

TABLE 1

Comparison of Individual, Majority, and Group Scores on the "Recognition of Valid Conclusions" Test

				t
Individual Decisions		Majority Decisions		
Means of average individual scores	17.5	"Deadlocks divided"	17.9	1.73
		"Deadlocks credited"	18.3	2.72*
Means of "superior" individual scores	18.8	"Deadlocks divided"	17.9	3.23†
		"Deadlocks credited"	18.3	1.66
Individual Decisions		Group Decisions		
Means of average individual scores	17.5	Mean scores of groups	21.9	9.46†
Means of "superior" individual scores	18.8			5.77†
Majority Decisions		Group Decisions		
"Deadlocks divided"	17.9	Mean scores of groups	21.9	6.60†
"Deadlocks credited"	18.3			5.95†

* Significant at .05 level.
† Significant at .01 level.

ited." The quality of group thinking was measured by computing the mean scores of experimental groups on the second form of the test when they were required to reach consensus on each of the test problems.

The mean scores obtained under the various experimental conditions and the *t* values they yield are summarized in Table 1. The average scores of members of the experimental groups working alone are not significantly larger or smaller than the mean of majority scores when the 22 deadlocks are counted as correct in half of the instances and incorrect in the other half. When all deadlocks are resolved in favor of the correct decision,

---

[1] The "superior" member of a homogeneous group is something of a misnomer. Experimental groups were made up of Ss whose initial scores differed by no more than a few points. In each case the "superior" member refers simply to the individual who made the highest individual score in the group despite its homogeneous character.

majority rule proves to be superior to the average performance of the individual group members. The "superior" members of the experimental groups, on the other hand, did significantly better than the majority when deadlocks were split, and as well as the majority when deadlocks were counted as correct solutions to the problems.

Group decisions were found to be clearly superior to individual decisions. As a result of discussion, experimental groups obtained mean scores that were significantly higher, at the .01 level, than "superior" members of the same groups were able to attain through individual effort. These findings also hold true when results for Form A and Form B are analyzed separately. Groups whose members scored initially near the upper limit of the test, 28 or 29 correct answers out of a possible 30, gained least from solving problems cooperatively. The largest gains were made by groups whose initial scores were low although nearly all of the experimental groups, with the exception of the highest scoring group in each class, made substantial gains as a result of group deliberation. Students in the lowest fifth of their classes as a group often rivalled the performance of the most brilliant member of the class working alone. In only two of the 29 experimental groups did students working together fail to outperform their own best member.[2]

When majority rule is compared with group consensus, the results show a similar large and significant advantage for group decision-making. Crediting all deadlocks from divided votes reduces the size of the group advantage over majority decisions, but its value is still highly significant.

The 31 control Ss had mean scores on the initial administration of the "Recognition of Valid Conclusions" test of 18.5. (Control Ss made an initial mean score of 18.8 on Form A and of 18.2 on Form B.) On the final test form their mean score was 18.7. (The final mean scores for control Ss were 18.9 on Form A and 18.6 on Form B.) This difference is not statistically significant and it is safe to assume that differences in mean scores of the experimental Ss were due to the experimental variables rather than differences in the test forms.

These data indicate that the members of homogeneous groups can achieve significantly better decisions by solving their problems cooperatively than they can through voting or by individual effort. Majority decisions, when all deadlocks can be successfully resolved, can produce better results than are obtained from the averaging of individual efforts. But in three out of four of the conditions observed in this experiment, majority decisions proved to be no better than, or inferior to, the decisions of individual members of the same groups.

---

[2] In both of these cases the groups contained individuals who received almost perfect initial scores.

DISCUSSION

The results of the first phase of this experiment need to be interpreted in the light of early research on collective judgments. Whether they explained the finding on statistical or psychological grounds, Watson (10), Gordon (3), Stroop (8), and Gurnee (4) found grouped judgments superior to those of the average individual and equal to those of the superior individual working alone. This conclusion is not supported by our data. When deadlocks are resolved on the basis of statistical probabilities, majority decisions are found to be no better than those of the average member of homogeneous groups.

The explanation for the difference in results seems to lie partly in the character of the tasks and partly in the methods of grouping data. Some of the problems used by these investigators involve what may be called additive activities. Whenever individual efforts are additive or cumulative, the larger the group the greater should be the advantage from combining individual data. Testing the accuracy of conclusions drawn from given arguments is not the same kind of problem. One answer simply cannot be added to another. A second explanation for the difference is found in the manner of grouping individual decisions. The pooling of data in previous studies combined the heterogeneous opinions of 10 to 100 individuals. In averaging data the greater the number and range of scores, the larger the gain from cancelling out individual errors. In this case, only four to six opinions from individuals of comparable ability determined the decision. Majority rule may prove a convenient political device for averaging individual preferences; but our results suggest that in small, homogeneous groups or committees, majority rule, when it precludes discussion or debate, is likely to be less effective than the personal judgment of superior members of the group.

After discussion, however, experimental groups produced decisions that were far superior to those of members working alone or through majority rule. Moreover, group decisions on the test problems were reached within the same period of time allotted to individuals.

Several hypotheses are offered in the literature for the high quality of group judgments. Watson found group decisions superior because of the influence of the ablest member.

In measuring the output of a group, either when working along cooperative group-thinking lines or when the project permits the simple compilation of individual efforts, it matters little about the ability of the poorest or even average member of the group. The results seem to show primarily what the few ablest in the group have produced (10, pp. 333–334).

This hypothesis, though generally tenable, seems inadequate to explain the results of this experiment. Groups were made up of students whose initial performance indicated a common aptitude for selecting logical conclusions from given arguments. The grading of items on the "Recognition of Valid Conclusions" test is such that persons who get similar scores are likely to possess not only the same level of ability but similar habits of thinking.

Another theory, suggested by Gurnee (4) and Thorndike (9), is that the better performance of the group is due to the social influence of the more confident group members who are more often right than wrong. It is difficult to see how this factor could have played a large part in the results. It would seem likely that students with similar patterns of right and wrong answers would share somewhat similar patterns of confidence about their answers. If so, this factor can be minimized.

It is necessary to go beyond these hypotheses to explain how correct solutions were reached by groups whose members made similar or identical errors when working alone. The diagnostic discussions and the analysis of recorded group sessions furnish additional clues to the psychological factors affecting the high level of group performance.

Membership in the experimental groups produced a higher level of interest in the successful completion of the task. Ss concentrated more intently on the assigned problems after being appointed to a group than they did when solving the problems individually. Group members found themselves more and more deeply involved as they proposed, and were forced to defend, their ideas. Participants identified with their own groups to such a degree that when some members became fatigued, others urged them to continue working.

Membership in the experimental groups had an inhibiting as well as facilitating effect. Knowledge that one's opinions were to be shared publicly made group members more cautious and deliberate in their own thinking. The necessity of explaining a conclusion forced many students to be more self-critical. Errors that might have been committed privately were checked before they were communicated to others.

Groups had greater critical resources than did individuals working alone. In spite of the uniform level of ability, group members saw different issues and a larger number of issues than a single person did working alone. A greater number of viewpoints increased the group's chances of selecting a valid one. Even the poorest members contributed significantly to the quality of the group product. Remarks that went no deeper than "I don't understand" or "That's absurd" often saved the group from error by forcing others to justify their opinions and in so doing disprove their own conclusions.

A more objective view of the problem resulted from competition between the private prejudices of group members. The test arguments were stated in loaded terms designed to make the choices between conclusions as difficult as possible. Each individual, however, brought a different set of values to his group. When arguments were stated so they appealed to persons of one persuasion, those in opposition were anxious to detect their error. In this way, liberals counteracted conservatives, Republicans offset Democrats, and "independents" guarded against critical lapses on the part of fraternity members. Groups were forced to become more objective, and this, of course, increased their chances of drawing valid conclusions. The significance of this one factor alone would be hard to overestimate.

Discussion of the test items also prevented other incidental mistakes from occurring. Some groups had to check their instructions several times because members had different interpretations of them. Discussion often led to a clarification of terms used in the test, and, where logical fallacies spring from ambiguous terms, this may account for some of the gains. A number of groups formulated general principles as they went along to help them avoid repeating errors in later problems.

What, then, prevented experimental groups from attaining even higher scores than they did? Analysis of the transcripts revealed two factors that together accounted for a majority of the group errors. The first was that group members agreed immediately and unanimously upon the wrong answer to a problem. Further study of the issue was then considered unnecessary and wasteful. This is the same factor that Jenness, following F. H. Allport, refers to as the "impression of universality" (5). Agreement becomes the criterion of correctness. Maier (7) suggests that provoking arguments under these circumstances leads to better judgments. The virtue of disagreement and the possible function of a "No-Man" in group deliberations, needs further testing.

The second factor was that groups, when they reached a deadlock, were unable to use their differences of opinion for their own advantage. When conflicts became intense they were resolved by surrender of the less aggressive members or by compromising on a third solution which was almost always incorrect but served to protect the egos of the parties to the controversy. Apparently disagreement stimulates thought up to a point; beyond that point, groups may lack the patience and skill to exploit it.

Discussion, as a preliminary to group decisions, causes groups to examine a problem more thoroughly and to consider a wider number of solutions. It encourages individuals to think more carefully and in sharing opinions to expose the logic of their position to the inspection of others. Membership in a group produces a sense of responsibility which intensifies and sustains effort. The biasing effect of private prejudice may be counteracted leading to a more objective view of the issues. The data of this study indicate that the answer to the question of whether group opinion is better than individual opinion because of the influence of the superior person or because of the discussion process itself is that discussion inherently contains psychological pressures and motivations which, if not abused, tend to produce superior judgments on complex intellectual problems. Individual decisions and collective judgments lack the additional ingredient supplied by interaction which permits a group to outperform its own members.

SUMMARY

The performance of individuals working alone, under majority rule, and as members of discussion groups were compared on a complex intellectual task. Individual judgment was measured by administering a test of ability to draw logical conclusions from given arguments. Individuals receiving similar scores were assigned to the same experimental groups so that the factor of distributed ability would be reduced to a minimum. The votes of members of the homogeneous groups were mathematically tallied to determine the results under conditions of majority rule. A second form of the test was completed as a group undertaking and the scores compared with individual and majority scores. The results indicated that:

1. Majority decisions, when deadlocks are evenly divided between right and wrong answers, are not significantly different from those made by the average individual and are inferior to those of the best member of the group working alone.

2. Group decisions, reached through cooperative deliberation, are significantly superior to decisions made by individual members working alone and to majority rule.

The superiority of group judgments was found not to be a reflection of the wisdom of the superior member of the group but a result of psychological factors inherent in discussion. Participation in a group led to more serious concentration on the task and to more enthusiastic individual effort. Group discussion was found to stimulate more careful thinking, to lead to a consideration of a wider range of ideas, and to provoke more objective and critical testing of conclusions.

References

1. Bradley, E. E. Formal validity in problem solving. Unpublished doctoral dissertation, Northwestern Univer., 1950.
2. Dashiell, J. F. Experimental studies of the influence of social situations on the behavior of human adults. In C. Murchison (Ed.), *Handbook of social psychology*. Worcester: Clark Univer. Press, 1935. Pp. 1097–1158.
3. Gordon, K. H. Group judgments in the field of lifted weights. *J. exp. Psychol.*, 1924, 7, 398–400.
4. Gurnee, H. A comparison of collective and individual judgments of fact. *J. exp. Psychol.*, 1937, 21, 106–112.
5. Jenness, A. The role of discussion in changing opinion regarding a matter of fact. *J. abnorm. soc. Psychol.*, 1932, 27, 279–296.
6. Kelley, H. H., & Thibaut, J. W. Experimental studies of group problem

solving and process. In G. Lindzey (ed.), *Handbook of social psychology*. Cambridge: Addison-Wesley, 1954. Pp. 735–785.

7. Maier, N. R. F., & Solem, A. R. The contribution of a discussion leader to the quality of group thinking. *Hum. Relat.*, 1952, 5, 277–288.

8. Stroop, J. R. Is the judgment of the group better than that of the average member of the group? *J. exp. Psychol.*, 1932, 15, 550–562.

9. Thorndike, R. L. The effect of discussion upon the correctness of group decisions, when the factor of majority influence is allowed for. *J. soc. Psychol.*, 1938, 9, 343–362.

10. Watson, G. B. Do groups think more efficiently than individuals? *J. abnorm. soc. Psychol.*, 1928, 23, 328–336.

18

Loyalty of Representatives to Ingroup Positions during Intergroup Competition[1]

ROBERT R. BLAKE and
JANE S. MOUTON
The University of Texas

A representative of a group may meet a representative of an opposing group to decide an issue under conditions which give victory to one of the sides and defeat to the other. International negotiation frequently takes this form, as do typical negotiations between labor and management in our own economic system. Military situations often arise in which the same pattern is present. Opposing groups seek a resolution of differences through interactions between representatives *within* the managerial branches of industrial, political and governmental units as well.

Resolution of intergroup conflict is sought most commonly through negotiations carried on by representatives. The rationale is that a spokesman is a *member* of the group he represents and, therefore, he knows the problem from an ingroup point of view (1).

Yet, a critical limitation is placed on a representative when intergroup relations are on a competitive basis or when they take a win-lose turn. From the standpoint of his own group membership, he is not entirely "free" to act in accord with fact or even to engage in compromise, for to do so would be interpreted by group members as bringing them "defeat." A previous study (2) has shown that the representative who exerts influence on the opposing representative, and in doing so obtains acceptance of his group's position, is accorded a "hero" reaction, and thereafter he enjoys increased status within his group. The representative who capitulates and thereby brings defeat to his group is treated as disloyal or traitorous by its members.

Examined from another point of view, in the negotiation situation, logical considerations may require that a representative renounce his group's

Reprinted from *Sociometry*, 24, 2 (June 1961), 177–183, by permission of the authors and The American Sociological Association.

[1] Studies reported concerned with intergroup behavior were partially supported by Grant M-2447 cl, Behavior of Group Representatives Under Pressure, National Institutes of Health, and by a grant from Esso Division, Humble Oil and Refining Company.

prior position in order to gain a valid resolution of the intergroup problem. But acting against the exercise of a logical and factually analytical attitude are group ties that require him to gain victory and, at whatever cost, to defend a point of view which protects his membership position.

The present study is designed to investigate the loyalty v. logic issue. The hypothesis is that, under conditions of win-lose competition, if the resolution of differences through representatives must result in acceptance of one position as "better" and another as "poorer" (no compromise possible), then it will more frequently end in deadlock (i.e., loyalty to a party line) than in capitulation (i.e., the application of logic in evaluating which position is better).

PROCEDURE

Setting and Subjects

All studies were undertaken in connection with human relations training programs (4), with laboratory populations ranging between 18 and 36 people each. A total of 520 participants served as members of 62 groups which engaged in a parallel sequence of activities centering on intergroup competition. The competition took place between pairs, trios and quartets of groups which ranged each in size from seven to twelve members.

Forty-six groups were composed of adults aged from 25 to 55, who were engaged in executive or supervisory positions. All were attending two-week human relations laboratory programs in which the experiment to be described was inserted to help participants gain insight regarding group action and the dynamics of intergroup relations under competitive conditions.

The remaining 16 groups were composed of junior and senior college students, both male and female, enrolled in social psychology. The sequence of activities paralleled those for the adult groups. All groups were matched in educational and occupational level for adult groups, and in class level and sex for college groups.

Sequence of Interactions

The arrangements for creating intergroup competition were:

Development of Autonomous Groups. Ten to twelve hours, divided into five or six two-hour sessions occurring over a three-day period, were devoted to autonomous ingroup activity. The purpose of having individuals meet together was to study decision making in groups through developing and then evaluating their own ingroup structures. The kind of group action involved in human relations training programs is described more fully elsewhere (3).

This basis of group organization was suitable for investigating intergroup conflict. First the grouping was intrinsically meaningful, since participants were engaged in studying internal group processes under their own responsibility and initiative. Cohesion generated quickly. Pride in membership was evidenced in quantitative measures of solidarity, which showed an increasing trend over the entire series of meetings. In addition, members sensed that their ability to perform as a group and their status as an effective unit were challenged when they were confronted with competition which would lead to victory or defeat. The result was a strong motive to win, shown by the fact that, when asked to indicate prospects of victory on a nine-point scale, all groups uniformly reported that they considered their own chance of victory better than the groups against whom they were pitted.

Creating Intergroup Competition. After completion of the first phase, each group had three hours to develop its own approach to the solution of an assigned problem. The problem, to be solved in the form of a two-page, double-spaced, typewritten memorandum, always concerned some basic issue with which members of the contending groups were equally familiar.

In the adult groups the problem used varied from occasion to occasion, but it always was related to an organizational situation, and typically it involved developing a statement of ways to improve the operation of the organization with respect to some specific issue, such as labor-management negotiations, relations between technical and practical personnel, the improvement of communications through levels within the organization hierarchy, and so on. For college groups the problem involved topics such as how to handle a deviant in a group, ways to deal with the integration issue, or developing a set of recommendations for the resolution of intergroup conflict.

Group members uniformly accepted the proposition that their performance provided an indication of their effectiveness as a problem-solving unit. The possibility of resolving differences between solutions by compromise or through an emergent product approach were unavailable. Group members were committed to the superiority of their own products, as shown by significant differences between ratings of the quality of their own solution and ratings of the quality of their solution by the opposing groups.

Clarification of Group Positions. On completion of the assigned task, the solutions were reproduced and exchanged for purposes of comparison. One to two hours were spent in ingroup discussion and evaluation of the merits of each solution. During this phase members were urged to increase their understanding of the position of the other group by noting similarities and differences between it and their own, and points needing clarification or elaboration.

At the beginning of this phase, representatives were elected by each group through a rank-ordering procedure. After the ingroup discussion, each representative explained and clarified his own group's solution in response to questions raised by the representative of the other group. The explanation and clarification phase lasted an additional two to four hours, depending on circumstances. This phase led to intensification of competition and to further elevation of estimates of the quality of one's own group's solution and devaluation of the solution of the competing group.

Winner and Loser Determined. Finally, through public interactions, the representatives attempted to reach a decision as to which solution was more adequate, and, therefore, the winner. Discussion between representatives continued until a decision was reached. If their efforts resulted in *deadlock*, impartial judges, either two or three in number, who had not participated in the earlier phases of competition and who did not know which groups produced which solutions, rendered the verdict. Before doing so, the judges had had a full opportunity to study the two solutions and then to gain any needed clarification from the representatives; these conferred in private and then answered queries in a "mechanical" order, so as to conceal the "ownership" of the solutions. The formal competition phase was completed after the verdict was announced.

RESULTS

The data summarized in Figure 6-1 show that it is extremely rare under the conditions described for a representative to capitulate. Only two out of 62 representatives voted against their group's position. The other 60 remained steadfastly loyal to their own group's point of view and deadlocked. In each case, impartial judges were able to decide upon a clear-cut winner. The repetitiveness of the phenomenon across competitions—on a probability basis, attributable to chance in only 1 in 10,000 times—demonstrates

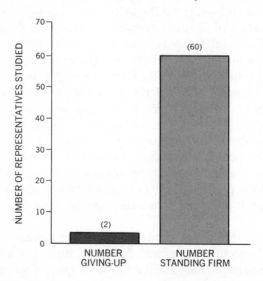

FIGURE 6-1

the strength of the motivation to win experienced by the person into whose hands is placed his group's fate. These results confirm that loyalty to an ingroup position replaces the exercise of logic when two group positions are evaluated under win-lose conditions.

The findings reported are generalizable to situations integrated around a win-lose outcome. Comparable results have also been obtained when representatives interacted in secrecy rather than under conditions where their behavior could be observed, and when representatives had no realistic basis for anticipating that the outcome of their interactions would be known to the group from which they came. In other words, confidence can be placed in these data as typifying a basic situation under which members from two autonomous groups confront one another when a win-lose outcome is to be expected from their interactions.

DISCUSSION

If relations between groups are on a win-lose basis, as happens when preferred positions have been publicly announced in advance, then the quest for a resolution by representatives is replete with obstacles.

The core of the difficulty seems to be in the fact that representatives are "committed" people. From the standpoint of their own group membership they do not appear to be free to apply a logical analysis, to weigh facts and balance relative units in developing a win-lose judgment. Rather, representatives act on loyalty and are motivated to win, or at least to avoid defeat, even though a judgment which would resolve an intergroup problem is sacrificed in the process. Where there is conflict of interest between groups, the situation is such that ingroup loyalty overwhelms logic. If a representative cannot win, then, through deadlocking, traitorous action can be avoided, and group defeat forestalled. In all but two of the competitive situations studied here, deadlock occurred. Judges had to be used to break the impasse.

Situations of competition in which mutually exclusive positions are taken are exceedingly common. The inability of representatives of groups to adjudicate differences in points of view has resulted in a number of "neutral" groups whose function is to give an impartial judgment. The use of a judge to render a verdict is one example. Within industry, stalemates between representatives of management and the union lead to the use of arbitration and mediation as a basis for resolving differences. When interaction, discussion, and problem solving between representatives of governments fail, alternatives to violence include Cold War and recourse to the United Nations.

In view of the results presented here, one question that might be posed is: What conditions are more conducive to representative interaction which will result in decisions rather than deadlock? Several suggestions can be made. The examples given above, as well as the experimental conditions, constitute situations where public positions are taken by *groups* in advance of negotiation, which is a routine procedure. Taking a position lays the groundwork for competition to enter, even when the groups would be expected to interact in a collaborative manner. For a representative to deviate from a fixed position means he is going against his group. If negotiations between representatives were to occur before a fixed position was taken, the possibility of reaching an acceptable solution might be increased (5). Another method of obtaining a resolution of differences in positions is through the use of superordinate goals (6). The superordinate goal approach aims at changing a win-lose situation into one where all parties stand to gain through the actions of each. Both of these procedures provide possible alternative approaches to resolving the sharply drawn conflict of interests representatives face when they are called upon to negotiate differences between groups within a logical frame of reference while at the same time remaining loyal to their own group's point of view.

SUMMARY

Five hundred and twenty persons, participating as members of 62 groups in human-relations training programs, engaged in a parallel sequence of ingroup and intergroup activities. Groups were placed in competition in pairs, trios and quartets, with the outcome of the win-lose competition resting on the negotiations of representatives from each of the groups. Results demonstrate that ingroup loyalty prevented the application of "objective" logic and only two of the 62 representatives capitulated to the opposition.

We interpret these data as supporting the proposition that negotiations by representatives can be an ineffectual basis for resolving a win-lose situation between contending groups.

References

1. Blake, R. R., "Psychology and the Crisis of Statesmanship," *The American Psychologist*, 1959, 14, 87–94.
2. ———, and Jane S. Mouton, "Heroes and Traitors: Two Patterns of Representing Groups in a Competitive Situation," *International Journal of Sociometry* (in press).
3. ———, *Training for Decision-Making in Groups*, New York: Putnam & Sons, 1960 (in press).
4. *Proceedings*, The Human Relations Training Laboratory, Austin, Texas: The University of Texas, 1960.
5. Rusk, D., "Parliamentary Diplomacy—Debate Versus Negotiation," *World Affairs Interpreter*, 1955, 26, 121–138.
6. Sherif, M., and Carolyn W. Sherif, *Groups in Harmony and Tension*, New York: Harpers, 1953.

For Further Reading

BOOKS

Cartwright, D., and Zander, A. (Eds.) *Group dynamics: research and theory* (Second Edition). Evanston, Illinois: Row, Peterson and Company, 1960.

A revision and updating of a 1956 work; the Lewinian tradition is the unifying theme.

Golembiewski, R. T. *The small group: an analysis of research concepts and operations.* Chicago: University of Chicago Press, 1962.

Over 1500 reports are reviewed in an attempt to provide a meaningful framework for small group analysis.

Hare, A. P., Borgatta, E. F. and Bales, R. F. (Eds.) *Small groups: studies in social interaction.* New York: Knopf, 1966.

Revision of a 1955 edition, with about a third of the selections being new. Contains early theory and research, current theory, social perception, group influence, and the group as a social system (equilibrium, group size, role differentiation, and leadership).

King, C. E. *The sociology of small groups.* New York: Pageant Press, 1962.

An elementary introduction to the topic of small groups.

Mills, T. M. *The sociology of small groups.* Englewood Cliffs, New Jersey: Prentice-Hall, 1967.

This paperback furnishes an excellent overview of research and theory in small groups.

Olmsted, M. S. *The small group.* San Francisco: Chandler Publishing Company, 1964.

An excellent introduction to the functions, culture, and structure of small groups; written for the layman.

Sherif, M. (Ed.). *Intergroup relations and leadership: approaches and research in industrial, ethnic, cultural and political areas.* New York: Wiley, 1962.

Introduction discusses the problem of multiple loyalties; theoretical papers by Sherif, Faris and Stogdill; Dubin on management-union relations; Blake and Mouton in win-or-lose conflict situations; Killian on leadership of minority groups; Klineberg and North on international relations; and others.

————, and Sherif, C. W. *Reference groups: exploration into conformity and deviation in adolescents.* New York: Harper and Row, 1964.

An interdisciplinary approach, reporting research and programs about reference groups.

ARTICLES

Bass, B. M., and Dunteman, G. Biases in the evaluation of one's own group, its allies and opponents. *J. Confl. Resol.*, 1963, 7 (1), 16–20. SA 14, B8339.

Other groups (in a sample of management personnel) were consistently underrated in worth.

Bates, A. P., and Babchuk, N. The primary group: a reappraisal. *Sociol. Quart.*, 1961, 2 (3), 181–191. PA 37, 1091.

Cooley's concept of the primary group should be clarified by noting sociological dimensions (such as size and homogeneity) and psychological dimensions (such as mutual attraction).

Blake, R. E., and Mouton, J. S. Overevaluation of own group's product in ingroup competition. *J. abnorm. soc. Psychol.*, 1962, 64 (3), 237–238. PA 38, 2580.

Competition resulted in group members evaluating their own group product above the judgments they accorded to the proposal from a comparison group.

Borgatta, M. L. The concept of the group: a brief consideration. *Sociol. soc. Res.*, 1958, 43 (2), 83–89. SA 9, 8848.

A brief review of the history of the concept, and illustrations of some present-day approaches to the study of the topic.

Bower, J. L. Group decision making: a report of an experimental study. *Behavioral Sci.*, 1965, 10 (3), 277–289. SA 15, C1882.

A report of an experiment on group decision-making that takes into account such variables as the decision rule used by the group, its information structure, and the relationship between individual goals and group goals.

Cervantes, L. F. Family background, primary relationships, and high school drop-outs. *J. Marr. Fam.*, 1965, 27 (2), 218–222. PA 39, 12167.

The family background of the dropout is less characterized by primary relationships than is the family background of the high school graduate.

DeFleur, M., and Quinney, R. A reformulation of Sutherland's Differential Association Theory and a strategy for empirical verification. *J. Research in Crime and Delinq.*, 1966, 3 (1), 1–21. SA 14, C1509.

An attempt is made to show some of the ways in which the approach of mathematical model-builders can yield new insights into old theories.

DeLamater, J., et al. Conceptual orientations of contemporary small group theory. *Psychol. Bull.*, 1965, 64 (6), 402–412. PA 40, 2809.

A review and categorization of research in small groups by (a) size of units studied; (b) social process levels with which they deal; and (c) the substantive content or the variables they employ.

Denzin, N. K. The Significant others of a college population. *Sociol. Quart.*, 1966, 7 (3), 298–310. SA 15, C4460.

Role specific significant others (G. H. Mead tradition) are important only in specific situations; orientational others (Manford Kuhn's formulation) are important regardless of role or situation.

Ferguson, C. K., and Kelley, H. H. Significant factors in over-evaluation of own-group's product. *J. abnorm. soc. Psychol.*, 1964, 69 (2), 223–228. SA 14, B8342.

Eleven pairs of small ad hoc groups worked on three tasks; the paired groups were within sight of each other but without instructions to compete. Marked preference for own-group product was found.

Fox, D. J., and Lorge, I. The relative quality of decisions written by individuals and by groups as the available time for problem solving is increased. *J. soc. Psychol.*, 1962, 57 (1), 227–242. PA 37, 3032.

With 50 minutes available, individuals wrote better solutions to human relations problems than did ad hoc groups; with more time, ad hoc groups write solutions as good (before instruction in group dynamics and problem solving). After instruction, solutions were better than those written by individuals.

Hagstrom, W. O., and Selvin, H. C. Two dimensions of cohesiveness in small groups. *Sociometry*, 1965, 28 (1), 30–43. PA 39, 9997.

A factor analysis of 19 possible indicators of cohesiveness yields two dimensions: "social stratification" and "sociometric cohesion"; these dimensions appear to reflect the distinction between the instrumental and intrinsic attractiveness of groups.

Hall, J., and Williams, M. S. A comparison of decision-making performances in established and ad hoc groups. *J. Personality soc. Psychol.*, 1966, 3 (2), 214–222. SA 15, C3478.

Established groups were significantly superior to ad hoc groups in decision performance relative to several criteria.

Hall, R. L., and Willerman, B. The educational influence of dormitory roommates. *Sociometry*, 1963, 26 (3), 294–318. SA 12, 9838.

The educational effects of roommates are powerfully mediated by (1) extent of course overlap between roommates and (2) the birth ordinal positions of the roommates in their respective families.

Hare, A. P. Interpersonal relations in the small group. In R. E. L. Faris (Ed.), *Handbook of modern sociology*. Chicago: Rand, McNally, 1964, pp. 217–271.

An excellent review of the literature.

Hyman, H. H. Reflections on reference groups. *Publ. Opinion Quart.*, 1963, 24 (3), 383–396. SA 10, A1667.

A short history of the concept from Hyman's coinage of the term to date, with suggestions for taking the concept more systematically into account.

Iwao, S. Internal versus external criticism of group standards. *Sociometry*, 1963, 26 (4), 410–421. PA 38, 5964.

Disagreement coming from an in-group member arouses more dissonance than the same disagreement from an out-group member.

Jansyn, L. R. Solidarity and delinquency in a street corner group. *Amer. sociol. Rev.*, 1966, 31 (5), 600–614. SA 15, C4659.

Observation of a severely delinquent street corner group showed that two thirds of the membership was relatively constant.

Kiesler, C. A. Attraction to the group and conformity to group norms. *J. Personality*, 1963, 31 (4), 559–569. PA 38, 8308.

Attraction to the group . . . varies directly with the level of acceptance of the individual by the group. The hypothesis of a curvilinear relationship between attraction to the group and conformity to group norms was supported.

Knutson, A. L. Quiet and vocal groups. *Sociometry*, 1960, 23 (1), 36–49. PA 35, 2120.

Members of more vocal groups were happier in their group assignments and more satisfied with their group experiences; the quiet groups clearly had a higher quality and more useful product.

Lambert, W. E., *et al*. The effect of increased salience of a membership group on pain tolerance. *J. Personality*, 1960, 28 (3), 350–357. PA 35, 2101.

Both Jewish and Christian subjects increased their pain tolerance when told their groups were typically inferior in regard to pain.

Schein, E. H. Man against man: brainwashing. *Correct. Psychiat.*, 1962, 8 (3), 90–97. PA 37, 4876.

Description of the Chinese Communist methods of producing change in behavior and attitudes. Social support is viewed as the key factor in the attitude change process.

Thomas, E. J., and Fink, C. F. Effects of group size. *Psychol. Bull.*, 1963, 60 (4), 371–384. PA 38, 878.

Group size is an important variable which should be taken into account in any theory of group behavior.

Thrasher, F. M. The gang. In M. B. Clinard and R. Quinney, *Criminal behavior systems*. New York: Holt, Rinehart and Winston, 1967. Pp. 336–359. SA 13, B6594.

A reprint of one of a now-classical study of juvenile delinquent gangs in Chicago.

Wallace, S. E. Reference group behavior in occupational role socialization. *Sociol. Quart.*, 1966, 7 (3), 366–372. SA 13, C4369.

Those students who have the legal profession as an occupational reference group have interaction primarily within the law school, are generally more interested in the profession and the law school, and have more favorable evaluations of the law school than did the students who did not have the legal profession as their reference group.

Wallace, W. L. Peer influences and undergraduates' aspirations for graduate study. *Sociol. of Educ.*, 1965, 38 (5), 375–393. SA 13, C1484.

Peer group aspiration climate had the greatest effect among those who had not yet chosen an occupation, moderate effect among those who had chosen relatively low occupations, least effect among those who had chosen high occupations.

Chapter Seven

Norms,
Conformity
and Deviance

The importance of norms in the analysis of social behavior can hardly be overestimated. While an extensive history of interest in the subject could be written, we may begin with Sumner's popularization of the term "folkways," in his book of the same title.[1] Through much of the history of social science, however, "normative behavior" has been indiscriminately utilized to refer either to values or to actions; more and more, however, sociologists are applying such distinctive terms as "ideal patterns" and "behavioral patterns,"[2] "ideal" and "typical" norms[3] or "ideal" and "real" norms[4] to differentiate between the collective sense of "ought" and actual practices.

While the concept of norm has a long history, the recent emphasis has been on *conformity*, a term as often used in a pejorative as in a descriptive sense. Like such concepts as institution, sanctions, rationalization and others that have widely divergent connotations in different disciplines, the term conformity has tended to imply simply acceptance of a norm when used by sociologists, and a more dynamic interpretation—almost an element of compulsiveness—when used by psychologists. While the terms *norms, conformity,* and *deviance* are often studied in isolation, it makes more sense to consider all simultaneously, for *conformity* or *deviance* must always be viewed in terms of specific norms. As Sherif has observed:

> Both conformity and deviation are relative to a range of tolerable behavior implied in a group norm. While conformity refers to behavior within this range, deviation implies that the behavior is at or beyond the limits of a range of tolerable behavior in the group. In short, deviation is not simply variation in behavior. It is variation of a type characterized by

[1] Sumner, W. G. *Folkways*. Boston: Ginn, 1906.

[2] "Kluckhohn has said that ideal patterns define what the people of a society would do or say in particular situations if they conformed completely to the standards set up by their culture. Behavioral patterns on the other hand, are derived from observations of how people actually behave in particular situations." In Beals, R. L. and Hoijer, H. *An introduction to anthropology*. New York: Macmillan, 1965, pp. 271ff.

[3] Dean, D. G., and Valdes, D. M., *Experiments in sociology*, 2nd ed., Instructor's Manual. New York: Appleton-Century-Crofts, 1967, p. 92.

[4] Martin, J. Ideal and typical norms. *Sociol. Inquiry*, 1964, 34 (1), 41–47.

other group members as "unwise," "threatening," "dangerous," or even "disloyal" or "traitorous." [5]

The first selection portrays a reaction to the public outcry against conformity so characteristic of the last few years. Marvin E. Wolfgang illustrates how extensive and widespread conformity has been throughout history—and indeed must be.

Another important aspect of the normative structure is delineated by Ephraim Mizruchi and Robert Perrucci in their interpretation of *norms* as prescription ("must") and proscription ("must not") values, using data on alcohol pathology for analysis. The importance of normative proscriptions is particularly vital to the understanding of *norm violation,* or *deviance.* For they suggest that "pathological drinking behavior is associated with a relative absence of directives for the act of drinking alcoholic beverages itself." [6] They ask whether the lack of "how to deviate" rules foster a greater deviation than where such prescriptions are absent.

Another explanation for lack of *conformity* is furnished in the selection by Richard A. Ball, who has studied the process by which delinquents come to deny the validity of the norms of the majority. He suggests that "neutralization" of society's norms is a precursor of deviant (in this case, delinquent) behavior. One's imagination should be stimulated to apply this approach for "goodness of fit" to such diverse topics as income tax evasion, premarital sex experiences, and "peace marchers" in our present social context.

Finally, for an article that points the way to further research, we have selected Richard H. Willis' "Two Dimensions of Conformity-Nonconformity," which declares that past models which view this behavior as a simple continuum are inadequate, and introduces a new variable, independence, as a third component of a triangular model.

[5] Sherif, M. and C. W. *An outline of social psychology.* New York: Harper and Row, 1956, p. 244.

[6] Mizruchi, E. and Perrucci, R. Norm qualities and differential effects of deviant behavior: an exploratory analysis. *Amer. Sociol. Rev.,* 1962, 27 (3), 395.

19

Conformity and
the Middle Class

MARVIN E. WOLFGANG
University of Pennsylvania

American writers of fiction, essay, and drama have long decried the middle class in our society, but especially since the last war has this numerically massive segment of our population been the subject of constant ridicule. The style of living, reading habits, consumption of household items, child-rearing practices, and the rituals of family living have been under unwarranted attack. The bourgeoisie, we are told, is a powerful force molding men to a similar pattern of conformity; yet few voices from this unfortunate group have risen above the increasing clamor of derision. It is time, therefore, to re-examine this middle class in order to see whether the prevailing sentiments of the intellectual literati are valid and to determine whether there are any middle-class virtues worth retaining.

It has become a standard cocktail joke to deride a particular form of behavior as "*so* bourgeois" or "decidedly middle class." So widespread is this type of phraseology that even the "decidedly middle class" has used it and has sought increasing but marginal differentiation in the consumption of goods (as David Riesman points out) in order to escape the heavy weight of conforming to patterned expectations of style, behavior, and furniture.

For decades literacy attacks have been made on what is referred to as the stolid, dull, conformistic mediocrity of the middle class. The justifiable concern of Sinclair Lewis with Babbitt only revived the general stream of essays deploring Philistinism and the inflexible reactionary. The *Death of A Salesman* by Miller and *The Organization Man* by Whyte point to the dangers of becoming a rutted, routinized conformist in industrial and other types of bureaucracies. But in the past few years there has been a *mentis gratissimus* error in the expansion and extension of these valid pronouncements of writers like Miller, Riesman, Whyte, *et al.*, for the entire middle class has become a label of conformity, a symbol of the Unimaginative Man. So far has this derision gone that recently Peter Viereck made a plea for the Unadjusted Man and invites us to escape from the mold of the masses.

How far we have come from the thirties and forties when the chief

Reprinted from *Sociology and Social Research*, 43, 6 (July–August 1959), 432–438, by permission of the author and the publisher.

goal of psychological training was Adjustment—always with a capital A! Perhaps our adjustment to the collective group has indeed become extreme, but these are relative judgments and may be found among the luxuries permitted to a prosperous nation not at war. Fighting against the fears of mass unemployment and fear itself during the thirties, and then against totalitarian aggression during the forties required a degree of social consciousness, *esprit de corps*, and acceptance of prescribed institutionalized roles of thought and action such as our nation had never before witnessed. The present cold war does not present an immediate, direct threat. There have been suggestions that for the remainder of this century our tense international relations will be suspended between the idealized peace held in 1945 and the speculated total destruction of another war. Under these circumstances there is less pressure than during national emergencies to conform to a national pattern, and we can enjoy the democratic luxury of self-criticism which views conformity with alarm.

But blind conformity should not be confused with belonging to the middle class. Adherence to middle class values is not the same as "over-adjustment," Philistinism, or mediocrity. Yet it is this kind of association between the middle class and the common criticisms about the organization man and the lonely crowd that is unwarrantedly made by an increasingly abundant number of people who seek variegated ways to "express their individuality" and to "escape the middle-class mold." My chief contentions, therefore, are, first, that identifying unimaginative conformity with the middle class is an error of association of ideas, a lack of proper perception; and, second, that the middle class with its system of values constitutes the basic framework of our harmoniously functioning society.

Excessive conformity to cultural expectations has been a phenomenon common to almost every major historical period through which Western civilization has passed. Toynbee speaks of the development of the Universal State as a symptom of civilizational decay, and of the need for a new or revived challenge to stimulate appropriate response. In the past, whenever similar expectations of behavior became excessively universal and the institutional demands for conformity too oppressive for the creative, dynamic individual, some one or some group always appeared on the cultural scene and was able to break through, to produce a revolution of thought or action. Shakespeare revolutionized the form of drama and theater. Cimabue and Giotto broke through the formal stylization of medieval art. So deeply embedded in astronomic and religious thought was the Ptolemaic conception of the universe that Copernicus and Galileo were revolutionaries of their time. Guido d'Arezzo, like Plato's philosopher bringing us out of the cave into sunlight, led us beyond the monochromatic scale into a polyphony of unlimited variation. In religion, architecture, law, and many other similar fields where cultural change occurred, the geniuses of history have deviated from the demands to conform when an institutional trait reached classic perfection of form and style, or when the requirements to conform became unbearable to the renascent spirit of man. Nonconformity of this type has always been an active, positive force—a voice of dignity and reason. Not always among the instances in which a few men revolutionized a style can it be claimed that the old form was something necessarily to be discarded. There is much delight derived from the classic Greek drama, the Gregorian chant, Gothic architecture, and from forms of art, thought, and behavioral expectations of earlier periods in our history. The old is not always totally displaced by the new.

Deviation, then, almost by definition appears to arise out of excessive conformity in a culture. Deviation that endures and becomes a pattern has been productive and pragmatically successful. Quacks, quirks, and phrenetic fringes have always been with us, and the heroes of history may have been labeled horrible heretics at the time of their innovations, but each was promulgating a positive thought or action based upon the virtuous elements of the traditions from which they sprang. When a religious, political, or other social innovator stepped out of the bounds of rigid conformity, he was pushed by the tyranny of the institution whose demands were too oppressive and pulled by the dynamic quality of the human spirit.

Perhaps it is true that one of the major battles man faces today is that of increasing depersonalization and mechanization, of trends toward centralization and overadjustment. These may be valid assertions; but, when we are told that it is the "middle-class morality that places chains of restrictions on individuality," that it is the "stultifying middle class" that is responsible for these social ills, and that "the pressure to conform is a middle-class phenomenon," then an unjustifiable connection is made between some real dangers in contemporary society and a social class that happens to be numerically the largest. Although bureaucracy may sometimes be an efficient means of organizational functioning, the resulting personality-damaging aspects of it that have been under attack should not be associated with the meaning given to the middle class nor the prevailing middle-class system of values. The creative, autonomous individual who is universally admired appears on all levels of the social class structure, and neither intellectuality nor intelligence owes allegiance to any particular class.

There are certain forms of middle-class behavior and thought that are most often derided. The delusions of happiness that are used to cover deep-seated, seething discontent and frustrations *do* undoubtedly occur among many middle-class families. The poignancy and directness of *Death of A Salesman* make this play one of the most important in the modern theater. There is perhaps a certain amount of drudgery and dull routine in which a middle-class Sisyphus daily participates. C. Wright Mills has portrayed many white-collar workers in this way. But it is presumptuous speculation to contend that the majority of the middle class is unhappy, despairing, confused, and drab. There is just as much evidence to propose an opposite contention. Furthermore, it may be that some social analysts who emphasize the despairing nature of the middle class project their own psyche into the life situations of the group they analyze and that they imagine how they (the writers) would respond as a typical white-collar worker in an executive job in American business.

Because the average American middle-class male goes to work every morning on the 8:02, sits at the same desk every day, works and lunches with the same office corps, is met on the 5:45 by his middle-class wife and preschool child in middle-class suburbia, it does not follow that he is bulging with frustrations and is following a life that leads nowhere. The bare outline of a daily routine fails to indicate the many pleasures that may be had at work, with associates, and within the family circle. What if he is one of thousands of similar commuters living in a housing development and has a middle-class automobile and two or three typically middle-class kids? The fact that he is doing some productive work, that he supports a family, that he is capable of providing decent clothing, shelter, and affection for his children should be viewed as more than a patterned mold of conformity. Moreover, this pattern may be a pattern simply *because* it provides an ease of living, harmony, and comfort that previous generations of strivers sought and failed to attain.

This middle-class male, his wife, and children may in fact be quite happy and do not seek more than marginal differentiation because of their contentment. Perhaps it is a life of some mediocrity for many, but there is merit in an abundance of middle-class mediocrity. (Webster defines *mediocre* as moderate excellence.) We are not, nor can we all be, geniuses, leaders, or President. Our open-class society permits sufficient striving and leaves open the door to leadership and achievement without causing mass anxiety about the inability to rise among the leading few. Only under the totalitarian restraints of a tyrannical set of conduct norms is the individual forced to seek refuge entirely outside the group. Within a democratic framework and an open-class society, there is adequate opportunity for flexibility and variation as well as for social mobility. If some kind of generalized conformity exists within this framework, perhaps it is not so horrendous or oppressive as is often suggested. If it were, the underlying strength that historically gave rise to the middle class would rescue the group.

There are basic values in American culture that find roots in the Judeo-Christian tradition, that were incorporated into the spirit of the Italian Renaissance and the Protestant Ethic, nepotized in the French and American revolutions. English common law borne by the colonial forefathers was part of the American rising middle-class structure. Norms of conduct stemming from these sources have produced the predominant value system in our society—and this is a middle-class value system.

There are semantic and other problems involved in any attempt to identify empirically the middle class, but included among middle-class norms is the ethic of rationality, forethought, planning. Emphasis is placed on respect for property and for the dignity of the person, which implies self-control and control of physical violence and aggression. The qualities of industry and thrift, of economic and occupational skills, of individual responsibility, resourcefulness, and self-reliance are considered admirable in themselves. Ambition, or the desire to "get ahead," has grown side by side with the striving middle class. The students of social class have detailed these middle-class values and have analyzed their relationship to a variety of economic and political aspects of American society. These norms constitute a value system that may not be the best of all possible worlds; they may be ideals imperfectly performed in reality. Whether they are proper norms is a dilemma for the absolutist. That they have provided a workable and harmoniously functioning society capable of withstanding onslaughts from without and weaknesses from within, history can record.

Conformity to this value system may, in this light, be desirable. The middle class has an ontological stability sufficiently tested and secure, composed of lasting values shared by most creative individuals and groups. These are not ephemeral values of the moment crying for attention and making demands for conformity to a less flexible set of norms. William Graham Sumner long ago pointed out that one can no more escape from the mores than he can from the laws of gravity. To divorce oneself from the prevailing mores simply means withdrawal into another set of mores. The middle-class mores have survived dynamic social change and have moved forward harmoniously with developments in the arts, science, and literature because one of the virtues of the middle-class value system is that it permits a wide range of behavior and attitude, including opportunities for innovation and change *within* the system.

What are the alternatives to this value system? The cult of the Beat and Angry men? As a way of life for a total society this kind of nihilism and vacuous negativism (which the middle class can tolerate quite easily) would result in mass nonproductive disorder. Some forms of Bohemian life are subcultural delights that provide refreshing vitality and constitute an expression of the alliance between the middle class and social and political freedom. It is interesting, however, how diffusive the prevailing middle-class value system is among many contemporary Bohemians and lesser sorts of deviants.

Another alternative, of course, is legal nonconformity—abrogation of middle-class norms that have been codified into law. Delinquency, crime, drug addiction, etc., certainly are deviations. The abiding interest the middle class has in literature, the cinema, and television that dwell on the themes of detective mysteries, crime and violence, indicates that the populace enjoys taking vicarious excursions into this type of nonconformity. We may smile at the vicariousness and economically profit from it; yet we are appalled at overt manifestations of this kind of nonconformity. When the delinquent or criminal is taken into custody, even the most ardent attackers of the "decidedly middle class" agree to the principle of reformation or rehabilitation. We seek to help the offender to adjust and to conform. And to what should he adjust? According to which set of values is he being reformed? We want him to conform to what kind of social expectations? Check the list of middle-class norms again and the answers are obvious. The reason society seeks to mold, to reform the delinquent and the criminal to this pattern is not only that it is the predominant pattern in American culture; it is also the pattern most likely to produce an integrated and socially useful human being.

The fight for individuality, personal differentiation, and the private life is a universal struggle. The genetic uniqueness of each individual and the wide range for personality development provided through middle-class values offer a continuity of optimism rather than despair. Conformity to this productive set of norms that results in social harmony and strength may be viewed as a virtue. Should the strictures toward conformity become too great or too rigid, the amorphous, unorganized, and flexible nature of the American middle class is such that it can permit changes to occur within the framework of the value system it supports.

20

Norm Qualities and Differential Effects of Deviant Behavior: An Exploratory Analysis*

EPHRAIM H. MIZRUCHI
Syracuse University

ROBERT PERRUCCI
Purdue University

INTRODUCTION

A major problem for contemporary sociologists revolves about the issue of long range vs. short range goals in the solution of perceived social problems. Should the sociologist concern himself primarily with abstract theory which is of a level of generality capable of application to many social settings, once developed and refined? Or, should he apply himself to a particular question yielding more immediate rewards for the process of solving seemingly urgent societal problems? In reality we find only a small number who clearly espouse either one position or the other. More typical of contemporary research is an effort to study the particular in order to cast light on the general.

The present paper attempts to illustrate how the study of normative and deviant drinking behavior yields hypotheses which are explicitly tied to more abstract generalizations which are applicable to a variety of social settings. Thus, research in the sphere of alcohol and society can make simultaneous contributions to the solution of immediate social problems and to the development of general theories of societal processes.

Our data in this paper are analyzed within a broad framework which embodies questions about the nature of normative integration, deviance, group reactions to deviance and social change.

Reprinted from *American Sociological Review*, 27, 3 (June 1962), pp. 391–399, by permission of the authors and The American Sociological Association.

* This version is an extension and revision of an earlier paper by the authors, "Norm Qualities and Differential Effects of Deviant Behavior," *American Sociological Review*, 27 (June 1962), pp. 391–399.

Completion of the revised version of this paper was supported by a travel agent from the Research Institute of Syracuse University.

The organizing concepts emerged both from a study of the data on cultural factors in drinking behavior and further induction into an appropriate theoretical model. The process includes the establishment of ideal type aspects of norms; providing data illustrating the significance of distinguishing these aspects from other norm qualities; and deriving *explicit* empirically testable hypotheses for the assessment of the original typology. Thus what is being attempted, in addition, is a study of how ideal-type method can be directly integrated with more formal empirical analysis.

NORMS AND NORMATIVE INTEGRATION

A fundamental notion embodied in the functional approach to social systems is that certain tasks must be performed in order that a given system may persist. Among the various tasks, or functional prerequisites, is the maintenance of a system of order. Many of the traditional dichotomies associated with the names of eminent forerunners of contemporary sociology reflect explicit and implicit concern with order. Durkheim's mechanical and organic solidarity (12), Tönnies' Gemeinschaft-Gesellschaft (33) Redfield's Folk-Urban (25) and Becker's Sacred-Secular (3) to name only a few, indicate a concern with the fundamental question of how society is organized and changed.

Though there are great divergences of viewpoint among contemporary sociologists regarding which factors are most significant in contrasting relatively simple and complex social organizations, few would disagree that the process of group adherence to shared norms represents an important dimension of order. Thus Durkheim (12) and Freedman *et al.* (13) have focused their attention on the contrast between normative and functional integration. These two dimensions as conceived by these writers are to be found in all group structures and represent ideal-typical states of systems. Thus contemporary urban communities, for example, would be expected to be integrated not only in terms of functional integration, i.e., integration based on the interrelated activities of heterogeneous groups, but normatively as well. The norms, consequently, represent crucial factors in the process of maintaining order.

Relatively little attention has been paid to the qualitative nature of the norms themselves as contrasted with the great concern associated with the direct effect of norms in controlling the activities of individuals in groups.[1] This is particularly the case with regard to the role played by the qualitative characteristics of norms in the process of normative integration and the utility of this dimension in empirical analysis.

---

[1] The most conspicuous exceptions are to be found in the work of William Graham Sumner (32), Talcott Parsons (22), Pitirim Sorokin (30), and Robin M. Williams, Jr. (36).

In terms of the sociocultural system, the problem of order may be analyzed with respect to the particular characteristics of the norms themselves, in addition to the control processes associated with the norms. In other words, the stability or integration of a system is not insured simply because the normative system is effectively transmitted (socialization) or collectively controlled (sanctions). The qualities of the norms themselves provide an inherent potential for system maintenance and system malintegration.

PROSCRIPTIVE AND PRESCRIPTIVE DIMENSIONS OF NORMS

Richard T. Morris (19), in a paper published a decade ago, suggested a classification of norms which focused on four significant aspects: their distribution; the mode of enforcement associated with a given norm; the transmission of norms; and the process of conformity to given norms. Robin M. Williams, Jr., has also incorporated this scheme in his systematic study of American society (36, pp. 26–27). Though there is no shortage of classificatory schemes in this important area of sociological theory, it would seem to the present writers that still another dimension is worthy of consideration as a possible addition to Morris' classification.

Indeed, Morris himself has suggested that "probably the most striking omission . . . [in his typology of norms] . . . is the content of the norms" (19, p. 612).

> "Content" is used here in two senses: classification of norms according to the area of behavior regulated . . . , or classification of norms according to the nature of action called for by the norms. . . . (19)

It is the latter to which we are addressing ourselves in this paper.

Our specific objective will be to present an additional typology, to illustrate its potential value by making reference to several sets of data related to the typology, and to suggest how greater attention to this dimension may prove fruitful in assessing the functional significance of certain aspects of norms in social systems.

In discussing norms in general, Williams points out that ". . . norms always carry some prescriptive or proscriptive *quality* . . ." (36, p. 26).[2] Talcott Parsons, in discussing the integration of social systems, has also directed attention to the significance of the proscriptive-prescriptive dimension. He states,

[2] It should be noted that we are not concerned here with *types* of norms as such, but only with specific *aspects* of norms. It should also be kept in mind that the proscriptive-prescriptive notions have existed in the anthropological literature for some time.

It is this integration by common values, manifested in the action of solidary groups or collectivities, which characterizes the partial or total integrations of social systems.

Social integration, however much it depends on internalized norms, cannot be achieved by these alone. It requires also some supplementary coordination provided by explicit *prescriptive* or *prohibitory* role-expectations (e.g., laws) (23, pp. 202–203).[3]

This particular dimension appears worthy of further exploration on the level of system-maintenance analysis. A preliminary ideal-typical description should prove sufficient for the first step in our analysis.

Norms in which the *proscriptive* element is most predominant are those which direct participants in the social structure to avoid, abstain, desist, and reject all forms of behavior associated with a particular potential type of activity. Examples of this dimension are the "thou shalt not" directives of the Ten Commandments and abstention from the pleasures of the flesh as directed by ascetic Protestantism.

The *prescriptive* dimension, on the other hand, directs participants to act in a particular way, spelling out the forms of behavior to which group members must conform. Typical of prescriptive directives are the norms requiring periodical church attendance and confession among Roman Catholics and the elaborate directives associated with the consumption of alcoholic beverages among the Orthodox Jews.

Thus the mandate of the predominantly proscriptive norm is "do not" while the mandate of the predominantly prescriptive norm is "do this" or "do that." The former provides only a goal viewed negatively; the latter provides a goal viewed positively, as well as a set of means for its attainment.

Whether this scheme is worthy of serious attention as a possible addition to the body of theory on norms would seem to depend upon its usefulness as an analytical tool, particularly as a means of organizing empirical findings. We have, with this in mind, selected some studies which help illustrate the possible utility of these notions in the process of relating theory to concrete data.

At least one area of patterned activity which particularly lends itself to analysis in this context has undergone extensive investigation.[4] The several sociological studies of the relationship between sociocultural factors and the consumption of alcoholic beverages should provide us with

[3] It should be noted also that the present writers do not view the significance of the prescriptive and proscriptive dimensions as operative on the external level alone, i.e., external to the internalized norms, as Parsons implies here, but on both the internalized and externalized levels of social control. Note also Robert K. Merton's awareness of the significance of these dimensions (17, p. 133).

[4] Note the similarity between our independently conceived approach and the earlier approach of Edwin M. Lemert (15, p. 33).

a "goodness of fit" criterion for our conceptual analysis.[5] The specific studies to which we refer are those of Straus and Bacon (31), Snyder (28), Skolnick (27), Mulford and Miller (21), Allardt, *et al.* (1), and more recently, Bruen and Hauge (6). All represent a high order of methodological procedure in terms of sampling, question design and data analysis. All of these studies focus on variations in drinking behavior among various social strata and ethnic groups, and provide a broad range of data on norms, beliefs, and sentiments concerning the uses of alcohol. Thus they are particularly valuable for codification. Our first problem, then, is to demonstrate whether the differences between prescriptive and proscriptive dimensions of norms are of significance in the analysis of concrete data.

The above studies report significant differences among the various groups with regard to pathological reactions resulting from differential patterns of alcohol consumption. By "pathological" we mean the extent to which these behaviors represent deviations which are threats to the personal well-being of group members, e.g., problem drinking or psychosis. We are suggesting that the extent to which these levels of pathology are present in a given system is directly related to problems of system maintenance although as we suggest below, these threats may also play a role in attaining greater short-run integration.

CULTURAL NORMS AND DRINKING PATHOLOGY

Three sets of data have been selected to demonstrate the existence of a relationship between types of normative system and drinking pathology. Snyder's study shows that intoxication is related to religio-ethnic group affiliation for college students.[6] As contrasted with the rates for the Jewish students, whose behavior is presumably directed by prescriptive norms, for example, the intoxication rate is much higher for the ascetic Protestant and Mormon groups, for whom the drinking of alcoholic beverages is proscribed. Snyder holds that,

> These data should not be construed as representing the comparative overall effectiveness of the norms of these groups in minimizing intoxication. The percentages . . . are based on the numbers of students in each group who have had some experience in using alcoholic beverages. They, therefore, do not reflect the large numbers of abstainers, especially in the Protestant group, who have never been intoxicated (29, p. 189).

[5] For a discussion of the "goodness of fit" concept in the verification of typologies, see, for example, James M. Beshers (5).

[6] Snyder's data were derived from original data gathered by Straus and Bacon for the college drinking study. See Snyder (29, p. 190).

We would hold that Snyder's interpretation is most meaningful within the context of the relationship between group affiliation and overall drinking behavior. However, it is precisely the question of the "overall effectiveness of the norms" for those who drink which concerns us here; this is the sphere in which the fundamental difference between our concern and that of the various analysts of drinking behavior manifests itself. While their focus is on the relationship between norms and specified features of the social structure, ours is on the qualitative nature of the norms themselves.

Skolnick's data[7] reveal even more sharply some of the consequences of normative deviation. When one compares the degree of social complications associated with religio-ethnic group affiliation, one finds that social complications tend to increase for selected groups of students. While social complications for the Jewish students are minimal, there is a marked increase for the ascetic Protestant groups. Thus, the data again reflect a relationship between ascetic Protestant affiliation and drinking pathology with respect to the extremities of deviant reactions for these groups.

Still other results that are significant in the context of the present study are the findings of Mulford and Miller in one of the most elaborate and extensive studies of the drinking behavior of an adult population. They approach questions similar to those posed by the other researchers from a social psychological viewpoint. Differentiating between drinking behavior that is directed by normative systems and that which involves idiosyncratic decisions regarding alcohol consumption, they developed a scale of "personal-effects definitions," which makes a distinction between relatively normative and non-normative drinking behavior (20, 2).

Mulford and Miller's interpretation of their findings is consistent with those of Straus and Bacon and Snyder with regard to the non-existence of group norms which characterizes the drinking behavior of respondents with abstinence backgrounds. From their results, it seems clear that the focus on "personal-effects" on the part of the drinker as contrasted with a more normative orientation is associated with problem drinking. An extensive statement by Mulford and Miller with regard to their findings reflects some points of convergence between their viewpoint and our own.

> The heavier consumption by the personal-effects drinker may also be a reflection of the *relative absence of social norms* in the situations where

---

[7] Skolnick's data were derived from original data gathered by Straus and Bacon for the college drinking study. The reader should note a possible objection associated with the groups on which *problem drinking* rates are based. For example, it has been pointed out that comparisons of alcoholism rates can be variously interpreted, depending upon whether the *base* of the comparison is the *total* membership of the two groups, or solely on the *drinkers* in the two groups. It should be clear, however, that (1) we are not speaking of *alcoholism* rates, but *problem drinking* rates; and (2) that we are primarily concerned with comparing alcohol pathology rates in different groups *for those who do drink*. For a discussion of these points, see Skolnick (27, p. 460).

he does much of his drinking. Persons who drink primarily for social effects may be presumed to do most of their drinking in more intimate group situations, involving family and friends, where restrictive norms are relatively effective; although, of course, the party norms may permit considerable latitude. The personal-effects drinker who attends parties probably is the one most likely to exceed the party norms, but as he does so repeatedly, he may find that he is not welcome and is then 'forced' to do more of his drinking alone and in public places where there is relative freedom from intimate group-norm restrictions.

Finally, the heavy drinking of the individual who is drinking mainly for the personal effects of alcohol may also reflect the likelihood that he does not carry in his mind a conception of *how many drinks* it takes to attain the desired effect, especially since such *prescriptions* are presumably not general in our culture. . . . (21, pp. 276–277).[8]

We can conclude from the above studies that normative systems play a role in the consumption of alcoholic beverages, and that pathological reactions to drinking tend to be greater for certain ascetic Protestant and Mormon groups, as compared with other religious groups. We would hold, in general, that pathological drinking behavior is associated with a relative absence of directives for the act of drinking alcoholic beverages itself. The important question then is: What is there about the nature of the normative systems of the ascetic Protestant and Mormon groups that predisposes their deviants to greater pathological reactions and, consequently, their structure to greater strain?

SIGNIFICANCE OF PRESCRIPTIVE AND PROSCRIPTIVE DIMENSION

We have indicated above that there is an absence of directives regarding drinking behavior among the ascetic Protestant and Mormon groups. In contrast to the prescriptive norms associated with drinking by Jews, for example, the ascetic Protestant and Mormon norms may be characterized as primarily *proscriptive*. Total abstinence is the norm for these groups. Hence, deviation from the abstinence pattern, even in what is ordinarily recognized as socially approved drinking in the larger society, e.g., before dinner, at parties, and like occasions, is associated with an almost complete absence of directives. As Straus and Bacon have pointed out in discussing the drinking behavior of Mormons, "If drinking behavior is adopted, variation must be the rule since there is no norm. Extremes are likely since the behavior itself represents rejection of social rules." (31, p. 144).[9]

---

[8] See also, Allardt (1), which provides additional data to support the hypothesis about the conditions associated with relative lack of drinking norms and our discussion below.

[9] Skolnick (27, p. 265), makes the point that extreme drinking behavior of those

Jewish drinking, as Snyder has shown, is patterned by an elaborate system of explicit directives as to what, when, where, with whom, how much, and why one is expected to consume alcoholic beverages. The norm is predominantly *prescriptive* in nature, and deviation from the drinking norms is associated with gradual and predictable patterns of deviant behavior. Thus Snyder's statistics show that tendencies to alcohol pathology increase in "step like" fashion from Orthodox Jewish drinking, which is associated with the relative absence of signs of pathology, to the Reform and Secular drinking pattern in which pathology is relatively high. Nevertheless, the highest rate still tends to remain lower than rates for the Protestant group (29, p. 197).

We would hold that it is inherent in the nature of the two sets of norms, the ascetic Protestant and Mormon norms, on the one hand, and the Jewish norms, on the other, that they predispose group members to different kinds of deviant reactions. The consequence of the differential deviant reactions is differential strain for the two sub-systems. Alcohol pathology represents not only personal problems, but problems for the group as well. The various efforts to cope with problems of alcohol on the part of different groups—governmental agencies, private welfare organizations, and religious groups, to name only a few—suggest that strain exists not only for the sub-systems in which they occur, but for larger social systems as well. In general, it can be noted that at least four types of group reactions to system strain can be isolated as indices of the extent of perceived threat to the system or its members. Group reactions may take the form of: (1) *Retrenchment*, in which all deviants are cast out of the group, leaving only a small hard core of adherents; (2) *Regeneration*, in which there is an attempt to revitalize the norm through a cultural renaissance; (3) *Rational-Scientific Innovation*, which includes efforts on the part of persons outside of the group as well as enlightened group participants to adapt new normative patterns to the pre-existing cultural system; and (4) *Permissiveness*, which involves individual determination of limits.[10] Examples of these types of reactions may be

---

exposed to abstinence teachings is a result of another norm derived from descriptions of the behavior of extreme drinkers, i.e., "the horrible example." Although we see the virtue of his notion of a "negative" role model, we would hold that theoretically, at least, a distinction must be made between role models—both positive and negative —role expectations, and norms. Thus, unless the expected behavior of the role model becomes generalized to the larger group, i.e., becomes an explicit, shared norm, it remains external to a given social system. In the case of drinking norms, Skolnick's observations need not lead to a rejection of our own explanation, since the negative role model, as we see it may represent an *additional* factor rather than an exclusive causal factor. However, the reader should keep in mind the fact that these notions— both Skolnick's and our own—represent hypotheses rather than conclusive generalizations.

[10] Merton and Parsons, it should be noted, have focused on deviant reactions to structured strain. Merton's typology is concerned with structured individual reactions to a disjunction between norms and success goals in American society. Parsons also

found reflected in behavior associated with deviant drinking activities. *Retrenchment* has manifested itself in the strong reactions to public intoxication on the part of the Chinese in the United States, who in the past, forced alcoholics and problem drinkers to return to the Chinese mainland if they failed to mend their ways, at the same time reinforcing the norms of individual responsibility to the group (14).[11] *Regeneration* is reflected in the abstinence movement in the United States. The *Rational-Scientific Innovation* reaction is exemplified in Mulford and Miller's suggestion that prescriptive drinking norms should replace proscriptive drinking norms for the ascetic Protestant groups in the United States (21, p. 498). And the persistence of patternless drinking in a good many American social contexts is a manifestation of *Permissiveness*.[12]

A TYPOLOGY OF NORMS

We have suggested above that the proscriptive and prescriptive dimensions of norms do make it possible for us to attain greater understanding of the dynamics of social pathology. We have, up to this point, discussed the two dimensions in very broad terms. To what extent can we specify the nature of these dimensions and place them in a context of

---

deals with individual deviant reactions in terms of motivational analysis. The typology presented here differs from both Merton and Parsons in the following respects: (1) our focus is on *collective* reactions rather than *individual* reactions; (2) this typology is concerned with *normative* reactions to strain rather than *deviant* reactions to strain; and (3) whereas Merton's focus is on *chronic* strain, i.e., a persistent element in the system, the above typology, at least in this context, is concerned with *acute* strain. Adding to the above approaches Williams' concept of "patterned norm evasion," we may derive the following classification of approaches to reactions to strain:

Deviant-Individual [a]   Normative-Individual [b]
Deviant-Group [c]   Normative-Group [d]

[a] See, for example, Robert K. Merton (17); Talcott Parsons (23, Ch. 7); Albert E. Cohen (11).

[b] This category is perhaps the most prevalent in the sociological literature. It is characterized by the following sequence: deviant act—group reaction—individual conformity. One of many examples may be found in Fritz J. Roethlisberger and William J. Dickson's description of "binging" as a negative sanction for nonconformity (26).

[c] See, for example, Robin M. Williams, Jr. (36). Chapter 10 is devoted in its entirety to norm evasion.

[d] In addition to our independently conceived notions concerning normative group reactions to strain, Howard Becker's posthumously published paper deals with similar types of problems (4).

[11] In the general context of group reactions to system strain, see Anthony F. C. Wallace (34).

[12] Our usage of "permissiveness," or individual determination of limits, represents what might otherwise be called unresolved *anomie*. However, since the group reactions described above are in effect reactions to an anomic condition, we have attempted to avoid using *anomie* for purposes of clarity. The significance of *permissiveness* as both a norm and as a type of *laissez faire* reaction is dealt with below.

TABLE 1

Qualitative Characteristics of Prescriptive and Proscriptive Norms

Characteristic of Norm	Proscriptive	Prescriptive
Elasticity	Inflexible: Behavior is defined as either compliant or deviant and there are no directives for action.	Flexible: Behavior is defined in degree of conformity and directives for how to act are explicit.
Elaboration	No ritual, no embellishment associated with act	Great deal of embellishment in ritualized and symbolic acts
Pervasiveness	Focus on a specific act applying to any and all contexts	Focus on a variety of similar acts in specified contexts
Functional interrelatedness	Norm tends to have few or no convergences with other norms in the larger system	Norm tends to converge with other norms in the larger system

social system analysis? With this perspective in view, norms may be classified ideal-typically in terms of the following descriptive characteristics which have emerged from our review of the various studies cited above: (1) the degree of elasticity; (2) the degree of elaboration; (3) the degree of pervasiveness; and (4) the degree of functional interrelatedness.

Table 1 describes those aspects of norms which make them classifiable as either proscriptive or prescriptive.[13] Table 2 shows how these factors are related, by way of illustration, to drinking behavior. The extent to

TABLE 2

Drinking Norms for Selected Groups by Qualitative Characteristics and Prescriptive-Proscriptive Dimension

	Elasticity	Elaboration	Pervasiveness	Functional Interrelatedness	
Prescriptive					
	++	++	++	++	Jews[1]
	+	++	+	++	Italians[2]
	−	−	−	+	Mormons[3]
Proscriptive					

[1] For an elaborate description of Orthodox Jewish drinking patterns, see Charles R. Snyder (28).

[2] Wine is viewed by Italians as both a food and as a beverage. It does not, however, embody the sacred element associated with Orthodox Jewish drinking. Italians do not recite blessing over the wine. See, for examples, Phyllis Williams and Robert Straus (35); and Giorgio Lolli, *et al.* (16).

[3] References to Mormon drinking may be found in Robert Straus and Selden Bacon (31).

which these factors, in varying degree, manifest themselves in given normative systems represents, in our judgment, a measure of the relative degree of predisposition to normative malintegration with respect to a given norm.

THE NORMATIVE AND THE FACTUAL

As we have suggested above, the overall effectiveness of norms in the process of system maintenance can be attributed to at least two characteristics: (1) the extent to which both internal and external sanctions effectively direct the behavior of group members; and (2) the nature of the norms themselves. It is the latter to which we have addressed ourselves in this paper. Although the two are undoubtedly related, we would

[13] In an initial classification of norms for general purposes, for example, norms may be classified as being predominantly proscriptive or prescriptive according to whether they enjoin or prohibit behavior. For a more complete understanding of the dynamics of normative behavior, especially with reference to problems of social control, a more intensive analysis of the norms themselves is necessary. Our hypothetical scheme, it should be noted, is derived from: (1) inspection of the various monographs cited in Table 2; (2) inspection of unpublished data on the Chinese; and (3) participant observation in various subcultural contexts.

hold that the qualitative nature of the norm is analytically distinct from the strength of sanctions attached to the norm. Thus, whether controls are internalized or externalized, or whether the sanctioning agents are informally or formally designated does not concern us here. The above data are consistent with our hypothesis that predominantly proscriptive norms are more likely than predominantly prescriptive norms to lead to extreme degrees of pathological reactions when deviation occurs.

It is possible to treat the whole matter of the relationship between norms and social pathology in terms of the relationship between the normative and factual orders. While we have indicated that our focus is on the qualitative nature of the norms themselves, our ultimate concern is with social control and group integration. The normative-factual orders lend themselves to analysis within the framework of the prescriptive-proscriptive dimension. Thus, one could interpret our discussion as an attempt to explore the consequences of situations in which the normative order and the factual order are more or less convergent or divergent. Rather than assume that it is simply the divergence between these two orders which is primarily productive of strain, we would hold that it is the quality of the normative order which determines the extent of strain in this context. The following suggestive scheme provides an illustration of a possible systematic approach to these dimensions. Thus, the following table describes a factual order, given a certain prescriptive-proscriptive normative order. The examples represent approximate empirical referents with regard to drinking norms.

TABLE 3

Norms

	Jewish *Italian*	*Mormon* *Methodist*
Normative Order	Highly Prescriptive	Highly Proscriptive
Factual Order	Deviation	Deviation
Level of Pathology	Low Level of Pathology	High Level of Pathology (Anomie)

As this preliminary scheme suggests, the following propositions can be formulated with respect to the aspects of norms referred to above:

1. Given a situation in which there is either *prescription* on the *normative* level and *deviation* on the factual level, pathology will be *high*.
2. Given a situation in which there is *prescription* on the *normative* level and *deviation* on the factual level, pathology will be *low*.

The above discussion implies that under certain normative conditions behavior which deviated from the norm does not threaten the system of order, while under other conditions it does. It should be added that the present analysis does not include a discussion of the relative effectiveness of each type of norm under conditions of normative integration without strain. Presumably, pathology is minimized as a result of conformity to both the predominantly proscriptive and prescriptive norms referred to above. Stated as a third proposition:

3. Given a situation in which there is *either* prescription or proscription on the *normative* level and *conformity* on the *factual* level, pathology will be *low*.

Thus, this approach is systematic and directly lends itself to empirical analysis.

PERMISSIVENESS AND ANOMIE

A third general aspect, to which we referred only briefly, is permissiveness. Although the evidence with respect to this pattern or lack of pattern is scanty, permissiveness appears to be characteristic of periods of normative transformation. Thus, in the United States the shift from proscription among Protestant abstentionist groups *without the provision of a corresponding set of clear directive* for drinking behavior appears to represent a period of *anomic* behavior which will, in time, become organized into a new pattern. In this context directives tend to be vague injunctions to avoid immoderate drinking and to "stay out of trouble." That this condition may persist over very long periods of time without becoming organized, thus enhancing the anomic condition and consequent deviant behavior, is illustrated by studies of Finnish drinking.

In Finland, where religious groups preach proscription and where the sale and distribution of alcohol is carefully controlled, the arrests for drunkenness rate in 1959 was 72.0 per 1000 inhabitants compared with 26.0 for Norway, 17.2 for Sweden and 6.3 for Denmark. Finland and Norway, it should be noted, are countries which had prohibition laws following World War I in contrast to Sweden which rejected prohibition as a solution to drinking problems and Denmark which did not even entertain the question of prohibition (6). Assuming that the behaviors associated with efforts to solve problems reflects underlying differences in normative orientations, it seems clear that arrests for drunkenness as a reflection of deviant behavior are higher where a background of proscription is greater.

Straus and Bacon (31), and Mulford and Miller (21), as we noted above, held that when those who were reared as abstainers drink there are no directives for how, when, how much and with whom to drink. Allardt (1) explored the intensity of attitude toward drinking in his Finnish sample and found what he described as an intensive negative attitude toward drinking (proscriptive) as contrasted with "an ambivalent one."

> The finding agrees very well with the intuitive picture one gets of the attitudes toward drinking in Finnish society. There are certain people with a strong negative attitude towards drinking, while most other people may show a very positive verbal attitude towards drinking and towards the functions of drinking, but this attitude is not consistent, and it is often expressed in a jocular way (1, p. 26).

Permissive attitudes toward drinking in Finland are also associated with acceptance of the value of occasional unrestrained drinking, suggesting still another link between permissiveness and deviance (1, p. 28). Thus the study of drinking in Finnish culture lends support to our original assumption regarding permissiveness and deviance.

We suggested above that permissiveness represents a condition of unresolved anomie. Recent research in the area of deviant behavior has focused on Merton's hypothesis that strains in social systems lead to deviant behavior and consequent anomie (17; 18, 29). More specifically, in American society the discrepancy between the American desire for success and differential opportunity for the attainment of success goals leads to deviant reactions and, ultimately, to anomie.

Although a thorough discussion of Merton's approach to anomie is beyond our primary concern here, it is well to comment briefly at this point since permissiveness and anomie represent aspects of the same phenomenon.

Our usage of anomie suggests that the source of the weakening of social controls on drinking is a reflection of general societal transformation related to industrialization and urbanization which were the foci of attention of the sociologists to whom we referred at the outset—Durkheim, Tönnies, Redfield and Becker. Given the kind of rapid transformation which characterizes the responses of sub-systems to increase in population, change in type of production and modification of family functions, to suggest only a few consequences of industrialization and urbanization, there is a simultaneous change in group attitudes toward the normative order. Thus, although there still tends to be an awareness of the rules limiting and directing man's desires, there is somewhat less certainty regarding whether or not adherence to these norms should be enforced. As social structures undergo change, so do normative systems. During periods of uncertainty a wider range of deviance is tolerated in the form of permissiveness, which, as we suggested above, allows the person rather than the group to determine the range of appropriate conduct. While all societies and groups must provide for flexibility in order to persist, periods during which permissiveness predominates do not always result in a reinforcement of the original normative system, as we noted above. Thus the uncertainty, i.e., associated with some of these periods is often the prelude to the emergence of new *normative patterns.*

With respect to drinking behavior in particular, however, the flexibility associated with change, if we are correct in our analysis of deviance, has more profound effects in systems undergoing change from proscription to other normative forms.

Similar to Merton's approach which deals directly with the group's response to deviance is our concern with what we have called permissiveness.

Recently several analysts of deviant drinking behavior, following Merton, have suggested that problem drinking represents a *retreatist* reaction to the strain associated with the discrepancy between success goals and opportunity to attain them. Thus the retreatist, having failed to reach his goal, withdraws from the race and turns to excessive drinking and, finally to problem drinking (29, pp. 202–205). This in turn leads to more deviant drinking on the part of others who observe the toleration of deviance. Given the paucity of empirical data on this aspect of anomie it is not possible to draw any conclusions at this time. If, however, patterns of deviant drinking can be linked to more general societal processes and their impact on normative systems then our objectives in this paper will have been served.

We have suggested that proscriptive and prescriptive dimensions are to be found in the analysis of other normative systems and data other than those dealing with alcohol pathology alone. We would suggest that sex behavior may be a fruitful area of investigation.[14] Some specific examples of other problems that would seem to lend themselves to this type of analysis would be studies of norms proscribing aggression among Jews; norms proscribing female pre-marital intercourse among Italians; and norms proscribing the acquisition of material luxuries among the Old Order Amish.

Finally, although we have abstracted norm qualities as our focus of attention and hold that they are an essential aspect of the processes enhancing and inhibiting deviance and pathology we do not feel that this approach is alone sufficient to understand these phenomena. Thus the subsequent experiences of persons reared in proscriptive cultures and subcultures play an important role in decisions to conform or deviate. Ernest Campbell (7, pp. 406–407) in a recent study, for example, presents data which indicate that college students who have internalized proscriptive drinking norms are more likely to form peer group associations that encourage personal abstinence and non-drinkers are less likely to pledge fraternities and sororities than drinkers. The study of the effects of drinking norms on behavior, then, also provides entree into the sphere of

[14] Christensen has noted the possible connection between proscription and extreme reactions, and has suggested that sex behavior and drinking behavior may be analogous in this respect. See Harold T. Christensen (8; 9).

group formation studies. In short, the study of drinking behavior is not only significant because it contributes directly to the solution of social problems but also for its contribution to the understanding of basic societal processes.

References

1. Allardt, E., T. Markanen, and M. Takala, *Drinking and Drinkers*, Helsinki: The Finnish Foundation for Alcohol Studies, 1963.
2. Bales, Robert F., "Cultural Differences in Rates of Alcoholism," *Quarterly Journal of Studies on Alcohol*, 6:400–499, 1946.
3. Becker, Howard, "Ionia and Athens: Studies in Secularization," Unpublished Ph.D. dissertation, University of Chicago, 1930.
4. ———, "Normative Reactions to Normlessness," *American Sociological Review*, 25:803–810, 1960.
5. Beshers, James M., "Pragmatic Criteria in Typology Construction," paper read at the annual meeting of the American Sociological Association, New York City, August, 1960.
6. Bruen, K. and R. Hauge, *Drinking of Northern Youth: A Cross-Cultural Survey*, Helsinki: The Finnish Foundation for Alcohol Studies, 1963.
7. Campbell, Ernest, "The Internalization of Moral Norms," *Sociometry*, 27:391–412, 1964.
8. Christensen, Harold T., "Cultural Relativism and Premarital Sex Norms," *ASR* 25:31–39, 1960.
9. ———, "Child Spacing Analysis Via Record Linkage," *Marriage and Family Living*, 25:272–280, 1963.
10. Clinard, Marshall (ed.), *Deviant Behavior and Anomie*, New York: The Free Press, 1964.
11. Cohen, Albert K., "The Study of Social Disorganization and Deviant Behavior," in Robert K. Merton, *et al.* (eds.), *Sociology Today*, New York: Basic Books, 1959.
12. Durkheim, Emile, *The Division of Labor in Society* (1893), translated by George Simpson, New York: Macmillan, 1933.
13. Freedman, Ronald et al., *Principles of Sociology*, New York: Holt, Rinehart and Winston, 1952.
14. Lee, Rose Hum and Ephraim H. Mizruchi, "A Study of Drinking Behavior and Attitudes Toward Alcohol of the Chinese in the United States," unpublished manuscript.
15. Lemert, Edwin M., *Social Pathology*, New York: McGraw-Hill, 1951.
16. Lolli, Giorgio, *Alcohol in Italian Culture*, Glencoe, Illinois: The Free Press, 1958.
17. Merton, Robert K., "Social Structure and Anomie," in *Social Theory and Social Structure*, Glencoe, Illinois: The Free Press, 1957.
18. Mizruchi, Ephraim H., *Success and Opportunity*, New York: The Free Press, 1964.
19. Morris, Richard T., "A Typology of Norms," *American Sociological Review*, 21:610–613, 1956.
20. Mulford, Harold A. and Donald A. Miller, "Drinking Behavior Related

to Definitions of Alcohol: A Report of Research in Progress," *American Sociological Review*, 24:385–389, 1959.

21. ———, "Drinking in Iowa," five articles appearing in separate numbers of Volume 21 (1960), *Quarterly Journal of Studies on Alcohol*.
22. Parsons, Talcott, *The Structure of Social Action*, New York: McGraw-Hill, 1937.
23. ———, *The Social System*, Glencoe, Illinois: The Free Press, 1951.
24. ———, "The Social System," in Talcott Parsons and Edward A. Shils, (eds.), *Toward a General Theory of Action*, Cambridge: Harvard University Press, 1951.
25. Redfield, Robert, *The Folk Culture of Yucatan*, Chicago: University of Chicago Press, 1941.
26. Roethlisberger, Fritz J. and William J. Dickson, *Management and the Worker*, Cambridge: Harvard University Press, 1939.
27. Skolnick, Jerome H., "Religious Affiliation and Drinking Behavior," *Quarterly Journal of Studies on Alcohol*, 19:452–470, 1958.
28. Snyder, Charles R., *Alcohol and the Jews*, Glencoe, Illinois: The Free Press, 1958.
29. ———, "Inebriety, Alcoholism and Anomie," in Marshall Clinard (ed.), *Deviant Behavior and Anomie*, New York: The Free Press, 1964.
30. Sorokin, Pitirim, *Society, Culture and Personality*, New York: Harper, 1947.
31. Straus, Robert and Seldon D. Bacon, *Drinking in College*, New Haven: Yale University Press, 1954.
32. Sumner, William Graham, *Folkways*, Boston: Ginn, 1906.
33. Tönnies, Ferdinand, *Gemeinschaft und Gesellschaft* (1887), translated by Charles P. Loomis as *Community and Society*, East Lansing, Michigan: Michigan State University Press, 1957.
34. Wallace, Anthony F. C., "Revitalization Movements," in Seymour M. Lipset and Neil J. Smelzer (eds.), *Sociology, The Progress of a Decade*, Englewood, New Jersey: Prentice-Hall, Inc., 1961.
35. Williams, Phyllis and Robert Straus, "Drinking Patterns of Italians in New Haven," *Quarterly Journal of Studies on Alcohol*, 11 (1950), 4 papers.
36. Williams, Jr., Robin M., *American Society*, New York: Knopf, 1960 revision.

21

An Empirical Exploration
of Neutralization Theory

RICHARD ALLEN BALL

West Virginia University

Sociological theories of crime and delinquency, emphasizing the etiological importance of social factors, have been characterized by one major deficiency: these theories do not satisfactorily explain why one individual does and another does not succumb to various pressures toward delinquency. This problem suggests that more adequate formulations must somehow take cognizance of personal factors. The persistent failure of sociological theories to deal with a "readiness" or "self" factor was explicitly recognized years ago. At that time, Reckless called for a reformulation of theories to take account of "differential response" to similar social pressures.[1]

A recent formulation which appears to incorporate the recognition of a self factor in delinquent behavior is the "neutralization theory" advanced by Sykes and Matza.[2] According to their statement, norms are not to be conceived as categorical imperatives but rather as qualified guidelines for a *zone* of acceptable behavior. The particular norms embodied in law have undergone considerable specification, and these specifications include completely or partially extenuating circumstances as, for example, in the principle of *mens rea*. Thus, the legal code itself supplies potential rationalizations for violation.

Sykes and Matza maintain that much delinquency is based upon such justifications.[3] They contend that, while excuses are usually considered to be rationalizations following violation, they might also be viewed as neutralizations which occur prior to deviant behavior. That is, the actor learns certain excuses or justifications for violation and is therefore able to violate the very norms to which he is at least partially committed. The following major "techniques of neutralization" were specified: (1) the

Reprinted from *Criminologica*, IV, 2 (August 1966), 22–32, by permission of the publisher and the author.

[1] Reckless, Walter C., *The Etiology of Delinquent and Criminal Behavior* (New York, Social Science Research Council, Bulletin 50, 1943), 51–52.

[2] Sykes, Gresham M., and David Matza, "Techniques of Neutralization: A Theory of Delinquency," *American Sociological Review*, 22, 6 (December, 1957), 664–673.

[3] A more recent exposition of Matza's thinking is presented in David Matza, *Delinquency and Drift* (New York: John Wiley and Sons, 1964). Certain valuable leads are contained there, but the present study is based explicitly on the original article.

denial of responsibility, (2) the denial of injury, (3) the denial of the victim, (4) the condemnation of the condemners, and (5) the appeal to higher loyalties.

The research reported here was designed as a preliminary exploration of the neutralization theory, and it must be emphasized that the study provides no complete test. The theory asserts that (a) delinquents accept the techniques of neutralization and (b) this acceptance facilitates violation by neutralizing the norms. The present study explores the first assertion. Assessment of the second will require a longitudinal design beyond the limitations of this study. The essential hypothesis was that delinquent boys would accept more justifications for violation of law than would nondelinquent boys. Since there is apparently no single conception of delinquency which satisfies all students of the problem, three of the more common definitions were employed. The use of such definitions seemed most suitable at this stage of research.

CONSTRUCTION OF A NEUTRALIZATION INVENTORY

Since Sykes and Matza describe the techniques of neutralization as ". . . a system of beliefs and attitudes . . . ," [4] it seemed most desirable to attempt to measure neutralization by means of an attitude inventory. Such inventories are frequently criticized on grounds that (1) they elicit responses to highly generalized items which respondents may interpret differently, and (2) that such general responses have too little relationship to the overt behavior of respondents. The present study adopts the view of attitude which insists upon closer specification of the subject-object referents. Thus, Sherif and Cantril have argued that "attitudes are always related to definite stimuli or stimulus situations." [5] The neutralization inventory was therefore constructed so as to present the respondent with fairly specific stimulus situations.

Ten specific situations were developed, each describing the commission of some offense by a sixteen-year-old boy. Both personal and property offenses were represented, and the offenses were intended to reflect a rough continuum of severity. These variations were considered especially desirable as a means of increasing sensitivity (discrimination). The situations were written for sixth grade reading level and checked against published reading lists. In order to locate these situations along the assumed continuum of severity, the schedule of 10 situations was administered to a sample of 203 college students. The students were asked to rank the 10 situations, in terms of "seriousness" *as they felt their mothers would rank them.* Per-

[4] *Ibid.,* p. 670.

[5] Sherif, Muzafer, and Hadley Cantril, *The Psychology of Ego-Involvements: Social Attitudes and Identification* (New York: John Wiley and Sons, 1947), 19.

ceived ranking by the mother was obtained because her opinion seemed more likely to reflect conventional morality.

An exhaustive set of 790 items was prepared, an average of approximately 80 items for each of the 10 situations. Each item presented an excuse (neutralization) for the infractious behavior specified in the particular situation to which it pertained.[6]

The 790 items were then submitted to five judges for a "jury opinion" as to validity.[7] Judges were requested to rate each item as follows: "VD" (very definitely indicates a neutralization technique), "D" (definitely indicates a neutralization technique), "F" (fair indication of a neutralization technique), "N" (does not indicate a neutralization technique), and "DN" (definitely does not indicate a neutralization technique). In addition, the judges were instructed to edit or eliminate any item considered "ambiguous, incomplete, verbose, irrelevant, inconsistent, or in any other way unsatisfactory." General comments and suggestions were solicited. An item was retained only if all judges agreed that it "definitely" or "very definitely" represented neutralization.

The final inventory was reduced to 4 situations representing different points along the continuum of offense "seriousness" as defined by the 203 students' perceptions of mothers' ranking. The 4 situations included an equal number of personal and property offenses. Ten items (with the highest "neutralization ratings" given by the judges) were listed under each of the behavior situations. The inventory was intensively pretested with 5 fifteen and sixteen-year-old boys in detention at the Juvenile Center, Columbus, Ohio, in order to determine their comprehension of the verbal statements and any reluctance to respond or to disguise attitudes.[8]

ADMINISTRATION

The completed neutralization inventory formed the first part of a schedule which also included a set of items from the M.M.P.I., the Srole

[6] No attempt was made to identify an item specifically with one of the five techniques of neutralization. It was feared that such a method might result in arbitrary rejection of potentially powerful items which fit the theory but overlapped two or more of the techniques.

[7] Judges came from the Department of Sociology and Anthropology, The Ohio State University. They included two professors with specialities in criminology and deviant behavior, two professors with special competencies in research methods, and one advanced graduate student specializing in criminology. Each judge was given a reproduction of Sykes and Matza's original article, the set of 790 items subsumed under the 10 situations, and a set of instructions requesting him to rate each item according to how well it indicated neutralization as defined by Sykes and Matza.

[8] The five boys were randomly selected. An intensive pretest with a careful probing of each boy's understanding of every item was considered more desirable than a cursory survey of responses from a large number of boys.

Scale (anomia), as "Index of Incipient Alienation," an inventory of self-reported delinquency, and a background information section.[9]

After completion of the neutralization inventory, and subsequent to its administration to the high school boys, the author learned that another attempt was being made to devise an index of neutralization, for administration to the institutionalized delinquents only. This instrument was attached to the original schedule.[10] It was felt that some additional evidence of validity might be gained from the correlation of scores on the two independently prepared measures.

Data were obtained for two separate groups of adolescent boys. One group consisted of 197 boys from Central High School, Columbus, Ohio. The second group included 200 boys enrolled in the academic program at the Fairfield School for Boys, Lancaster, Ohio. (The latter is a state institution for male juvenile delinquents.) It was felt that a more meaningful comparison could be made by sampling from this particular segment of the institutionalized population. The two groups, with age ranges from fifteen to eighteen, were virtually identical in age distribution. All respondents were working class boys; the North-Hatt Score distributions were nearly identical for the two groups.[11]

Since even an initial exploration of hypotheses regarding neutralization would be of little value without a reasonably reliable and valid measure of neutralization, an analysis of the neutralization inventory was undertaken

[9] Hathaway and Monachesi have reported the specific M.M.P.I. items as those discovered to be most closely associated with delinquency. See Hathaway, Starke R., and Elio D. Monachesi, *Adolescent Personality and Behavior* (Minneapolis: The University of Minnesota Press, 1963), 89–90.

The Srole Scale (anomia) is widely used to determine the degree to which the individual feels that (1) social leaders are indifferent to his problems, (2) there is little chance for accomplishment in what is an unpredictable society, (3) goals are receding from him, (4) no one can really be counted on to support him, and (5) life itself is meaningless and futile. See Leo Srole, "Social Integration and Certain Corollaries: An Exploratory Study," *American Sociological Review*, Vol. 21, No. 6 (December, 1956), 709–716.

The "Index of Incipient Alienation" is designed to indicate early development stages of alienation in which the adolescent becomes estranged from proximate social system. See Jarrett, William H., and Archibald O. Haller, "Situational and Personal Antecedents of Incipient Alienation: An Exploratory Study," *Genetic Psychology Monographs*, Vol. 69 (1964), 670–677.

The inventory of self-reported delinquency was based on a 7-item scale developed by Nye and Short. One item of the 7-item scale had to be deleted to insure that the instrument could be used with the intended respondents. The abridged inventory was used as one operational measure of delinquency. See Nye, F. Ivan, and James F. Short, Jr., "Scaling Delinquent Behavior," *American Sociological Review*, Vol. 22, No. 3 (June, 1957), 326–331.

[10] This instrument was prepared by Terry Nesbit, Ohio University, Athens, Ohio.

[11] For purposes of the study, working class was defined as a score of 70 or below on an interpolated North-Hatt Scale. See "The North-Hatt Scale" (mimeographed report, The Ohio State University, Columbus, n.d.).

prior to testing of hypotheses. Reliability was established by use of the Kuder Richardson Formula.[12]

Although, according to the consensus of the judges, the inventory appeared to possess face validity, additional evidence was sought. Correlations, obtained between the neutralization inventory and the various measures discussed above, tended to substantiate the claim for reasonable validity of the former.[13]

FINDINGS

The essence of Sykes and Matza's theory lies in the hypothesized connection between two variables—neutralization and delinquency. Neutralization was operationally defined in terms of scores on the neutralization inventory; for purposes of this study three different definitions of delinquency were employed, each of which represents an admittedly oversimplified dichotomy of "delinquents" and "nondelinquents." Again, it seemed advisable to employ these gross distinctions during an initial exploration. For similar reasons, two-tailed t-tests were used throughout as difference tests.

Following a simple dichotomy between boys committed to an institution (delinquents) and those not in such an institution (nondelinquents), comparisons were made between the Central High School group and the Fairfield School group. The institutionalized delinquents scored significantly higher $(P < .001)$ on the neutralization inventory, and on each of its four subscales, than did the high school boys. There was no significant difference between the scores of older (17–18 years old) and younger (15–16 years old) boys within each group. Negro boys tended to score somewhat higher than did the white boys in the same group, but

[12] Kuder, G. F., and M. W. Richardson, "The Theory of Estimation of Test Reliability," *Psychometrika*, 1957, 151–160. Reliability coefficients were computed for the total neutralization inventory and for each of the four subscales (individual situations with a set of ten items respectively). The reliability coefficient for the entire inventory was .98; reliability coefficients for the subscales were .91, .95, .92, and .94 respectively.

[13] Since neutralization is theoretically associated with other variables, scores on a valid neutralization inventory should be positively correlated with scores on inventories designed to measure these other variables (assuming their validity). On the other hand, extremely high correlations might suggest that the inventories were measuring essentially the same variable. To provide some modest supplementary evidence regarding validity, Pearsonian correlation coefficients were computed for the two samples separately. For the high school boys correlation between the neutralization inventory and the M.M.P.I. items, Index of Incipient Alienation, and the Srole Scale were .46, .17, and .33 respectively. For the institutionalized delinquents correlation between the neutralization inventory and the other measures were .36, .28, and .41 respectively. The coefficients are statistically significant $(P < .05)$. It appears that these instruments do measure variables related to, but different from, that measured by the neutralization inventory, although correlations between the latter and the Index of Incipient Alienation were lower than expected.

the difference was statistically significant $(P < .05)$ on two subscales only. Since the computation of so many difference tests increases the probability of obtaining one or more which will be statistically significant, these findings were regarded as highly tentative.

While they do not establish any clear connection between neutralization and race, the findings do suggest that race should be controlled in the analysis of neutralization scores. Taking white boys only, the results showed that the institutionalized delinquents scored significantly higher $(P < .01)$ on the neutralization inventory, and each of its four subscales, than did the high school boys. Similarly, the Negro institutionalized delinquents scored significantly higher $(P < .01)$ on the neutralization inventory, and on each subscale, than did the Negro high school boys. The differences apparently hold regardless of race.

Fifty of the 197 high school boys, while not meeting the criterion of institutionalization, did themselves report juvenile court appearances. Since delinquency has frequently been defined in terms of juvenile court appearances, a second definition was employed. The second definition of delinquency was based not only upon institutionalization, but also upon self reported court appearances.

The neutralization theory would lead one to hypothesize significant differences between the high school boys reporting court appearances and those reporting none. This hypothesis was substantiated; the high school boys reporting juvenile court appearances scored significantly higher $(P < .001)$ on the neutralization inventory, and on each of its subscales, than did the high school boys reporting no appearances. The Negro high school boys reporting court appearances scored significantly higher $(P < .01)$ than those Negro boys reporting no appearances; the white high school boys reporting appearances scored significantly higher $(P < .01)$ than those white boys reporting no such appearances. The differences then, hold within each racial category.

In an effort to explore further than relation of court appearances to neutralization, the institutionalized delinquents were subdivided into two groups, by dichotomizing at the median number of reported juvenile court appearances. No significant differences appeared, either on the neutralization inventory or any of its four subscales, between the institutionalized boys reporting "many" and those reporting "few" juvenile court appearances. There were no significant differences between the Negro institutionalized delinquents with "few" and those with "many" appearances, and there were no significant differences between the white institutionalized delinquents with "few" and those with "many" court appearances.

To probe still further, comparisons were made between the scores of all high school boys reporting some juvenile court appearances and the institutionalized delinquents reporting few (below the median number for all the institutionalized boys) such appearances. Again, no significant differences appeared. The findings were essentially the same when the two racial categories were kept separate. There were no significant differences, either on the total neutralization inventory or on any of its four subscales, between the Negro high school boys reporting some appearances and Negro institutionalized delinquents reporting few appearances. No significant difference appeared between the two groups of white boys, with one exception. A significant difference (P < .05) appeared on one subscale only. This single exception offers no substantial support for a hypothesis of neutralization differences, especially in view of the increased probability resulting from so many computations.

Since both institutional commitment and self reported court involvements fail to take account of intervening variables such as detection, willingness to report, and willingness to hold for court action, a third definition of delinquency was also employed. The third definition of delinquency was based on self reported involvement in delinquent behavior. The problem of the delinquent-nondelinquent dichotomy becomes especially obvious here, since few of the boys were expected to be so "good" as to report no violations at all.

To provide for direct comparison with the findings previously discussed, all 397 boys were placed in one of two categories by dichotomizing at the median of scores on the abridged Nye-Short scale of self reported delinquency. These two categories were referred to as "more seriously delinquent" boys and "less seriously delinquent" boys, respectively.

The neutralization theory would lead one to expect a significant difference in neutralization scores for the two groups of boys. This hypothesis is supported by the findings. The boys with many self reported delinquent acts scored significantly higher (P < .001) on the neutralization inventory, and on each of its four subscales, than did the boys with few self reported violations.

Since it seemed conceivable that these differences might hold for one racial category but not another, separate tests were again made for white and Negro boys. All white boys in the study were divided into two categories, by dichotomizing the white respondents at the median scores on the abridged Nye-Short scale. The findings indicated that the more seriously delinquent white boys (above the median for whites) scored significantly higher (P < .001) on the neutralization inventory and on each of the four subscales, than did the less seriously delinquent (below the median for whites) white boys. The more seriously delinquent Negro boys (above the median Negro score on the abridged Nye-Short scale) scored significantly higher (P < .001) on the neutralization inventory and on each of its four subscales than did their less seriously delinquent (below the median) counterparts. The differences, then, hold within each racial category.

CONCLUSIONS

Summarized in terms of an admittedly oversimplified dichotomy, the results of this study reinforce the general argument that "delinquents" tend to accept more excuses for a variety of offenses than do "nondelinquents." Specifically, the differences appear for both personal and property offenses, and along a continuum of severity, no matter whether the "delinquent" is defined as a boy who has been committed to an institution or one who has reported a high incidence of delinquent behavior. If juvenile court appearances are used to define delinquency, the findings suggest greater acceptance of these excuses for boys with such appearances, but no significant differences with the occurrance of institutionalization or between institutionalized boys with "few" and those with "many" appearances.[14] It may be that acceptance of excuses facilitates initial stages of delinquency, while other factors more adequately explain the persistence and severity of delinquency.

These findings, then, support Sykes and Matza's assertion that delinquents will accept the techniques of neutralization more than will nondelinquents. The data do not allow us to specify whether the excuses are accepted before, during, or after delinquency. The next logical step would be to investigate the assertion that acceptance of these excuses precedes delinquency and makes it possible.

Sykes and Matza's statement is not only a theory of neutralization: it is also an explicit denial of Cohen's "delinquency subculture" thesis. The neutralization theory maintains that most delinquents do not adhere to a different (subcultural) set of norms, but rather that they basically adhere to the conventional norms while accepting many justifications for deviance. In this sense, the norms have been "eroded" but not substantially replaced. The findings tend to support this position. Possible scores on the neutralization inventory range from 40 to 200, yet the mean score for all institutionalized delinquents was only 111. While these findings cannot be generalized to the entire population of institutionalized delinquents, they indicate that the attitudes of boys in the specific sample were not as deviant as the "delinquent subculture" thesis suggests. In fact, if adherence to a set of norms is viewed as a continuum extending from total commitment to rejection and substitution, the boys' attitudes were not even as far into "neutralization" as might have been expected.[15]

[14] Although the distribution of self-reported appearances did reflect what was known from the records of the boys, the requirement of respondent anonymity made it impossible to verify the self reports individually. No attempt was made to identify the nature of the offense which led to a specific court appearance. It is, of course, possible to argue that a boy reporting one appearance for a serious offense is "more delinquent" than another boy reporting five appearances for minor offenses (who may have actually been innocent of one or more charges). The reported court appearance is thus a very gross index of delinquency, but one suitable for exploration.

[15] Matza has recently suggested that the individual delinquent may not be as com-

While referring to techniques of neutralization as a "theory" of delinquency, Sykes and Matza clearly recognized that neutralization could be considered as one component of some more general "theory." Differential association theory was mentioned in the original article, but Matza has come to view this and other sociological theories as overly deterministic.[16] Actually, certain theoretical clarifications make it *possible* to incorporate neutralization into at least one more general theory of delinquency, and to use the above data as an indirect test of this more general theory.

The support for Sykes and Matza's neutralization theory may be interpreted as support for Reckless' and Shoham's "norm erosion" thesis, and at a more general level, as support for Reckless' "containment theory." [17] The containment theory stresses the chances of becoming involved in delinquency or crime. The basic contribution of this approach lies in its blending of self factors (inner containment) with social factors (outer containment). The theory is regarded as non-causal; "good" inner and "good" outer containments minimize the chance of delinquency involvement, while "poor" inner and "poor" outer containments produce the highest expectancy for delinquency. Containment theory applies only to the broad "middle range" of delinquency: "extreme personal disorders and extreme identification with a delinquent subculture" are specifically excluded.[18]

Containment theory has been cast at a very general level. The subsuming nature of the approach is an asset: it attempts to pull together previously separate and ostensibly discordant explanations. Yet such efforts at generalization often end in deceptive generality.

The "theory" which purports to explain so much may explain nothing. Any explanation should be divisible into connected propositions which may be posed as researchable hypotheses. Thus, attempts have been made to identify, measure, and relate the various self factors which together form "inner containment." [19] The theory has never been considered as complete and "closed."

---

mitted to delinquency as he appears, but may rather be responding to misunderstandings which have led him to believe that his companions are highly committed. (See Matza, *op. cit.*, pp. 50–59.)

[16] *Ibid.*, pp. 1–32.

[17] Reckless, Walter C., *The Crime Problem* (New York: Appleton-Century-Crofts, 1961), pp. 332–333; Reckless, Walter C., "A Non-causal Explanation: Containment Theory," *Excerpta Criminologica*, Vol. 2, No. 2, 1962, pp. 131–134; Reckless, Walter C., and Shlomo Shoham, "Norm Containment Theory as Applied to Delinquency and Crime," *Excerpta Criminologica*, Vol. 3, No. 6, 1963, pp. 1–9.

[18] Some confusion may be resolved by emphasizing that containment theory is built on the concept of "risk" rather than pure determinism.

[19] Reckless, Walter C., Simon Dinitz, and Ellen Murray, "Self Concept as an Insulator Against Delinquency," *American Sociological Review*, 21, 6 (December, 1956), pp. 744–746; Dinitz, Simon, Frank R. Scarpitti, and Walter C. Reckless, "Delinquency

Reckless and Shoham have recently suggested that "norm erosion" (the sloughing off of the moral significance of norms, the neutralization of the oughtness, the emancipation from internalized norms, etc.) is one important factor operating to reduce the holding power of inner containment. A variety of processes (e.g., incipient alienation, alienation, anomia, neutralization, etc.) might be expected to contribute to any such erosion, and the major source of this erosion might vary with different categories of actors.

Rather than indicating that neutralization is the single factor leading to delinquency, the findings may be interpreted as suggesting that *neutralization is one self factor which, in contributing to norm erosion, weakens inner containment and increases the risk of delinquency.*[20] This conclusion seems preferable. Delinquency consists of many different kinds of behavior, and it seems probable that different combinations of self factors, along with outer containments, will be associated with these different forms of delinquency. It is possible that neutralization is the most significant of these self factors for certain forms of gang delinquency (where the excuses may be learned and accepted) but less important as an explanation of lone delinquency. It is possible that neutralization will characterize some gang members, while a few may actually have inverted the norms in the manner suggested by Cohen's delinquent subculture hypothesis.

This study is considered only a rough preliminary step to further investigation of neutralization. Such research will probably require improved measures of neutralization, more sophisticated definitions of delinquency, and statistical techniques beyond simple difference tests. Above all, further research must specify whether acceptance of various justifications does in fact precede and effectively facilitate delinquency.

Vulnerability: A Cross Group and Longitudinal Analysis," *American Sociological Review*, 27, 4 (August, 1962), pp. 515–517; Scarpitti, Frank R., "Differential Socialization: The Delinquent Versus the Nondelinquent" (unpublished doctoral thesis, The Ohio State University, 1962); Landis, Judson R., "Social Class Differentials in Self, Value, and Opportunity Orientation as Related to Delinquency Potential" (unpublished doctoral thesis, The Ohio State University, 1962).

[20] This conclusion is supported by the findings, which show that the M.M.P.I. items, the Srole Scale, and the Index of Incipient Alienation also distinguished between the high school boys and the institutionalized delinquents. Other studies have discovered still different self factors which seem to be associated with delinquency, and some investigations have indicated that self factors may actually vary among types of delinquents. See, for example, Kinch, John W., "Self Conceptions of Types of Delinquents," *Sociological Inquiry*, 32 (Spring, 1962), pp. 228–234.

22

Two Dimensions of Conformity-Nonconformity

RICHARD H. WILLIS

Washington University

Walker and Heyns[1] have recently proposed a conceptualization of social influence which contrasts conformity with nonconformity. Others, such as Asch[2] and Jahoda,[3] prefer to contrast conformity with independence. In either case it is assumed that reactions to social pressures can be described in terms of a single response dimension.

Such unidimensional approaches have maintained a virtual monopoly on thinking in the areas of social influence and attitude change, but dissatisfaction has been expressed in some quarters recently. Kretch, Crutchfield, and Ballachey[4] introduce the concept of *counterformity*, which appears to be the obverse of conformity, and on page 507 comment: "Conformity, independence, and counterformity are thus not to be thought of as three points along a single continuum. Rather they represent vertices of a triangle."

Elsewhere[5] the author has advocated a conceptual framework which is similar in some ways to that of Kretch, Crutchfield, and Ballachey. The term *anticonformity* is used instead of counterformity. More importantly, two dimensions of response are introduced in order to specify precisely the interrelations among the three vertices of the triangle. The first of these dimensions is that of *dependence-independence*, while the second is that of *conformity-anticonformity*.

The purpose of this paper is to explicate an experimental technique which allows the simultaneous measurement of these two dimensions of

Reprinted from *Sociometry*, 26, 4 (December 1963), 499–513, by permission of the author and The American Sociological Association.

[1] Edward L. Walker and Roger W. Heyns, *An Anatomy for Conformity*, Englewood Cliffs, N.J.: Prentice-Hall, 1962.

[2] Solomon E. Asch, "Studies of Independence and Conformity: A Minority of One Against a Unanimous Majority," *Psychological Monographs*, 70 (No. 9, Whole No. 416, 1956).

[3] Marie Jahoda, "Conformity and Independence: A Psychological Analysis," *Human Relations*, 12 (April, 1959), pp. 99–120.

[4] David Kretch, Richard S. Crutchfield, and Egerton L. Ballachey, *Individual in Society*, New York: McGraw-Hill, 1962.

[5] Richard H. Willis, "Conformity, Independence, and Anticonformity," submitted for publication.

response. The underlying logic will be considered, and an example will be provided.

THE MEASURES

The two dimensions are represented as orthogonal [6] to one another, as shown in Figure 7-1. The dependence-independence (or independence) di-

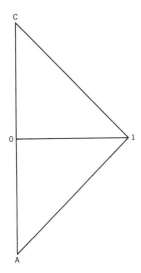

FIGURE 7-1
Relationships between conformity, independence, and anticonformity

mension is the horizontal axis, while the vertical axis is the conformity-anticonformity (or net conformity) dimension. The three vertices represent *conformity* (Point C), *independence* (Point I), and *anticonformity* (Point A). These three basic ways of responding to felt social pressures are referred to as *modes of response.*

Pure dependence behavior can fall anywhere along Line CA. Points along Line CI represent various combinations of conformity and independence, with no trace of anticonformity. Points within the triangle correspond to possible combinations of all three modes of response. That the figure is triangular, converging as it does at Point I, reflects the fact that the more independent an individual is, the less conformity or anticonformity he can exhibit. The completely independent person may *happen* to behave in ways which are prescribed or proscribed by the norms of his group, but this is incidental. It should also be noted that pure anti-

---

[6] Representing the two dimensions as orthogonal does not, of course, imply that the two sets of scores will necessarily be uncorrelated.

conformity behavior, like pure conformity behavior, is pure dependence behavior.

The conceptual scheme embodied in Figure 7-1 has considerable intuitive appeal, but in order for its potentialities to be realized, it is necessary to specify operations whereby subjects can be assigned positions along each of the two dimensions.

For purposes of simplicity, consider the simplest social situation, the dyad. Assume that both individuals are required to make binary judgments about identical stimuli. The usual procedure in a social influence experiment would be to require one of the subjects, S, to follow the other on each trial. Call this other, going first on each trial, the model, M. It would be customary in such a situation to define operationally the conformity of S as the frequency with which S agrees with M over that expected by chance. Almost exactly this procedure was employed by Croner and Willis,[7] and literally hundreds of studies have been conducted which equate conformity with level of congruence between the behavior of S and that of one or more others.

This "conformity as congruence" approach can be criticized for failing to differentiate between *intended* agreement and *incidental* agreement. Under certain circumstances it is reasonable to assume that S exhibits behavior like that of M just because each has independently formulated similar conclusions. Likewise, S may behave differently from M just because he has independently arrived at different attitudes or beliefs. Another way of phrasing essentially the same criticism is to say that this approach is unidimensional, failing to distinguish between the two dimensions of response diagrammed in Figure 1. It is relevant in this connection to recall that, to the extent that one is independent, one cannot exhibit either conformity or anticonformity, although an independent S can show any degree of overt agreement with M. The problem, then, is to develop procedures which do distinguish between intended and incidental agreement.

Leverage on the problem can be gained by collecting more data on each trial. Let S make the first judgment, M the second, and finally give S an opportunity to change his initial response. Further assume that M is a confederate of the experimenter.

With three binary responses per trial, there are eight possible outcomes on each, and considerations of symmetry allow these to be grouped into four basic *response patterns:*

$$C: +-- \text{ or } -++$$
$$I: +-+ \text{ or } -+-$$
$$A: ++- \text{ or } --+$$
$$U: +++ \text{ or } ---$$

[7] Melvyn D. Croner and Richard H. Willis, "Perceived Differences in Task Competency and Asymmetry of Dyadic Influence," *Journal of Abnormal and Social Psychology*, 62 (May, 1961), pp. 705–708.

C, I, and A stand for conformity, independence, and anticonformity, respectively, for reasons which should be fairly apparent. Thus, for the trial outcome $+--$, M disagrees with the initial judgment of S, and on his second response S changes his judgment so as to agree with that of M. This is clearly describable as conformity behavior on the part of S. Response pattern U cannot be given such a clear-cut interpretation. It appears to be an equivocal hybrid of conformity and independence, and it is therefore assigned the noncommittal label of U for uniformity.

If M agrees and disagrees equally often with the initial responses of S, and let us assume that this is the case,[8] then the sum of the frequencies for the C and I patterns will equal the sum of the frequencies for the A and U frequencies. This is true because C and I patterns appear on disagreement-trials while A and U patterns appear on agreement-trials.

In other words, if M disagrees with his initial response, S must choose between displaying a C pattern or an I pattern. If M agrees, the choice is between A and U patterns. In order to determine the proportion of times S resolves each of these two kinds of decisions in each of the two possible ways, the frequencies C, I, A, and U are converted into proportions of maximum values; designate these proportions c, i, a, and u. For example, assume that on the disagreement-trials S chooses the C pattern 15 times and the I pattern 35 times; c would be .30 and i would be .70.

Now consider an "obvious" method of computing scores. Let the independence score be equal to i and the net conformity score be equal to $c - a$. These equations seem plausible enough at first glance. Still, on reflection one might wonder why the proportion u does not appear in either one of them, since each of the four response patterns has the same logical status.

A more specific (and less visceral) objection is that these equations do not yield the relationships required by the conceptual framework of Figure 1. Consider, for example, the S who invariably disagrees on his second response with the response given by M. Such behavior, which is describable as pure anticonformity behavior, produces the following proportions: $c = .00$, $i = 1.00$, $a = 1.00$, and $u = .00$. Applying the above equations yields a net conformity score of -1.00 and an independence score of 1.00. The subject shows maximal anticonformity, but, at the same time, maximal independence! This is in contradiction to the conceptual framework of Figure 1, for there is no place in the figure for such a combination of scores. The problem which must be solved is that of determining a scoring system which allows only those combinations of scores specified by the model.

In order to derive a more satisfactory set of scoring formulas, it is convenient to introduce the concept of *boundary strategies*. One such bound-

[8] It is not necessary that M agree and disagree equally often with the subject's initial responses, but fulfilling this condition has the advantage of optimizing the accuracy with which response pattern proportions are estimated.

ary strategy has just been described, that of always disagreeing with M. There are three other such boundary strategies whereby S can determine his second response—always agreeing with M, always agreeing with his own initial response, and always disagreeing with his own initial response. The defining conditions of these boundary strategies, the response patterns generated by each, and corresponding locations in Figure 1 are as follows:

Strategy	Condition	Response Patterns	Location
S_e	$s_2 = m$	C and U	Point C
S_i	$s_2 = s_1$	I and U	Point I
S_a	$s_2 \neq m$	A and I	Point A
S_o	$s_2 \neq s_1$	C and A	Point O

The assignments of locations in Figure 1 are based on psychological considerations. For example, if S invariably agrees with M, this is clearly interpretable as pure conformity behavior, and assignment to Point C is consequently made. Similarly, always agreeing with one's initial response and always disagreeing with M are interpretable, respectively, as pure independence behavior and pure anticonformity behavior. Points I and A are accordingly assigned.

Boundary strategy S_o is a bit special. One interpretation is that of self-anticonformity, or inconsistency, since S insists on disagreeing with his initial response at every opportunity. The likelihood of such a motive operating with any force seems remote, however. An alternate interpretation is to consider this kind of behavior as an equal mixture of conformity and anti-conformity, since it leads to an equal proportion of Patterns C and A. This suggests that such behavior be located midway along Line CA, at Point O.

If it is granted that the four boundary strategies correspond to the locations on Triangle CIA as indicated, then how are intermediate cases to be dealt with? Consider the case in which no patterns of type A occur. This implies $a = 0$ and $u = 1$; as always, $c + i = 1$. Since points C and I both correspond to $u = 1$, it is reasonable to locate cases for which $a = 0$ and $u = 1$ along Line CI at a distance from C proportionate to the magnitude of i. This is represented by Point U in Figure 7-2. In a similar manner, cases for which $a = 1$ and $u = 0$ are located between Points O and A at a distance from O proportionate to the magnitude of i. This appears as Point V in Figure 2. In brief, the magnitude of i (or c, which is $1 - i$) determines the location of Line UV. Cases for which $1 > a > 0$ (or for which $0 < u < 1$), can be located along Line UV at a distance from U proportionate to the magnitude of a. This general case is labelled $P(x,y)$ in Figure 7-2.

It remains to express the coordinates of P algebraically. Letting the

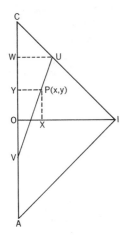

FIGURE 7-2
Construction for deriving the x and y scores

distance from the origin at O to any vertex equal unity, $OV = i$. This follows from the rule for locating V. Construct WU, parallel to OI. From the rule for locating U, $CU/CI = CU/\sqrt{2} = i$. It can furthermore be shown that the triangle CWU is isosceles, and thus $CW = WU = i$. Therefore, $WV = 1$, and $UV = \sqrt{1^2 + i^2}$. From the procedure for locating $P(x,y)$ along UV, $VP = u\sqrt{1^2 + i^2}$. By similar triangles, $YP/WU = u\sqrt{1^2 + i^2}/\sqrt{1^2 + i^2}$, or $x/i = u$. Consequently,

$$x = ui. \tag{1}$$

By the Pythagorean theorem, $VY^2 = u^2(1^2 + i^2) - u^2i^2 = u^2$. Therefore, $VY = u$, and $y = u - i$. Because $u = 1 - a$, and $i = 1 - c$, this can be re-written as

$$y = c - a. \tag{2}$$

Formula (2) is identical with the "obvious" formula for net conformity considered above, but Formula (1), for the independence score, has acquired a u as a coefficient. The revised formulas not only give u a role equally prominent to those given the proportions for the other response patterns (thus pleasing symmetrophiles), but they also yield the relationships required by the conceptual framework. Each possible combination of values of x and y corresponds to a location within or along the perimeter of Triangle CIA, and, conversely, each such location corresponds to a possible score combination.

Consider again the subject who caused so much trouble above by invariably disagreeing with the responses of the model. His net conformity score is still -1.00, but his independence score, by Formula (1), is zero. There is now a place for this subject, namely at Point A.

The changing slope of UV is of significance. When $c = 1$ and $i = 0$, the slope of UV is positive infinity. This means that response patterns of type U are, in effect, interpreted as indicative of pure conformity, for an increase in u produces an equal increase in y. Conversely, type A response patterns are interpreted as indicative of pure anticonformity, and an increase in a results in an equal decrease in y. The value of x remains constant at zero.

At the other extreme, when $c = 0$ and $i = 1$, the slope of UV is $+1$. Now each occurrence of the type U response pattern increments x and y equally. The type U pattern is interpreted psychologically as representing an equal mixture of conformity and independence behaviors. Response patterns of type A are now taken as equally indicative of anticonformity and dependence behaviors, for an increase in a produces equal decrements of x and y.

It is also possible to demonstrate that response patterns of type C and I affect x and y scores in a variable manner, depending upon the relative frequencies of u and a. This can be done by deriving the equations for x and y in an alternate way. A point S is located on CO at a distance from C proportionate to a, and a point T is located on IA at a distance from I also proportionate to a. $P(x,y)$ is then located on line ST at a distance from S proportionate to i (ST is not shown in Figure 2). Considerations of symmetry make it clear that the equations for x and y will be the same as those derived by the first method.

When $u = 0$ and $a = 1$, the slope of line ST will be negative infinity. Then type C response patterns will contribute positively to the y score, while type I patterns will diminish the value of y. The type C patterns are interpreted as pure conformity, while the type I patterns are interpreted as pure anticonformity. Neither type of pattern will have an effect on x, which remains equal to 0. When $u = 1$ and $a = 0$, the slope of ST equals -1. Type C patterns will then decrease x and increase y, while type I patterns will have the exact opposite effect. The former are interpreted as an equal mixture of independence and anticonformity.

A careful consideration of the nature of these interdependencies leads to the conclusion that the assumptions underlying Formulas (1) and (2) are tenable from a psychological point of view. Thus, as we have seen, when S exhibits maximum conformity on disagreement-trials, the ambiguous type U pattern is interpreted wholly as conformity, whereas maximum independence on disagreement-trials leads to an interpretation of the type U pattern as an equal mixture of conformity and independence. Similarly, maximal anticonformity on agreement trials implies an interpretation of type I patterns as pure anticonformity, while minimal anticonformity on agreement-trials leads to an interpretation of type *I* patterns as an equal mixture of independence and anticonformity.

AN EXPERIMENTAL ILLUSTRATION

An experiment was conducted with two basic objectives in mind.[9] The first was to test the technique detailed above for practicality and convenience. The second was to demonstrate results not accommodated by a unidimensional framework.

Ss were 54 lower division students at Washington University. Thirty-six were run in a 2 × 2 factorial design, while the remaining 18 constituted a control group. Two levels each of perceived task competency of *M*, and liking for *M*, were employed. All Ss were run with an *M* of the same sex and by an experimenter of the same sex. *M* was, of course, a confederate of the experimenter.

Stimuli were 100 lines drawn on cardboard. Under each line appeared a numerically expressed comparison length. The task was to judge whether the line was longer or shorter than the comparison length. In actuality, each line was *exactly equal* to the comparison length, but Ss were told that lines would be longer and shorter equally often.

On each trial S made an initial response, followed by *M*'s response, followed by S's second response. *M*'s responses were programmed to agree and disagree equally often with the initial responses of S. *M* was allowed to observe the initial responses of S, but second responses were made behind a screen.

The experiment was presented to S as an attempt to develop a technique for increasing the accuracy of perceptual judgments by the use of two observers instead of one. He was told that making reports of the highest possible accuracy was his primary responsibility, and that he was free to make as much or as little use as he wished of his partner's judgments.

Level of liking of *M* by S was manipulated by means of an exchange of notes prior to presentation of stimuli. The experimenter explained that people sometimes work better together if not totally unacquainted, and requested S and *M* to write *self descriptions* of about 100 words, using "whatever terms you feel are most appropriate for conveying an accurate impression of yourself to your partner." In the exchange, S received a prewritten note. In the high liking condition *M* described himself in favorable but modest terms, while in the low liking condition he revealed himself to be a despicable snob.

[9] Experimenters, other than the author, were Daniel Abbott, Jane Brownstone, Virginia Carpenter, Ruth Cotter, William Feigelman, Alston Kirk, David Ludwig, and Carl Pitts. The author would like to take this opportunity to acknowledge the substantial contributions made by these seminar participants to the design and execution of the experiment. A paper based on this experiment was presented at the Midwestern Psychological Association meeting in Chicago, May 1963.

The experimenter then requested S and M each to write a short *impression of partner*. It was implied that these would not be exchanged, to facilitate credibility, and when the experimenter collected the notes and exchanged them, M said "I thought you said these were to be confidential." The experimenter replied "I'm sorry if you misunderstood." The note read by S in the high liking condition was quite complimentary, while that in the low liking condition was definitely on the insulting side.

Perception of partner's task competency was manipulated by means of a note to S from the experimenter. When notes concerning impressions of partner were exchanged, the experimenter inserted a mimeographed form inside the note handed to S. This contained false information about the level of skill of M in making judgments of the same kind, presumably determined from his participation in an earlier experiment, plus a rationale for revealing this information to S. In the high perceived competency condition, M was said to be in the highest 2 per cent of college students, while in the low perceived competency condition, he was said to be in the lowest 2 per cent.

Following the experimental manipulations, S and M responded to the 100 stimuli, and finally a short post-experimental questionnaire was administered. The procedure used with Ss in the control group was exactly the same, except for the omission of the experimental manipulations.

From the standpoint of workability, this initial test of the technique was quite gratifying. The method was found to be both practicable and convenient, while more recent work (discussed in brief below) has shown it to possess a high degree of flexibility.

Results. A simple between-within analysis of variance indicated that the mean x-scores for the four experimental conditions did not differ significantly from one another. Moreover, a Duncan multiple range test[10] indicated that the largest and the smallest of these means did not differ significantly. The conclusion is warranted that the experimental manipu-

TABLE 1

Mean Independence of Partner (x-scores)

	Perceived Task Competency of Partner		
Liking for Partner	*Low*	*High*	*Mean*
High	.620	.449	.534
Low	.625	.620	.622
Mean	.622	.534	.578
Control group			.623

[10] David B. Duncan, "Multiple range and multiple F tests," *Biometrics*, 11 (March, 1955), pp. 1–42; Allen L. Edwards, *Experimental Design in Psychological Research*, Rev. ed., New York: Rinehart, 1960, see pp. 136–140.

lations had no significant effect on the extent to which Ss depended upon their partners in making their second judgments.

Analysis of variance applied to the y-scores yielded one significant effect. Extent of net conformity was significantly greater in the high than in the low perceived competency condition ($F = 6.35$, $df = 1/32$, p<.02. A Duncan multiple range test revealed significantly (p<.01) less net conformity in the low liking, lower perceived task competency condition than in the high liking, high perceived task competency condition. All other pairs of differences were not significantly different by the Duncan test.[11]

TABLE 2

Mean Net Conformity (y-scores)

	Perceived Task Competency of Partner		
Liking for Partner	*Low*	*High*	*Mean*
High	.284	.544	.414
Low	.258	.338	.298
Mean	.271	.441	.356
Control group			.340

The mean x-score for the control group was almost identical to those for the experimental conditions other than high liking, high perceived competency. The mean y-score for the control group was very nearly that for all four experimental conditions combined. In brief, the means for the control group did not differ appreciably from the corresponding overall means for experimental groups.

Discussion. If the one-dimensional model of Asch and Jahoda is adequate, the x- and y-scores will be perfectly and inversely correlated. The Asch/Jahoda model implies $a = 0$, and $u = 1$, which in turn implies $x = i$, and $y = c = 1 - i$. It would then make no difference which kind of scores were used, for both would lead to the same conclusions. The fact that x-

---

[11] The lack of any significant effects associated with levels of liking raises a question as to the success of this experimental manipulation. Two questions on the post-judgmental questionnaire allow a definite answer: the manipulation was outstandingly successful. Question 1 inquired directly about the degree of liking S had for M. The between-groups difference was in the appropriate direction and highly significant ($F = 42.55$, $df = 1/32$, $p < .0001$). Question 4 asked S to say how well he thought M liked him. Again the difference was in the appropriate direction and highly significant ($F = 53.15$, $df = 1/32$, $p < .0001$). In the planning of the experiment, it was hypothesized that the subject's liking for his partner could be manipulated by manipulating his perception of M's feelings towards him, and responses to Questions 1 and 4 are highly congruent with this hypothesis. Additional support for this hypothesis derives from the high correlation ($+.81$) between the two questions; this is significant beyond the .0001 level. An interesting characteristic of the scatter diagram was a pronounced "ceiling effect." In 52 of the 54 cases, the subject indicated that he liked M as well or better than M liked him in turn.

and y-scores yielded two distinctly different patterns of differences among group means demonstrates the insufficiency of the unidimensional model.

If anticonformity tendencies are absent—that is, if $a = 0$—the unidimensional model applies. All points $P(x, y)$ then lie along line CI. This single dimension, intersecting both axes at a 45 degree angle, suffices for plotting differences among Ss whose behavior contains no admixture of anticonformity. From this it can be seen that the conformity-independence-anticonformity model is not in strict opposition to the conformity-independence model. It is, rather, a generalization of it.

Despite the fact that the amount of anticonformity behavior present was sufficient to invalidate the unidimensional approach, such anticonformity tendencies were slight relative to the theoretical maximum. In a follow-up experiment by Willis and Hollander,[12] more pronounced differences were obtained. Each of the three experimental groups was run under conditions designed to elicit one of the three modes of response. In the case of the Independence group, the theoretical limit was closely approached. The Conformity and Anticonformity groups did not so closely approach their respective theoretical limits, but did display a considerable amount of movement over blocks of trials in the appropriate directions. Because between-group differences along *both* axes were highly significant, the results of this follow-up study demonstrate beyond any reasonable doubt the inadequacy of the unidimensional model.

The results of the present experiment are of some interest quite aside from the question of response dimensionality. Level of liking for partner had no significant effect on behavior, yet previous studies have almost invariably found conformity to be positively related to such factors as interpersonal attraction and group cohesiveness.[13] In fact, it is taken as axiomatic in Festinger's theory of informal social communication[14] that members of a group will conform to the extent to which they are attracted to the group. Why, then, does this usually efficacious variable fail to exert an effect here? In light of the highly successful experimental manipulation (see Footnote 11), this question demands an answer.

One obvious factor is that of group size. In a dyad the individual constitutes half the group; he cannot be put into the position of a minority. Furthermore, the subject interacted with his partner over a relatively short

[12] Richard H. Willis and E. P. Hollander, "An Experimental study of three response modes in social influence situations," *Journal of Abnormal and Social Psychology* (in press).

[13] E.g., Harold B. Gerard, "The Anchorage of Opinions in Face-to-Face Groups," *Human Relations*, 7 (August, 1954), pp. 313–325; Jay M. Jackson and Herbert D. Saltzstein, "The Effect of Person-Group Relationships on Conformity Processes," *Journal of Abnormal and Social Psychology*, 57 (July, 1958), pp. 17–24; Theodore M. Newcomb, *Personality and Social Change: Attitude Formation in a Student Community*, New York: Dryden, 1943.

[14] Leon Festinger, "Informal Social Communication," *Psychological Review*, 57 (September, 1950), pp. 271–282.

period of time—about an hour—and involvement with the partner was very likely superficial. He could be disliked, even intensely, but this dislike was probably of no great importance to the typical subject.

Because level of liking was manipulated in part by means of perceived acceptance by partner, and because liking and perceived acceptance were found to be highly correlated, some results of Argyle become relevant.[15] Also employing a dyadic social influence situation, he found no relationship between amount of influence and extent of perceived rejection by partner. This finding underscores the probable importance of the size of the group.

Another factor militating against the effect of liking for partner, probably a very important one, was the emphasis placed by the instructions on making accurate judgments. Thibaut and Strickland [16] found that a "task set" is accompanied by a greater resistance to social pressures than a "group set." In the present experiment a motivation to be accurate would make it reasonable to accept influence from a presumably skilled partner, but liking would be irrelevant.

An insightful perspective can be obtained by considering the group to be a triad rather than a dyad, with the experimenter being the third member. Even in the high perceived competency condition, the experimenter is viewed by the subject as being the ultimate authority. Thus, when the experimenter informs the subject that accuracy is the most important consideration, it is only to be expected that the subject adopts a "task set" rather than a "group set." Presumably, if the experimenter had suggested that the interpersonal relationship was the most important factor, and especially if the partner were allowed to observe the subject's second responses, level of liking would have been a more potent variable.

In any case, the assumption is usually made that interpersonal relations invariably affect susceptibility to social influence, but the present findings, as well as those of Argyle,[17] indicate that this assumption is not valid under all conditions.

VARIANTS OF THE TECHNIQUE

A few of the many possible modifications of the general procedure have been tried out in subsequent experimentation. A study by Landsbaum[18] employed a pseudo-interaction situation in which both members of the dyad were true subjects. The impression was created that the experimenter was transmitting information between subjects about initial responses on

[15] Michael Argyle, "Social Pressures in Public and Private Situations," *Journal of Abnormal and Social Psychology*, 54 (March, 1957), pp. 172–175.

[16] John W. Thibaut and Lloyd H. Strickland, "Psychological Set and Social Conformity," *Journal of Personality*, 25 (December, 1956), pp. 115–129.

[17] Argyle, *op. cit.*

[18] Jane Brownstone Landsbaum, MA thesis, in preparation, Washington University.

each trial, but in actuality the responses transmitted were predetermined. An obvious advantage of this variant is that subjects can be run twice as fast as the use of a confederate as model allows.

The study by Willis and Hollander[19] employed a pseudo-interaction situation and, in addition, provided feedback concerning the presumed correct answers after each trial. As might be expected, such feedback was found to be capable of producing powerful effects.

Yet another variation, not yet tested, is the use of multiple models displaying varying degrees of consensus among themselves. Problems of control and sequencing become considerably more complex with multiple models, however, and it is anticipated that the construction of special apparatus will be necessary before work can proceed in this direction.

[19] Willis and Hollander, *op. cit.*

For Further Reading

BOOKS

Berg, I. A., and Bass, B. M. (Eds.). *Conformity and deviation*. New York: Harper and Brothers, 1961.

A collection of papers which report current research and suggest ways of further study.

Walker, E. L., and Heyns, R. W. *An anatomy of conformity*. Englewood Cliffs, New Jersey: Prentice-Hall, 1962.

A study of the conditions under which conforming behavior is likely to occur.

ARTICLES

Allen, V. L., and Crutchfield, R. Generalization of experimentally reinforced conformity. *J. of abnorm. soc. Psychol.*, 1963, 67 (4), 326–333. PA 38, 4188.

Experimentally reinforced objective conformity did not generalize to some types of subjective material.

Asch, S. E. Issues in the study of social influences on judgment. In I. A. Berg and B. M. Bass (Eds.), *Conformity and deviation*. New York: Harper and Brothers, 1961, 143–158. PA 36, 4GE43A.

A description of some of the historical and recent issues involved in the topic, which includes a number of heterogeneous conditions.

Bass, B. M. Conformity, deviation, and a general theory of interpersonal behavior. In Berg and Bass, *Conformity and deviation*. Pp. 38–100. PA 36, 4GE38B.

Presents 37 theorems about conforming and deviant behavior.

Blake, J. and Davis, K. Norms, values and sanctions. Chapter 13, in R. F. L. Faris (Ed.), *Handbook of modern sociology*. Chicago: Rand, McNally, 1964. Pp. 456–484.

A good theoretical analysis.

Brittain, C. V. Adolescent choices and parent-peer pressures. *Amer. sociol. Review*, 1963, 28 (3), 385–391. PA 38, 2472.

Explores the conditions under which adolescents are peer-conforming and when parent-conforming.

Campbell, E. Q. The internalization of moral norms. *Sociometry*, 1964, 27 (4), 391–412. PA 39, 7489.

This paper reports the use of a semiprojective story completion technique to measure the internalization of an abstinence norm by high school seniors.

DiVesta, F. J. and Cox, L. Some dispositional correlates of conformity behavior. *J. of soc. Psychol.*, 1960, 52 (2), 259–268. PA 35, 4813.

Suggests that affiliative orientation, need achievement, ideology, sex and other variables are related to conformity.

Elliot, R. Use of a "Conformity" scale to assess vocational interests of undergraduates. *Psychol. Rep.*, 1965, *16* (3), 969–975. PA 39, 15228.

A conformity scale discriminates graduates from undergraduates and relates to postgraduate plans.

Endler, N. S. Conformity analyzed and related to personality. *J. of soc. Psychol.*, 1961, *53* (2), 273–283. PA 36, 1GE71.

Conformity is a function of the degree of social pressure and individual differences.

—— The effects of verbal reinforcement on conformity and deviant behavior. *J. of soc. Psychol.*, 1965, *66* (1), 147–154. PA 39, 15031.

Conformity is greatest when subjects are verbally reinforced by the experimenter for agreeing with a contrived group consensus, least when they are reinforced for disagreeing with the group; greatest in regard to verbal items, least regarding attitude items, with geometrical items in between.

Freedman, M. The dangers of nonconformism. *Amer. Scholar*, 1958–1959, *28* (1), 25–32, *passim*.

"One man's conformism may be another man's heresy," that is, to what is one conforming? An amusing article on how some who attack conformity conform in most of their behavior.

Gerard, H. Conformity and commitment to the group. *J. abnorm. soc. Psychol.*, 1964, *68* (2), 209–all. SA 13, B6756.

An individual who asserts his independence at the outset of an experiment, in public commitment, tends to continue to be independent.

Gibbs, J. P. Norms: the problem of definition and classification. *Amer. J. Sociol.*, 1965, *70* (5), 586–594. PA 39, 9875.

A critical appraisal of the concept and a proposed typology.

Gorfein, D. S., and Anderson, L. M. A note on the validity of the Bernberg Human Relations Inventory. *J. Psychol.*, 1962, *54* (1), 65–68. PA 37, 3008.

The Bernberg Human Relations Inventory was only partially supported as a measurement of conformity.

Hare, A. P. Interview responses: personality or conformity? *Publ. Opinion Quart.*, 1960, *24* (4), 679–685. SA 10, A2145.

Determined that personality differences of a sample of Negro and white mothers were due largely to the tendency of the Negro women to conform, that is to agree with items.

Hartley, R. E. Norm compatability, norm preference, and the acceptance of new reference groups. *J. of soc. Psychol.*, 1960, *52* (1), 87–95. PA 35, 6340.

An investigation of the relationship between perceptions of norm-congruity and the acceptance of a new group (freshmen) as a reference group.

Hawkins, N. E., and Meyer, M. E. Social values and conformity, *Psychonomic Science*, 1965, *2* (2), 31–32. PA 39, 7634.

On the basis of Allport-Vernon-Lindzey Scale of Values scores, a control and an experimental group were selected; contrived social pressure resulted in changes of values.

Hollander, E. P. Competence and conformity in the acceptance of influence. *J. Abnorm. soc. Psychol.*, 1960, *61* (2), 365–369. PA 36, 2GE65H.

Competency on a group task was associated with other's tendency to conform to the "leader"; past conformity was also related to present conformity.

——— Reconsidering the issue of conformity in personality. In H. P. David and J. C. Brengelmann, *Perspectives in personality research*. New York: Springer, 1960. Pp. 210–225. PA 35, 2116.

Laboratory studies of conformity are criticized. Conformity serves to maintain or increase status; but after status is established, greater freedom is permitted.

Hunt, R. G. *et al.* "Some Demographic Factors in Conforming Behavior." *Sociol. soc. Res.*, 1958, *42* (3), 196–198. SA 8, 7468.

Conformity was more apparent in students from relatively higher-income families; sex and religious affiliation were not related.

Kassarjian, W. M. and H. H. Conformity of judgment in a group situation. *Psychol. Rep.*, 1962, *10* (2), 491–494. PA 37, 3037.

Describes an attempt to conduct an experiment in conformity by a group rather than Asch's individual approach.

Katz, E. *et al.* Status mobility and reactions to deviance and subsequent conformity. *Sociometry*, 1964, *27* (3), 245–260. PA 39, 4745.

High status members whose rank is threatened by the conformity of a previously-deviant member do not reward the conforming behavior.

Lott, A. J. and B. E. Group cohesiveness, communication level, and conformity. *J. Abnorm. soc. Psychol.*, 1961, *62* (2), 408–412. PA 36, 4GE08L.

Both communication level and conformity behavior within groups vary positively with the degree of group cohesiveness.

Luchins, A. S. and E. H. On conformity with judgments of a majority or an authority. *J. soc. Psychol.*, 1961, *53* (2), 308–316. PA 36, 1GE03L.

Least correct responses (judgment of the length of lines) occurred when both the (instructed) majority and "authority" opposed the evidence; authority proved more effective than the majority.

Martin, J. G. Ideal and typical social norms. *Sociol. Inquiry*, 1964, *34* (1), 41–47. SA 13, B6694.

Ideal norms refer to how one ought to behave and typical norms refers to the actual behaviors of people.

Milgram, S. Liberating effects of group pressure. *J. Personality soc. Psychol.*, 1965, *1* (2), 127–134. SA 13, B6759.

This experiment shows that in specifiable circumstances, group pressure enables a person to resolve conflicting forces in a direction congruent with his values; that is, conformity may be constructive.

——— Nationality and conformity. *Scientific Amer.*, 1961, *205* (6), 45–52. PA 36, 4GB45M.

Conformity was found to be higher in Norway than in France.

Pepinsky, P. N. Social exceptions that prove the rule. In Berg and Bass, *op. cit.*, 380–411. PA 36, 4GE80P.

A report of several studies of socially constructive nonconformity.

Rosenberg, L. A. Conformity as a function of confidence in self and confidence in partner. *Hum. Relat.*, 1965, *16* (2), 131–139. PA 38, 5889.

Conformity is positively associated with increasing self-error and decreasing partner-error.

───── Group size, prior experience, and conformity. *J. abnorm. soc. Psychol.*, 1961, *63* (2), 436–437. PA 37, 1111.

There is a curvilinear relationship between the size of the group and the influence on the subject to conform; prior experience in judging length of lines is also related to accuracy of judgment.

Sherif, M. Conformity-deviation, norms and group relations. In Berg and Bass, *op. cit.*, 159–188. PA 36, 4GE59S.

Stresses the importance of thinking of conformity in relation to specific practices, values, moral standards, norms and the differences between laboratory situations and natural situations.

Slocum, W. L. and Stone, C. L. A method for measuring family images held by teen-agers. *Marriage Fam. Living*, 1959, *21* (3), 245–250. PA 36, 2FG45S.

There is a relationship between the images which teenagers have of their families and conforming behavior.

Smith, S. A. Conformity in cooperative and competitive groups. *J. of soc. Psychol.*, 1965, *65* (2), 337–350. PA 39, 15065.

People in a cooperative-group setting will conform more than people in a competitive-group setting.

Strickland, B. R., and Crowne, D. P. Conformity under conditions of simulated group pressure as a function of the need for social approval. *J. soc. Psychol.*, 1962, *58* (1), 171–181. PA 37, 6619.

Subjects with a high need for social approval conform significantly more often than those with a weaker need.

Turk, H. An inquiry into the undersocialized conception of man. *Social Forces*, 1965, *43* (4), 518–521. PA 39, 12155.

The behavior of an individual is governed by internalized norms and by the pressures of the social system. Members of the social system can agree more about what another member of the system should do than about what each should do himself.

Vaughan, G. M., Mangan, G. L. Conformity to group pressure in relation to the value of the task material. *J. abnorm. soc. Psychol.*, 1963, *66* (2), 179–183. PA 37, 6621.

Group pressure is resisted when highly valued material is utilized; susceptibility to influence increases with pressure.

Videbeck, R. Norm and status in sociological theory. *Sociol. Quart.*, 1964, *5* (3), 221–230. SA 13, B4893.

Norms are social, not individual; the percent of members who hold a particular normative opinion is important.

Vidulich, R. N., and Stabene, F. P. "Source certainty as a variable in conformity behavior." *J. soc. Psychol.*, 1965, *66* (2), 323–330. PA 39, 13587.

In an autokinetic experiment, a confederate who expressed high assurance induced greater conformity in the subject than when he expressed low assurance.

Wrench, D. and Endicott, K. Denial of affect and conformity. *J. Personality and soc. Psychol.*, 1965, 1 (5), 484–486. PA 39, 10013.

> Subjects who perceived a situation as having less emotional significance conformed more to group pressure.

Zelditch, M., "Values" institutionalized in the family. *Antioch Review*, 1957, 17 (4), 455–468. SA 7, 5898.

> A discussion of the sociological character of a norm and of the means by which norms are bound to the social life of a society through a process of institutionalization.

Chapter Eight

Values

One of the most ubiquitous, yet elusive concepts in social science is that of values. In its most elemental usage, a *value* is some attribute or object highly prized by the members of a society. Kluckhohn has proposed this definition: "A value is a conception, explicit or implicit, distinctive of an individual or characteristic of a group, of the desirable which influences the selection from available modes, means, and ends of action." [1] It has been the expectation that a knowledge of the values of a society or of individuals would make feasible the prediction of individual behavior and of social change, for values logically are virtually identical to the major goals or long-term desires of a group or persons, and means inconsistent towards those ends could not help but introduce strains into the social system.

We forego a systematic attempt at definition, deferring to the rather exhaustive survey by Allen Barton. In this selection, he (1) delineates the various conceptualizations of the topic proposed by several authorities; (2) discusses various research projects in which attempts have been made to measure values and finally (3) presents an annotated bibliography of articles and scales for measuring values. While this selection is of considerably greater length than are most in this collection, it is so complete a discussion that any student comprehending it will have an excellent understanding of the concept.

The other two selections are of more conventional length—and are also conventional social science; that is, both challenge long-held beliefs or "knowledge." In the article by Ernest Q. Campbell, the Myrdal hypothesis of "American Dilemma" (incongruity between the ideals of democracy and actual behavior indicating prejudice and discrimination) is seriously questioned. Campbell argues that in any case, "The American Creed" is not the only set of relevant norms, as other values may conflict with the equality dimension of our American culture, and thus make support of

---

[1] Kluckhohn, C. *et al.* "Values and value-orientations in the theory of action," pp. 388–433. In T. Parsons and E. A. Shils (Eds.), *Toward a general theory of action,* Cambridge, Massachusetts: Harvard University Press, 1951.

segregation possible without any accompanying sense of guilt. A reassessment of Myrdal's interpretation is forced upon us. Students will surely find this paper interesting both for the social issue with which it deals and the intriguing methodology which was employed.

Finally, Fred I. Greenstein effectively challenges the widely-held view that American values are in process of dramatic change. If the criteria of good research is that it raises more questions than it answers, then Campbell and Greenstein must indeed be accorded accolades.

23

Measuring the Values of Individuals

ALLEN BARTON

Bureau of Applied Social Research,
Columbia University

INTRODUCTION: VALUE-TRANSMITTERS, SOCIAL SCIENTISTS, AND METHODOLOGISTS

In all societies there are specialists concerned with the transmission of the culturally approved values to the younger generation, and their maintenance among the adult members of society. These processes in most cultures are highly traditional, and involve rituals full of deep emotional meaning. In modern scientifically oriented cultures the transmission and expression of values become the subject of scientific research. In this research two groups are especially involved: the social scientists, and the specialists in education and moral indoctrination—educators, churchmen, psychiatrists, social workers, correctional workers, and, occasionally, the mass-media communicators. The professional value-transmitters want the answers to practical problems, and sponsor and use applied research. The professional social scientists are called in to provide this applied research, at the same time as they carry on more basic research to develop general theories and methods for understanding and predicting the behavior of individuals, groups, and social systems. Between the practitioners and the scientists there is a partial (but not complete) common interest. The applied research called for by practitioners is often valuable to the scientists, and the basic research of the scientist in the long run is necessary to the improvement of applied research and applied technique. By judicious cooperation, the scientists can get resources and access to their human subjects of study, indispensable conditions for social research, while the practitioners get better research methods and theoretical guidance. Striking a fair bargain between theoretical and applied interests is, of course, a real problem, as is the application of scientific objectivity to what people hold most dear.

This paper discusses methodological problems in the measurement of

Reprinted from *Religious Education*, 57, 4 (July–August 1962), (Research Supplement), S 62–97, by permission of the author and The Religious Education Association, New York City.

the values of individuals. A very large number of studies have tried to make such measurements; educational research abounds with them, and journals of psychology, sociology, and anthropology continually publish them. This abundance of actual attempts makes it possible to undertake a methodological examination, since the methodologist is essentially a specialist in classifying, clarifying, and evaluating the research operations of other scientists. This work is related to the analysis of theory, but it is not identical, since it concentrates on the basic formal characteristics of the operations of measurement and analysis of data, rather than on the construction of systematic theories from the data. At a certain stage in the growth of research in a field, critical examination of methods is essential to the further development both of theory and research; without it, research will proliferate without improving, and theory may develop unanalyzed abstractions not translatable into research operations.

This paper consists of three parts. The first considers the conceptions of "values" used in social science research, in order to avoid purely terminological confusions, to delimit the area under consideration, and to distinguish several types of value-concepts. The second considers the types of observable indicators which are used, and how they are combined into measuring devices relevant to the various conceptions or types of values. The third, made up of two appendices, contains annotated references to (I) recent writings discussing the social science concept of values and (II) scales or questionnaires which have been used in studies relating to values.

THE DEFINITION OF VALUES

Discussions of values are difficult enough without confusion over the use of words. Unfortunately, a number of rather different terminologies are now widely employed. A group which is concerned with understanding a problem should not spend much time arguing over terminology, provided the underlying meanings can be clearly distinguished and labelled in some mutually comprehensible way.

I would like to indicate the main categories of things to which the noun "values" has been applied, and establish as a convention of this discussion a set of terms for these things. This can be done by making a series of distinctions:

*Distinction 1: Values as attributes of people
or attributes of objects*

Social scientists are in the habit of talking about people as "having values" in the sense of standards or tendencies of choice, located in the minds of men. Values in this sense are a kind of attitude.

Some writers, however, refer to the objects which people seek as "values." Stuart Dodd proposes:

Let a "value" be defined as a desideratum, i.e., anything desired or chosen by someone sometime (Dodd, 646).

Still others consider values as a kind of object in themselves:

Values are considered as absolutes, existing in the mind of God as eternal ideas, as independent validities, etc. (Adler, 272).

In either case, the value is outside the person whose behavior is studied.

There are clearly two things involved in any discussion of values: the objects which are valued, and the tendency or standard within the person to behave in certain ways toward these objects. In other words, there are "valued objects or attributes," and there are "value-standards" of people. Neither is understandable without reference to the other.

Here I will use the word "values" as a shorthand for value-standards, because it seems convenient in a discussion where the people are being measured, not the things.

Distinction 2: Values as attributes of individuals
or of collectives

Some social scientists speak habitually of the values of an individual; others prefer to restrict the term to those standards which are "shared" within a group, or at least held by an effective majority or dominant segment. The logical relationships between attributes of individuals and of collective units composed of individuals—groups, organizations, communities, regions, societies—are complicated. A clarifying discussion is found in a paper by Lazarsfeld and Menzel, "On the Relation Between Individual and Collective Properties" (P. F. Lazarsfeld and H. Menzel, in Amitai Etzioni, ed., *Complex Organizations*. New York: Holt, Rinehart, and Winston, 1961).

Here I will use the word to refer to an attribute of individuals, just like motives, attitudes, and habits. The question of whether an individual's values correspond to those of larger groups, of how much consensus there is within larger groups regarding values, and which values are effectively supported by organized incentive and sanctioning systems, will be left open. This individualistic definition of values is most convenient if we are studying the ways in which value-shaping institutions (schools, correctional institutions, churches, psychiatric institutions, communications media) influence people.

The study of the value-attributes of collective units is, of course, a central problem for sociology and anthropology: what is the influence of group norms, established social institutions, and cultural traditions upon the values of individuals, and how do these collective attributes maintain themselves or change. A clear understanding of these problems requires much more precise analysis of the relationship between individual attributes and conceptualizations of collective units and their properties. Terms like "the values of an organization," "the values of a society," or "institutionalized values" may sometimes be a useful shorthand for some such ideas as "the values held by a majority of the members" or "the values actually rewarded by the social system," but they can also be used to conceal a failure to think through the actual social processes involved in the interaction of individuals within collective units (Barton 1961).

Distinction 3: Values as conscious and verbalized standards of the individual, or as inferential constructs made by the research from observed behavior

The leading current social-science definition of value, that of the anthropologist Clyde Kluckhohn, raises the question of whether values are abstract generalizations made by the researcher from observed behavior of the subject, and attempts to compromise. (It also accepts the term as applying either to individuals or groups.)

> A value is a conception, explicit or implicit, distinctive of an individual or characteristic of a group, of the desirable which influences the selection from available modes, means and ends of action (Kluckhohn, 395).

Kluckhohn offers a commentary on each term in this definition. The terms "conception" and "explicit or implicit" are crucial to the present distinction.

> A *conception* identifies value as a logical construct comparable to culture or social structure. That is, values are not directly observable any more than culture is. Both values and culture are based upon what is said and done by individuals but represent inferences and abstractions from the immediate sense-data. . . . In its analytic meaning, the locus of value is neither in the organism nor in the immediately observable world; its locus is rather that of all scientific abstractions. Concretely, of course, any given value is in some sense "built into" the apperceptive mass or neural nets of the persons who hold that value—in the same way that a culture is "built into" its carriers. However, the social science abstraction "value" is not abstracted from neurological properties but from verbal and nonverbal behavioral events (Kluckhohn, 395–396).

To identify value as "a conception" requires that someone hold the conception. Is it a conception in the mind of the researcher—as suggested by his reference to it as a "scientific abstraction"—or is it also a conception in the mind of the person under study?

> The phrase *explicit or implicit* is necessary to our definition since it is an induction from experience that some of the deepest and most pervasive of personal and cultural values are only partially or occasionally verbalized and

in some instances must be inferential constructs on the part of the observer to explain consistencies in behavior. An implicit value is, however, almost always potentially expressible in rational language by actor as well as by observer. On the other hand, the fact that everybody cannot readily verbalize such conceptions does not remove them from the realm of value. It may legitimately be asked, "Can a conception be implicit?" The answer is that "verbalizable" is not to be equated with "clearly and habitually verbalized." The actor's values are often inchoate, incompletely or inadequately verbalized by him. But implicit values remain "conceptions" in the sense that they are abstract and generalized notions which can be put into words by the observer and then agreed to or dissented to by the actor. Verbalizability is a necessary test of value.

This is perhaps a way of saying that such matters as instinctual behavior and needs are below the level of abstraction and hence not part—directly —of the realm of value. Values must be susceptible of abstraction by the observer and formulable by the observer in such terms that the subject can understand and agree or disagree. The subject's own ordinary verbalization with respect to values will often be oblique or indirect, and implicit values will be manifested only in behavior and through verbalizations that do not directly state the pertinent values (Kluckhohn, 397–398).

Kluckhohn here insists that the value-standard be "verbalizable" in some general, abstract terms; the kinds of measures which this "necessary test" excludes are presumably those un-nameable "X-factors" of factor analysis, composed of items which empirically tend to be found in the same people, but for which no meaningful term in "rational language" can be found. Moreover, the standard must be verbalizable in terms understandable to the subject—although it is apparently not necessary that he accept the verbal formulation of the actual tendencies of his conduct.

It seems best for this discussion to allow both explicit standards (which may or may not correspond to persistent tendencies in behavior) and implicit standards (which may or may not be verbally stated or accepted by the actor) to bear the label "values," and to distinguish them by the modifiers explicit and implicit. The relation between these two types of values is a question for empirical research. The two conceptions point to two rather different sets of observable indicators.

Distinction 4: Values as desires or as obligations

Values are frequently identified with preferences, desires, motives, or interests.

Valuing may then be defined as actions which show a person's intensity of desire for various desiderata, or the amount of his "motivation" to pursue them. . . . The noun "value" has usually been used to imply some code or standard which persists through time, and provides a criterion by which people order their intensities of desiring various desiderata (Catton, 310, 311).

This broad definition embracing all preferences and desires (or at least all relatively persistent ones) ignores a distinction which some people want to preserve, between the feeling of liking and the feeling of obligation, between "I want to" and "I ought to" or "I feel he ought to." Kluckhohn expresses this somewhat awkwardly as the distinction between the desired and what is conceived as "desirable."

> A value is not just a preference but is a preference which is felt and/or considered to be justified—"morally" or by reasoning or by aesthetic judgments, usually by two or all three of these. Even if a value remains implicit, behavior with reference to this *conception* indicates an undertone of the desirable—not just the desired. The desirable is what it is felt or thought proper to want (Kluckhohn, 396).

Here again we have two conceptions, pointing to two different sets of indicators. The conception of values as any and all preferences tends to go with the conception of values as implicit and manifested by observable choices in behavior. The conception of values as standards which we feel are justified, to which people *should* adhere, focusses attention on verbal statements, and particularly on verbalizations which distinguish internal feelings of "ought" from those of "liking." The "sense of obligation" or "sense of value" is what distinguishes "normative values" in this sense from "mere preferences."

It is sometimes said that "introspection" or "verstehen"—the understanding of other people's behavior through the scientist's knowledge of his own feelings—is not a valid source of social science data. However, whenever we discuss our inner experiences with others, we find confirmation that those which we feel also take place in other people, just as we find confirmation of our external sense impressions. If it is possible to obtain better scientific measurements and predictions by using verbalizations of inner feelings as indicators, there can hardly be a scientific objection. The expressions of a sense of duty, a sense of guilt, a feeling of approval or of indignation toward others, are worth examining as scientific data. It may also be useful to preserve the distinction which most of us seem to feel, and which is manifested in our language, between these "normative" feelings of what "should" be, and purely "preferential" feelings of what we like.

There also appear to be behavioral indicators which distinguish the two kinds of values; people act differently depending on whether a certain choice is defined as a "matter of taste" or as a matter of obligation. It is only in the obligatory sense that values can be used to judge other people's conduct as right or wrong, worthy of respect or "worthless," rather than simply as pleasing or unpleasing to us. Much interpersonal behavior involving judging, condemning, and praising indicates normative values. And in making the distinction between preferences and feelings of obligation, we raise the possibility of conflict between the two; most of us have experienced such conflicts within ourselves, and have heard others describe experiencing them. The behavior of people who refuse to do what they would like to do and do what they should (or vice versa) has certain observable aspects.

Normative feelings, whether applied to oneself or to others, are of different degrees of "requiredness." Some standards are mandatory: one absolutely must, or absolutely must not. Others are in varying degrees normatively preferred but not absolutely required: a person preferably should be brave or generous or devout, but it is not absolutely required of most people. (Soldiers are required to be brave, the wealthy—in some societies —to be generous, and the priests to be devout, otherwise they will be bad soldiers, miserly rich men, wicked priests.) No one is required to be a doctor, but doctors are highly respected as compared with factory workers. (A few may consider being a factory worker positively degrading, but for most people it is simply a less valued occupation than certain others.) Religious or educational activities are generally considered more worthy of respect and approval than "wasting one's time" in amusement or drinking (which again a few consider positively evil, but most simply as less valuable activities). Some ideal standards are so utopian that few can live up to them; those who do are regarded at heroes or saints, but those who do not are not blamed. Thus we might consider normativeness or the feeling of moral obligation as a continuum, ranging from the mandatory through the morally preferred down to the absolute zero of matters of taste or purely personal preferences.

The obligatory values are especially significant for, and probably arise out of, the requirements of living together in a group and a society. It is true that much of the social control which produces a stable social system operates through the socialization of preferences, to make people like to do what is functional for the system. But this socialization does not always succeed, and the system therefore falls back both on external restraints (organized rewards and punishments) and internal restraints (feelings of obligation) to insure an adequate degree of conformity to social requirements. This set of feelings or compulsions are conceived by personality theory as the conscience or superego.

It is quite possible that the feelings of right and wrong, good and bad, obligatory and forbidden, worthy and unworthy, derive from rather different sources in different people and cultures. Some values, for some people, may reflect an introjected punitive parent (who may be projected as a wrathful god). Some may reflect internalized group sentiments, emphasizing shame rather than guilt. Some may derive from individual empathy with the feelings of other individuals, a sense of identification with others generally. The feelings of obligation and respect which define normative standards may thus be subjectively rather different for different people. It may be possible to distinguish their verbal and nonverbal behavior by pursuing these differences in origin and feeling-tone, even when the standard is abstractly the same. There may be a Puritanical, a humanistic, and a Buddhist version of the norms prohibiting theft, willful injury to others, and adultery, and requiring help to the afflicted.

Here we will apply the term "values" to both kinds of motives or feelings—the normative and the purely preferential. People's lives are shaped by major, enduring preferences among choices equally acceptable to the individual's conscience and the moral judgment of his fellows—for activity rather than passivity, for dealing with people rather than with things or abstractions, for enjoying nature rather than artificial surroundings, and so on. At the same time the sense of obligation also shapes people's lives and permits society to exist. We will try to preserve the distinction by talking about two kinds of values: preference-values (likings, needs, desires, or interests) and normative values (obligatory, ought, or moral values).

*Distinction 5: Values as a few basic, general standards
or tendencies of choice, or as all specific preferences or standards*

Those who define values as "all preferences" or as indicated by all actions must deal with the problem of multiplicity. Stuart Dodd speaks of the "myriad values of men," of "billions of objects of positive and negative desiring which we call values. . . ." Ralph White speaks of human wants as "almost infinitely varied," and notes that the problem applies as well to verbal as to behavioral indicators:

> If verbal data consisted of nothing but "I want this" or "that is good," the complexity would indeed be infinite, and verbal data could not be used to simplify in any way the vast chaos of our knowledge of human wants (White, 10).

Another approach is to distinguish "basic values" from the myriad specific wants, preferences, norms, or valuings. The basic values are assumed to be a relatively small number of general principles or tendencies which underlie the specific verbal or behavioral indicators, and are relatively stable. It is necessary to search for such relatively general, stable sources of regularity if human behavior is to be understood at all; millions of variables are neither practically nor scientifically manageable.

In this paper the term "values" will be reserved for a relatively small number of basic tendencies or principles; for the more specific items we can use the term "attitudes." Thus we can talk about people's attitudes toward tomatoes, lawnmowers, Turks, judges, murder, Edsels, stamp collecting, and so on, ad infinitum. One can have as many attitudes as there are items in the Sears Roebuck catalogue. Attitudes in this sense need not be long enduring; they can change from day to day in response to experience and social stimuli. Market research on specific products and audience research on television program choices deal in attitudes. The development of scientific theories of human behavior requires that some more general stable variables be identified.

There are two ways of proceeding to identify general or basic values. One is to ask the actors to verbalize the general standards which underlie specific behavior or verbal preferences; the other is to obtain large sets of verbal or nonverbal behavior and mathematically analyze them to see which specifics tend to vary together.

Ralph White proposes the first procedure as a remedy for the problem of multiplicity of specific choices:

A man wants to marry *this* girl, to rent *this* house, to vote for *this* presidential candidate; and the variety of girls, houses, and candidates, to say nothing of beefsteaks and cigarettes, is, for practical purposes, literally infinite.

.   .   .

Fortunately, however, people not only say *what* they want; they also often indicate reasons (which may or may not be the real reason) *why* they want it. A person says, "this girl is beautiful," or "this house is cheap," or "this candidate is honest"; and in doing so he ordinarily assumes that his listener, like himself, approves of beauty in women, cheapness in houses, and honesty in candidates. In other words, he invokes a value which, in the eyes of his culture, appears to be "self-evident." And *the number of such self-evident values is by no means unlimited.* Their number would be unmanageably large if all of the finer distinctions were taken into account (e.g., the distinction between beauty and prettiness, or between honesty and truthfulness) and for some purposes these finer distinctions do need to be taken into account. For other purposes, however, it is permissible to focus on whole groups of near-synonyms (White, 10).

The study of explicit values, of values as conscious and verbalized standards, therefore reduces the problem of multiplicity; and by grouping together concepts of similar meaning we can achieve any desired level of fewness-and-generality. Whether the resulting concepts have predictive value and form useful theories will depend on whether the ready-made abstractions found in the language of the society correspond to real patternings of behavior in that society.

This brings us to the second approach, that of factor analysis and similar techniques. By examining which specific choices tend to appear together, sets of items to which large numbers of people respond alike can be found. People who listen to classical music tend also to look at paintings, attend the theater, and engage in various other aesthetic activities more often than those who do not listen to classical music; the art-lovers also tend to go to the theater more than non-art-lovers, and so on. These items empirically form a positively correlated cluster. Because of the correlations of these interests with income, they will also probably have positive correlations with yachting, big-game hunting, driving an expensive car, and having servants. However, this latter cluster will relate much more closely to one another than to the first group, since you can be an art-lover, music-lover, even a theater-lover without having a high income, while it is much more difficult to engage in the latter activities unless you belong to the wealthier class. Factor analysis, latent structure analysis, and various forms of scale analysis represent formal mathematical attempts to identify underlying factors among such observable clusters of correlations.

The clusters or factors discovered by looking at what items tend to be found together, in the same groups of people, define both the groups of people and the sets of items at the same time. The naming of the factors and of the groups of people then becomes a problem. It is an empirical question of great importance whether the ready-made abstractions provided by the culture correspond to these clusters of jointly-occurring indicators or to these groups of similar-behavior people. It seems likely that the process by which the culture has created abstract concepts for describing human behavior, such as honesty, aesthetic interest, fairness, altruism, was a collective and informal form of factor analysis, refined by thinkers who perceived finer distinctions than most people commonly do. In the natural sciences, as more refined observations were made, the common-sense concepts of the language of the people did not suffice. The same may be true in the social sciences once their methods become better, on the average, than those of the public at large. Therefore it may be possible and necessary to conceptualize actual clusterings of behavior which are

TABLE 1

*Types of Concepts of the Basic Values of Individuals**

	VERBALIZED BY ACTOR	INFERRED BY RESEARCHER	
	A	B	
PREFERENCES	Explicit standards of preference	Implicit preference tendencies	A + B: All preferences
	C	D	
FEELINGS OF OBLIGATION	Explicit normative standards	Implicit normative tendencies	C + D: All normative values
	A + C: All explicit standards	B + D: All implicit tendencies	

* Another way of describing these types is:
  A. Explicit preferential values.
  B. Implicit preferential values.
  C. Explicit normative values.
  D. Implicit normative values.

not clearly recognized in the language—and to find implicit values which do not have standardized verbal expressions.

A Working Definition and Typology of Values

Our decisions concerning these distinctions can be summed up as follows: values will be defined here as general and stable dispositions of individuals, verbalized by them or inferred by the researcher, involving preference or a sense of obligation. The either-or components of this definition give us a typology of value-concepts.

The category of "preferences" can be defined in two ways: to cover all preferences, including those which have normative force or justification; or to include only "mere preferences" for which no additional justification is felt or claimed. Those who speak of values as preferences generally mean the first, inclusive definition; they do not mean to exclude normative values, although they may not distinguish them from other preferences.

Other Characteristics of Individuals Relevant to the Study of Values

A book which has had considerable impact on thinking about the "values" of young people is Philip Jacob's *Changing Values in College*, a summary and commentary on available research on the effects of going to college. I have written a methodological analysis of the problem of "Studying the Effects of College Education" based on the Jacob book. A careful reading shows that Jacob was concerned with much more than just "values" as he formally defined them ("a standard for decision-making, held by an individual student, and normally to be identified when it is articulated in (a) an expressed verbal statement or (b) overt conduct"). These additional things I have classified as:

    a. Critically examined vs. unexamined values
    b. Knowledge vs. ignorance
    c. Sensitivity of feeling for people and for beauty
    d. Philosophical or religious commitments.

It may be useful to discuss briefly these other characteristics of individuals which became involved in Jacob's discussion of value change, since they are likely to be important in any discussion of values.

a. Critically examined vs. unexamined values

It turns out that many of the criticisms Jacob makes of the colleges refer to their failure to give their students the capacity for and the commitment to independent, rational, penetrating thinking as opposed to conformist, stereotyped, uncritical thinking. Even where there have been major changes in attitudes, Jacob complains that they are induced by mere group conformity.

> The changes which do occur bring greater consistency into the value-patterns of the students and fit these patterns to a well-established standard of what a college graduate in American society is expected to believe and do. But the college student is not front-runner in a broad forward movement of values within the culture at large. If anything the "typical" college graduate is a cultural rubber stamp for the social heritage as it stands rather than the instigator of new patterns of thought and new standards of conduct. College socializes, but does not really liberalize the student.

The values of most people in the world are undoubtedly "cultural rubber stamps for the social heritage as it stands." Only in a society with an unusual toleration for rationality, individualism, and progress would anyone think of complaining about this. However, the question of whether values are arrived at in the individual through examination of one's own feelings and motives, critical examination of the social consequences of accepted values, and rational consideration of alternative standards in the light of both conscience and social consequences, is of great interest. The feeling that this *should* be done is a basic value of at least one school of liberal education. There is nothing in the definition of values which says that they should be arrived at in this way. It makes more sense to measure this as a separate variable which characterizes individuals' valuing-behavior: the extent to which their values have been arrived at through critical, independent thinking and feeling.

b. Knowledge vs. ignorance

Another aspect of the effect of college or any other educational institution is its effect on "beliefs." Jacob defines his problem in these terms:

> Such an approach to the study of values implies examination both of the actual behavioral choices of students and of the structure of beliefs to which such choices are related. The impact of social science curricula upon a student's conviction of what man is, and the nature of the world in which men live, might be a vital factor in altering his choices of conduct (Jacob, xiii).

Many of the empirical measures discussed by Jacob included a large number of questions about "beliefs." This ambiguous term includes several kinds of questions, but one category is clearly fact issues, at least potentially subject to empirical verification. People who are ignorant of the past and of communities, social groups, and cultures other than their own, are likely to behave differently and to have different kinds of values from those with more broad and "liberal" education and experience. The breadth of knowledge and cultural experience should be measured to explore its relationship to values; however, it should be kept conceptually distinct. Some studies mix knowledge items and value items indiscriminately in the effort to encompass entire personality "syndromes" such as "authoritarianism" or "conservatism."

c. Sensitivity of feeling for people and for beauty

This aspect was less frequently mentioned by Jacob, but it is widely recognized in literature on liberal education. This is the idea that "something more" should be produced by liberal education than intellectual skills and abstract or factual knowledge. Jacob speaks of the need for "sensitizing their feelings toward others" and "of arousing sympathetic concern for others."

It seems possible that this is a major influence on individual values in a society where old and rigid traditions are being abandoned. Measures of this attribute are only now being developed.

d. Philosophical or religious commitments

Many of the "beliefs" discussed by Jacob are simply beliefs as to facts, which are at least potentially verifiable by operations of science or common observation. Another sense of the word "belief" makes it identical with an attitude or a value: "I believe in equal rights for all races," "I believe in honesty." There remains a third category of statements labelled "beliefs" which are neither scientifically verifiable in any simple sense, nor simple evaluative statements about what one approves or disapproves. This third kind of beliefs might be termed "philosophical commitments." They include religious and metaphysical assumptions about the universe and the bases of human knowledge and experience. Typical items (not necessarily good ones) used to measure these beliefs are:

There is a source of knowledge beyond human experience.

I believe in God.

Most of the important things that happen to people are the result of circumstances beyond their control.

The so-called universal mysteries are ultimately knowable according to scientific method.

The relation of such philosophical commitments to values on the one hand, and to factual knowledge on the other, is a deep and complicated question. It is possible to investigate empirically what kinds of philosophical commitments go with what values and what factual beliefs, and how a change in one influences the others. This can only be done, however, if we keep these areas conceptually distinct and form independent measures of them. Recent work in anthropology has begun to develop measures of these "world-views" along with measures of values.

Cognitive beliefs about the nature of the world are included in the definition of "value orientations" by Clyde and Florence Kluckhohn. Clyde Kluckhohn writes:

> There is a philosophy behind the way of life of each individual and of every relatively homogeneous group at any given point in their histories. This gives, with varying degrees of explicitness or implications, some sense of coherence or unity both in cognitive and affective dimensions. (C. Kluckhohn 1951, 409)

In their major study, *Variations in Value Orientation*, Florence Kluckhohn and Fred Strodtbeck give their formal definition:

> Value orientations are complex but definitely patterned (rank-ordered) principles, resulting from the transactional interplay of three analytically distinguishable elements of the evaluative process—the cognitive, the affective, and the directive elements—which give order and direction to the everflowing stream of human acts and thoughts as these relate to the solution of "common human" problems (F. Kluckhohn and F. Strodtbeck 1961, 4).

Although they indicate that these three elements are analytically distinguishable, their research instruments do not so distinguish them, and the problem of the relation of the cognitive to the "affective and directive" is left open.

We can sum up this list of interrelated variables in the following scheme:

FIGURE 8-1

Factors Related to Individual Values

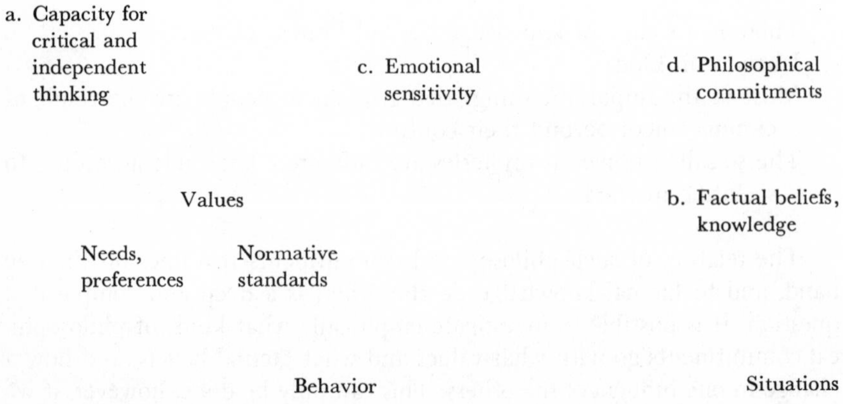

a. Capacity for critical and independent thinking

c. Emotional sensitivity

d. Philosophical commitments

Values

b. Factual beliefs, knowledge

Needs, preferences   Normative standards

Behavior   Situations

Behavior is, of course, required, facilitated, or limited by situational factors. Within a given situation, people will behave differently according to their factual beliefs about the situation and their values. Factual beliefs and values are considered to be influenced by three categories of intellectual and emotional factors: capacity for critical thinking, emotional sensitivity, and philosophical commitments.

INDICATORS OF VALUES

We have now roughly defined what people want to measure when they talk about the values of individuals. We have distinguished normative values, which involve some feeling of obligation or justification,' from preferential values, which are "matters of taste" and not necessarily felt to be obligatory or justifiable. We have restricted the term "values" to relatively general and enduring preferences, normative rules, or tendencies of choice which underlie the myriad specific preferences, rules and decisions which occur in daily life. Now we can raise the question, what indicators should we look for in people if we want to construct measurements of their values?

The indicators actually used in research can be divided into four main classes in terms of their form:

1. Explicit abstract elements of standards, criteria, or goals
2. Specific evaluative statements about particular objects
3. Statements of probable behavior in hypothetical situations
4. Reported or observed behavior

The first class attempts to obtain direct verbalizations of general values as explicit standards. The other three classes provide indicators from which implicit, underlying standards may be inferred. The indicators must be combined in some way to measure the underlying values in which we are interested. To do this we must have some way of deciding which indicators go together, and what to call the resulting measurement, problems which were discussed in the previous section.

The first class of indicators, depending on their wording, can indicate either normative or preferential values or some unspecified combination, depending on whether people are asked for standards of what they like or prefer, standards of what is right and wrong or good or bad, or standards of what is "important" to them.

Specific evaluative statements which use words like "enjoy," "like," "interested in," or "am pleased by" would be considered indicators of preferential rather than normative values. Those containing words like "should," "must," "ought to," "good," "bad," and "worthwhile" would be generally considered indicators of normative values. Some words are ambiguous, like "prefer" or "is important"; we cannot tell from their use whether a purely personal preference or a normative feeling is involved. Statements of either hypothetical or actual behavior do not indicate, on their face, whether normative or preferential values underlie the choice of conduct.

Combining the methodological classification with the conceptual distinctions of normative and preferential values, and explicit versus implicit standards, we can make the following typology of value indicators:

	Methodological Type of Indicator	a. Normative Values	b. Preferential Values Only	c. Norms and/or Preferences
VALUES AS EXPLICIT STANDARDS	1. Explicit statements of standards, criteria, goals	1-a	1-b	1-c
VALUES AS IMPLICIT STANDARDS	2. Specific evaluative statements	2-a	2-b	2-c
	3. Statements of future or hypothetical behavior			3-c
	4. Observations or reports of actual behavior			4-c

1. Abstract Value Statements

1.1 General values

The most direct approach to the measurement of basic values is represented by such methods as the "Inventory of Students' General Goals in Life," devised by the Cooperative Study in General Education. Twenty highly general goals were presented to the students in the form of a long series of paired comparisons, each goal against each other goal. Students were asked which in each pair they considered more important, for themselves. This formulation does not distinguish between goals which are personal preferences and those which are considered morally binding on people generally; the responses suggest some mixture of the two.

The goals are listed here in the average rank order assigned them by over 2,000 students at approximately sixteen colleges.

The results suggest some of the difficulties of this head-on approach as applied to values at the most general level of "goals in life." People are undoubtedly idealizing themselves along conventional lines. Still, it is interesting to know that "serving God" is given first rank, while "self-sacrifice for the sake of a better world" ranks 12th out of 20. (Is this because the latter is presented as involving self-sacrifice while the former is not? It is surely biasing to include self-sacrifice as part of the goal itself in one case, and not the other.) It is also interesting that among egoistic goals, "self-development—becoming a real, genuine person" (whatever that means) is

TABLE 2

Average Rank Given to "General Goals in Life"

1. Serving God, doing God's will.
2. Self-development—becoming a real, genuine person.
3. Promoting the most deep and lasting pleasures for the greatest number of people.
4. Fine relations with other persons.
5. Handling the specific problems of life as they arise.
6. Being able to "take it"; brave and uncomplaining acceptance of what circumstances bring.
7. Doing my duty.
8. Serving the community of which I am a part.
9. Overcoming my irrational emotions and sensuous desires.
10. Getting as many deep and lasting pleasures out of life as I can.
11. Peace of mind, contentment, stillness of spirit.
12. Self-sacrifice for the sake of a better world.
13. Making a place for myself in the world; getting ahead.
14. Finding my place in life and accepting it.
15. Security—protecting my way of life against adverse changes.
16. Realizing that I cannot change the bad features of the world, and doing the best I can for myself and those dear to me.
17. Achieving personal immortality in heaven.
18. Survival; continued existence.
19. Power; control over people and things.
20. Living for the pleasure of the moment.

the favorite of these adolescent respondents, along with "fine relations with other persons," "being able to take it," and "handling the specific problems of life as they arise." Power, security, and getting ahead fall far below these. This suggests that these "values" represent the concerns of young people at a certain difficult period of their growing up, rather than more permanent concerns.

The coverage of values in this Inventory is rather arbitrary. The authors of the Inventory report that they selected values to represent both "the great historical traditions of philosophy and religion" and the "cracker-barrel philosophy" of Americans generally, omitting those historically important goals which would rarely be found among American students. However, they have omitted intellectual values, aesthetic values, justice, and nationalism; and sensuality appears only as something to be "overcome" along with irrational emotions. A useful feature, although a time-consuming one, is the use of paired comparisons, forcing the respondent to choose between two values at a time. This provides information not only about the ranking but about the internal consistency of each individual's verbal choices. Such verbal consistency is the minimum criterion which expressions of abstract standards must meet if they are to be considered indicators of basic values.

A much more sophisticated attempt to obtain explicit general standards of value is the "Ways to Live" questionnaire devised by Charles Morris. Thirteen ways of life are described, each in a paragraph-long statement. The paragraphs include general personal preferences, norms of conduct, preferences for social policies, and some specific experiences, activities or situations, as well as general philosophical statements about the nature of the world and the trend of history. An example is:

> 6. Life continuously tends to stagnate, to become "comfortable," to become sicklied o'er with the pale cast of thought. Against these tendencies, a person must stress the need of constant activity—physical action, adventure, the realistic solution of specific problems as they appear, the improvement of techniques for controlling the world and society. Man's future depends primarily on what he does, not on what he feels or on his speculations. New problems constantly arise and always will arise. Improvements must always be made if man is to progress. We can't just follow the past or dream of what the future might be. We have to work resolutely and continually if control is to be gained over the forces which threaten us. Man should rely on technical advances made possible by scientific knowledge. He should find his goal in the solution of his problems. The good is the enemy of the better.

Respondents both rate each "Way" on a seven-point scale indicating their absolute degree of liking or disliking, but they also rank all thirteen in order of their preference. The responses are not combined, but form a 13-dimensional profile of values. Morris has attempted to construct the Ways to represent combinations of three components:

> The dionysian component is made up of the tendencies to release and indulge existing desires. . . . The promethean component of personality is the sum of . . . active tendencies to manipulate and remake the world. . . . The buddhistic component of personality comprises those tendencies in the self to regulate itself by holding in check its desires.

By taking all combinations of these three dimensions in which one is high, one medium, and one low, he obtains six types, to which he adds a seventh, which is medium on all three. The sixth Way quoted above was high on promethean, medium on dionysian, and low on buddhistic tendencies. The derivation of his remaining six Ways is not explained in the book, but they may represent other combinations in which one component is high and two are low, two high and one low, etc., from the possible 27 combinations of three three-valued items.

It should be clear from the example that each Way is in fact a very complex mixture of elements. People may respond to one sentence or phrase but not to others. A simple content analysis of the 13 paragraphs distinguishes at least 14 elements, most of them appearing in several Ways, but none of them explicitly dealt with in all of them.

In the Table each element is described as being highly emphasized, moderately emphasized, or given low emphasis in the different Ways. A blank indicates that the paragraph is not explicit on the point.

TABLE 3

An analysis of Morris' Ways to Live into component elements

	Ways to Live												
Elements	1	2	3	4	5	6	7	8	9	10	11	12	13
Social Policy													
a. Social-political concern	H			L		H							
b. Social progress and reform	M					H							
c. Technological progress						H							
Interpersonal Relations													
d. Intimate friendship, affection	M	L	H	L				M					H
e. Sociability, gregariousness	L	L		M	H				L				
f. Concern for others, sympathy			H		H			L	L				H
g. Power, manipulation of others			L	L							L		
h. Independence, self-reliance		H	L							H			L
Personal Experiences													
i. Sensuous enjoyment, expression of emotions	M	L	L	H	H		M	M		L			
j. Physical activity, making things		L	L		H	H		L	L			H	
k. Concern with material possessions		L	L		L								
l. Enjoyment of nature				H	L	L	M						H
m. Reflection, self-knowledge		H		H					H		H		
n. Intellectual concern, knowledge					M				L				
	1	2	3	4	5	6	7	8	9	10	11	12	13

Morris' thirteen Ways clearly do not exhaust all possible combinations of these elements. They do not permit respondents to discriminate certain elements which they like within a Way from others which they do not. The result is that a very wide-ranging and evocative set of stimuli are presented, but the modes of response are restricted. In practice, several of the Ways got little support from any nationality of students, and the high ratings were concentrated on a few. (In the United States the highest rating went to the Way which was "medium" on the three philosophical components, offering "a little of everything.")

If some method were devised to permit separate ratings on the component elements of the 13 Ways of Life, and certain gaps were filled in (such as the value of intellectual activities, and values at the level of social rather than individual goals, which are neglected), the results might be much more flexible and useful. Such a method has in fact been invented by a value-research whose technique will be discussed later on: permitting the respondent to indicate in the margin his approval or disapproval, or liking or disliking, of each particular element in a text. This would permit the Ways of Living to generate perhaps a couple of hundred separate responses. These could be analyzed to see which items go together and form dimensions, and a set of types could be found by taking various combinations of these dimensions which would have much more empirical relevance than Morris' a priori thirteen Ways.

Florence Kluckhohn and Fred Strodtbeck report a still more systematic method of presenting basic value components to respondents for them to rate. A set of twenty-two questions was prepared covering four areas: relational orientation, man-nature orientation, time orientation, and activity orientation. In each area three alternative directives for choice were offered. The alternatives took the form of short paragraphs, expressing what "some people said" or did about a situation. For example, in the relational area, lineal, collateral, and individualistic orientations are indicated by the alternatives in this question:

2. Well Arrangements
When a community has to make arrangements for water, such as drill a well, there are three different ways they can decide to arrange things like location, and who is going to do the work.

A (Lin) There are some communities where it is mainly the older or recognized leaders of the important families who decide the plans. Everyone usually accepts what they say without much discussion since they are the ones who are used to deciding such things and are the ones who have had the most experience.

B (Coll) There are some communities where most people in the group have a part in making the plans. Lots of different people talk, but nothing is done until *almost* everyone comes to agree as to what is best to be done.

 C   There are some communities where everyone holds to his own
(Ind)   opinion, and they decide the matter by vote. They do what the
     largest number want even though there are still a very great many
     people who disagree and object to the action.

Which way do you think is usually best in such cases?
Which of the other two ways do you think is better?
Which way of all three ways do you think most other persons in ——
  would usually think is best?

The items include, in accordance with their definition, both value and
cognitive elements. The items on relation of man to nature appear mainly
cognitive. Among the value items those dealing with *relationships* among
people are mainly normative, while those concerning *activity orientation*
are mainly preferential. Time orientation items are partly normative and
partly cognitive, if one analyzes the detailed language for "should" vs.
"is" statements.

   The results of the rankings are expressed as a value profile on several
dimensions.

   It is also possible to explore people's general, abstract values by asking
them to formulate them themselves, in response to open-ended questions.
Scott's study of "The Empirical Assessment of Values and Ideologies"
used this approach. A random sample of residents of a suburban town,
students at a state university, and students at a fundamentalist denominational college were asked to express their criteria for judging people as
good or bad.

  I wonder if you would think about your various friends and pick out two
  that you admire most. Now, what is it about the first person that you particularly admire? Anything else? . . .

  What is it about any person that makes him good? Anything else? What
  kinds of things about a person would make him especially bad?

  Suppose you wanted to raise your children to become the finest possible
  people. What are the important things you would try to teach them?

  What about yourself do you like? What about yourself do you not like?

The answers to the two general questions about what makes people
good or bad were used as the basis for value measurement. Although the
wording of the responses was very diverse, it was possible to get reasonably
high agreement on their classification into 21 categories which appeared
relatively frequently in the samples studied. (Altogether sixty categories
were discriminated, but the low-frequency ones were then combined into
wider categories.) Each person could therefore be classified as mentioning
or not mentioning each of these categories; he could be given a 21-dimen-
sioned value profile.

   The responses on these two questions about people in general were then checked against responses to the other questions on standards applied to friends, to bringing up children, and to one's self, and were significantly related, although we are not told how high the correlation was. A retest after a three months' interval on 50 respondents was also used to obtain an estimate of test-retest reliability; on many categories this was quite low, suggesting that as a measure of individual traits the method is not very effective. Possibly this could be improved by basing the classification of respondents on the full range of questions. Open-ended responses only to two questions about what makes people good or bad apparently do not produce a large enough "sample" of a person's values at any one time to be reliable.

It should be noted that these values are actually limited to criteria used in judging individuals ("moral ideals"), and omit those used in evaluating groups, communities, societies, or material objects. They also are clearly normative values, rather than personal preferences for ways of life.

In spite of the rather low individual test-retest reliabilities, the results show striking and understandable differences between the three populations studied. Listed in order of their frequency in the adult sample from the suburban community, the categories derived by the researchers and their frequency of mention in the three samples are shown in Table 4.

TABLE 4

Normative Criteria for Judging Individuals Expressed by Three Samples Responding to Open-Ended Questions

	Suburb	State Univ.	Fundamentalist College
Love of people	50%(1)	35%(2)	55%(2)
Honesty	49 (2)	25 (8)	28 (11)
Individual dignity	32 (3)	8 (16)	26 (13)
Generosity	31 (4)	13 (13)	23 (14)
Self-control, etc.	26 (5)	24 (6)	55 (3)
Genuineness	26 (6)	27 (5)	17 (17)
Social skills	19 (7)	43 (1)	66 (1)
Friendliness	18 (8)	15 (11)	55 (4)
Dependability	18 (9)	13 (14)	17 (18)
Religiousness	18 (10)	1 (20)	49 (5)
Happiness	17 (11)	20 (9)	43 (7)
Fairness	16 (12)	7 (18)	15 (19)
Humility	15 (13)	16 (10)	43 (8)
Integrity	12 (14)	15 (12)	21 (15)
Hard work	12 (15)	13 (15)	28 (12)
Loyalty	12 (16)	4 (19)	21 (16)
Intelligence	11 (17)	31 (4)	9 (20)
Respect for authority	10 (18)	6 (18)	38 (9)
Individuality; self-sufficiency; independence	5 (19)	32 (3)	32 (10)
Achievement; striving to do well	4 (20)	24 (7)	6 (21)
Being liked by others	1 (21)	0 (21)	47 (6)

A further effort to analyze the structure of values in these three populations was made by a cluster analysis on these 21 categories of values. The correlation between the presence of each pair of "moral ideals" was calculated, and those which were statistically significant were plotted in a matrix; it was then possible to order the items so that they fell into five clusters whose items were significantly related to one another, and not to items in other clusters. One cluster was composed of honesty, integrity, and genuineness, and was labelled "individual integrity." A second was intelligence, dependability, and fairness, which the researcher labelled "trustworthiness." (Could these items be related largely because they are applied to men, or by men? The relation of criteria for judging individuals to sex roles was not considered.) Religiousness and self-control made up a third factor. Love of people, individual dignity, generosity, and friendliness made up a fourth, labelled "people orientation." A fifth comprised happiness, respect for authority, social skills and humility, and was labelled "interpersonal opportunism." Other items had too low frequencies or did not correlate significantly with any others.

The same clusters appeared with certain shifts in items among the State University students, along with a sixth composed of hard work and achievement. Among the fundamentalist college students, however, these clusters do not appear; the structure of values is quite different. Instead, a large cluster centers around friendliness and happiness, and includes being liked, independence, hard work, and, marginally, respect for authority. Social skills, self-control, and humility form a second cluster. Both of these are considered related to the "interpersonal opportunism" pattern. The relatively simple structure is considered evidence of the value-homogeneity of the fundamentalist college students. Interestingly enough, "religiousness" as a criterion for judging others, although professed by about half of the students, has no significant relationship to any other value.

The same investigator developed a set of eight Guttman scales based on some of these values:

self-control	religiousness
intellectualism	independence
kindness to people	status
social skills	loyalty

The scales derive from a checklist of 41 attributes of people: the respondent must indicate whether he always admires them in other people, always dislikes them, or might do either depending on the situation. Scott was able to show relations between these values applying to individuals, and eight scales representing the same general values applied to foreign policy. Thus "self-control" correlated with the desire to avoid war, kindness to people with the desire to help other countries, and so on. Seven

TABLE 5

Importance of Various Criteria for an Ideal Job

Criterion	Ranked First	Other Highly Important	Medium	Low	
Provide an opportunity to use my special abilities	27	51	20	2	100%
Enable me to look forward to a stable, secure future	24	37	31	8	100%
Permit me to be creative and original	10	38	39	13	100%
Give me an opportunity to be helpful to others	10	33	44	13	100%
Provide me with a chance to earn a great deal of money	10	29	48	13	100%
Give me an opportunity to work with people rather than things	7	37	36	20	100%
Give me a chance to exercise leadership	4	28	53	15	100%
Leave me relatively free of supervision by others	3	35	48	14	100%
Give me social status and prestige	2	24	53	21	100%
Provide me with adventure	1	15	40	44	100%

of the eight values had highly significant correlations with the corresponding foreign-policy goals.

1.2 Values in particular areas of life

A very useful method of measuring values applicable to particular areas of life was developed by the Cornell study of college student values (Goldsen, et al.). In the area of occupational choice, for example, they were presented with a list of abstract criteria for "the ideal job for me." Each criterion was to be rated as highly important, of medium importance, or of little or no importance, irrelevant, or distasteful (these latter all combined). Furthermore, those rated as "highly important" were to be ranked in numerical order of their importance to the respondent. This provided an absolute rating; it also ranked the top few criteria without the burden of having to rank a long list or go through a large number of paired comparisons.

The results of this question for students at eleven universities are shown in Table 5 (Goldsen, et al., 27).

These are predominately preferential values. An element of social evaluation or obligation may influence certain choices (for example, being helpful to others, or being free of supervision), but there is no clearcut normative quality to most. Indeed, the question "personalizes" these values by specifying that they are to be rated in terms of the ideal job "for me."

With this rather simple device it was possible to measure values of students which were related—although by no means perfectly—to their occupational plans (Table 6).

There is not a one-to-one matching of verbally expressed criteria and job choices. Some occupations, like law, medicine, and business, seem to recruit people with widely varied values. These occupations actually permit a wide range of activities embodying various goals, and some people decide to enter them partly on the basis of situational pressures. The highest correspondence of values and choice appears among those planning to enter artistic fields; valuing creativity is almost a *sine qua non* for architects and artists. Likewise, a lack of concern with "earning a great deal of money" is almost a necessary condition for entering teaching. It will also be noted that some occupations involve particular patterns; the food, hotel, and restaurant group emphasize both money and being helpful to others, as is appropriate for a service industry; even the sales and promotion people are rather interested in "being helpful." The advertising, public relations, and journalism people are notable in combining creativity with an interest in making a great deal of money; the teachers combine an interest in creativity with wanting to be helpful. All of these results make sense and suggest that the value-measuring device is working in the aggregate, although it may not be too good a predictor for any one individual.

TABLE 6

Criteria for Desirable Occupation

	Percentage Rating as "Highly Important"		
Planned Occupation	*Chance to Earn a Great Deal of Money*	*Permit Me to Be Creative and Original*	*Opportunity to Be Helpful to Others*
Highest on "money"			
Food, restaurant, hotel	77	45	65
Business, real estate, finance	58	36	30
Sales, promotion	54	36	45
Law	50	43	45
Highest on "creativity"			
Architecture	31	86	29
Advertising, public relations, journalism	56	83	31
Artistic and related fields	49	81	28
Natural science	30	64	30
Teaching	17	59	47
Engineering	38	52	28
Farming	31	48	22
Highest on "helping others"			
Personnel	41	41	75
Medicine	33	34	53

It may be argued that the correspondence of values and occupational plans comes about in reverse, that people adjust their stated desires to the careers which they have entered on through chance or force of circumstance. To answer this argument we would have to know which came first, the "criterion" or the choice. Fortunately, we have this information for some members of a sample of Cornell students who were asked about both criteria and choices twice, two years apart (Rosenberg). This permits us to look at the relationship between values professed in 1950 and subsequent changes in occupational plans by 1952. The results of this analysis are rather striking. Results are reported for two groups—those planning to be teachers and those planning to be businessmen. For purposes of this analysis, the two criteria "be helpful to others" and "working with people rather than things" were considered "people-oriented" values, and all others as "non-people-oriented." For the analysis of the potential businessmen, "the chance to earn a great deal of money" or "give me social status and prestige" were combined as "money-status values."

There is a good deal of shifting of occupational plans among these students in any case; but those whose values are not congruent with the type of occupation they initially plan to enter are much more likely to change.

The total picture of changes both of plans and of values is presented

TABLE 7

Values Related to Subsequent Changes in Occupational Plans

	Those Planning to Be Teachers in 1950	
	People-oriented	*Non-people-oriented*
Still planning to be teachers in 1952:	57	19
No longer planning to be teachers in 1952:	43	81
	100%	100%
	(82)	(26)

	Those Planning to Be Businessmen in 1950	
	Money-status Oriented	*Not Money-status Oriented*
Still planning to be businessmen in 1952:	57	32
No longer planning to be businessmen in 1952:	43	68
	100%	100%
	(42)	(37)

in highly amplified form when both values and occupations are classified crudely as "people-oriented" or "not people-oriented," and people are classified by their position at two points in time.

This "sixteen-fold Table" tells us six things:

1. Initial consistency: There is a modest relationship between occupational choice and values early in the college career (64% choose occupations consistent with their values).
2. Trends in values and in choices: The overall division of the group on both values and choices has remained virtually unchanged over the two years. (There was a *slight* falling off of people-oriented occupations, from 44% to 41%.)
3. Turnover in values and in choices: In spite of this surface stability there has been a good deal of individual change in both directions. (Six per cent have changed both their values and their choice, 33% have changed one of these, and only 61% remain exactly as they were, even with respect to such a broad two-fold classification as is used here.)
4. Trend toward consistency: There is a slight increase in consistency of occupational choice with values as students go through college (after two years 69% choose consistently as against 64% earlier).
5. Turnover of consistency: The 5% net gain in consistency was the result of fairly large counter-movements (19% moved from inconsistent, but 14% moved the other way).

TABLE 8

Occupational Values and Choices of College Students at Two Points in Time

Occ. Choices and Values in 1952	Occupational Choices and Values in 1950				
		(inconsistent)			
	P.O. Occ. P.O. Value	P.O. Occ. NPO Value	NPO Occ. P.O. Value	NPO Occ. NPO Value	1952 Totals
P.O. Occ. P.O. Value	Remain consistent 22.9	Become consistent 3.0	5.1	Consistent change .8	31.7
P.O. Occ. NPO Val. (Inconsistent)	Become inconsistent 2.1	Remain inconsistent 4.1	1.1	Become inconsistent 2.0	9.3
NPO Occ. P.O. Val. (Inconsistent)	4.2	1.1	10.3	6.0	21.6
NPO Occ. NPO Val.	Consistent change 2.5	Become consistent 4.4	6.9	Remain consistent 23.6	37.4
1950 *Totals*	31.7	12.5	23.3	32.4	100.0 (712)

6. Relative strength of the two variables: Those who moved toward consistency did so just as frequently by changing their values as by changing their occupational choice. (Of the 19% who became consistent, 10% did so by changing their values, and 9% by changing their choices.) Likewise, those who became inconsistent did so about as often by changing their values as by changing choices. (Of the 14% who became inconsistent, 8% did so because of a change in values, and 6% because of a change in choices.)

Of these results, the first, second, and fourth could have been obtained by interviewing different samples at a two-year interval (a "trend study"), but the third, fifth, and sixth results could only be obtained by a "panel study" such as this one, following the same individuals over time.

The method of rating and ranking abstract criteria for particular areas of choice or evaluation was applied to other fields as well by the Cornell study. These included the goals of college education, the characteristics of an ideal mate, those of an ideal religious or ethical system, and those of an ideal government (Goldsen, et al., 7, 90, 128–129, 165).

The researchers were not able in these other fields to provide a neat validation of the values scales as in the occupational field, since the relevant behavior or choices were either inaccessible to study or would not become apparent until much later in the students' lives. However, the question about the characteristics of an ideal government could be related to certain specific policy questions. On this topic the attempt to measure values by rating of abstract criteria seems to have worked rather badly, since the abstract criteria have little relation to concrete policies verbally advocated on other questions.

Among the characteristics of an ideal government endorsed by large majorities were:

Unrestricted freedom to practice one's own religion, for everybody. (92% rate this "highly important")

Freedom to express or communicate any opinion on any subject, for everyone. (76% consider this "highly important")

The unrelated policy questions concerned the suppression of "dangerous" ideas and "unwholesome" religions. About one-fifth of all students favored suppression, and almost all of these students had endorsed "unrestricted freedom for everyone" in the abstract.

The contrast between the relative success and failure of ratings of abstract value-criteria to predict related specific behavior in these two areas illustrates the problem. Many more such studies will have to be made before we can predict in what areas or situations the abstract expressions are likely to relate to concrete choices. An article by John Dollard entitled "Under What Conditions Do Opinions Predict Behavior?" contains a useful discussion of the problem.

It might be suggested, however, that the following conditions favored the validity of the occupational values scale compared with that of political values:

a. Occupational choice is a salient personal problem for all college students; they must make a number of real and far-reaching decisions on the subject at this stage of their lives. Choice of an ideal government is not a real problem for them as it was for the delegates to the Constitutional Convention, and while opportunities to take action in support of civil liberties were occasionally available, the vast majority of students could ignore the issue if they so desired, unlike occupational decisions.

b. The culture from which the students come makes slogans about "freedom" part of the ritual of school life ("with liberty and justice for all"), of election campaigns, and of other patriotic celebrations, with very little emphasis on concrete application. Students are indoctrinated with the slogans of "freedom." In the occupational area the amount of "official morality" is much less, since the decline of the Horatio Alger myth.

c. In the political area the society not only does not make its slogans

TABLE 9

Abstract values and concrete policies

	Freedom to Express or Communicate Any Opinion on Any Subject for Everyone		
	Highly Important	*Medium, Low, or Irrelevant*	
People should be kept from spreading dangerous ideas because they might influence others to adopt them			
Agree	85	15	100%(562)
Disagree	94	6	100%(1832)
Uncertain	90	10	100%(352)

	Unrestricted Freedom to Practice One's Own Religion for Everyone		
	Highly Important	*Medium, Low, or Irrelevant*	
Religions which preach unwholesome ideas should be suppressed			
Agree	88	12	100%(515)
Disagree	94	6	100%(1578)
Uncertain	94	6	100%(644)

about freedom concrete but engages in behavior directly contradicting them. In recent years a large amount of public and private activity has been devoted to the suppression of certain groups and expressions, with a great deal of support from the press, political leaders, patriotic societies, and churches. Not only the Communist party but all kinds of radicals have been subjected to this treatment; as have magazines, books and motion pictures suspected of being immoral.

2. Specific Evaluative Statements as Indicators of Basic Values

Instead of asking people for their general goals in life, or for the attributes of an ideal job, mate, government, or religion, we may ask people long lists of specific questions and try to derive general underlying values from the responses.

2.1 Personal likes and dislikes

One outstanding example of this technique is the Activities Index (Stern, Stein, and Bloom). This consists of "like-dislike" responses to a list of 300 activities, such as the following:

Arguing with an instructor or supervisor.
Disregarding rules and regulations that seem unfair, even though I may suffer for it.
Organizing a protest meeting.
Studying the music of particular composers, such as Bach, Beethoven, etc.
Doing things with my hands: manual labor, manipulation, or construction.
Managing a store or business.
Walking along a dark street in the rain.
Making up and eating odd sandwiches.
Eating soft-boiled eggs.

The 300 activities were selected to represent the 32 "basic needs" proposed by Henry Murray in *Explorations in Personality*. Whether in fact they form 32 clusters or factors corresponding to the hypothesized basic needs has not yet been demonstrated. Scores obtained on the 32 a priori "scales" have been factor analyzed, and certain broad personality factors derived in this way. The items obviously do not have to be classified according to the 32-need scheme. The richness and scope of this questionnaire suggest that it might be used as a general measure of non-normative values. The formulation of the question as "liking or disliking" clearly puts the emphasis on personal preference rather than normative values.

2.2 Judgments on social issues

An example of the use of specific evaluative statements containing an element of moral approval or disapproval is the Inventory of Beliefs (Cooperative Study of Evaluation in General Education; also Stern, Stein, and Bloom). This is a set of 100 items (in the revised form T) to which the respondent is asked to agree or disagree. Many of the items do not express a value judgment at all but take the form of factual beliefs, for instance:

> "Lowering tariffs to admit more foreign goods into this country tends to raise our standard of living."
> "Foreign films emphasize sex more than American films do."

These beliefs, while they may be empirically related to values, are not in form statements of preference or obligation. However, 56 items on the Inventory do deal with what *should* be. Examples are:

> "It is only natural and right for each person to think that his family is better than any other."
> "Speak softly, but carry a big stick."
> "Picket lines ought to be respected and never crossed."
> "No world organization should have the right to tell Americans what they can or cannot do."
> "Literature should not question the basic moral concepts of society."
> "Europeans have no faults as bad as the provincial smugness and intolerance of Americans."

The content of these 56 items can be classified as follows:

14 norms applicable to people in general
(see the first three examples above)
10 statements of what government policies should be
(example four above)
13 statements of what literature, art, science, and education should or should not do
(example five)
15 judgments on various social groups such as Americans, foreigners, nudists, etc.
(example six above)
4 aesthetic preferences (concerning modern art, music, etc.)

In spite of their almost bizarre variety, the content of these items is mainly concerned with the themes of ethnic prejudice, traditionalistic sex morality, and nationalism—hardly a broad coverage of social issues. This corresponds indeed to the intention of its makers; the Inventory of Beliefs was intended to measure "stereopathic thinking," a personality or intellectual syndrome which liberal education was supposed to combat. The model of the "stereopath" seems to have been the student who adheres to a certain American pattern of small-town conservatism, fundamentalism, and prejudice, as opposed to the attitudes of the cosmopolitan liberal intellectual.

Other measures focus on special areas of public policy. The scales of "liberalism-conservatism" in recent years are largely concerned with attitudes toward Keynesian antidepression policies and the welfare state. A broader coverage of public issues is found in some studies. The West survey of college graduates divided the area of social-policy values into three segments: ethnocentrism (prejudice), internationalism, and attitudes toward the welfare state or planning *vs.* laissez-faire (Havemann and West). The Cornell study of college students devised three scales: civil liberties attitude, attitude toward organized labor, and, again, laissez-faire *vs.* government planning and welfare policies (Goldsen et al.). There does not appear to exist any wide-spectrum, rationally selected inventory of public-policy attitudes which is up to date. Such an inventory would probably tap such basic political-economic values as:

Ethnic prejudice
Internationalism-nationalism
Civil liberties *vs.* repression of deviants
Welfare state and planning *vs.* laissez-faire
Attitude toward organized labor
Attitude toward big business

Whether these would in fact emerge as the underlying clusters of items remains to be seen. Berelson, Lazarsfeld, and McPhee in *Voting* distinguish "position issues" (related to class interests) from "style issues" (related to cultural and personal interests and tastes). The former include most economic issues; the latter, religious, racial, civil liberties, and international issues. Lipset in *Political Man* has pointed out the lack of correlation between welfare-state issues and civil liberties issues in an essay on "Working-Class Authoritarianism." The Cornell study (Goldsen et al.) and Martin Trow's study of support for McCarthy have shown the lack of a close correlation between attitudes toward big business and attitudes toward labor unions: a significant number of people are hostile both toward big business and toward the big-labor, big-government institutions, while another group are favorable to both. Building upon these various distinctions, it may be possible to create a useful multi-dimensional measure of social-policy values, covering a broad range of issues. Certainly the notion of a single "liberalism-conservatism" dimension must be thrown out for present-day studies. There is urgent need for a more sophisticated approach to political attitudes.

An unusual procedure for covering a wide range of social policy issues was devised by Carter. He sets up a "projective situation" in which several explorers come upon an ideal unpopulated country never before discovered. They engage in a dialogue concerning the best society for the future population of this country, which they name Kolomon. The dialogue contains about 70 substantive paragraphs. A sample is as follows:

TOKAL: I think it would be better if the government owned all the land. If private ownership is allowed, the inevitable will happen and some men will get too much, and others will get too little.

LANOR: History has shown, I beg to remind my friend, that production is always higher in countries where private ownership is allowed. A man will work harder if he owns his own land and has a chance to make a profit from the fruits of his own labor.

IVA: Perhaps the solution lies in letting each man own the land during his lifetime and having it go back to the government when he dies.

LANOR: I disagree. What good is a man's work and sweat, if he cannot pass on his property to his children? I repeat: without private ownership of land, there is little incentive for a man to produce as much as he can.

The discussion covers many areas besides land ownership: education, social organization, moral code, foreign investment, industrialization, religion, etc. Respondents read through the dialogue, marking the margin with + +, +, ±, −, or − − to indicate agreement, disagreement, or ambivalence with respect to each statement. These indications of opinion are then summarized into 24 scores indicating the social value profile of the individual.

The technique produced meaningful group differences between samples of Indian, Filipino, and American students attending colleges in the U. S., and correlated highly with another test devised by the investigator which presented social-policy goals in abstract form as paired comparisons.

Respondents were reported as highly interested in the material. A large number of issues could be covered with minimum strain and boredom, compared to a prolonged questionnaire. The method is, of course, easily adaptable to almost any topic under the sun—one can devise dialogue on any issues taking place among appropriate people. It permits either specific or abstract values to be presented. It also may permit more adequate presentation of complex issues than a simple series of questions. Arguments can be developed, and distinctions made, in a way which is impossible in the questionnaire form. More work needs to be done using this form, but it is possibly a more humane and intelligent form of communication than the usual questionnaire.

Another way of getting away from slogans and unreal abstractions is the "story" technique. As shown by the example of the Cornell student study concerning slogans of "freedom," the individual respondent may respond quite superficially to an abstract policy question. He may have never made a personal decision on the subject; he may have thought little about it; and his answer may have little resemblance to his behavior in more concrete situations. The story method tries to present him with a more concrete situation. One of the best examples is A. W. Jones' study of "attitude toward corporate property rights," entitled *Life, Liberty, and Property.* Feeling that "property rights" was too abstract and sloganized a concept to ask about directly, Jones formulated a set of concrete situations in which dispossessed farmers in the depression, unemployed coal miners, workers whose employers refused to negotiate with a union, and similar aggrieved groups took actions which infringed the corporate property rights of banks, mine owners, and large corporations.

In each situation the respondent was asked whether he approved or disapproved the action taken, and his answers scored from 0 to 4 in intensity of acceptance of the property rights involved. The vividness and realism of the stories not only made the questionnaire more palatable, but presumably obtained more valid responses. The stories more nearly resembled the actual situations in which the respondent might have to make judgments or take actions involving respect for corporate property rights than would a set of abstract questions.

The results of the use of this questionnaire in Akron, Ohio, during the height of the labor conflict of the late 1930's suggest its usefulness.

TABLE 10

Attitude Toward Corporate Property Rights in Situations When They Conflicted with "Human Rights"

Score	C.I.O. Rubber Workers	Business Leaders	Middle Groups	Random Sample
0–3	39%	0%	10%	18%
4–7	29	0	10	15
8–11	17	0	15	18
12–15	6	0	15	14
16–19	6	0	17	14
20–23	3	6	16	9
24–27	—	11	9	5
28–32	—	83	7	7
	100%	100%	100%	100%
	(193)	(18)	(239)	(303)

The author points out that although the industrial labor and management groups most directly concerned with the struggles over unionization and wages are extremely polarized, presenting virtually non-overlapping distributions, the middle groups (consisting of chemists, office workers, teachers, ministers, and small merchants) lie mainly in the middle score range. Therefore a random sample of the city population does not present an extreme polarization, but tended to support compromise, which did in fact eventually take place.

2.3 Norms of personal conduct

A similar technique for measuring one particular value-dimension in the area of personal conduct was employed by Stouffer and Toby. Students were presented with situations of conflict between friendship obligations and general moral principles. They were asked whether the friend *has a right* to expect special treatment. Four situations were presented, putting the respondent in the roles of witness to an accident, drama critic reviewing a play, doctor examining an insurance prospect, and corporation director. Scores derived from these items were highly correlated with answers to similar questions about situations from college life with which the student might be directly confronted: as an examination grader, library assistant, and proctor at an examination.

The Stouffer questionnaire measured one of Parsons' pattern-variables, universalism-particularism. Strodtbeck has measured orientation toward achievement versus familism, by the same method of asking what a person should do in a set of choice situations, and found significant differences between different ethnic groups. A number of other scales for measuring particular value-dimensions have been devised which employ the method of obtaining responses to a number of specific situations or proposals, either in terms of what the respondent likes and dislikes, or what he thinks should or should not be done. Presumably some combination of a large number of these scales would provide a general value profile of the individual.

3. Statements of Future or Hypothetical Behavior

Still closer to the observation of actual behavior is a type of questioning in which the respondent is confronted with hypothetical but realistic situations, and asked how he thinks he *would* behave. The Stouffer study which asked what a person *should do* also asked what the respondent thought he *would do* in the situations. The results were not always the same.

The effort is to present the respondent with a sufficiently concrete and realistically described situation that he will be more likely to respond in the way he would actually act. The questions should duplicate as closely as possible the kind of value-testing situations which we would like to observe if we only have access to them or were willing to wait half a life time for them to occur.

There seem to be relatively few examples of this technique. The Allport "future autobiography" comes close, in the form of a completely unstructured essay on how the respondent plans to spend his life (Gillespie and Allport). In describing his "expectations, plans and aspirations for the future," the respondent is free to say what he will do in his major life decisions—what career he will enter, what his avocations will be, how he will bring up his children, how much he will participate in public affairs, how he will decide all of the major choices a person must make.

The Cooperative Study of Evaluation in General Education used a set of realistic hypothetical situations in its "Problems of Human Relations" test. The respondent is asked what he would do in a variety of situations—as a school teacher, in an apartment-sharing arrangement, in a friendship relation. (A few of the items for some reason ask what he *should* do.) The two test-writers found difficulty in making up items for which the "right" answer in terms of middle-class American norms was not invariably chosen; and the items actually used raise questions of values and social tactics which are very difficult to separate. The alternatives supposedly represent a "democratic," an "authoritarian," a "laissez-faire," and a "resort to experts" approach to human relations. The instrument did not achieve high reliability.

An attempt to use the method of hypotheticals in a particular area is the "Legal Ethics Questionnaire" used in several ongoing studies of lawyers and law students by Carlin and Barton. Here lawyers and law students were asked how they would behave in a set of concrete situations involving possible conflicts between self-interest and client interest, client interest and the public interest, and self-interest and the rights of lawyer colleagues. An effort was made to validate the items by the following technique: ratings as to their overall "ethicality" were obtained on a group of about 60 lawyers from other lawyers who knew them well. The 60 lawyers were given the questionnaire, and their scores on the "client," "colleague," and "justice" scales compared with the rating of the lawyer-"judges" who knew them. A rather good relationship was obtained for most "client" items, some relationship for the "colleague" items, and only a few significant relationships for the "public interest" items. This suggested that the judges themselves were placing less stress on the public interest as a component in ethicality, or that the respondents were more likely to falsify their behavior in this area.

The hypothetical-situation technique could be used for a wide range of ethical issues. We might ask people who are, or expect to become, businessmen how they would behave in a set of situations involving conflict between interest of the firm and adherence to ethical standards, or between self-interest and ethical conduct. Other sets of situations could be presented to people in other professions; and for almost everyone sets relating to conduct in family and friendship relations, consumer behavior, leisure-time activities, or citizenship activities would be relevant. Klausner has developed a "Faith Scale" which asks people what they would do in

situations of varying danger and threat which pose an obligation to help
another person.

Of course there is a great distance between saying that you would be
honorable or brave, and actually behaving in these ways. But at least these
questions go beyond generalities and slogans, by asking for concrete decisions in specific, realistic situations which the respondent may have been
in or may expect to be in. Short of studying actual behavior, this "story"
method would seem to have the closest correspondence to the notion that
basic values are those which influence real-life decisions. It would appear
worth further investigation.

4. Reports or Observations of Actual Behavior

If basic values are those which influence people's important real-life
decisions, as distinct from purely verbal responses in the artificial situation of an interview or a test, the most valid way to measure people's
values would be to measure their actual behavior: how they conduct themselves in their various social roles, and their choice of roles and activities.

One of the best examples of actual behavior measures is found in
Havemann and West's *They Went to College.* A sample of alumni from
American colleges generally were asked about their activities in the following fields: local community affairs; political activity; and intellectual
activity. The indicators were questions about how much they read about
various topics; how often they discussed them; whether they contributed
money or belonged to organizations in these fields; and whether they took
action by voting, writing letters to government officials, or calling on officials to influence them. The resulting measures correlated with the type
of college program which the graduates had taken.

A major problem in interpreting behavioral indicators is that behavior
is influenced by *situational factors* as well as by the internal dispositions
of the actor. Furthermore, the internal dispositions include not only values,
but also knowledge, beliefs, and abilities. A man may be politically active
because the system of rewards makes it profitable, or because he is in a
position to see that his self-interest is affected by government policies, as
well as because he places a high value on community or national welfare.
Likewise a man may be politically inactive because of the severity of the
penalties which expressing his opinions might entail, or because his other
roles demand all his available time. It is only with "other things being
equal" that behavior clearly indicates values to the observer. To use behavior as an indicator of values requires that we know and hold constant
—by manipulation of situations or by statistical operations—the other factors which influence behavior in addition to values.

Thus the differences in activity of college graduates found by West
might have been caused by the different situations which confront people in different occupations. Scientists, doctors, or salaried persons work-

ing for big corporations may find civic and political action of many kinds not only inconvenient but economically harmful. Lawyers, on the other hand, find in political activity one of their few legitimate ways of advertising, and independent businessmen or top management people may find civic or political action both an economic advantage and a strongly enforced group obligation.

By comparing *within each occupation* those with a liberal and those with a specialized education, many of these situational pressures could be held constant, and the differences which remained could be reasonably attributed to the internal dispositions of the graduates, related (either through self-selection or impact) to their course of study.

The use of behavioral indicators of values also involves difficult problems of data-collection. The kinds of behavior on which we can obtain information simply by asking people are limited. The West study inquired into such relatively accepted or innocuous behavior as engaging in civic and political activity in general. Attempts to study participation in deviant or radical political activity do not always meet with such success. And suppose we wanted to find out how honest or socially responsible people were in their occupational activities, or in their friendship and family relations? Suppose we want to find out how altruistic they are, how concerned with the brotherhood of man, how strong their sense of justice is, *in practice?* These are presumably basic values, but they are sensitive issues on which a man is not a very good witness or judge of his own conduct. To study such values "in action" requires intensive examination of particular institutions or situations, to obtain detailed and verified information about people's behavior from others as well as themselves. Community studies, studies of trade union leadership, of political organizations, of professionals, of business management, might obtain sufficient information to characterize the values of the participants.

The study by Lazarsfeld and Thielens of the behavior of social-science teachers under the stress of the McCarthy period tried to obtain behavior indicators of "caution" in performing the role of academic intellectual. Various ingenious methods were used to verify reports of situational pressures and incidents, and to check on the reported cautious behavior. The current Columbia study of the bar of a large city, mentioned earlier, attempted to validate its "ethics scale" by use of ratings by well-informed colleagues on a preliminary sample of respondents (Carlin et al.). Whenever a study takes not an atomistic sample but complete segments or groups as its subjects, it becomes possible to use respondents not only to report on themselves but as informants or judges with respect to other members of the sample. Whether such "reputational indicators" are more valid than self-reports is not always obvious, but the use of several possible bases of judgment is usually an advantage. Thus a study of law students' "sense of justice" compared scores based on self-reports (of information and activity concerning individual and social injustices) with ratings of two groups: faculty members and other students. The two groups of raters did not entirely agree; their disagreements, however, tended to be systematic and explainable in terms of different standards and different opportunities for observation of the subjects.

Reports of how people spend their time and money, or of the frequency with which they engage in certain activities, can also be used to indicate their values, subject to the possible influence of other factors. A study of farm family values used data on actual expenditures for various purposes, material possessions, and amount of education of family members as indicators of values, along with hypothetical choices in spending time and money, direct questioning about how much various specific items were desired, and questions (both open-ended and using ranking of given criteria) concerning explicit general values (Wilkening). One must, of course, consider the influence of situational factors such as the amount of income and the availability of facilities for engaging in various activities; but within a given income group, considering family size, and within a given community, differences in leisure-time activities or expenditure patterns are obvious indicators of values.

A very useful "behavioral" measure is possible if we have obtained information from an entire interacting social group, like a student body or an entire organization staff. We can then ask respondents sociometric questions: whom they like, whom they admire, who they consider would best represent the group at a convention, who are the leaders of the group. We can then see what the values of the chosen people are. Presumably members choose people who best embody the accepted values of the group. Newcomb used this technique in his study of attitude change among Bennington college girls, and found that those chosen as leaders were the most liberal and politically active girls. This confirmed the evidence of attitude scales which showed a consistent change toward liberalism and political activity over time. Christie and Merton used the same technique to explore the values of medical students. Values of faculty members or organizational leaders can likewise be studied through examining the characteristics of those whom they rate highly, promote, or recommend. Coleman has measured the value climates of high schools by examining the attributes of those designated as "the leading crowd."

Finally, there should be mentioned the possibility of observing actual behavior in contrived situations, which control factors other than values. By holding knowledge, rewards and punishments, and similar situational factors constant, relatively pure measures of the influence of values can be obtained. By making direct observations we avoid the errors and biases of self-reporting or reporting by participants on others. However, this controlled manipulation and observation have rarely been done in the study of values. The "studies in deceit" by Hartshorne and May in the late 1920's, in which children were presented with apparent opportunities to cheat which were, in fact, detectable by the investigators as a means of measuring honesty, remain an almost unique example.

The values indicated by actual behavior can be either preference-values or normative values. Most expenditures or uses of leisure reflect preference-values. Certain types may reflect a sense of obligation: participating in community-welfare, religious, or political activities. However, all such activities can be engaged in for reasons of sociability, social conformity, careerist motives, and other extrinsic reasons; it requires a close analysis of each specific community situation to be able to estimate the extent to which the behavior reflects a real sense of obligation on the part of the actor. The best test situations are those "where the chips are down," where engaging in a certain behavior will obviously not bring advantage and may bring penalties. "The summer soldier and the sunshine patriot" then depart, while the people who have internalized the values remain.

If words can be falsified, actions can be misinterpreted. Actions speak louder than words only when their situational context is known and understood.

Summary

We have shown that, in certain cases at least, the explicit, abstract standards which people verbalize are related to actual, important behavior (for example, occupational choice). We have also shown that it is possible to obtain useful results by presenting respondents with sets of particular statements, and inferring underlying values from their patterns of response. We have suggested that one particularly useful method may be to present the subject with hypothetical situations described as concretely as possible, and ask him to predict his probable action. From a set of such predicted actions in hypothetical but realistic situations, both preferences and norms of conduct may be inferred. Finally, where it is possible to obtain reports of actual behavior and to analyze it to hold constant disturbing situational factors, such information can be most useful indicators of values.

The problems of how indicators should be combined into factors or dimensions, how much each indicator should be weighted in a total score, and how much reliability should be demanded of measures, have not been discussed here. Recent developments promise to solve a number of the more troublesome technical and intellectual problems in these areas. These include factor analysis, latent structure analysis, stochastic models of turnover, and other new techniques in scaling. Those interested can find an introductory discussion in *The Handbook of Social Psychology*, and a more advanced discussion in W. S. Torgerson's monograph on the theory and methods of scaling.

A general conclusion from this examination of methods used to discover and measure the values of individuals might be that it appears possible to do it, and that present methods work in certain areas, with moderate reliability and validity. Much more needs to be done before the concepts and measurements of values are developed sufficiently to permit us to measure whatever values we are interested in in any group.

Appendix I

Recent writings discussing the concept of values in the social sciences

Franz Adler, "The Value Concept in Sociology," v. 62, *American Journal of Sociology*, 1956, 272–279.

Distinguishes four concepts:

A. "Values are considered as absolutes, existing in the mind of God as eternal ideas, as independent validities, etc.
B. Values are considered as being in the object, material or non-material.
C. Values are seen as located in man, originating in his biological needs or in his mind. Man by himself or man in the aggregate, variously referred to as group, society, culture, state, class, is seen as 'holding' values.
D. Values are equated with actions."

Type A is "not accessible to sense perception" and, consequently, not suited to study by the methods of natural science. Type B involves a circularity in that the value "in the object" can only be defined with reference to the needs or desires of man. "Values according to C are as inaccessible to the methods of the natural sciences (at the present state of our knowledge concerning internal mental and emotional phenomena) as values according to A and B." Therefore D is the only possible definition.

C. S. Belshaw, "The Identification of Values in Anthropology," v. 64, *American Journal of Sociology*, 1959, 555–562.

Distinguishes three types of concepts:

A. "Values are *ideas about* worthwhileness," mainly "ideals or expressions about the dictates of moral obligation," but including aesthetic judgments also.
B. Values as "social imperatives," as "an idea of worthwhileness . . . consistently applied to the various occasions of acting," as "an explanation of dominant traits of civilization in terms of cultural choice."
C. "The third, or Type C, approach begins with the analysis of individual preferences as expressed through behavior (whether or not verbalized) by the actor."

William R. Catton, Jr., "A Theory of Value," v. 24, *American Sociological Review*, 1959, 310–317.

Valuing as preferring. Refers to Kluckhohn's definition of values as preferences "felt and/or considered to be justified," but asserts that there is no way to empirically measure this. He confuses "the feeling of being justified" with the metaphysical notion of "objective justification."

Stuart A. Dodd, "On Classifying Human Values," v. 16, *American Sociological Review*, 1951, 645–653.

"Let 'a value' be defined as a desideratum, i.e., anything desired or chosen by someone sometime."

Bertha B. Friedman, *Foundations of the Measurement of Values*. Teachers College, Columbia University, 1946, Chapter V: "The Definition of Value"; Ch. VI: "The Location of Values."

A collection of definitions; discussion of the indicators.

Clyde Kluckhohn, "Values and Value-Orientations in the Theory of Action: An Exploration in Definition and Classification," in Talcott Parsons and Edward Shils, eds., *Toward a General Theory of Action*, Harvard, 1951, 388–433.

> This is the clearest social-science discussion; it makes the essential distinctions, although in the end it tries to harmonize too many points in a single definition of what values are, rather than making a typology.

Charles Morris, *Varieties of Human Value*. University of Chicago Press, 1956.

> Distinguishes "operative values," what people actually choose, "conceived values," what people conceive as desirable or preferable, and "object values," what is preferable regardless of whether it is preferred or conceived as preferable. "Preferential behavior would then define the value field, and the various employments of the term 'value' would be explicated not as referring to different entities . . . but as delineating different aspects of the value field."

Ralph Barton Perry, *Realms of Value: A Critique of Human Civilization*. Harvard, 1954, Chapter I: "The Definition of Value in Terms of Interest," and Chapter VI: "The Meaning of Morality."

> "A thing—any thing—has value, or is valuable, in the original and generic sense when it is the object of an interest—any interest."

Appendix II

Value Scales and Related Indices

T. W. Adorno, Else Frenkel-Brunswik, Daniel J. Levinson, and R. Nevitt Sanford, *The Authoritarian Personality*, New York: Harper, 1950.

> *The F-scale* in its final form consisted of 30 statements to which the respondent could register strong, moderate, or slight agreement or disagreement. All of the statements were presumed to indicate authoritarian tendencies. 16 were factual-belief items, and 14 were evaluative in form. They deal with general norms of human relations, perceptions of human nature, social policy issues, and some philosophic issues such as belief in science. Provides an authoritarianism score (subject to problems of response-set). Recent revisions include half authoritarian and half "democratic" statements.

> *The E-scale* in its final form consisted of 20 items measuring ethnocentrism. 6 concerned Jews, 6 concerned Negroes, and 8 concerned other minorities and chauvinistic nationalism. Provides an ethnocentrism score. (Response-set problems same as F-scale.)

> *The Politico-Economic Conservatism* (PEC) *Scale* was a set of statements dealing mainly with the issue of laissez-faire vs. the welfare state. The initial form had 16, a revised form 14, and a short form 5 items. Interestingly, these scales are balanced, containing both liberal and conservative statements. Provides a liberalism-conservatism score.

G. W. Allport, P. E. Vernon, and Gardner Lindzey, *Study of Values*, revised edition. Boston: Houghton Mifflin Co., 1951.

> 45-item questionnaire with 30 agree-disagree or two-way choice items, 15 items with multiple alternatives to be ranked. Answers are combined to give six value scores: theoretical, economic, aesthetic, social, political, and religious.

Allen H. Barton, *Studying the Effects of College Education*. New Haven: The Edward W. Hazen Foundation, 1959.

Contains an examination of the concepts, measures, and analytic procedures used in Philip E. Jacob's *Changing Values in College*. An appendix contains an analysis of a number of specific scales and questionnaires.

———, *Organizational Measurement*. New York: College Entrance Examination Board, 1961.

Chapter on "Attitudes" contains an examination of studies which have tried to measure the value climates, norms, and goals of organizations, including educational institutions.

———, and Saul Mendlovitz, "The experience of injustice as a research problem," 13 *Journal of Legal Education*, 1960.

An exploratory attempt to construct a measurement of "concern with justice" in personal and in public affairs, using information, attitudes, and reported activities questions.

Bernard Berelson, Paul F. Lazarsfeld, and William McPhee, *Voting*. University of Chicago Press, 1954.

Chapter 9 analyzes the role of issues in the 1948 campaign and makes a distinction between position (class) issues and style (cultural) issues. It also presents scales of domestic and international liberalism-conservatism, which combine to produce a four-fold typology.

Jerome Carlin, Allen Barton, Saul Mendlovitz, and Wagner Thielens, studies on lawyers and law students, in progress, Bureau of Applied Social Research, Columbia University.

Roy E. Carter, "An experiment in value measurement," 21 *American Sociological Review*, 1956, 156–163.

A dialogue concerning the most desirable society to create in a newly discovered country, with about 70 paragraphs each putting forward a viewpoint on some social issues. Respondents read through the dialogue and indicate their agreement or disagreement with each paragraph on a five-point scale. Responses are coded into institutional areas such as education, social organization, moral code, land ownership, religion, etc., to give 24 scores. No overall score is made.

R. Christie and M. Jahoda, eds., *Studies in the Scope and Method of "The Authoritarian Personality."* Glencoe, Illinois: The Free Press, 1954.

———, and P. Cook, "A guide to published literature relating to the authoritarian personality," 45 *Journal of Psychology*, 1958, 171–199.

———, J. Havel, and B. Seidenberg, "Is the F-scale Irreversible? 56 *Journal of Abnormal and Social Psychology*, 1958, 143–159.

Analyses and critiques of the F-scale.

———, and Robert K. Merton, "Procedures for the sociological study of the values climate of medical schools," 33 *Journal of Medical Education*, 1958, No. 10, part 2, ch. 6.

"Semantic differential"—a seven-point rating scale—is used to measure the ideal characteristics of physicians as seen by medical students.

Inferring of values from the qualities of students selected by fellow students as friends and as representatives of the school, and from qualities of students considered "outstanding" by faculty.

Machiavellianism scale used to measure "a conception of human nature as fallible and weak, a lack of affect (i.e., the value of detachment in dealing with people), and the uses of expedient procedures in social relations." Scale as used here consisted of four agree-disagree items.

James S. Coleman, "The adolescent subculture and academic achievement," 65 *American Journal of Sociology*, 1951, 337–347.

Direct measures of student values using the question, "How would you most like to be remembered in school: as an athletic star, a brilliant student, or most popular?" for boys; "a leader in extracurricular activities" substitutes for athletics for the girls. Indirect measures of value climates were obtained by taking the answers of those who were designated as members of the "leading crowd" by other students.

Cooperative Study of Evaluation in General Education, Inventory of Beliefs. Washington: American Council on Education, 1951. Form T, revised by George G. Stern, Department of Psychology, Syracuse University.

A set of 100 statements on social, political, and other issues to which people respond on a four-point scale of agreement or disagreement. 46 of the items are purely factual in form; the rest are evaluative. An overall scale of "stereopathy" is derived from it. The revised form also permits a scoring of the response set, "tendency to agree or disagree."

Cooperative Study of Evaluation in General Education, Problems in Human Relations. Washington: American Council on Education, 1953.

30 hypothetical situations, involving a problem in dealing with people in personal or organizational activities. In 19 of them respondents are asked what they would do, in the rest what should be done or what he would like. Each is provided with a democratic, authoritarian, laissez-faire, and resort-to-experts response. Provides a profile of relative preference for these four modes of solving human problems.

Cooperative Study in General Education, *Cooperation in General Education*. Washington: American Council on Education, 1947. See also, Harold B. Dunkel, *General Education in the Humanities*. Washington: American Council on Education, 1947.

Inventory of Students' General Goals in Life. 20 general goals, ranked in a set of paired comparisons, each against each. The result is a rank-order on each goal for each respondent—a kind of 20-dimensioned value-profile.

Paul Diederich and Ruth Ekstrom, "Values expressed in judgments of the behavior of others," *Educational Testing Service Bulletin*, 1959, 59–63.

Open-ended question to children in grades 4, 7, 10, and 13: "Tell something a person did that made you like him better" and likewise like him less.

John Dollard, "Under what conditions do opinions predict behavior?" 12 *Public Opinion Quarterly*, 1948–49, 623–632.

Seven propositions are suggested for conditions under which verbal opinions are related to action.

James M. Gillespie and Gordon W. Allport, *Youth's Outlook on the Future*. Garden City: Doubleday, 1955.

Two instruments are reported here: the Autobiography from Now to 2000 A.D., an essay in which young people express their "expectations, plans, and aspirations for the future," and a questionnaire which contains, besides background items and factual expectations, 26 evaluative questions. No overall scoring is used on either.

Rose K. Goldsen, Morris Rosenberg, Robin M. Williams, Jr., and Edward A. Suchman, *What College Students Think*. New York: Van Nostrand, 1960.

Educational goals rating involves six goals of education.

Occupational values rating involves rating ten criteria for the "ideal job" for the respondent.

Philosophy of government scale is based on four items concerning government-intervention vs. laissez-faire, scored to give a five class liberalism-conservatism classification.

Ideal government rating involves rating 16 rights or privileges as to how important it is that the government should guarantee them.

Faith in human nature scale is a Guttman scale with 5 items dealing with trust in other people to be helpful and not take advantage. The items are factual rather than evaluative in form, and are intended to reveal "the individual's global attitude toward human nature."

Religiousness scale is a Guttman scale based on four items concerning need for religious faith, belief in a divine God, attitude toward one's church or religion, and commitment to religion as a major source of satisfaction in life. It gives a five-point scale of religiousness.

Characteristics of an ideal religious or ethical system. This is a rating of ten characteristics in terms of how important they are to the respondent; they include nature of the beliefs, personal and social functions, and organizational attributes.

Absolute religious belief scale is derived from the ratings of five of the characteristics of an ideal religion; it correlates very highly with the religiousness scale, but is based on doctrinal beliefs, while the religiousness scale is based largely on questions of personal saliency of religion without doctrines being spelled out.

H. Hartshorne and M. May, *Studies in Deceit.* New York: Macmillan, 1928.

A set of situational tests of children's honesty, involving honesty in school test situations and honesty with money. Correlations between test-honesty and money-honesty were low, suggesting that honesty was not an over-all trait but a set of specific habits formed in particular situations.

Ernest Havemann and Patricia Salter West, *They Went to College.* New York: Harcourt, Brace, 1952.

The College Alumni Questionnaire included three scales of social-political attitudes: internationalism, ethnocentrism, and economic liberalism-conservatism. It also includes scales of political participation, community participation, and cultural activity based on sets of questions reporting actual behavior in these areas. Fuller details of the study are available in an unpublished doctoral dissertation, *The College Graduate in American Society.* Columbia University, 1951.

Glenn R. Hawkes, "A study of the personal values of elementary school children." 12 *Educational and Psychological Measurement,* 1952.

90 activities presented in sets of threes to be ranked in terms of "which looks best to you." Items are assumed to represent ten values: beauty, comfort, excitement, family life, friendship, personal improvement, physical freedom, power, privacy, and recognition.

J. S. Himes, "A value profile in mate selection among Negroes," *Marriage and Family Living,* 1954, 244–247.

68 items, scored to produce a "value profile" of eight criteria for mate selection: economic status, educational status, family and social status, family relations, leisure interests, moral standards, personality traits, and physical appearance.

Alfred Winslow Jones, *Life, Liberty, and Property.* Philadelphia: Lippincott, 1941.

Scale of attitudes toward corporate property rights, based on seven "situations" of conflict between property rights and human needs. Respondents asked whether they approved or disapproved actions of people in the situations.

Samuel Klausner, Faith Scale. Bureau of Applied Social Research, Columbia University.

Florence R. Kluckhohn and Fred L. Strodtbeck, *Variations in Value Orientations.* Evanston: Row, Peterson, 1961.

"The instrument created for the testing of the differences and similarities in the rank ordering of the value-orientation alternatives in the five cultures is a schedule of twenty-two items which are divided among the orientations as follows: *relational* orientation, seven items; *man-nature* and *time orientations,* five items each; *activity* orientation, five items which can be counted as six since one has two parts. The items used for testing the *relational, man-nature,* and *time* orientations test for the ordering of three alternatives. Those which test on the *activity* orientation seek only for the preference between the Doing and Being alternatives. Limitations of time and research funds prevented the development of items which would test all three alternatives of this orientation and also precluded any consideration of the *human nature* orientation.

"Each item of the schedule first delineates a type of life situation which we believe to be common to most rural, or folk, societies and then poses alternatives of solution for the problem which derive from and give expression to the theoretically postulated alternatives of the value orientation in question. For example, each of the items developed for testing on the *relational* orientation contains alternatives of solution of a very general problem situation which express the Lineal, Collateral, and Individualistic variations."

A detailed analysis of the language used suggests that the activity-orientation items are mainly *preferential* values; the relational items are mainly normative, and the man-nature items mainly cognitive. The time orientation items were rather ambiguous or mixed as between normative and cognitive wording. The query, "which way of (handling the situation) do you think is best?" does not clearly distinguish "most effective" from "morally correct." The cognitive items occasionally use "is true" instead of "is best," or "is the best idea" instead of "is the best way of (doing so-and-so)."

Melvin L. Kohn, "Social class and parental values," 64 *American Journal of Sociology,* 1959, 337–351.

Checklist of 17 characteristics; parents asked which three are most important in a boy or girl of fifth-grade age.

Paul F. Lazarsfeld and Wagner Thielens, *The Academic Mind.* Glencoe, Illinois: The Free Press, 1958.

A study of college social science professors; this includes a variety of measures relevant to values: an index of caution, an index of concern with civil liberties, an index of political permissiveness in the campus setting, along with measures of external pressures and supports.

S. M. Lipset, *Political Man.* Garden City: Doubleday, 1960.

Chapter 4 contains a discussion of working-class authoritarianism as measured by various indicators; Chapter 5 examines middle-class authoritarianism as one form of "political extremism."

Charles Morris, *Varieties of Human Value.* University of Chicago Press, 1956.

The "Ways to live" questionnaire describes 13 ways to live in a paragraph each.

Respondents rate each Way on a seven-point scale of degrees of liking, and also rank the 13 in order of preference. This gives a 13-dimensioned profile.

Henry Murray, *Explorations in Personality*. New York: Oxford University Press, 1938.

An attempt to formulate a set of basic "needs." Contains discussions of the Thematic Apperception Test along with a wide variety of other tests, questionnaires, observations, etc.

Gwynn Nettler, "A measure of alienation," 22 *American Sociological Review*, 1957, 672–677.

17 items concerning both participation in common social activities and attitudes toward mass culture and present social institutions, which people respond to on a five-point scale of agreement or disagreement. These items give a single alienation score.

Theodore M. Newcomb, *Personality and Social Change*. New York: Dryden, 1943.

A set of items on social and political issues of the 1930's, to which respondents could indicate 5 degrees of agreement. An overall scale of liberalism-conservatism is derived from it.

C. Ramsey, R. S. Polson, and G. E. Spencer, "Values and adoption of practice," 24 *Rural Sociology*, 1959, 35–47.

120-item test measures 12 values: achievement, belief in science, belief in progress, efficiency, external conformity, familism, farming as a way of life, hard work, individualism, material comfort, security, traditionalism. Certain of these values were significantly related to adoption of new farming practices.

Morris Rosenberg, *Occupations and Values*. Glencoe, Illinois: The Free Press, 1957.

Analysis of the occupational value data from the Cornell Survey.

H. K. Schwartzenweller, "Value orientations in educational and occupational choices," 24 *Rural Sociology*, 1959, 246–256.

21 questions requiring ranking of four occupational goals in terms of "importance" to the respondent. Provides scores on 12 assumed values: achievement, creative work, external conformity, familism, friendship, hard work, individualism, material comfort, mental work, security, service to society, working with people.

William S. Scott, "International ideology and interpersonal ideology," 24 *Public Opinion Quarterly*, 1960, 419–435.

Guttman scales for eight criteria of judging people, based on traits "admired" or "disliked." Guttman scales for eight foreign policy goals.

Leo Srole, "Social integration and certain corollaries," 21 *American Sociological Review*, 1956, 709–716.

The Anomie scale consists of five items representing different aspects of individual malintegration with society: beliefs that public officials are not responsive to the citizens, that one can't plan for the future, that the average man is becoming worse off, that the future is so black that it isn't fair to bring children into the world, and that other people can't be counted on.

Buford Stefflre, "Concurrent validity of the Vocational Values Inventory," 52 *Journal of Educational Research*, 1959, 339–341.

168 forced-choice questions scored to yield 7 postulated vocational values: altruism, control, job freedom, money, prestige, security, and self-realization.

George G. Stern, Morris I. Stein, and Benjamin S. Bloom, *Methods in Personality Assessment*. Glencoe, Illinois: The Free Press, 1956.

The Activities Index consists of 300 activities to which people respond whether they like or dislike them. The results are combined into 32 assumed "basic need" scores, and are further combined by factor analysis to give a personality profile.

Samuel Stouffer, *Communism, Conformity and Civil Liberties*. New York: Doubleday, 1955.

Tolerance scale measures permissiveness toward people with deviant social and political ideologies—communists, socialists, atheists—in exercising rights of freedom of speech, press, and assembly.

————, and Jackson Toby, "Role-conflict and personality," 56 *American Journal of Sociology*, 1951, 395–406.

Seven hypothetical situations involving conflict between adherence to universalistic norms of honesty and loyalty to a friend. For each situation the respondent was asked both what he would do, and what his friend would have a right to expect. Four situations form an approximate Guttman scale of universalism-particularism.

Fred Strodtbeck, "Family interaction, values, and achievement," in D. C. McClelland, A. L. Baldwin, U. Bronfenbrenner, and F. L. Strodtbeck, *Talent and Society*. Princeton, New Jersey: Van Nostrand, 1958.

Measures of achievement orientation among two immigrant ethnic groups, studied in connection with observational measurements of family interaction patterns.

Martin Trow, "Small businessmen, political intolerance, and support for McCarthy," 64 *American Journal of Sociology*, 1958, 270–281.

This study employs a fourfold typology of political orientations toward the dominant economic institutions, based on questions as to whether big business has too much power and whether unions are good or bad. The types resulting were favorable to both big institutions, pro-union and anti-business, pro-business and anti-union, and anti both big institutions. A *scale of political tolerance* was also used, based on willingness to allow newspapers to criticize our form of government, to allow socialists to publish newspapers, and to allow Communists to speak on the radio. These two measures were examined in relation to support for "Senator McCarthy's methods of investigation."

E. A. Wilkening, "Techniques of assessing farm family values," *Rural Sociology*, 1954, 39–49.

Study used five ways of measuring values: open-ended questions on family goals, verbal ranking of five main goals, direct questions on how much certain items were desired, hypothetical choices in the use of time or money, and actual behavior (what material possessions were owned, how much education family members had gotten, expenditure patterns).

24

Moral Discomfort and Racial Segregation— An Examination of the Myrdal Hypothesis*

ERNEST Q. CAMPBELL

University of North Carolina

INTRODUCTION

It is a common assumption in the sociological and psychological literature on American race relations that there is a large amount of guilt among majority group members regarding a segregated social system. The major reference work by Gunnar Myrdal is the classic statement of this viewpoint: "[The Negro problem] makes for moral uneasiness." [1] "The moral struggle goes on within people and not only between them." [2] "The American Negro problem is a problem in the heart of the American. It is there that the interracial struggle goes on. The 'American Dilemma' . . . is the ever-raging conflict between, on the one hand, the valuations preserved on the general plane which we shall call the 'American Creed,' where the American thinks, talks, and acts under the influence of high national and Christian precepts, and, on the other hand, the valuations on specific planes of individual and group living, where personal and local interests; economic, social, and sexual jealousies; considerations of community prestige and conformity; group prejudice against particular persons or types of people; and all sorts of miscellaneous wants, impulses, and habits dominate his outlook." [3]

The same theme is emphasized in Arnold Rose's summary presentation of the Myrdal study. Rose says of our nation that "it labors persistently with its moral problems. It is taking its Creed very seriously indeed." [4] Or

Reprinted from *Social Forces*, 39, 3 (March 1961), 228–234, by permission of the author and The University of North Carolina Press.

* Paper presented at the twenty-third annual meeting of the Southern Sociological Society in Atlanta, Georgia, April 8, 1960.

[1] Gunnar Myrdal, *An American Dilemma* (New York: Harper and Bros., 1944), p. xiv.

[2] *Ibid.*, p. xlviii.

[3] *Ibid.*, p. xlvii.

[4] Arnold Rose, *The Negro in America* (New York: Harper and Bros., 1944), p. 8.

again: "Even a poor and uneducated white person in some isolated and backward rural region in the Deep South, who is violently prejudiced against the Negro and intent upon depriving him of civic rights and human independence, has also a compartment in his mind housing the entire American Creed of liberty, equality, justice, and fair opportunity for everybody." [5]

But the Myrdal-Rose position is by no means an alien voice. Rather, it represents an almost unanimous theme in both the professional and semi-popular literature. Simpson and Yinger, for example, conclude that "Although there may be some gains [from prejudice], there are, from the point of view of the interests and values of the prejudiced person himself, far more losses in the long run. One could scarcely expect otherwise among a people who proclaim a democratic ideology with great fervor. . . ." [6] Allport argues that ". . . prejudice in a life is more likely than not to arouse some compunction, at least some of the time. It is almost impossible to integrate it consistently with affiliative needs and humane values." [7] And Dollard observes that "It is characteristic of the human self, as Sumner has shown it to be of society, that the individual attempts to show a consistent front toward his fellow men; he does not like to be caught in inconsistencies. . . . It is a great mistake to think that the equalitarian ideal does not function in the South as well as in the North. . . . But there is more conflict over the ideal in Southerntown because it is more frequently and flagrantly violated. This is undoubtedly perceived as painful by middle-class white people; . . . ." [8] These are but illustrative of an abundant literature.

The position has not gone unchallenged. Golightly contends, for example, that guilt results from the violation of group ideals and that caste is not such a violation. He observes further that society itself provides mechanisms for reducing such incidental guilt feelings as may arise in the minds of the sophisticated and sceptical.[9] Campbell and Pettigrew, in a study of the performance of ministers during the Little Rock crisis in 1957 and 1958, conclude that neither the small sect minister, typically segregationist and vocal, nor the denomination minister, typically integrationist and silent, give significant evidence of guilt. They reason that social isolation and hostile attitudes shelter the former from communications that might force the moral issue, and that a well articulated Creed

[5] *Ibid.*, p. 10.

[6] G. E. Simpson and J. M. Yinger, *Racial and Cultural Minorities: An Analysis of Prejudice and Discrimination* (rev. ed.; New York: Harper and Bros., 1958), p. 287.

[7] Gordon W. Allport, *The Nature of Prejudice* (New York: Doubleday & Co., Inc. [Anchor Edition], 1958), pp. 312–313.

[8] John Dollard, *Caste and Class in a Southern Town* (New York: Doubleday & Co., Inc. [Anchor Edition], 1949), pp. 365–366.

[9] C. L. Golightly, "Race, Values, and Guilt," *Social Forces*, 26 (December 1947), pp. 125–139.

of Segregation further protects him. Those ministers who failed to defend a sensed moral imperative during crisis, on the other hand, held a set of values and beliefs centered around their occupational role obligations, the effect of which was to quiet any self-aggression that otherwise might develop.[10] And Merton observes that for one of his types, the all-weather illiberal (or prejudiced discriminator), "it is clear that one 'ought' to accord a Negro and a white different treatment in a wide diversity of situations, as it is clear to the population at large that one 'ought' to accord a child and an adult different treatment in many situations. . . . For the confirmed illiberal, ethnic discrimination does *not* represent a discrepancy between *his* ideals and *his* behavior. His ideals proclaim the right, even the duty, of discrimination." [11] Such challenges and qualifications constitute a minor fragment of the total, however.

The absence of quantitative empirical data is a uniform characteristic of the pertinent literature. There can be no doubt that a strict logical analysis reveals incompatibilities between the tenets of segregation and those of the American Creed. But we need not be satisfied with analysis at this level. Is the inconsistency an experiential phenomenon? What are its consequences for personality integration? What are its potentials for social change? What proportion of the population experiences the discrepancy as a significant source of discomfort? Can we distinguish those who do from those who do not? We cannot assume the answers to these empirical questions from a demonstration of the rational incompatibility of segregation and equalitarian values. The present paper reports an exploratory effort to measure the incidence and correlates of racial guilt.

DESIGN AND PROCEDURE

Data were secured from 279 students in social science and introductory sociology courses in 1957 at a public university in what is geographically if not culturally a Deep South state. Questionnaires were administered as schedules (for research purposes unrelated to this report) by research personnel to approximately half the total.[12] The others were completed as questionnaires in routine classroom situations. Four students did not complete the forms, reducing the working N to 275. The sample is 57 percent freshmen and 27 percent sophomore, the remainder being juniors

[10] Ernest Q. Campbell and Thomas F. Pettigrew, *Christians in Racial Crisis: A Study of The Little Rock Ministry* (Washington, D.C.: The Public Affairs Press, 1959), chaps. 3 and 4. See also "Racial and Moral Crisis: The Role of Little Rock Ministers," *American Journal of Sociology*, 64 (March 1959), pp. 509–516.

[11] R. K. Merton, "Discrimination and The American Creed," in R. M. MacIver (ed.), *Discrimination and National Welfare* (New York: Harper & Bros., 1949), p. 109.

[12] The assistance of Charles M. Grigg and his students is acknowledged with appreciation.

and seniors. Sixty-five percent were born in a Deep South state. Forty-three percent had fathers with some college education, while 36 percent of the fathers had not finished high school.

The material on which the analysis is based appeared in the form of four situations and was presented as "an exercise in role taking" in which the student would "imagine yourself in a situation you have not experienced." The first situation placed the student as a junior in a (unspecified) high school in the state, to which it had just been announced that Negro students, totalling perhaps 10 percent of the student body, would be admitted for the coming year. Seven agree-disagree items, taken from a Guttman scale built with a quite different population,[13] were then presented. The subject then turned the page and received a new set of instructions. These placed him near the end of his *senior* year in a state high school to which Negro students had been admitted the previous September. Their performance was described in favorable terms: "You have observed that [they] are generally friendly and polite, that they dress neatly, and that they study their lessons and perform well in class." The subject was asked to respond to the same seven items presented on the previous page and instructed not to be concerned about the comparability of his responses.

A third set of instructions placed the respondent in the same (i.e., senior year) situation except that the Negro students were described unfavorably: Some were said to have poor manners and shoddy clothing, to be unfriendly and such poor scholars that "sometimes the entire class is held back while the teacher tries to help them." Again the items were repeated.

Finally, the situation was structured as in the first presentation, with the student a high school *junior* just having learned of plans to desegregate. Instructions were different, however: "This time, respond to the items in terms of *how you think you ought to feel* about desegregation in public schools, regardless of how you actually feel about it. Although how you feel may correspond to how you think you ought to feel, do not be concerned with whether your responses coincide with those on any previous page."

The measures are called respectively the Before, the Good Performance, the Poor Performance, and the Ought. Two of the seven items were dropped before analysis began: one because it becomes a factual item in the Good Performance and Poor Performance situations, the other because in agreeing with it one must express hostility toward liberal whites as well as Negroes. The five remaining items were processed according to Guttman scale procedures.

As shown in Table 1, the items meet most scale criteria satisfactorily in each of the four situations, although in one or two instances adjacent

---

[13] See Ernest Q. Campbell, The Attitude Effects of Education Desegregation in a Southern Community: A Methodological Study in Scale Analysis (unpublished Ph.D. dissertation, Vanderbilt University, 1956).

TABLE 1

Cumulative Scale Properties, School Desegregation Attitudes in Four Hypothetical Situations (N of 275)

	Before[a]		Good[b]		Poor		Ought[c]	
	Obs.	*Ch.[d]*	*Obs.*	*Ch.*	*Obs.*	*Ch.*	*Obs.*	*Ch.*
C. of Reproducibility	.964	.852	.957	.849	.961	.863	.948	.840
C. of Scalability								
By individual marginals	.788	—	.737	—	.776	—	.622	—
By item marginals	.895	—	.876	—	.867	—	.853	—
Non-error Cases	.829	.387	.804	.370	.825	.422	.756	.345

[a] The response pattern (PNPPP) (where P is positive, N is negative) includes 17 cases, or 6.2 percent of the total. This exceeds the 5 percent limit usually used.
[b] The response pattern (PNPPP) includes 15 cases, or 5.5 percent of the total.
[c] The response pattern (PNPPP) includes 20 cases, or 7.5 percent of the total.
[d] "Obs." is an abbreviation for "observed," "ch." an abbreviation for "chance."

marginals become quite closely bunched. The number of pure scale types is encouragingly high in all cases. Furthermore, Table 2 indicates

TABLE 2

Percentage of Respondents Giving Positive Responses to Individual Items by Type of Measurement Situation (N of 275)

		Type of Situation			
Level of Difficulty	Item Number	Before	Good	Poor	Ought
Most	3	25.4	35.5	19.4	53.0
	5	29.0	46.6	21.9	53.4
	1	43.7	65.2	34.8	66.7
	6	52.3	69.9	39.1	69.1
Least	7	71.0	73.8	62.0	81.4

that the items maintain their same order of difficulty in the several situations, supporting an earlier finding that Guttman scales—at least when small numbers of items are used—can be used in attitude change studies.[14]

Upon this proof of satisfactory scale performance, subjects were given a simple score determined by the number of items answered positively. The range is from zero to five on each scale, with higher scores representing relative favorableness toward desegregation.

ANALYSIS OF THE FINDINGS

The *Before* scale is used here to constitute a base, or control, for certain comparisons. Both the *Poor* and the *Good* scales are assumed to measure response to hypothetically possible real situations accompanying school desegregation. They should reflect the application of *performance* norms to the situations as described. The *Ought* scale is used to measure the respondent's conception of the proper, right, or appropriate reaction that should characterize his response to the desegregation. It relates to whatever *moral* norms are operative in the situation.

Our first substantive issue is to determine what changes from the Before score appear on the several hypothetical measures. Appropriate data appear in Tables 3 and 4. They are presented in the form of averages for all respondents, together with a change-to-possible-change ratio designed to control the ceiling effect. Two important comparisons can be made: (1) A substantial difference between mean scale scores on the Before and Ought measures does appear, consistent with the Myrdal hypothesis; (2) The difference between Before and Ought means is greater than that be-

[14] *Ibid.*, chap. IV.

TABLE 3

Distribution of Scale Scores by Type of Measurement Situation

	Scale Scores						
Measurement Situation	*0*	*1*	*2*	*3*	*4*	*5*	*Total*
Before	78	46	34	48	29	40	275
Good	54	20	26	53	51	71	275
Poor	96	55	34	38	29	23	275
Ought	43	23	23	43	32	111	275

tween the Before and Good means. We are able thus to show that moral uneasiness does seem to operate in the system, and that, indeed, hypothesized excellent conduct by Negro students is not a sufficiently strong stimulus to induce response as tolerant as that given when one answers as he "should."

These are group data. Arbitrary criteria must be used in classifying individual respondents as to whether they show guilt on the issue. The Guilty are defined operationally as those whose scale scores shift at least two positions in a tolerant direction on the Ought as compared to the Before scale. In the case of those with scale scores of 4 on the Before scale, these are considered guilty if they shift to the maximum score of 5 on the Ought measure. Since the 5's on the Before scale cannot increase their tolerance, no analysis is possible and they are not included in further discussion. This procedure gives us 123 respondents classified as Guilty and 112 classified as Not Guilty. Our next task is to determine whether the Guilty perform differently on other variables measured in the study or possess other characteristics that distinguish them from the Not Guilty.

TABLE 4

Average Score, and Change-to-Possible-Change Ratio by Scale Score on Before Measure

	Good Performance		Poor Performance[b]		Moral Ought	
Before Score	*Av. Score*	*Change Ratio*[a]	*Av. Score*	*Change Ratio*[a]	*Av. Score*	*Change Ratio*[a]
0	.88	.176	—	—	1.53	.306
1	2.48	.370	1.17	−.170	3.26	.565
2	3.26	.420	1.35	.325	3.62	.540
3	3.88	.440	2.38	.207	3.75	.375
4	4.21	.210	3.14	.215	4.55	.550
5	—	—	3.88	.224	—	—
Total	2.87	.268	1.70	.187	3.20	.381

[a] The change ratio is computed by dividing the actual change in scores by the possible change. For example, those who score 2 on the Before measure have a possible change of 3 (up to 5) on the Good Performance. They show in fact a change of 1.26 (up to 3.26). The change ratio, .420, is determined by dividing 3 into 1.26.

[b] The change ratio on the Poor Performance scale is computed from the observed movement toward the intolerant end of the scale. For the other two scales, the measurement base is movement toward the tolerant end.

Place of Origin

One should not be expected to experience guilt independent of the source of the accusation that his values or conduct are morally unbecoming. Protestants are not likely to feel guilty about birth control despite Catholic moral indignation on the subject, nor are citizens in capitalist countries made guilty about the pursuit of profit by the allegations of Marxists that it is brutal and vicious. Minimal requirements for the arousal of guilt would seem to include the *presentation* of a message dissonant with one's accepted values by a valued source under conditions in which neither personal needs, group associations, nor cultural setting jam or filter the message enough to seriously distort its content and implications.

Our measures of relative exposure to norms contradicting the premises of segregation are most crude. We assume that residents of the Deep South are less likely to encounter the American Creed in its untempered form than are those from other parts of the United States. We assume also that residents of rural areas are more isolated from currents of thoughts and information incompatible with segregation patterns, hence that they less frequently than urbanites will experience guilt concerning race injustice. Since the rural-urban dimension is not independent of region of origin, a control on the latter variable is imposed in examining the relationships.

Data support these expectations, though neither consistently nor strongly. Those born in the Deep South are indeed less likely to be classified as guilty. And the tendency is in the expected direction when we compare those from farms and small towns (less than 10,000 population) with those from larger towns and cities. When we control on region, those from farms and small towns of the Deep South show less guilt; no such pattern holds, however, for those from other parts of the nation.

Sex of Respondent

We have no strong reason for expecting a difference in guilt by sex. Although a literature consistently argues that sexual exploitation of Negro females, and a strong sexual interest in forbidden Negroes, lie at the base of racial guilt, this literature is too speculative and nonempirical in framework to be pertinent. So we do not claim a theoretical basis nor a clear hypothesis regarding direction of association.

Data indicate that females are more likely to have a discrepancy between their Before and their Ought scale scores. If we analyze separately for each Before scale position, on four of the five possible tests the females show greater frequency of guilt. For the total sample, however, the chi square value is significant only at the .10 level.

Generalized Guilt

We wish to examine the possibility that guilt as measured in this study is a component part of a more general tendency to experience guilt (or at least to admit experiencing it). Perhaps the person who shows a discrepancy between his Ought attitudes is the person who in a series of every-day experiences is more likely to respond with some form of self-aggression.[15] Hence the following question was asked: "During this school year would you say that you have had guilt feelings (that is, felt guilty about something that you have done or thought of doing that is wrong) frequently, sometimes, once or twice, or not at all?" Those saying "frequently" or "sometimes" are said to show generalized guilt. The results suggest that a general tendency to experience sensations of guilt is more apparent among those showing a Do-Ought discrepancy on the racial scale.

Females are more likely than males among these respondents to report generalized guilt. They are also more likely to be tolerant on the Before measure and to show guilt on the Before-Ought comparisons. Since the association between generalized guilt and race guilt, then, may be a function of sex, separate analysis of males and females is undertaken. Among males, the (statistically insignificant) association reverses the expected one, with the racially guilty tending to report generalized guilt less often. But among females, the positive association between generalized and race guilt is significant at the .02 level by the chi square test.

Performance Norms vs. Moral Norms

Inspection of Table 4 indicates that attitude change as a proportion of possible attitude change is greater on the Ought measure than on the Good measure. In other words, within the limits of these data students seem to change less in response to a high quality of performance by Negro students than when indicating their conceptions of a morally proper attitude to take. The question arises whether the Guilty are either more or less responsive than the Not Guilty to good performance by Negro students. In other words, does their guilt possibly create a sensitivity to rational supports for a liberal attitude? Analysis indicates that the guilty are indeed more responsive to competent performance. Sixty-two percent of the Guilty and only 31 percent of the Not Guilty show greater tolerance on the Good Performance than on the Before scale. The relationship holds at every Before scale level but is most apparent at the lower extreme. If we consider only those with Before scores of 0, 1, and 2, 72 percent of the Guilty respond favorably to the good performance, compared to but 24 percent among the Not Guilty.

[15] We choose not to view any such relationship between the two measures as a criterion measure or validation of the use of the Do-Ought distinction as a guilt measure.

We have shown that those with Before-Ought discrepancies show greater Before-Good discrepancies, suggesting that the Guilty are especially sensitive to good performance by Negroes. We next raise the question whether this greater responsiveness to a performance factor also appears on the Poor Performance scale. Do the Guilty more readily than the Not Guilty shift to the negative end of the scale when Negroes perform in stereotypical style and impede the education of whites? Or do the Guilty display perhaps a compulsive need to remain relatively tolerant in spite of empirical evidence that conceivably may justify an intolerant position? Inspection shows that there is no difference between the Guilty and the Not Guilty in response to the Poor Performance.

The effect of guilt as a determinant of response to empirical stimuli is demonstrated more clearly in Table 5. Respondents are classified into

TABLE 5

Relation of Racial Guilt to Response Flexibility Among the Tolerant and the Intolerant

	Intolerant[a]		Tolerant[b]	
	Rigid	*Flexible*	*Rigid*	*Flexible*
Guilty	23	60	24	16
Not guilty	57	18	24	13

[a] χ^2 of 36.75, significant at .001 level.
[b] χ^2 insignificant.

four categories. The Before scale types 0, 1, and 2 [16] are called the Rigid Intolerant if the scale score does not increase on the Good Performance measure and the Flexible Intolerant if it does increase. The Before scale types 3, 4, and 5 are called the Rigid Tolerant if the scale score does not decrease on the Poor Performance scale and the Flexible Tolerant if it does. It is apparent from the first two columns of Table 5 that the Guilty respond to the Good Performance situation and the Not Guilty do not; and it is also apparent from the last two columns that this greater responsiveness is not more typical of the guilty on the Poor Performance items.

DISCUSSION AND IMPLICATIONS

Gunnar Myrdal performed a disservice to our understanding of segregated social systems by his drastic simplification of the normative dimensions of the issue. His position that the race issue must be understood as a conflict between the base and the idealistic elements of man's nature—

[16] This cutting point is determined by intensity analysis of separate intensity questions.

man's self-seeking, selfish interests in profiting from segregation versus his affective commitment to the ideals of the American Creed—undoubtedly is deficient in describing significantly large elements of the white population. Further, the clear implication that an awareness of the discrepancy will supply the motive force for attitude and social change—hence that certain outcomes in the unfolding drama of race relations in the South and the nation are more probable because the ultimate implementation of the Creed is inevitable—may suggest relatively ineffectual strategies of social action. It seems apparent that the American Creed simply is not transmitted to many people as a set of values pertinent to racial issues. Further, a segregated system provides its own set of counter-norms, a rationale that justifies the system while it helps the actor in the system to compartmentalize or re-interpret the American Creed. But perhaps most important, the Creed is not the only set of perfectly legitimate and acceptable norms relevant to the prediction and implementation of racial change. Certain virtues valued especially in middle and upper class white culture operate to check the pace of social change that the flow of guilt would initiate were these other things not valued. The Myrdalian emphasis leads us to see the support of segregation, or hesitancy to change from it, as a set of rationalizations, as defenses used to protect the person from an otherwise sure awareness that he is wrong. And when one is "troubled" about race relations, we make of this a "troubled conscience." Such does not follow.

Perhaps we can move from the abstract to the example. These are not hard to find. A tolerant parent is concerned about the effect of desegregation on educational quality in the public schools. A tolerant citizen is concerned that minority groups who get the vote will be bloc-voted and he believes this to be an improper exercise of privilege. A tolerant family wonders whether it is right to shift its patronage from Company A to Company B just because Negro pickets are concentrating their protest on Company A; Company B doesn't serve Negroes at lunch counters either. A racially tolerant white wants to condemn the racially intolerant and wonders whether he ought not show the same tolerance of the intolerant he expects them to show toward Negroes. A tolerant minister is prudently silent during a racial crisis for fear that he cannot hold his church together if he becomes a partisan. Education, fairness, citizenship, tolerance, unity —valuing these things may soften one's attack on segregation. For the person to whom racial justice as well as these are valued, there is a moral conflict—i.e., a conflict between opposed sets of legitimate, moral norms— that to ignore is to imperil our understanding, and that the Myrdalian argument encourages us to ignore. We encounter a similar risk in interpreting the data presented in this paper.

The data show that guilt, as herein defined, characterizes many respondents, though by no means all of them. We argue that this constitutes an "isness"-"oughtness" incongruity that is the "problem in the heart of the American" in the Myrdalian conception. But we are severely restricted in the fact that we have measured but one dimension in a multi-dimensional field. Maybe, had we asked another set of questions, we would have shown that many people are intolerant of their friends' intolerance but feel they ought not be. Maybe some people experience a moral obligation to conform to custom, i.e. to respect the will of the majority. Seen from this perspective, belief in racial justice and an accepting attitude toward desegregation become only one in a complex *set* of "oughts." Components of this set may or may not produce consistent behavioral outcomes; that is, they may or may not reinforce each other. Only if we assume that they do may we use measures of racial guilt as predictors of individual behavior or of social change.

There are other cautions to be raised. These are, after all, only paper and pencil reports. Furthermore, the responses are to imaginary situations; we know that there are wide individual differences in empathic ability and that the capacity to imaginatively create a social situation is not uniformly distributed. But perhaps the major restriction is the fact that our respondents were college students. We believe that they are more likely than most to be exposed to communications that define the dilemma and present sets of values rationally incongruous with contemporary race patterns. Probably they are also better equipped intellectually to bring the full measure of the incompatibility into their consciousness and attempt to deal with it. We assume, in other words, that those who do not enter college exist in personal and social environments less likely to induce guilt; consequently the present results cannot be generalized.

25

New Light on Changing
American Values:
A Forgotten Body
of Survey Data*

FRED I. GREENSTEIN
Wesleyan University

The values held by Americans are commonly believed to have undergone a radical change since the turn of the century. Americans, it is said,
have come increasingly to prize leisure over work, accommodation to
their fellows over individual achievement, in general, passivity over activity. The best known statement of the many variations on this theme
is probably that of David Riesman and his associates. Riesman's thesis
was presented in terms of changes in social structure and "social character"; changes from an "age of production" to an "age of consumption,"
which he believed had been accompanied by a shift from "inner-" to
"other-direction" in the sources of Americans' "modes of conformity." [1]
William Whyte's well-publicized comments on "The Declining Protestant
Ethic" parallel Riesman's assertions at many points.[2]

The views of Riesman and Whyte are widely accepted. Clyde Kluckhohn reaches similar though not identical conclusions on the basis of
a "massive" review of several hundred "empirical and impressionistic
writings on American culture and especially American values by social
scientists and others." [3] Much of the literature Kluckhohn was able to find

Reprinted from *Social Forces*, 42, 4 (May 1964), 441–450, by permission of the
author and The University of North Carolina Press.

* Helpful comments on earlier drafts of this paper were made by a number of
readers, including Arthur J. Brodbeck, Jurgen Herbst, Elton F. Jackson, Robert E.
Lane, Stanley Lebergott, Nelson Polsby, Josef Silverstein, Vladimir Stoikov, and Barbara and Raymond Wolfinger.

[1] David Riesman with Nathan Glazer and Reuel Denney, *The Lonely Crowd: A
Study of the Changing American Character* (New Haven, Conn.: Yale University
Press, 1950), hereafter attributed for the sake of brevity to the senior author. A num-
ber of commentators on Riesman's work have pointed out that his discussion is less of
changing character than of changing values and practices. See, for example, the articles
by Sheldon L. Messinger and Burton R. Clark and by Robert Gutman and Dennis
Wrong in Seymour M. Lipset and Leo Lowenthal, eds., *Culture and Social Character:
The Work of David Riesman* (New York: The Free Press of Glencoe, 1961).

[2] *The Organization Man* (New York: Simon and Schuster, 1956).

[3] "Have There Been Discernible Shifts in American Values During the Past Gen-

had been "produced by writers . . . who based their reflections on their own experience rather than upon specifically pointed and systematic research." [4] Granting that these observations did not meet satisfactory standards of evidence, Kluckhohn nevertheless was impressed by the amount of broad agreement with Riesman and Whyte, although he felt it necessary to point to "the possibility that the consonance derives from Zeitgiest or from parrotings—with variations—of a few popular formulations." [5]

In addition to impressionistic accounts of changing American values, Kluckhohn was able to draw upon several studies which presented "hard" data—analyses of various indirect indices of value change, such as the variations over the years in the content of the lyrics of popular songs, best selling novels, and religious literature. The findings of a number of these studies seem to support the assertions of Riesman and Whyte. For example, after observing differences in the types of individuals who served as topics of popular magazine biographies between 1901 and 1941,[6] Leo Lowenthal concluded that contemporary audiences were being exposed to "idols of consumption" (e.g., film stars) rather than the "idols of production" (e.g., business magnates) of earlier years. Lowenthal's findings were drawn upon by Riesman to support the thesis of *The Lonely Crowd*. A more recent example of the analysis of value changes in cultural products is the study by de Charms and Moeller of a century-and-a-half of grade school textbooks.[7] Noting that "achievement imagery" in children's readers had declined consistently after the 1880's, de Charms and Moeller concluded that their findings "correspond very well" with those of Riesman and other commentators.

Lately, however, objections have been raised to the argument that one of the major twentieth century developments has been the supplanting of the Protestant Ethic with what Whyte calls "the Social Ethic." Lipset, for example, after a detailed examination of comments on the United States by nineteenth century foreign visitors, asserts that the "traits of the other-directed man have to a considerable extent always existed in the American character and that the values of achievement and individualism persist in American Society." [8] Parsons and White argue that

---

eration?" in Elting E. Morison, ed., *The American Style* (New York: Harper and Brothers, 1958), pp. 145–217.

[4] *Ibid.*, p. 148.

[5] *Ibid.*, p. 182.

[6] Leo Lowenthal, "Biographies in Popular Magazines," in Paul F. Lazarsfeld and Frank N. Stanton, eds., *Radio Research 1942–43* (New York: Duell, Sloan and Pearce, 1944), pp. 507–548.

[7] Richard de Charms and Gerald H. Moeller, "Values Expressed in American Children's Readers: 1800–1950," *Journal of Abnormal and Social Psychology*, 64 (1962), pp. 136–142.

[8] Seymour M. Lipset, "A Changing American Character?" in Lipset and Lowenthal, *op. cit.*, p. 140.

the American "value-system has . . . remained stable . . ." and that "a major part of the phenomena that form the center of the analyses of Riesman, Kluckhohn, and others" consists merely of "new *specifications* of the [unchanged] general value system, in relation to new structural and situational conditions." [9]

Ideally one would hope to resolve such disagreements by direct observation of trends over the years in people's values (a research tactic which is becoming increasingly practical as historical survey data accumulate), rather than by impressionistic reports or indirect indices of value change. As Riesman and Glazer comment, referring to questionnaires which have been devised to test Riesman's hypotheses, "we wish there were ways of finding out how nineteenth-century young people might have responded to such questionnaires . . . but history buries its dead . . . ." [10]

A FORGOTTEN BODY OF SURVEY DATA

The present article analyzes a forgotten body of survey data going back to the 1890's. Between 1896 and 1910, students of education conducted numerous investigations of the "ideals" of children and adolescents—i.e., of their statements about "what person you would most like to resemble." In later years a number of additional studies of children's exemplars were carried out, one in the 1920's and several since 1944. [11] Thus evidence is available over a 50-year period on trends in juvenile heroes and hero-wor-

[9] Talcott Parsons and Winston White, "The Link between Character and Society," in Lipset and Lowenthal, *op. cit.*, p. 103. Also see Winston White, *Beyond Conformity* (New York: The Free Press of Glencoe, 1961).

[10] David Riesman with the collaboration of Nathan Glazer, "*The Lonely Crowd*: A Reconsideration in 1960," in Lipset and Lowenthal, *op. cit.*, p. 429.

[11] This paper draws mainly on the studies indicated with asterisks below. Following each in parentheses is the estimated or actual date of field work. In the text of the paper, these studies are indicated by date of field work rather than date of publication.

* Estelle M. Darrah, "A Study of Children's Ideals," *Popular Science Monthly*, 53 (May 1898), pp. 88–98 (Field work 1896); Earl Barnes, "Type Study on Ideals," *Studies in Education*, 2 (1902), pp. 36–42, 78–82, 115–122, 157–162, 198–202, 237–242; * Will G. Chambers, "The Evolution of Ideals," *The Pedagogical Seminary*, 10 (March 1903), pp. 101–143 (Field work *ca.* May 1902); * David S. Hill, "Comparative Study of Children's Ideals," *Pedagogical Seminary*, 18 (June 1911), pp. 219–231 (Field work *ca.* 1910); * David S. Hill, "Personification of Ideals by Urban Children," *Journal of Social Psychology*, 1 (August 1930), pp. 379–393 (Field work *ca.* 1928); * M. Louise Stoughton and Alice M. Ray, "A Study of Children's Heroes and Ideals," *The Journal of Experimental Education*, 15 (December 1946), pp. 156–160 (Field work *ca.* 1944); Robert J. Havighurst, et al., "The Development of the Ideal Self in Childhood and Adolescence," *Journal of Educational Research*, 40 (December 1946), pp. 241–257; J. B. Winkler, "Age Trends and Sex Differences in the Wishes, Identifications, Activities, and Fears of Children," *Child Development*, 20 (1949), pp. 191–200; * Fred I. Greenstein, *Children's Political Perspectives: A Study of the Development of Political Awareness and Preferences Among Pre-Adolescents*, unpublished

ship. These data, which are probably the longest time series of reasonably reliable and comparable questionnaire findings, have the merit of providing us with a direct index of values in the general population. In view of the emphasis by Riesman, among others, on changing socialization practices as one determinant of value changes, it is especially interesting that the data are on the values of young people.

Several factors make possible the use of these data from a period before acceptable standards for survey research had been developed. First, although not based on random sampling, the studies draw on exceedingly large and diversified populations of children. For both the pre-World War I and the post-1944 periods (which are most important for our purposes) several studies are available from widely dispersed geographical areas, and for both periods there is enough impressionistic information about respondents' social characteristics to make it clear that the populations studied were broadly heterogeneous. Secondly, raw data are available from five of the studies—two from the early period, one from the 1920's, and two from the later period—making possible secondary analysis in terms of categories which are more revealing than those used in the original studies. In these five studies complete or nearly complete inventories of all the individuals referred to by the respondents were reported. Therefore re-analysis was possible once the identities of some of the more obscure names (ranging from turn-of-the-century Congressmen to silent screen performers) were established and a number of minor estimates were made to fill in slight gaps. Finally, the pattern of findings emerging from all the studies, a pattern which, as we shall see, supports the thesis that values have *not* changed markedly in the directions suggested by Riesman, is sufficiently clear-cut and internally consistent to eliminate doubts about the representativeness of the data.

Since the studies are of hero-worship it is useful to juxtapose them with Lowenthal's findings on changing heroes of popular biography and to discuss them in the context of both Lowenthal's and Riesman's interpretations of the former's findings.

---

doctoral dissertation, Yale University Library, 1959, pp. 77–102 (Field work January through March, 1958).

Chambers, *op. cit.*, presents a bibliography of a number of additional early studies. Not considered in the present discussion are several early studies of the "ideals" of foreign children, most of which are cited in Chambers' bibliography, and a study of parochial school children by Sister Mary Inez Phelan, *An Empirical Study of the Ideals of Adolescent Boys and Girls* (Washington, D.C.: Catholic University of America, 1936). A discussion of the findings in several of the early studies with respect to sex differences appears in Herbert Hyman, *Political Socialization* (Glencoe, Ill.: The Free Press, 1959), pp. 30–31. I am indebted to Hyman's book for bringing these studies to my attention.

LOWENTHAL AND RIESMAN ON
CHANGING VALUES

Lowenthal's conclusion that "idols of consumption" had taken the place of "idols of production" was based on rather striking differences in the occupations of magazine biography subjects before and after World War I. Three major changes were found in "the professional distribution of . . . 'heroes' "; changes which Riesman saw as fitting snugly into the conclusions of *The Lonely Crowd:*

1. Perhaps the most clear-cut change followed close upon the growth in the second decade of the century of spectator sports and the mass entertainment industry. During the period before the Great War, 77 percent of the biographies of entertainers were of representatives of "serious arts" (i.e., literature, fine arts, music, dance, theatre). For each successive time period sampled there was a consistent shift in the direction of representatives of athletics and of what Lowenthal refers to as "the sphere of cheap or mass entertainment," until by 1940–41 "serious artists" made up only 9 percent of the entertainers about whom biographies were written. In all, entertainers ("serious" and "non-serious") accounted for only a fourth of the pre-World War I biographies as opposed to one-half of the post-war biographies. Lowenthal concluded that "the [contemporary] idols of the masses are not, as they were in the past, the leading names in the battle of production, but the headliners of the movies, the ballparks, and the night clubs." [12]

2. The over-all decline in biographies of leaders "in the battle of production" was not as sharp as the overall increase in biographies of entertainers. Leaders of production made up 28 percent of the pre-1914 biographies and an average of about 17 percent of the biographies in the three later time-periods sampled by Lowenthal. But here also the differences were greater if one took account of the degree to which the biographical subjects represented the "serious side" of life. Early biographies were of bankers and railroad executives; the later ones concentrated on such figures as the owner of a vacation resort, a man who had organized a roadside restaurant chain, and a professional model.

3. Finally, consistent with the assertion in *The Lonely Crowd* that with the advent of other-direction politics increasingly has become a passive spectator activity rather than an arena in which to vent intense feelings,[13] biographies of political leaders were less common after World

---

[12] Lowenthal, *op. cit.*, p. 517. In a brief aside, Lowenthal raises the possibility that the subjects of magazine biographies were representative merely of the "ideology" of the time, *ibid.*, p. 513. Riesman, however, seems to assume that they represent attitudes in the general population. ("Surveys of content in the mass media show a shift in the kinds of information about business and political leaders that audiences ask for.") *The Lonely Crowd, op. cit.*, p. 237.

[13] *The Lonely Crowd, op. cit.*, chap. 8.

War I. Forty-six percent of the early biographies were of people in political life; less than 30 percent of the later biographies were of politicians.

Both Lowenthal and Riesman interpret the shifts in biographical heroes since the turn of the century in terms of a decline in popular aspiration levels. Biographies during the early period were "to be looked upon as examples of success which can be imitated," Lowenthal suggests. Taking note of the rhetoric in the biographies as well as the individuals who were their subjects, he concludes that during the early period such magazine articles served as "educational models." They reflected a period of "rugged individualism . . . characterized by eagerness and confidence that the social ladder may be scaled on a mass basis." The later biographies, on the other hand, "seem to lead to a dream world of the masses who no longer are capable or willing to conceive of biographies primarily as a means of orientation and education." [14]

Riesman agrees that biographies during the early period served as models which were within the aspirations of their readers, whereas today the individual "cannot imagine himself in the work role of the president of the United States or the head of a big company." However, he suggests that the contemporary biographies also are models; but these are new, other-directed models of taste, life-style, and leisure-time pursuit—"the frontiers on which the reader can himself compete. . . . ." [15]

Besides using the data on trends in children's exemplars to determine whether Lowenthal's content analysis findings are valid indicators of changes in "the idols of the masses," they also may be used to establish whether one other shift in the type of exemplar chosen by children which might be anticipated from speculations in *The Lonely Crowd* has taken place.

4. Riesman suggests that identification with national heroes served an important function in the socialization of children during the period when society was "dependent on inner direction."

> [In] the George Washington myth . . . [N]ot only are the little boys told in the period of inner direction that they may grow up to be president but they are given scales by which to measure and discipline themselves for the job during boyhood. If they do not tell lies, if they work hard, and so on— if, that is, they act in their boyhoods as the legendary Washington acted in his—then they may succeed to his adult role.[16]

Although Riesman does not explicitly state that the use of national heroes as childhood models has declined over the years, this conclusion is consistent with this discussion.

[14] Lowenthal, *op. cit.*, p. 517.
[15] *The Lonely Crowd, op. cit.*, p. 273.
[16] *Ibid.*, p. 96.

TRENDS IN CHILDREN'S HEROES SINCE
THE TURN OF THE CENTURY

In addition to drawing on the five studies (summarized in Table 1) which were suitable for retabulation, the following analysis makes impressionistic use of other internal evidence from the studies, including lengthy but not exhaustive inventories of children's statements about why they chose to be like their hero, and additional studies which did not supply sufficiently comparable or detailed data for retabulation. We shall be concerned with (1) whether the direct questionnaire data confirm the trends in "hero-worship" suggested by Lowenthal's indirect data, and (2), more fundamentally, with whether the pattern of findings in the various direct studies of children is consistent with the belief that popular aspiration levels have declined.

The first four studies summarized in Table 1 (as well as the other early studies referred to in the text and notes) employed the following item, or some slight variation thereof: "Of all persons whom you have heard, or read about, or seen, whom would you most care to be like or resemble? Why?" [17]

The fifth study used a somewhat different question: "Name a famous person you want to be like." [18]

The earlier item produced references to figures from the immediate environment by between about one-fifth and two-fifths of the respondents; the item used in 1958 produced very few such references. Therefore the latter wording may inflate the proportion of children referring to public figures, although in 1958 failure to respond is much more common than in the earlier studies. As will be seen, the variation in item and response pattern is not a serious drawback for the analysis.[19]

1. Entertainers

Following Lowenthal, I have defined "entertainer" in "the broadest sense of the word" to encompass not only popular performers such as film stars and professional athletes, but also all representatives of literature and

---

[17] This is the wording used by Hill, "Personification of Ideals by Urban Children," *op. cit.* The item was worded as follows in the other studies: "What person of whom you have heard or read would you most like to be? "Why?" Chambers, *op. cit.*; "Which person (among those you have seen, or thought of, or heard of, or read about) would you most like to resemble? Why?" Hill, "Comparative Study of Children's Ideals," *op. cit.*; "Of all the persons whom you have known, or heard about, or read about, whom would you most wish to be like? And why do you like this person?" Stoughton and Ray, *op. cit.*

[18] Greenstein, *op. cit.*, p. 76.

[19] When no response and immediate environment categories in Table 1 are dropped and percentages are computed for all studies on the basis only of responses to wider environment exemplars, there is no change in the findings discussed below.

the arts. Included are figures from the past (e.g., Longfellow and even Mozart) as well as those who were living at the times of the various studies.

The long-run trends in children's responses are generally consistent with Lowenthal's findings. In particular, the change he observed in the ratio of "serious" and "non-serious" artists is clearly evident. Before World War I both the percentages in Table 1 and the author's discussions of their findings indicate that children rarely referred to popular performers. By 1928, the proportion of popular figures referred to (e.g., Clara Bow, Rudolph Valentino, Ty Cobb, Paul Whiteman) is double that of "serious" artists; in the post-1944 samples, references to the latter category virtually disappear.[20] Because the decline of "serious artists" is accompanied by an increase in "non-serious" artists and because of the possibility that the phrasing of the 1958 item "increased" the frequency of reference to entertainers, it is not possible to determine with certainty whether overall references to entertainers have increased.

2. Businessmen, Industrialists, Financiers

Lowenthal's procedure was to combine business and professional occupations into a single category, the latter including such disparate types as a college president and an inventor of gadgets. Then he further analyzed the occupations in terms of whether they were "serious" or "non-serious" and whether they represented production or consumption spheres of life.

In Table 1, I have reported only the proportion of references to "captains of industry" (industrialists, financiers, and businessmen in general). This avoids a great many troublesome coding decisions about whether a profession is "serious" and at the same time provides a clear-cut test of whether veneration of "idols of production" has declined.

The findings summarized in Table 1 cast serious doubt on the assump-

---

[20] Evidently none of the 1944 children referred to "serious" artists. The findings of Havighurst, et al. although presented in categories which are not strictly comparable to the present ones, provide supporting evidence that children have tended to choose popular entertainers as their exemplars in recent decades. Their study, which was of nine different populations of children and adolescents—most of them Midwesterners —seems to have been conducted in 1944 or 1945. The total number of respondents is 1,147. Havighurst, et al. present a category of exemplars labeled "glamorous adults," including "people with a romantic or ephemeral fame, due to the more superficial qualities of appearance and behavior; e.g., movie stars, military figures, athletes," as well as "characters in comic strips or radio dramas." Their discussion suggests that most of the references coded in this category were to popular entertainers. In three of the populations they studied, references to "glamorous adults" exceeded 30 percent and in four they exceeded 20 percent. In the remaining two the percentages were 14 and 2. The item used in this study permitted references both to individuals personally known by the respondents and to imaginary "composite characters," as well as to public figures. The inclusion of the "composite" category (numerous responses were classified under this heading) presumably reduces references to figures in the wider environment and therefore makes Havighurst's estimate of the frequency of "glamorous" exemplars conservative.

TABLE 1

Percent of Children and Adolescents Choosing Various Classes of Public Figures as Exemplars: 1902–1958*

Exemplars	Place, Approximate Date of Field Work, and Investigator				
	1902 New Castle, Penna.	1910 Nashville, Tenn.	1928 Birmingham, Montgomery, Mobile, Ala.	1944 Springfield, Mass.	1958 New Haven, Conn.
	Chambers	Hill	Hill	Stoughton, Ray	Greenstein
Entertainment					
"Serious"	4.1	4.1	5.1	—	1.8
"Non-Serious"	.6	.3	10.4	8.1	36.1
Business	1.6	1.0	1.0	—	.6
Contemporary Political					
Incumbent President	3.3	.9	.2	2.7	3.3
Other	9.2	1.4	2.2	.4	3.0
National Hero					
Washington	29.2	22.0	19.9	4.9	3.2
Lincoln	3.4	.6	2.4	1.5	3.6
Other	3.0	9.6	5.1	4.6	3.6

Miscellaneous Figures from Wider Environment	17.2	20.6	15.6	33.4	14.8
Immediate Environment Figures	22.4	39.5	33.8	44.4	2.0
No Response or Invalid Response	6.0	—	4.3	—	28.0
Total	100.0	100.0	100.0	100.0	100.0
Ages Included in Present Tabulation	7–16	7–15	6–20	9 and 11	9–15
Number of Cases	2333	1431	8813	259	659

* A number of the percentages in Table 1 are estimates of the percentages which would have resulted if certain minor gaps in the data did not exist. All estimates are between a fraction of a percent and about three percent of what would have been found if full data were available, with the exception of the 1902 statistic for "other national heroes," which is—to some unknown degree—larger than the 3 percent indicated in the table. In each case where an estimate has been made the estimate is conservative with respect to the interpretation of the table in the text, so that any other estimate would have further strengthened the conclusions. (For example, the highest possible estimate is used for "other contemporary political figures" in 1902, and the lowest possible estimate in 1944.) Further information about the five studies summarized here, along with a discussion of the techniques of retabulation and estimation, is contained in a mimeographed technical appendix available from the author. The "miscellaneous figures from wider environment" category is residual. It includes, among others, scientists, inventors, military leaders, religious figures, and characters from fiction, as well as a small number of responses which could not be classified because the names of the exemplars were not listed or were unidentifiable.

Invalid responses (e.g., references to an occupation rather than an individual; illegible questionnaires; etc.) were eliminated from the 1910 study prior to analysis. These made up about three percent of the original 1910 sample. There is no discussion of invalid responses or of failures to respond in the 1944 study, and none are reported. The 1944 study was of second grade (age 7), fourth grade (age 9), and sixth grade (age 11) children; I have retabulated the percentages, eliminating the second grade subsample in order to bring the mean age closer to that of the other studies. Even after retabulation the mean age of this sample is still somewhat lower than that of the other samples. This evidently accounts for the greater tendency of 1944 respondants to refer to immediate environment exemplars. The size of the residual "miscellaneous" category in this study is a function partly of war-time references to military heroes and partly of a somewhat larger number of unidentified exemplars.

tion that the frequent pre-World War I magazine biographies of captains of industry were an accurate indication of mass aspirations at the time. If such goals were prevalent in the population, it is difficult to believe that they would not have been reflected in children's statements about who they would "care to be like or resemble." But only a minute proportion (less than 2 percent) of the children in the early studies referred to men like Carnegie, Rockefeller, and Morgan as their "ideals." It is true that still fewer contemporary children make such choices (none seem to have in the 1944 study). But the decline is within an exceedingly small range.

3. Contemporary Political Figures

The incumbent president and other living politicians have been placed in this category, plus individuals who were active during the adult lifetimes of parents of the children studied. Thus for the 1958 respondents, Franklin D. Roosevelt is treated as "contemporary"; Woodrow Wilson and Theodore Roosevelt have the same status for the 1928 children.

The data on contemporary political figures also cast doubt on the adequacy of Lowenthal's index. During all periods very few children chose the incumbent president. The proportion of 1902 references to Theodore Roosevelt, for example, is virtually identical with the proportion of 1944 references to Franklin Roosevelt, and in general there is no significant variation over the half-century in references to the chief executive. Studies of children's occupational goals, which were conducted around the turn of the century, further support the finding that children of that period rarely developed presidential aspirations.[21]

[21] If log cabin-to-White House mythology ever had much of an impact on children's aspirations, this must have been in the period before the 1890's, judging from the early occupational preference studies. For example, in a study of the responses of 1,065 five through 16-year-old Brooklyn, New York, Long Branch, New Jersey, and Melrose, Mass. children to the question, "What would you like to be when you grow up?" only 11 references to the presidency emerged. Adelaide E. Wyckoff, "Children's Ideals," *The Pedagogical Seminary*, 8 (December 1901), pp. 482–492. In another early study, in which the field work took place in 1893, 1,234 Santa Rosa and San Jose, California public school children were read an anecdote describing a group of children expressing their occupational preferences. Included in the occupations listed was president. Some children made this choice, but apparently too few to be included in a table which lists occupations referred to as infrequently as six times. Hatti M. Willard, "Children's Ambitions," *Studies in Education*, 1 (January 1897), pp. 243–253. The discussions of two other early studies, neither of which present tabulations, also suggest that when children in the 1890's were asked "What would you like to be?" few of them mentioned the presidency. Will S. Monroe, "Vocational Interests of Children," *Education*, 18 (January 1898), pp. 259–264, a study of 1,755 eight to 16-year-old school children from a number of Connecticut River Valley communities in Massachusetts; and J. P. Taylor, "A Preliminary Study of Children's Hopes," *Forty-Second Annual Report of the State Superintendent for the School Year Ending July 31, 1895*, Vol. II, State of New York Department of Public Instruction, pp. 987–1015, a study of 2,000 school children from various New York State communities. These occupational preference studies present

At first glance there seems to be partial support for Lowenthal's thesis in the finding that "other contemporary political figures" were chosen by about nine percent of the 1902 respondents, in contrast to less than three percent of the respondents in later studies. But two-thirds of the "other" 1902 references were to the recently assassinated President McKinley and there is evidence that during the period immediately after his death, McKinley's "martyrdom" led to a widespread idolization of him on the part of children, as well as adults.[22]

4. National Heroes

Riesman's discussion of the erstwhile role of national heroes in children's socialization leads us to expect that references to the *dramatis personae* of American patriotic lore will have declined. And this indeed is the case. Over 35 percent of the 1902 responses and only about 10 percent of the post-1944 responses fell in this category. In the first of the reports on children's exemplars, Darrah's 1896 study of 1440 St. Paul, Minnesota and San Mateo County, California children, references to Washington and Lincoln alone (by far the most frequently mentioned patriotic figures in all of the studies) were made by 40 percent of the ten- to sixteen-year-old respondents.[23] The breakdown of national heroes reported in Table 1 leads to a further observation: one individual—George Washington—seems to account for the entire declining trend in references to national heroes.

To recapitulate, the direct data on children's exemplars are consistent with only one of the three trends reported by Lowenthal. The ratio of popular over "serious" entertainers has increased over the years in roughly the same way that the content of magazine biographies has shifted. But changes in magazine biographies of "heroes of production" and of political leaders are not reflected in the direct observations of public exemplars. The direct data also support Riesman's hypothesis that contemporary children are less likely than their predecessors to identify with national heroes. We may now consider the implications of these findings.

---

extensive quotations of children's responses and therefore are of considerable impressionistic interest. Unfortunately, they are not suitable for systematic secondary analysis.

[22] A few weeks after McKinley's assassination, Earl Barnes asked 1,800 seven through 17-year-old Long Branch, New Jersey and Winfield, New York children to write essays on the topic, "Would you wish to be like Mr. McKinley? Why?" Ninety-two percent of the responses were positive and the remaining eight percent apparently consisted not of personal rejections of McKinley, but rather of statements such as "I would not like to have the care he had on his mind all the time." Earl Barnes, "Political Ideas of American Children," *Studies in Education*, 2 (1902), pp. 25–30. Barnes' discussion of his findings makes it clear that the positive responses were in the nature of vague, eulogistic statements about McKinley's character; they were not assertions of the child's desire some day to become president.

[23] Darrah, *op. cit.*, p. 94.

DISCUSSION

In general, the body of "forgotten" data discussed here provides little if any support for the notion that Americans have placed a declining value on achievement. It is true that when one compares "official" emanations (for example, addresses to high school and college graduating classes) of the past with those of today "the decline of the Protestant ethic" seems plentifully evident. But this comparison may merely confound *fin de siècle* rationalizations with reality.[24] De Charms and Moeller find that between 1880 and 1910 "achievement imagery" in children's text books was about twice as common as it is in the contemporary period. This, they imply, indicates that achievement values were more prevalent then than now, a factor which they feel helps to explain industrial growth during those years.[25] Yet, in view of the consistently low rate of choice of businessmen as exemplars, it is difficult to believe that turn-of-the-century young people exceeded contemporary youths in the desire to excel in economic enterprise. The absence of business exemplars is especially striking in the face of what, on Lowenthal's showing, seems to have been a concerted attempt in the media to display businessmen as models for popular emulation.[26]

Similarly, rhetoric suggesting that "every boy is a potential President of the United States" abounded 60 years ago. Consider, for example, the statement by the author of one of the early studies that this "feeling . . . is one of our prized possessions. Our school literature is full of it; no address before children is complete which fails to remind them that each is on his way to the presidential chair." [27] As we have seen, the rhetoric seems to have had little impact on children's felt aspirations—choice of the incumbent president as an exemplar was exceedingly rare.

The two classes of exemplar which *did* shift over the half-century—entertainers and national heroes—are quite ambiguous indicators of aspiration levels. There is no *a priori* reason for assuming that the individual who wants to be like Enrico Caruso or Lily Pons is more driven to succeed than someone who sets up Frank Sinatra or Debbie Reynolds as an "ideal." The reverse could as easily be true. The decline in reference to national heroes (or, more precisely, references to Washington) is equally difficult

[24] For one likely intellectual source of such rationalizations, see Richard Hofstadter, *Social Darwinism in American Thought: 1860–1915* (Philadelphia: University of Pennsylvania Press, 1944). Cf. also, R. Richard Wohl, "The 'Rags to Riches Story': An Episode of Secular Idealism," in Reinhard Bendix and Seymour M. Lipset, eds., *Class Status and Power* (Glencoe, Ill.: The Free Press, 1953), pp. 388–395.

[25] De Charms and Moeller, *op. cit.*, pp. 193 and 141. For additional uses of children's text books as indices of achievement motivation see David C. McClelland, *The Achieving Society* (Princeton, N.J.: Van Nostrand, 1961).

[26] Further research would be desirable to determine whether the two magazines sampled by Lowenthal, *Saturday Evening Post* and *Collier's*, were representative of other periodicals of the time.

[27] Barnes, "Political Ideas of American Children," *op. cit.*, p. 27.

to interpret. One hypothesis, which at first seems credible, is that identification with a hero such as Washington serves to channel a child's aspirations in the direction of political achievement. This seems to have been Riesman's assumption in the passage quoted above about the function of the George Washington myth in the period "dependent upon inner direction." His remarks continue: "The [presidential] role, moreover, by its very nature, is a continuing one; somebody is always president. . . . In fantasy, the little boy not only identifies with the young Washington in the French and Indian wars but also with the adult role of president. . . . " [28] If this were the case we would expect—contrary to the present findings—that populations which were high in identification with figures such as Washington also would be high in reference to incumbent presidents.[29]

Unfortunately, in the early studies respondents' explanations of why they chose to be like their exemplars were not presented exhaustively. Therefore they cannot be retabulated. However, the extensive quotations which are given also fail to support the Riesmanian conception of an era in which the socialization process instilled in children lofty aspirations—*ad astra per aspera*.[30]

The responses reported in the early studies are not couched in the language of personal striving, nor do they carry the implication that the child expected personally to assume the role of the individual to whom he referred. The largest proportion of statements seem simply to ascribe to the child's hero what one of the early writers called "rather vague moral qualities." [31] ("I want to be like George Washington because he was good.") Other responses stress the fame of the child's exemplar, his wealth (but without the implication that by emulating his hero the child expects personally to obtain riches), his physical appearance.

[28] *The Lonely Crowd, op. cit.*, p. 96.

[29] We might also expect that age breakdowns would show identifications with Washington to be common among young children and to decline among older children, accompanied by a compensatory increase in reference to the incumbent president. Fragmentary evidence from the two earliest studies summarized in Table 1 suggests that references to Washington did indeed decrease with age, but that there was no age variation in the infrequent identifications with the incumbent president.

The discussion of trends in references to entertainers and national heroes carries no implication that the changes reported in Table 1 are irrelevant to understanding shifts in American values; it *is* being suggested that the trends do not support the thesis that there has been a shift in the direction of greater mass passivity. In explaining the changes in children's exemplars, at the very least one would have to take account of the enormously great visibility of popular entertainers to contemporary Americans as a consequence of technological change in mass communication, and of curricular changes in public education, including the advent of "social studies" as a substitute for history. On the latter see Wilhelmina Hill, *Social Studies in the Elementary School Program* (Washington, D.C.: Department of Health, Education, and Welfare, 1960), p. 24.

[30] *The Lonely Crowd, op. cit.*, pp. 118–120.

[31] Barnes, "Political Ideas of American Children," *op. cit.*, p. 28.

Even the earliest of the studies (1896) contains quotations which, with slight alterations in prose style, might have served as epigraphs for chapters in *The Lonely Crowd* on the other-directed way of life. For example, a fifteen-year-old boy explained shortly before the election of 1896 that he wanted to be like William Jennings Bryan because Bryan "is well proportioned and well built, a good looking gentleman, and one of the smartest men in the United States . . . and is, without an exception, the greatest orator on the face of the globe." [32] In the same study, a fourteen-year-old boy selected as his idol a man he wanted to resemble "because he has not very hard work, and he has a good time and plenty of money. . . ." [33]

The assumption that achievement values have changed may, as Lipset's remarks suggest, simply be the result of inaccurate conceptions of nineteenth century America. Writers who emphasize the passivity of contemporary Americans usually at least tacitly picture a much more vigorous, optimistic, upwardly striving folk who populated what Lowenthal calls the "open-minded liberal society" at the beginning of the century. But commentators on the present often find it tempting to idealize the past.[34] Certain mistaken notions about structural changes in American society in the present century probably have contributed to the widely held belief that American aspiration levels have declined. For example, until recently it was widely assumed that upward occupation mobility has diminished in the United States. This assumption has been severely challenged by recent research.[35] Similarly, questionable assertions about the debilitating effects of contemporary "mass society" may have predisposed observers to accept over-simplified, if not erroneous hypotheses about value change.[36]

[32] Darrah, *op. cit.*, pp. 90–91.

[33] *Ibid.*, p. 92. Similar statements may be found in the numerous quotations of children's reasons for preferring occupations reported in the studies cited in footnote 21.

[34] It is interesting to compare Lowenthal's characterization of turn-of-the-century American society with the following observation by one of the early students of children's occupational preferences: "The small number of extravagant impossible hopings [among the respondents] seems quite remarkable. The apparent contentment with the lot nature has given them, the genuine delight with which the poorer children look forward to the severe monotonous labors that the future holds in store, the glad willingness to share the heavy burdens of supporting their father's family, all are witnesses to the triumph of childhood's hope and idealism over the toil and pain of the world." Taylor, *op. cit.*, p. 999. Children during this period doubtless were not devoid of mobility aspirations. Cf. the comparisons of Massachusetts children's occupational preferences with parental occupations by Monroe, *op. cit.*, which suggest, for example, that children of unskilled laborers tended to aspire toward skilled trades.

[35] Natalie Rogoff, *Recent Trends in Occupational Mobility* (Glencoe, Ill.: The Free Press, 1953); Seymour M. Lipset and Reinhard Bendix, *Social Mobility in Industrial Society* (Berkeley and Los Angeles: University of California Press, 1959).

[36] Cf., for example, Daniel Bell, "America as a Mass Society: A Critique," *Commentary*, 32 (July 1956), 75–83; Scott Greer and Peter Orleans, "Mass Society and Parapolitical Structure," *American Sociological Review*, 27 (1962), pp. 634–646.

SUMMARY

A secondary analysis of trends in children's exemplars over a period of approximately 60 years fails to support the hypothesis that American values have changed in the directions suggested by such commentators as David Riesman. Identifications with business leaders and political leaders are rare today, but were equally rare at the turn of the century. Children are less likely today to choose national heroes; more likely to choose popular entertainment figures. However, there is no reason to interpret these changes as evidence of declining aspiration levels. In general, examination of this body of studies suggests that commentators who point to the increasing passivity of contemporary Americans are able to do so only by idealizing the American past.

For Further Reading

BOOKS

Allport, G. W., Vernon, P. E., and Lindzey, G., A *study of values* (3d Ed.), Boston: Houghton Mifflin, 1960.

A revision and updating of the 1931 work; presents a measure of the relative prominence of six basic interests or motives in personality.

Kluckhohn, F. R. and Strodtbeck, F. L., *Variations in value orientations*, Evanston: Row, Peterson and Company, 1961.

A study of the patterns, or principles of the cultures of five contrasting ethnic groups: The Spanish-Americans of Texas; a group of homesteaders in Texas; the Rimrock Mormons; the Navaho and the Zuni tribes.

ARTICLES

Angell, R. C. Social values of Soviet and American elites: content analysis of elite media. *J. Conflict Resolution*, 1964, 8 (4), 331–385.

Bender, I. E. Changes in religious interest: a retest after 15 years. *J. abnorm. soc. Psychol.*, 1958, 57 (1), 41–46. SA 9, A0180.

A significant increase in the religious values (Allport-Vernon) was found in a sample of 84 Dartmouth men after a 15-year interval.

Berrien, F. K. Japanese versus American values. *J. soc. Psychol.*, 1965, 65 (2), 181–191. PA 39, 14861.

Studies reviewed here portray the Japanese as being more deferent and more willing to work long hours; however, external democratic values are not internalized.

Bidwell, C. E., and Vreeland, R. S. College education and moral orientations: an organizational approach. *Adm. Sci. Quart.* 1962, 8 (2), 166–191. PA 38, 5835.

Existing research presents both positive and negative evidence that colleges serve as agents of moral socialization. Presents a typology of organizations which do and do not induct their clients into the organization.

Bronfenbrenner, U. The role of age, sex, class, and culture in studies of moral development. *Religious Educ.*, 1962, 57 (4), 3–17. PA 37, 4678.

The acquisition of values and character, as a function of the above variables, is discussed.

Burton, R. V. Generality of honesty reconsidered. *Psychol. Review*, 1963, 70 (6), 481–499. PA 38, 5839.

A reanalysis of the Hartshorne and May 1928 findings, using factor analysis and Guttman's simplex model. There is some underlying generality in moral behavior, though there is still much of the variance of the honesty tests due to specific test determinants.

Catton, W. R. A retest of the measurability of certain human values. *Amer. sociol. Review*, 1956, 21 (3), 357–359. SA 5, 3113.

A report of a study of the measurement of "infinite" values among a group of ministers.

Dackawich, S. J. An analysis of the values of a modern Midwestern community. *Sociol. soc. Res.*, 1959, 44 (1), 18–26. SA 11, A4244.

An analysis of such values as love of people, dignity, integrity, fairness, mentality, happiness, humility, religion, sobriety and genuineness, by sex, occupation and education.

Davis, J. A. Intellectual climates in 135 American colleges and universities: a study in "social psychophysics." *Sociology of Educ.*, 1963, 37 (2), 110–128. SA 12, B0494.

Students' perceptions of intellectual values are distorted toward their own value positions.

De Charms, R., and Moeller, G. H. Values expressed in American children's readers: 1800–1950. *J. Abnorm. soc. Psychol.*, 1962, 64 (2), 136–142. SA 11, A6119.

Content analysis demonstrated a rise in achievement imagery from 1800 to about 1900 and then a steady decline.

Dunham, Vera S. Social values of Soviet and American elites: insights from Soviet literature. *J. Confl. Resol.*, 1964, 8 (4), 386–423.

Content analysis is used to determine Soviet and American values, as reflected in official or elite literature.

Edwards, J. B. Some studies of the moral development of children. *Educ. Research*, 1965, 7 (3), 200–211. PA 40, 1394.

Observes that more research is carried out on intellectual rather than moral development of children and urges more research of the latter.

Eister, A. W. Comment on the Kolb-Parsons discussion of man's freedom. *J. for scientific Study of Religion*, 1963, 3 (1), 107–108. SA 13, B6687.

A discussion of the effects of the institutional system and the cultural structuring of values on the freedom of men.

Goldstein, B., and Eichhorn, R. L. The changing Protestant ethic: rural patterns in health, work, and leisure. *Amer. Sociol. Review*, 1961, 26 (4), 557–565. PA 36, 3GB57G.

High work-oriented farmers were more individualistic, more ascetic, but their economic behavior appeared to be less rational.

Gorlow, L. and Barocas, R. Value preference and interpersonal behavior. *J. soc. Psychol.*, 1965, 66 (2), 271–280. PA 39, 14949.

Morris' *Ways to Live* document, in Q sort form, was given to 50 young adults; six value orientations were related to behavior.

Hartley, Ruth E. Relationships between perceived values and acceptance of a new reference group. *J. soc. Psychol.*, 1960, 51 (1), 181–190. PA 36, 3GE81H.

The greater the compatability between the values of the individual and the perceived values of the new group (college freshmen) the more likely the individual is to accept the new group as a reference group.

Hilton, T. L., and Korn, J. H. Measured change in personal values. *Educ. Psychol. Measmt.*, 1964, 24 (3), 609–622. PA 39, 4800.

Reliability for values tests given monthly ranged from .74 for the political scale to .89 for the religious scale.

Huntley, C. W. Changes in study of values scores during the four years of college. *Genetic Psychol. Monog.*, 1965, 71 (2), 349–383. PA 39, 14957.

Allport-Vernon-Lindzey Study of Values was given to 1,027 men at college entrance and at graduation. Nine curriculum groups revealed different patterns of change.

Jones, L. V. and Bock, R. D. Multiple discriminant analysis applied to "Ways to Live" ratings from six cultural groups. *Sociometry*, 1960, 23 (2), 162–176. PA 35, 2057.

A comparison of United States white, Negro, Indian, Japanese, Chinese, and Norwegian students in response to Morris' schedule.

Kilby, R. W. Personal values of Indian and American university students. *J. humanist. Psychol.*, 1963, 3 (2), 108–146. PA 39, 4706.

Morris' "Ways to Live" scale was stable within Indian and American groups; a number of value differences were found between the groups.

Kirby, John D. Are morals subversive? *Amer. J. of Econ. & Sociol.*, 1955, 14 (4), 335–346. SA 4, 2054.

The new morality of individualism helped undermine the old order of Hellenic Greece; in recent Western culture, the new morality is social while our institutions are individualistic.

Kluckhohn, C. Have there been discernible shifts in American values during the past generation. In E. E. Morison (ed.), *The American style: Essays in value and performance*; New York: Harper and Brothers, 1958. Pp. 145–217.

Larson, R. F. Measuring "Infinite" Values. *Amer. Catholic sociol. Rev.*, 1959, 20 (3), 194–202. SA 9, 0182.

Catholic and Protestant ministers rank the values almost identically.

Lang, G. E., and Lang, K. Van Doren as victim: student reaction. *Studies in pub. Communication*, 1961, 3, 50–58. SA 14, C3055.

Lacking objective moral norms, students fell back on particularistic standards . . . poor understanding of social determinism leads students to locate responsibility in external circumstances.

Lehmann, I. J. Some socio-cultural differences in attitudes and values. *J. educ. Sociol.*, 1962, 36 (1), 1–9. SA 11, A4646.

Rural subjects were more traditionally-value-oriented than urban; high social class homes were less traditional; women were more religious; aesthetic and social-value-oriented.

Lipset, S. M. The value patterns of democracy: a case study in comparative analysis. *Amer. Sociol. Rev.*, 1943, 28 (4), 515–531. SA 12, A7993.

Analysis of the value systems of the four largest English-speaking democracies illustrates the similarity of the core values.

Lynd, R. S. Assumptions in American life, from *Knowledge for what?* Princeton, New Jersey: Princeton U. Press, 1939. Pp. 60–62. Reprinted in R. W.

O'Brien, C. C. Schiag, and W. T. Martin Eds., *Readings in general sociology*. (Boston: Houghton Mifflin, 1957, 2nd Ed.) Reprinted in this text in Selection 30.

An amusing confrontation of logically inconsistent values typically held by Americans.

McLaughlin, B. Values in behavioral science. *J. Relig. and Hlth.*, 1965, 4 (3), 258–276.

Values are a part of behavioral science, and are categories of intentionality.

Morris, C. Values, problematic and unproblematic, and science. *J. of Communication*, 1961, 11 (4), 205–210. PA 36, 5GD05M.

There is a dynamic interaction of science and evaluation, of knowledge and values —the "is" and the "ought to be."

Pyron, B. Belief Q-Sort, Allport-Vernon Study of Values and religion. *Psychol. Reports*, 1961, 8 (3), 399–400. PA 36, 2GD99P.

Three religious groups were significantly different on this scale of values.

Rettig, S. Invariance of factor structure of ethical judgments by Indian and American college students. *Sociometry*, 1964, 27 (1), 96–113. PA 38, 8290.

Despite cultural differences, the "invariance coefficients" exceeded .80 on 5 of the 6 factors extracted; moral relativism had a lower invariance factor because Indian students subsumed it under various family practices.

————, and Pasamanick, B. Invariance in factor structure of moral value judgments from American and Korean college students. *Sociometry*, 1962, 25 (1), 73–84. PA 37, 1078.

The structure of moral judgments is considerably invariant across two very different cultures. The thesis of complete ethical relativity appears to be seriously challenged.

———— and ————. Moral value structure and social class. *Sociometry*, 1961, 24 (1), 21–35. PA 36, 1GC21R.

A hypothesis of a curvilinear relationship between severity of moral judgment and social class on moral issues was supported in the general and economic dimension but not in the family and religious morality (which varied inversely with social class).

Rodman, H. The lower-class value stretch. *Social Forces*, 1963, 42 (2), 205–215. SA 12, BO600.

The lower-class value stretch refers to the wider range of values and the lower degree of commitment among this class of people; it is hypothesized that this is a response to deprivation.

Rogers, C. R. Toward a modern approach to values: the valuing process in the mature person. *J. abnorm. soc. Psychol.*, 1964, 68 (2), 160–167. SA 11, B6740.

Relates personal, physical, and mental growth to the development of values.

Rose, P. I., The myth of unanimity: student opinions on critical issues. *Sociol Educ.*, 1963, 37 (2), 129–149. SA 12, BO509.

Challenges Jacob's generalization of a homogeneity of basic values among college students; questionnaires provide data that do not support the idea of unanimity.

Scott, W. A. Empirical assessment of values and ideologies. *Amer. sociol. Rev.*, 1959, *24* (3), 299–310. SA 7, 6772.

Procedures developed for assessing values of social groups by interviews or questionnaires; these involve content analysis of responses to standardized questions concerning traits which the subject admires in other people.

Shartle, C. L., Brumback, G. B., and Rizzo, J. R. An approach to dimensions of values. *J. Psychol.*, 1964, *57* (1), 101–111. PA 39, 1446.

Relates the concept of value into types of organizational behavior—in this study, business, foreign and military service.

Spaulding, I. A. Of human values. *Sociol. soc. Res.*, 1963, *47* (2), 169–178. PA 38, 2536.

Values are essential for the integration of the social system; relates internal and environmental values.

Taguiri, R. Value orientations and the relationship of managers and scientists. *Adm. Sci. Quart.*, 1965, *10* (1), 39–51. PA 13, 16495.

Value orientations of the two groups were relatively similar, although the scientists were more interested in theoretical values (Allport-Vernon-Lindzey).

Vaughan, G. M. and Mangan, G. L. Conformity to group pressure in relation to the value of the task material. *J. abnorm. soc. Psychol.*, 1963, *66* (2), 179–183. PA 37, 6621.

Group pressure is resisted when highly valued material is utilized.

Zurcher, Louis A., *et al.* Value orientation, role conflict, and alienation from work: A cross-cultural study. *Amer. sociol. Rev.*, 1963, *30* (4), 539–548.

Mexican workers in a Texas bank were more oriented toward "particularism" than Anglo-American employees; since the bank is a universalistically-oriented work organization, alienation was more characteristic of the Mexican workers.

Chapter Nine

Role

The concept of role has frequently served as a bridge for psychology and sociology. This topic is especially congenial to teamwork because the construct involves the definition of rights, obligations, and expected behavior of people in interaction. Role expectancies are socially defined, though individuals interpret these directives with varying degrees of accuracy and comply with varying degrees of acceptance. Because it is almost impossible to contemplate the subject without being acutely aware of both social prescriptions (or proscriptions) and individual performance, the concept of role has been the focus for innumerable studies in both disciplines.

Simply defined, *role* is the behavior expected of an individual occupying any given social position. Sports fans are familiar with diagrams of football plays: the assignment is to the occupant of a specific position, regardless of the specific individual who happens to be the role-occupant at the moment. That there are variations in the capability, commitment, and enthusiasm of role occupants hardly needs to be elaborated.

Because of the seemingly precise definition of the concept of role, social scientists have paid insufficient attention to the empirical assessment of role expectancies. In the first selection, Charles L. Mulford reports research in which he found (rather than simply taking for granted) an extremely high consensus among segments of a general population as to what the behavior and attitudes of community leaders should be.

A quite different situation is described by Ernest Q. Campbell and Thomas F. Pettigrew, who document the incompatible expectations that faced the ministers in the Little Rock integration crisis. They found one set of expectations held by the national denominational authorities, another by congregational and community members, and sometimes still another held by the ministers themselves. This type of situation is usually designated by the term *role conflict*.

A theoretical analysis of the basis of role expectation—sharpened because the analysis is in terms of conflicting claims—is presented by John T. Gullahorn and Jeanne E. Gullahorn, with interpretations of the ways in which an individual may resolve conflicting expectancies. They differentiate between *status-produced role conflict* (which involves different expectations by significant others) and *contingent role conflict* (which results from simultaneous occupancy of two statuses or roles, both of which have legitimate expectations that cannot be fulfilled at the same time). Elsewhere these have been labeled *intra-* and *inter-role* conflict, respectively.

Another closely-related aspect, but one for which we do not have an article, has been termed *role ambiguity*. Melvin Seeman,[1] in his study of the role of school superintendents, determined that the teachers in the school system coveted primary- or peer-type relationships with the superintendent, while at the same time desiring salary raises (and to obtain these, it was necessary for him to spend a considerable amount of time cultivating the understanding and good will of the leaders of the community). To illustrate role ambiguity, from time to time the editor has informally requested his students to state preferences regarding the conduct of a course, of which the following was one item:

A professor is a better teacher if he:

a. gives lectures that are well-ordered and timed
b. allows time for students to ask questions, etc.

Invariably there has been a lack of consensus. The percentage favoring the first response has varied from about 35 percent to nearly 50 percent.[2]

Perhaps the reader can readily furnish examples of role ambiguity from his own adolescence—that period of life when one is half-child, half-man, neither fish nor fowl, too old to gain admission to sports events at half-price but not old enough to drive the family car!

Finally, we turn to Howard J. Ehrlich, James W. Rinehart, and John C. Howell for a discussion of some problems in conducting research in role conflict. They introduce some new variables in their analysis: the legitimacy of expectations of others; the sanctions which various relevant groups might apply; the intensity with which others hold their expectations; and the personal preferences of the role-occupant. Note how it is particularly clear in this selection that good research proceeds from past reports, profits by them, and attempts to integrate findings, or when unable to do so seeks a suitable explanation or proposes further research to clarify the discrepancy.

[1] Seeman, M., Role Conflict and Ambivalence in Leadership. *Amer. Sociol. Rev.*, 1953, 18 (4), 373–380.

[2] The full scale may be found in D. G. Dean and D. M. Valdes, *Experiments in sociology*. 2nd ed. New York: Appleton-Century-Crofts, 1967.

26

On Role Consensus About Community Leaders

CHARLES L. MULFORD

Iowa State University

Recent community studies have been criticized for emphasizing the power or prestige of leader positions and slighting the *roles* which their incumbents are expected to play.[1] "Expected" implies a type of mutual recognition and normative legitimation which is felt to be crucial to the continuity and orderly operation of a social system.[2] Though potentially important in this way, our current knowledge of the images and attitudes which are attached to public leaders has been said to suffer from overgeneralization and conceptual unclarity. More particularly, the possibility of variable role expectations among different community subgroups has been singled out as requiring further investigation.[3] A modest and preliminary response to this need will be reported here. We ask what is the degree of consensus that exists within and between status and residential categories about the obligations and desired attributes of community leaders?

RESEARCH DESIGN

Three sets of respondents were interviewed in Western County, Iowa: a simple random sample of 134 household heads (farm operators) from the rural areas of the county, a simple random sample of 195 household heads from a nonrural community of 15,000 persons, and the 36 persons who were designated as "influential" by 5 or more respondents in the nonrural sample. The first two samples were also subdivided into status categories, using education as the criterion.

The questionnaire included a checklist of 34 "obligations a community

Reprinted from *Sociological Inquiry*, 36, 1 (Winter 1966), 15–18, by permission of the author and the publisher.

[1] For a summary of such criticism, see Raymond E. Wolfinger, "The Study of Community Power," *American Sociological Review*, 25 (October, 1960), pp. 636–644.

[2] See Ralph M. Stogdill, *Individual Behavior and Group Achievement*, New York: Oxford University Press, 1959.

[3] See Wendell Bell, Richard J. Hill, and Charles R. Wright, *Public Leadership*, San Francisco: Chandler Publishing Company, 1961, p. 151.

leader has," each accompanied by the following five-point scale: "(1) absolutely must, (2) preferably should, (3) may or may not, (4) preferably should not, (5) absolutely must not." The same scale alternatives were used in eliciting responses to a second checklist, one of 38 "qualities important for a community leader." Both lists were derived from earlier, open-end interviews with public officials in the same county.

Mean scale scores provided the basis for rank ordering the items within each checklist for each category of respondent to be considered. Spearman coefficients of rank order correlation were used to compare the rank orderings with one another as to amount of agreement about leader roles. Using this computationally most manageable method precluded the assessment of consensus within categories. Our study is thus restricted to discovering whether certain frequent sources of difference in orientation were operative —namely those between rural and nonrural; between high, medium, and low status; between combinations of residential and status categories; and between influential and noninfluentials.

RESULTS AND DISCUSSION

Tables 1 and 2 show a strikingly high level of agreement among rural and nonrural respondents about what a community leader is obligated to do and what he should be like. The overall correlation between rural and nonrural rank orderings of obligations was .97. The correlation between the nonrural random sample and the nonrural influential rank orderings

TABLE 1

Intercorrelations Among Rank Orderings of Leader Obligations Provided by Different Categories of Respondent

	Rural Low Status* (n = 36)	Rural Middle Status (n = 72)	Rural High Status (n = 26)	Nonrural Low Status (n = 26)	Nonrural Middle Status (n = 107)	Nonrural High Status (n = 62)
Rural Low Status	x	.96	.86	.90	.92	.92
Rural Middle Status		x	.94	.94	.95	.94
Rural High Status			x	.89	.93	.93
Nonrural Low Status				x	.91	.94
Nonrural Middle Status					x	.96
Nonrural High Status						x

* Low, middle, and high status were defined, respectively, as 0–8, 9–12, and 13 or more years of formal education.

TABLE 2

Intercorrelations Among Rank Orderings of Leader Qualities Provided by Different Categories of Respondent

	Rural Low Status* (n = 36)	Rural Middle Status (n = 72)	Rural High Status (n = 26)	Nonrural Low Status (n = 26)	Nonrural Middle Status (n = 107)	Nonrural High Status (n = 62)
Rural Low Status	x	.88	.86	.84	.88	.78
Rural Middle Status		x	.92	.91	.91	.90
Rural High Status			x	.96	.89	.98
Nonrural Low Status				x	.82	.80
Nonrural Middle Status					x	.95
Nonrural High Status						x

* See footnote to Table 1.

for obligations was .94, indicating that community influentials also concurred in these expectations. The overall correlation between rural and nonrural rank orderings of desirable qualities was .94, and the correlation of the nonrural random sample with the nonrural influentials was .95 in this respect.

Role consensus appeared to exist across several lines which are otherwise often productive of differences in orientation. Had we asked which members of which kinds of groups were most likely to attain this ideal, however, we would very likely have discovered cleavages. In such an event, the often neglected distinction we have made between consensus about power *positions* and consensus about who are rightfully the powerful persons would become crucial.

Turning to the *content* of the observed role consensus, we find that the following kinds of obligation received mean ranks of from 1 to 10 in the nonrural sample and between 1 and 13 in the rural sample:

> Investigates all problems thoroughly before making a decision; be willing to change your mind as new evidence is available; actively seek able people to participate in community affairs; take a definite and open stand on public issues; consult specialists before making a decision about a community problem; have a great interest in people; keep the community fully informed about what is going on; listen carefully to all complaints; cooperate with all organizations in the community; take an active interest in state and national affairs.

The following obligations received the 10 lowest ranks in the nonrural sample and were among the 13 lowest in the rural sample:

Avoid being controversial; be careful not to offend important groups in the community; defend past policy; engage in public debates with those who oppose him; take a neutral stand on any issue on which the community is evenly split; try to settle community issues quietly, behind the scenes; occasionally compromise with local pressure groups; vigorously change the way things are done; use influence to further personal ambitions; make major changes without seeking public support.

It appears as though both "instrumental" and "expressive" obligations[4] were included among those ranked high. Whether the same leaders were expected to meet both kinds of obligation, however, is beyond the scope of the present study. This observation (and attendant proviso) is also supported when leader *qualities* are taken into consideration. The following eight received ranks between 1 and 10 in the nonrural sample, and between 1 and 11 in the rural sample:

Of sound judgment; a hard worker; practical; a man of vision; sincere; able to work with others; tactful; skilled in public relations.

The two most marked disagreements occurred between the two samples over the items, "able to express ideas clearly," and "objective." The rural sample ranked these qualities 11 and 10 positions lower than did the nonrural sample. Both of these qualities appear to refer to instrumental roles; it is tempting though premature to speculate whether the *Gesellschaftlich* component may not be weaker in rural sentiment. More refined analyses may permit exploration of this possibility.

Attributes which ranked among the ten lowest within both samples were:

In favor of welfare state; outspoken; a Republican; quiet; a Democrat; young; female; a bachelor; easy-going; over 60 years of age.

Given the role consensus about community leaders which appears to exist over various societal subsets, at least in the present case, the next step should be an inquiry into the expected division of labor, if any, among *different* leader roles.

[4] For a description of the use of this typology, see Talcott Parsons, Robert F. Bales *et al.*, editors, *Family: Socialization and Interaction Process*, Glencoe: The Free Press, 1955, *passim*. For employment of a related typology at the level of community leadership, see Amitai Etzioni, "The Functional Differentiation of Elites in the Kibbutz," *American Journal of Sociology*, 64 (March, 1959), pp. 476–487.

27

Racial and Moral Crisis:
The Role of
Little Rock Ministers*

ERNEST Q. CAMPBELL and
THOMAS F. PETTIGREW
University of North Carolina and
Harvard University

This paper analyzes the conduct of the ministers in established denominations in Little Rock, Arkansas, during the crisis over the admission of Negro students to the Central High School in the fall of 1957. How do ministers behave in racial crisis, caught between integrationist and segregationist forces?

One might expect that Little Rock's clergymen would favor school integration. All the major national Protestant bodies have adopted forceful declarations commending the Supreme Court's desegregation decision of 1954 and urging their members to comply with it. And southern pastors have voted in favor of these statements at their church conferences—and sometimes have even issued similar pronouncements to their own congregations.[1] But the southern man of God faces serious congregational opposition if he attempts to express his integrationist beliefs publicly in the local community. The vast majority of southern whites—even those living in the Middle South—are definitely against racial desegregation.[2]

Reprinted from *American Journal of Sociology*, 64, 5 (March 1959), 509–516, by permission of the authors and The University of Chicago Press. Copyright, 1959, by the University of Chicago.

* This study was supported by a grant from the Laboratory of Social Relations, Harvard University. The authors wish to express their gratitude to Professor Samuel A. Stouffer for his suggestions. Two brief popular accounts of aspects of this study have appeared previously: "Men of God in Racial Crisis," *Christian Century*, LXXV (June 4, 1958), 163–165, and "Vignettes from Little Rock," *Christianity and Crisis*, XVIII (September 29, 1958), 118–136.

[1] For example, local ministerial groups issued such statements in New Orleans, Louisiana; Richmond, Virginia; Dallas and Houston, Texas; and Atlanta, Macon, and Columbus, Georgia. For a review of national church statements see "Protestantism Speaks on Justice and Integration," *Christian Century*, LXXV (February 5, 1958), 164–166.

[2] A 1956 National Opinion Research Center poll indicated that only one in every seven white southerners approves school integration (H. H. Hyman and P. B. Sheatsley, "Attitudes toward Desegregation," *Scientific American*, CXCV [December, 1956], 35–39). A 1956 survey by the American Institute of Public Opinion showed that in

The purpose of this study is to determine how the ministers of established denominations in Little Rock behaved in the conflict. In analyzing their behavior, we treat self-expectations as an independent variable. This is contrary to the usual course, in which the actor is important analytically only because he is caught between contradictory *external* expectations. The standard model of role conflict treats ego as forced to decide between the incompatible norms of groups that can impose sanctions for nonconformity. This model—which is essentially what Lazarsfeld means by cross-pressures —skirts the issue of whether ego imposes expectations on itself and punishes deviations. Pressure and sanction are external to the actor. Hence the typical model tends to be ahistorical in the sense that a finite number of cross-pressuring groups are used to predict the actor's behavior. It is assumed that the actor cannot have developed from periods of prior socialization any normative expectations for his behavior which would have an independent existence.[3] This additional variable—the actor's expectations of himself—is especially meaningful in the analysis.

Though it is a city of approximately 125,000, Little Rock has much of the atmosphere and easy communication of a small town. It is located in almost the geometric center of the state, and physically and culturally it borders on both the Deep South-like delta country to the east and south and the Mountain South-like hill country to the west and north. Thus Little Rock is not a city of the Deep South. Its public transportation had been successfully integrated in 1956, and its voters, as late as March, 1957, had elected two men to the school board who supported the board's plan for token integration of Central High School. And yet Little Rock is a southern city, with southern traditions of race relations. These patterns became of world-wide interest after Governor Faubus called out the National Guard to prevent desegregation and thereby set off the most publicized and the most critical chain of events in the integration process to date.

Only two ministers devoted their sermons to the impending change on the Sunday before the fateful opening of school in September, 1957. Both warmly approved of the step and hoped for its success. Other ministers

the Middle South—including Arkansas—only one in five whites approved of school integration (M. M. Tumin, *Segregation and Desegregation* [New York: Anti-Defamation League of B'nai B'rith, 1957], p. 109).

[3] By showing that the actor may have a predisposition toward either a particularistic or a universalistic "solution" to role conflicts in instances where the particularistic-universalistic dimension is relevant, Stouffer and Toby link the study of personality to that of role obligations in a way rarely done (Samuel A. Stouffer and Jackson Toby, "Role Conflict and Personality," *American Journal of Sociology*, LVI [March, 1951], 395–406). This study, however, treats the personal predisposition as a determinant of conflict resolution rather than a factor in conflict development. Much the same is true of Gross's analysis (Neal Gross, Ward S. Mason, and Alexander McEachern, *Explorations in Role Analysis: Studies of the School Superintendency Role* [New York: John Wiley & Sons, 1958], esp. chaps. xv, xvi, and xvii).

alluded to it in prayer or comment. It was commonly believed that a majority of the leading denominations' clergy favored the school board's "gradual" plan. This impression seemed confirmed when immediately after Governor Faubus had surrounded Central High with troops fifteen of the city's most prominent ministers issued a protest in, according to the local *Arkansas Gazette*, "the strongest language permissible to men of God."

When Negro students appeared at the high school for the first time, they were escorted by four white Protestant ministers and a number of prominent Negro leaders. Two of the four whites are local clergymen, one being the president of the biracial ministerial association, the other, president of the local Human Relations Council. Many of the more influential ministers of the city had been asked the night before to join this escort. Some demurred; others said they would try to come. Only two appeared.

On September 23, the day of the rioting near Central High School, several leaders of the ministerial association personally urged immediate counteraction on the mayor and the chief of police. Later, support was solicited from selected ministers in the state to issue a declaration of Christian principle, but dissension over the statement prevented its publication. Indeed, *no* systematic attempts were made by the clergy to appeal to the conscience of the community. Such statements as individual ministers did express were usually—though not always—appeals for "law and order" rather than a Christian defense of the principle of desegregation.

Several weeks after the rioting, plans for a community-wide prayer service began to develop. Care was taken to present this service in as neutral terms as possible. Compromise and reconciliation were stressed: never was it described as organized prayers for integration. And indorsements came from both sides of the controversy—from President Eisenhower and from Governor Faubus. As one of the sponsors put it: "Good Christians can honestly disagree on the question of segregation or integration. But we can all join together in prayers for guidance, that peace may return to our city." The services in the co-operating churches were held on Columbus Day, October 12. All the leading churches participated, with only the working-class sects conspicuously missing. The services varied widely from informal prayers to elaborate programs, and attendances varied widely, too, and totaled perhaps six thousand.

These "prayers for peace" may best be viewed as a ritualistic termination of any attempts by the clergy to direct the course of events in the racial crisis. The prayers had met the national demand for ministerial action and the ministers' own need to act; and they had completed the whole unpleasant business. Despite sporadic efforts by a small number to undertake more effective steps, the ministers lapsed into a general silence that continued throughout the school year.

We began our work in Little Rock in the week after the peace prayers. Following a series of background interviews and a careful analysis of ministerial action as recorded in the press, twenty-nine detailed interviews with ministers were held.[4] Twenty-seven of them are Protestants and two are Jewish; the Roman Catholics did not co-operate.

This sample was not selected randomly; the so-called "snowball technique" was used in order to include the most influential church leaders. This involves asking each interviewee to name the members of the Little Rock clergy that he considers to be "the most influential." The first interview was made with an announced leader of the peace prayers, and interviewing was continued with all the men mentioned as influential until no new names were suggested. We added a number of ministers who were not named but who had taken strongly liberal positions during the crisis. Thus our sample is most heavily weighted with the pastors of the larger churches with the greatest prestige and the pastors of smaller churches who had assumed active roles in the conflict. These two groups, we anticipated, would have to contend with the greatest amount of incompatibility in role.

Most of the interviews were held in the church offices. Rapport, which was generally excellent, was partly secured by the authors' identification with southern educational institutions. A detailed summary, as nearly as possible a verbatim account, was placed on Audograph recording equipment shortly after the completion of each interview. Information in three broad areas was sought, and to this end a series of open-ended questions was developed. A series of questions was aimed at determining whether the respondent was a segregationist or an integrationist. A segregationist here is defined as one who prefers racial barriers as presently constituted; an integrationist is one to whom the removal of legal and artificial barriers to racial contact is morally preferable to the present system.[5]

Each interviewee was asked to give a complete account of what he had done and said in both his parish and in the community at large regarding the racial crisis. If he had not been active or vocal, we probed him for the reason and to learn if he had felt guilty over his failure to state the moral imperatives.

A final set of questions dealt with the pastor's perception of his congregation's reaction to whatever stand he had taken. If pressure had been applied on him by his parishioners, we probed him to learn exactly what pressure had been used and how.

The segregationist.—Only five of the twenty-nine clergymen we interviewed were segregationists by our definition. None was avidly so, and, unlike segregationist ministers of the sects, none depended on "chapter-

---

[4] Thirteen additional interviews were held with the sect leaders of an openly pro-segregation prayer service. None of these were members of the ministerial association or were in personal contact with any ministers of the established denominations. A detailed report on them will be published.

[5] Using the interview, three judges, the two authors and a graduate assistant, independently rated each respondent as either a segregationist or an integrationist. Agreement between the three raters was complete for twenty-seven of the twenty-nine cases.

and-verse Scripture" to defend his stand. All men in their late fifties or sixties, they did not think that the crisis was a religious matter. One of them was a supervising administrator in a denominational hierarchy. Although all five were affiliated with prominent denominations, they were not among the leaders of the local ministerial body.

These five men have not been publicly active in defending segregation.[6] Each was opposed to violence, and none showed evidence of internal discomfort or conflict. All five co-operated with the neutrally toned prayers for peace. As one of them commented, "You certainly can't go wrong by praying. Praying can't hurt you on anything."

The inactive integrationist.—Inactive integrationists had done enough —or believed they had done enough—to acquaint their congregations with their sympathy with racial tolerance and integration, but during the crucial weeks of the crisis they were generally silent. These, representing as they do all major denominations, varied considerably as to age and size of church served. Included among them were virtually all the ministers of high prestige, many of whom had signed the protest against Governor Faubus at the start of the crisis and later were advocates of the peace prayer services. Some had spoken out in favor of "law and order" and in criticism of violence. They had not, however, defended the continued attendance of the Negro students in the high school, and they had not challenged their members to defend educational desegregation as a Christian obligation. They were publicly viewed as integrationists only because they had supported "law and order" and had not defended segregation.

Altogether, the inactive integrationists comprise sixteen out of the twenty-nine of our sample. Because it was not a random sample, we cannot draw inferences regarding the division of the total ministerial community or of ministers of established denominations into integrationist and segregationist camps. However, since the sample underrepresents the uninfluential minister who had not been in the public eye during the crisis, we may conclude that a large majority of Little Rock's men of God did not encourage their members to define the issue as religious, nor did they initiate actions or participate in programs aimed at integration.

The active integrationist.—Eight of our respondents can be designated as active integrationists because they continued to defend integration in principle and to insist that support of racial integration is nothing less than a Christian imperative. They were, on the whole, young men who have headed their small churches for only a few years. Most were disturbed that the churches of the city were segregated; some have urged their churches to admit Negroes.

Most of the active integrationists had serious difficulty with their members because of their activities, evidence of which was lowered Sunday-

---

[6] Again, this is in contrast to the sect segregationists. One sect minister is president and another is the chaplain of the local Citizens' Council.

morning attendance, requests for transfer, diminished giving, personal snubs and insults, and rumors of sentiment for their dismissal. One had concluded that his usefulness to his congregation had ended and accordingly had requested to be transferred. By the end of 1958, several others had been removed from their pulpits.

One thing all twenty-nine of the sample had in common was a segregationist congregation.[7] Without exception, they believed that the majority of their members were strong opponents of racial integration. The highest estimate given by any integrationist of the proportion of his congregation which supported his views was 40 per cent; the median estimate for segregation was 75 per cent. Only three interviewees thought that a majority of their members would "accept" a strong public defense of integration by their minister.

Personal integrity, alone, would lead the liberal Little Rock minister to defend integration and condemn those who support segregation. However, the minister is obligated to consider the expectations of his church membership, especially inasmuch as the members' reactions bear upon his own effectiveness.

When an individual is responsible to a public, we distinguish three systems as relevant to his behavior: the self-reference system (SRS), the professional reference system (PRS), and the membership reference system (MRS). The SRS consists of the actor's demands, expectations, and images regarding himself. It may be thought of as what the actor would do in the absence of sanctions from external sources. We have already seen that typically the SRS would support racial integration.[8] The PRS consists of several sources mutually related to his occupational role yet independent of his congregation: national and regional church bodies, the local ecclesiastical hierarchy, if any, the local ministerial association, personal contacts and friendships with fellow ministers, and, probably, an image of "my church." Finally, the MRS consists simply of the minister's congregation. We have already seen that it favored segregation or at least ministerial neutrality.

The net effect of three reference systems seems to favor the cause of integration. Were they equal in strength, and were there no contrary forces internal to any of them, this conclusion is obvious. The minister would then feel committed to support the official national policy of his denomination; his knowledge that fellow ministers were similarly committed would support him, and the local hierarchy would encourage him to make this

---

[7] Our study of a modest sample of church members bore out the ministers' estimates of predominantly pro-segregation sentiment in their congregations.

[8] Although groups make demands, impose sanctions, and significantly affect the actors' self-expectations and self-sanctions, nevertheless, we treat the self-reference system as an independent variable in role conflict. This system seems especially significant where personal action is contrary to the pressure of known and significant groups.

decision and reassure him should his congregation threaten disaffection. These external influences would reinforce his own values, resulting in forthright action in stating and urging the Christian imperatives. However, internal inconsistencies in the PRS and the SRS restrain what on first examination appears to be an influence toward the defense of integration.

The professional reference system.—Two overriding characteristics of the PRS minimize its liberalizing influence. First, most of its components cannot or do not impose sanctions for non-conformity to their expectations. Second, those parts of the PRS that can impose sanctions also impose other demands on the minister, inconsistent with the defense of racial integration before members who, in large part, believe in racial separation and whose beliefs are profoundly emotional.

The inability to impose sanctions.—The national and regional associations that serve as the official "voice of the church" are not organized to confer effective rewards or punishments on individual ministers. Especially is this true in the case of failure to espouse national racial policy or to act decisively in the presence of racial tension. This is even more true of the local ministerial association; it does not presume to censure or praise its members. Conversely, the local church hierarchy is an immediate source of sanctions. It has the responsibility of recommending or assigning parishes, and of assisting the pastor in expanding the program of his church.

The probability and the nature of sanctions from fellow ministers among whom one has personal contacts and friends are somewhat more difficult to specify. However, it does not appear likely that he is subject to sanctions if he does not conform to their expectations by liberal behavior on racial matters. Should he indorse and actively support segregationist and violent elements, this would be another matter. If he is silent or guarded, however, it is not likely to subject him to sanction. The active integrationists in Little Rock expressed disappointment at the inaction of their associates while at the same time suggesting possible mitigating circumstances. There is no evidence that personal or professional ties had been damaged.

Among the various components of the PRS, then, only the local ecclesiastica, which does not exist for some, and, to a considerably lesser extent, fellow ministers, are conceivable sources influencing the minister's decision to be silent, restrained, or forthright.

Conflicting expectations and mitigated pressures.—The role of the minister as community reformer is not as institutionalized (i.e., it does not have as significant a built-in system of rewards and punishments) as are certain other roles associated with the ministry. The minister is responsible for the over-all conduct of the affairs of the church and is judged successful or unsuccessful according to how they prosper. He must encourage co-operative endeavor, reconciling differences, and bring people together. Vigor and high morale of the membership are reflected in increased financial support and a growing membership, and his fellow ministers and his church superiors are keenly sensitive to these evidences of his effectiveness. His goal, elusive though it may be, is maximum support from all members of an ever growing congregation.

The church hierarchy keeps records. It hears reports and rumors. It does not like to see divided congregations, alienated ministers, reduced membership, or decreased contributions. Responsible as it is for the destiny of the denomination in a given territory, it compares its changing fortunes with those of rival churches. In assigning ministers to parishes, it rewards some with prominent pulpits and punishes others with posts of low prestige or little promise. However exalted the moral virtue the minister expounds, the hierarchy does not wish him to damn his listeners to hell—unless somehow he gets them back in time to attend service next Sunday. Promotions for him are determined far less by the number of times he defends unpopular causes, however virtuous their merit, than by the state of the physical plant and the state of the coffer.

Now it is especially commendable if the minister can defend the cause and the state the imperative with such tact or imprint that cleavages are not opened or loyalties alienated. If, however, the moral imperative and church cohesion are mutually incompatible, there is little doubt that the church superiors favor the latter. One administrator told two of his ministers, "It's o.k. to be liberal, boys; just don't stick your neck out." Indeed, ecclesiastical officials advised younger ministers, systematically, to "go slow," reminding them of the possibility of permanent damage to the church through rash action.

Under these circumstances pressure from the national church to take an advanced position on racial matters loses much of its force. The minister is rewarded *only* if his efforts do not endanger the membership of the church: "Don't lose your congregation." Similarly, the prospect of an unfavorable response from his congregation protects him from the (possibly liberal) church hierarchy; he need only point to what happened to Pastor X, who did not heed the rumblings in his congregation. The higher officials, themselves keenly aware of local values and customs, will understand. And his fellow ministers, too, are, after all, in the same boat. They give him sympathy, not censure, if he says, "My hands are tied." An informal rationale develops that reassures the pastor: "These things take time," "You can't change people overnight," "You can't talk to people when they won't listen." There is strong sympathy for the forthright pastor who is in real trouble, but he is looked on as an object lesson. Thus the ministers reinforce each other in inaction, despite their common antipathy to segregation.

The self-reference system.—We still must reckon with the demands the minister imposes upon himself. It is obvious that the actor has the power of self-sanction, through guilt. A threatening sense of unworthiness, of inadequacy in God's sight, cannot be taken lightly. Similarly, to grant one's self the biblical commendation "Well done" is a significant reward. We have said that the self is an influence favoring action in support of desegregation. Can the inactive integrationist, then, either avoid or control the sense of guilt?

Our data are not entirely appropriate to the question. Nevertheless, four circumstances—all of which permit of generalization to other cases— appear at least partially to prevent the sense of guilt. These include major characteristics of the ministerial role, several ministerial values and "working propositions," certain techniques for communicating without explicit commitment, and the gratifying reactions of extreme opposition forces.

The role structure.—The church, as an institutional structure, sets criteria by which the minister may assess his management of the religious enterprise; it does *not* offer criteria by which to evaluate his stand on controversial issues.[9] This encourages, even compels, the minister to base his self-image, hence his sense of worth or unworth, on his success in managing his church. Thus, if church members do not share his goals, three types of institutionalized responsibilities restrain him in reform.

In the first place, the minister is required to be a cohesive force, to "maintain a fellowship in peace, harmony, and Christian love," rather than to promote dissension. Thus some ministers prayed during the Columbus Day services that members "carry no opinion to the point of disrupting the Christian fellowship."

Second, he is expected to show a progressive increase in the membership of his church. Pro-integration activity, lacking mass support, is likely to drive members to other churches.

Finally, his task is to encourage maximum annual giving and to plan for the improvement and expansion of the plant. It is hardly surprising that several inactive integrationists who were engaged in vital fund-raising campaigns shrank from action that might endanger their success.

Working propositions.—The minister makes certain assumptions about his work that reduce the likelihood of guilt when he does not defend moral convictions that his members reject. He is, first, a devotee of education, by which he means the gradual growth and development of spiritual assets —in contrast to his counterpart of an earlier period, who was more likely to believe in sudden change through conversion. He also believes that communication with the sinner must be preserved at all costs ("You can't teach those you can't reach") and for long enough to effect gradual change in attitude and behavior. A crisis, when feelings run high, is not the time to risk alienating those one wishes to change. For example, Pastor X acted decisively but, in so doing, damaged or lost his pastorate: "Look at him; he can't do any good now."

Communication techniques.—The minister may avoid committing himself unequivocally.[10] Some use the "every man a priest" technique, for

---

[9] Blizzard does not find a "community reformer" or "social critic" role in the ministry (see Samuel W. Blizzard, "The Minister's Dilemma," *Christian Century*, LXXIII [April 25, 1956], 508–510).

[10] For a full description and illustration of such techniques as used in Little Rock

example, the stating of his own opinion while expressing tolerance for contradictory ones and reminding his listeners that their access to God's truth is equal with his. Others use the "deeper issues" approach; generalities such as the brotherhood of man, brotherly love, humility, and universal justice are discussed without specific reference to the race issue, in the hope that the listener may make the association himself. Still another course is to remind listeners that "God is watching," that the question of race has religious significance and therefore they should "act like Christians." There is also the method of deriding the avowed segregationists without supporting their opposites. The "exaggerated southerner" technique, which may be supplementary to any of the others, involves a heavy southern drawl and, where possible, reference to an aristocratic line of planter descent.

These techniques do not demand belief in integration as a Christian imperative. Further, except for the "every man a priest" technique, they do not commit the speaker to integrationist goals as religious values; the listener may make applications as he chooses. The speaker, on the other hand, can assure himself that the connections are there to be made; he supplies, as it were, a do-it-yourself moral kit.

Reaction of the opposition.—The ministerial body in Little Rock, except for pastors to dissident fundamentalist sects, is defined by agitated segregationists as a bunch of "race-mixers" and "nigger-lovers." For example, the charge was made that the peace prayers were intended to "further integration under a hypocritical veneer of prayer" and that the sect pastors sponsored prayers for segregation "to show that not all of the city's ministers believe in mixing the races." Indeed, ministers of major denominations were charged with having "race on the mind" so that they were straying from, even rejecting, the biblical standard to further their un-Christian goals.

The effect of opposition by segregation extremists was to convince certain inactive integrationists that indeed they *had* been courageous and forthright. The minister, having actually appropriated the opposition's evaluation of his behavior, reversing its affective tone found the reassurance he needed that his personal convictions had been adequately and forcefully expressed.

Were the force of the membership reference system not what it is, the professional reference system and the self-reference system would supply support to integration that was not limited to "law and order" appeals and the denunciation of violence. However, since "Don't lose your congregation" is itself a strong professional and personal demand, the force of the PRS is neutralized, and the pressure from the SRS becomes confused and conflicting. Inaction is a typical response to conflicting pressures within both the internal and the external system.

It is not surprising, then, that most Little Rock ministers have been

---

see our *Christian in Racial Crisis: A Study of Little Rock's Ministers* (Washington, D. C.: Public Affairs Press, 1959).

far less active and vocal in the racial crisis than the policies of their national church bodies and their sense of identification with them, as well as their own value systems, would lead one to expect. Rather, what is surprising is that a small number continued to express vigorously the moral imperative as they saw it, in the face of congregational disaffection, threatened reprisal, and the lukewarm support or quiet discouragement of their superiors and peers.

28

Role Conflict and
Its Resolution*

JOHN T. GULLAHORN and
JEANNE E. GULLAHORN
Michigan State University

With the increasing complexity of modern society, the ubiquitous communication channels impinging on civilized man, and the heightened frequency and intensity of interaction in urban living, men today are confronted more often than ever before with those moral dilemmas sociologists
call role conflicts. We propose to discuss types of role conflict in terms of
the specific definitions of social status and social role developed herein and
then to present a brief statement of methods of role conflict resolution.

STATUS-ROLE DEFINITION

"Social status" refers to a position within a social system as it is defined
in terms of the configuration of expectations relating the position to the
system as a whole and to each of the other positions within the system.[1]
"Social role" refers to the incumbent's set of expectations associated with
occupancy of a specific status.

Reprinted from *Sociological Quarterly*, 4, 1 (Winter 1963), 32–48, by permission
of the authors and the publisher.

* Revision of a paper read in part at the annual meeting of the American Sociological Association, September, 1959. We wish to acknowledge the helpful comments
and criticisms of Professors Charles P. Loomis, Wilbur Brookover, Idus Murphree,
and the late Samuel A. Stouffer. Our indebtedness to the works of Talcott Parsons
and George Homans is evident throughout the paper. Appreciation is also due the
Jacob Wertheim Committee of Harvard University for support during the early part
of the analysis on which this paper is based. We are also grateful to System Development Corporation for continued support.

[1] Our definition of status in terms of expectations differs from that presented by
Gross and his associates, who treat status as position *qua* position—N. Gross, W. S.
Mason, and A. W. McEachern, *Explorations in Role Analysis: Studies of the School
Superintendency Role* (New York: Wiley, 1958). The expectations or evaluative
standards applied to any status incumbent may be characterized in terms of *behaviors*
(what the incumbent should do), particularly the direction (what he should or should
not do) and the intensity (what he must do, ought to do, might possibly do, etc.)
of these expected behaviors as opposed to expectations defined in terms of *attributes*
(what the incumbent should be, as a consequence of ascriptive qualities or achievement qualifications). The expectations may also be specified in terms of *rights* (what
the incumbent may expect from others) vs. *duties* (what others may expect from
him) and in terms of the specificity or diffuseness of these rights and duties.—Cf. T.
Parsons and E. A. Shils, "Values, Motives, and Systems of Action," in Parsons and

The meanings of these definitions may be clarified by considering how they were derived. In the Model for Role Analysis (Figure 9-1), all parts of the diagram to the left of the vertical line pertain to Ego as the reference person.[2] The right side of the diagram relates to Alters as points of reference. Included among these Alters are those individuals or groups interacting with Ego within the social system in which he holds the given status, as well as Ego's reference groups having legitimate concern with the social system under consideration.[3]

In Figure 9-1 the term "General Status," in the circle farthest to the

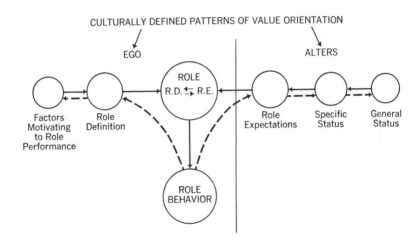

FIGURE 9-1
Culturally Defined Patterns of Valve Orientation

right, designates the general expectations applied to anyone occupying a given position in a group. For example, certain qualities and behavior patterns are expected of the president of an organization, and on the basis

---

Shils (eds.), *Toward a General Theory of Action* (Cambridge, Mass.: Harvard Univ. Press, 1951). Still another way of characterizing the standards concerns the *responsibility* (the range of performances expected of an incumbent) vs. the *authority* (the degree of freedom the incumbent may exercise in initiating performance and interaction) involved in the status.—Cf. R. M. Stogdill, *Individual Behavior and Group Achievement* (New York: Oxford Univ. Press, 1959), pp. 129–132. Furthermore, the expectations may be described in terms of who the "expecters" are and what degree of neutrality or affectivity is involved in their sentiment relationship with the status incumbent.—Cf. Parsons and Shils, *op. cit.*

[2] Throughout the paper the terms Ego and Alter are used in the anthropological sense. Ego is the person who is the current point of reference; Alter is any person or group with whom Ego is interacting or whom he takes as point of reference.

[3] Cf. W. B. Brookover, "Research on Teacher and Administrator Roles," *Journal of Educational Sociology*, 29:2–13 (1955).

of these general expectations most individuals can discriminate reliably between the president and his secretary. The general status of president thus pertains to the position or office of president in any formal system, including the expectations applying alike to the presidency of a union, a corporation, a Rotary Club, etc.[4]

"Specific Status," in the second circle from the right, refers to the expectations of significant Alters for behavior and qualities appropriate to a particular position in a specific social system. Certain expectations apply to the status of President, Local Union 429, regardless of who the president is. While many of the expectations for this specific status will coincide with those for the general status of president of an organization, others will be unique to the particular union social system. Furthermore, in contrast to the relatively large set of Alters defining expectations for the general status of president, only a small subset, belonging to the union-company social system, has a legitimate right to specify behavior for the local union presidency. The obverse of this limitation in the number of Alters is that a more clearly defined network of expectations becomes possible for the specific status.

When a person has been selected as incumbent in a specific status, a new pattern of expectations may emerge; that is, the Alters may modify their definition of the specific status to accommodate certain personal characteristics, qualifications, or limitations of this individual (Ego). This set of definitions is labeled "Role Expectations." For certain positions—e.g., that of a laborer on an assembly line—the configuration of rights and obligations defined at the level of Role Expectations may conform, by and large, with the patterning of expectations defined at the level of Specific Status. For other statuses, however, differences may be observed at these two levels. For example, the role expectations for a union business agent who happens to have a law degree may differ from those for other status incumbents who precede or follow him.

Let us now consider Ego as the social system point of reference. In Figure 9-1, the circle farthest to the left designates Factors Motivating to Role Performance. This level refers to conative aspects of Ego's personality organization, particularly his patterning of need-dispositions. From the viewpoint of action within the social system, the crucial personality variable underlying role performance appears to be a generalized learned need-disposition toward some degree of conformity to the culturally defined patterns of value orientation.[5] Given this generalized motivation for participation in the social system, we may predict that more specific need-dispositions will influence and be influenced by Ego's recruitment (or

---

[4] Cf. E. C. Hughes, "Dilemmas and Contradictions of Status," *American Journal of Sociology,* 50:353–359 (Mar., 1945); "Institutional Office and the Person," *American Journal of Sociology,* 43:404–413 (Nov., 1937).

[5] Cf. Parsons and Shils, *op. cit.*

self-recruitment) in specific status-roles.[6] Furthermore, these particular need-dispositions may determine Ego's individual style of role performance.

"Role Definition," in the second circle from the left in Figure 9-1 refers to Ego's perception of the configuration of expectations associated with incumbency in the status. Emphasis here is on a more cognitive level of personality organization, focusing on Ego's assessment of what he perceives, in a relatively veridical manner, to be the reality of the situation. Of course, in varying degrees motivational factors will influence Ego's perceptions. However, at this level we assume that Ego's definition of the situation is based on symbolic reality testing, involving cognitive evaluation of the congruence between personal need-dispositions and the exigencies of the situation. Before Ego has actually engaged in behavior as status incumbent, his definition of the role will be influenced by such factors as his reference groups, past experience in other statuses, and interaction with Alters in comparable statuses.

Prior to entering the position, Ego is engaged in role definition. As he becomes an incumbent he must achieve some conclusion regarding the total configuration of expectations defining the specific status. To do this Ego indulges in what Mead terms "role taking," that is, adopting the perspective of the significant Alters.[7] "Role" is defined as the union Ego achieves between the set of elements comprising his own role definition and the set of elements comprising the role expectations of the Alters who form his reference groups for this status. Role thus represents an interaction of the personality system with the social system. As Parsons notes, the integration of the personality and the social systems at the level of role is possible because the need-dispositions of the former and the pattern variables of role expectations of the latter were both derived from a common set of culturally defined value orientations.[8] The shared system of cultural values provides a reference framework for normative control by defining legitimate expectations for role relationships.

"Role Behavior" refers to Ego's performance as incumbent in the specific status—that is, his behavior based on a cognitive organization of his own role definition and his perception of the Alters' expectations.[9]

[6] Cf. A. Davis, "The Motivation of Underprivileged Workers," in W. F. Whyte (ed.), *Industry and Society* (New York: McGraw-Hill, 1946); William E. Henry, "The Business Executive: Dynamics of a Social Role," *American Journal of Sociology,* 54:286–291 (Jan., 1949); Robert K. Merton, *Social Theory and Social Structure* (Glencoe, Ill.: The Free Press, 1957); T. R. Sarbin, "Role Theory," in G. Lindzey (ed.), *Handbook of Social Psychology,* I (Cambridge, Mass.: Addison-Wesley, 1954).

[7] G. H. Mead, *Mind, Self, and Society* (Chicago: Univ. of Chicago Press, 1934).

[8] T. Parsons, "An Approach to Psychological Theory in Terms of the Theory of Action," in S. Koch (ed.), *Psychology: A Study of a Science,* 3, *Formulations of the Person and the Social Context* (New York: McGraw-Hill, 1959); *The Social System* (Glencoe, Ill.: The Free Press, 1951).

[9] The term "role behavior" is equivalent to Mead's "role playing." It is also comparable to Sarbin's "role enactment," which includes "among other segments of behavior, gross skeletal movements, the performance of verbal and motoric gestures,

Obviously, the role expectations of Alter and the role definition of Ego will have points of overlap and of conflict. As these differences are reconciled and as new contingencies are encountered in role behavior, role undergoes some degree of redefinition. That is, Alter's positive sanctions reinforce certain aspects of Ego's role behavior, whereas his negative sanctions tend to modify other role responses. Alter's reactions thus provide feedback enabling Ego to redefine his role and to assess what Homans would term the balance of rewards and investments resulting from continued status incumbency.[10] Such information also influences Ego's commitment to adequate role performance.[11]

If Alter's manipulation of sanctions elicits overt role behavior that is at variance with Ego's values, Ego may experience considerable cognitive dissonance. According to Festinger's reformulation of Heider's theory, the presence of cognitive dissonance generates pressures to reduce that dissonance, and a relatively direct means of accomplishing this reduction is by changing one or more of the elements involved in the dissonant relation.[12] Thus Ego could withdraw from his status and thereby avoid further role behavior which would be incongruent with his values. However, should Ego decide that the rewards from status incumbency exceed the costs, then he could reduce his cognitive dissonance by modifying some of his old beliefs. To bolster this change he might also shift reference groups. In this manner Ego would not only reduce his dissonance but also increase his social profit from role interaction since his costs in terms of foregone values would be diminished.[13] Ultimately such a modification in beliefs and change in reference groups may engender a cognitive reorganization in Ego, influencing the strengths or saliencies of particular need-dispositions.[14] Illustrations of this effect of role behavior appear in Merton's analysis of the bureaucratic personality which may become "fit, with an unfit fitness," as well as in Homans' treatment of social control.[15] Thus, as the arrows in Figure 9-1 indicate, personality not only influences but is also influenced by role behavior.

---

posture and gait, styles of speech and accent, the wearing of certain forms of dress and costume, the use of material objects, the wearing of emblems or ornamentation, including tattoos, etc. In short, role enactment embraces what may be called the mechanics of the role-taking process" (op. cit., p. 232).

[10] G. C. Homans, Social Behavior: Its Elementary Forms (New York: Harcourt, Brace & World, 1961); "Status among Clerical Workers," Human Organization, 12:5–10 (1953).

[11] A. Zaleznik, C. R. Christensen, and F. J. Roethlisberger, The Motivation, Productivity, and Satisfaction of Workers: A Prediction Study (Boston: Division of Research, Harvard University Graduate School of Business Administration, 1958).

[12] L. Festinger, A Theory of Cognitive Dissonance (Evanston, Ill.: Row, Peterson, 1957); cf. F. Heider, The Psychology of Interpersonal Relations (New York: Wiley, 1958), ch. 7 et passim.

[13] Cf. Homans, Social Behavior.

[14] Cf. Parsons, "An Approach to Psychological Theory"; The Social System.

[15] Merton, op cit., chs. 6 and 7; Homans, Social Behavior.

In discussing role interaction we have elaborated upon certain effects of Alter's reactions to Ego's role behavior. Let us turn now to the obverse situation. Ego's role behavior and manipulation of sanctions provides feedback to Alter and may influence Alter's definition of his own role as well as his expectations vis-à-vis Ego's role. Ultimately, modifications in significant Alters' role expectations may influence the definitions of the specific status or even of the general status. Up to the last point, our treatment of the double-contingency of role interaction was premised on the assumption that Ego and Alter were behaving in terms of a shared system of relatively clearly defined patterns of value orientation. Should Ego succeed, however, in modifying expectations at the level of the specific or the general status, then Ego may have "transcended" the values of his particular social system by influencing "morality" so that it reflects to some extent his own nature and potentialities.[16] Riesman's "autonomous" man also represents such an independent and value-producing type, as does the charismatic leader.[17]

ROLE CONFLICT ANALYSIS

Role conflict is defined as a situation characterized by all of the following conditions: (1) A decision is required of a person whose role is such that he is expected to decide; (2) the decision is between two or more response alternatives, each of which will fulfill the legitimate expectations of an Alter with claims upon the person; (3) no decision open to the person will satisfy the requirements imposed upon him by *all* of the expectations or obligations in conflict. In general, no matter what Ego decides he will fail to fulfill some of the legitimate expectations imposed upon him by his role(s).

We may distinguish two types of role conflict: (1) *status-produced role conflict*, developing from incumbency in a single status subject to incompatible expectations or obligations; and (2) *contingent role conflict*, resulting from incumbency in two statuses, both of whose legitimate sets of expectations cannot be fulfilled simultaneously.

Status-Produced Role Conflict. We may further analyze this type of role conflict in terms of two subtypes. One of these, depicted in Figure 9-2, develops from lack of consensus among status definers.[18]

---

[16] Cf. E. Fromm, *Man for Himself* (New York: Farrar and Rinehart, 1947).

[17] David Riesman, Nathan Glazer, and Reuel Denney, *The Lonely Crowd* (New Haven: Yale Univ. Press, 1950); Max Weber, "The Sociology of Charismatic Authority," in H. H. Gerth and C. Wright Mills (eds.), *From Max Weber: Essays in Sociology* (New York: Oxford Univ. Press, 1946), ch. 9; "The Meaning of Discipline," *ibid.*, ch. 10; *The Theory of Social and Economic Organization* (New York: Oxford Univ. Press, 1947), ch. 3.

[18] The present treatment is a refinement of the distinction between status-produced and contingent role conflict made by the senior author in a previous paper concerning role conflict among union leaders.—J. T. Gullahorn, "Role Conflict among Union

In our previous discussion and diagrammatic presentation of status and role we treated the *total set* of expectations and obligations at each level of status definition. If we divide these total sets into subsets according to the different Alters or groups of Alters defining the status at each level, the potentiality of conflict arising from divergent or incompatible expectations among the relevant Alters becomes apparent. A simple illustration is presented in Figure 9-2, where the top circle at each level of status definition represents the set of expectations of one Alter and the bottom circle, the set of expectations of another Alter. The hatched section of overlap of the circles includes those components of the status definition which are identical within both groups. The size of this intersection thus represents the extent of consensus between two status definers.

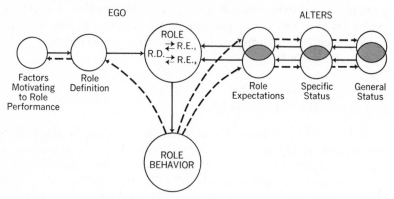

FIGURE 9-2

Conversely, the areas in the circles outside the hatched intersections represent the components of status definitions which differ for each group of Alters. These areas indicate the extent of lack of consensus among the status definers. Lack of consensus, per se, need not lead to role conflict. Role conflict is likely to ensue for Ego only when the differing expectations of the Alters are actually incompatible *and* are elicited simultaneously in the context of a specific situation.

For example, the regional representative of an international union often confronts a status-produced role conflict developing from incompatible expectations of different status definers. Officers of each local union within his region tend to perceive his major responsibility to involve defending their interests and mobilizing the power of the international union for this purpose if necessary. The officers of the international union, however, consider his primary responsibility to be the maintenance of the best interests of the international in all situations arising in the region. At times it may be impossible for the representative to act in accord with all of these

Leaders" (paper presented at the annual meeting of the American Sociological Society, September, 1954). Status-produced role conflict is comparable to what Gross and his associates term "intrarole conflict."—Gross, Mason, and McEachern, *op. cit.*, pp. 248 f.

potentially incompatible expectations. Similarly, the foreman in industry, the noncommissioned officer in the military services, the superintendent or principal in a school system, and other "men in the middle" may anticipate recurrent conflicts among legitimate expectations.[19]

The other subtype of status-produced role conflict develops from incompatible obligations included in one specific status. In this situation the expectations of the relevant Alters may be relatively congruent; however, the decision confronting Ego is such that he cannot fulfill all of the obligations involved in his status. Figure 9-3 depicts this type of role conflict in

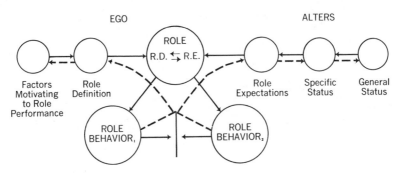

FIGURE 9-3

which the inherent contradictions among responsibilities united in one status result in incompatible response alternatives for role performance.

This type of role dilemma occasionally confronts a union business agent whose responsibilities involve the welfare of the local as a whole and of each group composing it. When he is required to make a decision concerning promotion policy, his obligations to one subgroup may be fulfilled at the expense of another. In this situation all relevant groups may agree in their role expectations vis-à-vis the business agent. That is, they may all accept his authority and expect his decision to be in the best interest of the union. The conflict arises at the level of role behavior because any action of the status incumbent will fail to comply with legitimate obligations to Alters for whose welfare he is responsible. This situation is comparable to that which Barnard treats as the moral dilemma inherent in executive positions.[20]

Contingent Role Conflict. The other principal type of role conflict arises

[19] This type of role conflict can be further analyzed in terms of Homans' concepts of external and internal systems.—G. C. Homans, *The Human Group* (New York: Harcourt, Brace, 1950), ch. 16 *et passim*. The foreman in an industrial plant may find that he cannot fulfill his obligations within the external system without support from the internal system. Therefore, the effective foreman must mobilize the sentiments of the internal system in support of the essential activities of the external system. As status incumbent he must operate discriminatingly and simultaneously in terms of the needs and norms of both systems.

[20] C. I. Barnard, *The Functions of the Executive* (Cambridge, Mass.: Harvard Univ. Press, 1938), ch. 17.

as a consequence of the multiplicity of statuses which Ego simultaneously occupies. Some elements in the different roles that Ego plays may be potentially incompatible so that occasionally he cannot fulfill simultaneously the expectations associated with all of the statuses. This type of conflict, depicted in Figure 9-4, has received extensive investigation.[21]

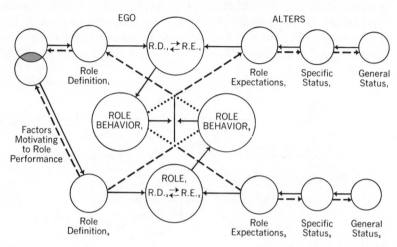

FIGURE 9-4

Contingent role conflict confronted a union officer who was offered a promotion into management at a time when his wife was ill and his family in need of additional income. The promotion would have meant $26.00 extra weekly salary. However, he and his fellow officers were convinced that his accepting management's offer would demoralize the newly organized union they had worked years to build. In this situation neither the status of union leader nor that of family man—considered independently —place impossible demands on this individual's role behavior. Conflict developed from and was contingent on his involvement in both statuses and on the necessity of giving precedence to one set of role expectations, since he could not fulfill both simultaneously.

Psychological and Sociological Role Conflict. Before proceeding to consider modes of role conflict resolution let us distinguish between person-

[21] J. W. Getzels and E. G. Guba, "Role, Role Conflict, and Effectiveness," *American Sociological Review*, 19:164–175 (Apr., 1954); Gross, Mason, and McEachern, *op. cit.*, ch. 17; J. T. Gullahorn, "Measuring Role Conflict," *American Journal of Sociology*, 61:299–303 (Jan., 1956); "Role Conflict among Union Leaders," *op. cit.*; "Social Tensions in Labor Union Relationships" (unpublished Ph.D. dissertation, Harvard University, 1953); Merton, *op. cit.*, pp. 371–380; Parsons, *The Social System*, ch. 7; Sarbin, *op. cit.*, pp. 252 f; Samuel A. Stouffer, "An Analysis of Conflicting Social Norms," *American Sociological Review*, 14:707–717 (Dec., 1949); Stouffer and J. Toby, "Role Conflict and Personality," *American Journal of Sociology*, 56:395–406 (Mar., 1951); J. P. Sutcliffe and M. Haberman, "Factors Influencing Choice in Role Conflict Situations," *American Sociological Review*, 21:695–703 (Dec., 1956).

alistically and sociologically defined role conflict. From a phenomenological viewpoint a role conflict exists only when Ego defines the situation as such and experiences tension in endeavoring to resolve his dilemma. With reference to Figures 9-2, 9-3, and 9-4, the loci of the conflict are in the large circles labeled Role. Should Ego so perceive the situation that he feels no conflict in deciding among apparently irreconcilable though legitimate obligations, then from a personality-system frame of reference he does not experience a role conflict.

In the previous example, the union officer who was offered a promotion into management during his wife's illness experienced considerable tension in making a decision which forced him to choose between the incompatible expectations resulting from simultaneous involvement in two roles, to both of which he was deeply committed. Thus he experienced a role conflict as defined from both a personalistic and a sociological viewpoint. Another union officer faced with a similar decision reacted differently: he accepted the promotion, apparently without question. What superficially appeared to be the same situation was not perceived in a similar manner by two different status incumbents in the union social system. The second officer had in fact deliberately, though surreptitiously, sought union office as an avenue into management. Therefore, he did not experience psychological role conflict.

Sociologically, however, different criteria are relevant. With reference again to Figures 9-2, 9-3, and 9-4, the locus of role conflict is in the set of circles labeled Role Expectations. The situation confronting the second officer fulfilled the conditions of role conflict noted previously. He faced incompatible legitimate expectations; his action could satisfy only one set of expectations at the expense of the other. Therefore, with respect to the union social system this status incumbent's hierarchy of value commitments and consequent behavior were deviant.

We have just discussed a situation in which Ego confronted a role conflict defined from a sociological but not from a personalistic viewpoint. The obverse may also occur. That is, Ego may encounter a situation which he perceives as a role conflict but which actually does not meet the sociological criteria for a role conflict. We may term this occurrence a pseudo role conflict since, contrary to Ego's perception of the situation, one or more of the previously defined conditions of role conflict are not fulfilled: (1) Ego actually is not expected or required to make a decision concerning the competing claims; (2) one or both of the conflicting claims on him are illegitimate;[22] (3) a creative solution satisfactory to the competing Alters is possible.

[22] Some authors include dilemmas involving illegitimate demands on a status incumbent in their treatment of role conflict (Gross, Mason, and McEachern, *op. cit.*; Sarbin, *op. cit.*). We prefer to consider such situations separately in terms of a power conflict among the Alters having repercussions on the stability of the social system in question as well as on the conformity of the particular status incumbent (cf. Parsons,

ROLE CONFLICT RESOLUTION

In this section we shall consider pseudo role conflict situations as well as role conflicts fulfilling the requirements of both a sociological and a psychological conceptualization.[23] Our reference point is Ego—his resolution of a role conflict in terms of his role behavior.

When Ego considers a situation to be a role conflict (whether or not it is one from a sociological viewpoint), there appear to be three possible means of resolving the dilemma. (1) He may accept the responsibility for decision and decide among the competing claims made on him; (2) he may delay the responsibility for decision; (3) he may reject the responsibility for decision.

An outline suggesting some of the conditions influencing Ego's selection among these three modes of role conflict resolution appears in the Appendix. Some of the conditions listed were derived from social system theory and from formulations regarding the resolution of cognitive dissonance; others emanated from empirical studies, particularly an investigation of role conflict among labor union leaders.[24] It is hoped the outline will suggest hypotheses for further research.

Considering role conflict situations in general we would expect the following rank-ordering in Ego's choice among the three modes of resolution: postponing responsibility for decision would be most preferred; rejecting responsibility by referring the decision to others would be next; and accepting responsibility and making the decision would be the last. The predicted rank order is based upon expectancies concerning relative costs to Ego of the decision alternatives.

Generally, postponing a decision is the least punitive response to a role conflict situation. When such a solution is adopted the rights of neither claimant need be denied; hence Ego avoids the consequences of failing in his obligations to any of the significant Alters. Thus Ego may postpone a decision solely because it is possible to do so. In formal systems, however, responsibility may be so structured that this alternative becomes impossible without further legitimation. Indeed, if Ego has frequent face-to-face contact with the claimants, he may not be able to persist in stalling on the excuse that insufficient data are available for decision. However, if Ego can evade pressure and continue to delay, one or both of the competing Alters may desist, or the conditions might change so that the problem can be re-

---

"An Approach to Psychological Theory"; *The Social System*, p. 280). Ego's resolution of such dilemmas necessarily involves consideration of the sanctioning power of the Alters pressing the illegitimate claims.

[23] In the case of sociologically defined role conflicts which Ego does not perceive as such, Ego may be forced to redefine the situation as a role conflict; or, if he acts in accord with his deviant definition of the situation, he may be subject to strong sanctions from the offended Alters.

[24] Gullahorn, *op. cit.*, fn. 21. "Social Tensions . . . ."

defined. Therefore, Ego may never make a decision on the conflict—except for the decision to keep postponing a commitment on it—or ultimately he may be able to redefine the problem so that a creative solution becomes possible. Barnard attaches great importance to the executive skill involved in knowing when to postpone decision and when not to decide.[25]

While delaying a decision seems to be a preferred action alternative, Ego probably can avail himself of this course only in situations where time pressure can be evaded and communication kept relatively indirect through bureaucratic channels. For example, in the case of a role conflict involving a local union and its national headquarters, a local union officer can stall on the problem by consuming time in correspondence.[26]

Resolving a role conflict by referring the responsibility for decision to others also protects Ego from direct responsibility for action against the claims of an Alter. This mode of resolution is likely to be possible mainly in the case of status-produced role conflicts where the competing Alters are part of a limited social system and therefore presumably share relevant values; where they can get together relatively easily to discuss the problem; and where they can accept common leadership. These conditions are less likely to be fulfilled in contingent role conflict situations. However, in certain social systems Ego may be able to resolve a contingent role conflict by referring the responsibility for decision to a functional authority such as a priest or rabbi whom the competing claimants regard as qualified to settle moral dilemmas.

When Ego accepts responsibility for decision and chooses between the competing claims made on him he pays the cost of possible sanctions from the disappointed Alters and also feelings of guilt because he cannot satisfy all those to whom he is obligated. But often these consequences must be accepted when Ego cannot evade the decision by stalling tactics or by referring it to others. Such is frequently the case when Ego confronts contingent role conflicts involving time pressures—for example, when a union officer's family expects him to attend a relative's birthday celebration on the evening of an executive committee meeting. The structuring of responsibility in a formal system might also be such that Ego must accept the burden of decision for resolving status-produced conflicts as well. If Ego has sufficient social capital that he can afford the cost of sanctions from the offended Alters, and if he has a sufficient sense of moral rectitude that he can tolerate the cognitive dissonance resulting from decisions regarding role conflicts, then his exercise of authority is not likely to threaten his continued status occupancy. However, individuals who occupy statuses subject to recurring role conflicts are likely to be lonely men. But, as Homans concludes in his discussion of authority, Ego "can best reconcile leadership and popularity if, first, he spends a good deal of time rewarding

---

[25] Barnard, *op. cit.*, ch. 13.
[26] Gullahorn, *op. cit.*, fn. 21.

them [Alters] as individuals relative to the amount of time he spends coordinating their joint actions, and second, he succeeds in attaining a goal highly rewarding to them, for then the reward will offset the costs he has made them incur in the process." [27]

Appendix

The following outline suggests some of the conditions influencing Ego's choice among three possible modes of role conflict resolution.

   I. Ego may accept the responsibility for decision and choose between the competing claims made on him when any of the following conditions prevail:[28]

   A. Values of both systems, of a more inclusive social system, or of the most significant reference groups are hierarchically ranked so that obligations to one of the competing Alters are recognized as having greater claim or legitimacy.[29]

   B. The data serving as a basis for decision give greater support to the legitimacy of one set of expectations.

   C. Ego's role definition is more nearly consonant with the role expectations of one competing Alter than with those of the other.

   D. Ego's commitment to one role or to one set of competing expectations is greater than to the other.

   II. Ego may delay the responsibility for decision when any of the following conditions prevail:

   A. Delay can be legitimized on the grounds that inadequate information is available for immediate decision.

   B. The threat of possible system disruption is less from delay than from immediate decision.

   C. Negative sanctions seem more probable from action favoring the system to which Ego is more deeply committed; positive sanctions seem more likely from decision favoring the system to which Ego is less deeply committed.[30]

[27] Homans, *Social Behavior*, p. 315.

[28] These conditions with their social system referent are comparable to what Abelson terms "bolstering" of one conflicting cognitive element in the resolution of belief dilemmas.—R. P. Abelson, "Modes of Resolution of Belief Dilemmas," *The Journal of Conflict Resolution*, 3:343–352 (1959).

[29] Cf. Stouffer, *op. cit.*; J. Toby, "Some Variables in Role Conflict Analysis," *Social Forces*, 30:323–327 (1953).

[30] Cf. Gullahorn, "Measuring Role Conflict," *American Journal of Sociology*, 61: 299–303 (January 1956).

III. Ego may reject the responsibility for decision.

    A. Ego may withdraw from the status(es) when he perceives certain of the following conditions:[31]

        1. Withdrawal would not so seriously repudiate the norms or be so detrimental to the system's welfare as would deciding against the claims of the system.

        2. Withdrawal would cast Ego in the role of sacrificing for the system and thus might strengthen his power within the system.

        3. The rewards ensuing from role behavior barely exceed Ego's investment; hence he is not deeply committed to the role.[32]

    B. Ego may shift the burden of responsibility for decision to the Alters involved in the conflict.

        1. Ego may refer the decision to *both of the competing Alters* when all of the following conditions are met:

            a. Alters in both groups share the same value orientations relevant to the decision in question.

            b. Adequate communication channels exist between the competitors.

            c. Ego believes the claims of both groups deserve equal consideration.

        2. Ego may refer the decision to *one of the competing Alters* when either of the following conditions prevails:

            a. Alters in one group can exert controlling power over the other.

            b. Ego expects Alters in one group to modify their role expectations.

    C. Ego may shift the burden of responsibility for decision to an Alter other than those pressing conflicting claims on him.

        1. Ego may refer the decision to a *higher authority* when any of following conditions occur:

            a. The location of Ego's position in the communication network precludes his gaining access to information necessary for decision.

            b. The decision would affect groups within the system over whom Ego has no legitimate authority.

            c. The endorsement of higher authority will be essential to legitimize the decision.

        2. Ego may refer the decision to an *authority in a subordinate status* when any of the following conditions prevail:

[31] The conditions listed refer to outright resignation from status incumbency. Ego may, however, withdraw temporarily by becoming ill. As Parsons has noted, illness is a relatively prevalent form of deviance from role performance.—*The Social System*, pp. 285–292.

[32] J. W. Thibaut and H. H. Kelley, *The Social Psychology of Groups* (New York: Wiley, 1959), ch. 6.

      a. Decision properly falls within the scope of the subordinate's status.

      b. The claimants have evaded established communication channels; therefore Ego may legitimately refer the problem to his subordinate.

      c. Using the subordinate as a scapegoat will be less damaging to the system (and to Ego) than will Ego's assuming responsibility for decision.

3. Ego may refer the decision to a *functional authority*—i.e., one accepted as qualified to make a technical or moral decision—when either of the following circumstances occurs:

      a. Ego does not possess adequate technical competence with reference to the problem.

      b. The opinion of the authority will be accepted as authoritative by both groups.

29

The Study of Role Conflict: Explorations in Methodology*

HOWARD J. EHRLICH and
JAMES W. RINEHART
The Ohio State University

JOHN C. HOWELL
Michigan State University

It is the purpose of this paper to report the results of two empirical studies of role conflict conducted by the authors and to compare the procedures and results of these studies with that conducted by Gross, Mason, and McEachern (2), and, where possible, those conducted by Shull and Miller (4). Primary focus will be placed upon the prediction of the resolution of role conflict and the diversity of the operations employed in making such predictions. We shall attempt to answer the following questions: (a) What is the relationship between the many predictor variables and the methods of operationalizing them in the studies under review? (b) What is the relative efficacy of these predictors of conflict resolution? and (c) What degree of stability do they manifest as predictors in the studies in which they have been employed?

THE RESEARCH PROCEDURES

Study I.

The context of this study is a large midwestern state police organization with the subjects of study being a seven per cent, stratified-cluster sample of police patrolmen. The patrolmen interviewed were presented with a series

Reprinted from *Sociometry*, 25, 1 (March 1962), 85–97, by permission of the authors and the American Sociological Association.

* The research reported here was supported by the Highway Traffic Safety Center of Michigan State University and in part by a grant (M-2957) from the United States Public Health Service. The authors wish to express their gratitude to Professor Jack J. Preiss of Duke University, who was primarily responsible for the initiation of the "Police Project" from which part of the materials reported herein were taken. The present paper is a revision of a briefer report presented at the American Sociological Association meetings, St. Louis, Missouri, September 2, 1961.

of four structured situations which, in the judgment of the researcher (on the basis of seven months of systematic and participant observation at Central Headquarters), represented real and *potential* conflict situations. The content of the four conflict situations may be summarized as follows: (a) the conflict between emphasizing or balancing traffic work and criminal investigation; (b) the conflict between leaving the job behind or preserving one's occupational role outside the job; (c) the conflict between being a "model citizen" or being a "good citizen"; (d) the conflict between overlooking or not overlooking the rules and regulations. Each situation included two or three contradictory alternatives for behavior which met the criteria of being mutually exclusive and exhaustive of all of the empirically possible alternatives.

Situation 2, by means of example, confronted the respondent with the following expectations:

A. *Expect me to be a policeman 24 hours a day.*
B. *Expect me to leave my job behind when I am off duty.*
C. *Have no expectations of me on this matter.*

The respondents were then asked to indicate which alternative "most nearly represented" what each of eleven audiences[1] expected of them. The list of audiences was standardized for all situations: Headquarters Command, District Command, Post Commander, Assistant Post Commanders, Patrolmen, Wife-Family, Personal Friends, Service Clubs, Fraternal Organizations, the Press, and Local and County Police. Finally the interviewer probed to determine other audiences whose expectations were perceived as salient in the situation. This check indicated that virtually all salient audiences had been tapped by the original listing. Full details and the distributions of responses by situation, audience, and expectation appear in Ehrlich (1).

If the respondent indicated that he would be confronted with contradictory expectations in a situation, the interviewer probed with focused ques-

[1] The term "audience group," introduced by Ralph Turner (5) as a special class of reference groups, refers to those groups by whom the actor sees his role performance observed and evaluated, and to whose expectations and evaluations he attends. The introduction here of the concept of audience group, however much refinement it may need, carries with it certain decided advantages: (a) Its usage proscribes the arbitrary assignment of "counter-roles" ("alters," "role partners," etc.) by the observer. (b) Recognition of the symbolic character of an audience group helps emphasize that the physical presence of others is neither a necessary nor a sufficient condition for role performance. (c) The conception of audience group is flexible enough to encompass idiosyncratic sources of expectancies and evaluation, e.g., "significant others," "role models," etc. (d) This conception is further flexible in that it does not carry with it the implication that the actor necessarily conforms to the expectations of his audience. (e) Finally, the use of the concept of audience group, despite the nascent state of reference group theory, hopefully directs attention to the possibility, or perhaps the necessity, of integrating reference group theory and role theory.

tions in order to ascertain, among other things, the legitimacy and obliga-
toriness of these expectations, as well as the respondent's mode of
resolution.

The interviews were conducted at four police stations in our sample
during a period of participant-observation. A period of sustained personal
contact with the prospective interviewees, ranging from one to three weeks,
was thus maintained prior to their being interviewed. In all, 51 interviews
on the four conflict situations were completed, yielding a total of 204
protocols for analysis. Of these, 138 were instances of role conflict (1).

Study II.

The subjects of the second study were 33 police trainees in the same
organization who had successfully completed the first eight months of their
training program. The role conflict situations employed in the first study
remained constant, but the interview schedule was modified to the form of
a self-administering questionnaire, and was group-administered. While the
procedure for reporting legitimacy and obligation remained constant, the
questionnaire form entailed two modifications. The number of audience
groups was reduced to nine, seven of which had been enumerated on the
first schedule. Secondly, conflict resolutions—elicited in the interview
situation by an open-ended question—were here determined by answers to
a structured question. Finally, questions concerning sanctions and personal
preference were added (3).

Studies I and II both yielded similar distributions of conflict and congruent responses. Moreover, these distributions are virtually identical to
those obtained in a third study which utilized a mail questionnaire sent to
a ten per cent systematic random sample of patrolmen not included in the
first study. The results of this latter study—undertaken for somewhat different research interests and not reported in this paper—are introduced here
to emphasize the stability of our findings. Thus the data-gathering procedures per se—interview schedule, group-administered questionnaire, and an
abbreviated and anonymous mail questionnaire—are not significant sources
of variation in our findings. Finally, we may assert that our samples are
truly representative of the population of police patrolmen in the subject
organization.

Gross, Mason, and McEachern

In the context of one of the most comprehensive attempts at system-
atizing and empirically testing the propositions of role theory, Gross and
his associates introduced a theory of role conflict resolution based on the
concepts of legitimacy, sanctions, and personal orientation to legitimacy and
sanctions. The subject population in which this theory was tested was a
50 per cent stratified sample of school superintendents (n = 105) in the

state of Massachusetts. The interview schedule employed was used as our model in Study I, and the interviews here took place in the context of an eight-hour interview situation in the researchers' offices. The four conflict situations dealt with: (a) the conflict between hiring and promoting personnel on the basis of professional criteria or on the basis of "special" considerations to the preferences of influential others; (b) the conflict between spending most evenings on school and community business or with families or friends; (c) the conflict between minimizing or maximizing teacher salary increases; and (d) the conflict between giving priority to the financial resources of the community in preparing the school budget or giving priority to its educational needs.

The alternatives which define the potential conflict situations both in this study and in our two studies represent abstracted elements of real and pervasive situations in the subject organizations. The situations themselves confront every school superintendent and every police patrolman in the discharge of his role obligations. They are contrived or artificial situations only in the limited sense that they do not provide in the interview schedules the full detail of a "real" situation. Finally, it ought to be noted here that in all of these studies we are dealing with the verbal reports of persons and not with direct observations of their role behavior.

Shull and Miller

In a study aimed at a further testing of the Gross, Mason, and McEachern theory of role conflict resolution, Shull and Miller studied two populations of business managers—first- and second-year groups enrolled in an executive training program at Indiana University, training directors of various Indiana firms who were members of a state chapter of the American Society of Training Directors, and international, state, and local labor leaders holding posts in and around Indianapolis. The data were secured through a mail questionnaire in the case of the training directors and resulted in 33 per cent returns. The questionnaires to the business and labor leaders were distributed "in a group setting and then later collected" and yielded 70 per cent and 90 per cent returns respectively. Their questionnaire form of Gross's interview schedule consisted of: (a) a structured situation that evoked the respondent's assessments of the legitimacy and sanctions dimensions of the given expectations; (b) the respondent's selection from among five alternatives for resolving the conflict; and (c) instructions to construct an actual role conflict situation he had encountered, and to report on the legitimacy and sanctions of the expectations involved as well as how he resolved the conflict. The single structured situation presented by Shull and Miller involved a conflict relating to the manner of setting up a supervisory training program, which has been requested by the president of the company; the training director believes it should be compulsory and on company time, whereas the general plant superintendent, who is operating under a heavy production schedule, insists on initiating the program on a voluntary basis and off company time. The president has said that the plant superintendent will be ordered to comply with the conditions specified by the training director. Respondents were asked to complete the questionnaire assuming that they were the training director.

LEGITIMACY

To Gross and his associates, "A legitimate expectation is one which the incumbent of a focal position feels others have a right to hold. An illegitimate expectation is one which he does not feel others have a right to hold" (2, p. 248). It was expected that individuals would be predisposed to conform to expectations which others have a right to hold and predisposed not to conform to expectations which others do not have a right to hold. It was further contended that "failure to conform to an expectation which is perceived as legitimate will result in negative internal sanctions" (2, p. 285). Legitimacy thus defined was operationalized by asking the respondent whether he thought the individual or group named has a right to expect him to do this. This operational procedure was included in both Studies I and II.

Shull and Miller, in their attempt at testing the Harvard group's theory, departed slightly from this operation by asking the respondents whether they thought a given individual's expectation was *"right and reasonable."*

Ehrlich has proposed an alternative definition of and procedure for operationalizing this concept. Legitimacy he defined as the institutionalized accountability of the actor to an audience group for his own acts and/or the acts of others (1, pp. 12–14). Respondents were asked, with reference to a given audience in a given situation, "Are you accountable to these persons for what you actually do?"

It is entirely probable that the three operationalizations of legitimacy would evoke three distinct sets of responses. We may visualize these three procedures as lying on an expectation-audience continuum. At the one end of the continuum we find Shull and Miller's definition which emphasizes the content of the expectation. Toward the midpoint of the continuum lies the construction of Gross and his associates which takes into consideration both content of the expectation and primarily the authority of the audience holding the position. Ehrlich's conception, at the other end of the continuum, focuses primarily upon the institutionalized structure of the actor-audience relationship.

For all studies, legitimacy was treated dichotomously. Gross considered an expectation legitimate if a respondent reported at least one audience as having a right to hold it. An expectation was considered illegitimate if *no* audiences were perceived as having a right to hold it. Predictions were

then made on the assumption that actors would conform to legitimate
expectations and reject or ignore those seen as illegitimate. Where only
one expectation was perceived as legitimate, then it was predicted that the
actor would conform to it. If both expectations were perceived as legitimate, a "compromise" behavior was predicted, i.e., it was assumed that the
actor would attempt to conform in part to both expectations through some
form of compromise. Finally, where neither expectation was legitimate, it
was assumed that the actor would attempt some form of avoidance behavior. Using these predictive policies, which we shall call Policy 1, Gross
achieved successful predictions in 63 per cent of his cases, and Shull and
Miller, 46 per cent correct predictions (Table 1).

TABLE 1

*The Proportion of Correct Predictions of Role Conflict Resolutions Achieved Through the Use
of Legitimacy and Sanctions as Predictors*

	Study I	Study II	Gross, Mason and McEachern	Shull and Miller
Legitimacy				
1. "right"				
(a) policy 1	.19	.35	.63	—
(b) policy 2	.56	.54	—	—
2. "accountable"	.54	—	—	—
3. "right and reasonable"	—	—	—	.46*
Sanctions				
4. "obligation"	.51	.48	—	—
5. "access"	—	.55	—	—
6. "exercise"	—	.54	—	—
7. "severity"	—	—	.82	—
8. "conditional"	—	—	—	—†
Combinations				
1(b)–4	.58	.52	—	—
2–4	.57	—	—	—
1(b)–5	—	.54	—	—
1(b)–6	—	.54	—	—
1(a)–7	—	—	.83	—
3–8	—	—	—	.52

* Our computation from their data.
† Cannot determine from their data.

In Studies I and II, using the same predictive policy, we achieved 19
per cent and 35 per cent correct predictions respectively. It is apparent that
we have failed to replicate this finding of Gross, Mason, and McEachern,
and that this policy decision is of little value in our studies.

Investigation of the disparity in these findings suggests quite strongly
that the applicability of this predictive policy depends upon (a) the degree

to which respondents report that those holding conflicting expectations have a right to hold each,[2] and (b) the degree to which they report actually engaging in compromise behavior. This can be seen below:

	Proportion of Compromise Resolutions		Proportionate Error
	Expected	Reported	
	(a)	(b)	(c)
Study I	.68	.08	.89
Study II	.52	.08	.84
Gross, Mason, McEachern	.31	.20	.36

Thus the policemen are more likely than the school superintendents to perceive the expectations of others as legitimate, but less likely to engage in compromise behavior. The proportionate error (c), which is derived from the ratio of the expected to the difference between reported and expected, is therefore more than twice as great in our studies.

Our own decisional criterion, Policy 2, is based on the assumption that the number of audiences perceived as legitimately holding a given expectation may be taken as the "degree of legitimacy" of an expectation. In a set of conflicting expectations, then, one expectation is construed as "more legitimate" than the others if the number of audiences the actor perceives as legitimately holding that expectation exceeds the number of audiences the actor perceives as legitimately holding the other expectations in the set. Prediction is, then, always in the direction of the greater degree of legitimacy.

For Gross and his associates, number is an irrelevant dimension. Under their policy, if ten audiences were perceived as legitimately holding expectation A and one audience legitimately holding expectation B, they would predict a compromise resolution. Under our policy, we would predict conformity to A. As can be seen in Table 1, the proportion of correct predictions achieved through our procedure manifests relatively stable results and is significantly greater than was achieved under the first procedure. The obtained proportion of correct predictions is here not significantly different from those obtained by Gross.

In Study I, legitimacy, in terms of both right and accountability, was asked of the respondent. Seventy-two per cent of the patrolmen perceived their audiences as having a right to the various expectations, but in only 57 per cent of the cases did they regard themselves as accountable to those audiences. Of the 1617 response pairs, 76 per cent yielded convergence in that the respondent indicated both right and accountability or neither. The two variables, as shown in Table 1, yield consistent predictions. Their high degree of association and consistent predictions strongly suggests that the two questions are measuring the same dimension.

[2] In this instance, using Gross's model, we would expect a compromise behavior.

SANCTIONS

In attempting to codify the dimensions of expectations, it was proposed that expectations may in part be construed as optional or obligatory (1, Chapter I). A role expectation was construed as obligatory if and only if failure to perform the role expected imposed negative sanctions upon the actor, while performance of the role expected did not incur negative sanctions. This was operationalized by two questions. First the respondent was asked, "Would they (the audience group) insist or demand that you do as they expect you to?" on the assumption that such insistence is a concomitant of obligation as defined. Then the respondent was asked, "What would they do if you didn't do as they expect?" to determine the content and nature of the imposed sanctions. Our quite unexpected finding was that the policemen in our sample could not answer this latter question. Even when they knew the audience group whose expectation they were not fulfilling would take some form of action, they were invariably uncertain as to what specifically it might do. Not only were the respondents unclear as to the informal sanctions that might be invoked by their fellow patrolmen or wives or friends, they were equally unclear as to what the formal sanctions within the organization might be.

It may well be the case that, in attempting to elicit the *specific* sanctions which the actor anticipated, we were imposing upon our respondents the task of discriminating elements of their phenomenal world which they otherwise do not discriminate. This is not to say that persons are not aware of at least some of the specific sanctions which they encounter as a consequence of selecting among behavioral alternatives. This is to suggest, rather, that such knowledge in some groups and in some situations is relatively unimportant; and, therefore, there is no well-developed vocabulary for its articulation.

In the school superintendent population, Gross, asking a similar question, apparently encountered no such difficulties in eliciting responses nor in classifying them on an *ad hoc* scale of severity of sanctions. It seems quite likely that the school superintendents are much more sensitive to the sanctions that their choice in role conflict situations may incur than are the patrolmen in our study, at least with respect to the situations under analysis.

In our second study, we included our question on "insistence" but shifted emphasis to two other dimensions of sanctions—access to sanctions and the likelihood of sanctions exercise. With respect to the former dimension the trainees were asked, "In what position are the persons in this category to apply pressure to try to make policemen do as they expect?" Sanctions exercise was ascertained by asking, "If policemen didn't act the way persons in this category who hold this view expect, what is the likelihood that such persons would actually do something to try to get policemen to act according to their view?"

Still another procedure was devised by Shull and Miller which we have taken the liberty of labeling *conditional sanction*. These researchers asked the question of the general form: What do you anticipate will happen to you if you ignore the given expectation and then fail to produce good results? Responses were recorded on a five-point scale where the alternatives ranged from "no disapproval" through "placed in a lower status position or discharged."

The results of our two studies in Table 1 are virtually identical. The report that an expectation is obligatory converges with both our access and exercise questions 81 per cent of the time; sanctions access and sanctions exercise converge 89 per cent of the time. This high degree of association is reflected in the relative constancy of correct predictions made with the use of these operations, and suggests quite strongly that they are tapping the same underlying dimension. The rather significantly greater degree of predictions obtained by the Harvard group is not difficult to understand, and supports our contention that the school superintendent is more concerned with sanctions than is the patrolman.

Finally, the range of correct predictions of conflict resolution achieved through use of the sanctions variables is approximately that achieved by use of the legitimacy variables in our studies but not in Gross's, again emphasizing the differential effects of sanctions here. In all of the studies, moreover, the various combinations of legitimacy and sanctions yield very little improvement in prediction.

INTENSITY ANALYSIS

The data of Study II, as analyzed and thus far reported here, are based on the treatment of legitimacy, obligation, sanctions access, and sanctions exercise as dichotomous attributes. This is to say that the perceived expectations of an audience were treated as being either legitimate or illegitimate, as being obligatory or not obligatory, and the audience perceived as having high or low access to sanctions and having a high or low likelihood of exercising those sanctions. The questionnaire responses, however, were secured on a five-point scale so as to obtain some measure of the intensity with which the actor regarded a given audience group's expectations. For example, the choice points constructed for legitimacy ranged from "has every right" on one extreme to "has no right" on the other extreme. Using these intensities and operating under Policy 2, the legitimacy and obligation variables showed an increase in prediction of 6 per cent each, while the sanctions access and exercise variables showed increases of 1 and 2 per cent respectively. It had been contended by both Gross and his associates and Shull and Miller that the use of such intensity measures would increase prediction. In this regard they were correct, but the increases in prediction we obtained over those reported in Table 1 were negligible.

PERSONAL DIMENSIONS

Few studies of role behavior have incorporated both personal and social dimensions. Gross and his associates attempted to handle this difficult task by introducing the assumption "that individuals may be differentiated according to their primacy of orientation to the legitimacy or to the sanctions dimensions of the expectations in the situation" (2, p. 289). Persons who, in role conflict situations, give primacy to the legitimacy dimension, that is, place stress on the right of others to hold a given expectation, were characterized as having a *moral orientation*. Those giving priority to the sanctions over the legitimacy dimension were characterized as *expedient* in their orientation. Finally, a *moral-expedient orientation* was introduced to encompass persons who do not give primacy to the legitimacy or sanctions dimension but who take both into a relatively equal accounting. The superintendent respondents were assigned to one of the three categories by the following procedure: Every respondent completed a 37-item questionnaire in which each item described the behavior which the superintendent may or may not be expected to engage in as the administrator of a public school. The response categories were structured on a five-point scale ranging from "absolutely must" through "absolutely must not" engage in the described behavior. Each absolute response was given a score of 1, and the scores obtained ranged from 1 through 30. The obtained distribution was divided approximately into thirds, with those in the lower third being defined as expedients, those in the upper third (who answered 19 to 30 of the items in absolute terms) considered moralists, and those who fell in the middle category categorized as moral-expedients. This done, predictions of conflict resolution were made on the basis of the *combined* dimensions of legitimacy, sanctions, and personal orientation. These three variables taken together, which the authors label as their role conflict theory, yield 91 per cent correct predictions. The addition of this variable results in an 8 per cent increase in prediction over the combination of legitimacy and sanctions.

In Study II we introduced into our questionnaire the variable of *personal preference*. We asked our trainees to indicate which of the given expectations they preferred each of the various audiences to hold of them. Using this procedure for determining personal preference, we achieved 47 per cent correct predictions of conflict resolution. When taken in combination with legitimacy and sanctions access, 56 per cent correct predictions were obtained. Thus, it should be noted that personal preference is approximately the same in predictive efficiency in these situations as the perception of legitimacy, obligation, and sanctions; and in combination with these variables does not appreciably increase prediction.

To recapitulate: In our two studies of role conflict conducted in the context of the same police organization and utilizing the same conflict situations but varying (a) in the data-gathering procedures (interviews, in which reports of conflict resolution were open-ended, vs. questionnaires, in which these reports were structured), (b) by the status of the respondent (police patrolmen vs. police trainees), (c) by the number and person of audiences the respondent was questioned about, and (d) the operational procedures by which legitimacy and sanctions were ascertained, we achieved a stable set of results with respect to the prediction of reported behavior in role conflict situations. This occurred despite our variation in the procedures of research employed; and neither the variables nor the alternative procedures of operationalization we employed affected the outcome of our predictions in any significant manner. Our proportion of successful predictions never exceeded .60, and this was consistently and significantly lower than that achieved by Gross, Mason, and McEachern. The findings of Shull and Miller similarly fall significantly below that of the school superintendent study, and are in most respects comparable to ours.

AN ALTERNATIVE PROCEDURE FOR PREDICTION

Before we proceed to a discussion of the further implications of the findings of these researches, we shall attempt to report in part on an alternative method for the prediction of role conflict resolution. At least one conceivable predictor, because of its all too obvious character, has not been given any significant attention: the audience group per se. Certainly, we may expect that the expectations of some audiences are of more importance to us than others. Corollary with this, it seems likely too that an actor will be more likely to conform to what he perceives to be the expectations of an audience of his "significant others" than to the expectations of any other audience group. We may easily subject this presumed predictor to test by determining the number of times there is a correspondence between the actor's perception of what a given audience, or combination of audiences, expects and what the actor reports doing. For two or more audiences, the predictions are made on the basis of the most frequently mentioned expectation; while expectations of equal frequency are counted as an error.

We shall concern ourselves in this report only with those audiences included in our schedule who occupy formal positions within the police organization. Our predictions based on these audiences taken together were, in Study I, 56 per cent correct, and in Study II, 58 per cent correct. We have achieved, therefore, relatively the same degree of correct prediction from the knowledge of what the respondent perceives is expected of him *independent* of attributions of legitimacy, sanctions, or even personal preference. Thus we are forced to the conclusion, within the confines of our studies, that the various research operations we have employed, which among themselves yield highly similar results, are certainly not parsimonious in the prediction of behavior in role conflict situations.

SUMMARY AND CONCLUSIONS

The results and methods of four role conflict studies were compared in an attempt to ascertain (a) the relative efficacy of various role conflict variables as predictors of role conflict resolution; (b) the effect of different operational definitions of these variables on the prediction of role conflict resolution; and (c) the degree of stability these variables manifest as predictors of conflict resolution in the four studies in which they have been employed.

The results of Studies I and II are remarkably stable despite the utilization of different methods of data collection and different samples taken from a single population. Such stability has afforded a firm base for comparing our results with those of two previously reported studies of role conflict.

None of the variables or possible combinations of variables—legitimacy, obligation, sanctions access, sanctions exercise or personal preference—were dominant in regard to their relative efficacy as predictors of role conflict resolution. The proportion of correct predictions of conflict resolution, utilizing the various and distinct operations reported, was found to be roughly commensurate, though a striking disparity is found between our studies and the Shull and Miller study on the one hand and that of Gross, Mason, and McEachern on the other.

It is our contention that, where our operations and procedures of analysis are comparable, the differences obtained between our findings and the findings of Gross and his associates are due in large measure to differences in the populations studied. Our research can by no means be taken as demonstration of this, but does indicate, at the very least, the necessity of further studies of the general applicability of these variables of role conflict analysis in other and diverse populations.

Finally, for both Studies I and II an alternative method for the prediction of role conflict resolution was reported. Utilizing the perceived expectations of certain audience groups as criteria, approximately the same degree of predictive accuracy was achieved as that achieved using role conflict variables as criteria. Thus the respondent's perception of what the other members of his organization expected of him was equally predictive of conflict resolution as the various attributions of these expectations—legitimacy, obligation, etc. The generally disappointing predictive accuracy reported by the authors seriously questions the efficacy of such variables as legitimacy and sanctions as predictors of role conflict resolution. Certainly the utilization of these variables did not appear in our studies as the most parsimonious technique available for prediction. Clearly, further investigation into the nature of the audience group and more general reference-group processes is in order.

References

1. Ehrlich, H. J., "The Analysis of Role Conflicts in a Complex Organization: The Police," Ph.D. Dissertation, Michigan State University, 1959.
2. Gross, N., W. S. Mason, and A. W. McEachern, *Explorations in Role Analysis: Studies of the School Superintendency Role*, New York: John Wiley and Sons, 1958.
3. Rinehart, J. W., "Analysis of Selected Role Conflict Variables," M.A. Thesis, Michigan State University, 1961.
4. Shull, F. A., Jr., and D. C. Miller, "Role Conflict Behavior in Administration: A Study in the Validation of a Theory of Role Conflict Resolution," Paper presented at the American Sociological Association meetings, 1960 (mimeographed).
5. Turner, R. H., "Role Taking, Role Standpoint, and Reference Group Behavior," *American Journal of Sociology*, 1956, 61, 316–328.

For Further Reading

BOOKS

Biddle, B. J., and Thomas, E. J. (Eds.). *Role theory: concepts and research.* New York: Wiley, 1966.

An anthology for which the editors prepared a short history of role theory and discuss concepts for classifying roles, concepts of role properties, and role variables.

Gross, N., Mason, W. S., and McEachern, A. W. *Explorations in role analysis: studies of the school superintendency.* New York: Wiley, 1958.

An unusually rigorous theoretical and methodological explication of this concept.

Haas, J. E. *Role conception and group consensus.* Columbus, Ohio: The Ohio State University, 1964. Research Monograph Number 117.

A report of a research studying the relationship of consensus of role to performance, sociometric preference, friction, and similarity of background.

ARTICLES

Arkoff, A., *et al.* Male-dominant and equalitarian attitudes in Japanese, Japanese-American, and Caucasian-American students. *J. soc. Psychol.*, 1964, *64* (2), 225–229. PA 39, 7547.

Japanese and Japanese-American students exhibited greater sex role differences than did Caucasian-American students.

Back, K. W., Hood, T. C. and Brehm, M. L. The subject role in small group experiments. *Social Forces*, 1964, *43* (2), 181–187. PA 39, 7486.

A discussion of the problems involved in the experimenter's and the subject's role.

Drabek, T. E. Student preferences in professor-student classroom role relations. *Sociol. Inquiry*, 1966, *36* (1), 87–97. SA 14, C1459.

Student preferences in professor-student classroom role relations were conceptualized as being on a continuum representing the degree to which students actively planned, directed, and participated in classroom activities. Six hypotheses confirmed.

Emmerich, W. Family role concepts of children ages six to ten. *Child Develpm.*, 1961, *32*, 609–624. PA 36, 5FGO9E.

The father was seen as more powerful than the mother; role perception is related to age.

Evans, T. Q. The brethren pastor: differential conceptions of an emerging role. *J. for the Scientific Study of Religion*, 1963, *3* (1), 43–51. PA 38, 8159.

There are significant differences between the pastoral role expectations of lay office-holders and pastors.

Goode, W. J. A theory of role strain. *Amer. sociol. Rev.*, 1960, *25* (4), 483–496. PA 35, 4043.

The individual cannot fully satisfy all role demands, and must move through a continuous sequence of role decisions and bargains.

Gross, E. and Stone, G. P. Embarrassment and the analysis of role requirements. *Amer. J. Sociol.*, 1964, 70 (1), 1–15. PA 39, 1484.

Since embarrassment incapacitates a person for continuing role performance, it can provide an indicator of basic requirements of role performance.

Janis, I. L. and Gilmore, J. B. The influence of incentive conditions on the success of role playing in modifying attitudes. *J. Personality soc. Psychol.*, 1965, 1 (1), 17–27. PA 39, 7592.

More attitude change occurred when overt role-playing was carried out under favorable sponsorship than under unfavorable sponsorship conditions.

Johnson, M. M. Sex role learning in the nuclear family. *Child Develpm.*, 1963, 34 (2), 319–333. PA 38, 8077.

Asserts that the key to sex role learning is identification with the father.

Knoff, W. F. Role: a concept linking society and personality. *Amer. J. Psychiat.*, 1961, 117 (11), 1010–1015. PA 36, 2GE10K.

A brief review of the concept is presented; attention is called to its possible integrative function in the study of sociological and psychological phenomena; implications and applications of role theory are discussed.

Lacognata, A. A., Faculty academic-role expectations. *J. soc. Psychol.*, 1965, 66 (2), 337–344. PA 39, 16312.

This study suggests high consensus among faculty, relatively independent of teaching functions and academic disciplines.

Lewis, D. J. Stimulus, response, and a social role. *J. soc. Psychol.*, 1959, 50 (1), 119–127. PA 35, 3314.

Purpose: to determine what antecedent and consequent (stimulus-response) the term "role" refers to. The term makes clear that the subject matter of large areas of the social sciences is the same.

Lopata, H. Z. A restatement of the relation between role and status. *Sociol. Soc. Res.*, 1964, 49 (1), 58–68. PA 39, 4747.

Argues for the recognition of factors other than status upon role behavior.

Mann, J. H. Studies of role performance. *Genetic Psychol. Monogr.*, 1961, 64, 213–307. PA 36, 3GA13M.

Can different role performances be efficiently described in terms of the same dimensions? Can an individual's performance in one role be used to predict his performance in other roles?

Moser, A. J. Marriage role expectations of high school students. *Marriage Fam. Living*, 1961, 23 (1), 42–43. PA 36, 3FH42M.

An inventory of marriage role expectations was administered to 354 twelfth graders; related to sex, status, religion and other variables.

Rosengren, W. R. Social instability and attitudes toward pregnancy as a social role. *Social Probl.*, 1962, 9 (4), 371–378. PA 37, 6588.

Found a negative association between self-esteem and sick role expectations; women with value conflicts tended to regard themselves as more sick than those without such conflicts.

Rushing, W. A. The role concept: assumptions and their methodological implications. *Sociol. Soc. Res.*, 1964, 49 (1), 46–57. SA 13, B6699.

Most formulations make two assumptions which have important methodological implications: the prescriptive and the complementarity.

Smith, V. I. Role conflicts in the position of a military education adviser. *Social Forces*, 1961, 40 (2), 176–178. SA 10, A3427.

The military education adviser is faced with inconsistencies between detailed job analysis that appoints her as general overseer for the school program, and army regulations which specifically state that her duties are advisory.

Snoek, J. D. Role strain in diversified role sets. *Amer. J. Sociol.*, 1966, 71 (4), 363–372. SA 14, C1876.

An important source of role strain is the requirement to maintain working relationships with persons in a wide variety of complementary roles.

Stuckert, R. F. Role perception and marital satisfaction—a configurational approach. *Marriage Fam. Living*, 1963, 25 (4), 415–419. SA 12, A9982.

Neither compatibility of role expectations nor accuracy of perception was uniformly related to marital satisfaction; husband's definition more important than the wife's (from his marital adjustment viewpoint); the accuracy with which the wife perceived the role concepts and expectations of her husband was of greater importance in marital satisfaction from the standpoint of the wife.

Webb, S. C., and Chueh, J. C. The effect of role taking on the judgment of attitudes. *J. of soc. Psychol.*, 1965, 65 (2), 279–292. PA 39, 15007.

Role-taking instructions produce a change in scale values for both Negroes and whites.

Wolfe, D. M., and Snoek, J. D. A study of tensions and adjustments under role conflict. *J. soc. Issues*, 1962, 18 (3), 102–121. SA 12, A8076.

Sources of role conflict may be organizational or personal; reactions include rejection of role "senders" or withdrawal from them.

Zurcher, L. A., Jr. The sailor aboard ship: a study of the role behavior in a total institution. *Social Forces*, 1965, 43 (3), 389–400. PA 39, 9940.

A study of the formal and informal shipboard organizations and the role expectations of the sailor, and his behavioral modification of the expected role.

Chapter Ten

Leadership

A continuous and absorbing fascination with the topic of leadership is a characteristic of the twentieth-century *Zeitgeist*, if not indeed a hallmark of democracy. Social scientists, as creatures of their culture, have had an intense and sustained interest in the theoretical and empirical aspects of leadership. Yet here, perhaps more than in regard to any other subject in this collection, there is *lack* of a clear-cut, consistent definition. Kenneth F. Janda, in the first selection, writes of the *delusion of sufficiency* (which incorporates many connotations in one concept) and *confusion by similarity* (which refers to one or more analytically distinct concepts sharing the same label). After reviewing how this situation has stymied the accumulation of scholarly research on leadership, he proposed that the term be restricted by referring only to legitimized power.

In the second article, Margaret W. Pryer, Austin W. Flint and Bernard M. Bass, define *leadership*—or more exactly, successful leadership—in terms of an individual's ability to solve the group's problems. Using an R.O.T.C. setting as a laboratory, they determined that contrary to their early hypothesis (that there would be less leadership change with continued experience of leaders among initially-effective groups) groups became or remained effective as long as they did not change leaders.

Finally, in the third selection, we turn to the community arena. Linton C. Freeman, Thomas J. Fararo, Warner Bloomberg, Jr., and Morris H. Sunshine studied the problem of defining the leaders in a community, and found that the same set of nominees did not always appear when different criteria were utilized. On the contrary, the list of leaders varied when decision-making, participation in voluntary activities, community reputation, or power position were considered. If we accept the axiomatic proposition that good research raises more questions than it answers, the task of definition of leadership—or rather, kinds of leadership—would appear sufficient to occupy a considerable number of man-hours for an indefinite future.

One may be tormented, in reading these articles, to ask whether "the leader" may be a different person in formal as contrasted with informal groups, in voluntary as opposed to production-oriented associations, in time of crisis as against routine situations, in the birth and in the dying throes of an organization. Fire, earth, water, phlogiston—are we having difficulty because of inadequate conceptualization?

30

Towards the Explication of the Concept of Leadership in Terms of the Concept of Power*

KENNETH F. JANDA

The task of this paper is to present a conception of leadership as a particular type of power relationship. By way of an introduction to this presentation, some remarks will first be made concerning concept construction and social research. Two approaches to the study of leadership will then be examined, setting the stage for a discussion about the development of the concept of leadership. After examining some of the conceptual difficulties which have plagued the study of leadership, this paper will comment briefly on the relationship between the study of leadership and the study of power. Finally, attention will be directed to the main task of considering leadership as a power phenomenon.

CONCEPT CONSTRUCTION AND SOCIAL RESEARCH

The development of a cumulative body of knowledge depends, in part, upon the development of a precise vocabulary which can provide exact descriptions for the specific phenomena under study. Prefatory to developing their own technical vocabulary for identifying the things they study, scientists generally utilize the common vocabulary of the language in which they communicate. Of course, as used in everyday language, a word will frequently have several quite different denotations, more than one of which might be related to the subject of study. Moreover, conventional words sometimes acquire additional connotations which add to their richness but subtract from their precision.

Reprinted from *Human Relations*, 13, 4 (November 1960), 345–363, by permission of the author and the publisher.

* This paper was produced during my research training period as a pre-doctoral Fellow of the Social Science Research Council. I wish to thank the Council for its support during this period. I am especially grateful to Dorwin Cartwright of the Research Center for Group Dynamics for his encouragement and helpful criticism regarding this paper. Also due for thanks are George Psathas and Henry Teune, both of Indiana University, whose cautious skepticism led to some valuable re-formulation of my arguments.

Notwithstanding these semantic barriers to precise understanding, scholars are often led, for a variety of reasons, to adopt a familiar word, associated with related but diverse meanings, and use it in a more restricted, technical sense from that in which it is normally used in ordinary conversation. When employed in a specialized sense as a nominal definition for an independently defined phenomenon, our conventional word becomes a label for a scientific concept and eventually comes to stand for that concept itself. These word-labels then become candidates for inclusion within the technical vocabulary associated with the field of study. "Leadership" and "power" (i.e. the concept of leadership and the concept of power) are examples of conventional words which have been incorporated into the technical vocabulary of those attempting to construct a systematic body of knowledge about social behavior.

Although obvious benefits accompany the practice of identifying a scientific concept with a word which possesses some related meaning in normal use, there are at least two difficulties attending the use of familiar words in this manner. The first will be called the *delusion of sufficiency*, pertaining to a premature satisfaction with the analytical utility of the concept being proposed. The delusion of sufficiency sometimes results in concepts which are not independently defined but which incorporate the wealth of denotations and connotations associated with the normal use of the word. At other times, the delusion of sufficiency might lead to the hasty adoption of a fairly explicit common meaning without consideration of the problems involved in utilizing that meaning to support rigorous analysis. However it arises, the delusion of sufficiency produces concepts which are not analytically tight and are therefore inadequate for exacting study.

The second difficulty, called *confusion by similarity*, relates to the entanglement of a carefully formulated concept with one or more other analytically distinct concepts that share the same label. A clear concept might be confused with one prepared under the delusion of sufficiency, or perhaps the confusion would result when alternative analytically tight concepts were similarly named. Both the delusion of sufficiency and confusion by similarity present obstacles to the development of a cumulative body of knowledge, and—in view of social scientists' disinclination to abandon common words for neologisms—both are particularly troublesome for the systematic study of social behavior.

Despite their special susceptibility to these two kinds of difficulty, the social sciences have only recently begun to grapple in earnest with the problems that these difficulties present. A great deal of fresh effort is now being directed to concept clarification in these disciplines. On the nature and function of concept clarification, Robert K. Merton (1957) has this to say:

> It is, then, one function of conceptual clarification to make explicit the character of data subsumed under a concept. . . .

In a similar fashion, conceptual analysis may often resolve apparent anti-monies in empirical findings by indicating that such contradictions are more apparent than real. This familiar phrase refers, in part, to the fact that initially crudely defined concepts have tacitly included significantly different elements so that data organized in terms of these concepts differ materially and thus exhibit apparently contradictory tendencies. The function of conceptual analysis in this instance is to maximize the likelihood of the comparability, in significant respects, of data which are to be included in research (pp. 90–91).

Unfortunately, the recent emphasis on conceptual clarification has lagged badly behind the development and application of methodological techniques used in operationizing concepts. As a result, our literature has become cluttered with a wealth of disparate findings on poorly defined, similarly named concepts. Both the study of leadership and the study of power offer prime examples of this conceptual-operational imbalance. However, the task of this paper will only be to inquire at length into the conceptual status of one of these, the study of leadership. A thorough treatment of the concept of power—the subject of another work—is precluded at this time. Nevertheless, the final portion of this paper will draw from the literature on power in an attempt to explicate a concept of leadership in terms of power. But, first, the study of leadership must be investigated in some detail.

APPROACHES TO THE STUDY OF LEADERSHIP

Anyone at all familiar with the literature of sociology and social psychology will readily grant that the topic of leadership has commanded considerable attention from students in these fields. However, it is not unfair to say that these disciplines have distinguished themselves more by accumulating *studies* on leadership than by cumulating *knowledge* on leadership.

The heroic efforts of some students to synthesize disparate findings by editing and categorizing these studies usually fail to satisfy anyone— including the persons who undertake the task. In a recent attempt to impose some order upon this literature, Browne and Cohn (1958) corroborate this general viewpoint of the study of leadership. They introduce their work with these comments:

> Through all of the subsequent history of man's attempts to record human experiences, leadership has been recognized to an increasingly greater extent as one of the significant aspects of human activity. As a result, there is now a great mass of "leadership literature" which, if it were to be assembled in one place, would fill many libraries. The great part of this mass, however, would have little organization; it would evidence little in the way

of common assumptions and hypotheses; it would vary widely in theoretical and methodological approaches. To a great extent, therefore, leadership is a mass of content without any coagulating substances to bring it together or to produce coordination and point out interrelationships (Introduction, first page).

The history of the study of leadership is somewhat less chaotic than the study itself. Most students have identified two main approaches used in studying leadership. The earlier is commonly known as the "trait" approach, and the other is usually called the "situational-interactional" approach.

The old trait approach originally considered the "leader" as a personality type that tends to assume a position of dominance in almost every social situation, and its early followers tried to discover the particular personality factors common to all such persons. With the acknowledgement that the same people do not always "lead" in every social situation, the focus of the trait approach was shifted to discover the different personality traits demanded of a leader by each situation, but students following this approach were still concerned with identifying and examining the personalities of individuals considered to be leaders.

The obvious limitations of this method of study caused some students to divert their attention from cataloguing personality traits and led them to study leadership in terms of "situational-interactional" factors. By focusing upon the interaction among individuals in their activities as group members, this approach removed personality traits of the leader from their determinant status and relegated them to the position of a contributing factor to be examined in conjunction with three other factors: (1) the social and physical nature of the environment within which the group must operate, (2) the nature of the group task, and (3) the personality characteristics of the other group members.

Whereas the student of the trait approach sought to account for the leadership phenomenon solely by studying the personality factors of the leader himself, situational-interactionalists argued that there were other relevant variables that had to be taken into account. The existence of these other variables could be advanced to account for the disturbing fact that individuals who possessed leadership "traits" frequently were not designated as leaders. The explanatory superiority of the situational-interactional approach demonstrated itself to the extent that current research on leadership is conducted almost exclusively in this framework.

THE CONCEPT OF LEADERSHIP,
THE DELUSION OF SUFFICIENCY,
AND CONFUSION BY SIMILARITY

The preceding section, while discussing two approaches to the study of leadership, used "approach" to refer to the evaluative framework within which variables are judged for importance and are selected for examination. However, the *concepts* employed in these approaches have not yet been examined for their adequacy in defining the leadership phenomenon in terms of general characteristics which can be used to identify the specific phenomena to be studied by these approaches.

It is usually much easier to discover what specific phenomena people have been studying than to find out what conceptions have guided the selection of these phenomena, for in many cases the conceptions are implicit whereas the items under examination are nearly always explicit. What basic conception underlies the entire body of leadership literature when this literature is viewed in the aggregate; i.e., what concept provides the lowest common denominator that can be used to accommodate the findings on leadership? First, it appears that all students would agree that leadership is some type of group phenomenon, for virtually no one writes on leadership apart from group behavior. Moreover, the leadership phenomenon would appear to be concerned with the activities of "salient" group members—those who could be positively differentiated from the other group members on the basis of behavior, perceptions, group structure, or personal factors. However, our common denominator cannot be reduced beyond this point and still be used to accommodate the entire body of literature on leadership; the collective conceptual and operational definitions advanced in the name of leadership are too disparate to be combined under a denomination more precise than that referring to some form of saliency attributable to individual members within a group.

In a general manner, the development of the concept of leadership can be traced through the trait approach and the situational-interactional approach in terms of the delusion of sufficiency and confusion by similarity. On the whole, it can be said that the concept used to guide inquiry into leadership under the trait approach was prepared almost completely under the delusion of sufficiency, as most inventories of leadership traits were conducted with only simple, commonsense notions of leadership. This point was brought out very clearly in Stogdill's review (1948), which noted that, in many cases, the notion of leadership was never independently defined. Instead, "leaders" were designated by some manner—Stogdill listed five primary methods—and then leadership was assumed to be operative because of the existence of an individual named as a leader. However, it was seldom made clear whether leadership then referred to (1) the behavior of this individual in interaction with other group members, (2) the behavior of this individual as a group member—perhaps with differentiated role functions to perform, (3) the behavior of other group members in interaction with the member designated as leader, (4) the social relationship which existed between the leader and other group members, (5) all of the above, or (6) none of the above.

Although many students following the situational-interactional approach also operated with dictionary definitions of leadership, some penetrated through the delusion of sufficiency to formulate more precise concepts of leadership. For example, R. B. Cattell (1952) has presented a conception of leadership which involves a group member's effect upon group syntality, and Stogdill (1953, p. 41) defined leadership as "the process (act) of influencing the activities of an organized group in its efforts toward goal setting and goal achievement." Each of these conceptions has a fairly explicit meaning, but they both bear different implications for research and theory. However, as they carry the same label, these conceptions are susceptible to confusion by similarity. The possibility of this confusion would not be bothersome if these were the only conceptions in competition, but of course there are many more. As a matter of fact, Stogdill (1957, p. 7) superseded his definition given above with another quite different one which views leadership as "the behavior of an individual when he is directing the activities of a group toward a shared goal." Furthermore, there are still many scholars writing on this topic who have yet to dispel the delusion of sufficiency and establish exactly what it is that they are studying. Their highly ambiguous ideas of leadership complicate the general concept even further.

Of course, these difficulties are not confined to the study of leadership; no doubt all disciplines are plagued by these problems. However, the case being made here is that the concept of leadership has been characterized by the delusion of sufficiency and confusion by similarity to such an extent as to render the accumulated literature on leadership almost valueless in the aggregate. Both difficulties have surrounded the concept of leadership with an ambiguity that is clearly reflected in the study of leadership. Regarding the chaotic state of this literature, Thibaut and Kelley (1959, p. 289) have this to say:

> Not much smaller than the bibliography on leadership is the diversity of views on the topic. Many of the studies essentially ask: what do people mean when they speak of a leader? Other studies begin with a conceptual or empirical definition of leadership and then proceed to determine the correlates or consequences of leadership so defined. Even a cursory review of these investigations show that leadership means many different things to different people.

In witness that leadership means "different things to different people," Shartle (1951) and Morris and Seeman (1950) offer similar listings of five criteria frequently used to identify leaders. According to Shartle's list, a leader has been identified as:

1. An individual who exercises positive influence acts upon others.
2. An individual who exercises more important positive influence acts than any other member of the group or organization he is in.
3. An individual who exercises most influence in goal-setting or goal-achievement of the group or organization.
4. An individual elected by the group as leader.
5. An individual in a given office or position of apparently high influence potential (Shartle, 1951, pp. 121–122).

Gibb's listing (1954) of leadership criteria includes all these under fewer headings and also adds two others:

6. The leader as a focus for the group.
7. The leader as one who engages in leadership behavior.

As to what is involved in "leadership behavior," Morris and Seeman would include:

A. Behavior involved in the execution of a given position.
B. All the behavior of an individual selected as leader.
C. Any positive influence act.
D. Behavior of any individual that makes a difference in the behavior or characteristics of the group.
E. Behavior of an individual when he is directing the activities of a group (p. 51).

The literature on leadership has, at one time or another, utilized all these criteria to identify "leaders." Although students of the subject are often troubled by the obvious differences in the phenomena selected for study by these various criteria, they reluctantly do what Festinger (1955, p. 208) did and include studies under a heading of leadership "only because those reporting such studies call it leadership."

CONCEPTUAL DIFFICULTIES AND
THE STUDY OF LEADERSHIP

The question might be raised, "Why *not* include all studies which purport to examine leadership under a general heading of 'leadership'?" Of course, the answer to this question involves considerations of a concept's utility for guiding research which can contribute to a cumulative body of knowledge about the phenomenon being studied. Simply put, research findings about different phenomena do not become additive merely by labelling these phenomena as if they were identical. Furthermore, this practice of indiscriminate labelling is a step *away* from concept clarification rather than a step toward it, and the study of leadership reflects enough muddy analysis because of conceptual difficulties without the need for further obfuscation.

In order to support this general indictment of the literature on leadership, four specific charges against this literature will be set forth along with their substantiating statements.

1. Little comparability exists among leadership studies in the aggregate, for these studies, being guided by widely differing notions of the phenomenon called leadership, have not concerned themselves with common phenomena.

Numerous reports (see Borgatta *et al.*, 1955; Cattell & Stice, 1954; Chowdhry & Newcomb, 1955; Gibb, 1954; Stogdill & Coons, 1957) have documented the easily understood fact that two or more operational definitions of a leader, applied to the same group, generally identify *different* individuals as the leaders of the group. As Cattell and Stice (1954) have shown with regard to personality factors, the specific criterion used to designate a leader conditions the findings about personality variables associated with the phenomenon of leadership. Nevertheless, findings on leadership are seldom categorized according to the operational definitions used to identify leaders but, instead, these incomparable findings have assumed a false compatibility under the general label of leadership.

As long as findings can be identified with specific criteria used to identify leaders, *some* measure of comparability is still maintained. However, even this thin thread, tying the operational measure to some common conceptual basis, is sometimes snipped off. Chowdhry and Newcomb (1955) were guilty of this act when they added together the scores from sociometric questions based on four criteria of leadership: those individuals most capable of acting as president of the group, those who most influence the decisions of others, those most worthy of acting as group representatives to a convention, and those most liked as friends—and then called the individuals receiving the highest one-fifth of the total choices the "leaders." This highly arbitrary procedure was also followed by Borgatta, Couch, and Bales (1955) but with different criteria and a different cut-off point. Both these studies became successful candidates for the literature on leadership simply by virtue of their titles.

2. Much of the research on leadership has been influenced by a conception which, upon inspection, blurs into another more fundamental concept employed in the study of group processes.

It has been suggested that the one thing which various leadership criteria have in common is their insistence upon some kind of saliency within the group. Clearly, a member cannot be salient unless he can be differentiated from other group members on one or more criteria, and, of course, almost every group member can be differentiated from other group members on the basis of one or more of these criteria. From this realization, it is just a short step to conclude that every group member can be, and often *is*, a leader. Moreover, this step has been taken by many students. For example, Bass (1960, p. 89) has claimed, "Any member of the group can exhibit some amount of leadership. Members will vary in the extent they do so." Again, Haythorn (1955) produced findings in express support of Cattell's hypothesis that every man in a group is to some extent a leader in so far as every man has some effect upon group syntality. Haythorn's conclusion was, "At least in small groups of this nature it seems probable that each individual member makes some contribution to the characteristics of the total group" (1955, p. 339). Finally, Cartwright and Zander (1953, p. 538) state that *if* "Leadership is viewed as the performance of those acts which help the group achieve its objectives," *then* "In principle, leadership may be performed by one or many members of the group."

Thus, we are confronted with a conception of leadership based on *quantitative* instead of *qualitative* considerations. Under this conception, the group is no longer studied to discover *who* leads, for *everybody* leads. The important thing to find out is how *much* they lead. In fact, this is the logical conclusion to an approach which equates leadership with contributions to group performance. Question: whatever became of the concept of group *membership*? Is there no residual of group activity left anywhere to attach to this concept? Apparently, "membership" now only identifies the particular group to which each leader belongs, although there was a time when group members were expected to contribute to group performance.

Of course, the point being made here is that the current use of "leadership behavior" is essentially the same as that of "membership behavior" in that both seem to refer to behavior which contributes to group performance. Although some articles on leadership are still bold enough to hold that "A group may or may not have leaders" (Stogdill, 1953, p. 41), the general conception of leadership has become sufficiently blurred into the concept of membership to produce a number of statements which contend that "Every group member is thus in some degree a leader" (Cattell, 1952, p. 182).

3. The study of leadership has suffered under a dubious distinction between "leadership" and "headship" which has adversely conditioned much of the conceptualizing about leadership.

The literature on leadership reflects a tendency to dissociate the concept from considerations of group structure. Stogdill (1953) is one of the few who have presented a conception of leadership as a function of group organization, and Stogdill's conception was attacked by Gibb (1954, p. 880) who contended that it "represents an unnecessary restriction on the

concept of leadership and has no operational advantage in research."
Alone, these words conceal the frame of reference Gibb undoubtedly used
in formulating this remark, for Gibb has held that leadership disappears
and headship results when group activity is conducted under structure and
organization. Gibb's criteria (1955a) for distinguishing between the concepts of headship and leadership are these:

1. The position of headship is maintained through an organized system
   and not by the spontaneous recognition of the individual contribution to the group goal.
2. In headship, the group goal is not internally determined.
3. Headship does not really involve *a group* at all, since there is no
   sense of shared feeling or joint action.
4. A situation of headship involves a wide social gap between the group
   members and the head, who works to maintain this distance.

Why does Gibb bother with four criteria when his third one alone
would suffice? If "groupness" is requisite for leadership and "non-group-
ness" is requisite for headship—where is the problem? Rarely can social
scientists deal with concepts which dovetail so well. However, these other
criteria of differentiation are erected to bolster a doubtful distinction.
Each criterion dissolves upon close examination and serious reflection.
Is leadership, however defined, predicated on "the spontaneous recognition
of the individual contribution to the group goal"? In leadership, is the
group goal always "internally determined"? Does leadership never involve
the maintenance of a "wide social gap"? A quick recollection of the literature reporting on research in leadership will produce a "no" to all three
of the above questions.

This is not the time or place to conduct an inquiry into this tangential
concept. Simply stated, the issue at hand is that the leadership-headship
dichotomy is not quite as sharp as frequently claimed. Perhaps the criteria
can be supplemented and adjusted to produce a conceptual distinction
between the terms which accords to an intuitional basis for that distinction.
The fact is, this still remains to be done, and studies of leadership in even
the most *formalized* social structures cannot be excluded purely on cries
of "headship."

No doubt some readers will interpret the debunking of headship as an
unnecessary parry of a fanciful thrust, but the thrust has a real basis in
the literature. Writings on leadership radiate a genuine feeling that studies
of leadership based on positional status in an organized group are somehow "missing" the *real* leaders of a group. Apparently, the presumption is
that such studies become so preoccupied with the investigation of relationships as they *should* be that they frequently overlook relationships as
they *are*. This has probably been done in the past and may be done in
the future, but the fact that some research has been conducted poorly

should not preclude efforts to pursue similar research properly. The tendency to explicitly dissociate the concept of leadership from group status is hardly fanciful; it is a real force.[1]

4. *The study of leadership has emerged as a separate field in the study of group processes and has been conducted as if leadership were a totally unique phenomenon, although virtually all of the existing conceptions of leadership can be explicated in terms of more basic concepts of social psychology.*

Normal usage of the word "leadership" has cloaked the term with a false concreteness which students have tried to capture in constructing conceptions of leadership. However, the intuitive notion of leadership is too ambiguous to elicit agreement upon any single conception; alternative conceptions appear equally satisfying to our commonsense ideas. Moreover, the conceptions of leadership which have been formulated can frequently be interpreted as special cases of phenomena associated with more basic concepts of social psychology. This assessment of the literature finds support in the comments of Thibaut and Kelley (1959, p. 289) who say that "among the complex aspects of leadership, there do not seem to be any properties unique to the phenomena. In virtually all cases leadership seems to be analyzable in terms of other, simpler concepts."

In order to substantiate this contention, let us review the previous listing of leadership criteria (p. 457). Criteria 1, 2, and 3 all employ the concept of influence in identifying leaders; criterion 4 is based on perception processes; and number 5 involves considerations of group structure and influence processes. Criterion 6—at least as proposed by Redl (1955) —is dependent upon concepts of group psychoanalysis. Within the set of criteria included under No. 7, leadership behavior, A and E are both concerned with concepts of role differentiation; B includes practically every notion used in the study of human behavior; D involves concepts which attend the study of groups in general; and C once more employs the concept of influence.

Among the different concepts utilized in formulating criteria to identify leaders, the most prominent one appears to be the concept of influence. Indeed, this concept is utilized to such an extent that the study of influence itself might be expected to command considerable attention from those studying leadership. However, the actual relationship between these areas of study does not match this expectation.

[1] See Gouldner (1950, p. 16) for the position of another student of leadership who is concerned over the implications for research and theory produced by the perpetuation of the "headship"-"leadership" distinction.

THE RELATIONSHIP BETWEEN
THE STUDY OF LEADERSHIP AND
THE STUDY OF POWER (INFLUENCE)[2]

The first thing to be noted in a comparative review of the literature on leadership and that on power is that *there is almost no overlap between the two.* Studies of leadership and studies of power have been conducted almost independently of each other. By this, it is meant that, in the main, those who write on leadership do not write on power and *vice versa.* Moreover, the number of cross-references between the two bodies of literature is amazingly small. Footnotes appearing in the literature on leadership *seldom* cite studies of power, and the reverse again holds true. Of course, verbal references to the other will be found in the literature on either concept, but these references are clearly of a superficial nature.

As an indication of the separation between the studies, consider the practice followed to 1959 in each volume of the *Annual Review of Psychology.* In each of these volumes, there is a chapter dealing with the literature on "Social Psychology and Group Processes." With the exception of the first volume of the *Review,* in which Jerome Bruner (1950) passed only very lightly over some general literature on "group dynamics," every subsequent chapter has, with minor modifications, devoted *separate* sections to the literature on "leadership" and that on "influence processes." Moreover, the literature cited in one section usually does not receive acknowledgement in the other. This practice was followed by Katz (1951), Smith (1952), Newcomb (1953), Crutchfield (1954), Festinger (1955), French (1956), Cartwright (1957), Heyns (1958) and Gilchrist (1959) from 1951 through 1959. Of these authors, only French explicitly refers the reader on leadership to the other section on influence processes.[3]

Furthermore, it may be said that, whenever the two concepts *are* considered together in the same work, one of the two clearly becomes the real subject for analysis, and the treatment accorded to the subordinated concept is usually quite sophomoric, ignoring relevant literature on the topic. In short, we have two separate, practically self-contained bodies of literature —one on leadership, the other on power. The remainder of this paper will

[2] Although both labels, "power" and "influence," have been employed by different students investigating the same type of social relationships, "power" has probably been used more frequently in the literature on the subject. However, an excellent case, based on the delusion of sufficiency and confusion by similarity, can be made for employing "influence" as a label for this concept while excluding all references to "power." Notwithstanding this fact, *for the purposes of this paper,* power and influence will be used synonymously.

[3] Riecken's recent chapter on "Social Psychology" in the 1960 volume of the *Annual Review* is the first to consider the literature under a heading of "Leadership and Power." However, Riecken reported mainly on research which examined the power variable in leadership behavior, and he did not review any works which attempted to relate the concepts.

attempt to relate these literatures by presenting a concept of leadership in terms of power.

LEADERSHIP AS A POWER PHENOMENON

The conceptual complexities surrounding the power phenomenon are too involved to be discussed in detail at this time, and reference will only be made to what recent writers (Cartwright, 1959; Dahl, 1957; March, 1955; Simon, 1953) might agree on as a conceptual definition of power. These writers would view the power phenomenon as a particular type of social relationship in which one person adjusts his behavior to conform with a pattern of behavior communicated to him by another person. This concept supports these specific definitions:

power, used as an adjective modifying "relationship"—a particular type of social relationship which demonstrates the features involved in the conceptual definition
power, noun—the ability to cause other persons to adjust their behavior in conformance with communicated behavior patterns
power-wielder—the individual who prescribes patterns of behavior which are followed by other individuals
power-recipient—the person who adjusts his behavior to conform with the prescribed pattern of behavior.

Regarding leadership and power, it should be immediately noted that this conceptual formulation of power is already close to some students' formulation of leadership. For example, Warriner (1955, p. 367) conceives leadership "as a form of relationship between persons [which] requires that one or several persons act in conformance with the request of another." According to this formulation, the concepts of leadership and power can hardly be differentiated from each other.

However, it is contended that a theoretically significant and operationally useful conception of leadership can be provided by considering leadership phenomena as a particular subset within the larger set of power phenomena. Thus, all leader-follower relationships are power-wielder–power-recipient relationships, but not all power relationships involve leadership. Leadership phenomena can be distinguished from other power phenomena when power relationships occur among members of the same group and when these relationships are based on the group members' perceptions that another group member may, with reference to their group activities, legitimately prescribe behavior patterns for them to follow. Thus, in a situation of leadership, the power-recipients do not object to the power-wielder's demands upon their behavior as group members. Essentially this same concept of leadership was advanced by Gouldner in 1950, but his presentation has not seemed to have much influence on the literature. In his words, "a leader would be an individual in a group who, in *some* situations, has the *right* to issue *certain* kinds of stimuli which tend to be accepted by others in the group as obligations" (Gouldner, 1950, p. 19).

In order to examine this idea of legitimacy further, we must first answer some basic questions about power relationships in general. Why does anyone "accept" influence? That is, why do power relationships exist at all? For now, the answer can be given that power relationships exist because some individuals can motivate other individuals to perform specific acts of behavior. Cartwright links motivation to power in this manner:

> . . . "motive base" refers to the sorts of phenomena variously referred to as "need," "motive," "drive," "tension system," or "instinct." The important feature of motive base as it relates to the conception of power is that an act of an agent must "tap" a motive base for it to activate a force (Cartwright, 1959, pp. 204–205).
>
> . . . In our formulation, O can activate a force on P only if some act of O can tap a motive base of P. In this sense, P's motive base may be thought of as a basis of O's power (ibid., p. 206).

According to the conception proposed in this paper, the base of a power relationship provides the identifying element for distinguishing leadership phenomena from power phenomena in general. Writing in the same volume of studies as Cartwright, French and Raven (1959, pp. 155–156) expand upon this notion of the bases of power:

> "By the basis of power we mean the relationship between O and P which is the source of that power. . . . Although there are undoubtedly many possible bases of power which may be distinguished, we shall here define five which seem especially common and important. These five bases of O's power are : (1) reward power, based on P's perception that O has the ability to mediate rewards for him; (2) coercive power, based on P's perception that O has the ability to mediate punishments for him; (3) legitimate power, based on the perception by P that O has a legitimate right to prescribe behavior for him; (4) referent power, based on P's identification with O; (5) expert power, based on the perception that O has some knowledge or expertness."

Now some students of leadership would probably call all intra-group power relationships "leadership," regardless of the power base used to support that relationship. Apparently, Warriner (1955) would subscribe to this position along with Bass (1960, p. 94), who contends that "leadership may be viewed as influence occurring among members of the same group." However, the conception of leadership offered in this paper obviously excludes reward, coercive, referent, and expert power from being considered as a basis of leadership. According to this paper's conception, leadership does not occur unless the power-wielder secures the desired behavior from the power-recipient on the basis of *legitimate* power—that is, when the influence attempt comes from a group member who is perceived as having the "right" to prescribe behavior for other group members to follow.

LEGITIMACY AS A POWER BASE
AND THE STUDY OF LEADERSHIP

At this point it must be emphasized that legitimate power *per se* is not sufficient to support this conception of leadership. Simple equation of leadership with legitimate power is essentially the conception proposed by Gouldner. However, this paper identifies leadership with a particular *type* of legitimate power. That is, the power-wielder must be perceived as having a particular right *with reference to the activities of power-recipients as group members* to prescribe behavior patterns for them to follow.

It is necessary to emphasize the association of leadership with a particular type of legitimate power, for legitimacy itself stems from different sources. French and Raven (1959, p. 160) disclose three important sub-bases for legitimate power:

> Cultural values constitute one common basis for the legitimate power of one individual over another. O has characteristics which are specified by the culture as giving him the right to prescribe behavior for P, who may not have these characteristics . . . .

> Acceptance of the social structure is another basis for legitimate power. If P accepts as right the social structure of his group, organization, or society, especially the social structure involving a hierarchy of authority, P will accept the legitimate authority of O who occupies a superior office in the hierarchy . . . .

> Designation by a legitimizing agent is a third basis for legitimate power. An influencer O may be seen as legitimate in prescribing behavior for P because he has been granted such power by a legitimizing agent whom P accepts . . . . An election is perhaps the most common example of a group's serving to legitimize the authority of one individual or office for other individuals in the group.

The inclusion of cultural values as a base of legitimacy reveals the necessity of adding a restriction to Gouldner's equation of leadership with legitimate power. Legitimate power based on cultural values includes power relationships that we would want to exclude from our conception of leadership, which would encompass only those power relationships produced by the power-recipient's perception that the power-wielder has the right to prescribe behavior for him as a member of a particular group.

We have not yet discussed the way in which group members develop perceptions of leaders. Acceptance of the social structure and designation by a legitimizing agent are obviously only operative in on-going groups of long duration. However, the leadership phenomenon can also be found in newly formed traditionless groups. In such groups, an individual may emerge as a leader because of his personality, abilities, resources, special knowledge, etc. In short, the group members identify his behavior requests with the group goal and, in the process of conforming to these requests, develop perceptions that this individual has the right to prescribe behavior patterns for them with reference to their activities as group members.

However, in on-going groups of long duration—which probably includes the groups of most interest to social scientists—the last two bases of legitimate power, acceptance of the social structure and designation by a legitimizing agent, assume great importance for students of leadership. A group member occupying a position in an accepted social structure or given formal status by a legitimizing agent may thereby acquire legitimate power and only need exercise that power base to demonstrate leadership. Of course, these two factors and leadership do not necessarily coincide. The extent to which these factors do coincide is, in fact, a subject for empirical examination. However, the literature dealing with leadership as a *concept*—apart from the literature reporting on *research*—distinctly subordinates the importance of these factors as determinants of leadership. Perhaps this failure can be attributed to the over-concern with promoting a distinction between "headship" and "leadership." In any case, the literature on power has not ignored investigating these factors, and some of these findings may be reviewed with profit for leadership.

French and Snyder (1959) have produced findings which, in general, support their contention that formal group status in itself is a source of power. Raven and French (1958b, p. 83), conducting research specifically designed to examine several aspects of legitimate power, claim to "have experimentally demonstrated that a member whose group has elected him to a position of authority will thereby achieve legitimate power over remaining members." Furthermore, in another article experimenting with differences in the degree of influence demonstrated by elected and non-elected supervisors, Raven and French (1958a) clearly establish the superior influence of the elected supervisor but discover an unexpected finding in the amount of influence demonstrated by the non-elected supervisor. They explained this observation by stating, "It thus seems likely that the very occupation of a key position in a structure lends legitimacy to the occupant" (ibid., p. 409).

In strong contrast to the literature conceptualizing about leadership, research studies provide an important place for formal group status, employing it as an indicator of the leadership phenomenon. The examinations of political leadership conducted by Seligman (1955) and Moos and Koslin (1951, 1952) are certainly studies of individuals possessing formal group status. Similarly, Seeman (1953) investigates role conflict among leaders by concentrating on the individuals who hold top positions in social institutions. Kahn and Katz (1953) are two more students of leadership concerned with persons who possess formal group status. Morris and Seeman (1950, p. 152), reporting on early progress in the Ohio State Leadership Studies Program, also state that "the method used to date in the various studies made by the staff has been the selection of individuals in high office as persons to examine for leadership. . . ."

The articles by Lewin and Lippitt (1955) and White and Lippitt (1953) utilize formal group status as a technique for inducing leadership, the type of which was then varied among "authoritarian," "democratic," and "laissez-faire" roles. Preston and Heintz (1953) and Hare (1955) also equated leadership with formal group status while varying the leader's role between "supervisory" and "participatory" leadership. Torrance's study (1955) differed in that his formal leadership was altered between "directive" and "non-directive" roles. Gibb (1955b) and Maier and Solem (1953), explicitly considering groups without formal leaders as "leaderless," examine the effect of leadership on group performance by comparing these groups with ones which elected leaders. Finally, the legitimization of the formal status of the conference chairman was specifically acknowledged by Berkowitz (1955).

As mentioned before, many studies identify "leadership" on the basis of criteria other than formal group status. It is suggested that the variations discovered in the behavior of formally designated leaders from that shown by other types of leaders might be due to the different bases of power upon which each can draw in establishing power relationships. The findings of Carter, Haythorn, Shriver, and Lanzetta (1953) on "emergent" versus "appointed" leaders would tend to indicate different bases of power were attached to each type. Maier and Solem also suggest a shift in the bases of power available to group members who still possess formal group status but who have suffered a loss in legitimate power. They hold, "The great limitation to autocratic leadership is that such a leader has difficulty in having his decisions accepted so that appropriate action will follow" (1953, p. 561).

SUMMARY AND CONCLUSION

This paper has presented a conception of leadership as a particular type of power relationship characterized by a group member's perception that another group member has the right to prescribe behavior patterns for the former regarding his activity as a member of a particular group. This conception carries certain implications which were not discussed in the text. Some of these implications are immediately obvious: different group members can perceive different individuals as leaders; the same member can perceive more than one individual as his leader; leadership may or may not exist in a given group; etc. It would seem that these implications, when expanded upon and drawn more sharply, can account for much of the diversity existing within the literature on leadership. The task of strengthening this concept through further delineations of its implications for research and theory is the subject of a future effort; this brief sketch of leadership in terms of power must suffice for now.[4]

For those students who *already* view leadership as involving power relationships, this paper can be interpreted as a recommendation for them to raise the concept of power from its subordinated position and conduct their study with a greater attention to power relationships in general. This would involve drawing distinctions as to the type of power relationship being studied under the heading of leadership and utilizing findings on power relevant to power relationships among group members. It seems inconceivable that students of leadership who define their conceptions in terms of power can afford to ignore the large and growing body of literature on this subject and fail to incorporate its findings in their study. One of the results of this redirection of emphasis would involve paying greater attention to the behavior of the follower than is normally given, for, as Katz (1951, p. 140) says, "Leadership is a relation involving two terms and it is impossible to study the influencing agent without also studying the people being influenced."

For those students of leadership who are not satisfied with a conception of leadership explicated in terms of power, this paper urges that they re-examine precisely what it is that they are studying. Admittedly, there is no monopoly granted for the exclusive use of labels, and if one person chooses to call something else "leadership", he is privileged to do so. Undoubtedly, we will always be subject to some degree of confusion by similarity as long as we are committed to the use of common words as labels for scientific concepts. However, this might be a small price to pay for retaining the benefits which accompany easy translation into common language.

As for the merits of other conceptions of leadership, the standard of utility must be the final arbiter, and the proof of utility must be borne by the advocates of these conceptions. As Cartwright (1959, p. 187) says, "One must rely in the long run upon a sort of inverse 'Gresham's law'

[4] Other "forms" of leadership cannot always be easily related to this conception based on legitimate power. For example, "leadership by coercion" contains a possibility of contradiction within the context of this conception, for this phrase appears to describe a power relationship based on coercive power *as well as* on legitimate power. Although it is generally thought that the operation of one base of power precludes the operation of another, this is, of course, an empirical question which must await a more precise formulation of the variables involved as well as further research on the nature of the bases of power, including the conditions under which they operate. However, the familiar concept of "charismatic leadership" can be accommodated within this conception with little difficulty by considering charismatic leadership as a particular type of leadership which can be characterized either by the strength of the power base available to the power-wielder or by his personal qualities which invoke the intense feelings of voluntary obedience within the group members.

which holds that good conceptual systems drive out bad." Indeed, the conception proposed in this paper must also win its way, if it is to be won, through such competition. Furthermore, it is not thought that this conception is in anywhere near a perfected stage; it can probably be improved now and most certainly will be improved in the future, as new findings on power are brought to light and as new thinking is conducted on the concept of legitimacy.

Nevertheless, it is thought that this specific conception of leadership has advantages which will yield rewards for its users. It seems apparent that this conception—as well as any—closely approximates an "intuitive" notion of leadership. As Seeman (1950, p. 41) said, "Though specific definitions of leadership may vary considerably, the core of the concept—regardless of whether we define leadership as 'acts which make a difference in group effectiveness'—is the idea of a stratification in terms of power or influence." If the association of leadership and legitimate power is adopted, the study of power can hardly be avoided in the study of leadership, which has been isolated, to a large extent, from other aspects of social psychology. In Seeman's words:

> The extent to which status attributes and leadership ideology are correlated has an important bearing on the extent to which we may profitably conceive of "leadership" as a distinct research "area" separable from the more general problems of power, influence, or social status. Myrdal has pointed out that the concern with "leadership" is a distinctly American phenomenon, and it may well be that our research *per se* simply reflects this "American bias," and that from a social scientific point of view our work might be more profitable if we adopted such a more general framework . . . (ibid., pp. 47–48).

The general attitude of this paper is mirrored by the concluding comments of Thibaut and Kelley in their recent book, *The Social Psychology of Groups* (1959, p. 290):

> It is our opinion that leadership research will be most fruitful when it adopts an indirect and analytical approach to its task. Rather than going directly into the complex phenomena and surplus-meaning-laden terminology encompassed by the term leadership, research must first be directed toward clarifying problems of power structures, norms and goals, task requirements, functional roles, etc., each of which is complex and challenging enough in its own right. In short, an understanding of leadership must rest on a more basic understanding of the structure and functioning of groups.

And this paper urges an approach to leadership which draws upon a basic understanding of power.

References

Back, Kurt W. (1951). Influence through social communication. *J. abnorm. soc. Psychol. 46*, January, 9–23.

Bass, Bernard M. (1960). *Leadership, psychology, and organizational behavior.* New York: Harper & Brothers.

Berkowitz, Leonard (1955). Sharing leadership in small, decision-making groups. In A. Paul Hare, Edgar F. Borgatta, & Robert F. Bales (Eds.), *Small groups: studies in social interaction.* New York: Alfred A. Knopf. Pp. 543–455.

Borgatta, Edgar F., Couch, Arthur S., & Bales, Robert F. (1955). Some findings relevant to the great man theory of leadership. In A. Paul Hare, Edgar F. Borgatta, & Robert F. Bales (Eds.), *Small groups: studies in social interaction.* New York: Alfred A. Knopf. Pp. 568–574.

Browne, C. G. & Cohn, Thomas S. (Eds.) (1958). *The study of leadership.* Danville, Illinois: The Interstate Printers and Publishers.

Bruner, Jerome S. (1950). Social psychology and group processes. In Calvin P. Stone (Ed.), *Annual review of psychology.* Stanford: Annual Reviews. Pp. 119–50.

Carter, Launor, Haythorn, William, Shriver, Beatrice, & Lanzetta, John. (1953). The behavior of leaders and other group members. In Dorwin Cartwright & Alvin Zander, *Group dynamics.* Evanston: Row, Peterson. Pp. 551–60.

Cartwright, Dorwin (1957). Social psychology and group processes. In Paul R. Farnsworth (Ed.), *Annual review of psychology.* Stanford: Annual Reviews. Pp. 211–236.

———— (1959). A field theoretical conception of power. In Dorwin Cartwright (Ed.), *Studies in social power.* Ann Arbor: Research Center for Group Dynamics, Institute for Social Research, University of Michigan. Pp. 183–219.

————, & Zander, Alvin (1953). Leadership: introduction. In Dorwin Cartwright & Alvin Zander, *Group dynamics.* Evanston: Row, Peterson. Pp. 535–550.

Cattell, Raymond B. (1952). New concepts for measuring leadership, in terms of group syntality. *Hum. Relat. 4*, 161–184.

————, & Stice, Glen F. (1954). Four formulae for selecting leaders on the basis of personality. *Hum. Relat. 7*, 493–507.

Chowdhry, Kamla, & Newcomb, Theodore M. (1955). The relative ability of leaders and non-leaders to estimate opinions of their own groups. In A. Paul Hare, Edgar F. Borgatta, & Robert F. Bales (Eds.), *Small groups: studies in social interaction.* New York: Alfred A. Knopf. Pp. 235–245.

Crutchfield, Richard S. (1954). Social psychology and group processes. In Calvin P. Stone (Ed.), *Annual review of psychology.* Stanford: Annual Reviews. Pp. 171–202.

Dahl, Robert A. (1957). The concept of power. *Behavioral science 2*, July, 201–215.

Festinger, Leon (1955). Social psychology and group processes. In Calvin P. Stone (Ed.), *Annual review of psychology.* Stanford: Annual Reviews. Pp. 187–216.

French, John R. P., Jr., & Raven, Bertram (1959). The bases of social power. In Dorwin Cartwright (Ed.), *Studies in social power*. Ann Arbor: Research Center for Group Dynamics, Institute for Social Research, University of Michigan. Pp. 150–167.

———, & Snyder, Richard (1959). Leadership and interpersonal power. In Dorwin Cartwright (Ed.), *Studies in social power*. Ann Arbor: Research Center for Group Dynamics, Institute for Social Research, University of Michigan. Pp. 118–149.

French, Robert L. (1956). Social psychology and group processes. In Paul R. Farnsworth (Ed.), *Annual review of psychology*. Stanford: Annual Reviews. Pp. 63–94.

Gibb, Cecil A. (1954). Chapter 24: Leadership. In Gardner Lindzey (Ed.), *Handbook of social psychology*, Vol. II. Cambridge, Mass.: Addison–Wesley. Pp. 877–920.

——— (1955a). The principles and traits of leadership. In A. Paul Hare, Edgar F. Borgatta, & Robert F. Bales (Eds.), *Small groups: studies in social interaction*. New York: Alfred A. Knopf. Pp. 87–95.

——— (1955b). The sociometry of leadership in temporary groups. In A. Paul Hare, Edgar F. Borgatta, & Robert F. Bales (Eds.), *Small groups: studies in social interaction*. New York: Alfred A. Knopf. Pp. 526–542.

Gilchrist, J. C. (1959). Social psychology and group processes. In Paul R. Farnsworth (Ed.), *Annual review of psychology*. Stanford: Annual Reviews. Pp. 233–264.

Gouldner, A. W. (Ed.) (1950). *Studies in leadership*. New York: Harper & Brothers.

Hare, A. Paul (1955). Small group discussion with participatory and supervisory leadership. In A. Paul Hare, Edgar F. Borgatta, & Robert F. Bales (Eds.), *Small groups: studies in social interaction*. New York: Alfred A. Knopf. Pp. 556–560.

Haythorn, William (1955). The influence of individual members on the characteristics of small groups. In A. Paul Hare, Edgar F. Borgatta, & Robert F. Bales (Eds.), *Small groups: studies in social interaction*. New York: Alfred A. Knopf. Pp. 330–341.

Heyns, Roger W. (1958). Social psychology and group processes. In Paul R. Farnsworth (Ed.), *Annual review of psychology*. Stanford: Annual Reviews. Pp. 419–452.

Kahn, Robert L., & Katz, Daniel (1953). Leadership practices in relation to productivity and morale. In Dorwin Cartwright & Alvin Zander, *Group dynamics*. Evanston: Row, Peterson. Pp. 612–628.

Katz, Daniel (1951). Social psychology and group processes. In Calvin P. Stone (Ed.), *Annual review of psychology*. Stanford: Annual Reviews. Pp. 137–172.

Lewin, Kurt, & Lippitt, Ronald (1955). An experimental approach to the study of autocracy and democracy: a preliminary note. In A. Paul Hare, Edgar F. Borgatta, & Robert F. Bales (Eds.), *Small groups: studies in social interaction*. New York: Alfred A. Knopf. Pp. 516–23.

Maier, Norman R. F., & Solem, Allen R. (1953). The contribution of a discussion leader to the quality of group thinking: the effective use of minority opinions. In Dorwin Cartwright & Alvin Zander, *Group dynamics*. Evanston: Row, Peterson. Pp. 561–572.

March, James G. (1955). An introduction to the theory and measurement of influence. *Amer. polit. Sci. Rev.* 49, June, 431–451. Reprinted in Heinz

Eulau, Samuel J. Eldersveld, & Morris Janowitz (Eds.), *Political behavior.* Glencoe, Illinois: The Free Press, 1956. Pp. 385–397.

Merton, Robert K. (1957). *Social theory and social structure.* Glencoe: The Free Press.

Moos, Malcolm, & Koslin, Bertram (1951). Political leadership re-examined: an experimental approach. *Public Opinion Quarterly 15,* Fall, 563–574.

——— (1952). Prestige suggestion and political leadership. *Public Opinion Quarterly 16,* Spring, 77–93.

Morris, Richard T., & Seeman, Melvin (1950). The problem of leadership: an interdisciplinary approach. *Amer. J. Sociol. 56,* September, 149–155.

Newcomb, Theodore M. (1953). Social psychology and group processes. In Calvin P. Stone (Ed.), *Annual review of psychology.* Stanford: Annual Reviews. Pp. 183–214.

Preston, Malcolm G. & Heintz, Roy K. (1953). Effects of participatory vs. supervisory leadership on group judgment. In Dorwin Cartwright & Alvin Zander, *Group dynamics.* Evanston: Row, Peterson. Pp. 573–584.

Raven, Bertram H., & French, John R. P., Jr. (1958a). Group support, legimate power, and social influence. *J. Personality 26,* September, 400–409.

——— (1958b). Legitimate power, coercive power, and observability in social influence. *Sociometry 21,* June, 83–97.

Redl, Fritz (1955). Group emotion and leadership. In A. Paul Hare, Edgar F. Borgatta, & Robert F. Bales (Eds.), *Small groups: studies in social interaction.* New York: Alfred A. Knopf. Pp. 71–86.

Riecken, Henry W. (1960). Social psychology. In Paul R. Farnsworth (Ed.), *Annual review of psychology.* Stanford: Annual Reviews. Pp. 479–510.

Seeman, Melvin (1950). Some status correlates of leadership. In Alonzo G. Grace (Ed.), *Leadership in American education.* (Proceedings of the Co-Operative Conference for Administrative Officers of Public and Private Schools.) Chicago: The University of Chicago Press. Pp. 40–50.

——— (1953). Role conflict and ambivalence in leadership. *Amer. sociol. Rev. 18,* August, 373–380.

Seligman, Lester G. (1955). Development in the presidency and the conception of political leadership. *Amer. sociol. Rev. 20,* December, 706–712.

Shartle, Carroll L. (1951). Studies in naval leadership. In Harold Guetzkow, *Groups, Leadership and Men.* Pittsburgh: Carnegie Press. Pp. 119–133.

Simon, Herbert A. (1957). Notes on the observation and measurement of political power. *J. of Politics 15,* November, 500–516. Reprinted in Herbert Simon, *Models of man, social and rational.* New York: John Wiley & Sons. Pp. 62–78.

Smith, M. Brewster (1952). Social psychology and group processes. In Calvin P. Stone (Ed.), *Annual review of psychology.* Stanford, Annual Reviews. Pp. 175–204.

Stogdill, Ralph M. (1948). Personal factors associated with leadership: a survey of the literature. *J. of Psychology 25,* 35–71.

——— (1953). Leadership, membership, and organization. In Dorwin Cartwright & Alvin Zander, *Group dynamics.* Evanston: Row, Peterson. Pp. 39–51.

———, & Coons, Alvin E. (1957). *Leader behavior: its description and measurement.* Columbus: Research Monograph Number 88, Bureau of Business, The Ohio State University.

Thibaut, John W., & Kelley, Harold H. (1959). *The social psychology of groups.* New York: John Wiley & Sons.

Torrance, E. Paul (1955). Methods of conducting critiques of group problem-solving performance. In A. Paul Hare, Edgar F. Borgatta, & Robert F. Bales (Eds.), *Small groups: studies in social interaction.* New York: Alfred A. Knopf. Pp. 560–567.

Warriner, Charles K. (1955). Leadership in the small group. *Amer. J. Sociol.* 60, January, 361–369.

White, Ralph, & Lippitt, Ronald (1953). Leader behavior and member reaction in three "Social Climates." In Dorwin Cartwright & Alvin Zander, *Group dynamics.* Evanston: Row, Peterson. Pp. 585–611.

31

Group Effectiveness and Consistency of Leadership*

MARGARET W. PRYER
State Colony, Pineville, Louisiana

AUSTIN W. FLINT
Metropolitan Life Insurance Co.

BERNARD M. BASS
University of Pittsburgh

The origins of leadership were examined in detail in *Leadership, Psychology and Organizational Behavior*.[1] Theorems were derived concerning the development of an individual's attempts to lead, his success in influencing others and his effectiveness, *i.e.*, how much those who accepted his leadership were rewarded and not punished.

An experiment was designed to examine the consequences of early success and leader effectiveness on subsequent leadership behavior, and to determine the extent to which leadership depends upon the ability of the would-be leader and his esteem among his peers.

It was assumed that a group member whose early leadership is *effective* will be especially *successful* in influencing others subsequently. Early *success* of a member as a leader should result in his subsequent attempts to lead, if the group is faced with similar problems. If I accept your suggestions and then I am rewarded or avoid punishment, I will be more likely to follow you again the next time you attempt to influence me. If you have been successful in influencing me, you will be more likely to attempt to do so again when we face another problem together. Conversely, *ineffectiveness* should result in reduced success subsequently; reduced success should result in fewer attempts to lead.

The theory proposes that a *successful* leader is likely to be *effective* if he knows how to solve the group's problem.[2] Experiments support this

Reprinted from *Sociometry*, 25, 4 (December 1962), 391–397, by permission of the authors and The American Sociological Association.

* Supported by Contract N7 onr 35609, Group Psychology Branch, Office of Naval Research. Bernard M. Bass was Visiting Professor of Psychology, University of California, for the period 1961–1962.

[1] Bernard M. Bass, *Leadership, Psychology and Organizational Behavior*, New York: Harper, 1960, pp. 83–205, 259–300.

[2] *Ibid.*, pp. 139–140.

proposition.[3] Once a member is identified as able to solve the group's problems, his subsequent attempts to lead are increasingly likely to be successful. That is, if he becomes highly valued as a person, or highly esteemed by his peers, he increases his likelihood of success as a leader. At the same time, he increases his attempts to lead as his evaluation of himself—his self-esteem—is enhanced by early success and effectiveness as a leader.

The purpose of the present analysis was to examine empirically the significance of early effectiveness on subsequent success as a leader.

HYPOTHESIS AND METHOD

Hypothesis. Estimation of the *effectiveness* of leadership requires that we examine the effectiveness of the group at the time *successful* leadership is displayed. It was reasoned that a member is likely to display successful leadership if he has been successful in an earlier similar situation where his influence resulted in *effective group performance, i.e.,* performance which is rewarding or reinforcing to the membership.[4] If a given member's leadership has resulted in effective group performance on an earlier occasion, a group should be more likely to respond favorably to his attempted leadership in the present situation. If the earlier result has been ineffective performance, a group should be more likely to turn to someone else. Therefore, there should be less change in leaders among initially effective groups than among initially ineffective groups. An experimental analysis tested the validity of the last two propositions. Effects emerged, but not as anticipated.

Subjects. Seventeen five-man groups of R.O.T.C. sophomores were tested for admission to advanced R.O.T.C. by an objective method for studying group behavior.[5] In these groups all members were equated in control over each other, so as to correspond to what are usually called "initially leaderless" groups. Members of nine of these groups were high in self-rated motivation to enter Advanced R.O.T.C., members of four were medium, and members of four were low in such motivation.[6]

---

[3] Bernard M. Bass, "Some Aspects of Attempted, Successful, and Effective Leadership," *Journal of Applied Psychology,* 45 (April, 1961), pp. 120–122.

[4] Reinforcements for problem solving laboratory groups are usually secondary or symbolic or mediated by irrelevant cues. Finding the correct answer, obtaining satisfactory knowledge of results, completing tasks as instructed, winning contests, receiving favorable judgments, may all serve as rewards to groups.

[5] Bernard M. Bass, Eugene L. Gaier, Francis J. Farese, and Austin W. Flint, "An Objective Method for Studying Behavior in Groups," *Psychological Reports Monograph,* 3 (June, 1957), pp. 265–280.

[6] The validity of the assessment of motivation of these cadets has been documented in Bernard M. Bass, Margaret W. Pryer, Eugene L. Gaier, and Austin W. Flint, "Interacting Effects of Control, Motivation, Group Practice and Problem Difficulty

Method. Each group worked on 10 problems. On each problem, members first privately ordered (X) a list of five words to try to match a true or criterion order (R) of the familiarity of the words to enlisted airmen.[7] The discussion was held to reach a group decision (G) on the proper ranking. Then, each member again privately ranked (Y) the five words. Finally, the group was informed of the criterion rank order (R) so that after each discussion each group could estimate how effective it had been. Members understood that the better their groups did, and the better they did individually, the higher grade they would earn for their overall performance.

For a single problem the rank difference correlations among the various rank orders produced by the group provided measures of accuracy and agreement. Indices of leadership and group effectiveness were calculated from these differences.

For a single trial, a single member, *i*'s, *successful public leadership* was based on four rank difference correlations: (1) the degree to which the group decision correlated with *i*'s initial decision $(^{\rho}GX_i)$; (2) plus the extent to which the group decision agreed with *i*'s final decision $(^{\rho}GY_i)$; (3) less the amount that the group decision agreed on the average with everyone else's initial rankings $(^{\bar{\rho}}GX_j)$; (4) less the amount that *i* agreed on the average with everyone else originally $(^{\bar{\rho}}X_iX_j)$. Member *i*'s *successful private leadership* was: (1) the degree to which his own rankings remained unchanged $(^{\rho}X_iX_i)$; (2) the average amount that everyone else's rankings shifted $(^{\bar{\rho}}X_jY_j)$; (3) *plus* the average extent to which everyone else agreed more with *i* finally $(^{\bar{\rho}}Y_iY_j)$ than they did initially $(^{\bar{\rho}}X_iX_j)$.

Public effectiveness was the increase in accuracy—how well the criterion was matched—by the public group decision compared to the accuracy of the average initial private decision by the members $(^{\rho}GR - ^{\bar{\rho}}RX)$. *Private effectiveness* was the average accuracy of the final private decisions of the members compared to the accuracy of their initial private decisions $(^{\bar{\rho}}RY - ^{\bar{\rho}}RX)$, or how much better the average member matched the criterion after a discussion than before.[8]

FINDINGS

Changing Leadership as a Function of Initial Ineffectiveness. In each of the 17 groups, successful public leadership exhibited on the first five trials by the five group members was correlated with their success pooled

on Attempted Leadership," *Journal of Abnormal and Social Psychology,* 56 (May, 1958), pp. 352–358.

[7] The criterion had been established by Clyde E. Noble, "The Meaning-familiarity Relationship," *Psychological Review,* 60 (March, 1953), pp. 89–98.

[8] For further details, see Bass, Gaier *et al., op cit.*

for the second five trials. Similar consistency correlations were obtained for successful private leadership.

TABLE 1

Subdivision of the 17 Groups According to Their Public Effectiveness on the First and Second Five Trials

First Five Trials		Second Five Trials		
Effectiveness	*N*	*Effectiveness*	*N*	*Code*
Above median effectiveness of 17 groups	9	Above median effectiveness of 9 groups	5	Hi-Hi
		Below median	4	Hi-Lo
Below median effectiveness of 17 groups	8	Above median effectiveness of 8 groups	4	Lo-Hi
		Below median	4	Lo-Lo

The 17 groups were subdivided as shown in Table 1 according to their total public effectiveness on the first five trials. Those nine groups above average in effectiveness on the first five trials were then subdivided into "effective" and "ineffective" on the second five trials. The same subdivision was made for those eight groups below average on the first five trials. Groups were dichotomized in private effectiveness in the same way.

The mean consistencies in public leadership were determined for the five "hi-hi" groups, the four "hi-lo" groups, the four "lo-hi" groups, and the four "lo-lo" groups. These mean values are displayed in Table 2.

TABLE 2

Consistency of Leadership as a Function of Changing Effectiveness

Public Effectiveness on the First Five Trials	Public Effectiveness on the Second Five Trials		
	High	*Low*	*Both*
High	.63	.08	.39
Low	.81	−.60	.21
Both	.73	−.30	—

Private Effectiveness on the First Five Trials	Private Effectiveness on the Second Five Trials		
	High	*Low*	*Both*
High	.40	.29	.35
Low	.35	.12	.24
Both	.38	.21	—

Inspection of Table 2 showed that whether a group was high or low in public effectiveness on the first five trials was not important in determining the consistency with which its members exhibited successful leadership. Groups, both high or low on the first five trials in effectiveness, were equally consistent (.63 and .81) in who led—*as long as they were above average in effectiveness on the second five trials!* On the other hand, regardless of public effectiveness on the first five trials, groups relatively lower in public effectiveness on the second five trials, showed no leadership consistency (.08) or actually reversed leadership (−.60) between the first and second five trials. Groups which changed least in leaders from the first five trials to the second five were those groups which were the most effective publicly on the second five trials regardless of whether they were high or low in effectiveness on the first five trials.

Similar but less dramatic effects emerged when private successful leadership was examined, as can be seen in Table 2.

To show these effects and to test their significance, the groups were rearranged according to their relative gain or loss in public effectiveness and in private effectiveness when their performance on the second five trials was compared with their performance on the first five trials.

Effectiveness as a Function of Consistent Leadership. The 17 groups were divided into those gaining in public effectiveness from the first five trials to the last five trials, and those losing in effectiveness. The successful public leadership consistency correlations were ranked for all groups and the Kruskal-Wallis H test was performed to determine if significant differences existed between the ranks for groups gaining in effectiveness compared with those losing. This analysis was repeated for the private measures of effectiveness and leadership.

Eight groups gained in public effectiveness. The median percentage increase was 108 per cent, *i.e.*, the median group more than doubled in effectiveness on the second five trials. Nine groups lost in public effectiveness. The median loss was 49 per cent. The median successful public leadership consistency correlation was .70 for the eight groups gaining in public effectiveness. The corresponding median correlation was −.08 for the nine groups losing in public effectiveness. An H of 8.90 was significant at the 1 per cent level of confidence with 1 degree of freedom.

The median increase in private effectiveness for the nine gaining groups was 178 per cent. The eight losing groups exhibited a median loss in private effectiveness of 52 per cent. The median successful private leadership consistency correlation was .33 for the nine groups gaining in private effectiveness. The median correlation for the eight groups losing in private effectiveness was .01. The H test of the difference in consistency of leadership was not significant although the differences were in the same direction as for public measures.

Interaction with Motivation. More of the highly motivated groups gained in effectiveness while more of the groups lower in motivation lost

TABLE 3

Groups Gaining or Losing in Effectiveness as a Function of Level of Motivation

| Motivation Level | Public Effectiveness | | |
	Number Gaining	Number Losing	Total
High	5	4	9
Medium	2	2	4
Low	1	3	4
All	8	9	17

	Private Effectiveness		
High	7	2	9
Medium	1	3	4
Low	1	3	4
All	9	8	17

in effectiveness. Table 3 exhibits these differences. These results are what might have been expected assuming that those highly motivated would maintain interest in the work while those low in motivation would be inclined toward boredom and apathy as work continued.

The small number of groups made a complex statistical analysis impossible. However, the groups of high motivation only were sorted into those which gained or lost in effectiveness from the first to the second five trials. Among these high motivation groups, the same differences in consistency of leadership emerged. With motivation held constantly high, the five groups gaining in public effectiveness showed a median leadership consistency of .69. The four losing groups exhibited a correlation of −.09. The H of 3.8 was significant at the 5 per cent level.

For private effectiveness and leadership, with motivation constantly high, the corresponding median correlations were .33 and −.15. We inferred that the same effects emerged where motivation was held constant and high as where motivation varied. Again the difference was in the expected direction, but the small number of groups which lost precluded any test of significance.

SUMMARY AND CONCLUSIONS

Our results suggest that groups are most likely to become more effective if they reach early agreement on who shall lead. Once this interaction problem is settled satisfactorily without further contest, the groups can move to a higher state of task effectiveness. The results fit with the comments by Carter, Haythorn *et al.*,[9] concerning the status struggle in initially leaderless groups as well as the political maxim, "Don't change horses in mid-stream."

This study began with the hypothesis that initially effective groups change leaders less than initially ineffective groups. The data supported another hypothesis: any groups became or remained effective as long as they did not change leaders. In groups which gained in effectiveness, leadership consistencies of .70 and .33 were found. Among groups that lost in effectiveness, consistency of leadership dropped to −.08 and .01. The hypothesis was also supported for groups high in motivation.

[9] Launor Carter, William Haythorn, Beatrice Shriver, and John Lanzetta, "The Behavior of Leaders and Other Group Members," *Journal of Abnormal and Social Psychology*, 46 (Oct., 1951), pp. 589–595.

32

Locating Leaders in Local Communities: A Comparison of Some Alternative Approaches*

LINTON C. FREEMAN,
THOMAS J. FARARO,
WARNER BLOOMBERG, JR.
and MORRIS H. SUNSHINE
Syracuse University†

Most investigators would probably agree that leadership refers to a complex process whereby a relatively small number of individuals in a collectivity behave in such a way that they effect (or effectively prevent) a change in the lives of a relatively large number. But agreement on theoretical details of the leadership process or on how it is to be studied is another matter. Much of the recent literature on community leadership has been critical.[1] Gibb has suggested that there are a great many *kinds* of leadership—many different ways in which changes may be effected. He has proposed that leaders be assigned to various types including "the initiator, energizer, harmonizer, expediter, and the like." [2] Banfield has stressed the importance of the distinction between intended and unintended

Reprinted from *American Sociological Review*, 28, 5 (October 1963), 791–798, by permission of the authors and The American Sociological Association.

* Support for this study was provided by a grant from the Fund for Adult Education to the University College of Syracuse University.

† In September, 1963, Warner Bloomberg, Jr., joined the faculty of the Department of Urban Affairs, University of Wisconsin at Milwaukee.

[1] Cecil A. Gibb, "Leadership," in Gardner Lindzey (ed.), *Handbook of Social Psychology*, Vol. 2, Cambridge, Mass.: Addison-Wesley, 1954, pp. 877–920; Edward C. Banfield, "The Concept 'Leadership' in Community Research," paper read before the Annual Meeting of the American Political Science Association, St. Louis, Missouri, 1958; Robert A. Dahl, "A Critique of the Ruling Elite Model," *American Political Science Review*, 52 (June, 1958), pp. 463–469; Nelson W. Polsby, "The Sociology of Community Power: A Reassessment," *Social Forces*, 37 (March, 1959), pp. 232–236; Nelson W. Polsby, "Three Problems in the Analysis of Community Power," *American Sociological Review*, 24 (December, 1959), pp. 798–803; Raymond E. Wolfinger, "Reputation and Reality in the Study of 'Community Power'," *American Sociological Review*, 25 (October, 1960), pp. 636–644.

[2] Cecil A. Gibb, *op. cit.*

leadership.[3] And both Dahl and Polsby have called attention to the desirability of considering the *extent* of the effect a given leader has in expediting a particular change and the *range* of changes over which his effect holds.[4] It seems evident, then, that although these critics might agree with the minimum definition presented above, they would all like to see some additional factors included within its scope.

Polsby has translated the comments of the critics into a set of operational guides for research.[5] He has suggested that a satisfactory study of community leadership must involve a detailed examination of the whole decision-making process as it is exhibited over a range of issues. Here we should have to specify each issue, the persons involved, their intentions, and the extent and nature of their influence if any. Such a program represents an ideal that might be used to think about the process of community leadership. But as a research strategy, this plan raises many problems.

In the first place, both influence and intention are concepts presenting great difficulty in empirical application. Both require that elaborate observational and interviewing procedures be developed, and both raise reliability problems.[6] May we, for example, take a person's word concerning his intentions, or must they be inferred from his behavior? And even when two persons interact and one subsequently changes his stated position in the direction of the views of the other, it is difficult to *prove* that influence has taken place. But even if these questions were eliminated, a practical problem would still remain. To follow the prescriptions listed above would be prohibitively expensive, requiring detailed observation of hundreds (or thousands) of individuals over an extended period. To record all interaction relevant to the decisions under study, it would be necessary to observe each person in a large number of varied situations, many of them quite private. Even then it would be difficult to evaluate the impact of the process of observation itself. Given these considerations, Polsby's ideal has never been reached. All existing studies of community leadership represent some compromise.

Most authors of community leadership studies would probably agree that the critics are on the right track. But most have been willing (or perhaps forced by circumstances) to make one or more basic assumptions in order to achieve a workable research design. Four types of compromise have been common. They will be discussed below.

  [3] Edward C. Banfield, *op. cit.*

  [4] Nelson W. Polsby, "The Sociology of Community Power: A Reassessment," *op. cit.* and Robert A. Dahl, *op. cit.*

  [5] Nelson W. Polsby, "The Sociology of Community Power," *op. cit.*

  [6] Herbert A. Simon, "Notes on the Observation and Measurement of Political Power," in his *Models of Man*, New York: John Wiley and Sons, 1957; James G. March, "An Introduction to the Theory and Measurement of Influence," *American Political Science Review*, 49 (June, 1955), pp. 431–451; James G. March, "Measurement Concepts in the Theory of Influence," *Journal of Politics*, 19 (May, 1957) pp. 202–226.

Perhaps the most realistic of the compromise studies are those based on the assumption that active participation in decision making *is* leadership. Typically, in such studies, one or a series of community decisions are either observed or reconstructed. In so doing, an attempt is made to identify the active participants in the decision-making process. These decision-making studies frequently are restricted to a small number of decisions, and they usually fail to present convincing evidence on the questions of intent and amount of impact. But they do provide a more or less direct index of participation. If they err it is by including individuals who, though present, had little or no impact on the decision. On the face of it this seems preferable to the likelihood of excluding important influentials.[7]

A second compromise approach is to assume that formal authority *is* leadership. Aside from arbitrarily defining which positions are "on top," these studies underestimate the impact of those not in official positions on the outcomes of the decision-making process.

The third approach assumes that leadership is a necessary consequence of social activity. This assumption leads to studies of social participation. Such studies have used everything from rough indexes of memberships in voluntary associations to carefully constructed scales of activity in such associations. In each case it is reasoned that community leadership results from a high degree of voluntary activity in community affairs. The social participation approach is thus the converse of the study of position. While the former stresses activity, the latter is concerned only with formal authority. But to the extent that activity in voluntary associations leads to having an impact upon community change, activists are leaders.

The final approach assumes that leadership is too complex to be indexed directly. Instead of examining leadership as such, proponents of this approach assess reputation for leadership. Their reasoning suggests that all of the more direct approaches neglect one or another key dimensions of the leadership process. They turn, therefore, to informants from the community itself. Often rather elaborate steps have been taken to insure that the informants are indeed informed. For example, positional leaders may be questioned in order to develop a list of reputed leaders or influentials; then the reported influentials are polled to determine the top influentials. In such cases it is reasonable to suppose that the grossly uninformed are ruled out.

Various critics have condemned the indeterminacy and subjectivity of this procedure.[8] But its defenders reason that the reputational approach is the only way to uncover the subtleties of intent, extent of impact, and the like in the leadership process. What, they ask, but a life-long involvement in the activities of a community could possibly yield sophisticated answers

---

[7] Numerous examples of this and other approaches to the study of leadership may be found in Wendell Bell, Richard J. Hill, and Charles R. Wright, *Public Leadership*, San Francisco: Chandler, 1961.

[8] See the articles by Dahl, Polsby, and Wolfinger cited above.

to the question "Who are the leaders?" The reputational approach, then, assumes the possibility of locating some individuals who unquestionably meet the criteria of community leadership, and who in turn will be able to name others not so visible to the outside observer.

Currently, the controversy continues. Proponents of one or another of these competing points of view argue for its inherent superiority and the obvious validity of its assumptions. Others take the view that all of these approaches get at leadership. But these are empirical questions; they can be answered only on the basis of comparison, not by faith or by rhetoric. A number of partial contrasts have been published, but so far no systematic overall comparison of these procedures has been reported. The present report represents such an attempt. An effort is made to determine the degree to which these several procedures agree or disagree in locating community leaders.

The data presented here represent a part of a larger study of leadership in the Syracuse, N.Y. metropolitan area. Two reports have been published,[9] and several additional papers are forthcoming.

DECISION-MAKING

The study of participation in the decision-making process was of central concern in the Syracuse study. The first major task of the project team was to select a set of community problems or issues which would provide a point of entry into a pool (or pools) of participants in the decision-making process. Interviews were conducted with 20 local specialists in community study and with 50 informants representing diverse segments of the city's population. Care was taken to include representatives of each group along the total range of interest and institutional commitment. These 70 interviews provided a list of about 250 community issues. The list was reduced to a set of 39 issues according to the following criteria:

1. Each issue must have been at least temporarily resolved by a decision.
2. The decision must be perceived as important by informants representing diverse segments of the community.
3. The decision must pertain to the development, distribution, and utilization of resources and facilities which have an impact on a large segment of the metropolitan population.
4. The decision must involve alternative lines of action. It must entail a certain degree of choice on the part of participants; and the outcome must not be predetermined.

[9] Linton C. Freeman, Warner Bloomberg, Jr., Stephen P. Koff, Morris H. Sunshine, and Thomas J. Fararo, *Local Community Leadership*, Syracuse: University College of Syracuse University, 1960; Linton C. Freeman, Thomas J. Fararo, Warner Bloomberg, Jr., and Morris H. Sunshine, *Metropolitan Decision-Making*, Syracuse: University College of Syracuse University, 1962.

5. The decision must be administered rather than made by individuals in "the market." For the purpose of this study, an administered decision was defined as one made by individuals holding top positions in organizational structures which empower them to make decisions affecting many people.
6. The decision must involve individuals and groups resident in the Syracuse Metropolitan Area. Decisions made outside the Metropolitan Area (e.g., by the state government), were excluded even though they might affect residents of the Metropolitan Area.
7. The decision must fall within the time period 1955–1960.
8. The set of decisions as a whole must affect the entire range of important institutional sectors, such as governmental, economic, political, educational, religious, ethnic, and the like.[10]

The next step in the research process required the determination of positional leaders or formal authorities for each of the set of 39 issues. The study began with those individuals who were formally responsible for the decisions. The element of arbitrary judgment usually involved in the positional approach was thus avoided. Here, the importance of a position was derived from its role in determining a choice among alternative lines of action rather than of being the consequence of an arbitrary assumption.

The responsible formal authorities were determined on the basis of documents pertinent to the 39 decisions. In addition, several attorneys were consulted to insure that correct determinations were made. The number of authorities responsible for making each of these decisions ranged from two to 57.

The interviews started with authoritative persons. Respondents were presented with a set of 39 cards, each of which identified a decision. They were asked to sort the cards into two piles: (1) "Those in which you participated; that is, where others involved in this decision would recognize you as being involved," and (2) "Those in which you were not a participant." For those issues in which they claimed participation, individuals were then asked to name all the others who were also involved. Here they were instructed to report on the basis of first-hand knowledge of participation rather than on hearsay. Respondents were also given a questionnaire covering their social backgrounds.

When the interviews with authorities were completed, their responses for those decisions on which they possessed authority were tabulated. Then, any person who had been nominated as a participant by two authorities for the same issue was designated as a first zone influential. Two nominations were deemed necessary in order to avoid bias due to accidental contacts, mistakes of memory, or a tendency to mention personal friends. In the final tabulations this same rule of two nominations was applied to

---

[10] The entire set of 39 issues is described in the earlier publications of the study group, *op cit.*

authorities also. Therefore, no person is counted as a participant unless he has two nominations by qualified nominators.

As the next step, all first zone influentials were interviewed using exactly the same procedures as those used for authorities. Their responses were tabulated for the decisions in which they had been involved, and any person nominated by one authority and one first zone influential was also classified as a first zone influential and interviewed. Then any person nominated by two first zone influentials was designated a second zone influential—two steps removed from formal authority but still involved. We did not interview beyond these second zone influentials. We might have continued with third and fourth zones and so on; but on the basis of qualitative data gathered during the interviews, we suspected we were moving well into the periphery of impact on the outcome of decision making.

In all, 628 interviews were completed. Of these, 550 qualified as participants. These participants, then, are the leaders as determined by the decision-making phase of the Syracuse study. They were ranked in terms of the number of decisions in which they were involved. For the present analysis the 32 most active participants are considered.

SOCIAL ACTIVITY

Each of the 550 participants uncovered by the decision-making study was asked to complete a questionnaire covering his social background and current activities. These questionnaires were returned by 506 informants. The answers included responses to a set of questions designed to elicit as much information as possible about voluntary association memberships. Specific questions were included to determine memberships in the following areas:

1. Committees formed to deal with community problems.
2. Community service organizations.
3. Business organizations.
4. Professional organizations.
5. Union organizations.
6. Clubs and social organizations.
7. Cultural organizations.
8. Religious organizations.
9. Political parties, organizations and clubs.
10. Veterans' and patriotic organizations.
11. Other clubs and organizations.

Memberships in these organizations were tabulated, and a rough overall index to voluntary activity was calculated by simply summing the number of memberships for each person. The respondents were ranked in terms of number of memberships, and the 32 most active organizational members were included in the present anlaysis.

REPUTATION

Each questionnaire also invited the respondent to list the most influential leaders in the community. Eight spaces were provided for answers. Nominations were tabulated and, following traditional procedures, the top 41 reputed leaders were listed. The responses of those 41 respondents were then tabulated separately. The top 32 were derived from their rankings. This was done in order to maximize the chances that our nominators would be informed. As it turned out, however, the top 32 nominations of the whole group and the top 32 provided by the top 41 were exactly the same persons and in the same order. For Syracuse these nominations showed remarkable consistency all along the line.

POSITION

In determining the top positional leaders it seemed desirable to avoid as much as possible making the usual arbitrary assumptions. Traditional usage of the positional approach dictated the determination of the titular heads of the major organizations in business, government, the professions, and the like. Within each of these institutional areas choice could be made in terms of size, but it was difficult to determine how many organizations should be selected in each area.

An empirical resolution for this problem was provided in a recent report by D'Antonio *et al.*[11] These authors provided data on the proportions of reputed leaders representing each of the seven relevant institutional areas in 10 previous studies. Since agreement on these relative proportions was reasonably close for the six middle-sized American communities reported, they were used to assign proportions in each institutional area in the present study. The proportions derived from D'Antonio and those used in the present study are reported in Table 1. In this case positional leaders are the titular heads of the largest organizations in each of the institutional areas, and each area is represented according to the proportion listed in Table 1. Thirty-two organizations were chosen in all. As a check on its validity, the list of organizations was shown to several local experts in community affairs. They were in substantial agreement that the organizations listed seemed consistent with their perceptions of the "top" organiza-

---

[11] William D'Antonio, William Form, Charles Loomis, and Eugene Erickson, "Institutional and Occupational Representatives in Eleven Community Influence Systems," *American Sociological Review*, 26 (June, 1961), pp. 440–446.

TABLE 1

Percentage of Leaders in Each Institutional Area

Institution	Six Cities	Syracuse
Business	57	59
Government	8	9
Professions	12	13
Education	5	6
Communications	8	6
Labor	4	3
Religion	5	3
Total	99	99

tions in Syracuse. The heads of these organizations might be expected to have formal control over much of the institutional system of the community.

These, then, are the raw materials of the current study. An attempt was made to determine the degree to which these several procedures would allocate the same persons to the top leadership category.

RESULTS

The several procedures for determining leaders did not converge on a single set of individuals. Top leaders according to one procedure were not necessarily the same as those indicated by another. An index of agreement for each pair was constructed by calculating the ratio of the actual number of agreements to their total possible number. Results are listed in Table 2.

TABLE 2

Percentage of Agreement in Determining Leaders by Four Traditional Procedures

Participation	Social activity	Reputation	Position
25			
33	25		
39	22	74	

It is possible that any of the methods used, if modified enough, would have yielded significantly different results.[12] The procedures we followed seem in their essentials to be like those followed in most of the studies so far published. (Those who believe they have altered the use of positions, nominations, memberships, or other indexes in such a way as to obtain a

[12] The choice of the top 32 leaders in each category, is, for example, somewhat arbitrary. When another number is used, the *absolute* percentages of agreement vary, but their standings *relative* to one another remain stable.

major difference in the output of the technique have only to demonstrate this by empirical comparisons.) Our impression is that most versions of each approach represent only vernier adjustments of the same device and thus can have only marginally differing results.

Table 2 suggests that there is far from perfect agreement in determining leaders by means of these four methods. In only one case do two of these methods concur in more than 50 per cent of their nominations. Reputation and position seem to be in substantial agreement in locating leaders. To a large degree, therefore, reputed leaders are the titular heads of major community organizations. They are not, however, themselves active as participants in decision making to any great extent.

Reputation for leadership seems to derive primarily from position, not from participation. But it appears unlikely that position itself constitutes a sufficient basis for reputation. The reputations, however, might belong to the organizations and not the individuals. In such a case, when an informant named John Smith as a leader what might have been intended was the fact that the Smith Snippel Company (of which John Smith was president) is influential in community decisions. Smith would thus have been named only because we had asked for a person's name. Our hypothesis, then, is that reputation should correspond with the participation rate of organizations rather than the participation rates of individuals.

On the basis of this hypothesis, the data on participation were retabulated. Each participant was classified according to his organization or place of employment. Then the head of each organization was credited not only with his own participation, but with the sum of the participation of his employees. In this manner an index of organizational participation was constructed and the top 30 organizational leaders were determined. Individuals so nominated were compared with those introduced by the earlier procedures. The results are shown in Table 3.

TABLE 3

Percentage of Agreement Between Organizational Participation and Four Traditional Procedures

Traditional Procedure	Percentage of Agreement
Participation	33
Social activity	25
Reputation	67
Position	80

The proportions shown in Table 3 support our hypothesis. Organizational participation seems to uncover substantially the same leaders as reputation and position. The top reputed leaders, therefore, though not active participants themselves, head up the largest organizations, and the personnel of these organizations have the highest participation rates.

This result accounts for a great deal of participation in community decision making. Since organizational participation provides a workable index, many participants must be employees of large community organizations. But this does not explain the most active class of individual participants—those who were picked up by the individual participation index. These people seem to be virtually full-time participants in community affairs. We know that they are not organizational heads, but we have not determined who they are.

In view of the sheer amount of their participation, the top participants must be professional participants of some sort. And, as a class, professional participants in community affairs should be government officials and employees or full-time professional executives of non-governmental agencies formally and primarily committed to intervention in community affairs. With this as our hypothesis, the individuals nominated as leaders by the four traditional indexes were all classified into either government and professional or non-professional categories. Then percentages of government personnel and professionals were calculated for all four indexes. The results are shown in Table 4.

TABLE 4

Percentage of Leaders According to Four Traditional Procedures Who Are Government Officials or Employees or Professional Participants

Traditional Procedure	Percentage of Government Personnel or Professional Participants
Participation	66
Social activity	20
Reputation	20
Position	28

Again the results support our hypothesis. The most active individual participants are typically government personnel.

The participation index thus gets at personnel quite different from those selected by reputational or positional indexes, or by social activity. These differing cadres of people seem to represent *different kinds* of leadership behavior with respect to the local community.

SUMMARY AND DISCUSSION OF RESULTS

These results indicate that at least in Syracuse "leadership" is not a homogeneous category. Which "leaders" are uncovered seems in large part to be a function of the mode of study. The several traditional indexes allow us to locate one or another of three basic types of "leaders."

First, there are those who enjoy the reputation for top leadership. These are very frequently the same individuals who are the heads of the largest and most actively participating business, industrial, governmental, political, professional, educational, labor and religious organizations in Syracuse. They are uncovered by studies of reputation, position, or organizational participation. In view of their formal command over the institutional structure and the symbolic value of their status as indexed by reputation, these individuals may be called the *Institutional Leaders* of Syracuse.

These Institutional Leaders, however, are for the most part not active participants in community affairs. There is no evidence that they have any direct impact on most decisions which take place. Their activity may be limited to that of lending prestige to or legitimizing the solutions provided by others. They might conceivably be participating decision makers in secret, but more likely they serve chiefly to provide access to the decision-making structure for their underlings: the *Effectors*.

The Effectors are located by studying participation. They are the active workers in the actual process of community decision making. Many of the most active Effectors are government personnel and professional participants, and the others are the employees of the large private corporations directed by the Institutional Leaders. In some cases, the Effectors are in touch with their employers, and it seems likely that their activities are frequently guided by what they view as company policy; but, judging from our data, they are often pretty much on their own. At any rate, these men carry most of the burden of effecting community change.

The third type of leader might be called the *Activists*. These people are active—and often hold office—in voluntary organizations, community service organizations, and clubs. Although they are not involved as often as the Effectors, the Activists do participate in decision making. For the most part they seem to lack the positional stature to be Institutional Leaders. Furthermore, they often work for or direct smaller organizations in the community. They lack the power base provided by association with government or one of the major industrial or business firms. Yet, seemingly by sheer commitment of time and effort to community affairs, these Activists do help shape the future of the community.

In conclusion, the various differing approaches to the study of community leadership seem to uncover different types of leaders. The study of reputation, position or organizational participation seems to get at the Institutional Leaders. Studies of participation in decision making, on the other hand, tap the Effectors of community action. And studies of social activity seem to seek out the Activists who gain entry by dint of sheer commitment, time, and energy.

In part, our results are dependent upon the Syracuse situation. It is likely that 25 years ago, when Syracuse was smaller and less diversified, the Institutional Leaders and the Effectors were the same people.[13] And 25

---

[13] For an interesting discussion of the development of a community leadership structure, see Robert O. Schulze, "The Bifurcation of Power in a Satellite City," in Morris Janowitz (ed.), *Community Political Systems*, Glencoe, Illinois: Free Press, 1961.

years from now this description will probably no longer hold. Other communities, in other stages of development and diversification will probably show different patterns. But until more comparative studies are done, conclusions of this kind are virtually guesses.

For Further Reading

BOOKS

Bass, B. M. *Leadership, psychology, and organizational behavior.* New York: Harper & Row, 1960.

Proposes a systematic theory of leadership and organizational behavior. Formulates operational definitions for such concepts as group effectiveness, group attractiveness, and leadership.

Beal, G. M., Bohlen, J. M. and Raudabaugh, J. N. *Leadership and dynamic group action.* Ames, Iowa: The Iowa State University Press, 1962.

A practical introduction to techniques for improving leadership; includes suggestions for handling groups under varying circumstances; suggestions for evaluation of leadership.

Bell, W., Hill, R. J. and Wright, C. R. *Public leadership: a critical review with special reference to adult education.* San Francisco: Chandler, 1961.

A report of a large number of surveys; discusses how "leadership" may vary when defined variously (formal leadership, reputation, opinion leadership, and so forth).

Bellows, R. *Creative leadership.* Englewood Cliffs, New Jersey: Prentice-Hall, 1959.

An eclectic theory of leadership with special attention to creativeness. Concepts and methods involved in the process of dynamic leadership are documented by empirical studies.

Dubin, R., Homans, G. C., Mann, F. C., and Miller, D. C. *Leadership and productivity: some facts of industrial life.* San Francisco: Chandler, 1965.

A study of the relationship between supervision and productivity, each author devoting his attention to different aspects of this topic.

Hollander, E. P. (Ed.). *Leaders, groups, and influence.* New York: Oxford University Press, 1964.

A collection of 20 papers by the editor and his colleagues; includes research on sociometric leadership and conformity.

Hunter, F. *Top leadership, U.S.A.* Chapel Hill: University of North Carolina Press, 1959.

Documents the concentration of decision-making in the hands of national leaders.

Mills, C. W. *The power elite.* New York: Oxford University Press, 1956.

Writing with the abandon of a novelist, Mills sees the ruling elite as made up of the executives of the largest corporations, the highest military officials, and the appointed executive staff of the President.

Petrullo, L. and Bass, B. M. *Leadership and interpersonal behavior.* New York: Holt, Rinehart and Winston, 1961.

Papers that were read in a symposium sponsored by the Office of Naval Research, including topics on theory, sociometry, leadership under stress, and leadership traits.

Seeman, M. *Social status and leadership: the case of the school executive.* Columbus, Ohio: Ohio State University Press, 1960.

Attempts to relate the style of leadership to status and the leadership role to the conflicts in American culture (the success ideology versus the equality mandate, universalistic criteria versus particularistic demands, and so forth).

Sherif, M. (Ed.). *Intergroup relations and leadership.* New York: Wiley, 1962.

Already annotated in "For Further Reading" section of Chapter Six.

Tannenbaum, R., Wechsler, I. R. and Massarik F. *Leadership and organization: a behavioral science approach.* New York: McGraw-Hill, 1961.

Emphasizes sensitivity training through small groups for the development of leadership and research on interpersonal relations within formal organizations.

ARTICLES

Barnlund, D. C. Consistency of emergent leadership in groups with changing tasks and members. *Speech Monograph,* 1962, 29 (1), 45–52.

Leadership was found to depend upon situational variables—there was little correlation in leadership when such varied tasks as solving problems relating to motor, artistic, mathematical, literary, social and spatial characteristics were involved.

Bass, B. M. Some aspects of attempted, successful, and effective leadership. *J. appl. Psychol.,* 1961, 45 (2), 120–122. PA 36, 3GF20B.

Successful leadership is related more to ability in effective than in ineffective groups; discrepancies between self-esteem and the esteem in which the member is held by the group are manifested in unsuccessful leadership.

Beer, M., *et al.* Some perceived properties of the difference between leaders and non-leaders. *J. Psychol.* 1959, 47 (1), 49–56. SA 9, A0547.

Leaders are significantly higher in confidence and realism, more willing to accept responsibility, more driving and arbitrary, more forceful and persuasive than non-leaders.

Bennis, W. G. Revisionist theory of leadership. *Harvard bus. Rev.,* 1961, 39 (1), 26–36. PA 36, 3GF26B.

An effective leader is viewed as one who is able to mediate between an organization and its members in such a way as to maximize the satisfactions of both. Conflicts between these two were resolved in favor of the organization by the "scientific management" school; in favor of the individual by the "human relations" approach. More recent research has faced the inevitable conflict more objectively.

Bonjean, C. M. Class, status, and power reputation. *Sociol. soc. Res.,* 1964, 49 (1), 69–75. SA 13, B7061.

Two hundred and ninety reputational leaders and economic dominants in four communities were asked to nominate and rank local leaders—three leadership types: visible leaders, concealed leaders, and symbolic leaders.

————, and Olson, D. M. Community leadership: directions of research. *Adm. Sci. Quart.,* 1964, 9 (3), PA 39, 7649.

A review of recent literature in which each of the main methods of identification of leadership (positional, reputational, and decisional) is described and criticized.

Bowers, D. G., and Seashore, S. E. Predicting organizational effectiveness with a four-factor theory of leadership. *Adm. Sci. Quart.*, 1966, *11* (2), 238–264. SA 15, C4155.

Four basic dimensions of leadership: support, interaction facilitation, goal emphasis, and work facilitation. Ability to predict is enhanced by taking simultaneous account of certain non-leadership variables.

Clifford, C., and Cohn, T. S. The relationship between leadership and personality attributes perceived by followers. *J. soc. Psychol.*, 1964, *64* (1), 57–64. PA 39, 4906.

Leadership is related to personal attributes as seen by the followers, with different attributes required in different leadership roles.

Cohn, T., *et al.* Leadership and predicting attitudes of others. *J. soc. Psychol.*, 1961, *55* (2), 199–206. PA 36, 3GF99C.

Groups of children in a summer camp were asked to predict attitudes of others and also select sociometric and elected leaders. No significant relationship was found between the ability to predict attitudes of others and indices of leadership.

DuBrin, A. J. Trait and situational approaches in the development of a leadership inventory. *J. indust. Psychol.*, 1963, *1* (1), 28–37. PA 38, 5979.

Reports the development and validation of a self-report type of leadership inventory and compares the relative contribution of "trait" and "situational" type items to inventory validity. Greater validity is obtained when both types of items are included in the predictor.

Frye, R. L. Relationship between rated leaders and the traits assigned to these leaders. *J. soc. Psychol.*, 1965, *66* (1), 95–99.

Determines that there is a stereotype regarding leaders.

Gibb, C. A. Leadership. In G. Lindzey (Ed.), *Handbook of social psychology.* Volume 2. (Cambridge, Massachusetts: Addison-Wesley, 1954.) Pp. 877–920.

An older but still one of the most comprehensive articles on the topic.

Goldman, M., and Fraas, L. A. The effects of leader selection on group performance. *Sociometry*, 1965, *28* (1), 82–88. SA 14, B9191.

There was a significant gap in problem-solving performance between groups that elected their leaders according to ability, as opposed to a leader arbitrarily selected by the experimenter or no leader appointed.

Gross, E. Dimensions of leadership. *Personn. J.*, 1961, *40* (5), 213–218. PA 36, 3GE13G.

Leaders may create or define goals, clarify and administer them, choose appropriate means, assign tasks and coordinate, motivate, create loyalty, represent their group, and spark its membership into action at the right moment. Leadership is situationally-relevant.

Greer, F. L. Leader indulgence and group performance. *Psychol. Monogr.*, 1961, *75* (12, Whole No. 516), PA 36, 5GF35G.

Tested and confirmed the hypothesis that the more a leader satisfies the needs of his men, the more effective group performance will be.

Lang, K. and Leaders, G. E.: Initiators and instigators. *Collective Dynamics.* New York: Thomas Y. Crowell, 1961. Pp. 231–254.

Discusses two different types of leadership pertinent to collective behavior.

Maier, N. R. F., and Hoffman, L. R. Acceptance and quality of solutions as related to leaders' attitudes toward disagreement in group problem solving. *J. appl. Behavioral Sci.*, 1965, 1 (4), 373–386. SA 14, C1896.

When the foreman most often reported having problem employees, solutions were least likely to be innovative and acceptance was relatively low; when the foreman perceived his subordinates as idea men, innovative solutions increased and satisfaction with the solution was greatest for all concerned.

Prentice, W. C. H. Understanding leadership. *Harvard Business Rev.*, 1961, 39 (5), 143–151. PA 37, 4893.

A leader must accomplish a group goal by providing some direction; by helping each to see how a personal motive can be satisfied in the process.

Roby, T. B. Group problem solving under two types of executive structure. *J. abnorm. soc. Psychol.*, 1963, 67 (6), 550–556. SA 13, B6763.

Problems requiring reaction to environmental changes are more quickly solved under the shared responsibility condition; problems involving coordination of action among operators (airmen) are more efficiently solved with a competent centralized authority. Designation of a low aptitude group member as leader produced inferior performance on both problem types.

Schlesinger, L., *et al.* Leader-member interaction in management committees. *J. abnorm. soc. Psychol.*, 1960, 61 (3), 360–364. PA 36, 2CF60S.

When a leader exerts effective (frequent but low magnitude) control, the group moves toward more successful resolutions of problems; when leaders are low in skillful control, group members begin to vie with one another for leadership.

Sollie, C. R. A comparison of reputational techniques for identifying community leaders. *Rural Sociol.*, 1966, 31 (3), 301–309. SA 15, C3492.

Four different reputational techniques—a panel of experts, community leaders identified by the experts, residents of the area contacted by use of the snowball technique, and a random sample—indicated a fairly high level of agreement. The relatively simple snowball technique may be as valid as the more complicated techniques.

Unesco, Leadership and economic growth. *Int. soc. Sci. J.*, 1964, 16 (2).

Entire issue is devoted to leadership in developing countries.

Chapter Eleven

Culture

The idea of *culture* is so all-encompassing that it might better be termed a perspective rather than a concept. Perhaps the most widely-quoted definition is that of Kroeber and Kluckhohn:

"Culture consists of patterns, explicit and implicit, of and for behavior acquired and transmitted by symbols, constituting the distinctive achievement of human groups, including their embodiments in artifacts; the essential core of culture consists of traditional (i.e., historically derived and selected) ideas and especially their attached values; culture systems may, on the one hand, be considered as products of action, on the other as conditioning elements of further action." [1]

For our introduction to the topic, we turn to a semipopular exposition, an excerpt from the familiar *The Proper Study of Mankind* by Stuart Chase. With a certain brashness and perhaps overdramatization, Chase vividly illustrates the importance of the culture concept in understanding human behavior.

The second selection is much more scientifically oriented, and brilliantly merges social-psychological (personality variables) and sociological (culture) emphases in an attempt to explain prejudice in two widely-separated societies: Southern United States and South Africa. Thomas F. Pettigrew's article introduces evidence that shows how extremely important it is to understand both the specific culture and personality dynamics in understanding human behavior (in this case, prejudice).

Finally, an article by J. Milton Yinger introduces the concept of *contraculture* to analyze the culture of small groups that are actually in opposition to the larger society's values, and not merely possessed of a distinguishing ethos (which is properly termed a *subculture*). One can imaginatively speculate what this contribution will add to studies of cultural comparison.

---

[1] Kroeber, A. A., and Kluckhohn, C. *Culture: a critical review of concepts and definitions*. Cambridge, Massachusetts: Harvard University Peabody Museum of American Archaeology and Ethnology Papers, Volume 47, Number 1, 1952. Also available in paperback (Vintage Books, 1963).

33

The Culture Concept*
STUART CHASE

The culture concept of anthropologists and sociologists is the corner-stone of the study of behavior. "The work of the social scientist," says Ralph Linton, "must begin with the investigation of cultures, the ways of life which are characteristic of particular societies." In this sense "culture" means far more than the arts and graces. Knowledge about it has been accumulating for more than a century in painstaking studies of hundreds of communities, both primitive and civilized. Here and in the next few chapters we shall examine this concept from various points of view.*

An understanding of human culture enlarges one's perspective. The effect is something like those amazing photographs taken from outer space which show the globe and its oceans and continents in perspective—one planet and one world. The culture concept shows us mankind in perspective. It deflates many a fixed idea and cherished notion about ourselves and our society. It takes us clean out of Western civilization and its values, and shows us what a Congo man, a Moscow man, and a Detroit man have in common—how all have similar needs, but meet those needs by habits, customs, and beliefs which vary spectacularly.

It shows how every human being is shaped by his culture in ways far below the level of consciousness. His language, his habits of thinking, his tool-using muscles, are developed in special patterns. To use them at all he must use them as he learned to do in childhood and in youth.

> Without the presence of culture, conserving past gains and shaping each succeeding generation . . . *homo sapiens* would be nothing more than a terrestrial anthropoid ape, slightly divergent in structure and slightly superior in intelligence, but a brother to the chimpanzee . . . .

So says Ralph Linton in *The Study of Man*, a brilliant inventory of the major findings in cultural anthropology. We have already referred to it and we shall do so often in the pages to come. Walter Bagehot, writing long before Linton, had invented the phrase, "the cake of custom." Presently Sumner published his epoch-making *Folkways*, a classic which has, I sup-

Reprinted from *The Proper Study of Mankind*, revised edition (New York: Harper and Row, 1956), 61–73 (Harper Colophon Books), by permission of the author and the publishers.

* In writing for a popular audience, the author evidently decided his presentation would be less formidable without the usual citations. (Ed.)

pose, influenced every social scientist working today. I read it just after leaving college, and it made a shambles of much that I had learned there. The first effect was to accent the differences in human customs around the world. It was pleasantly shocking to learn that this tribe consider it immodest to wear anything above the waist, while that tribe customarily killed, with due ceremony, the ailing aged.

The initial shock, however, soon gives way to something more fundamental. To the adult mind, the great lesson is not human differences, but *similarities.* Common needs persist in human behavior everywhere. They are the universals which govern Homo sapiens, from green tropical jungles to the jungles of Manhattan. To solve our current problems, . . . generalizations and theories will have to be grounded on the principles which affect all societies, the common denominators of human living.

Although no scientist can study his own species with the objectivity he applies to a colony of ants, he can study villages in Borneo more impersonally than villages on Cape Cod. He must learn not to be surprised at anything, not even when wives in a harem belligerently defend the institution of polygamy (or polygyny, if you want to be technical). Some groups, says Linton, not only tolerate epileptics, they honor them as agents of the higher powers. Many an inmate of our mental hospitals might be not only free but a respected oracle in some other society.

The investigator develops that tolerant sophistication which is characteristic of anthropologists: "Well, some do and some don't." Instead of applying his own moral values to a given custom, he concentrates on trying to understand its local meaning in that particular culture. Such an attitude may be depressing to missionary zeal, but it is a great help in acquiring dependable knowledge about human behavior. Any culture can develop antisocial customs—and most do—but no culture can continue them in a big way without running the risk of extinction. There is a tribe in New Guinea described by Margaret Mead which has been pushing head-hunting to dangerous extremes. Ultimate survival is the sanction hanging over every behavior pattern—including the use of atomic bombs.

Alexander Leighton[1] describes what he calls the "parachute technique" developed by a training school in the American Southwest. After a student has been instructed for some weeks in the culture concept, using local Indian and Spanish materials, he is sent to a remote Indian village to make his way, beginning with sign language. He must find his own lodging and food. Trainees are invariably astonished at their success in adjusting to a totally different situation. They discover basic questions which must be answered in approaching any culture, and how to find the answers.

It would be a fine idea to put technical assistance (Point Four) administrators through the "parachute technique" before they set out to improve local conditions in Burma or the Sudan.

_____
[1] In a talk at the Washington Seminar, May 14, 1952.

When enough investigators have collected data from enough places, and comparative studies are made, the universal patterns begin to appear: the needs and functions which *all* tribes share, civilized as well as primitive. These common denominators, when adequately checked by competent observers, give vital information about human behavior, information which statesmen neglect at their peril. How, for instance, is it possible even to think intelligently about ending war, or about strengthening the United Nations, without an understanding of such universals?

DEFINING CULTURE

Along with eating and sleeping, one universal habit of our species is forming ourselves into bands, tribes, societies. We then evolve various ways and means for holding the group together and giving it structure.

A *society* refers to a group of people who have learned to work and live together.

A *culture* refers to the way of life which the group follows.

Culture is the cement which binds the group together. Without it, a group is not a society but a mob, an aggregate, a milling mass. Social scientists divide a culture into three chief parts:

1. *Habits*, customs, ways of behaving, which a child begins to learn almost as soon as he is born. How to keep clean, how to eat his food properly, how to dress, how to comport himself in church and school. The most important habit of all is how to communicate, including the unique gift of speech. He is born with large speech centers in his brain, but language must always be learned.

2. *Belief* systems, to give him his ideas of right and wrong. Religion, magic, patriotism, property standards, all the accepted symbols and credos of his society.

3. *Artifacts*, the tools, utensils, constructions, machines, which the society has developed or borrowed from other societies. The catalogue of a large mail order house gives us some idea of the artifacts loose in the American culture today. In 1800, it is safe to say, such a catalogue would not have been a tenth the size.

Customs and belief systems vary inside a culture, depending on the status of subgroups. In Europe, until recently at least, royalty had a different set of rules from those of the middle classes, and both differed from the rules for peasants and laborers. In the United States and Canada, while classes are very fluid, rich people do not observe quite the same pattern as journeymen plumbers—even though President Eisenhower's original cabinet in 1953 was composed of "a plumber and eight millionaires."

Journalists and fiction writers speak of the "unwritten law," by which they must mean the culture of the tribe. Culture comes ages before formal law. Nature peoples like the Eskimo have no formal law at all; there are no courts or statutes or jails, but the living law or culture may enjoin the death penalty just the same. Unless the formal law is in line with the living law, it cannot be enforced. The Prohibition law in the United States banning alcoholic beverages was an instructive example. One difficulty in setting up a formal international law today is that there is as yet no international *living* law, no planetary culture.

Dwelling together in groups is as characteristic of man as the shape of his teeth or his inclination to laugh. "A social organism," said William James, "is what it is because each member proceeds to his own duty with a trust that the other members will simultaneously do theirs. A government, an army, a commercial system, a ship, a college, an athletic team, all exist on this condition without which not only is nothing achieved, but nothing is even attempted."

It is difficult to overemphasize the importance of this observation—yet not many of us understand it. If most people were dishonest, if they failed to do what they promised to do, if they did not take care of the children, help others in crisis, society would fall apart. Most people are "good," just as the charge account statistics prove; they pay their bills, they can be trusted. The culture concept makes it plain why this must be so. If any considerable fraction—say more than 5 percent—could *not* be trusted to do what was expected of them, there would be no dependable culture, no living, growing society—just a prisoner-of-war camp, with a polyglot mixture of prisoners. A functioning society must be self-disciplining. When we talk about "dictators," "democracy," "the state," "freedom," we often forget this underlying condition.

In Homo sapiens, society rather than the individual has become the primary unit in the struggle for existence. For centuries in the West, philosophers, theologians, educators, businessmen, have concentrated on the individual. They have affirmed that he alone was responsible for his sins, his sufferings, his triumphs, and his defeats. Social scientists find that the individual is not that kind of organism, and cannot be understood in such a conceptual frame. He is a product of his culture; he is a living part of his group, and can be understood only in relation to it. To judge him outside this matrix is like trying to understand a fish without reference to water.

A comprehension of the *double role* of the individual, observes Linton, as a separate person and as a unit in society, provides a key to many problems of human behavior. "Until the psychologist knows what the norms of behavior imposed by a particular society are, and can discount them as indicators of personality, he will be unable to penetrate behind the façade of social conformity and cultural uniformity to reach the authentic individual." Dr. William C. Menninger made the same point about mental health. . . .

Social scientists are a long way from working out *all* the relationships between the individual and his culture, but they have led the study of man out of a blind alley. They have begun to ask the right questions, and have demonstrated that man is a social animal to a degree hitherto unappreciated. Apparently he has always been one since he came down from trees. Sometimes his group comprises only a few families, living under the most primitive conditions. Sometimes it fills a continent; but it is always there.

On this broad base, the science of man begins. A baby snake can fend for itself about as soon as it can squirm. A human baby, without a group behind it, either starves immediately, or if natural food is by some miracle available, comes to resemble a gibbering idiot. Civilized man can do more things than the savage because he has the opportunity to learn more things; his culture is richer; it accumulates like compound interest. The innate ability of the savage, however, may be just as great.

TRANSFERRING CULTURES

Darwin, in the *Voyage of the Beagle,* tells of delivering two young people, Jemmy and Fuegia, back to their savage and naked clan on Tierra del Fuego. Although the children had been exposed to British culture for only a few years, they had learned to speak both English and Spanish, were neat in their dress and table manners, quick with their minds, and favorites with the crew.

> It was interesting to watch the conduct of the savages when we landed toward Jemmy Button: they immediately perceived the difference between him and ourselves, and held much conversation one with another on the subject. The old man addressed a long harangue to Jemmy, which it seems was to invite him to stay with them. But Jemmy understood very little of their language, and was, moreover, thoroughly ashamed of his countrymen.

The picture Darwin draws is memorable and tragic—the terrified children in their neat British dress being forced back to a bleak and primitive life on one of the most forbidding islands on earth. Kind people in England had felt that they would be happier there, but, innocent of the culture concept, they were inflicting a cruel punishment on Jemmy and Fuegia. Either the children should not have been kidnaped in the first place, or once taken, they should have been adopted for life.

Here is Fung Kwok Keung, born Joseph Rinehart on Long Island, New York. Scheinfeld describes how he was taken to China at a tender age and brought up as a Chinese boy. He comes back to America as a young man, and we find him before the blackboard painfully learning English in an "Americanization" class. "He had become so thoroughly Chinese in manner, speech, habit, and outlook that he was distinguishable from members of the race only by his features." [2] This is not something strange and abnormal; it will *always* happen when a baby is transferred to another culture.

NEW PERSPECTIVE ON HISTORY

The culture concept gives us a new perspective on history as well as on ourselves. A culture is a process of gradual change without beginning or end. "The spectacular rise and fall of certain civilizations," says Linton, "should not blind us to the fact that most cultures have never fallen." Our own American culture, for example, can be viewed as a continuum extending back unbroken through written history, through archeological time, through the unrecorded dark, to the very dawn of the race. If the chain had once been broken, you and I would not be here.

Individuals are born and die, the culture slowly shifts under the pressure of climate, new invention, internal need; the *group* moves east or south, over Bering Strait, down the Mexican plateau, down to Tierra del Fuego. But always the children are protected, loved, and taught; always the group closes in against its natural enemies; the cord is unbroken for a million years. The group is deathless and timeless. The individual may not be able to adjust to outside realities; the group eventually must.

With our accent on the individual in America, we are normally little aware of the society in which we have our being. In war and disaster the realization breaks through. A forest fire, a child lost in the New Hampshire woods, a flood on the Ohio River, a hurricane in Florida, a plane crash in the Rocky Mountains—and the community swings into action without thought of payment or prestige.

The culture concept gives us the closest fit to the truth about mankind yet discovered by the scientific method. Truths discovered by other methods do not concern us here. History as customarily written, from Herodotus to the present day, seldom focuses on this truth, but rather on kings, generals, popes, presidents, prime ministers, prophets, the great men who rise out of the group, often to torment it. "While the popular view is that the leader makes the times," says Ogburn, "a realistic view emphasizes the exact opposite."

Formal history, with its Caesars and Napoleons, tends to be a record of the abnormal, the geniuses, sports, freaks, and misfits, the glandular cases of mankind. It stands the social pyramid on its apex. The culture concept puts it back upon its base. The kings and the warriors are dramatic, true enough, but the real story concerns the society which sheltered its children, accumulated invention, and wrung a living from nature down through the ages.

[2] A. Scheinfeld, *You and Heredity.*

TIMETABLE FOR REFORMERS

The culture concept focuses a strong lens, too, on measures for economic and social reform. What, after all, can even the most inspired agitators and propagandists do to a society embedded in the gigantic toils of age-old patterns? They can do something, but not as much as they think they can. Kluckhohn and Kelly point out that many social planners neglect the facts of culture. They think they can somehow wipe the slate clean and start afresh. It is impossible. "Every human being is born into a world defined by already existing cultural patterns." The red government of China, one suspects, is now learning this stubborn truth.

The idea that a group can suddenly be emancipated from its past habits is no more sensible than the idea that a man who flaps his arms rapidly enough can fly. If the group could change as fast as some reformers hope, it would have dashed itself to pieces some time in the Old Stone Age. The group's main task is survival through reproduction and nourishment. The young can be protected, and a food supply secured, only in the momentum of established procedures.

One of my strongest impressions when I visited the U.S.S.R. ten years after the "ten days that shook the world," was how little things had probably changed. Where was this great revolution they talked about? The streets, the shops, the houses, the peasants in the fields, the factory workers, all looked like the photographs taken in czarist days. A Baedeker guide of 1907 described the railroads and local officials of 1927 with apparent accuracy. Power had shifted at the apex, but the base of the social pyramid seemed almost unmoved. Perhaps the common people *felt* differently from their predecessors; but who could tell? I doubted if 5 percent of their day-by-day behavior had been altered by the revolution. But is this not what one would expect in the light of the culture concept? The news we get in the headlines, the accounts by historians, scarcely touch this monolithic continuity.

The adoption of the Weimar Constitution in Germany in 1919 was an attempt to make Germans as democratic as Vermonters, in defiance of a thousand years of German cultural momentum. Naturally it collapsed and in the ensuing vacuum Hitler found his opportunity. There should be a lesson here for those vocal Americans who want to make "democracy" —on the Corn Belt model—the price of aid to hungry people East and West. Can we expect the reforms in Germany after World War II to last longer? It is possible that the people's sufferings did in fact weaken the culture and make it more responsive to change. We must wait for history to give the final answer in Germany. So too in Japan, where some postwar reforms were politely accepted and later abandoned. No reform can bear fruit unless it is grafted successfully to the living tree of culture.

An understanding of the culture concept produces a curious paradox. A given institution in one's culture—say the United States banking system

—comes to seem at once weaker and stronger. One can no longer stand in awe of it as an eternal verity, for one knows it is man-made and bound to change with external circumstances. The gold standard has already ceased to be an eternal verity. But for the short view the institution commands increased respect. If one kicks it too hard, one is extremely likely to break some bones.

All this sheds quite a different light on the fears of those congressmen who believed that social science meant wild reforms, strange -isms and -ologies. We find that the social scientists have described the most massive brake on wild reforms possible to imagine; more effective than whole armies of FBI agents and secret police. The senators can relax.

THE FORMATIVE YEARS

The saying that if the church has a boy until he is six he will be a good communicant for life, has strong support from social scientists. The demonstration that any healthy infant can adjust to any culture—if he is not discriminated against because of the color of his skin—emphasizes the vast importance of the earliest years. Five branches of social science are joining today to drive home this conclusion—the anthropologists, linguists, sociologists, psychologists, and psychiatrists.

The *anthropologists* say that since Cro-Magnon days, at least, children of any nation or race have had practically the same inborn equipment. But from birth every experience helps to shape a child to the culture in which he finds himself. Even by the age of three or four he has learned hundreds of habits, and received thousands of impressions, which he will not consciously remember later in life, but which already stamp him as a member of Eskimo or Japanese or American society.

The *linguists* demonstrate that by the time he is six, a child has absorbed the structure of his language, and that this structure will shape his whole system of thought throughout his life.

The *sociologists* emphasize the institutional and community aspects of the culture.

The *psychologists* study the responses of young children, aided with all manner of laboratory equipment—cameras, sound tracks, one-way windows. They analyze the vital process by which an individual becomes a culture-carrier.

The *psychiatrists* emphasize emotional influences on children, showing how early experiences may mold an individual's character, and perhaps produce a mental breakdown in later years.

Scientists talk more and more about the vital importance of security and affection, the feeling of belonging, in early years. A lack of emotional security in childhood may bring serious results, examples of which can be seen in any mental hospital and in outbreaks of juvenile delinquency.

OPTIMISTIC NOTE

Finally, the culture concept gives us hope that many of our problems can be solved. If people were bad by virtue of their "blood," or their genes, or their innate characters, there would not be much we could do about it. But if people depend on their group, and a given problem lies primarily in an adjustment of culture patterns, or an adjustment *to* culture patterns, a good deal can be done about it.

Theoretically, a society could be completely made over in something like 15 years—the time it takes to educate a rising crop of youngsters. But such a theory assumes that parents, nurses, teachers, have all been re-educated themselves—which, as Euclid used to say, is absurd. But it helps, I think, to know that the trouble does not all come from an erring and invariant human nature packaged at birth. It comes mostly from culture patterns built into the plastic human nervous system. Culture patterns do change, and can be changed.

These are some of the stimulating vistas which anthropology and sociology open to the inquiring layman. My image of the photograph taken from outer space may not be so exaggerated after all. If we let this knowledge flow into our minds, the world can never look the same again. Furthermore, it is not a doctrine, a philosophical system, a prophet's message, it is *social science*, where reasonable proof has been established.

The laws of culture are something like Boyle's law of gases. An individual person, like a molecule of hydrogen, is unpredictable. But there is a definite pattern which the whole group will follow, and which can be statistically described. We know, for instance, how many will be born, how many will marry, how many classrooms will be needed in the years ahead. If an observer charts the pattern, he can predict behavior with reasonable probability.

I have repeatedly put the idea of culture to work on my personal problems, and used it to help evaluate the news that comes over the air waves every morning. It throws a flood of light on matters which had puzzled me before. It helps explain some of the difficulties in American foreign policy, troubles in Korea, China, Israel, the roots of McCarthyism, the limits of "coexistence" between East and West, the real barriers to world peace, barriers to a universal language, to world government.

It has clarified my ideas on how to bring up children, why they have to be disciplined—not because they are "naughty," but to prepare them for the environment in which they must live. It has broadened my ideas about schools and education, about meetings, participation, democracy. It has given new insight into the importance of symbols and ceremonials, such as weddings, funerals, parades, ticker tape rides up Broadway. I used to sniff at some of these displays, but I sniff no longer. It has made me, I think, a better judge of novels, stories, plays. Has the author run off the track imposed by the culture? As an example, it seems to me that Steinbeck runs off the track from time to time in his otherwise delightful *Cannery Row*. Too many people break too many rules to make a viable society—like those head-hunters in New Guinea. The culture concept has certainly reinforced for me the cardinal importance of religion in a society.

Finally, when one becomes aware how he personally is culture-bound, by a curious paradox he is freed a little from his bonds. He can look over the walls of his own culture and see the other peoples of the world behind their walls. He can for the first time in his life begin to understand people of an alien culture. How strange that science should be the cause of a deep ethical experience!

34

Personality and Sociocultural Factors in Intergroup Attitudes: A Cross-national Comparison*

THOMAS F. PETTIGREW

Harvard University

I. INTRODUCTION

Along the continuum of prejudice theories, two extreme positions have been popular. One strongly emphasizes the personality of the bigot and neglects his cultural milieu; the other views intolerance as a mere reflection of cultural norms and neglects individual differences. Recent evidence lends little support to either pole. As further data are gathered with more refined research tools, it becomes increasingly apparent that the psychological and sociological correlates of prejudice are elaborately intertwined and that both are essential to provide an adequate theoretical framework for this complex phenomenon.

Carrying this viewpoint further, Smith, Bruner, and White (38, pp. 41–44) have delineated three functions that attitudes may serve for an individual. First, there is the *object-appraisal* function; attitudes aid in the process of understanding "reality" as it is defined by the culture. Second, attitudes can play a *social-adjustment* role by contributing to the individual's identification with, or differentiation from, various reference groups. It should be noted that both these functions—object appraisal and social adjustment—are important reflections on the personality level of sociocultural conditions. But the most studied function of attitudes, *externalization,* is somewhat unique. "Externalization occurs when an individual, often responding unconsciously, senses an analogy between a perceived environmental event and some unresolved inner problem . . . [and] adopts

Reprinted from *Journal of Conflict Resolution*, 2, 1 (March 1958), 29–42, by permission of the author and the publisher.

* This article is a revision of a paper delivered in September, 1957, at the New York meetings of the American Psychological Association. The author wishes to express his deep appreciation to Professor Gordon W. Allport for his advice and encouragement and to Dr. Herbert Kelman, this issue's special editor, for his theoretical and editorial suggestions.

an attitude . . . which is a transformed version of his way of dealing with his inner difficulty." Such a process may serve to reduce anxiety. The principal psychological theories of prejudice—frustration-aggression (9), psychoanalytic (20), and authoritarianism (1)—all deal chiefly with this third process.

External expression of inner conflict is relatively more independent of sociocultural factors than are the other functions of attitudes. Indeed, a heuristic distinction between externalized personality variables and sociological variables contributes to our understanding of much that is known about intergroup conflict.

Minard's observations of race relations in the coal-mining county of McDowell, West Virginia, serve as a direct illustration of the point (26). The general pattern in this region consists of white and Negro miners being integrated below the ground and almost completely segregated above the ground. Minard estimates that roughly 60 per cent of the white miners manage to reverse roles almost completely; they can accept Negroes as equals in the mines but cannot accept them as equals elsewhere. Furthermore, he feels that, at one extreme, about 20 per cent accept the black miners as equals in both situations, while, at the other extreme, about 20 per cent never accept them in either situation. In our terms, the behavior of the majority of these whites studied by Minard can be predicted largely by sociocultural expectations, and the behavior of the consistent minorities can be accounted for largely by externalized personality variables.

The research literature abounds with further examples in which a separation of psychological and sociological factors is helpful. The many papers on interracial contact in housing (7, 40), at work (11), and in the army (39) show the marked effects that can be brought about by certain changes in the social situation between races. But personality factors are still operating. Usually these studies report that some individuals hold favorable attitudes toward minorities even before the contact and that other individuals still hold unfavorable attitudes after the contact. Many of these studies also find the changes brought about by the contact are quite specific and delimited in nature. That is, the intergroup changes occur only under a narrow range of conditions, since the basic personality orientations of the participants have not changed fundamentally. Thus white department-store employees become more accepting of Negroes in the work situation after equal status contact but not in other situations (11). And the attitudes of white army personnel toward the Negro as a fighting man improve after equal status contact in combat, but their attitudes toward the Negro as a social companion do not change (39).

Desegregation findings furnish further illustrations where the distinction is useful. Social demands for racial desegregation and the irresistible trend of the times are counteracting personality predispositions in many communities. Thus a 1954 public opinion survey in Oklahoma found an overwhelming majority of the residents sternly against desegregation, and yet today mixed schools have become accepted throughout most of the state without incident (17). And in Wilmington, Delaware, two years after successful school integration without apparent public opposition, a poll indicated that only a minority approved of the school desegregation decision of the Supreme Court (17). Indeed, this discrepancy between opinions and demands is a general phenomenon throughout the border states. Hyman and Sheatsley (16) report that only 31 per cent of the white population in those border areas that have already integrated their school systems endorse desegregation.

This conflict between authority-supported cultural changes and personal preferences is underscored by another finding that public opinion polls have uncovered in the South. Several investigators have independently shown that respondents themselves make a distinction between what they individually favor and what they expect to happen in their community. Thus the huge majority of southern whites favor racial segregation, but most of them also feel that desegregation is inevitable (16, 28).

Finally, the work originally done by La Piere (19) in 1934 and more recently replicated in different contexts by Saenger and Gilbert (34) and by Kutner, Wilkins, and Yarrow (18) furnishes further justification for a theoretical separation of social and externalization aspects of intergroup conflict. These investigations illustrate the results of conflicting personality predispositions and actual social situations with minority-group members; frequently the face-to-face conditions override previous practices.

Such work has led several authorities in the field to make the socio-cultural and personality differentiation. Psychologist G. W. Allport discusses the two classes of factors separately in his definitive volume, *The Nature of Prejudice* (2), and sociologist Arnold Rose makes a similar distinction in a recent theoretical article on intergroup relations (33).

The present paper is a summary report on research conducted chiefly to gain cross-national perspective on these two sets of prejudice factors. The studies were made in two parts of the world where racial conflict today is highlighted and cultural sanctions of intolerance are intense and explicit: the Union of South Africa and the southern United States. First, a more detailed report of previously unpublished data will be presented on the South African study. Following this, a comparison will be made with the southern United States based on a summary of data presented in detail elsewhere (29).

II. RACIAL PREJUDICE IN THE UNION OF SOUTH AFRICA[1]

The limited evidence available supports the general belief that white South Africans are unusually prejudiced against Africans (14, 21, 24). This

[1] This investigation was conducted during 1956 when the author was an honorary research associate of the University of Natal's Institute for Social Research. The study

raises the intriguing question as to whether this increased hostility represents (a) more externalizing personality potential for prejudice among South Africans, (b) the effects of different cultural norms and pressures, or (c) both of these.

To provide a tentative answer, a questionnaire study was undertaken of the racial attitudes of students at the English-speaking University of Natal in the Union of South Africa. A non-random sample of 627 undergraduates—approximately one-third of the entire university—completed an anonymous instrument containing three scales and a number of background items.[2] The three scales are a thirteen-item measure of authoritarianism (F scale) whose statements are shown in Table 2, a sixteen-item measure of social conformity (C scale) whose statements are shown in Table 3, and an eighteen-item measure of anti-African attitudes (A scale) whose statements are shown in Table 8.[3] Background information includes place of birth, political party preference, father's occupation, and ethnic-group membership.

Taken as a group, these students evidence considerable hostility toward Africans, accepting in large degree the white-supremacy ideology so adamantly propounded by the present government of their country. Thus 72 per cent of the sample agree that "there is something inherently primitive and uncivilized in the native, as shown in his music and extreme aggressiveness"; and 69 per cent agree that "manual labor seems to fit the native mentality better than more skilled and responsible work." And yet their F-scale responses are roughly comparable to those of American student populations.[4] Thus these South Africans are sharply prejudiced against blacks without possessing any greater externalizing personality potential for intolerance than peoples in more tolerant areas.

---

would not have been possible without the aid of the institute's co-operative staff, particularly Professor Arnold Lloyd (now of the University of Witwatersrand), Dr. Hamish Dickie-Clark, Miss Len Kuyper, Dr. Jack Mann, and Professor Max Marwick (now of the University of Witwatersrand).

[2] Comparisons between this one-third sample and the total student body of the University of Natal reveal that, in terms of sex, age, and field of concentration, the sample's distributions are quite similar to the student body at large.

[3] All thirteen of the F-scale items are from the original California study on authoritarianism (1, pp. 255–257); the C scale is a new scale composed of both new items and adaptations from the conformity measures of Hoffman (15) and MacCrone (22); and fourteen of the A-scale items are new, while four are adaptations from the E scale (1, items 8, 31, and 34 on p. 105 and item 29 on p. 117).

[4] Comparisons across diverse groups with varying forms of the F scale are difficult and tenuous at best. American college samples generally average slightly below the neutral point on F-scale statements, while the present South African sample averages slightly above the neutral point. This small difference can probably be accounted for by (a) the use of a disproportionate number of high-agreement items in the thirteen-item F scale employed with the South African sample and (b) the inclusion in the South African group of fields of concentration not usually included in tested American college groups (e.g., agriculture) whose members tend to score high on the F scale (due probably to social class factors).

In addition, authoritarianism correlates with anti-African attitudes at a level comparable to relationships between authoritarianism and prejudice in other parts of the world. Table 1 shows that the A and F scales correlate

TABLE 1

Correlations Between Anti-African Scale (A) and Authoritarianism (F) and Conformity (C) Scales*

| Variables | Ethnic Group† | |
	Afrikaners	English
N	50	513
A and F	+0.56	+0.46
A and C	+0.42	+0.46

* All four of these product-moment correlations are significantly different from zero at better than the 1 per cent level of confidence. The scale scores that were correlated vary between 0 and 10. They were calculated on the basis of +4 for agree strongly, +3 for agree, +2 for omitted response, +1 for disagree and 0 for disagree strongly for each item, and then the total scores were collapsed into the 0–10 categories for machine analysis.

† Separate analyses by ethnic group are made necessary by the sharply divergent A-scale means of the two groups (see Table 7).

+0.56 among the Afrikaans-speaking members of the sample and +0.46 among the English-speaking members. Similar scales typically correlate in the fifties in American college samples.[5] The C-scale measure of social conformity—employed for the first time in this investigation—relates to the A-scale scores significantly, too, in both ethnic groups (Table 1).

More detailed analyses of the F and C scales' relationships with anti-African attitudes are provided in Tables 2 and 3. Each of the thirteen authoritarian statements separates the less and more prejudiced halves of the sample in the predicted direction, seven of the differences proving to be significant at better than the 0.001 level of confidence. The sixteen C-scale items predict almost as well; the more anti-African students in every case agree more often than the less prejudiced. Perhaps the conforming attitude of the bigots is capsuled in the first item of Table 3. While only a third of the tolerant members of the group agree with the statement, over half the prejudiced students feel that "it's better to go along with the crowd than to be a martyr."

These personality relationships suggest (*a*) that personality factors are as important correlates of prejudice in this sample as they are in other, non-South African samples; (*b*) that social conformity (as measured by the C scale) is a particularly crucial personality variable in this sample's

[5] Again, comparisons are difficult. Correlations between long-form F scales and ethnocentrism scales (measuring prejudice against a variety of out-groups) have sometimes reached the sixties and even occasionally the seventies in American college samples (1, 2, 5). But correlations of the magnitude found in this study have been consistently reported when—as in this study—a short-form F scale and a prejudice scale against a single out-group are related.

TABLE 2
Anti-African Prejudice and F-Scale Items

F-Scale Item	Percentage Agreement*		$2 \times 2\chi^2$	p
	Less Prejudiced Half	*More Prejudiced Half*		
a. Nowadays when so many different kinds of people move around and mix together so much, a person has to be especially careful not to catch an infection or disease from them	13.6	33.2	33.5	0.001
b. There is hardly anything lower than a person who does not feel a great love and respect for his parents	52.6	70.5	21.2	.001
c. People can be put into two distinct classes: the weak and the strong	23.5	37.8	15.1	.001
d. Most of our social problems would be solved if we could somehow get rid of the immoral, crooked, and feebleminded people	45.4	60.6	14.8	.001
e. The most important thing a child should learn is obedience to his parents	79.8	90.2	13.2	.001
f. Every person should have faith in some supernatural power whose decisions he obeys without question	46.7	60.9	13.0	.001
g. When a person has a problem or worry, it is best for him not to think about it, but to keep busy with more cheerful things	39.4	53.2	11.8	.001
h. Nowadays more and more people are prying into matters that should remain private and personal	63.5	74.5	8.6	.01
i. If people would talk less and work more, everybody would be better off	67.8	78.2	8.3	.01
j. An insult to our honor should always be punished	31.8	40.3	4.7	.05
k. No sane, normal person would ever think of hurting a close friend or relative	67.9	76.6	4.3	.05
l. Science has its place, but there are many important things that can never possibly be understood by the human mind	80.7	85.8	2.9	0.10
m. Some day it will probably be shown that astrology can explain a lot of things	44.4	48.0	0.9	n.s.

* The respondent was given four categories: agree strongly, agree, disagree, and disagree strongly. Percentage agreement is calculated by combining the first two of these replies.

TABLE 3

Anti-African Prejudice and C-Scale Items

C-Scale Item	Percentage Agreement*		$2 \times 2\chi^2$	p
	Less Prejudiced Half	More Prejudiced Half		
a. It's better to go along with the crowd than to be a martyr	34.8	53.2	21.8	0.001
b. When almost everyone agrees on something, there is little reason to oppose it	16.6	31.1	18.5	.001
c. Adherence to convention produces the best kind of citizen	31.8	46.8	14.9	.001
d. To be successful, a group's members must act and think alike	45.7	60.0	12.5	.001
e. It is important for friends to have similar opinions	28.5	42.2	12.1	.001
f. It is more important to be loyal and conform to our own group than to try to co-operate with other groups	25.6	38.5	11.7	.001
g. We should alter our needs to fit society's demands rather than change society to fit our needs	42.4	55.1	11.4	.001
h. A good group member should agree with the other members	21.2	33.2	11.1	.001
i. It is best not to express your views when in the company of friends who disagree with you	23.8	32.9	6.1	.02
j. Before a person does something, he should try to consider how friends will react to it	54.6	63.1	4.4	.05
k. To become a success these days, a person has to act in the way that others expect him to act	33.2	41.5	4.2	.05
l. A group cannot expect to maintain its identity unless its members all think and feel in very much the same way	59.3	66.8	3.9	.05
m. It is one's duty to conform to the passing demands of the world and to suppress those personal desires that do not fit these demands	43.7	51.1	3.4	.10
n. A person should adapt his ideas and his behavior to the group that happens to be with him at the time	45.7	52.6	3.1	.10
o. It is extremely uncomfortable to go accidentally to a formal party in street clothes	78.5	83.1	2.0	.20
p. To get along well in a group, you have to follow the lead of others	27.2	31.1	1.1	0.30

* Percentage agreement calculated as in Table 2.

attitudes toward Africans; and (c) that personality components do not in themselves account for the heightened intolerance of this sample.

We must turn to sociocultural factors to explain the extreme prejudice of these respondents, and the unusual importance of these variables is made clear by the data. For instance, the 560 students who were born on the African continent are significantly more intolerant of Africans than the remaining 65, but they are *not* more authoritarian. Table 4 shows that

TABLE 4

*Place of Birth and Anti-African Prejudice**

		Place of Birth	
Anti-African Attitudes†	*N*	*On African Continent*	*Not on African Continent*
		560	65
Least prejudiced	176	28%	29%
Medium prejudiced	246	38%	54%
Most prejudiced	203	34%	17%

* 2 × 3 chi-square = 9.33; $p < 0.01$.

† The least prejudiced are the students who rated A-scale scores from 0 through 4 by disagreeing with a heavy majority of the items; the medium prejudiced received scores of either 5 or 6 by agreeing with roughly half of the 18 A-scale items; and the most prejudiced obtained scores of 7 through 10 by agreeing with a majority of the statements.

those not born in Africa are much less likely to fall into the most prejudiced third of the distribution than other sample members. And yet the two groups do not differ significantly in their F-scale scores. More thoroughly influenced throughout their lives by the culture's definition of the white man's situation in Africa, students born on the Dark Continent are more anti-African without the usual personality concomitants of ethnocentrism.

Another such relationship involves students who support the Nationalist party—the pro-*Apartheid* political faction that is presently in power. Table 5 indicates that these respondents score significantly higher on the

TABLE 5

*Political Party Preference and Anti-African Prejudice**

		Political Party Preference†	
Anti-African Attitudes	*N*	*Nationalist Party*	*Other Parties*
		72	483
Least prejudiced	157	8%	35%
Medium prejudiced	210	26%	36%
Most prejudiced	188	66%	29%

* 2 × 3 chi-square = 38.60; $p < 0.001$.

† Seventy-two of the 627 students did not indicate any political preference.

A scale than their fellow undergraduates, but these two groups do not differ on the F scale. Again a prejudice difference is not accompanied by a personality potential difference. These relationships with political party preference and prejudice hold for each of the major ethnic groups—Afrikaners and English—considered separately.

Two other comparisons yield statistically significant differences in both authoritarianism and anti-African prejudice. Table 6 indicates that those

TABLE 6

Father's Occupational Status and Anti-African Prejudice*

		Father's Occupational Status†	
Anti-African Attitudes	*N*	*Manual*	*Non-manual*
		146	417
Less prejudiced half	280	34%	55%
More prejudiced half	283	66%	45%

* 2 × 2 chi-square = 18.90; $p < 0.001$.
† Sixty-four of the 627 students did not indicate their fathers' occupations.

sample members whose fathers are manually employed are significantly more intolerant of the African than those whose fathers are non-manually employed. The two groups differ in the same manner in their F-scale scores. But when authoritarianism is controlled for, the groups still differ significantly in their attitudes toward blacks.[6] In other words, the children of manual fathers are more prejudiced and more authoritarian than other students, and they remain more prejudiced even after the difference in authoritarianism is partialed out of the relationship. These upwardly mobile students must be carefully in step with the mores to establish firmly their rise in the social structure, and the mores of South Africa lead to intolerance.

Table 7 shows the sharp difference between the Afrikaner and English subjects in the sample. Afrikaners are both more anti-African and more authoritarian, and, when the F-scale differences are corrected for, they remain significantly more hostile to the African.[7] These 50 students are di-

---

[6] Authoritarianism can be controlled out in two ways. First, separate chi-square analyses of father's employment and anti-African attitudes were made for low and high F-scale halves. Second, the A- and F-scale scores were employed in an analysis of covariance that partialed out F scores. Both analyses indicate that father's employment is a significant correlate of anti-African attitudes even after authoritarianism is controlled out of the relationship.

[7] Authoritarianism was controlled out by both of the analyses described in the previous footnote. With their F-scale differences corrected for, Afrikaners in the sample are still significantly more hostile to the African than the English students. The cultural determination of this ethnic-group difference is made apparent when we survey the attitudes of the English students toward the Indians of South Africa. In sharp contrast to their African attitudes, the English members of the sample are considerably more anti-Indian—one-fifth of them "wish someone would kill all of them."

TABLE 7
Ethnic Group and Anti-African Prejudice*

| Anti-African Attitudes | N | Ethnic Group† | |
		Afrikaners	English
		50	513
Less prejudiced half	264	14%	50%
More prejudiced half	299	86%	50%

* 2 × 2 chi-square = 23.7; $p < 0.001$.

† Ethnic group is determined by both the student's own ethnic identification and the principal language spoken in his home. Sixty-four of the students identified with other groups (e.g., Jewish, French, German) and are not included in this analysis.

rectly subject to the national ethos and have no conflicting national reference, as many English-speaking South Africans have in Great Britain. Like the upwardly mobile, they are in roles that demand unusual conformity.

Table 8 clarifies further ethnic differences in attitudes toward the African. Sixteen of the A scale's eighteen statements significantly separate the Afrikaners from the English, the former scoring higher in all cases. And, moreover, there is a definite trend in these differences. The five items which discriminate poorest between the ethnic groups (items *n* through *r*) are all stereotyped-belief statements; they refer to the standard traits frequently associated with Africans—lazy, primitive, happy-go-lucky, and bad-smelling. Conversely, five of the six best discriminators (items *b* through *f*) are all exclusion-discrimination statements; they deny equal rights to Africans in employment, housing, and voting. Afrikaans-speaking and English-speaking students, then, do not differ sharply in the degree to which they harbor the traditional stereotype of the African, but they do possess markedly divergent views on discrimination against the African. A key to these differences may be provided in the lone exception to this trend, item *a*. Seven out of every ten Afrikaners, as compared with only a third of the English, believe that the "natives will always have a greater tendency toward crimes of violence than Europeans." Strong projection may be operating for those agreeing with this statement, but, in any event, it suggests that physical fear of the black man is especially prevalent among our Afrikaans-speaking respondents and that this may be the fundamental motivation for their emphasis on excluding and discriminating against the African.

All these findings point to the crucial role of the cultural milieu in shaping the attitudes of the white South African toward the blacks in his midst. While externalizing personality factors do not account for the students' unusually prejudiced attitudes concerning Africans, variables which reflect the dominant norms of the white society prove to be important. Students who are especially responsive to these norms—those who were born in Africa, those who identify with the Nationalist party, those who are upwardly mobile, and those who have been molded by the conservative traditions of the Afrikaans-speaking people—tend to be intolerant of Africans to some degree, regardless of their basic personality structure.

III. RACIAL PREJUDICE
IN THE SOUTHERN UNITED STATES

Similar considerations led to an earlier comparative study of anti-Negro prejudice in the southern and northern United States. While considerable evidence indicates that white southerners are typically more intolerant of the Negro than white northerners (16, 27, 30, 35, 36, 39), little work has been focused on the factors underlying this difference. But, like the South African data, the scant data available suggest that sociocultural and not externalization factors may be the crucial determinants of the contrasting regional attitudes toward the Negro.

Thus, if the South did have more externalizing personality potential for prejudice than other American areas, it should also be more anti-Semitic.[8] But Roper (31, 32) has twice found in his national polls that the South is one of the most tolerant regions toward Jews, and Prothro (30) has noted that 40 per cent of his adult white Louisiana sample is at the same time favorable in its attitudes toward Jews and highly anti-Negro. Furthermore, there is no evidence that the stern family pattern associated with "prejudiced personalities" (1, 12) is more prevalent in the South than in the North (6, 8). And, finally, the few white southern populations that have been given the F scale have obtained means that fall easily within the range of means reported for non-southern populations (1, 25, 37).

Rose categorically concludes: "There is no evidence that 'authoritarian personality' or frustration-aggression or scapegoating, or any known source of 'prejudice' in the psychological sense, is any more prevalent in the South than in the North" (33). And Prothro adds: "Situational, historical and cultural factors appear to be of considerable, perhaps major, import in addition to personality dynamics" in determining anti-Negro attitudes in the South (30).

In testing these ideas in the two regions, different methods were employed than those used in South Africa. Public opinion polling techniques were utilized with 366 randomly selected white adults in eight roughly matched communities in the North and South. The four small southern towns, located in Georgia and North Carolina, were chosen to have Negro population percentages ranging from 10 to 45 per cent, while the small

---

[8] This is true because the prejudiced personality is predisposed to disliking all socially recognized out-groups—Negroes, Jews, Catholics, etc.—and not just one. Being functionally necessary, prejudice generalizes to out-groups of all varieties (1, 2, 13).

TABLE 8

Ethnic-Group Differences on A-Scale Items

A-Scale Item	Percentage Agreement*		$2 \times 2\chi^2$	p
	Afrikaners	English		
a. Because of their primitive background, natives will always have a greater tendency toward crimes of violence than Europeans	70.0	34.9	33.6	0.001
b. Native musicians are sometimes as good as Europeans at swing music and jazz, but it is a mistake to have mixed native-European bands	86.0	54.2	18.8	.001
c. Most of the natives would become officious, overbearing, and disagreeable if not kept in their place	80.0	48.3	18.2	.001
d. Laws which would force equal employment opportunities for both the natives and Europeans would not be fair to European employers	74.0	44.2	16.2	.001
e. The natives have their rights, but it is best to keep them in their own districts and schools and to prevent too much contact with Europeans	86.0	63.7	9.9	.01
f. The natives do not deserve the right to vote	64.0	41.3	9.5	.01
g. The natives will never have the intelligence and organizing ability to run a modern industrial society	42.0	23.2	8.7	.01

h. As the native will never properly absorb our civilization, the only solution is to let him develop along his own lines	68.0	46.3	8.6	.01
i. Manual labor seems to fit the native mentality better than more skilled and responsible work	88.0	68.9	8.0	.01
j. Seldom, if ever, is a native superior to most Europeans intellectually	72.0	52.2	7.1	.01
k. The natives tend to be overly emotional	66.0	46.5	7.1	.01
l. Because of his immaturity, the South African native is likely to be led into all sorts of mischief and should therefore be strictly controlled in his own best interests	92.0	75.6	6.9	.01
m. The granting of wide educational opportunities to natives is a dangerous thing	36.0	19.9	6.9	.01
n. Most natives are lazy and lack ambition	60.0	44.1	4.6	.05
o. There is something inherently primitive and uncivilized in the native, as shown in his music and extreme aggressiveness	86.0	72.1	4.4	.05
p. Due to the differences in innate endowment, the Bantu race will always be inferior to the white race	54.0	39.6	4.0	.05
q. Most of the natives are happy-go-lucky and irresponsible	70.0	60.0	1.9	0.20
r. In spite of what some claim, the natives do have a different and more pronounced body odor than Europeans	84.0	81.5	0.2	n.s.

* Percentage agreement calculated as in Table 2.

northern towns, all located in New England, have less than 1 per cent Negroes each.

The interview schedule contained a ten-item measure of authoritarianism (F scale), an eight-item measure of anti-Semitism (A-S scale), and a twelve-item measure of anti-Negro prejudice (N scale), together with numerous background questions.[9] The poll purported to be concerned with the effects of the mass media upon public opinion, and it seems largely due to this guise that the blatantly phrased prejudice statements caused no interview breakoffs.

Of greatest immediate interest is the striking similarity in these results with those of the South African investigation. First, the southern sample is considerably more anti-Negro than the northern sample but is *not* more authoritarian. Similar to the Afrikaner-English differences (Table 8), the southerners respond in the more prejudiced direction on each of the N-scale statements but are most unique in their extreme attitudes concerning excluding and discriminating against the Negro. That is, southerners and northerners in the samples both share in large degree the lazy, primitive, happy-go-lucky, and bad-smelling stereotype of the Negro, but southerners far more than northerners wish to deny equal rights to the Negro in employment, housing, and voting. And yet there is no difference in the externalization potential for intolerance; the F-scale means of the two samples are almost identical.

Further similarities to the South African data support the contention that personality dynamics, such as authoritarianism, are not responsible for the sharp North-South divergence in attitudes toward the Negro. When age and education are partialed out,[10] the N and F scales correlate to a comparable degree in the two populations. Moreover, with age and education partialed out again, the N and A-S scales relate at equivalent levels in the two regional samples. In other words, the externalizing prejudiced personality as tapped by the F and A-S scales does not account for any more of the anti-Negro variance in the southern sample than it does in

[9] There is considerable overlap in items used in the two investigations. Again, all ten of the F items are taken from the work of Adorno *et al.* (1); seven were used in South Africa (Table 2, items *a*, *b*, *c*, *f*, *h*, *i*, and *k*); and the others are items 1, 13, and 21 of p. 255 in *The Authoritarian Personality* (1). The A-S items are all from the California investigations, too (1, items 3, 4, 13, 15, 22, and 24 on pp. 68–69 and items 4 and 15 on p. 70). Save for the word substitutions of "white" for "European" and "Negro" for "native," all twelve N-scale items were used in the South African A scale (Table 8, items *b*, *c*, *d*, *e*, *f*, *j*, *k*, *m*, *n*, *o*, *q*, and *r*). That virtually the same prejudice and authoritarian statements can be successfully used in the Union of South Africa and in the northern and southern United States suggests that racial prejudice and its personality concomitants take extremely similar forms in many parts of the Western world.

[10] This was not necessary in the South African data because the college sample is relatively homogeneous in terms of age and education. In heterogeneous, randomly drawn adult samples, however, age and education must be controlled, since both authoritarianism and prejudice are positively related to age and negatively related to education (2, 5, 16, 23).

the northern sample. This finding, combined with the previously mentioned fact that the two groups do not differ in their F-scale responses, indicates that externalization factors do not explain the heightened bigotry of the southerners. As with the South African results, we must turn to social variables in an effort to account for the regional discrepancy in attitudes toward the Negro.

All six of the sociocultural dimensions tested yield meaningful relationships with Negro prejudice in the southern sample: sex, church attendance, social mobility, political party identification, armed service, and education. These variables reflect southern culture in a manner similar to the social variables tested in the South African study. And as in South Africa, those southerners, who by their roles in the social structure can be anticipated to be conforming to the dictates of the culture, prove to be more prejudiced against Negroes than their counterparts. For example, females, the "carriers of culture," are significantly more anti-Negro than men in the southern sample but *not* in the northern sample.

Two other groups of southerners who manifest conforming behavior in other areas are also more intolerant of Negroes.[11] Respondents who have been to church within the week are significantly more anti-Negro than those who have not been within the month, and there is a tendency (though not statistically significant) for the upwardly mobile to be more anti-Negro than others in the non-manual occupational class. The latter result recalls the finding in the South African study that students whose fathers are manual workers tend to be more anti-African (Table 6). In the northern sample, no such trends appear. Protestant churchgoers in the North tend to be more tolerant of the Negro than Protestant non-attenders, and no relationship between upward mobility and attitudes toward Negroes is discernible. Conformity to northern norms—unlike conformity to southern or South African norms—is not associated with hostility for the black man.

In contrast to the conformers, southerners who evidence deviance from the mores in some area of social life tend to be *less* anti-Negro. Non-attenders of church furnish one example. Another example are respondents who explicitly identify themselves as political independents, which also represents a degree of deviance: they tend to be considerably more tolerant of the Negro than are southerners who consider themselves either Democrats or Republicans.[12] Again, no such discrepancy occurs in the northern population.

[11] The church attendance, social mobility, political party identification, and armed service findings reported here were all established with matched-pair analyses. This design made it possible to control the age, education, and sex variables out of these relationships. The detailed results are published elsewhere (29).

[12] It might be thought that Republican party membership in the South constitutes deviance, too. Actually, the "solid South" is not that politically solid; three of the four southern communities polled have favored some Republican candidates in recent elections.

Downward mobility has been noted by other investigators to be positively related to intolerance in the North (3, 10), and this finding is replicated in the present northern data. But in the southern data a striking
reversal occurs. The downwardly mobile in the South are much less anti-
Negro than other manually employed respondents, though the two groups
do not differ in authoritarianism. Perhaps in a culture that emphasizes
status and family background, that makes a sharp distinction between
"poor whites" and "respectable whites," and that cherishes its aristocratic
traditions (4, 6, 8), the downwardly mobile southerner learns to reject
much of his culture. And rejecting the culture's stress on tradition and
status makes it easier to reject also the culture's dicta concerning the
Negro.

Two groups of southerners—armed service veterans and the highly
educated—are potential deviants from southern culture simply because
their special experience and study have brought them into contact with
other ways of life. And, as we might expect, we find that both veterans
and college-educated southerners are considerably more tolerant of the
Negro than non-veterans and the poorly educated. Veterans in both regions prove to be more authoritarian than non-veterans,[13] and, consistent
with this, northern veterans are less tolerant of Negroes than northerners
who had not served. Education is negatively related to N-scale scores in the
northern sample, too, but significantly less than in the southern sample.
Exposure to non-southern culture leads to deviance from the strict southern
norms concerning the Negro; little wonder that southerners who have been
out of the region for any considerable length of time are generally viewed
as suspect by their neighbors upon return.

These consistent relationships with social factors in the southern data
have been interpreted in terms of conformity and deviance from the narrowly prescribed mores of small-town southern life. Evidence for such an
analysis comes from a final intra-southern difference. Southern communities with high Negro population ratios (38 and 45 per cent) have significantly higher N-scale means than the other communities sampled in the
South with low Negro ratios (10 and 18 per cent), though they are *not*
different in authoritarianism or anti-Semitism. In southern areas with the
most intensely anti-Negro norms, prejudice against the black southerner is
greater, even though there is not a greater amount of externalizing personality potential for prejudice.

Though limited by the restricted samples employed, this evidence indicates that sociocultural factors—as in the South African sample—are
indeed the key to the regional difference in attitudes toward the Negro.
In spite of the marked contrast in samples and method between the two
investigations, both the South African and the southern results underline

---

[13] Presumably this increased authoritarianism of veterans is related to their service
experience in authoritarian environments, though Christie (5) failed to note an increase
in F scores of army recruits after six weeks of infantry basic training.

the unique importance of social variables in prejudice that is sanctioned by the cultural norms.

IV. SUMMARY AND CONCLUSIONS

Finely interwoven personality and sociocultural variables together form the foundation upon which a broad and satisfactory theory of racial prejudice must be built. Neither set of factors can be neglected, but a heuristic separation between the relatively culture-free externalization factors and social factors aids analysis. The present paper uses this distinction to interpret prejudice data from two parts of the world with tense racial conflict —the Union of South Africa and the southern United States.

Externalization factors such as authoritarianism are associated with prejudice in both the South African and the southern samples at levels roughly comparable with other areas. Data from the South African students hint, however, that susceptibility to conform may be an unusually important psychological component of prejudice in regions where the cultural norms positively sanction intolerance. In addition, there is no indication in either of these samples that there is any more externalizing personality potential for prejudice in these areas than in more tolerant parts of the globe.

The extensive racial prejudice of the South African and southern groups seems directly linked with the antiblack dictates of the two cultures. Sociocultural factors which reflect the mores consistently relate to prejudice—place of birth, political party preference, upward mobility, and ethnic-group membership in the South African data and sex, church attendance, social mobility, political party identification, armed service, and education in the southern data. The pattern is clear: conformity to South African or southern mores is associated with racial intolerance, while deviance from these mores is associated with racial tolerance.

Taken together with other published work, these limited results suggest a broad, cross-national hypothesis:

In areas with historically imbedded traditions of racial intolerance, externalizing personality factors underlying prejudice remain important, but sociocultural factors are unusually crucial and account for the heightened racial hostility.

Should future, more extensive, research support such a hypothesis, its implications for prejudice theory would be considerable. Regions or peoples with heightened prejudice against a particular outgroup would not necessarily be thought of as harboring more authoritarianism; the special conflict may reflect the operation of particular historical, cultural, and social factors. Such a prospect may be encouraging to many action programs— efforts which typically are more successful at changing a person's relation to his culture than they are at changing basic personality structure. Desegregation is a case in point. The success of the movement in the South does not depend—this hypothesis would contend—on changing the deeply ingrained orientations of prejudice-prone personalities; rather, it rests on the effectiveness with which racial integration now going on in the South can restructure the mores to which so many culturally intolerant southerners conform.

A second implication of the hypothesis is that personality factors such as authoritarianism and susceptibility to conform cannot be overlooked in understanding bigotry even in parts of the world like the Union of South Africa and the southern United States. Most psychological approaches to prejudice, it has been noted, are concerned chiefly with the externalization function of attitudes. Perhaps, as the object-appraisal and social-adjustment functions of attitudes are studied in more detail, the direct personality concomitants of cultural pressures will be isolated and better understood.

References

1. Adorno, T. W., Frenkel-Brunswik, Else, Levinson, D. J., and Sanford, R. N. *The Authoritarian Personality*. New York: Harper & Bros., 1950.
2. Allport, G. W. *The Nature of Prejudice*. Cambridge, Mass: Addison-Wesley Press, 1954.
3. Bettelheim, B., and Janowitz, M. *Dynamics of Prejudice*. New York: Harper & Bros., 1950.
4. Cash, W. *The Mind of the South*. New York: Knopf, 1941.
5. Christie, R. "Authoritarianism Re-examined." In R. Christie and M. Jahoda (eds.), *Studies in the Scope and Method of "The Authoritarian Personality,"* pp. 123–196. Glencoe, Ill.: Free Press, 1954.
6. Davis, A., Gardner, B., and Gardner, Mary. *Deep South*. Chicago: University of Chicago Press, 1941.
7. Deutsch, M., and Collins, M. *Interracial Housing*. Minneapolis: University of Minnesota Press, 1951.
8. Dollard, J. *Caste and Class in a Southern Town*. New Haven, Conn.: Yale University Press, 1937.
9. ————, Doob, L., Miller, N., Mowrer, O., and Sears, R. *Frustration and Aggression*. New Haven, Conn.: Yale University Press, 1939.
10. Greenblum, J., and Pearlin, L. "Vertical Mobility and Prejudice: A Sociopsychological Analysis." In R. Bendix and S. Lipset (eds.), *Class, Status, and Power*, pp. 480–491. Glencoe, Ill.: Free Press, 1953.
11. Harding, J., and Hogrefe, R. "Attitudes of White Department Store Employees toward Negro Co-workers," *Journal of Social Issues*, VIII, No. 1 (1952), 18–28.
12. Harris, D. B., Gough, H. G., and Martin, W. E. "Children's Ethnic Attitudes. II. Relationship to Parental Beliefs concerning Child Training," *Child Development*, XXI (1950), 169–181.
13. Hartley, E. L. *Problems in Prejudice*. New York: Kings Crown Press, 1946.
14. Hellmann, Ellen (ed.). *Handbook on Race Relations in South Africa*. Cape Town, South Africa: Oxford University Press, 1949.

15. Hoffman, M. L. "Some Psychodynamic Factors in Compulsive Conformity," *Journal of Abnormal and Social Psychology*, XLVIII (1953), 383–393.
16. Hyman, H. H., and Sheatsley, P. B. "Attitudes toward Desegregation," *Scientific American*, CXCV (1956), 35–39.
17. Jones, E. "City Limits." In D. Shoemaker (ed.), *With All Deliberate Speed*, pp. 71–87. New York: Harper & Bros., 1957.
18. Kutner, B., Wilkins, Carol, and Yarrow, Penny. "Verbal Attitudes and Overt Behavior Involving Racial Prejudice," *Journal of Abnormal and Social Psychology*, XLVII (1952), 649–52.
19. La Piere, R. T. "Attitudes versus Actions," *Social Forces*, XIII (1934), 230–237.
20. McLean, Helen V. "Psychodynamic Factors in Racial Relations," *Annals of the American Academy of Political and Social Science*, CCXLIV (1946), 159–166.
21. MacCrone, I. D. *Race Attitudes in South Africa*. London: Oxford University Press, 1937.
22. ———. "Ethnocentric Ideology and Ethnocentrism," *Proceedings of the South African Psychological Association*, IV (1953), 21–24.
23. MacKinnon, W. J., and Centers, R. "Authoritarianism and Urban Stratification," *American Journal of Sociology*, XLI (1956), 610–620.
24. Malherbe, E. G. *Race Attitudes and Education*. Johannesburg, South Africa: Institute of Race Relations, 1946.
25. Milton, O. "Presidential Choice and Performance on a Scale of Authoritarianism," *American Psychologist*, VII (1952), 597–598.
26. Minard, R. D. "Race Relations in the Pocahontas Coal Field," *Journal of Social Issues*, VIII, No. 1 (1952), 29–44.
27. Myrdal, G. *An American Dilemma*. New York: Harper & Bros., 1944.
28. Pettigrew, T. F. "Desegregation and Its Chances for Success: Northern and Southern Views," *Social Forces*, XXXV (1957), 339–344.
29. ———. "Regional Differences in Anti-Negro Prejudice" (manuscript presently submitted for publication).
30. Prothro, E. T. "Ethnocentrism and Anti-Negro Attitudes in the Deep South," *Journal of Abnormal and Social Psychology*, XLVII (1952), 105–108.
31. Roper, E. "United States Anti-Semites," *Fortune*, XXXIII (1946), 257–260.
32. ———. "United States Anti-Semites," *Fortune*, XXXVI (1947), 5–10.
33. Rose, A. M. "Intergroup Relations vs. Prejudice: Pertinent Theory for the Study of Social Change," *Social Problems*, IV (1956), 173–176.
34. Saenger, G., and Gilbert, Emily. "Customer Reactions to the Integration of Negro Sales Personnel," *International Journal of Opinion and Attitude Research*, IV (1950), 57–76.
35. Samelson, Babette. "The Patterning of Attitudes and Beliefs Regarding the American Negro: An Analysis of Public Opinion." Unpublished doctoral dissertation, Radcliffe College, 1945.
36. Sims, V. M., and Patrick, J. R. "Attitude towards the Negro of Northern and Southern College Students," *Journal of Social Psychology*, VII (1936), 192–204.
37. Smith, C. U., and Prothro, J. W. "Ethnic Differences in Authoritarian Personality," *Social Forces*, XXXV (1957), 334–338.

38. Smith, M. B., Bruner, J. S., and White, R. W. *Opinions and Personality.* New York: John Wiley & Sons, 1956.
39. Stouffer, S. A., Suchman, E. A., DeVinney, L. C., Star, Shirley A., and Williams, R. M., Jr. *The American Soldier: Adjustment during Army Life.* ("Studies in Social Psychology in World War II," Vol. I.) Princeton: Princeton University Press, 1949.
40. Wilner, D. M., Walkley, R. P., and Cook, S. W. "Residential Proximity and Intergroup Relations in Public Housing Projects," *Journal of Social Issues,* VIII, No. 1 (1952), 45–69.

35

Contraculture and Subculture

J. MILTON YINGER
Oberlin College

In recent years there has been widespread and fruitful employment of the concept of subculture in sociological and anthropological research. The term has been used to focus attention not only on the wide diversity of norms to be found in many societies but on the normative aspects of deviant behavior. The ease with which the term has been adopted, with little study of its exact meaning or its values and its difficulties, is indicative of its utility in emphasizing a sociological point of view in research that has been strongly influenced both by individualistic and moralistic interpretations. To describe the normative qualities of an occupation, to contrast the value systems of social classes, or to emphasize the controlling power of the code of a delinquent gang is to underline a sociological aspect of these phenomena that is often disregarded.

In the early days of sociology and anthropology, a key task was to document the enormous variability of culture from society to society and to explore the significance of the overly simplified but useful idea that "the mores can make anything right." In recent years that task has been extended to the study of the enormous variability of culture *within* some societies. It is unfortunate that "subculture," a central concept in this process, has seldom been adequately defined.[1] It has been used as an *ad*

Reprinted from *American Sociological Review*, 25, 5 (October 1960) 625–635, by permission of the author and The American Sociological Association.

[1] There are a few formal definitions. For example: "The term 'subculture' refers in this paper to 'cultural variants displayed by certain segments of the population.' Subcultures are distinguished not by one or two isolated traits—they constitute relatively cohesive cultural systems. They are worlds within the larger world of our national culture." (Mirra Komarovsky and S. S. Sargent, "Research into Subcultural Influences upon Personality," in S. S. Sargent and M. W. Smith, editors, *Culture and Personality*, New York: The Viking Fund, 1949, p. 143.) These authors then refer to class, race, occupation, residence, and region. After referring to sub-group values and language, Kimball Young and Raymond W. Mack state: "Such shared learned behaviors which are common to a specific group or category are called *subcultures*." (*Sociology and Social Life*, New York: American Book, 1959, p. 49.) They refer then to ethnic, occupational, and regional variations. Blaine Mercer writes: "A society contains numerous subgroups, each with its own characteristic ways of thinking and acting. These cultures within a culture are called *subcultures*." (*The Study of Society*, New York: Harcourt-Brace, 1958, p. 34.) Thereafter he discusses Whyte's *Streetcorner Society*. Although these definitions are helpful, they fail to make several distinctions which are developed below.

hoc concept whenever a writer wished to emphasize the normative aspects of behavior that differed from some general standard. The result has been a blurring of the meaning of the term, confusion with other terms, and a failure frequently to distinguish between two levels of social causation.

THREE USAGES OF SUBCULTURE

Few concepts appear so often in current sociological writing. In the course of twelve months, I have noted over 100 books and articles that make some use, from incidental to elaborate, of the idea of "subculture." The usages vary so widely, however, that the value of the term is severely limited. If chemists had only one word to refer to all colorless liquids and this led them to pay attention to only the two characteristics shared in common, their analysis would be exceedingly primitive. Such an analogy overstates the diversity of ideas covered by "subculture," but the range is very wide. Nevertheless three distinct meanings can be described.

In some anthropological work, subculture refers to certain universal tendencies that seem to occur in all societies. They underlie culture, precede it, and set limits to the range of its variation. Thus Kroeber writes: "Indeed, such more or less recurrent near-regularities of form or process as have to date been formulated for culture are actually subcultural in nature. They are limits set to culture by physical or organic factors." [2] In *The Study of Man*, Linton uses subculture to refer to various pan-human phenomena that seem to occur everywhere. Thus goodnatured and tyrannical parents may be found in societies that differ widely in their family patterns.[3] This use shades off into other concepts that are similar but not identical: Edward Sapir's "precultural" and Cooley's "human nature" refer to biological and social influences that underlie all cultures.[4] Since subculture is only rarely used today to refer to this series of ideas, I shall exclude them from further consideration, with the suggestion that the use of Sapir's term "precultural" might well clarify our thinking.

Two other usages of subculture represent a much more serious confusion. The term is often used to point to the normative systems of groups

[2] A. L. Kroeber, "The Concept of Culture in Science," *Journal of General Education*, 3 (April, 1949), p. 187. See also Clyde Kluckhohn's reference to this idea in "Culture and Behavior," in Gardner Lindzey, editor, *Handbook of Social Psychology*, Cambridge: Addison-Wesley, 1954, Vol. 2, p. 954; and A. L. Kroeber in "Problems of Process: Results," in Sol Tax *et al.*, editors, *An Appraisal of Anthropology Today*, Chicago: University of Chicago Press, 1953, p. 119.

[3] Ralph Linton, *The Study of Man*, New York: Appleton-Century, 1936, p. 486. See also his *The Cultural Background of Personality*, New York: Appleton-Century-Crofts, 1945, pp. 148–151. Elsewhere in *The Study of Man*, Linton uses subculture in a different sense, similar to the second usage described below.

[4] Edward Sapir, "Personality," in *Encyclopedia of the Social Sciences*, New York: Macmillan, 1931, Vol. 12, p. 86; Charles H. Cooley, *Human Nature and the Social Order*, revised edition, New York: Scribner, 1922.

smaller than a society, to give emphasis to the way these groups differ in such things as language, values, religion, diet, and style of life from the larger society of which they are a part. Perhaps the most common referent in this usage is an ethnic enclave (French Canadians in Maine) or a region (the subculture of the South),[5] but the distinctive norms of much smaller and more temporary groups (even a particular friendship group) may be described as a subculture. Kluckhohn, for example, refers to "the subculture of anthropologists" and Riesman to "subcultures among the faculty."

This second meaning, which itself contains some ambiguities, as we shall see, must be distinguished from a third meaning associated with it when the reference is to norms that arise specifically from a frustrating situation or from conflict between a group and the larger society. Thus the emergent norms of a delinquent gang or the standards of an adolescent peer group have often been designated "subcultural." In addition to a cultural dimension, this third usage introduces a social-psychological dimension, for there is direct reference to the personality factors involved in the development and maintenance of the norms. Specifically, such personality tendencies as frustration, anxiety, feelings of role ambiguity, and resentment are shown to be involved in the creation of the subculture. The mutual influence of personality and culture is not a distinctive characteristic of this type of subculture, of course, for they are everywhere interactive. Thus:

> Tendencies for parents to respond harshly to their children's aggressive behavior, for instance, if common to the members of a society, are to be referred equally to the culture and to the modal personality of the parents. But the result in the developing child is not a foregone conclusion: present knowledge suggests that under specifiable conditions outcomes as different as rigid politeness or touchy latent hostility may follow. These consequences in turn may lead to cultural elaborations that seem superficially remote from the cultural starting point, yet are dynamically linked with it . . . .[6]

[5] See, e.g., John K. Morland, *Millways of Kent*, Chapel Hill: University of North Carolina Press, 1958; Julian Steward, *The People of Puerto Rico*, Champaign: University of Illinois Press, 1956; Charles Wagley and Marvin Harris, "A Typology of Latin American Subcultures," *American Anthropologist*, 57 (June, 1955), pp. 428–451; Evon Z. Vogt, "American Subcultural *Continua* as Exemplified by the Mormons and Texans," *American Anthropologist*, 57 (December, 1955), pp. 1163–1172; Murray Straus, "Subcultural Variations in Ceylonese Mental Ability: A Study in National Character," *Journal of Social Psychology*, 39 (February, 1954), pp. 129–141; Joel B. Montague and Edgar G. Epps, "Attitudes Toward Social Mobility as Revealed by Samples of Negro and White Boys," *Pacific Sociological Review*, 1 (Fall, 1958), pp. 81–84; Hylan Lewis, *Blackways of Kent*, Chapel Hill: University of North Carolina Press, 1955; Robin M. Williams, Jr., *American Society*, New York: Knopf, 1951, Chapter 10; T. S. Langner, "A Test of Intergroup Prejudice Which Takes Account of Individual and Group Differences in Values," *Journal of Abnormal and Social Psychology*, 48 (October, 1953), pp. 548–554.

[6] Brewster Smith, "Anthropology and Psychology," in John Gillin, editor, *For a Science of Social Man*, New York: Macmillan, 1954, p. 61. See also Talcott Parsons

As this quotation suggests, culture and personality are always empirically tied together. Yet the nature of the relation is not the same in all
cases. The term subculture, when used in the third way described here,
raises to a position of prominence one particular kind of dynamic linkage
between norms and personality: the creation of a series of inverse or
counter values (opposed to those of the surrounding society) in face of
serious frustration or conflict. To call attention to the special aspects of
this kind of normative system, I suggest the term *contraculture*. Before
exploring the relationship between subculture and contraculture, however, the range of meanings given subculture even when it is limited to
the second usage requires comment.

SUBCULTURE AND ROLE

The variety of referents for the term subculture is very wide because
the normative systems of sub-societies can be differentiated on many
grounds. The groups involved may range from a large regional subdivision
to a religious sect with only one small congregation. The distinctive norms
may involve many aspects of life—religion, language, diet, moral values—
or, for example, only a few separate practices among the members of an
occupational group. Further distinctions among subcultures might be made
on the basis of time (has the subculture persisted through a number of
generations?), origin (by migration, absorption, by a dominant society,
social or physical segregation, occupational specialization, and other
sources) and by the mode of relationship to the surrounding culture (from
indifference to conflict). Such wide variation in the phenomena covered
by a term can be handled by careful specification of the several grounds for
subclassification. Confusion has arisen not so much from the scope of the
term subculture as from its use as a substitute for "role." Only with great
effort is some degree of clarity being achieved in the use of the role concept and the related terms "position" and "role behavior." [7] Were this
development retarded by confusion of role with subculture it would be
unfortunate. All societies have differentiating roles, but only heterogeneous
societies have subcultures. Role is *that part of* a full culture that is as-

---

and Edward A. Shils, editors, *Toward A General Theory of Action*, Cambridge: Harvard
University Press, 1951, esp. the monograph by the editors; and Ralph Linton's preface
to Abram Kardiner, *The Psychological Frontiers of Society*, New York: Columbia University Press, 1945.

[7] See, e.g., Neal Gross, Ward S. Mason, and A. W. McEachern, *Explorations in
Role Analysis*, New York: Wiley, 1958; F. L. Bates, "Position, Role, and Status: A Reformulation of Concepts," *Social Forces*, 34 (May, 1956), pp. 313–321; Robert K.
Merton, "The Role-Set: Problems in Sociological Theory," *British Journal of Sociology*, 8 (June, 1957), pp. 106–120; S. F. Nadel, *The Theory of Social Structure*, Glencoe, Ill.: Free Press, 1957; Theodore R. Sarbin, "Role Theory," in *Handbook of Social
Psychology, op. cit.*, Vol. 1, Chapter 6.

signed, as the appropriate rights and duties, to those occupying a given position.[8] These rights and duties usually interlock into a system with those of persons who occupy other positions. They are known to and accepted by all those who share the culture. Thus the role of a physician is known, at least in vague outline, by most persons in a society and it is seen as part of the total culture. (This is not to prejudge the question of role consensus, for there may be many non-role aspects of being a physician.) But subculture is not tied in this way into the larger cultural complex: it refers to norms that set a group apart from, not those that integrate a group with, the total society. Subcultural norms, as contrasted with role norms, are unknown to, looked down upon, or thought of as separating forces by the other members of a society. There are doubtless subcultural aspects of being a physician—normative influences affecting his behavior that are not part of his role, not culturally designated rights and duties. But the empirical mixture should not obscure the need for this analytic distinction.

Along with confusion with the role concept, subculture carries many of the ambiguities associated with the parent concept of culture. In much social scientific writing it is not at all clear whether culture refers to norms, that is, to expected or valued behavior, or to behavior that is widely followed and therefore normal in a statistical sense only. This dual referent is particularly likely to be found in the work of anthropologists. Perhaps because their concepts are derived largely from the study of relatively more stable and homogeneous societies, they draw less sharply the distinction between the statistically normal and the normative. Sociologists are more apt to find it necessary to explore the tensions between the social order and culture, to be alert to deviations, and they are therefore more likely to define culture abstractly as a shared normative system. Yet much of the commentary on subculture refers to behavior. In my judgment this identification is unwise. Behavior is the result of the convergence of many forces. One should not assume, when the members of a group behave in similar ways, that cultural norms produce this result. Collective behavior theory and personality theory may also help to account for the similarities.

CONTRACULTURE

Failure to distinguish between role and subculture and vagueness in the concept of culture itself are not the only difficulties in the use of the idea of subculture. Perhaps more serious is the tendency to obscure, under this one term, two levels of explanation, one sociological and the other social-psychological, with a resulting failure to understand the causal forces at work. On few topics can one get wider agreement among sociologists

---

[8] It is possible, of course, for a subculture to specify roles within its own system.

than on the dangers of reductionism. If a psychologist attempts to explain social facts by psychological theories, we throw the book (probably Durkheim) at him; we emphasize the "fallacy of misplaced concreteness." In view of the widespread neglect of socio-cultural factors in the explanation of behavior, this is a necessary task. It makes vitally important, however, keen awareness by sociologists that they also deal with an abstract model. Perhaps we can reverse Durkheim's dictum to say: Do not try to explain social psychological facts by sociological theories; or, more adequately, do not try to explain *behavior* (a product of the interaction of sociocultural and personality influences) by a sociological theory alone. Yablonsky has recently reminded us that an excessively sociological theory of gangs can result in our seeing a definite group structure and a clear pattern of norms where in fact there is a "near-group," with an imprecise definition of boundaries and limited agreement on norms.[9] Carelessly used, our concepts can obscure the facts we seek to understand.

To see the cultural element in delinquency or in the domination of an individual by his adolescent group, phenomena that on the surface are non-cultural or even "anti-cultural," was a long step forward in their explanation. But it is also necessary to see the non-cultural aspects of some "norms"—phenomena that on the surface seem thoroughly cultural. Our vocabulary needs to be rich enough to help us to deal with these differences. The tendency to use the same term to refer to phenomena that share *some* elements in common, disregarding important differences, is to be content with phyla names when we need also to designate genus and species.

To sharpen our analysis, I suggest the use of the term contraculture wherever the normative system of a group contains, as a primary element, a theme of conflict with the values of the total society, where personality variables are directly involved in the development and maintenance of the group's values, and wherever its norms can be understood only by reference to the relationships of the group to a surrounding dominant culture.[10] None of these criteria definitely separates contraculture from

---

[9] Lewis Yablonsky, "The Delinquent Gang as a Near-Group," *Social Problems*, 7 (Fall, 1959), pp. 108–117.

[10] By the noun in "contraculture" I seek to call attention to the normative aspects of the phenomena under study and by the qualifying prefix to call attention to the conflict aspects. Similar terms are occasionally found in the literature, but they are either defined only by their use in context or are used differently from the meaning assigned to contraculture in this paper. Harold D. Lasswell uses the term "countermores" to refer to "culture patterns which appeal mainly to the *id* . . . ." (*World Politics and Personal Insecurity*, New York: McGraw-Hill, 1935, p. 64). He then designates "revolutionists, prostitutes, prisoners, obscene and subversive talk"—which scarcely suggest a clear analytic category. In *World Revolutionary Propaganda*, New York: Knopf, 1939, Lasswell and Dorothy Blumenstock discuss the use of inverse values as a revolutionary propaganda weapon and comment on the presumed vulnerability of deprived persons to the countermores stressed in this propaganda. In *Power and Society*, New Haven: Yale University Press, 1950, p. 49, Lasswell uses the term somewhat differently: "*Counter-*

subculture because each is a continuum. Sub-societies fall along a range with respect to each criterion. The values of most subcultures probably conflict in some measure with the larger culture. In a contraculture, however, the conflict element is central; many of the values, indeed, are specifically contradictions of the values of the dominant culture. Similarly, personality variables are involved in the development and maintenance of all cultures and subcultures, but usually the influence of personality is by way of variations around a theme that is part of the culture. In a contraculture, on the other hand, the theme itself expresses the tendencies of the persons who compose it. Finally, the norms of all subcultures are doubtless affected in some degree by the nature of the relationship with the larger culture. A subculture, as a pure type, however, does not require, for its understanding, intensive analysis of interaction with the larger culture; that is, its norms are not, to any significant degree, a product of that interaction. But a contraculture can be understood only by giving full attention to the interaction of the group which is its bearer with the larger society. It is one thing to say that the subculture of the rural, lower-class Negro encourages slow, inefficient work. It is another thing to say, with Charles S. Johnson, that such a norm represents "pseudo-ignorant malingering," a contracultural way of describing the same phenomenon. Johnson stressed the conflict element, the extent to which the norm was a product of interaction of white and Negro. There is certainly value in emphasizing the subcultural source of some of the values of southern Negroes. Against racist views or individual explanations, the sociologist opposes the subcultural: If they strive less, have different sexual mores, or otherwise vary from standards of the dominant society, it is in part because they have been socialized in accordance with different norms. But this is not enough, for their similar behavior may be interpreted in part as a shared response to a frustrating environment.

Empirically, subcultural and contracultural influences may be mixed, of course. Delinquency and adolescent behavior almost certainly manifest both influences. The need, however, is to develop a clean analytic distinc-

---

mores are culture traits symbolized by the group as deviations from the mores, and yet are expected to occur." A certain amount of bribery, for example, is "normal" "and must be included by the candid observer as part of culture."

At various points, Talcott Parsons more nearly approaches the meaning of the concept contraculture as used here, although more by implication than by direct definition, and without distinguishing it from the concept of subculture. Referring to the ideological aspects of a subculture, he writes: "In such cases of an open break with the value-system and ideology of the wider society we may speak of a 'counter-ideology.'" (*The Social System*, Glencoe, Ill.: Free Press, 1951, p. 355.) And later: "If, however, the culture of the deviant group, like that of the delinquent gang, remains a 'counter-culture' it is difficult to find the bridges by which it can acquire influence over wider circles" (p. 522). It is not clear from these uses how counter-ideology and counter-culture are to be defined; but the important place Parsons gives to the element of ambivalence in his use of the concept subculture suggests that he has in mind something similar to our concept of contraculture in his use of these various terms. (See *ibid.*, p. 286.)

tion between the two in order to interpret the wide variations in their mixture.

ADOLESCENT SUBCULTURE AND
CONTRACULTURE

The utility of the distinction between contraculture and subculture can be tested by applying it to several research problems where the concept of subculture has been widely used. There is an extensive literature that interprets the behavior of adolescents substantially in these terms.[11] In the words of Havighurst and Taba: "Recent studies of adolescents have emphasized the fact that boys and girls in their teens have a culture of their own with moral standards and with moral pressures behind those standards. This culture has been called the 'adolescent peer culture.'"[12] Or Riesman: "All the morality is the group's. Indeed, even the fact that it is a morality is concealed by the confusing notion that the function of the group is to have fun, to play. . . ."[13] A close reading of the literature on adolescent culture reveals at least four different levels of interpretation, often only partially distinguished:

1. There is a cultural level, in which the roles of adolescent boys and girls are described, or the specialties (in Linton's sense) are designated. There is no reason to introduce concepts other than role or specialty to refer to norms that are generally accepted by elders and youths alike as appropriate to youth.

2. On the subcultural level, there are norms that manifest some separate system of values accepted within the adolescent group. These norms are not part of the role of youth. In part they are unknown to the elders; in part they conflict with standards accepted by the elders. They are learned, not by socialization in the total society, but by interaction within the sub-society of youth. Thus interests, games, speech patterns, and

---

[11] See Talcott Parsons, *Essays in Sociological Theory Pure and Applied*, Glencoe, Ill.: Free Press, 1949, Chapter 5; Howard Becker, *German Youth: Bond or Free*, New York: Oxford, 1946; S. N. Eisenstadt, *From Generation to Generation. Age Groups and the Social Structure*, Glencoe, Ill.: Free Press, 1956; David Riesman et al., *The Lonely Crowd*, New Haven: Yale University Press, 1950; R. J. Havighurst and Hilda Taba, *Adolescent Character and Personality*, New York: Wiley, 1949; Kingsley Davis, "The Sociology of Parent-Youth Conflict," *American Sociological Review*, 5 (August, 1940), pp. 523–534; Ralph Linton, "Age and Sex Categories," *American Sociological Review*, 7 (October, 1942), pp. 589–603; Joseph R. Gusfield, "The Problem of Generations in an Organizational Structure," *Social Forces*, 35 (May, 1957), pp. 323–330. For some contradictory evidence, see W. A. Westley and Frederick Elkin, "The Protective Environment and Adolescent Socialization," *Social Forces*, 35 (March, 1957), pp. 243–249; and Elkin and Westley, "The Myth of Adolescent Culture," *American Sociological Review*, 20 (December, 1955), pp. 680–684.

[12] *Op. cit.*, p. 35.

[13] *Op. cit.*, p. 72.

aesthetic tastes may be communicated among an age-group with little reference to the larger culture.

3. There are currents of fashion or of other collective behavior that sweep through an adolescent group, strongly influencing the behavior of its members.[14] Although it is difficult to distinguish fashion from culture —many empirical phenomena have aspects of both—it is wise to keep them apart conceptually. This is not always done. The terminology of Riesman is closer to that of fashion than of culture, but the net impression of his analysis is that he is thinking of control by the peer group primarily as a cultural phenomenon.[15] And the sentence following the one quoted above from Havighurst and Taba reads: "Boys and girls, desiring the approval of their age mates, follow the fashions of the peer culture in morals, dress, and speech. . . ." If the peer group influence stems from fashion, then strictly speaking it is not culture. The two differ to some degree in their origins, their functions, and their consequences.[16]

4. Many analyses of the control exercised by a youth group over its members employ the *concept* of contraculture, although the terminology and the assumptions are often those of subculture or culture. There is emphasis on the cross-pressures which young people feel: they want to be adults, yet fear to leave the securities of childhood; they experience contradictory adult treatment—a demand for grownup behavior here, the prevention of it there; ambiguity of self-image leads to efforts to prove oneself a full-fledged adult; there is sexual frustration. The peer group may help one to struggle with these cross-pressures, as described by Parsons: "Perhaps the best single point of reference for characterizing the youth culture lies in its contrast with the dominant pattern of the adult male role. By contrast with emphasis on responsibility in this role, the orientation of the youth culture is more or less specifically irresponsible." [17] This irresponsibility cannot be understood simply as another cultural norm, as part of the "role" of youth, although these are Parsons' terms. It must be studied in the context of strain, of role ambiguity. Some sociologists explain this irresponsibility as merely a manifestation of the youth culture, thus obscuring the personality factors also involved. The description and analysis of an adolescent subculture, to be sure, are an important contri-

[14] See Harold Finestone, "Cats, Kicks, and Color," *Social Problems*, 5 (July, 1957), pp. 3–13. Here the "cat" among some Negroes is seen as "the personal counterpart of an expressive social movement."

[15] See Riesman, *op. cit.*, esp. Chapter 3, "A Jury of Their Peers."

[16] The desirability of keeping distinct the analytic concepts of culture and collective behavior, including fashion, cannot be elaborated here. See Herbert Blumer, "Collective Behavior," in A. M. Lee, editor, *Principles of Sociology*, New York: Barnes and Nobel, 1951; Ralph H. Turner and Lewis M. Killian, *Collective Behavior*, Englewood Cliffs, N. J.: Prentice-Hall, 1957; Edward Sapir, "Fashion," *Encyclopedia of the Social Sciences*, New York: Macmillan, 1931, Vol. 6, pp. 139–144; Georg Simmel, "Fashion," *American Journal of Sociology*, 62 (May, 1957), pp. 541–558.

[17] Parsons, *op. cit. Essays* . . . , p. 92.

bution to the sociology of youth. Many adolescents spend a great deal of time in groups that sustain norms different from those of the adult world; and adults often respond to the behavior that follows these norms in an "ethnocentric" way. To rely on a subcultural explanation alone, however, is to disregard the emergent quality of many of the standards and to minimize the fact that they are often in direct conflict with adult standards (which most adolescents themselves will soon accept).

This sharp conflict of values requires explanation. Parsons states the facts clearly: "Negatively, there is a strong tendency to repudiate interests in adult things, and to feel at least a certain recalcitrance to the pressure of adult expectations and disciplines. . . . Thus the youth culture is not only, as is true of the curricular aspects of formal education, a matter of age status as such but also shows signs of being a product of tensions in the relationship of younger people and adults." [18] At several other points Parsons develops the "reaction" theme and later uses the concept of "reaction-formation." [19] Should these various phenomena be subsumed under the concept of culture? It is one thing for a society to train its youth to certain ways of behaving. It is quite another for a youth group to develop inverse values in an effort to struggle with role ambiguities and strains. The adolescent may experience both as normative sanctions; but that should scarcely lead the social analyst to disregard their differences. I suggest the term contraculture in order to indicate the normative *and* the conflict aspects of this type of situation.

DELINQUENT CONTRACULTURE

The usefulness of separating subcultural and contracultural influences is seen particularly clearly in the analysis of delinquency and of criminality generally. Perhaps in no other field were there more substantial gains in understanding made possible by the introduction of a sociological point of view to supplement and to correct individualistic and moralistic interpretations. There is little need to review the extensive literature, from *Delinquent Gangs* to *Delinquent Boys*, to establish the importance of the normative element in criminal and delinquent behavior. It is a mistake, however, to try to stretch a useful concept into a total theory. A "complex-adequate" analysis[20] may seem less sharp and definitive than one based on one factor, but it is likely to be far more useful. Cohen's excellent work,[21] although labelled as a study of the culture of the gang, does

[18] *Ibid.*, pp. 92–93.

[19] See *ibid.*, pp. 101–102, 189–190, 342–345, 355.

[20] See Robin M. Williams, Jr., "Continuity and Change in Sociological Study," *American Sociological Review*, 23 (December, 1958), pp. 619–633.

[21] Albert K. Cohen, *Delinquent Boys*, Glencoe, Ill.: Free Press, 1955.

not overlook the psychogenic sources of delinquency. In fact, his explanation of the origins of the subculture (contraculture) and its functions for the lower class male makes clear that the norms of the gang are not learned, accepted, and taught in the same way that we learn what foods to eat, what clothes to wear, what language to speak. The very existence of the gang is a sign, in part, of blocked ambition. Because tensions set in motion by this blockage cannot be resolved by achievement of dominant values, such values are repressed, their importance denied, counter-values affirmed. The gang member is often ambivalent. Thwarted in his desire to achieve higher status by the criteria of the dominant society, he accepts criteria he can meet; but the reaction-formation in this response is indicated by the content of the delinquent norms—non-utilitarian, malicious, and negativistic, in Cohen's terms. This negative polarity represents the need to repress his own tendencies to accept the dominant cultural standards. This is not to say that the values of the gang cannot be explained partially by cultural analysis, by some extension of the idea that "the mores can make anything right." But I suggest that Cohen's multiple-factor analysis might have been clearer, and less subject to mis-interpretation, had he introduced the concept of contraculture alongside the concept of subculture. One reviewer, for example, completely disregards the "negative polarity" theme:

> In an overall summary, cultural delinquency is a phenomenon of culture, society, and sociocultural experience. It is a positive thing: members of the several social classes are socialized, but there is a differential content in the socialization. Delinquency is not a negative thing; it is not a result of the breakdown of society, nor of the failure to curb criminal instincts, nor of the failure of the family, the church, or the school. The same set of concepts, the same social processes, and the same set of logical assumptions account for both delinquency and lawfulness. Since delinquency is of this character, it is unnecessary to invent any pathology to account for it.[22]

This statement neither adequately represents Cohen's thesis nor encourages us to explore a number of important questions: Why do only some of those who are exposed to the delinquent "subculture" learn it? [23] Why do those who follow the subculture often manifest ambivalence and guilt feelings? [24] Why do many of the same patterns of behavior occur in areas

[22] Frank Hartung, in a review of *Delinquent Boys, American Sociological Review*, 20 (December, 1955), p. 752.

[23] See Solomon Kobrin, "The Conflict of Values in Delinquency Areas," *American Sociological Review*, 16 (October, 1951), pp. 653–661; Alex Inkeles, "Personality and Social Structure," in Robert K. Merton *et al.*, editors, *Sociology Today*, New York: Basic Books, 1959, p. 254.

[24] See Gresham M. Sykes and David Matza, "Techniques of Neutralization: A Theory of Delinquency," *American Sociological Review*, 22 (December, 1957), pp. 664–670.

and among groups where the presence of the subculture is much less clear
(middle-class delinquency)? [25] What is the significance of the fact that
the delinquent subculture is not only different from but in part at least
a reversal of the values of the dominant culture? The use of a purely subcultural model of analysis discourages or even prevents the raising of these
questions and thus precludes adequate answers to them.

Cohen and Short have dealt with several of these issues by suggesting
the need for a typology. Specifically for the study of delinquency, they
propose five types of subcultures: the parent male (the central pattern
described in *Delinquent Boys*), the conflict-oriented, the drug addict, the
semi-professional theft, and the middle-class subcultures.[26] Although the
criteria of classification are not entirely clear, these categories are primarily
descriptive. The concept of contraculture might be added to this list as
a type of subculture, if the one distinctive criterion used to designate a
subculture is the presence in a sub-society of a normative system that
separates it from the total society. Such a procedure does not seem, however, to produce an adequate taxonomy. If the shift is made from description to analysis, or from an interest in the content of norms to their
etiology, an important difference emerges between subculture and contraculture: the one set of norms derives from standard socialization in a
sub-society; the other stems from conflict and frustration in the experience
of those who share many of the values of the whole society but are
thwarted in their efforts to achieve those values.

It should be stressed once more that these are analytic concepts, no
one of which is adequate to handle the empirical variations of delinquent
behavior. Failure to recognize the abstract quality of our conceptual tools
leads to unnecessary disagreements. When Miller describes the "Lower
Class Culture as a Generating Milieu of Gang Delinquency," for example, he points to an important series of influences that derive from the
value system of the lower-class community.[27] In his effort to emphasize
this aspect of the etiology of delinquency, however, he tends to overlook
the kind of evidence reported by Sykes and Matza, Cohen, Finestone,
Yablonsky, the McCords, and others concerning collective behavior and
personality variables.[28] Surely the evidence is now rich enough for us to
state definitively that delinquency is a multi-variable product. The task
ahead is not to prove that it stems largely from cultural or subcultural or

[25] John I. Kitsuse and David C. Dietrick, *"Delinquent Boys: A Critique," American
Sociological Review*, 24 (April, 1959), pp. 208–215.

[26] See Albert Cohen and James Short, "Research in Delinquent Subcultures," *The
Journal of Social Issues*, 14, 3 (1958), pp. 20–37.

[27] Walter B. Miller, "Lower Class Culture as a Generating Milieu of Gang Delinquency," *The Journal of Social Issues*, 14, 3 (1958), pp. 5–19.

[28] In addition to the studies of Sykes and Matza, Cohen, Finestone, and Yablonsky
cited above, see William McCord and Joan McCord, *Origins of Crime. A New Evaluation of the Cambridge-Somerville Youth Study*, New York: Columbia University
Press, 1959.

contracultural influences, but to spell out the conditions under which these and other factors will be found in various empirical mixtures.[29]

CONTRACULTURAL ASPECTS OF
CLASS AND OCCUPATION

The same admixture of the concepts of culture, subculture, and contraculture is found in the extensive literature on occupations and classes. Doubtless all three forces are found in many instances, and the research task is to untangle their various influences. It may stretch the meaning of the term too far to speak of the *position* of the "middle-class member," with its culturally designated role specifications; although in relatively stable societies the usage seems appropriate. In such societies, many of the rights and obligations of various status levels are culturally defined. In more mobile class systems, however, subcultural and contracultural norms become important. Our understanding of the American class system has certainly been deepened in the last twenty years by the descriptions of differences, among classes, in value perspectives, time orientations, levels of aspiration, leisure-time styles, and child rearing practices.[30]

---

[29] In a recent manuscript, Sykes and Matza suggest that delinquent behavior can profitably be studied as an exaggerated expression of certain "subterranean values" of the dominant society (the search for excitement, the use of "pull" to get by without too much work, and aggression). This idea deserves careful study. The main research task is to discover the conditions which promote selective and exaggerated attention to these values at the cost of neglect of the more prominent "public" values. It seems likely that this task will lead to the incorporation of the "subterranean values" thesis into the larger complex of theories of delinquency. The thesis raises a question of terminology in connection with the present paper: At what point does exaggerated emphasis on a value become a counter-value by virtue of the exaggeration? *Some* cultural support can be found in complex society for many patterns of behavior that are not fully valued. A society may accept or even applaud a pattern that is used to a limited degree while condemning its extravagant use. And the meaning of the pattern in the life of the individual when found in culturally approved degree differs from what it is when the pattern becomes a dominant theme. To discover why some subterranean values are raised into a style of life, therefore, requires more than cultural analysis. (See Gresham M. Sykes and David Matza, "Juvenile Delinquency and Subterranean Values," unpublished manuscript, 1960.)

[30] Of the many studies in this area, see Charles McArthur, "Personality Differences Between Middle and Upper Classes," *Journal of Abnormal and Social Psychology*, 50 (March, 1955), pp. 247–254; Melvin L. Kohn, "Social Class and Parental Values," *American Journal of Sociology*, 64 (January, 1959), pp. 337–351; A. B. Hollingshead and Frederick C. Redlich, *Social Class and Mental Illness*, New York: Wiley, 1958; Clyde R. White, "Social Class Differences in the Uses of Leisure," *American Journal of Sociology*, 61 (September, 1955), pp. 145–151; John A. Clausen and Melvin L. Kohn, "The Ecological Approach in Social Psychiatry," *American Journal of Sociology*, 60 (September, 1954), pp. 140–151; A. B. Hollingshead, *Elmtown's Youth*, New York: Wiley, 1949; Louis Schneider and Sverre Lysgaard, "The Deferred Gratification Pattern: A Preliminary Study," *American Sociological Review*, 18 (April, 1953), pp. 142–149; Urie Bronfenbrenner, "Socialization and Social Class Through Time and

The introduction of the concept of subculture has helped to avoid class derived biases in the interpretation of the wide variations in these phenomena. In class analysis as in the study of deviations, however, there may be some over-compensation in the effort to eliminate the distortions of a middle-class and often rural perspective.[31] There is evidence to suggest that differences between classes are based less upon different values and norms than the subcultural approach suggests. The "innovations" of lower-class members, to use Merton's term, are not simply subcultural acts defined as innovative by middle-class persons. They are in part responses to a frustrating situation. They are efforts to deal with the disjunction of means and ends. When the disjunction is reduced, the variations in value and behavior are reduced. Thus Rosen found, "surprisingly," that Negroes in the Northeast made higher scores on an "achievement value" test than his description of Negro "culture" led him to expect. This may indicate that the low achievement response is less the result of a subcultural norm than a protest against a difficult situation. If the situation improves, the achievement value changes.[32] Stephenson's discovery that occupational plans of lower-class youth are considerably below those of higher-class youth, but that their aspirations are only slightly lower, bears on this same point. His data suggest that the classes differ not only in norms, but also in opportunity.[33] Differences in behavior, therefore, are only partly a result of subcultural contrasts. The lower educational aspirations of lower-class members are also found to be in part situationally induced, not simply normatively induced. When the situation changes, values and behavior change, as Mulligan found in his study of the response of the sons of blue-collar workers to the educational opportunities of the GI Bill, and as Wilson reports in his investigation of the aspirations of lower-class boys attending higher-class schools and upper-class boys attending lower-class schools.[34]

In short, our thinking about differences in behavior among social

---

Space," in Eleanor E. Maccoby et al., editors, Readings in Social Psychology, New York: Holt, 1958, pp. 400–425.

[31] C. Wright Mills, "The Professional Ideology of Social Pathologists," American Journal of Sociology, 49 (September, 1943), pp. 165–180.

[32] Bernard C. Rosen, "Race, Ethnicity, and the Achievement Syndrome," American Sociological Review, 24 (February, 1959), pp. 47–60. It is highly important, in aspiration studies, to compare, not absolute levels, but the extent of aspiration above the existing level of individuals or their families. A low absolute target for lower-class members may require a larger reach than a higher target for middle-class persons. See Leonard Reissman, "Levels of Aspiration and Social Class," American Sociological Review, 18 (June, 1953), pp. 233–242.

[33] Richard M. Stephenson, "Mobility Orientation and Stratification of 1,000 Ninth Graders," American Sociological Review, 22 (April, 1957), pp. 204–212.

[34] Raymond A. Mulligan, "Socio-Economic Background and College Enrollment," American Sociological Review, 16 (April, 1951), pp. 188–196; Alan B. Wilson, "Residential Segregation of Social Classes and Aspirations of High School Boys," American Sociological Review, 24 (December, 1959), pp. 836–845.

classes will be sharpened if we distinguish among those differences that derive from role influences, those based on subcultural variations, and those that express contracultural responses to deprivation. The proportions will vary from society to society; the research task is to specify the conditions under which various distributions occur. One would expect, to propose one hypothesis, to find more contracultural norms among lower-class members of an open society than in a similar group in a closed society.

The interpretation of differential behavior among the members of various occupational categories can also be strengthened by the distinctions made above. Here the contrast between role and subculture is especially useful. The role of a teacher consists of the rights and duties that *integrate* him into a system of expected and established relationships with others. The teaching subculture, on the other hand, insofar as it exists, *separates* teachers from the cultural world of others. It is either unknown to others or, if known, a source of disagreement and perhaps of conflict with others. There are also contracultural aspects of some occupational styles of life. In interpreting the differences between the values of jazz musicians and "squares," for example, Becker writes: "their rejection of commercialism in music and squares in social life was part of the casting aside of the total American culture by men who could enjoy privileged status but who were unable to achieve a satisfactory personal adjustment within it." [35] Their style of life, in other words, can be understood only by supplementing the cultural and subcultural dimensions with the conflict theme. Cameron develops the same point. Although he makes no use of the term subculture, he describes the differentiating norms of the dance-band group, presumably a result of the "esoteric" aspects of their art, the differences in their time schedule, and the like. But he also describes the *contra* aspects of some of the norms, and suggests that they derive from the fact that early recruitment ties the jazz musician to the adolescence problem.[36]

CONCLUSION

Poorly defined terms plague research in many areas, particularly in the specification of relationships between sociological and social psychological levels of analysis. Thus "anomie" is still used to refer both to a social structural fact and to a personality fact, although this confusion is gradually being reduced. "Role" may refer, alternately, to rights and duties prescribed for the occupants of a position or to individual performance of that position. And subculture, I have suggested, is used to designate both the traditional norms of a sub-society and the emergent norms of a group

[35] Howard S. Becker, "The Professional Dance Musician and His Audience," *American Journal of Sociology*, 57 (September, 1951), pp. 136–144.

[36] W. B. Cameron, "Sociological Notes on the Jam Session," *Social Forces*, 33 (December, 1954), pp. 177–182.

caught in a frustrating and conflict-laden situation. This paper indicates that there are differences in the origin, function, and perpetuation of traditional and emergent norms, and suggests that the use of the concept contraculture for the latter might improve sociological analysis.

Hypotheses to guide the study of subculture can most profitably be derived from a general theory of culture. As an illustration, it may be hypothesized that a subculture will appear, in the first instance, as a result of mobility or an extension of communication that brings groups of different cultural background into membership in the same society, followed by physical or social isolation or both that prevents full assimilation.

Hypotheses concerning contracultures, on the other hand, can best be derived from social psychological theory—from the study of collective behavior, the frustration-aggression thesis, or the theory of group formation. One might hypothesize, for example, that under conditions of deprivation and frustration of major values (in a context where the deprivation is obvious because of extensive communication with the dominant group), and where value confusion and weak social controls obtain, contracultural norms will appear. One would expect to find, according to these propositions, many subcultural values among southern rural Negroes. Among first and second generation urban Negroes, however, one would expect an increase in contracultural norms. Both groups are deprived, but in the urban situation there is more "value leakage" from the dominant group, more value confusion, and weakened social controls.[37]

The subculture of the sociologist requires sophistication about the full range of human behavior. This desideratum has led to the proposition that the vast diversity of norms believed in and acted upon by the members of a modern society is not a sign of value confusion and breakdown but rather an indication that urban life brings into one system of interaction persons drawn from many cultural worlds. One unanticipated consequence of the sociological subculture may be that we exaggerate the normative insulation and solidarity of these various worlds. An important empirical question concerns the extent and results of their interaction.

[37] There are numerous alternative ways in which the protest against deprivation can be expressed. Delinquency and drug addiction often have a contracultural aspect; but somewhat less clearly, political and religious movements among disprivileged groups may also invert the values of the influential but inaccessible dominant group. Thus the concept of contraculture may help us to understand, for example, the Garveyite movement, the Ras Tafari cult, and some aspects of the value schemes of lower-class sects. (See, e.g., Liston Pope, *Millhands and Preachers*, New Haven: Yale University Press, 1942; and George E. Simpson, "The Ras Tafari Movement in Jamaica: A Study of Race and Class Conflict," *Social Forces*, 34 (December, 1955), pp. 167–170.)

For Further Reading

BOOKS

Chase, S. *The proper study of mankind*. Rev. ed. New York: Harper and Row, 1956. Available in paperback, Harper Colophon Books.

Revision of an earlier work which gained wide acceptance as an interpreter of social science: a vivid and highly-readable introduction.

Hsu, F. L. K. (Ed.). *Psychological anthropology*. Homewood, Illinois: Dorsey Press, 1961.

This anthology attempts to combine psychology and anthropology in an approach to culture and personality.

Kluckhohn, R. (Ed.). *Culture and behavior. Collected Essays of Clyde Kluckhohn*. New York: Free Press, 1962.

A collection of 21 articles, mainly from inaccessible journals, spanning the range of Kluckhohn's interests—from archaeology to culture and personality. An excellent article on field methodology and one on the limitations of functionalism.

Thompson, L. *Toward a science of mankind*. New York: McGraw-Hill, 1961.

Attempts to present a theory for anthropological studies.

Whiting, B. B. (Ed.). *Six cultures: studies in child rearing*. New York: John Wiley, 1963.

Reports investigations designed in 1953. Using a common field manual, sites were chosen to maximize cultural differences—Mexico, northern India, Luzon, Okinawa, Kenya and New England—using psychoanalytic variables in the study of childrearing.

ARTICLES

Alfert, E. A multiple score personality test administered to German and Austrian students: cross-cultural vs. intra-cultural differences. *J. soc. Psychol.*, 1959, 50 (1), 37–46. PA 35, 3318.

German, Austrian, and Vassar students differed less from group to group than within each culture.

Arnhoff, F. N., Leon, H. V., and Lorge, I. Cross-cultural acceptance of stereotypes toward aging. *J. soc. Psychol.*, 1964, 63 (1), 41–58. PA 39, 1465.

Significant differences in attitudes toward aging were found among college students in the United States, England, Japan, Sweden, Greece and Puerto Rico.

Ayal, E. B. Value systems and economic development in Japan and Thailand. *J. soc. Issues*, 1963, 19 (1), 35–51. PA 38, 716.

Suggests that value differences between the cultures of Japan and Thailand can explain the economic development of Japan in contrast to that of Thailand.

Bharucha-Reid, R. P. Appearance and reality in culture. *J. soc. Psychol.*, 1962, 57 (1), 169–193. PA 37, 2975.

A critical appraisal of some cross-cultural studies.

Christensen, H. T., and Carpenter, G. R. Timing patterns in the development of sexual intimacy: an attitudinal report on three modern Western societies, *Marriage Fam. Living*, 1962, 24 (1), 30–35. PA 37, 1044.

A comparison of attitudes toward premarital coitus in a (college) sample of Midwestern United States, Inter-mountain United States (Mormon), and Denmark.

Elder, G. H., Jr. Role relations, sociocultural environments and autocratic family ideology, *Sociometry*, 1965, 28 (2), 173–196. PA 39, 12083.

Parent-youth relations, education, residential patterns and work settings were found to be related to autocratic ideology in the cultures of the United States, Great Britain, West Germany, Mexico and Italy.

Foa, E. Cross-cultural similarity and difference in inter-personal behavior. *J. abnorm. soc. Psychol.*, 1964, 68 (5), 517–522. PA 39, 4698.

It is suggested that certain aspects of interpersonal behavior are common to different cultures, while certain other aspects change from culture to culture. Data compares two groups in Jerusalem, Israel, one originating from Europe and the other from the Middle East.

Freedman, M. B. Changes in six decades of some attitudes and values held by educated women. *J. soc. Issues*, 1961, 17 (1), 19–28. PA 37, 1051.

Comparison of six decades of Vassar alumni; significant differences in attitudes were found. Present-day attitudes are more flexible (F scale).

Haber, L. D. Age and integration setting: a re-appraisal of "The Changing American Parent," *Amer. sociol. Rev.*, 1967, 27 (5), 682–689. PA 37, 4748.

The differences between entrepreneurial and bureaucratic families in childrearing practices presented in the Detroit study are predictable from the fact that the two groups differ in age.

Hsu, L. K., et al. Culture pattern and adolescent behavior. *Int. J. soc. Psychiat.*, 1961, 7 (1), 33–53. PA 36, 4FH33H.

Hawaiian youth have a much smoother transition from childhood to adulthood than do Chicago adolescents.

Jahoda, M. A social-psychological approach to the study of culture. *Hum. Relat.*, 1961, 14 (1), 23–30. PA 36, 2GB23J.

Relates the concept of culture to social-psychological thinking by introducing the concept of "fit."

Matsumoto, M., and Smith, H. T. Japanese and American children's perception of parents. *J. genet. Psychol.*, 1961, 98 (1), 83–88. PA 35, 6157.

There was greater psychological distance between parents and children, and clearer differentiation between maternal and paternal roles in Japan, than among American fifth- and sixth-grade students.

Rapp, D. W. Child-rearing attitudes of mothers in Germany and the United States. *Child Develpm.*, 1961, 32 (4), 669–678. PA 36, 5FG68R.

United States (124 Florida) mothers showed significantly less concern with controlling children than did 124 German mothers.

Remmers, H. H. Cross-cultural studies of teenagers' problems. *J. educ. Psychol.*, 1962, 53 (6), 254–261. PA 37, 4767.

Stratified samples of more than 5000 teenagers in the United States, Puerto Rico, West Germany and India indicated similar rankings of problem areas; health problems are of least concern and post-high school problems are of most concern.

Rosen, B. C. Socialization and achievement motivation in Brazil. *Amer. sociol. Rev.*, 1962, 27 (5), 612–624. PA 37, 4827.

Brazilian mothers were less likely to train their sons in self-reliance, autonomy and achievement than were American mothers.

Sebald, H. Studying national character through comparative content analysis. *Social Forces*, 1962, 40 (4), 318–322. SA 11, A4663.

Using elementary school song books (1940), the author determined that German song books emphasized the needs of the society over the needs of the individual, glorified authority and a patriot's death (as opposed to song books used in the United States).

Triandis, H. C. and L. M. A cross-cultural study of social distance. *Psychol. Monogr.: General and Applied*, 1962, 76 (Whole Number 540). PA 38, 5905.

Nationality and religion were the two most important variables explaining social distance for a Greek sample, while race and religion were the predominant factors for an American group.

Turner, R. H. Preoccupation with competitiveness and social acceptance among American and English boys. *Sociometry*, 1960, 23 (3), 307–325. PA 35, 2064.

English and American students were found to be similar with regard to preoccupation with competitiveness and a resultant exaggerated seeking for love.

Zurcher, L. A., *et al.* Value orientation, role conflict and alienation from work. *Amer. sociol. Rev.*, 1963, 30 (4), 539–548.

Mexican employees, in contrast to Anglo-American employees of a Texas bank, were more oriented toward "particularism"; since the bank is a universalistically-oriented work organization, alienation was more characteristic of the Mexican workers.

Chapter Twelve

Collective Behavior

Collective behavior is not really a concept but rather a term for a rather wide range of topics which social scientists have studied. Fads, fashions, rumor, panic, disasters, race riots, and social movements are a few of the situations that have loosely been associated under the general rubric of collective behavior.

As Stansfeld Sargent and Robert Williamson have observed,[1] the interest in the field has waxed and waned. Beginning with the impressionistic writings of Gabriel Le Tarde and Gustave Le Bon, the subject was largely discredited in the reaction to the "group mind fallacy," and fell into disinterest about the time of World War II. However, as they have noted, collective behavior has had a recrudescence recently, in part because of a growing concern about disasters and riots.

The term collective behavior is an unfortunate one, for it is quite imprecise and undescriptive. In a sense, nearly all of human behavior is shared, or "collective": certainly many of the concepts which we have studied—such as attitudes, norms, values, roles, culture, and so on—do not exist in private worlds; but, on the contrary make possible, and result from, human interaction. Even activities often assumed to be strictly personal—prayer, dreams, posture, personal hygiene, and the like—take a characteristic bent in different cultures.

By general consent, however, collective behavior usually refers to conditions which are not routine, to situations in which the normal processes of social living are inoperative, where "the existing social organization either collapses or does not apply."[2] We follow, then, the conventional definition, which may be expressed by Sherif:

> In a general sense, collective interaction means behavior in social situations in which a number of individuals or groups actively participate and react to one another. In the literature, the term "collective behavior" refers

---

[1] Sargent, S. S. and Williamson, R. C. *Social Psychology.* (3rd ed.) New York: The Ronald Press, 1966, 533.

[2] Deutscher, I. and Kong-ming, P. *Functional analysis of collective behavior in a disaster. Sociol. Quart.*, 1961, 2 (1), 34.

to extreme cases of interaction exemplified by mobs engaged in lynching, by a riot launched against another group, by crowds carrying out a hunger march or a revolutionary move, by rallies voicing some mass protest in support of their demands, by crowds vowing that the last drop of their blood is committed to the incorporation of some territory within the bounds of their motherland . . .[3]

Even in these disruptive situations, however, order is not entirely lacking. As William Form and his colleagues noted after their research in a tornado, flood and a bombing situation, "Far from having a condition of social anomie, social systems continue to operate through all of the disaster stages, new systems emerge, and continuity is found between the old and the emergent social systems." [4]

As Donald M. Valdes and Dwight G. Dean have suggested,[5] what is customarily called "collective behavior" may be schematically represented as one end of an arc which includes unorganized or disorganized situations, through social organization (institutionalized ways of meeting basic human needs), to bureaucracy which may ultimately end in overorganization or the minute prescription of rules to cover every conceivable situation.

It would take an exhaustively long book to encompass adequately the myriad types of behavior subsumed under the general heading of collective behavior. Gradually, sociologists and psychologists have discovered that even in nonroutine situations where there appears to be disorganization, human behavior is not chaotic. From at least the time of Frederic Thrasher's publication of *The Gang*,[6] social science has documented the fact that order is not lacking in those areas of cities that have been termed disorganized.

We have chosen articles that illustrate the contemporary concerns of social scientists in both theoretical and practical aspects, rather than present an encyclopedia-like perusal of the literature. These selections might all be viewed as attempts to discern patterns, regularities, predictabilities in what at first seemed random and chaotic behavior.

Perhaps the first step in gaining knowledge is to come to realize that what has heretofore been assumed to be true may upon research turn out not to be so. Enrico L. Quarantelli, using disasters as a common reference point, determined that the commonly held images (images, that is, of panic withdrawal, of dependence upon outside direction, and of the

[3] Sherif, M. and C. W. *An outline of social psychology.* (Rev. ed.) (New York: Harper and Row, 1956), p. 337.

[4] Form, W. H., Loomis, C. P., *et al. The persistence and emergence of social and cultural systems in disasters. Amer. Sociol. Rev.* 1956, 21, 181.

[5] Valdes, D. M., and Dean, D. G. *Sociology in use.* New York: Macmillan, 1965. Pp. 234 ff.

[6] Thrasher, Frederic, *The Gang* (Chicago: University of Chicago Press, 1936).

inability of authorities to control the situation) are simply without foundation. In contrast to the distortions produced by the mass media, he again and again cites studies that prove that in crises most individuals do not react randomly or chaotically but proceed with what must be regarded as remarkable calm to "pick up the pieces" after a disaster.

That there is already a considerable body of substantiated knowledge is documented in the report by Robert Shellow and Derek V. Roemer. They specifically cite research findings which they utilized for their recommendations to police for the avoidance of a riot accompanying a visit by motorcyclists.

The selection by Stanley Lieberson and Arnold R. Silverman is valuable not only for the factual data it presents, but also for its illustration of an imaginative approach studying race riots in absentia, as it were. They have attempted to determine the underlying conditions or precipitants of such phenomena. One can only imagine the social benefits that might accrue if accurate predictions of future trouble spots could be made, and acted upon.

Finally, Thomas E. Drabek and Enrico L. Quarantelli, in their study of "Blame in Disaster," make intriguing suggestions as to the social necessity for a scapegoat, or blameworthy persons, and raise provocative questions concerning the relationship of collective behavior (at least in its blame-manifestation aspects), to the ongoing social structure, or social organization of a society. This selection vividly illustrates that our culture's emphasis upon the individual may foreclose the possibility of looking at problems from a sociological perspective and therefore fail to deal with problems adequately.

These four readings may lay the basis for an appreciation of the antecedents, accompaniments, and consequences of those tension-laden circumstances commonly called collective behavior. They hint at the possibility of an understanding that some day may make the presently unexpected predictable. It may be possible to analyze what such situations have in common, so that what is presently merely a field of interest, may eventually evolve into a concept, a description of social processes discernible in the efforts of groups and individuals to repair the ruptured social structure.

36

Images of Withdrawal
Behavior in Disasters:
Some Basic Misconceptions

ENRICO L. QUARANTELLI*

The Ohio State University

In the last decade, the research efforts of social scientists have increasingly been directed to the reaction of people and communities in disaster situations (1, 2, 3, 4, 5). Much of the research has been stimulated by the threat posed for American society by nuclear warfare and the necessity of deriving civilian defense measures (6, 7). However, disasters are not confined to wartime and research in the area has theoretical as well as practical implications. The present paper assumes this larger framework.

Various studies have uncovered basic misconceptions about human behavior in disasters. This paper brings together such findings concerning one selected kind of disaster reaction. Our starting point is the perspective of those persons or organizations who are most involved in disaster control and relief activities. Most agencies and officials assume victim populations withdraw as soon as possible from impact areas (8). This assumption involves three not altogether consistent images of withdrawal behavior. One image is that of "panic"; another is that of "dependency." Additionally superimposed on these two images is another one of "control." That is, whether withdrawal be thought of in the form of panic and/or dependency, the assumption is made that such behavior can be controlled. Certain misconceptions about all three images will be examined.

THE "PANIC" IMAGE

Withdrawal behavior is often visualized as taking the form of highly disorganized flight by hysterical individuals who have stampeded at the

Reprinted from *Social Problems*, 8, 1 (Summer 1960) 68–79, by permission of the author and the publisher.

* The author has in the past worked as a member of the Disaster Team of the National Opinion Research Center, and as a consultant to the Committee on Disaster Studies (now called the Disaster Research Group) of the National Research Council. Some of the examples used, and part of the analysis set forth, were obtained as a result of this work. However, the views expressed and the interpretations of the data are solely the responsibility of the author. They do not necessarily reflect the opinions of any of these organizations.

sight of actual or potential danger. The flight is pictured as marked by irrational decisions, illogical actions, and an anti-social disregard for others. In general, the expectation is one of widespread personal and social chaos as the disaster victims flee.

As depicted, this image might appear extreme. However it is the implicit image that is operative in many cases. This can be seen in what officials and administrators assume in their planning and thinking, as well as in what they do and decide about disaster problems.

The expectation of a panicky form of withdrawal is illustrated, for instance, in a recent statement on community disasters prepared for the guidance of nurses. Panic is stated as being one of the five most common reactions to disasters, if not the most common. The behavior is said to be characterized by a:

> . . . "blind flight" reaction, manifested by wild running about . . . or otherwise disorganized hysterical behavior. Absence of judgment and logical thinking will be conspicuous. Such an individual requires prompt and effective action, both to protect him from the consequences of his undirected behavior and to prevent his panic from spreading throughout the group (9).

Also indicative of the image held is the failure of responsible officials, at times, to take appropriate actions during pre-impact periods of possible disasters because of their anxiety about initiating panic. For example, city officials and state police refused to order the evacuation of an eastern ocean resort, despite the urgent recommendations of the Weather Bureau and the Coast Guard, because they feared such action on their part would precipitate a panicky flight. They preferred to chance the danger of inaction, even though they knew the intensity of the hurricane heading for their low lying area, and the likelihood that the two routes from the city would become impassable if the storm were of the magnitude predicted (10).

Concern over evoking panicky reactions sometimes hinders even the alerting of people to possible dangers. Thus during the Rio Grande floods, some Mexican and American officials felt that they had to play down warnings otherwise people would panic (11). Because of a similar concern, forecasts of tornado conditions were not issued prior to the Worcester tornado (12). In a much more circumscribed crisis situation but because of this same fear of initiating panic, alarm bells were not rung on the collision-doomed *Andrea Doria* (13).

Much civilian defense planning in this country also assumes that not only will withdrawal be inevitable, but that it will be markedly maladaptive, unthinking, and contagious behavior. The major control problem is seen as one of stopping a panicky exodus. This is manifested in official articles (one by the former Civil Defense [CD] head very aptly illustrating our point by being called—*Panic, the Ultimate Weapon?*) (14), manuals, conferences, committee reports, and the literature distributed by many state and local CD agencies (15, 16, 17, 18, 19, 20). The narrowness of the focus is pinpointed by the observation made in a critique of a CD walkout exercise that "the problem of evacuation has largely been visualized up to now as being one of holding back the public from fleeing the city in a rout" (21).

This is not a distinctively American cultural reaction. Prior to World War II, British planners also proceeded on the assumption that in the event of war:

> . . . a large exodus from London and other cities was inevitable; panic would send the people out and unless the Government took firm control . . . chaos and confusion were bound to ensue. . . . In its deliberations, the question was viewed not as a problem of getting people away, but as a problem of preventing panic flight. This led . . . to the suggestion that the [police] force should be enlarged and a cordon thrown round London. So convinced was the committee . . . that a "disorderly general flight" would take place that it felt it could not carry its study further until a decision had been reached on "how control of the population was to be exercised." (22).

Nothing remotely approaching these expectations materialized. People showed a great reluctance to leave. For example, only 37 per cent of the total evacuable number of mothers and children left London (23). This is the actual problem in most peace and wartime disasters—that of getting movement rather than preventing it. This should not be surprising. Human beings have a very strong tendency to continue with their on-going lines of action in preference to initiating new courses of activity.

Where the disaster threat is slow moving as in the instance of floods, this tendency inevitably poses a task of major magnitude for control officials. Studies of and reports about dozens of floods in American society consistently mention a reluctance to withdraw (24). However, this is not a peculiarly American cultural trait. It has similarly been reported for flood-threatened Mexican, English, Dutch, and Italian groups. In some of these instances, even the threat of force and coercive measures were not enough to motivate all inhabitants to leave their endangered areas (25).

Nor is this tendency to remain in threatened locations confined to flood situations. An unwillingness to withdraw has been documented for disasters ranging from maritime catastrophes to air attacks on metropolitan areas to avalanches advancing on mountain villages (26, 27, 28, 29). It also has been reported for threats which endure and increase in intensity like epidemics, and for those marked by brief violent impact such as explosions (30, 31).

Sometimes even when their physical world is literally disintegrating around them, substantial number of individuals refuse to withdraw from the impact area. What may appear to be an objectively impossible stress situation to an outsider, may not be so subjectively defined by the persons involved. For example, Bootle, England, a city of about 55,000 people was bombed nightly for a week. Sixty per cent of all houses were damaged at least twice, and only 10 per cent escaped serious damage. Community facilities were shattered and all the main roads for motor transportation were blocked. Yet despite this extensive damage, with all its consequent effects on food distribution, gas, water, and public services in general, around one fourth of the population remained to sleep in their homes throughout the raids (32).

Mass media accounts frequently report "thousands" or whole communities fleeing upon the receipt of hurricane warnings. However, systematic studies of such situations do not bear out these accounts. Thus despite intensive warnings about Hurricane Florence, 66 per cent of the interviewed respondents in a Florida town did not leave their homes. Only about 17 per cent went to the shelters prepared by authorities (33). In a New England city hit by Hurricane Carol and Edna in quick succession, only 4 per cent of the inhabitants evacuated each time (34). The evidence suggests that such withdrawal behavior as does occur, is by transients such as tourists and not by the resident population (35).

Just as disaster agencies generally overestimate withdrawal because of the panic image, so do the mass communication agencies. This is true even when the news sources are present in the impact area. For example, there was an exodus from flood stricken Port Jervis, New York, when a false rumor spread about a dam break. Local newspaper accounts said "most of the city" of 9,000 inhabitants had fled. An actual field study showed that at a very maximum perhaps one fourth might have evacuated (36).

People not only do not bolt from endangered areas; they sometimes return to them if they have left even though the threat is still existent. This is well illustrated in the return to their home towns by many German and English war-time evacuees. Over 60 per cent of the British government-sponsored evacuees had returned four months after their initial evacuation (37). This drift back continued at a steady rate and despite official pleas, to areas that were prime targets for air and rocket attacks. At a time when the city was being bombed every night, even children were being brought back to London at nearly as rapid a rate as they were being evacuated (38). Similarly in Germany, children were brought back in the face of governmental efforts to discourage it by refusing to provide schooling or ration cards (39). The same drift back to threatened areas has also been reported for prolonged epidemics (40). To be sure, if severity of threat continues to increase as in the instance of the air attacks on Japan, there is a gradual increase in withdrawal with fewer return movements (41). Nevertheless, the overall picture is clearly far from one of people wildly fleeing upon a sign of danger.

Scientific studies of disasters do not bear out the existence of pandemonium and chaos, or the extensive panicstricken reactions frequently reported in journalistic and popular accounts, or by involved observers (e.g., relief personnel). Much of the discrepancy between the two versions lies in the failure of the non-scientist to note a distinction between personal and social disorganization. As W. I. Thomas pointed out long ago, one can be present without the other. In disasters there often is *relatively* widespread social or community disorganization concurrent with lack of disorganization at the individual and small group level.

Thus Clifford in his study of the Rio Grande flood, noted that organized rescue and evacuation by community agencies in the areas of greatest danger all but totally collapsed. Less than 5 per cent of the 30,000 evacuees from Piedras Negras, Mexico were helped by any organization at all (42). However, in the absence of community wide coordination the inhabitants continued to act out their family and friendship roles. At the individual and small group level there was relatively deliberate behavior and much mutual assistance in evacuating the area. Thus on the American side, in Eagle Pass, 26 per cent of the respondents received help in evacuating from their immediate family, 20 per cent from other relatives, and 50 per cent from friends and neighbors (43). In this and in drastically different kinds of disasters (e.g., the Texas City explosion) (44), below the community level, there was not the disorganization in fleeing from the disaster scene that is assumed in the panic image.

In addition to confusing social and personal disorganization, there is also a frequent failure to recognize that involved individuals and groups are often acting on the basis of different definitions of the disaster situation. This is illustrated in the behavior exhibited during a series of house explosions in a Rochester, New York suburb. Viewed from the vantage point of an airplane, the withdrawal that was occurring might seem chaotic, and generally analogous to the helter-skelter observable if an ant hill is toppled over. However, a study revealed that viewed from the perspective of participants, there was relatively reasoned, controlled, logical and adaptive withdrawing from specific points of danger. In the course of interacting with others, divergent definitions of places of safety were developed, and accordingly led to different withdrawal patterns. As the NORC report stated:

> Although people engaged in a crowdlike behavior . . . all critical judgment was not lost. People talked over the merits of moving from one place to another. They discussed the advisability of fleeing from the area altogether. There was a tendency to respond rather quickly to some suggestion on the part of others, but on the whole, people remained somewhat discriminating—taking into consideration various aspects of the situation as they saw them.
>
> By far the most common activity that emerged out of the interaction of members of milling groups was a type of withdrawal behavior. As people talked over the event among themselves they would decide that some particular location, such as a backyard or the lawn in front of an all electric

house, was a position of relative safety. On the basis of the group consensus they would then move to those places. . . . Some people left the area . . . because they felt the area in general to be an unsafe place with houses exploding all around them (45).

Another reason why the overall picture of withdrawal behavior that emerges from various disaster studies is drastically different from that implied in the "panic" image, is because the latter image fails to note the difference between flight and panic flight. The two are not equivalent. Panic is flight where the individual ceases to play any social role whatsoever and merely flees (46, 47, 48). Withdrawal that assumes this form is extremely rare. Most withdrawal behavior involves definite role playing especially along lines of primary group ties. Thus in the precipitous so-called "panic flight" from Port Jervis (mentioned earlier) there was no solitary flight, and 23 per cent of those fleeting even made attempts to assist community members other than those who were in their own original fleeing group (49).

Additionally, when panic does occur it is very seldom on a large scale. Panic flights are almost always highly localized episodes, with few participants, and of short duration. In fact, except for some instances involving armies, the author after eight years of intensively seeking for such cases, can not cite a single clear cut instance where more than three or four score people were involved. The often cited case of the invasion from Mars broadcast did not involve withdrawal leading to cessation of all role playing or much flight for that matter. (Even the Cantril study reported that around 84 per cent of the audience was in no way disturbed by the broadcast [5].) Many supposed cases of "mass panic," upon examination turn out to be crisis situations where behavior other than flight was manifested.

Even in those rare situations where panic does occur, the majority of participants in the situation seldom engage in panic flight. Here again as in the instance of the Martian broadcast, incorrect versions prevail regarding what happened in historically famous cases like the Cocoanut Grove night club fire or the Iroquois theatre fire. The available evidence fairly clearly suggests that panic was not the model form of withdrawal even in those highly circumscribed situations (51). More systematic studies of very extensive disasters like the California earthquake of 1952, or the two atomic bombings definitely indicate that the overwhelming majority of persons did not panic in such cataclysmic circumstances either. Only very isolated instances of such flight behavior were found (52, 53).

The evidence is conclusive that when withdrawal does occur, it does not manifest itself in the way implied in the "panic" image. Such narrow emphasis on and concern with panic is actually dysfunctional. It results in a failure to predict and to be responsive to the stress behaviors that do occur. It leads to the overlooking of more important problems that do arise in connection with withdrawal.

THE "DEPENDENCY" IMAGE

In contrast to the hyperactivity assumed in the "panic" image, the "dependency" image embodies the idea of passivity. Withdrawal is visualized as taking the form of officially guided evacuations by helpless victims, who are so devoid of initiative that everything has to be done for them. The picture is one of docile and impotent individuals, waiting childlike for someone to take care of them. In general, the expectation is almost one of apathetic dependency on "Big Brothers" in the guise of relief workers and welfare planners.

Here again the image might appear overdrawn. However, it is an implicit one that clearly guides the thinking and planning of many disaster-concerned organizations and their personnel. Field procedures of various agencies and designers of disaster plans generally assume that the bulk of disaster victims will attain personal safety and comfort mostly through the resources of official sources. Or in the words of a former Red Cross president, agency help is needed because disasters create:

> shock . . . uncertainty, crippling anxiety, loss of confidence, discouragement, dependence . . . at the very time when the needs for social helpfulness are greatest and most acute, the normal protective and helping processes are inoperative or disrupted (54).

There is some limited evidence of a "disaster syndrome." The initial stages of this reaction involve a state of apathy or shock leading to a regression in normal cognitive processes. It has been reported occurring following relatively sudden, violent-type catastrophes (55, 56).

However the "disaster syndrome" appears only in the more traumatic kinds of disasters, is confined to the post impact period, and is of short duration (its initial stage seldom enduring more than minutes or hours) (57, 58). More important, the reaction does not occur on a large scale. Some disaster researchers have speculated that it might affect anywhere from 33 to 75 per cent of disaster victims (59, 60). But one of the few disaster studies that used an area probability sample, found that only 14 per cent of all respondents may have manifested the initial stages of the syndrome (61). In the Flint-Beecher, Michigan tornado a figure of less than 20 per cent was reported (62). There is evidence too that the reaction is culturally structured. It has not been observed in studies of responses to typhoons on Yap nor in reactions to explosive and destructive volcanic eruptions among the Orokaivas in New Guinea (63, 64).

Disaster victims react in an active manner, not passively as implied in the dependency image. They do not just wait around for offers of aid by organizations. They act on their own, sometimes even contrary to the expressed wishes of formal agencies and public authorities. On a large scale, once they have started to react to the crisis, victims show personal initiative and a pattern of self and informal mutual help. Observations of flood evacuees in India suggest this is true even in societies passively oriented towards nature, and with a fatalistic attitude about personal crises and problems (65).

In general, disaster victims work out their own private withdrawal arrangements. For example, when a tornado hit Worcester, approximately 10,000 persons were made homeless. However, only about 50 individuals were housed by the public authorities. Displaced persons instead moved in with other family members, intimates, neighbors, and generally ignored the formal agencies (66). Such behavior additionally suggests an exaggeration of the belief regarding weakened kinship and primary ties in modern mass societies, and the full transfer of protective functions from the family to large scale organizations (67).

Viewed cross-culturally, the network of informal social relationships of societies seems to come especially to the fore in situations of this kind. Extensive mutual and self help and disregard of official sources has been documented for English flood evacuees and Japanese bombing refugees (68, 69). In one Mexican flood only 4.7 per cent of around 40,000 of those who evacuated received aid of an official organization. They relied instead on the help of friends and neighbors (70). Data from wartime evacuations also report the same strong independent and avoidance behavior. Of around 1,400,000 persons made homeless in the London region, only about one in seven passed through the official rest centers provided (71).

Even when the housing facilities of a whole community undergo complete or great destruction, there is still no inevitable movement towards emergency mass shelters. When 55 per cent of Eagle Pass, Texas, a city of 10,000 was inundated and other sections were threatened, only 350 persons made use of the available mass shelters in safe public buildings (72). Similarly in the 1955 California floods, in the hardest hit area, over 50,000 people had to evacuate their homes. However, 38 Red Cross shelters in 13 towns registered only 9,260 persons, around 18 per cent of all the evacuees (73).

Mass shelters are seldom used for the purpose for which they are originally established. For instance, from 15,000 to 20,000 persons were forced by a flash flood to evacuate Vanport, Oregon. Less than 15 per cent of the evacuees, however, went to the more than 20 public shelters set up in nearby Portland (74). These shelters were therefore transformed into temporary food and clothing distribution centers. This often happens in disaster situations and could be viewed positively. What otherwise might not be available (i.e., distribution centers), are frequently ready at hand to be used as relief and rehabilitation activities are commenced. In this way perhaps, the misconception of dependency might be considered as having at least one positive latent function for relief operations.

In general, as in the instance of the expectation of "panic," an anticipation of "dependency" leads to a looking for what does not occur, with a consequent misdirection of organizational activity, and a failure to foresee and adequately provide for that which does occur. Thus in an Arkansas tornado, since the destruction of housing in some towns was close to 100 per cent, extensive preparations were made to receive and house evacuees in dormitories and public buildings. However, all but 2 per cent of the victims went elsewhere. There was little relationship between the time, energy, and personnel mobilized to prepare the emergency quarters and the actual usage of those facilities. In the process furthermore, crucial needs· were ignored—e.g., the necessity of a centralized clearing house of information regarding whereabouts and conditions of evacuated victims (75). In many disasters moreover, the dependency image is actively dysfunctional in that it often leads to the duplication of unnecessary efforts and an intensification of the already existing societal confusion.

The pattern of mutual and self help also prevails in other withdrawal activities besides that of obtaining shelter. Victims repeatedly show an ability, particularly when working in small informal groups, to cope with most immediate disaster problems (except those requiring highly specialized skills or special equipment as in some kinds of medical treatment). In the Flint-Beecher tornado the victim and fringe population, with almost no aid from formal agencies were able within 3 to 4 hours to rescue and bring to nearby hospitals from two thirds to three fourths of the 927 casualties. In fact, less than a fifth of the disaster-struck population had *any* contact at all with organizations during the early hours of the emergency period (76).

Even in the most extensive disasters the formal agencies contact but a relative fraction of all victims. Thus the official statistics of the American Red Cross clearly show that emergency mass care was given to but a relatively small proportion of victims in any of its principal disaster relief operations from 1906 to 1955 (77). Similarly, in a systematic study NORC found that in a post-tornado impact period of three weeks, only around a third of the respondents had had contact of any kiņd with either the Red Cross or the Salvation Army (78).

The evidence is fairly strong that far from seeking and being dependent on formal disaster organizations, these are the last source that people turn to for help when seeking to cope with crisis-created problems. Rosow has well depicted the hierarchy of assistance seeking. He noted:

> . . . the hierarchy of orientation in seeking and giving help ran from informal, intimate groups to formal, less familiar agencies. . . .
>
> Sources of help could be ranked in an order of preference or closeness to the person. People sought help first from family and intimates. Then they turned to larger membership groups where they felt a sense of belonging (*viz.*, church, occasionally place of work, etc.). They looked next to other individual members of the community (casual acquaintances and strangers). Only then, fourth, did they turn to more impersonal formal organizations. These were almost invariably the most familiar, established

community institutions (*viz.*, radio stations, police, welfare department, etc.). Their final source was the group of special disaster agencies (*viz.*, Red Cross, Civil Defense, etc.).

   . . . the general responses . . . characterized by *informal self help and spontaneous mutual aid* rather than a reliance on public services . . . caused inexperienced authorities to over-estimate the welfare needs in food, housing and clothing which they would be called upon to provide (79).

To emphasize the reasonable and striving behavior of persons in withdrawal is not to deny the importance and fundamental need for planning and actions by formal agencies. Under most circumstances, and especially the wider the scope of the disaster, organizations can do much to ameliorate and soften the problems involved in any sort of withdrawal. Nevertheless, it is a fact that responsible agencies and officials often have the incorrect images of "panic" and/or "dependency" discussed above with consequent inefficiencies and dysfunctionalities in their operations.[1]

In summary, even under very severe stress people do not become completely irresponsible or totally impotent; rather they seek in conjunction with others to solve their withdrawal problems in those ways that appear most reasonable to them as they view the situation. Generally the same can be said of them that has been said of combat soldiers: "Under the most harrowing circumstances, they are able to control fear or anxiety, to think clearly and to make appropriate decisions with rapidity" (81).

THE "CONTROL" IMAGE

Whether it be thought in terms of the "panic" and/or "dependency" images, it is also implicitly assumed by most disaster authorities that withdrawal can be controlled to a very high degree. Many formal disaster plans specify in fine details the supposed ways of controlling all but the most ephemeral of withdrawal behavior. Rather extensive structuring of the behavior is envisioned as possible, actually as well as ideally.

Unlike the other two this image might not appear overdrawn but simply obvious. This is the image disaster agencies would be expected to have. However, this is just the point. Seldom in the thinking and planning of disaster administrators, is any question raised about the basic feasibility of such social engineering. The objective is taken for granted and it is assumed that means can be devised to achieve it.

---

[1] That misconceptions are not the monopoly of organizational personnel and the general populace only, can be illustrated by noting this statement in a 1956 text on social control:

   In times of crisis such as induced by tornado, fire, flood, explosion, or destruction by war, the old habits of life are suddenly destroyed, and all existing systems of control . . . are temporarily thrown out of gear. The entire social mechanism is thrown out of line. General chaos reigns. . . . Orderly rescue work and reconstruction are impossible until some authority takes charge (p. 80).

There is even a tendency to view any "unplanned" withdrawal as unfortunate and disruptive behavior. As one agency official remarked about some upper New York state flood victims: "These darn people going off and doing things for themselves are just making a mess out of things. We can't send them off the right way and keep proper track of them" (82). A similar attitude was more formally expressed by an advisory committee for civil defense which stated that:

> After civilian disaster due to enemy action, unregulated evacuation should be de-emphasized and rigidly controlled. Any but the most carefully regulated and disciplined evacuation will tend to disrupt transport, clog roads, dissolve group and family ties, and tear the individual away from any useful group role in disaster control and restoration of the community (83).

Any formal organization or governmental agency with enough physical force at its disposal can move relatively rapidly large blocs of people. However, this has happened only where the reactions of the people involved were of no great import, and where the circumstances were defined as unusual even for a time of crisis. Thus during World War II, the U. S. government evacuated around 100,000 Japanese-Americans from the West Coast and the Soviet government transplanted certain ethnic groups from southern Russia to its Eastern areas, in both cases the moves being justified on the grounds of suspected disloyalty (84, 85).

Apart from such unusual situations, however, even totalitarian governments using compulsory measures during wartime, have found it exceedingly difficult to initiate or prevent withdrawal. Frequently orders have had to be rescinded in the face of widespread violations or violent objections. In Germany, for example, the authorities had to abandon direct and indirect attempts to prevent through official regulations, the return by children to cities from which they had been evacuated (86). Different social systems have had similar difficulties in enforcing compulsory measures. The British government in both World Wars initially banned the use of subway stations as overnight shelters from air raids. Both times, however, people continued to withdraw to the stations. The official regulations had to be changed (87). No greater success was obtained from an order aimed at preventing treacking behavior (i.e., the overnight withdrawal from a city which in the case of Plymouth, for instance, involved at one time a nightly movement of between 30,000 to 50,000 people) (88).

Lack of compliance with orders characterizes peacetime disasters too. In Zierikzee, Holland, an order to withdraw from the partially flooded city led not only to protests but an attempt to stay the order through legal court action. Nearly 3,000 of the residents never did leave but remained in defiance of repeated commands to leave and the threat of physical force (89). Likewise, orders not to withdraw from an area as sometimes have been issued in cases of epidemics have also been often disregarded (90).

When people feel they have a legitimate reason for non-compliance, the issuance of an order has no more effect than the existence of unpopular laws against gambling prevent such activity. Disaster situations in themselves do not necessarily make people more pliable to direct organizational control than they normally are.

Scientific studies of disasters clearly show that at best outside agencies impose only a very relative and segmental ordering on the withdrawal behavior of disaster victims. It is a very different picture from what organizations believe possible. In part the discrepancy derives from the "panic" and "dependency" images discussed. These being incorrect, so is the belief that stems from them about the possibility of extensive control.

However, other factors are also involved. Most disaster organizations, because of their selectivity of perception on limited objectives or atypical followers, do not perceive disregard even of official proclamations as a challenge to their basic presupposition about being able to structure withdrawal. As Fritz and Mathewson have noted: "Disaster control and relief agencies often gain a false sense of power and omnipotence over population movements by virtue of structuring one segment of the total field (91). For example, an alarm was sounded over a possible tidal wave hitting a California city. Officials issued an order and were able to clear the downtown area rather quickly. The evacuation was called a "success." However, many of those who left went to the beach to look for the wave! Successful control of movement was evaluated in terms of getting people to withdraw from a specific area, not whether the withdrawal was to a place of safety (92). More often, officials simply observe just those persons who follow their orders and advice, and take it as evidence of their command of the total situation.

Organizations also appear immune to contradictory evidence regarding their presupposition of control, because the perceived failure of victims to follow orders is interpreted in part as institutional weaknesses in the means used. Lack of extensive control is attributed to inadequacies in advance planning or inexperience in administrative skills. The problem is thus defined as a failure in procedural means and not whether the end objective is one that can actually be realized. Frequent perceptions of lack of organizational control therefore do not serve to shake the belief in possible control (somewhat in the same manner as "exceptions to the rule" seldom ever change the perception of racial and other stereotypes).

Another underlying reason for the organizational viewpoint is the belief that social norms and values undergo major changes during a disaster situation. It is believed that there occurs a relaxation or breakdown of pre-disaster taboos and values regarding modesty, privacy, intergroup relations, social class differences, etc. (93). Given relative absence of norms, it is assumed it becomes much more possible than would otherwise be the case to direct the behavior of people along certain organizationally desired lines.

However, the evidence indicates that at best there is only temporary and limited suspension of some norms. This fact is confused by the tendency in popular accounts and unsystematic observations to single out atypical happenings as if they were the model case. Thus, instances can be found of housing being shared by American Negro and white evacuees (94). There is, however, no data showing that this is ever a widespread disaster pattern. In fact, a study of a Louisiana area hit by Hurricane Audrey indicates that any such apparent deviation from norms actually may be part of the latent normative pattern, for "in times of impending danger or stress . . . it is customary [for Negroes] to seek refuge at the homes of friendly white employers" (95). Only limited changes in pre-impact norms occur in other societies also. In the Holland flood evacuations, there were no major breeches of fundamental values and mores and but a temporary setting aside of a few secondary norms (96).

This is what would be sociologically expected. It is difficult to conceive how lifetime socialization could be reversed in a very short time period, or how social interaction could proceed without assuming the predictability given by the usual norms of any group. As Clifford in his cross-cultural study has noted:

> It is unrealistic to assume that in disaster situations major values of a system will lose their force or be displaced by other values. [Such values] are important in disaster action if they are important in normal situations in the community. The way in which patterns of social action and relationships are structured tend to persist as action components (p. 97, italics removed).

Disaster organizations consequently do not have as normlessness a situation in which to structure withdrawal behavior as they seem to think they have.

Very extensive control of withdrawal might possibly be imposed by formal organizations in a situation approaching total social unorganization. However, while it is evident that there is more social or community than personal or small group disruption, disasters do not create situations of total social anomie. Only some of the customary large scale behavior patterns are rendered ineffectual, and this usually only in relatively extensive and devastating crises. And in such situations new social patterns quickly emerge after impact to restore a social equilibrium. Or as Form and Loomis have stated: "Far from having a condition of social *anomie*, social systems continue to operate through *all* of the disaster stages, new systems emerge, and continuity is found between the old and the emergent social systems" (98). Under such conditions, it is impossible that an outside framework of extensive control could be imposed on withdrawal.

Apart from being impossible, full control of withdrawal behavior is not necessarily desirable. It would for instance, be highly dysfunctional if impact populations let the burden of withdrawing fall exclusively on the efforts of disaster control agencies. It is apparent that in any but crises of the smallest scale, organizations would not be able to handle the task. The independent and striving behavior of victims represents a way pressure is taken off the security agencies of a social system, and displaced to those parts of the social structure, particularly the informal social groups, which can relatively adequately deal with the problem.

References

1. Chapman, D. (ed.), "Human behavior in disaster: a new field of social research," *J. of Soc. Issues*, 1954, 10, 3.
2. Demerath, N. and Wallace, A. (eds.), "Human adaptation to disaster," *Hum. Org.* 1956, 16.
3. Fritz, C. and Williams, H., "The human being in disasters: a research perspective," *Annals of the American Academy of Political and Social Science*, 1957, 309, 42–51.
4. Marks, E. *et al.*, Human reactions in disaster situations (Unpublished report, National Opinion Research Center, 1954).
5. Moore, H., *Tornadoes over Texas* (Austin, University of Texas Press, 1957).
6. Hirshleifer, J., "Some thoughts on the social structure after a bombing disaster," *World Politics*, 1956, 8, 206–227.
7. Toryakian, E., "Aftermath of a thermonuclear attack on the United States: some sociological considerations," *Social Probs.* 1959, 6, 291–303.
8. Ikle, F., Quarantelli, E., Rayner, J. and Withey, S., *Withdrawal Behavior in Disasters: Escape, Flight and Evaluation* (Washington: Committee on Disaster Studies, 1958).
9. "Psychological first aid in disasters," *Am. J. of Nursing*, 1955, 55, 437.
10. ———, and Kincaid, H., *Some Social Aspects of Wartime Evacuation of American Cities* (Washington: Committee on Disaster Studies, 1956, 5.
11. Clifford, R., *Informal Group Actions in the Rio Flood* (Preliminary report to the Committee on Disaster Studies, February, 1955).
12. ———, Control Problems in Disasters (unpublished paper).
13. ———, "An analysis of panic behavior" (unpublished paper).
14. Peterson, V., "Panic, the ultimate weapon?" *Collier's*, August 21, 1953.
15. Federal Civil Defense Administration, *The Problem of Panic* (Washington: Government Printing Office, 1955).
16. ———, *The Role of the Warden in Panic Prevention* (Washington: Government Printing Office, 1954).
17. Fritz, C. and Mathewson, J., *Convergence Behavior in Disasters: A Problem in Social Control* (Washington: Committee on Disaster Studies, 1957).
18. Galdston, I. (ed.), *Panic and Morale* (New York: Academy of Medicine, 1958).
19. Ikle, F. and Kincaid, H., *op. cit.*
20. *Information and Training for Civil Defense* (Part IX of Project East River) (New York: Associated Universities Inc., 1952).
21. Ikle, F., Quarantelli, E., Rayner, J. and Withey, S., *op. cit.*, 7.
22. Titmus, R., *Problems of Social Policy* (London: Longmans Co., 1950), 23.

23. Ikle, F., *Social Impact of Bomb Destruction* (Norman: University of Oklahoma Press, 1958), 79.
24. *Information and Training for Civil Defense, op. cit.*
25. Ikle, F. *et al., op. cit.*
26. Fritz, C. and Mathewson, J., *op. cit.*
27. Ikle, F., *op. cit.*
28. ———, "An analysis of panic behavior," *op. cit.*
29. Titmus, R., *op. cit.*
30. Ikle, F. *et al., op. cit.*
31. Marks, E., *et al., op. cit.*
32. Titmus, R., *op. cit.*, 311.
33. Ikle, F., *et al., op. cit.*, 8.
34. Prell, A., "Successive hurricanes and cultural defenses in a New England City," paper read at the August 1955 annual meeting of the American Sociological Society.
35. Ikle, F., *et al., op. cit.*
36. Danzig, E., Thayer, P. and Galanter, L., *The Effects of a Threatening Rumor on A Disaster Stricken Community: The Port Jervis Study* (Washington: Committee on Disaster Studies, 1958), 10.
37. Ikle, F., *op. cit.*, 10.
38. Titmus, R., *op. cit.*
39. Ikle, F., *op. cit.*, 90.
40. Ikle, F., *et al., op. cit.*
41. Ikle, F., *op. cit.*
42. ———, "The Rio Grande Flood . . ." *op. cit.*, 84.
43. ———, *op. cit.*, 118.
44. Logan, L., Killian, L., and Mars, W., *A Study of the Effects of Catastrophe on Social Disorganization* (Chevy Chase: Operations Research Office, 1952).
45. Marks, E., *et al., op. cit.*, 135–136.
46. Ikle, F., "An analysis of panic behavior," *op. cit.*
47. Marks, E., "The behavior of panic participants," *Sociol. and Social Res.* 1957, 41, 187–194.
48. ———, "The nature and conditions of panic," *Am. J. of Sociol.*, 1954, 60:267–275.
49. Danzig, E., Thayer, P., and Galanter, L., *op. cit.*
50. Cantril, H., Gaudet, H., and Hertzog, H., *The Invasion from Mars* (Princeton: Princeton University Press, 1940).
51. Ikle, F., "An analysis of panic behavior," *op. cit.*
52. ———, *op. cit.*
53. ———, "An analysis of panic behavior," *op. cit.*
54. Bunker, E., "The voluntary effort in disaster relief," *Annals of the American Academy of Political and Social Science*, 1957, 309:110.
55. Tyhurst, J., "The role of transition states—including disasters—in mental illness," in Walter Reed Army Institute of Research, *Symposium on Preventive and Social Psychiatry* (Washington: Government Printing Office, 1945).
56. Wallace, A., *Tornado in Worcester* (Washington: Committee on Disaster Studies, 1956).
57. Demerath, N. and Wallace, A., *op. cit.*
58. Ikle, F. *et al., op. cit.*
59. Tyhurst, J., *op. cit.*, 152.

60. Wallace, A., *op. cit.*, 110.
61. Fritz, C. and Marks, E., "The NORC studies of human behavior in disaster," *J. of Social Issues*, 1954, 10:39.
62. Form, W., and Nosow, S., *Community in Disaster* (New York: Harper, 1958), 86.
63. Kessing, F., "The papuan orokaiva vs. Mt. Lamington: Cultural shock and its aftermath," *Hum. Org.*, 1952, 11:16–22.
64. Schneider, C., "Typhoons on Yap," *Hum. Org.*, 1957, 16: 10–15.
65. Ikle, F., "An analysis of panic behavior," *op. cit.*
66. Rosow, I., *Authority in Natural Disasters* (to be published by the Committee on Disaster Studies).
67. Quarantelli, E., "Note on the protective function of the family in disasters," *Marriage and Family Living* (in press).
68. Ikle, F., *et al.*, *op. cit.*
69. Young, M., "The role of the extended family in a disaster," *Hum. Relations*, 1954, 3:383–391.
70. ———, "The Rio Grande Flood . . ." *op. cit.*, 84.
71. Titmus, R., *op. cit.*, 301.
72. Clifford, R., *op. cit.*
73. Stile, W., "How a community met a disaster: Yuba city flood," *Annals of the American Academy of Political and Social Science*, 1957, 309:163.
74. American National Red Cross, Shelters: *Disaster Preparedness Leaflet No. 6*, 1948.
75. Ikle, F., *et al.*, *op. cit.*
76. Form, W. and Nosow, S., *op. cit.*, 117.
77. Smith, D., "Emergency mass care," *Annals of the American Academy of Political and Social Science*, 1957, 309:121–122.
78. Marks, E. *et al.*, *op. cit.*
79. Rosow, I., *op. cit.*, 87–88.
80. Landis, P., *Social Control* (New York: Lippincott, 1956), 399.
81. Grinker, R. and Spiegel, J., *Men Under Stress* (Philadelphia: Blakiston, 1945), 53–54.
82. Ikle, F., "An analysis of panic behavior," *op. cit.*
83. *An Introduction to the Psychiatric Aspects of Civil Defense* (Topeka: Group for the Advancement of Psychiatry, 1951), 4.
84. Peterson, W., "A general typology of migration," *Am. Sociol. Rev.*, 1958, 23:256–265.
85. Thomas, D., *The Salvage* (Berkeley: University of California, 1952).
86. U. S. Strategic Bombing Survey, *The Effects of Strategic Bombing on German Morale* (Washington: Government Printing Office, 1945).
87. Clifford, R., "Control Problems in Disasters," *op. cit.*
88. Titmus, R., *op. cit.*, 308.
89. Clifford, R., "Control problems in disasters," *op. cit.*
90. Ikle, F., *et al.*, *op. cit.*
91. Fritz, C. and Mathewson, J., *op. cit.*, 80.
92. Clifford, R., "Control problems in disasters," *op. cit.*
93. Fritz, C. and Williams, H., *op. cit.*, 42–51.
94. Perry, S., Siler, E. and Bloch, D., *The Child and His Family in Disaster: A Study of the 1953 Vicksburg Tornado* (Washington: Committee on Disaster Studies, 1956).
95. Fogleman, C. and Parenton, V., "Disaster and aftermath: selected aspects

of individual and group behavior in critical situations," *Social Forces*, 1959, 38:130.

96. Clifford, R., "Control problems in disasters," *op. cit.*
97. ——, "The Rio Grande Flood . . . ," *op. cit.*, 127.
98. Form, W., *et al.*, "The persistence and emergence of social and cultural systems in disasters," *Amer. Sociol. Review*, 1956, 21:18.

37

The Riot That Didn't
Happen

ROBERT SHELLOW and
DEREK V. ROEMER*

Although citizens traditionally rely upon police for prevention and control of civil riot, most police departments have only limited experience in coping with large crowds, much less full riot conditions. Moreover, it seems likely that police will be called to serve in this capacity with growing frequency as public streets become more and more the stage on which social protests and counter-protests are acted out.

This growing threat to civil order poses questions of specific relevance for social scientists. Can the approach and theories of social science be put to use in communities facing the threat or fact of civil disorder? Can social scientists study riot behavior as it develops, while at the same time sharing the responsibility for its prevention?

The authors of this paper were confronted by these two questions in the summer of 1965. A national motorcycle race was scheduled for the Labor Day weekend at Upper Marlboro, the County seat of Prince George's County, Maryland. This county of 500,000 population is adjacent to Washington, D.C., and is partly suburban, partly rural. Upper Marlboro is in a rural sector, but is only about 15 miles from well-populated suburbs.

Our involvement in what later turned out to be six weeks of planning for riot prevention began as a casual conversation between one of the authors and a detective lieutenant.[1] The news media had reported all the

Reprinted from *Social Problems*, (Fall 1966), 14:221–233, by permission of the authors and the publishers.

* Chief and Project Director respectively, Adolescent Process Section, Mental Health Study Center, National Institute of Mental Health. The two authors constitute the "staff" referred to in the paper.

The authors wish to acknowledge the contribution of senior officers and men of the Prince George's County Police Department whose decisions and actions were ultimately responsible for the project's success. In this regard, we wish to cite especially Inspector Roland Sweitzer, Deputy Chief Vincent Free, and Captain Thomas Rogato, who carried the burden of planning and daily command decisions, and Chief George Panagoulis whose sanction of the project guaranteed the necessary flexibility in the assignment of men and equipment throughout the Labor Day weekend. We also wish to express our gratitude to the following motorcycle clubs: the D. C. Strokers, the Saddle Squires, the Draggin' Gypsies and the D. C. Ramblers whose members were kind enough to introduce us into the world of motorcycling.

[1] We had been consulting and collaborating with the County police on a variety

gory details of the Weir's Beach riot which followed the National Championship motorcycle races near Laconia, New Hampshire. The first details of the July 4th resort riots were still Page One news. The lieutenant reported that shortly after the Weir's Beach episode three motorcyclists, claiming to be "Hell's Angels," were arrested and jailed for disorderly conduct by town policemen in Prince George's County. Angered by being forced to bathe for court, the cyclists threatened to return in force over Labor Day to "tear up the County."

Wishing to be kept posted on the local situation, we spoke to the Inspector responsible for police action over Labor Day. He was concerned, but he wasn't sure how seriously to take the possibility of violence. We all agreed that very little was known about the "Hell's Angels" and how they were likely to behave among several thousand motorcyclists amassed for a big race. Our professional curiosity aroused, we offered to try to chase down the rumors, and bring the results of our inquiries back to the police. But two weeks of search failed to turn up so much as one Hell's Angel, though the rumors of invasion and destruction were persistent and proliferating.[2]

When we reviewed accounts of a number of recent riots and disturbances in connection with recreational or sporting events,[3] we noted several factors which seemed to be significant in all of them. Though they are not based on a systematic review of the relevant sociological literature, we have found that the following generalizations fit rather well with at least one major theoretical analysis:[4]

1. An influx of outsiders into a small town or circumscribed amusement area, where the number of outsiders was large relative to the number of local inhabitants and control personnel.
2. The outsiders were distinguished from "locals" by some common feature such as an intense interest (e.g., motorcycling), an age group (e.g., college youth), place of residence (e.g., urban areas), race, etc.

---

of matters for some years, and had developed informal, first-name relationships with many officers.

[2] We managed to track down one individual who was alleged to be acquainted with genuine "Hell's Angels." He said he could see no earthly reason why Hell's Angels or anyone else would want to leave California and come to Prince George's County. In mid-August we learned he himself had left for California on his "motor," and did not intend to return before Spring, if at all.

[3] Most of these accounts were from newspapers, with the exception of a very informative report and analysis of a 1963 riot at Garnett, Kansas in connection with a sports car race. The report was prepared by Bill D. Schul, Juvenile Director, and is available from the Office of the Attorney General of Kansas, in Topeka.

[4] R. H. Turner and L. M. Killian, *Collective Behavior*, Englewood Cliffs, N.J.: Prentice-Hall, 1957; R. H. Turner, "Collective Behavior," in E. L. Faris (ed.), *Handbook of Modern Sociology*, Chicago: Rand McNally, 1964. Though all the events referred to above occurred in recreational settings on major holidays or at national sports events, similarities to many of the race riots and political disturbances discussed by these authors can be discerned.

3. The distinction between "locals" and "outsiders" was often made more visible by differences between the two in dress, argot, and other expressive behavior.

The specific conditions under which exuberance and rowdiness exploded into rioting seemed to be the following:

1. Recreational, service and control facilities were "flooded" by overwhelming numbers of visitors who were then left at loose ends, ready for any kind of "action."
2. Ineffectual, often provocative attempts at control and expression of authority by police or officials.
3. Development of a sense of group solidarity among members of the crowd.

Often the locals, including the authorities, contributed to the developing cohesion by perceiving the visitors as a homogeneous mass, attributing negative characteristics to them as a class, labelling them, e.g., as "hoodlums" or "young punks," and then treating them accordingly. The effect of opposition or attack in increasing group cohesion is well documented.[5] If the opposition is ineffectual as well, many members of the developing mob begin to sense its potential power. (Several reports of disturbances attributed careful preplanning to a small cadre of dedicated instigators, who allegedly circulated rumors before the event and selected targets on the scene. Actual proof of "planning," however, as opposed to mere repetition of common rumors, is difficult to obtain.)

It had become obvious that in order to prepare for the Labor Day weekend, much information would be needed about the organization of motorcycling, as a sport and as a way of life. Moving from one enthusiast to another and making contacts at the local Harley-Davidson dealer, we made a number of discoveries.

Motorcyclists come from all walks of life. The majority are employed, and need to be, since as much as $3,000 may be tied up in a "motor." The devotees insist that the size of the machine separates the men from the boys. Those who own enormous Harley-Davidsons and the large Triumphs or BSA's, and who engage in competitive events such as races, "field events" and "hill climbs," see themselves as a breed apart from the "candy ass" owners of Hondas and the lightweights. For the former group, the motorcycle often serves as the fulcrum of social and even family life. They enjoy being able to take off any evening at a moment's notice and ride, say, from Washington, D.C. to Atlantic City, returning as the sun rises.

    [5] F. M. Thrasher, The Gang, Chicago: University of Chicago Press, 1927; M. Sherif and C. W. Sherif, Reference Groups: Exploration into Conformity and Deviation of Adolescents, New York: Harper and Row, 1964.

They travel regularly to weekend field meets and races, usually camping overnight on the scene.

Like many hobby-sports, motorcycling has its formal organization, The American Motorcycle Association (AMA) and its "sanctioned" members. AMA clubs have tight rules and tolerate little deviance. There are other clubs, some of which aspire to AMA membership and some of which suit those who enjoy a more relaxed and casual organization. The latter require only that members not seriously embarrass the club in public. They tend to be more tolerant in their attitudes regarding noisy mufflers and styling, and less regimented during group expeditions. All get classified by the AMA as "outlaws."

Aside from these more or less conforming clubs, the "outlaw" class also includes groups of dedicated rowdies who pride themselves on their ability to intimidate and destroy. The *Hell's Angels Motorcycle Club of California* is such a group, as are the *Gooses,* from New York and New Jersey, or the *Pagans,* from the Washington area. Some groups and individuals trade on the established reputation of the "Hell's Angels," imitating their insignia, the "winged death's head and wheel." [6]

Spokesmen for the motorcycling "Establishment" often refer to the "one percent who cause all the trouble," and give the sport a bad image. The rowdies have proudly accepted "one percenter" as an honorific epithet, and often have it emblazoned on their costume as a badge of commitment. It is the "one percenter" who personifies the popular stereotype of the motorcycle gang member, as portrayed by Marlon Brando in "The Wild Ones." Current styles among these individuals include long hair, beards, earrings, oily dungarees which are never washed, and an enormous variety of bizarre, highly personalized regalia. Some affect the habit attributed to "beatniks" of never bathing.

Regardless of their reference group or status within it, motorcyclists are of one voice in complaining of police persecution, and they all report victimization on the streets by ordinary motorists. Many respectable motorcyclists, like the "rowdy outlaws," see themselves as a persecuted minority. [7]

With regard to the Labor Day weekend itself, we learned that the schedule of events was more complex than we or the police had thought. Aside from the big race on Sunday, the "Ninth Annual Tobacco Trail Classic" at the Upper Marlboro track, there were lesser races at the same track on Saturday. The main race was for the first time a National Championship event, with top riders competing for points toward the national title. At the Vista track, 14 miles away but within the same police jurisdiction,

[6] Jackets with insignia, often brought back as souvenirs of a California trip, can be traded around from one motorcyclist to another, each taking his turn as a "Hell's Angel" and enjoying all the rights and privileges attendant thereto.

[7] One suspects that even respectable enthusiasts found attractive as well as abhorrent elements in the outlaw image, even though they resented and suffered from its indiscriminate application to all motorcyclists by the general public.

there were to be "field events" (drag races, "riding the plank," "sack races," etc.) on Saturday and Sunday and an AMA-sanctioned race meet Monday. The sponsors of the Upper Marlboro races had also scheduled a Saturday night race, at a track 30 miles away in the Baltimore suburbs, "to give people something to do and keep them out of trouble."

The Vista track had in the past operated as an "outlaw" track without AMA sanction, and most or all of the competitors and spectators had been Negroes. However, in 1965 it achieved sanctioned status, and its events were now listed in the national calendar. A dance hall, popular with Washington area Negroes, was located in the track infield and would be operating every night of the weekend. Very likely large proportions of those attending the motorcycle events at Vista would be Negroes. The crowd at the Marlboro track was expected to be between 3,000 and 6,000; a much smaller crowd was anticipated at Vista. Most motorcyclists we spoke to thought there would be a great deal of migration during the weekend from one track to another and among the various camping areas (assuming there were more than one), the taverns, and other recreation spots. Easy mobility is the essence of motorcycling.

Concluding that our staff enjoyed a special and privileged relationship with motorcyclists, the police asked us whether or not the race should be called off. We did not feel we could take responsibility for the decision, but we joined in the deliberations. To cancel a public event on the basis of thin rumor alone was a dangerous precedent to set, yet to knowingly jeopardize the safety of innocent people was unthinkable. Finally it was decided to permit the race to be run as scheduled, with every effort being made to avert violence. Our shift in role from outside consultant to partnership with the police in this project tied us much closer to the action and events of the weekend than would have been true in the role of detached scientist-observer.

GOALS AND STRATEGIES

The decision to permit the race made, we then developed a set of major goals which we felt should guide our own planning and that of the police.

First of all we encouraged sober planning for all the events and contingencies of the long weekend. Naturally, advance planning was not foreign to a professional police department. Nonetheless we felt that the unsettled state of the "Hell's Angels" rumors, plus our refusal to make pseudo-authoritative pronouncements on the probable course of events, helped maintain a degree of controlled anxiety among police officials. This limited anxiety went far to prevent a premature resolution of the planning process, either through panicky reliance on harshness or toughness on the one hand, or complacent relaxation on the other. Planning, we felt, should have three major objectives: first, anticipation of the kinds, numbers and distribution of motorcyclists and spectators, as well as the activities they would engage in and the amount of localized roving to be expected; second, the disposition of police officers and their instructions both as to general attitude and specific actions in various contingencies; third, coordination of the several police departments concerned, including the State Police, and the local police of nearby towns and counties to which the motorcyclists might travel in search of recreation. We relied on the County police to make contact with the other departments.

The second goal was to avoid a polarization of relations between the authorities on the one hand and motorcyclists in general on the other.[8] We addressed our efforts to both groups. As we explored the "culture" of motorcycling, we tried to keep the police informed and interested in what we learned. We arranged a meeting between some local motorcyclists and police officials; films of sport motorcycling were shown, and afterwards each group gave frank expression to its gripes concerning the other. Our educational goals with the police were: 1) to show them that motorcyclists are not essentially different from other citizens, and need not be treated as a breed apart; 2) to inform them that motorcyclists are not a homogeneous class but come in a variety of shapes and sizes, some innocuous, some potentially troublesome; 3) to impress upon them that indiscriminate harsh treatment of all motorcyclists would confirm the latter's sense of persecution, increase group solidarity among them, and go far toward creating the very polarization we wished to avoid.

In working with local motorcyclists, we had two objectives: 1) to involve the organized groups in the actual control effort, asking them not only to refrain from participating in or serving as passive audience to rowdiness, but to help actively in identifying potential trouble areas, keeping police informed of large group movements, etc.; 2) to weaken the respectable motorcyclists' sense of solidarity with the "one percenters" through reinforcing their existing concern for the deteriorating "image" of motorcycling and pointing up their vested interest in a peaceful race meet.[9]

Our third major goal was to ensure that adequate facilities were provided for the visiting motorcyclists, with an eye to both containment and entertainment. The object here was to inhibit milling behavior, a usual precursor to crowd disturbances. Specifically, we suggested that adequate and convenient camping facilities were customary and essential at motorcycle meets, and that certain informal and rather dangerous recreations (such as drag racing and stunt riding in the camp grounds), which do not

---

[8] Cf. use of this term in J. S. Coleman, *Community Conflict*, Glencoe, Ill.: Free Press, 1957.

[9] Organized motorcyclists viewed with alarm the possibility of wholesale cancelling of scheduled events. A major meet had been cancelled only a few weeks previously, in Pennsylvania. We ascertained that the cancellation was due to past, and threatened rowdyism.

impinge on the non-motorcycling citizenry, are also customary and ought to be permitted.[10]

Finally, our fourth major objective was to monitor the events of the weekend and keep a continuous flow of intelligence coming into command headquarters, so that the senior officer could make effective decisions. Here we served in something of a combined research and undercover capacity, checking out rumors, keeping current with the temper of various groups, clubs and gangs among the motorcyclists, and observing events such as fights or accidents as they occurred. We made a point of spending time in places where the County police could not routinely go.

EVENTS LEADING UP TO THE WEEKEND

Rumors of the arrival *en masse* of the Hell's Angels of California persisted through Saturday of the three-day weekend and were *never* clearly proved or disproved. However, we learned Hell's Angels were anticipated in resorts all the way from Ocean City, Maryland, 140 miles away, to the Pacific coast. Three scattered locations (a tavern, the race track and a whole town) in Prince George's County were to be wrecked. All these rumors seemed to be circulating mostly among youth and motorcyclists. We began to see that the Hell's Angels were assuming a mythical character. They had become folk heroes, functioning both as vicarious exemplars of behavior most youth could only fantasy (unless swept away in mob activity), and as legendary champions who could come to the rescue of the oppressed and persecuted.[11] An older motorcyclist, witnessing police harassment of his fellows at a town outside Prince George's County, was heard to remark, "Just wait 'til the Angels hear about this when they come in tomorrow. They'll come down here and tear this place apart."

The police never did accept the idea of actively involving local motorcycle clubs in the control effort, even though we offered to do all the leg work in getting club representatives together for a meeting. An exception was the large club that sponsored the Marlboro races. The Inspector warned them severely that any trouble this weekend would greatly reduce the likelihood of the race being permitted next year.[12] However, he emphasized

---

[10] We had noted that at Laconia the only permissible camping area was 40 to 50 miles from the track. The campers were reluctant to set out on the long return trip after each day's racing, some preferring simply to stay up all night. Thus they remained in the town of Weir's Beach long past the time when they might ordinarily have returned to secluded camping areas for an evening of drag-racing, motor-revving and beer-drinking in mutually acceptable segregation from the rest of the citizenry.

[11] O. E. Klapp, *Heroes, Villains, and Fools,* Englewood Cliffs, N.J.: Prentice-Hall (Spectrum), 1962.

[12] The earlier possibility of the race being cancelled had upset the sponsoring club considerably. This was the most important national race yet scheduled here, and a substantial sum had been invested in publicity, etc. Even the national office of the AMA

that the department would not discriminate in any way against motor-cyclists, and that they by no means classified all motorcyclists with the Hell's Angels. The Inspector convinced the sponsoring club of the necessity of hiring uniformed guards for the race track. The club also assured us that adequate camping facilities would be provided.

There was little advance coordination among the various police departments in the area. The State Police initially announced a policy of "keep them moving," and said they would "get tough" with any rowdy-looking types they encountered, but later they did conform to the approach of the County police. The detailed cooperation between departments that we had envisioned, like involvement of the motorcycle clubs in police planning, was probably considered too far outside normal practice to be warranted by the situation.

Among these largely negative circumstances, one particularly positive development stood out. At each police roll call prior to the Labor Day weekend, all the uniformed men were instructed to treat all motorcyclists just as they would any motorist visiting the County. They were told that only a very small minority of motorcyclists were troublemakers, and that only the behavior, not the style of dress, haircut or bodily cleanliness was a matter of police concern. Thus the professional police attitude of neutrality and commitment to impartial law-enforcement, characteristic of the department's work in other special situations, was reinforced with respect to a new group.[13]

On Saturday morning of the race weekend we and the police were quite disturbed to learn that the sponsoring AMA club had reneged on its promise to provide public camping facilities. Apparently they wished to avoid the expense of renting portable outhouses, which were likely to be broken up for firewood in the course of the weekend. We were further disturbed to learn that early arrivals, some of whom were pretty ragged and rough looking, had already set up camp in the large field usually rented for that purpose. This created a tricky problem for the police. They could not legitimately enter the field, which was private property, unless the owner complained or a violation of law occurred which was visible from the public highway. If the police officially notified the owner, he would be bound to ask that the trespassers be removed, because of his liability for damages incurred by people who were on his property with his implied permission. Eviction of the growing crowd of squatters would have meant removing a noisy, potentially troublesome group from a location remote from residences and businesses where the amount of property they could damage was limited. Furthermore they were not, at that time, visibly violating laws. There was no way to predict where they would go if evicted,

---

was moved to write an angry letter citing numerous motorcycle events attracting much larger crowds which had been held during the year without incident.

[13] R. Shellow, "Reinforcing Police Neutrality in Civil Rights Confrontations," *Journal of Applied Behavioral Science*, 1 (July–August–September, 1965), pp. 243–254.

but obviously they would not go home, so early in the weekend. The problem might simply have been scattered all over the County, aggravating the difficulties of control while at the same time provoking resentment which could have been turned against innocent citizens.

It was decided that notification of the owner of the field was not warranted and that there were tactical advantages in keeping the field open, since it seemed to be attracting and holding the rowdier element. So long as they were all in one place, surveillance would be simple and response to trouble could be quick.

The activities on the field were kept under continuous but unobtrusive observation. Police cars were continually passing the field, occasionally pausing near the entrance; the people on the field were thus kept aware of the police presence in the general area, but not so heavily as to arouse feelings of persecution. The 45-man Civil Disturbance Unit (CDU), trained in riot control but lacking experience in full riot conditions, had been mobilized and sent out on the road the night before (Friday). Only a few motorcyclists were seen in the County and the Unit was dismissed around midnight. The usual dance at the Vista track was held without incident.

From Saturday through Monday the entire force, including the CDU, was ordered on 12-hour shifts. The men were kept on the road except when responding to trouble calls, thus providing extra control for the normally heavy holiday beach traffic. We felt that the men would have been able to respond more quickly to large-scale trouble if they had been concentrated in two or three central stand-by locations rather than dispersed over the County's 486 square miles. However, police officials judged that the disadvantage of a possible delay in mobilization of force was offset by the double payoff from the same investment in overtime pay—more extensive traffic control as well as riot prevention.

An elaborate communications system was set up, employing the police radio (monitored by newspapers and wire services) and also a Civil Defense band which permitted more detailed discussion and open references to likely trouble spots. A special radio code was established so that squad cars using the police band could notify headquarters briefly and in confidence of the presence of groups of motorcyclists.

THE WEEKEND AS IT DEVELOPED

On Saturday, only a few hundred spectators attended the scheduled lightweight and novice races at Marlboro. Across the highway those squatters, dusty out-of-towners and locals who preferred the role of contestant to that of passive onlooker conducted their own impromptu field games.[14]

---

[14] The vast majority of motorcyclists who came to see the 75-mile National race never entered the field. There was virtually no contact between those on the field and

The entire center of the squatters' field, despite its ruts and hummocks, became a drag strip. Groups, clubs, even families had set up camp sites around the periphery of the field in a broken crescent.

Groups and couples who settled on the extreme ends of the crescent appeared to have expensive camping equipment and rather conventional dress. Dead center at the head of the drag strip, the most ragged troop of squatters set up headquarters in a large army tent, its center pole flying a red flag. Sullen young men and girls milled around this command post drinking beer and making menacing noises at curiosity seekers. Clusters of jackets marked "Hell's Angels," "Pagans," or "The Gooses," were seen. Individuals sported a nose ring, a swastika, a Halloween wig, or gold cross earrings; many wore their hair in shoulder-length manes.

A group of mostly short-haired locals, more or less neat in T-Shirts and jeans, tried to introduce some order into the drag races. One tried to control racing by flagging each pair of racers to a start. He was successful for several hours but finally the enormous quantities of beer, hard liquor, and green wine consumed by participants began to undermine his authority. Racers roared past him without waiting for the flag. He shouted for order, but few responded. Non-racers criss-crossed the drag strip, narrowly escaping collision. The proximity of the self-appointed track superintendents to the encampment of long-haired outsiders and locals became abrasive. Accidents began to occur; and finally a fight broke out between a very wobbly Pagan and a helmeted short-haired local. The short-haired hero punched the Pagan unconscious, and was then successfully protected by his associates from assault by the rest of the Pagans. The victor had the poor taste and bad judgment to sit triumphantly astride the hood of a truck, waving his beer can in bravado challenge. Now all the "one percenters" joined in a confederation and charged *en masse* toward the short-haired locals. Just at that moment a drunken cyclist lost his machine to a rut in the track. His mishap was noted by police on the highway who dispatched an ambulance along with five police cruisers. The vehicles poured onto the field and fanned out in a half-circle around the casualty, thus coincidentally presenting the crowd with an array of flashing red lights. The unexpected show of power was so sudden and instantaneous that the would-be warriors at the head of the strip broke ranks and returned to their staging area. Unknowingly (since the conflict had not reached a stage where observers off the field could distinguish it as such), the police had put a stop to what might have been a bloody war, for the local motorcycle enthusiasts were far outnumbered by the combined force of Pagans, "Hell's Angels," [15] and

---

the ten times greater number of persons who remained at the track. A busy high-speed dual-lane highway separated the two areas.

[15] Note that "Hell's Angels" appears in quotes wherever the reference is to participants in local events. It was never established that any bona fide members of the Hell's Angels Motorcycle Club of California were present in Prince George's County. None of the persons wearing Hell's Angels insignia who were arrested in the County

Gooses. Quite fortuitously, those spoiling for trouble got the message that there was a large force of police nearby, ready for action on a moment's notice.

Following the withdrawal of the police, twenty "Hell's Angels" and Gooses set out to replenish their beer supply at the Old Tavern nearby. Just as they started to throw their weight around in the bar and threaten the owner, a police sergeant and another officer entered the room. The group quieted down and waited for the action. Three cyclists moved to the window to assess the size of the sergeant's force; four cruisers were visible. The sergeant opened with, "I hope you all are behaving yourselves." Remembering from a conversation with us that motorcycle chains worn loosely over the hips rather than through belt loops should be considered weapons, he asked, "What's that chain for?" "Hey, man, I lock up my motor with it." "Well, aren't you afraid someone'll steal your motor, not being locked up and all? You better come with me while we put that chain on right, son." The group tensed, then relaxed as the young man elected to go quietly and do as the sergeant suggested. Shortly after this low-key encounter the group roared back to the field and the Old Tavern was prematurely closed for the weekend.

At eleven that evening about 75 cyclists were seen by one of our staff at a Rock 'n' Roll beach resort in a neighboring county. The Chief of Police there had already advised the press of his intention to lock up any rowdy motorcyclists who showed up. He arranged for the State Police to back him up. Twenty state troopers in riot dress with five dogs were lined up on the main street across from the crowd of motorcycle riders, while six local policemen pushed and poked with night sticks, arresting several who took exception to their tactics. By 1:30 A.M. most of the motorcyclists had left town. Statements to the press by the Chief greatly exaggerated the numbers present and arrested, thus giving an unwarranted notoriety to the evening.

By Sunday morning 300 motorcyclists had settled on the field at Marlboro. Those who had been driven from the beach resort were in a mean mood. Under the direction of the unofficial starter drag racing resumed at a more frantic tempo than on the day before. Across the highway a steady stream of spectators poured onto the track for the afternoon race. Few took notice of the accidents that were beginning to occur on the field.

At two in the afternoon a fire was set in a railroad caboose on a siding behind the field. Fire equipment and police responded quickly; no attempt was made to find the arsonists. At three o'clock a crane was started on an adjacent construction site and tools were stolen from its cab. At four-thirty, coinciding with the Tobacco Trail Classic across the road, a young man removed the license plates from his dilapidated old car and set it afire.

---

gave California addresses. In any case there were less than ten people in the entire crowd wearing such insignia.

With another sportsman straddling the hood, the owner drove onto the drag strip and jumped free. The car rammed an accelerating motorcycle. Both hood rider and motorcyclist were thrown on impact, both suffering broken legs. A fire truck arrived to put out the fire amid jeers from spectators. A police lieutenant supervised aid to the injured, making humorous asides to cool the excited crowd and enable the ambulance to remove the casualties to the hospital.

About six o'clock the long-haired groups demanded that the locals turn over the starting flag to a "Hell's Angel" who appeared to be one of their leaders. Fighting broke out but subsided immediately when one squad of the CDU (10 men) drove onto the field. This time the police had riot equipment visible—helmets, clubs, shotguns, gas masks. The crowd dispersed; the squad withdrew. Since tension on the field seemed to be building, command officers set up an observation post on a cloverleaf approach overlooking the field. At six-thirty the flagman and a delegation from his club came up to plead with command officers to clear the field of hoodlums; they threatened to bring in their own weapons if police didn't protect them. Since the delegation could not agree on who should be charged with what, police action was delayed.

At seven several men broke away from the milling crowd at the center of the field and ran to their machines. From the observation post, it was clear they were returning with bars, chains and other weapons. The entire CDU was sent on to the field where they quickly assembled in riot formation. The Inspector drawled out over the bull-horn, "All right men, you've had your fun, now it's time to go home." Before he finished his sentence motorcycles began to move out of the field. Within twenty minutes the area was clear except for some peaceful campers who were allowed to finish their dinner.

Up to this time, the importance of containing trouble makers on the field was dominant in the minds of commanding officers. But if the crowd were allowed to remain overnight, fighting probably would continue, but now under cover of darkness. Dispersing the squatters while it was still light would, hopefully, send them on their way home. The alternative, isolating and removing the instigators and mob leaders, was complicated by the fact that police could not remain on the field, and by the inability or unwillingness of cyclists to serve as complainants.

Fifteen minutes after the field was vacated, ten men and a girl were arrested outside the Old Tavern, where they had started to break windows. Within minutes, another ten, including the leading "Hell's Angel," were arrested as trespassers at a filling station where they refused to make way for customers. There was no further trouble in the County, at the Vista track, or at the beach resort, though an anxious lookout was maintained till early the next morning. By Monday it was obvious that the danger had passed. The final races at Vista were held without incident, although some "Hell's Angels" and Pagans were rumored to be among the spectators.

REACTION TO THE WEEKEND

Both the command officers and the County Commissioner responsible for police matters were satisfied that the police had conducted themselves effectively and that the control effort had been a success. They felt, however, that the situation had not warranted the extra expense and trouble. Estimates of cost ranged from $6,000 to $10,000, but certainly some of the overtime pay would have been necessary for a Labor Day weekend even without motorcyclists. The Commissioner announced that he couldn't see why the County had "to put up year after year with the influx of motorcycle tramps who camp out, drink and fight among themselves." [16]

Like the Commissioner, most of the police leadership was opposed to permitting the race next year. We refrained from offering unsolicited and premature advice on the issue of future races. The club sponsoring the Marlboro races was considering cutting down the meet to a one-day event and preventing camping altogether, in the hope that this would make the event more acceptable to authorities.

Since we were unable to maintain contacts among Pagans, Gooses, or "Hell's Angels," we could not ascertain *their* reactions to police policy and procedure. We did talk to our acquaintance at the local Harley-Davidson dealership, which provides service and parts for many out-of-town motorcyclists. He reported that for the first time in nine years of race meets he had heard none of the usual atrocity stories of police mistreatment of motorcyclists in the County. The local short-haired motorcyclists who had been in the fighting on the field felt that the police had exercised entirely too much restraint in dealing with that situation. They did not know, until we told them, that the field had not been rented this year.

CONCLUSION

There was no riot in Prince George's County. The citizens and their property emerged almost unscathed. The races and field events were held. The campers drank, dragged and scuffled undisturbed for a longer period than any of them probably expected.

Was all the concern, planning and extra police activity justified? Would the Gooses, Pagans and alleged "Hell's Angels" have been just as peaceful anyway, despite their frightening appearance? We think not, and cite the forays against the Old Tavern, the crane and the caboose, the incinerated car, and the brawling which broke out repeatedly on the field as evidence that, if unhindered and undaunted, the hoodlum element sooner or later would have left the camping area and sought glory and reputation in new arenas, before new audiences. These seem to be people

[16] Quoted in *The Prince George's Post*, Thursday, September 9, 1965, p. 9.

who need and seek the stimulation of collective action, excitement, and violence. Without it they become depressed and demoralized. They have an affinity for the romantic role of outlaw, which is perhaps the only status in which they feel they can stand out as individuals. In it they approach the dramatic, larger-than-life identity of the mythic Hell's Angel. And only the self-justifying power of mob action could support such a heroic identity for youths such as these. We see them, then as mob seekers and mob creators.

We consider four factors to have been critical in preventing the spread of violence to the local citizenry.

Most important was *the general police policy of strength, fairness and neutrality,* which influenced all the tactics employed. Law violations were dealt with immediately and firmly, but motorcyclists were not harassed or deliberately antagonized. The availability of overwhelming force, literally on a moment's notice, was demonstrated but not over-dramatized. Thus potential mob leaders were deprived of the rallying point of "police brutality," the potential followers never developed the sense of mob power that results from evidence of police weakness. Well-behaved motorcyclists, whatever their appearance, were not mistreated and thus were not given reason for aligning themselves with the trouble-seekers and against the police.

The decision not to interfere with the motorcyclists camping and drag racing on private property, until extreme violence impended, was also of critical importance, for several reasons. In the field the potential trouble-makers were all contained in an open area where their activities, their comings and goings, could be easily observed. They were segregated by the broad highway and differentiated from the much larger mass of spectators at the track, and thus deprived of both victims and audience.[17] The amount of property vulnerable to damage was relatively small. Finally, they were allowed to occupy their time with activities which were both customary and satisfying (drinking, dragging, showing off, etc.) while not annoying other citizens. This business of "keeping them occupied" is not trivial. Mob action, except in a catastrophe, is usually preceded by a period of "milling," wherein people whose customary lines of action are blocked or inappropriate to the situation seek new guidelines. They engage in seemingly aimless behavior, which is actually exchange of fact and rumor, and movement toward consensus. It is during such periods that mob leaders can seize the initiative in directing the crowd toward specific objectives.[18]

A third important factor was *the continuous flow of intelligence,* both during the weekend and over the preceding weeks. We feel that our investigations and discussions before the holiday, aside from their obvious

---

[17] The presence of a large group of onlookers would also have been a serious impediment to swift police response in case of trouble.

[18] Turner and Killian, *op. cit.*

utility in planning, helped break down police stereotypes concerning motorcyclists and reinforced an attitude of impartiality toward them.

Last but far from least was plain and simple *good luck,* which favored
us on several occasions. Undoubtedly there was an element of luck in
the fact that the "hoodlum element" chose to remain at the campground
rather than roam the County. The factional dispute between the short-
haired locals and the "one percenters" may have been fortunate, in that it
kept the warlike elements busy and precluded any alliance between the
two groups. It was especially fortunate that when it finally became necessary
to clear the field, most of the rowdier motorcyclists left the County
entirely. The Vista track, even with its nightly dances, did not attract
them. The isolation of the campground from the racetrack and from
settled areas was another helpful accident.

As noted above, certain policies which we considered advisable were
not carried out. We believe that the trouble which did occur can be
attributed in part to those omissions.

The failure of the sponsoring club to provide camping facilities at
Marlboro, as promised in the race publicity, might well have had more
serious consequences than it did. Depriving the visitors of the activities
ordinarily organized around campsites logically means they will seek
others; they become a group of potential malcontents, at loose ends, away
from home, and with a grievance. Violence in such a situation need not
be entirely spontaneous; norms from similar past situations (e.g., New
Hampshire) exist to guide the group to it (see Turner, 1964 on norms in
crowd behavior).

The fighting on the field might not have gone as far as it did if the local
motorcycle clubs had all been actively involved in the control effort. The
"short-hairs" who were brawling with the "one percenters" were all members of one club. In addition to avoiding trouble and reporting it when
they saw it, local groups could have helped operate the camping area (if
it was formally rented), directed the informal drag races with official
sanction, and set up a registry of all groups entering the campground. Such
a registry (including motorcycle tag numbers) might have destroyed the
anonymity which allows people away from home and in a group to violate
law and convention and feel safe about it.

Once coordination with the State Police contingent assigned to the
County was achieved, the lack of involvement of other departments in the
planning was of no consequence for the County department. It might
have been, had the motorcyclists chosen to roam more. Town police at the
Rock 'n' Roll beach resort might have benefitted from coordination and
consultation with the County department.

As social scientists we tried to apply in this situation the specialized
knowledge and theory of our field, and found it useful. The police, logically,
focus on the apprehension of persons who violate laws, protection of
citizens from the acts of such persons, prevention of specifically violative

behavior, and the deployment of strength in accordance with those goals. As social scientists we focused on the collection of data, the analysis of differences and similarities, the understanding of group and individual behavior, and the communication and exchange of fact and opinion.[19]

Though the events of Labor Day, 1965 in Prince George's County were of little national or long-term import in themselves, we consider the principles applied and the lessons learned to have far broader relevance—a significant practice for things to come.

[19] The clarity with which these distinctions are drawn is not meant to deny that there are policemen who think like social scientists, and vice versa.

38

The Precipitants and Underlying Conditions of Race Riots*

STANLEY LIEBERSON and
ARNOLD R. SILVERMAN
University of Wisconsin

The immediate precipitants and underlying conditions of race riots in the U.S. during the past half century are the subject of this paper. Using both "hard" and "soft" data, employing journalistic accounts as well as census data, we consider in a somewhat more systematic fashion the influence of diverse factors suggested as causes of riots in sociological case studies and texts on collective behavior.[1] Riots, as distinguished from lynchings and other forms of collective violence, involve an assault on persons and property simply because they are part of a given subgroup of the community. In contrast, lynchings and other types of violence are directed toward a particular individual as a collective response to some specific act. In practice, this distinction is sometimes difficult to apply, particularly in deciding when a localized racial incident has become a riot.[2] We have excluded some of the housing "riots" from our analysis because

Reprinted from *American Sociological Review*, 30, 6 (December 1965), 887–898, by permission of the author and The American Sociological Association.

* The comments of Alma and Karl Taeuber, and David Heise are gratefully acknowledged.

[1] Herbert Blumer, "Collective Behavior," in Alfred McClung Lee (ed.), *New Outline of the Principles of Sociology*, New York: Barnes and Noble, 1951, pp. 165–222; Chicago Commission on Race Relations, *The Negro in Chicago*, Chicago: University of Chicago Press, 1922, pp. 1–78; Allen D. Grimshaw, "Three Major Cases of Colour Violence in the United States," *Race*, 5 (1963), pp. 76–86 and "Factors Contributing to Colour Violence in the United States and Britain," *ibid.*, 3 (May, 1962), pp. 3–19; Allen D. Grimshaw, "Urban Racial Violence in the United States; Changing Ecological Considerations," *American Journal of Sociology*, 66 (1960), pp. 109–119; Kurt Lang and Gladys Engel Lang, *Collective Dynamics*, New York: Thomas Y. Crowell, 1961; Alfred McClung Lee and Norman Daymond Humphrey, *Race Riot*, New York: Dryden Press, 1943; Elliott M. Rudwick, *Race Riot at East St. Louis, July 2, 1917*, Carbondale: Southern Illinois University Press, 1964; Neil J. Smelser, *Theory of Collective Behavior*, New York: Free Press of Glencoe, 1963; Ralph H. Turner and Lewis M. Killian, *Collective Behavior*, Englewood Cliffs, N.J.: Prentice-Hall, 1957; Ralph H. Turner and Samuel J. Surace, "Zoot-Suiters and Mexicans: Symbols in Crowd Behavior," *American Journal of Sociology*, 62 (1956), pp. 14–20.

[2] Lynchings, for example, are sometimes followed by riots. No doubt we would have included some of these events and excluded others had more detail been available.

they were directed specifically at Negroes attempting to move into an area rather than at Negroes *per se* or some other more generalized target.

Using the *New York Times Index* for the period between 1913 and 1963, we found 72 different events that might be properly classified as Negro-white race riots. Descriptions of riots in various editions of the *Negro Yearbook* supplemented some of the *Times* reports and also provided reports of four additional riots. In several instances, magazines and local newspapers were used for further information. Finally, we employed the sociological descriptions available for some race riots. Reliance on journalistic accounts for our basic sample of riots means the study is vulnerable to any selectivity in the riots actually reported in the newspaper. Our analysis of the immediate precipitants of race riots is similarly limited by the brevity of some of the descriptive accounts as well as by possible distortions in reporting.[3] For the underlying community conditions of riots, we relied largely on census data.

As one might expect, race riots are usually sparked by a provocation involving members of the two races. At most only four of the 76 riots occurred without a precipitating event, and even in these few cases, the apparent lack of precipitant may be due to the scantiness of the accounts rather than the absence of an immediate cause. In riots, life and property are treated with an indifference and recklessness contrary to basic values in western society (except in wartime); and it is therefore important to ask what kind of events precipitate such an acute breakdown of social control, and whether these precipitants are uncommon occurrences of an exceptionally provocative nature.

Although lynchings are not riots, data gathered on the immediate causes of the 3,700 lynchings in the U.S. between 1889 and 1930 are illuminating. Of the known accusations, more than a third (37.7 per cent) were murder; in nearly a quarter (23.4 per cent) the accusation was rape or attempted rape; assault was the charge in 5.8 per cent and theft in 7.1 per cent.[4] Compared with the frequency of these felonies in the South, murder and rape—violations of strong social taboos—are greatly over-represented as precipitants of lynchings.

In the same fashion, we suggest, the immediate precipitants of race riots almost always involve some confrontation between the groups in which members of one race are deeply "wronged" in fact or in rumor by members of the other. Precipitants tend to be transgressions of strongly held mores by a representative of the other group. The difficulty is to obtain an independent judgment of the severity of offenses that precipitate riots.

For two rather frequent types of precipitants, we can offer some in-

---

[3] See, for example, Raoul Naroll, *Data Quality Control—A New Research Technique*, New York: Free Press of Glencoe, 1962.

[4] Arthur F. Raper, *The Tragedy of Lynching*, Chapel Hill: University of North Carolina Press, 1933, p. 36.

dependent evidence of their intensity. First, riots are often precipitated in the U.S. by crimes—particularly alleged crimes against persons rather than property alone, or the public order. Murder, rape, assault, manslaughter, and theft by means of violence or intimidation arouse the greatest concern and receive the most publicity in the mass media.[5] In 1950, the median sentence received by men found guilty of offenses against persons was 9.9 years, whereas it was 3.9 years for those charged with other felonies.[6] Even excluding murder, sentences for other felonies against persons were more than twice as long as those for offenses solely against property or the public order. Since punishment reflects the public's values with respect to the intrinsic "evil" of various acts, it is in this sense an independent measure of the severity of acts that precipitate race riots.

Another class of events that apparently violate strongly held norms involve Negroes crossing the various segregation barriers erected against them. Particularly frequent as precipitants in recent years, these acts are "bad" only because Negro-white interaction occurs in a form generally prohibited, e.g., when Negroes use the same swimming pool as whites.[7]

We have classified the 72 riots for which data are available in terms

TABLE 1

Immediate Precipitants of Race Riots, 1913–1963

Rape, murder, attack, or hold-up of white women by Negro men	10
Killings, arrest, interference, assault, or search of Negro men by white policemen	15
Other inter-racial murder or shooting	11
Inter-racial fight, no mention of lethal weapons	16
Civil liberties, public facilities, segregation, political events, and housing	14
Negro strikebreakers, upgrading, or other job-based conflicts	5
Burning of an American flag by Negroes	1
No information available	4
Total number	76

[5] Marshall B. Clinard, *Sociology of Deviant Behavior*, New York: Holt, Rinehart and Winston, 1957, p. 196. We include robbery as a crime against persons throughout this analysis.

[6] Based on data reported in Federal Bureau of Prisons, *National Prisoner Statistics: Prisoners in State and Federal Institutions, 1950*, Leavenworth, Kansas: U.S. Penitentiary, 1954, Tables 37 and 38. Determinate and maximum indeterminate sentences are combined.

[7] Myrdal hypothesizes a rank order of discrimination in which whites object most strongly to close personal contact with Negroes. See Gunnar Myrdal, *An American Dilemma*, New York: Harper, 1944, pp. 60–61. Although a follow-up study suggested some modifications of this thesis, the areas of highest white resistance to Negroes remained unaltered. See Lewis M. Killian and Charles M. Grigg, "Rank Orders of Discrimination of Negroes and Whites in a Southern City," *Social Forces*, 39 (1961), p. 238.

of the nature of the immediate precipitant of the violence. (See Table 1.) The reader should recognize that it is not always clear which event triggered a riot, especially when a chain of inter-related events occurs. Not only is it difficult to specify where the riot begins and the precipitant ends, but often there are several precipitants. In these cases we have determined whether at least some of the events involve offenses against relatively sacred values.

A sizable majority of the precipitants do involve an actual or rumored violation of one group by a member of the other. The ten cases in which white women were attacked by Negro men are highly inflammatory; apparently these involve violations of an extremely strong taboo. Highly charged acts to begin with, the murder, rape, or assault of women is even more serious an offense when offender and victim are of different races. Negroes were almost half of all persons executed for murder by civil authorities in the United States between 1930 and 1952 and nearly 90 per cent of those executed for rape.[8] In their analysis of the 1943 Los Angeles zoot-suiter riot, Turner and Surace describe sexual assault as the dominant trigger:

> The most prominent charge from each side was that the other had molested its girls. It was reported that sailors became enraged by the rumor that zoot-suiters were guilty of "assaults on female relatives of servicemen." Similarly, the claim against sailors was that they persisted in molesting and insulting Mexican girls. While many other charges were reported in the newspapers, including unsubstantiated suggestions of sabotage of the war effort, the sex charges dominated the precipitating context.[9]

The second type of precipitant, offenses committed by white law-enforcement officials against Negroes, involves white transgression of norms no less sacred than those involved in the rape of white women by Negro men. The Harlem riot during World War II started when a Negro woman was arrested by a white policeman for disorderly conduct. A Negro soldier, on leave, tried to stop him and the ensuing fight ended with both men in the hospital, the policeman with a battered head and the soldier with a pistol wound in the shoulder. Of greatest interest here is the account of the incident that spread through the Negro community: a Negro soldier was said to have been shot in the back and killed by a white policeman in the presence of the Negro's mother.[10]

The Harlem riot of July, 1964 was precipitated by a demonstration protesting the slaying of a 15-year old Negro boy by a white policeman, an act viewed as a wanton exercise of police brutality. The Bedford-Stuyvesant, Rochester, Jersey City, and Philadelphia riots of 1964—also out-

---

[8] Federal Bureau of Prisons, *op. cit.*, pp. 30–31.
[9] Turner and Surace, *op. cit.*, pp. 16–17.
[10] *Time*, August 9, 1943, p. 19; *New Republic*, August 16, 1943, pp. 220–222.

side the period covered in our study—were also precipitated by arrests or the presence of police.[11]

Both the fatal shooting of the boy and the rumored treacherous shooting of a soldier during wartime, in front of his mother, are highly inflammatory acts because they arouse some of the strongest sentiments the population holds, and they are especially inflammatory because they were committed by members of one race against another. In addition, offenses committed by white law enforcement officials, highly inflammatory in themselves, are aggravated when they involve actual or alleged wrongdoing on the part of officials expected to uphold and administer the law in an impartial manner. A number of recent race riots over civil-rights issues have been precipitated by police behavior, particularly in breaking up demonstrations.[12] We shall have more to say about the role of the police in our discussion of the underlying conditions of race riots.

The next category of precipitants, "Other inter-racial murder or shooting," calls for little additional comment. The shooting of white policemen by Negro men (three cases), although intrinsically not as inflammatory as inter-racial offenses against women and children, nevertheless involves murder or attempted murder of a representative of the government. The rumored beating to death of a Negro boy in a New York department store after he was seized for shoplifting, and the rumors of brutal assaults on women and children that circulated among both races during the Detroit race riot of World War II, are clearly in accord with our thesis that the precipitants tend to be violations of important mores. In two cases rumors of impending violence precipitated actual riots. In one instance there was a rumor of a forthcoming riot and in the other, anticipation of a lynching. In both instances, the rumors involved interracial violation of rights widely accepted as fundamental. Finally, two of the other four inter-racial murders or shootings were accompanied by Negro offenses against white women: as we noted earlier, more than one element may be involved in the precipitation of a race riot. In one of these incidents, a white man was murdered by three Negroes and a rumor arose that he had been trying to protect a white woman from these men.[13] In the other, a Negro had made derogatory statements about a white woman over whom a Negro had been lynched some weeks before.[14]

Most of the 16 race riots precipitated by inter-racial fights without the use of lethal weapons do not appear to involve offenses of the most in-

---

[11] "Background of Northern Negro Riots," New York Times, September 27, 1964, p. 81.

[12] This is particularly evident in the South.

[13] New York Times, September 21, 1920, p. 1; Chicago Daily Tribune, September 21, 1920, pp. 1–2.

[14] Monroe N. Work (ed.), Negro Yearbook, 1921–1922, Tuskegee Institute, Ala. Negro Yearbook Publishing Co., p. 75.

tense nature. One difficulty here is that the accounts of these riots are so scanty that we do not know whether rumors existed, over what issue the fights started, or other features that may have made the incident especially inflammatory, e.g., a young adult attacking an elderly person or a cripple. A fairly common element in riots with this type of precipitant is a chain of events in which members of each racial group come to the assistance of others already engaged in the fight. This tends to excite the onlookers who arrive after the initial provocation, particularly if members of one race appear to be receiving the worse part of the battle.

"Civil liberties, public facilities, segregation, political events, and housing" is a residual category involving diverse precipitants. Some of the precipitants fit the thesis that sacred values were violated. For example, a riot in upstate New York in the mid-thirties was precipitated by whites attempting to break up a meeting called to rally support for a Negro accused of attacking a white girl.[15] From the white point of view this involves the not uncommon theme of sexual molesting; from the other side, it is a white attempt to prevent Negroes' efforts to insure fair treatment for a Negro accused of a provocative act. A riot in Athens, Ala. in 1946 involved whites protesting police favoritism after a brawl for which two whites had been arrested and a Negro escaped.[16] But for the most part, it is difficult to establish conclusively the extent to which the precipitants in this category were offenses against inter-racial mores. In some cases we are tempted to say that they were—the two just mentioned, or the Negro boy attempting to dance with a white girl at a city-sponsored dance—but in others, we are less certain about the nature of the acts.

Of the five job-based riots, three involved the allegation that Negroes were or had been strike breakers, one was over the up-grading of jobs held by Negroes, and one was simply in an industrial setting. Taking a conservative stance, we would not be inclined to label these as violations of sacred norms.

Burning an American flag is a different type of offense, for it violates neither the person nor any segregation taboo, but it is clearly an offense against one of the nation's most sacred symbols. We shall say more about this type of precipitant, which is unusual for riots in the U.S., when we discuss racial and ethnic riots elsewhere in the world.

In brief, at least a sizable proportion of the immediate precipitants of race riots appear to involve inter-racial violations of intense societal norms. Noteworthy are the large number of events in which bodily injury is the precipitant as well as the smaller number of cases precipitated by violations of inter-racial segregation taboos.

[15] *New York Times*, August 28, 1934, p. 3.

[16] Charles R. Lawrence, Jr., "Race Riots in the United States 1942–1946" in Jessie Parkhurst Guzman (ed.), *Negro Yearbook, 1941–1946*, Tuskegee Institute, Ala.: Department of Records and Research, 1947, pp. 253–254.

UNDERLYING CONDITIONS

Applying Durkheim's typology, we observe that many of the immediate precipitants were acts that call for repressive sanctions, that is, they "consisted essentially in an act contrary to strong and defined states of the common conscience." [17] Repressive sanctions are normally administered under penal law by courts in the U.S. For example, murder, rape, and other acts of physical violence are strongly disapproved and severely punished in our society. Many, though not all, of the violations of segregation taboos in the period studied were also punishable through law enforcement, but in these instances, at least some members of either or both racial populations were unable to accept the institutions normally used for handling such offenses. Instead a riot occurred, involving, by definition, a generalized response directed at a collectivity rather than the offender—indeed, the actual offender was often untouched.

Although the immediate precipitants were highly inflammatory, we may still ask why a riot occurred rather than the normal processes of arrest, trial, and punishment, for interracial friction occurs far more often than the small number of occasions that erupted into race riots indicates. Why did violence break out where it did rather than at other places where similar incidents occurred? Or to put it another way, the types of violation described earlier probably occur almost daily, yet in most instances they do not lead to collective violence. Are there special circumstances that increase or decrease the chances of a riot ensuing?

One possible interpretation of the location and timing of riots is simply that riots are randomly distributed. Any precipitating incident of this type increase the chances of a riot, but there is no systematic reason why riots occur when and where they do, other than possible differences among cities in the frequency of precipitating incidents. A second approach is based on the notion that certain social conditions in the community increase the probability that a precipitating incident will lead to a riot. From this perspective, we can ask whether cities experiencing riots differ from other cities with regard to the institutional conditions suggested as increasing the chances of a riot.

Poisson distribution. To evaluate the first interpretation, that is, whether riots are randomly distributed in time and place, we used the Poisson distribution, which the low frequency of race riots (1.5 per year between 1913 and 1963) makes appropriate for comparing the actual frequency of riots with what would be expected in a random distribution.[18]

[17] Emile Durkheim, *The Division of Labor in Society*, Glencoe, Ill.: Free Press, 1933, p. 105.

[18] For discussions of the application of the Poisson distribution, see G. Udny Yule and M. G. Kendall, *An Introduction to the Theory of Statistics*, London: Charles Griffin, 1950, pp. 189–194; M. J. Moroney, *Facts From Figures*, Harmondsworth, Middlesex: Penguin Books, 1951, Ch. 8.

Columns 2 and 3 of Table 2 show, respectively, the actual and expected number of riots per year in the 51 years from 1913 through 1963. Inspection indicates that the Poisson distribution yields a poor fit. For example, in 26 of the years no riot was reported though the theoretical distribution would lead us to expect only 11 such years. Applying the appropriate chi-square test for goodness of fit, we conclude that we cannot accept the assumption that the probability of riots is equal each year.[19]

In similar fashion, we can consider the concentration of riots in cities. Restricting ourselves to the 333 cities with 50,000 or more population in 1960, we have compared the actual and expected frequencies of cities experiencing a specified number of riots. There are more cities without any

TABLE 2

Race Riots: Actual and Expected Frequencies

By Year			By City		
Riots per Year (1)	*Observed Frequency* (2)	*Poisson Frequency* (3)	*Riots per Year* (4)	*Observed Frequency* (5)	*Poisson Frequency* (6)
0	26	11.4	0	300	281.2
1	10	17.1	1	25	47.2
2	7	12.8	2	3	4.3
3	2	6.4	3	3	0.3
4	1	2.4	4	1	0.0
5	0	0.7	5–14	1	0.0
6	0	0.2			
7	2	0.0			
8	1	0.0			
9	1	0.0			
10	0	0.0			
11	1	0.0			
Total years	51	51.0	Total cities	333	333.0

riots, and more with several, than would be expected on the basis of the Poisson distribution (columns 5 and 6): riots occurred in only 33 of these cities. The goodness-of-fit test confirms our impression that the theoretical distribution does not fit the actual distribution of riots in cities.

Two types of sampling bias may have influenced these results. First, newspapers probably fluctuate in their propensity to report riots, so that the frequency of riots at a given point in time increases the probability that riots occurring shortly afterwards will be reported. This is analogous to the tendency of newspapers to make the frequency of rapes or other events into a crime wave when in fact the major variable is the frequency of

[19] Our computation of chi-square is based on the adjustments suggested in Helen M. Walker and Joseph Lev, *Statistical Inference*, New York: Henry Holt, 1953, pp. 105–107.

reporting such events.[20] A second possible bias arises from the fact that our primary source is the *New York Times*. Milder forms of racial violence in metropolitan New York and the mid-Atlantic area are more likely to be covered than riots of equivalent severity elsewhere. This would lead to a distribution of repeated riots different from that expected on the basis of the Poisson formula. Also, note that our test refers only to riots, not to precipitating incidents *per se*. Therefore we can reach no conclusions with respect to the distribution of precipitants by time or place. These difficulties notwithstanding, the results give us no reason to think riots are random with respect to time and place.

A COMPARATIVE ANALYSIS

Since the type of event that precipitates riots is far more common than actual riots, we ask whether this form of collective violence is due to underlying conditions that keep at least one segment of the population from accepting the normal institutional response to a provocative incident. From this perspective, precipitants are a necessary but not sufficient cause of riots.

A rather wide-ranging array of interpretations have been advanced after the occurrence of riots in particular communities. Such factors as rapidly expanding Negro population, economic hardships, police brutality, job ceilings, Negro competition with whites, slums, unsympathetic city officials, contagion, communist elements, agitators, warm weather, unruly elements, and others have figured in popular and semi-popular interpretations of race riots. Although case studies of race riots are extremely valuable where they provide an accurate description of events before and during a riot, obviously it is impossible to determine which factors are critical on the basis of one city's experience.

When we move from the presentation of *plausible* reasons to a systematic empirical test of the actual importance of various attributes in increasing the chances of riots, we encounter serious difficulties. Not only do we have a plethora of independent variables, but their actual significance is very difficult to test. Quantitative data on many of these characteristics are scarce, and in any case it is difficult to know how much causal significance to attribute anyway. For example, a riot may occur in a city containing a Negro slum area. The cruel truth is that housing conditions for Negroes are inferior in virtually every city in the U.S. To infer a causal link, one must determine not whether Negro slums exist in the riot city, but whether that city is worse in this respect than others where no riots occurred. Similarly, in any large city unemployed whites and Ne-

[20] See, for example, Nahum Z. Medalia and Otto N. Larsen, "Diffusion and Belief in a Collective Delusion: The Seattle Windshield Pitting Epidemic," *American Sociological Review*, 23 (1958), pp. 180–186.

groes might respond to an opportunity for a racial riot. Again the question is whether an unusually large number of such people live in one community compared with another.

Our requirements for quantitative data covering at least part of a 50-year span limit the causal hypotheses we can test. For the most part we have relied on U.S. censuses of the past six decades for data bearing on some of the propositions encountered in case studies and popular interpretations of race riots. This part of our study, therefore, necessarily has a certain *ad hoc* quality.

Method. To examine the influence of variables others have suggested as underlying causes of race riots, we used a paired-comparison analysis. Each city experiencing a riot was compared with a city as similar as possible in size and region which had no riot in the ten years preceding or following the riot date.[21] Preference was given to the city in the same state closest in population size, with the provision that it have at least half but no more than twice the population of the riot city. Where no such city existed we selected the city closest in size in the same subregion or region.[22] We compared the very largest cities, such as New York, Chicago, and Los Angeles, with other leading centers in the nation closest in population, regardless of region.

Using the nonparametric sign test, we evaluated the extent to which riot cities differ from their control cities in the direction hypothesized. When a given city experienced more than one riot, it was included as many times as the number of riots. Because census data by size of place and decade were not always available, our "N" in most cases is considerably less than the 76 riots discussed earlier. For convenience in presentation, we have divided the hypotheses into four major categories: population growth and composition; work situation; housing; and government.

DEMOGRAPHIC FACTORS

The rapid influx of Negroes and sometimes whites into cities is certainly one of the most frequently cited reasons for the occurrence of race riots. Although large-scale migration is not usually viewed as a sufficient cause for a riot, it is commonly considered important because rapid influx disrupts the on-going social order and creates various problems in the Negro community. For 66 riots we could determine the growth of the Negro and white populations between the census years preceding and following the race riot, for each riot city and for a comparable community.

[21] For the most recent riots we could not apply the ten-year limit into the future in selecting control cities, but such cities were included in our analysis.

[22] See U.S. Bureau of the Census, *U.S. Census of Population: 1960. Selected Area Reports, Standard Metropolitan Statistical Areas.* Washington, D.C.: U.S. Government Printing Office, 1963, pp. xvi–xvii.

For 66 riots we could determine the growth of the Negro and white populations between the census years preceding and following the race riot, for each riot city and for a comparable community selected at the beginning of the decade. We thus have data for 66 pairs of cities, each pair consisting of a riot city and a control city.

In about half the cases, percentage increases in both total and white population were smaller in the riot cities than in the non-riot cities. Moreover, in 56 per cent of the comparisons the control cities experienced greater percentage increases in Negro population than the riot cities did. Our results clearly fail to support the contention that rapid population change accompanies riots. For the years between 1917 and 1921—a period marked by both Negro migration and numerous riots—we found no sizable difference between riot and control cities in their percentage gains in Negro population during the decades. Also contrary to expectation are the differences in racial composition of riot and control cities. Again for 66 pairs, we find that in exactly half the comparisons, the proportion of Negroes is smaller in the riot city than in its control city.

Since this comparative approach is used with succeeding hypotheses, we should consider briefly the implications of these findings. First, we draw no conclusions about whether Negro population growth in riot cities differs from its growth elsewhere in the U.S. Riot cities have experienced more rapid growth than the remainder of the nation simply because Negro population movement has been largely from rural to urban areas. Similarly, since our method is designed to compare riot cities only with other cities similar in size and region, we make no inferences about differences between riot cities and all other U.S. cities. What we do conclude is that riot cities do not differ from non-riot cities of the same size and region in their rates of population increase, and therefore that increases in population fail to explain the occurrence of outbreaks in one city rather than another.[23]

WORK SITUATION

Traditional occupations. The occupational world of Negroes is far more restricted than that of whites. In particular, certain occupational pursuits have been more or less "traditional" for urban Negroes. These are generally lower in both status and income. Accordingly, wherever possible we determined the proportion of Negro men in the labor force

[23] See Robin Williams, Jr., in collaboration with John P. Dean and Edward A. Suchman, *Strangers Next Door*, Englewood Cliffs, N.J.: Prentice-Hall, 1964, pp. 135–137. In a study based on a nationwide sample of cities, they find the general level of race conflict and tension no higher in cities with rapid population growth and high mobility than in those with relatively stable populations. In short, our method gets at the question of why riots occur in the particular cities they do, rather than in comparable urban centers.

who are employed either as laborers or in domestic and service occupations. Needless to say, we were forced to use some rather crude measures as well as broad categories which undoubtedly include some occupations outside the "traditional" rubric. A serious difficulty is created by contradictory hypotheses that depend on which group appears to be the aggressor. On the one hand, we might expect greater antagonism on the part of Negroes in cities where they are relatively restricted in occupational opportunities, i.e., where most Negroes are in traditional pursuits. On the other hand, we might well expect that where Negroes fare relatively well in their efforts to break through the job restrictions, whites' hostility might be greater and hence riots more likely to ensue.

For 43 riots we were able to determine the Negro occupational distribution in both the riot and control city during the closest census period. In 65 per cent of these paired comparisons ($N = 28$), the percentage of Negro men holding traditional occupations is lower in the riot city.[24] This suggests that riots are due to the relative threat to whites where Negroes are less concentrated in their traditional pursuits. If such were the case, then we might expect the white and Negro percentages in these occupations to be more alike in the riot city than in the control city. This is precisely what we find: in 30 of the 43 paired comparisons, the *difference* between whites and Negroes, in proportions engaged in laboring, domestic, and service occupations, is smaller in the riot city.[25] The encroachment of Negroes in the white occupational world evidently tends to increase the chances of a riot, although we must also consider the possibility that Negro militancy increases as Negroes move out of their traditional niche.

Store owners. A more specific occupational factor sometimes associated with riots—particularly ghetto riots—is the low frequency of store ownership in Negro areas and the consequent resentment of white store owners in these areas. We are unable to get at these data directly. If we assume, however, that virtually all Negro store owners are located in the ghetto, then we can simply examine the percentage of employed Negro men who are self-employed in various facets of retail trade, such as store, restaurant, or tavern owners. Although differences between riot and control cities tend to be slight, nevertheless in 24 of 39 riots, the percentage of Negroes who are store owners is larger in the nonriot city.[26] Results might be even stronger had it been possible to subcategorize riots. For instance, the absence of Negro store owners would presumably contribute to Negroes' rioting but would contribute relatively little to white assaults.

Unemployment. As was the case for traditional occupations, unemployment presents contradictory possibilities, so that we might well expect riots when either Negroes or whites have relatively high unemployment

[24] Using a two-tailed test, p = .0672.

[25] p = .0073, single-tailed test.

[26] These differences are significant at the .10 level.

rates. Our analysis is even cruder here, since unemployment is far more volatile from year to year, and we are able to use data only for the closest census year.[27] First, the white unemployment rate appears to have no influence on the likelihood of a riot. In 12 comparisons white unemployment rates were higher in the city experiencing the riot, and in 13 cases, higher in the control city. For Negro unemployment, results tend to run counter to what we might expect. Negro unemployment is higher in the control than in the riot city in 15 out of 25 comparisons. And Negro-white *differences* are lower in the riot than in the control city in 15 out of 25 comparisons.[28]

These results do not confirm our expectations: high white unemployment apparently does not increase the chances of a riot, nor is high Negro unemployment associated with riots in the direction expected. On an aggregate basis, the number of riots during the Great Depression of the thirties was not unusually large. In view of the weakness of the data—particularly the fact that we do not have unemployment rates for the specific year in which the riots take place—all we can conclude is that we have failed to confirm the hypothesis, not that we have disproved it.

Income. Since the influence of income on riots may reflect either group's position, our problem is similar to that discussed in connection with Negro occupational composition. Median income data are available for only 12 riots and their controls. In six comparisons Negro income is higher in the control city and in the other six it is higher in the riot city. In 11 of the 12 cases, however, white income in the riot city is lower than in the control.[29] The *difference* between Negro and white income was larger in the city without a riot in ten of the 12 cases.[30] The small number precludes analysis of these findings in greater detail, but we can observe that riots tend to occur in cities where white income is lower than that of whites in comparable areas. The lower white income also means that Negro-white differences tend to be smaller in these cities than in the control areas. Thus, the results, though extremely limited in time and place, do not support the notion that race riots are a consequence either of low Negro income or of relatively large Negro-white discrepancies in income.

HOUSING

Ghetto riots in particular are often attributed to the poor housing conditions of Negroes, but our data fail to disclose any tendency whatsoever for housing to be of lower quality in cities that have experienced riots. For

[27] Although data are available for other years, to our knowledge none can be obtained by race for specific cities.

[28] $p = .212$, single-tailed test.

[29] $p < .01$, single-tailed test.

[30] $p = .038$, two-tailed test.

20 paired comparisons we could determine which city had a larger percentage of Negro families in sub-standard housing (using the census categories of "dilapidated" in 1950 and 1960 and "needing major repairs" in 1940). In ten cases the non-riot city had poorer Negro housing than the riot city. Although obviously not all riots could be considered ghetto riots, surely we should find some tendency for Negroes in cities experiencing riots to have poorer dwellings than they do in cities without riots, if it were true that poorer housing quality increases the likelihood of a race riot. Very likely, Negro housing is poor in so many locales that it cannot distinguish cities experiencing riots from those that do not.

GOVERNMENT

Police. Local government is one of the most important institutions to consider in an analysis of race riots. Municipal policies, particularly with respect to police, can greatly influence the chances of a race riot. Earlier, we observed that many of the precipitating incidents involve white police behavior toward Negroes, and adequate police training and tactics often prevent incipient riots from developing.[31] Moreover, police activities reflect the policies, sympathies, and attitudes of the local municipal government.

One often-cited factor in race riots is the lack of Negro policemen. First, one major complaint on the part of Negroes is that of white police brutality. So far as the police are Negroes, actual brutality will probably not arouse strong racial feelings. Second, police in some riots have encouraged or tolerated white violence toward Negroes, so that we might expect stronger police control where the force is mixed, as well as greater confidence in police protection among Negroes. Finally, since the number of Negro policemen is for the most part controlled by the city administration, the representation of Negroes is an indicator of city policies toward race relations in general.

Data are hard to obtain and for 1950 and 1960 we have been obliged to use census reports for entire metropolitan areas. Also, for some decades policemen are not reported separately from closely related occupations such as sheriffs and marshals. Nevertheless, of 38 pairs of cities, in 24 the city without the riot had more Negro policemen per thousand Negroes than did the matched city that experienced a riot.[32] Although differences between riot and control cities are rather slight, these results do suggest that police force composition influences the likelihood of a riot.

City council. We hypothesize that the manner in which councilmen are elected and the relative size of the city council will influence the occur-

---

[31] Joseph D. Lohman, *The Police and Minority Groups*, Chicago: Chicago Park District, 1947, pp. 80–93; Smelser, *op. cit.*, pp. 261–268.

[32] $p = .07$, single-tailed test.

rence of riots. Our reasoning is based on several assumptions. The election of councilmen at large gives numerically smaller groups a greater handicap in expressing their interests than they encounter in communities where councilmen are elected directly from spatial districts.[33] In cities where the average size of a councilman's constituency is small, we assume that representatives are more responsive to the wishes of the population and therefore that members of the community have a more adequate mechanism for transmitting their interests and concerns. This implies that more diverse interests will be expressed in the city's governing body.

Our hypothesis is that the more direct the relation between voter and government, the less likely are riots to occur. A more responsive government makes riots less likely because it provides regular institutional channels for expressing grievances. Small districts provide more responsive government than large districts, and large districts, more than elections at large. In comparisons between a city with a city-wide election system and one where councilmen are elected both at large and by district, we classified the latter situation as the less likely to lead to riots. Where both cities have the same form of election, we computed the mean population per councilman. (Comparisons involving Deep South cities were based on the white population only.) Thus, we gave form of election priority over size of constituency in our causal hypothesis.

In 14 of 22 pairs, population per councilman was larger in the city experiencing the riot than in the control city, or elections at large were used in the riot city and direct election of representatives in the control city.[34] Considering our inability to take into account the degree of gerrymandering in cities with direct representation, these results offer an encouraging degree of support for our hypothesis.

DISCUSSION

Our analysis of the precipitating and underlying conditions of race riots suggests several generalizations about their evolution. First, precipitating incidents often involve highly charged offenses committed by members of one group against the other, such as attacks on women, police brutality and interference, murder, and assault. In recent years, violation of segregation taboos by Negroes as well as white resistance have been increasingly frequent precipitants. Riots are generalized responses in which there is categorical assault on persons and property by virtue of their racial membership. Such violence is not restricted and may even exclude the specific antagonists responsible for the precipitating event.

The diffuse response generated by the precipitating event, as well as

---

[33] James Q. Wilson, *Negro Politics*, Glencoe, Ill.: Free Press, 1960, pp. 25–33.

[34] Though p is not significant (.143), the relationship is in the predicted direction.

the fact that often the alleged offenses are of the sort normally dealt with by appropriate communal institutions, suggests that additional factors channel the inflammatory act into a riot. Since there are usually a number of factors that could have contributed to a riot in any given community, we used a comparative approach to determine why riots occur in some cities and not in others of comparable size and location.

Going beyond our data and trying to place our findings in a broad framework, we suggest that riots are more likely to occur when social institutions function inadequately, or when grievances are not resolved, or cannot be resolved under the existing institutional arrangements. Populations are predisposed or prone to riot; they are not simply neutral aggregates transformed into a violent mob by the agitation or charisma of individuals. Indeed, the immediate precipitant simply ignites prior community tensions revolving about basic institutional difficulties. The failure of functionaries to perform the roles expected by one or both of the racial groups, cross-pressures, or the absence of an institution capable of handling a community problem involving inter-racial relations will create the conditions under which riots are most likely. Many riots are precipitated by offenses that arouse considerable interest and concern. When members of the victimized race are dubious about the intention or capacity of relevant functionaries to achieve justice or a "fair" solution, then the normal social controls are greatly weakened by the lack of faith in the community's institutions.

Our evidence supports the proposition that the functioning of local community government is important in determining whether a riot will follow a precipitating incident. Prompt police action can prevent riots from developing; their inaction or actual encouragement can increase the chances of a race riot. Riot cities not only employ fewer Negro policemen, but they are also communities whose electoral systems tend to be less sensitive to the demands of the electorate. Local government illustrates the possibility that riots occur when a community institution is malfunctioning, from the perspective of one or both racial segments.

Our finding that Negroes are less likely to be store owners in riot cities illustrates the problem arising when no social institution exists for handling the difficulties faced by a racial group. Small merchants require credit, skill and sophistication in operating and locating their stores, ability to obtain leases, and so on. To our knowledge no widely operating social institution is designed to achieve these goals for the disadvantaged Negro. Similarly, our finding that riots are more likely where Negroes are closer to whites in their proportions in "traditional" Negro occupations, and where Negro-white income differences are smaller, suggests that a conflict of interests between the races is inherent in the economic world.

Our use of significance tests requires further comment. Many of the relationships are in the direction predicted but fail to meet the normal standards for significance. Several extenuating circumstances help account for this. First, many of our hypotheses refer to specific types of riots: for example, some riots are clearly "white riots;" others, equally clearly, are Negro; and many are both, in the sense that extensive attacks are directed at both groups. Were the data in an ideal form, we could separate the ghetto riots, the white assaults, and the interracial warfare into separate categories, and then apply our hypotheses to specific subsets of riots. Because our sample is small and the accounts of many riots are very scanty, we are prepared to accept these weaker associations as at least consistent with our approach to the underlying conditions of race riots.

Several implications of our results are relevant to riots elsewhere. Racial and ethnic incidents in other parts of the world are also frequently precipitated by physical violence. Dahlke's description of the Kishinew pogrom in Russia ascribes considerable importance as a precipitant to the widespread legend that Jews annually kill Christian children, as a part of their religious rites.[35] The extensive riots in Ceylon in 1958 included a number of highly provocative rumors of inter-ethnic violations. For example, "a Sinhalese baby had been snatched from its mother's arms and immersed in a barrel of boiling tar." [36] The Durban riots of 1949 were precipitated by an incident in which an African youth was knocked over by an Indian trader.[37]

A number of other riots, however, are precipitated by violations of symbols rather than persons or taboos. The burning of an American flag by Negroes triggered a race riot in the United States. Our impression is that this type of precipitant is more common in some other parts of the world. Riots in Kashmir, West Bengal, and East Pakistan in late 1963 and early 1964, for example, were precipitated by the theft of a hair of the prophet Mohammed from a Mosque in Kashmir.[38] One of the precipitants of the Chinese-Thai riots of 1945, the Yaorawat Incident, was the Chinese tendency to fly Chinese flags without also flying the Thai flag of the nation.[39] Jews tore down the czar's crown from the town hall and damaged portraits of various rulers prior to Kiev's pogrom in 1905.[40]

Our results also suggest that race riots are frequently misunderstood. We have encountered a number of accounts in the popular literature at-

---

[35] H. Otto Dahlke, "Race and Minority Riots—A Study in the Typology of Violence," *Social Forces*, 30 (1952), p. 421.

[36] Tarzie Vittachi, *Emergency '58: The Story of the Ceylon Race Riots*, London: Andre Deutsch, 1958, p. 48.

[37] Anthony H. Richmond, *The Colour Problem* (rev. ed.), Harmondsworth, Middlesex: Pelican Books, 1961, p. 123.

[38] *New York Times*, January 16, 1964, p. 17; January 19, p. 6; January 20, p. 6; January 24, p. 2; January 26, p. 15.

[39] G. William Skinner, *Chinese Society in Thailand: An Analytical History*, Ithaca, N. Y.: Cornell University Press, 1957, p. 279.

[40] From the diary of Shulgin, in *Source Book for History* 2.1, Vol. 2, "History of Western Civilization," Brooklyn, N.Y.: Brooklyn College, Department of History, 1949, Ch. 31.

tributing riots to communist influence, hoodlums, or rabble-rousers. Although lower-class youths and young adults are undoubtedly active during riots, potential participants of this type are probably available in almost any community. What interests us is the community failure to see the riot in terms of institutional malfunctioning or a racial difficulty which is not met—and perhaps cannot be—by existing social institutions. Many riots in other parts of the world revolve about national political institutions such that a disadvantaged segment is unable to obtain recognition of its interests and concerns through normal political channels. While this type of riot is not common in the U.S., the same basic conditions exist when either whites or Negroes are unable to use existing institutions to satisfy their needs and interests.

39

Blame In Disaster: Another Look, Another Viewpoint*

THOMAS E. DRABEK
University of Denver

ENRICO L. QUARANTELLI
Ohio State University

Two major viewpoints have been presented in the literature to explain the assignment of blame to individuals following disasters. One viewpoint characterizes the process as a guilt-reducing search for scapegoats. It is assumed that this is a typical response to catastrophes and essentially irrational in nature. In contrast, the other viewpoint suggests that the attribution of personal blame following disasters is a relatively rare phenomenon which occurs only under quite specific conditions. Blame assignment is seen as rationally motivated by desires to prevent future recurrence of similar disasters.

In this paper, after first detailing these two different views, we present a brief description of the events leading up to the assignment of blame after the Indianapolis Coliseum explosion. Both of the major viewpoints which purport to explain such phenomena are then evaluated in light of data gathered in a field study by the Ohio State University Disaster Research Center.[1] The data are not inconsistent with the second formulation, but suggest the usefulness of a broader view.

Thus, we conclude the paper with the presentation of a third interpretation of the process of blaming persons after disasters. From this perspective blame assignment is seen first, as a process which is rooted in certain institutional frameworks, and second, as a mechanism for obscuring defects in social structures and distracting attention from a "faulty" system. Historical examples, however, additionally suggest that the process of blame assignment may serve primarily to retard rather than to prevent changes in social structure. Thus, this third viewpoint attempts to show

---

* Paper presented at the 1966 Annual Meeting of the American Sociological Association at Miami, Florida. Published by permission of the authors.

[1] For details both as to field procedures and findings see the monograph by Thomas E. Drabek, *Disaster in Aisle 13: A Case Study of the Coliseum Explosion at the Indiana State Fairgrounds, October 31, 1963*, published by the Disaster Research Center at Ohio State University. Details of the disaster set forth later in this paper are drawn from the monograph.

the functioning of a social psychological process in the dynamics as well as the maintenance of social systems.

THE TWO MAJOR VIEWPOINTS

Reflecting the general lack of research on community disasters, there have been few studies into the process of blame assignment. Veltfort and Lee analyzed post-disaster public reactions to the 1942 Cocoanut Grove night club fire in Boston.[2] While the fire was relatively minor, exiting patrons found some emergency doors sealed shut and also jammed a revolving door. Many of the nearly 500 casualties were killed in the resulting panic flight.[3]

Veltfort and Lee take the position that the public affixing of blame in the days following this disaster was primarily an unconscious effort to relieve blocked emotional reactions to what had occurred. There was no immediate public attack on Boston's lax and insufficient laws. Instead, members of the City Council or public officials were blamed for having failed to pass more stringent legislation or to enforce existing statutes. After a month of investigation, the County Grand Jury indicted ten men.

This personalization is viewed by Veltfort and Lee as an essential characteristic of the scapegoating process. They state that "the immediate and desired objective of the scapegoaters was to relieve their feelings of frustration, of fear, of hostility, of guilt, by legally fixing the responsibility on the guilty so that they might be punished." [4] Hence, their conclusion is that the attempt to relieve unconscious guilt feelings resulted in irrational behavior; i.e., there was the selection of a series of scapegoats rather than a demand for more strict laws.

However, these researchers point out that certain potential candidates were not chosen as scapegoats. For example, no blame was attached to the sixteen year old club employee whose action in striking a match to obtain more light, while trying to replace a missing bulb, was the specific cause of the fire. Why? According to Veltfort and Lee, because there was public admiration of his straightforward, voluntary admission of having started the fire. His teachers testified he was a model young man from an impoverished family. His youth, and the fact that his mother was seriously ill, also prevented him from being accepted as a scapegoat. A prankster, who presumably had removed the bulb, was not selected because he was

---

[2] Helene Rank Veltfort and George F. Lee, "The Cocoanut Grove Fire: A Study in Scapegoating," *The Journal of Abnormal and Social Psychology*, 38, Clinical Supplement (April, 1943), pp. 138–154.

[3] A general description of the event is given in Paul Benzaquin, *Holocaust!* New York: Holt, 1959.

[4] Veltfort and Lee, *op. cit.*, p. 151.

not identified and also because his act certainly was not the direct cause of the fire.

More importantly however, according to Veltfort and Lee, those seeking someone to blame had been exposed to "more satisfying" scapegoats to relieve their guilt feelings. Ten prominent persons and officials were indicted and charged with a variety of offenses, e.g., conspiracy to violate building codes, failure to enforce fire laws, failure to report violations of the building laws, and so forth. All ten had high status in their respective groups, e.g., the owners of the club and the Boston Building Commissioner. Veltfort and Lee state that these persons were selected because "collectively they were 'the rascals,' for among certain elements of the public there is a deep-rooted, perhaps unrecognized latent hostility toward all political authority, toward those 'higher up'." [5] Likewise, all past hostilities which had accumulated against "political bigwigs" and "money czars" could be focused on the two classes of scapegoats, the owners and public officials. Hence, ". . . elements of the public may have found opportunity to *enhance* their own self-conceived prestige; they could, by scapegoating, feel, at least momentarily, superior to these so-called 'higher ups'." [6] In essence, this formulation is a variant of the frustration-aggression hypothesis.

In a similar vein Wolfenstein, after reviewing relevant disaster literature, takes the position that individuals cannot blame those who died. In the Cocoanut Grove Fire, no one blamed the panic of the victims which led to the fatal crush and the blocking of exits. Similarly in a 1955 French race track disaster, a driver who crashed into the spectators was viewed as a savior rather than an "agent of destruction" in that he saved the lives of the other drivers by avoiding collisions with them.[7] Wolfenstein concludes that an individual who survives disaster feels guilty for not having died himself. "Probably the more latent hostility there is present in an individual the greater will be his need to blame either himself or others for destructive happenings." [8]

From this perspective then, attribution of blame following disaster is motivated by unconscious guilt and related feelings. Such motivations produce a variety of irrational behaviors among which scapegoating is common. "Innocent" persons are selected on the basis of latent hostilities to receive irrational attacks from a guilt-ridden populace.

In sharp contrast to the above viewpoint is the position advanced by Bucher.[9] She analyzed responses of residents of Elizabeth, New Jersey in

[5] *Ibid.*, p. 146.

[6] *Ibid.*, p. 150.

[7] Martha Wolfenstein, *Disaster, A Psychological Essay*, Chicago: The Free Press, 1957, pp. 214–215.

[8] *Ibid.*, p. 219.

[9] Rue Bucher, "Blame and Hostility in Disaster," *The American Journal of Sociology*, 62 (March, 1957), pp. 467–475.

1951–1952 to three consecutive airplane crashes within a three month period. Rather than being a common feature of disasters, Bucher suggests that attribution of blame to individuals will result only when certain specific conditions are present. Persons must first define the situation sufficiently to assess responsibility. This only occurs when conventional explanations are not available. For example, in present day Western society, probably no person will be assigned direct responsibility for destruction caused by tornados, floods, and hurricanes. Damage and deaths from such events can be conventionally accounted for in non-personal and naturalistic terms.

According to Bucher, even though conventional explanations are not available, two additional conditions must also be present before personal blame will be affixed: 1) ". . . those who blame the agents of responsibility are convinced that the agents will not of their own volition take action which will remedy the situation;" and 2) ". . . those responsible must be perceived as violating moral standards, as standing in opposition to basic values." [10]

Bucher placed primary emphasis on futurity, i.e., the assignment of blame is done in an effort to insure that a future recurrence might be prevented. As a consequence, the attribution of responsibility tends to be shifted upward in the hierarchy of authority. Persons who may have had a direct hand in the catastrophe, such as the airline pilots, are not blamed. Thus, in the instance of the plane crashes, Bucher interprets attribution of responsibility as being ". . . laid where people thought the power resided to alleviate the conditions underlying the crashes. It was not instrumentality in causing the crashes which determined responsibility but ability to do something to prevent their recurrence. The problem was who had control over these conditions and who had the power to see that they were corrected." [11]

In Elizabeth, there actually was never any blame placed on specific authorities. The blamers did not go beyond articulating a generalized "they" as responsible for failing to take action. Bucher attributes the greater lack of specificity to the limited knowledge of her lower and middle class respondents about airlines, airports and the whole range of industries and agencies, public as well as private, associated therewith. From this perspective then, assessment of responsibility and the affixing of personal blame are viewed as processes partaking at least of subjective rationality. Only when causation can be assigned to non-conventional explanations will responsibility be assessed. If it is felt that appropriate action will not be taken by the "agents of responsibility," then blame will be assigned. Such assignments are made to those who are perceived to have the power to correct existing conditions. Specificity depends on the degree of sophisti-

[10] *Ibid.*, pp. 472–473.
[11] *Ibid.*, p. 471.

cated knowledge about persons and groups that blamers can bring to bear.

While there are marked theoretical differences in the two viewpoints described, these differences are largely in the interpretation of the behavioral events which occurred. There is a close parallel between some of the posited general categories of post-disaster behavior. Similar events can also be seen in what occurred following the Indianapolis Coliseum explosion.

THE INDIANAPOLIS COLISEUM EXPLOSION

At 11:06 P.M., October 31, 1963, a violent explosion suddenly ended the performance of the "Holiday on Ice" show being presented at the State Fairgrounds Coliseum in Indianapolis, Indiana. Fifty-four persons were killed immediately. Nearly four hundred others were injured. Twenty-seven of the injured later died, raising the final death count to eighty-one, the highest single death toll ever to occur in an Indiana disaster.

Newspaper, radio and television coverage of the disaster was almost instantaneous. While immediate reports were focused on the rescue operations, descriptions of what had happened, and identification of the victims, mass media attention slowly shifted towards accounting for the disaster. Once it became public knowledge that fire liquid petroleum gas tanks found in the rubble were suspected of being the cause of the explosion, representatives of the mass media quickly pressed inquiries along these lines.

Interest in the cause of the explosion was intensified throughout the night, and the three major Indianapolis newspapers had the following headlines on their first editions after the disaster:

"FIRE CHIEF RAPS GAS TANK USAGE IN THE COLISEUM" [12]

"PROBE PRESSED IN BLAST THAT KILLED 62 HERE" [13]

"65 KILLED, HUNDREDS HURT IN COLISEUM GAS EXPLOSION." [14]

The Marion County Prosecutor, on November 1, requested the Grand Jury to begin an immediate investigation, which they did.

The mass communication system kept the spotlight relentlessly focused on possible responsibility for the explosion. For instance, the evening following the explosion the State Fire Marshal was pressed to admit in a televised interview that apparently no one had applied or obtained the necessary permit to use liquid gas inside the Coliseum.

Eventually, formal investigations into the cause of the explosion were conducted by at least nine different organizations including: The Indian-

[12] *The Indianapolis Times,* November 1, 1963, p. 1.
[13] *The Indianapolis News,* November 1, 1963, p. 1.
[14] *The Indianapolis Star,* November 1, 1963, p. 1.

apolis Fire Department, the Indianapolis Police Department, the State Police, the County Sheriff's Office, the State Administrative Building Council, the State Fire Marshal, The County Coroner's Office, and the company insuring the State Fair Board and the Indiana Coliseum Corporation. Almost all these groups focused their efforts on determining the physical cause of the explosion. In part, this was a response to inquiries by representatives of the mass media as to possible personal responsibility.[15]

After five weeks of inquiry during which repeated trips to the scene of the disaster were made, and thirty-two witnesses were questioned, the Grand Jury completed its investigation in early December. LP gas, illegally stored inside the Coliseum, was judged to be the cause of the explosion. These findings of the violation of legal norms led to the assignment of responsibility. Seven persons were indicted, three officials of the firm who supplied the tanks, the General Manager and the Concession Manager of the Indiana Coliseum Corporation, the State Fire Marshal, and the Indianapolis Fire Chief.

Data from the Coliseum disaster related to blame can effectively be interpreted within the framework suggested by Bucher. It was almost immediately clear that human responsibility would be assessed in this instance. The presence of the five LP gas tanks quickly focalized discussions of cause. The illegality of the presence of the tanks was stressed by the mass media which also identified the public and private officials who had been directly or indirectly involved in their installation. A personal and nonnaturalistic explanation of the explosion became a definite possibility.

Two additional elements were also present. First, newspaper accounts suggested that previous warnings had not resulted in action. For example, *The Indianapolis Star*[16] reported that a check of official records indicated that the Fire Marshal's Office had been warned of leaking propane gas in the Coliseum on September 3, 1959, at which time they stopped its use. On September 4, inspectors were again notified of leaking LP gas at the Coliseum. This resulted in a declaration by the Chief Inspector from the Fire Marshal's Office that he did not have an adequate staff to police fire regulations properly. Such articles were countered with statements by representatives from the Coliseum who stated that LP gas tanks had been openly used for ten years, during which time they had never been told anything about the need for a permit for such use. Hence, it was implied that the "agents of responsibility" might not correct existing conditions.

Some open official criticism of the Grand Jury action would not have challenged this implication. For instance, the then Governor of the state publicly declared that the indictment against the Fire Marshal was unfair. He alleged that the Grand Jury had used public officials as "scapegoats."

---

[15] Detailed discussion of the physical cause of the blast is presented in Wilbur L. Walls, "Indianapolis Coliseum Explosion," *Quarterly of the National Fire Protection Association*, 57 (April, 1964), pp. 392–398.

[16] *The Indianapolis Star*, November 2, 1963.

The Governor further added that the Fire Marshal had brought some improvement to his agency, and that he would remain as the State Fire Marshal.

Of course, from a sociological viewpoint the issue is not the factual accuracy or the lack of accuracy of specific charges or countercharges made. What scientifically has to be taken into account is what was publicly aired, and the perception of this by people in general. It is after all an old axiom in sociology that "if a situation is defined as real, it is real insofar as consequences are concerned." In this particular situation, press reports clearly implied that some of those in a position to do so might not make changes which would help reduce the probability of similar kinds of future events.

Words used in the indictments by the Grand Jury also implied that the "agents of responsibility" were in opposition to basic cultural values. For example, the jury felt some control over future uses of LP gas was needed to ". . . guarantee that the desire for profit on the part of a few will never again relegate the matter of public safety to a point of reckless indifference." [17] The report further stated that "the Fire Marshal was considered (political) patronage and he acted the part." Thus, all of the elements suggested by Bucher as being necessary for blame were present in this instance.

Furthermore, the attribution of blame was focused high in the authority structure of each organization. Indictments were directed at the Fire Chief, not the City Fire Inspectors; the State Fire Marshal, not his agents; top executives of the firm supplying the tanks, not the individuals who actually installed the illegal tanks; and the executives of the Coliseum Corporation, not the concessionaires who used the tanks.

Yet could this not be interpreted as another example of irrational scapegoating? Since there is a similarity in category to those indicted following the Cocoanut Grove fire, were not these persons selected because of irrational latent hostilities against authority figures and "money czars"?

Further reading of the Grand Jury report, however, renders such an interpretation difficult to defend. Consistently there is reference to the need for changes in existing law such as might provide new requirements whereby on-site inspection would occur on the day of any large public gathering, and possibly stand-by inspection during actual performances. The jury report also labeled the permit system, then used, as "archaic and useless" and further suggested that the entire State Fire Marshal's Office should be reorganized "from top to bottom." Finally, the Grand Jury urged that consideration be given to legislation which would make violation of regulations by the Fire Marshal a punishable crime.

Thus, it appears that the prime desire of the Grand Jury was for structural and normative changes so as to prevent a recurrence of the Coliseum

[17] This and the following quotations from the Grand Jury report are as reported in *The Indianapolis Times*, December 10, 1963.

disaster or any similar to it. It might be argued that if this is the intent, why did the jury then not take steps regarding such changes rather than indicting persons? The answer is in the very nature of legal institutions. The Grand Jury visualized things about the system as being at fault but such legal groups can only deal with *persons* if something is amiss; they can not indict social structures and cultural norms.

ANOTHER VIEWPOINT

The last observation suggests a possible extension of the Bucher formulation which seems adequate as far as it goes. We wish to suggest as alluded to above, that personal blame assignment in American society is rooted in the institutional framework. Investigative agencies are constrained by a legal pattern which requires them to "point the finger" at persons who are potentially legally prosecutable. The institutional structure is such that only personal blame can be assessed.

This was the situation after the disaster at Indianapolis. While there was in one sense some indication of awareness of a systemic problem, its solution was approached in the usual and almost necessary way. That is, given traditional American patterns of coping with difficulties of this kind, only the legal processes (i.e., a Grand Jury, indictments, trials and so forth) were utilized. The social machinery for coping with these kinds of situations was not geared towards doing anything about defects in the social system. The political-legal processes could only condemn individuals and ask for their punishment. The verbal assault in the mass media probably also served as another institutionalized pressure on the Grand Jury to indict individuals and thus weakened the call for corrective actions.

A basic assumption underlying this position is that socially disapproved behavior can best be deterred by punishing "guilty" individuals so that others will be warned against committing similar acts. However, many sociologists have suggested that this whole orientation with its focus on individual responsibility, "guilt" and "innocence," may well attack only the *symptoms* of such problems and thereby serve to delay changes necessary to alleviate those conditions contributing to the social difficulty. For instance, Horton and Leslie note that in looking at social problems there frequently is "a search for the villain instead of a search for insight. To many people, 'doing something' about a social problem means finding and punishing the 'bad' people." [18] The consequence of this, as these authors state, is that "punishing the 'bad' people, . . . will have very little permanent effect upon the problem." [19]

[18] Paul B. Horton and Gerald R. Leslie, *The Sociology of Social Problems*, New York: Appleton-Century-Crofts, Inc., 1960, p. 8.

[19] *Ibid.*, p. 8. This point frequently appears in the sociological literature, e.g., see C. Wright Mills, *The Sociological Imagination*, New York: Oxford University Press,

We would suggest that analysis of the process whereby blame was affixed following the Indianapolis disaster clearly illustrated this very point.

A basic structural element within the social system was inadequate—this was the inspection procedure. For example, only twelve investigators were assigned the responsibility to provide inspection for the entire state of Indiana. One inspector had a district of 4,000 square miles. Power of the inspectors was limited to impotent "cease and desist" orders. Political patronage rather than a merit system was the basis of selection of both the Fire Marshal and the State Inspectors. No selection criteria existed for either type of position. Yet the attack on persons drew attention away from all of this.

Basically, it is our contention that if other persons had been in the same positions in the existing faulty structure, they could have done little except behave as did those individuals charged with being "guilty" of a misdeed. For example, insufficient staff, both in number and quality, rendered meaningful preventive action by the Fire Marshal, a physical impossibility. Similarly, safety training for the employees who installed or utilized the LP gas tanks was inadequate. Economic considerations were reported to have been a major factor.

In essence, we are saying that the efficacy of the entire procedure utilized by the Indianapolis community to remedy those conditions which resulted in the disaster may well be questioned. In raising questions of efficacy we are essentially expanding on the position expressed by Merton and Nesbit that there are latent social problems that may not always be recognized as such by the members of the group involved.[20] They point out that if sociologists were to restrict themselves only to these social conditions which a majority of people regard as undesirable, this would "exclude study of all manners of other conditions that are in fact at odds with the declared value and purposes of those who accept or endorse these conditions."[21] As Merton and Nesbit further add, not all "processes of society inimical to the values of men are recognized as such by them."[22]

Not only does blame attribution after a disaster draw attention from structural problems, but it actually might give an illusion that corrective action of some sort is being taken. This too is dysfunctional in the same sense that Lazarsfeld and Merton a number of years ago indicated that developments in the then emerging mass media has a narcotizing function.[23] They noted that while most Americans were becoming better

1959, pp. 8–11; Lawrence K. Frank, "Society as the Patient," *American Journal of Sociology,* 42 (1936), pp. 335–334.

[20] Robert K. Merton and Robert A. Nesbit, *Contemporary Social Problems,* New York: Harcourt, Brace and World, Inc., 1961, pp. 705–709.

[21] *Ibid.,* p. 708.

[22] *Ibid.*

[23] Paul F. Lazarsfeld and Robert K. Merton, "Mass Communication, Popular Taste

politically informed than ever before, "exposure to this flood of information may serve to narcotize rather than to energize the average reader or listener. As an increasing need of time is devoted to reading and listening, a decreasing share is available for organized action." [24] Hence, while seemingly better informed about societal problems, citizens might become increasingly more apathetic toward civic action. Similarly, public attention focused on the punishment of "guilty" individuals, does not encourage actions to correct structural flaws. In the particular example we used, the issue of an inadequate inspection procedure remained submerged, hidden by the search for "guilty" individuals.

It is of more than passing interest that in another major disaster studied by the Disaster Research Center, the absence of personal blame attribution for the event was accompanied by relatively rapid and major structural changes. On November 23, 1963, a nursing home fire in Ohio resulted in the death of 63 patients. Several investigations revealed many of the same, if not even greater, general weaknesses in the fire inspection procedures found in Indiana. However, there was very little movement in the direction of looking for the individuals supposedly to "blame" for the tragedy. A Grand Jury failed to indict anyone; no persons or officials were held responsible; and everyone connected with the event was exonerated. Yet within a few months, major and stringent new rules and regulations were put into effect in the state of Ohio; nursing homes not meeting the new standards were forced to close. Had this event not occurred, it is doubtful that new standards would have been enacted.[25]

By contrast, in Indiana, more than two years after the disaster, not even the attribution of personal blame had been settled. In early 1966 all legal cases were still pending except those against the Indianapolis Fire Chief and the general manager of the firm that supplied the tanks. The case of the former had been dismissed; the charge against the latter had been reduced from involuntary manslaughter to assault and battery, and he had been sentenced to 150 days on the state prison farm. The other five persons charged still remained under indictment. Thus, months, going on years, after the disaster, the issue of personal blame itself remained.

As for any structural changes in the involved organizations and community, relatively little had occurred. There had been a few procedural changes instituted in the State Fire Marshal's office but nothing of a substantial nature. The relatively low attendance at Coliseum events after the building was reopened seemed to indicate that some public conscious-

---

and Organized Social Action," pp. 459–480, in Wilbur Schramm, ed., *Mass Communications*, Urbana: The University of Illinois Press, 1949.

[24] *Ibid.*, p. 469.

[25] As indicated by the date, the disaster occurred the day after the assassination of President Kennedy; a time at which few were interested in the nursing home disaster. Thus, the fire was not spotlighted by the mass communication system as it would have been had the fire occurred at a different time. This may have influenced the response in a way than otherwise would have been the case.

ness of the event lingered on. Within a year after the disaster, however, capacity and standing room audiences attended some shows. Thus, except for those most directly involved in suits and the like, the community appeared to have returned to its pre-disaster patterns.

It would be premature to argue that personal blame assignment besides deflecting attention away from structural faults, always prevents structural changes. There is indeed some historical evidence to suggest that some disastrous events eventually have an impact on the institutional framework. For example, the first international code of maritime safety laws came in 1914, two years after the sinking of the *Titanic*; the latest in 1960, four years after the loss of the *Andrea Doria*. In the famous Triangle Waist factory in New York City, 147 workers were killed and the owners were indicted for manslaughter; yet within months new laws were passed, giving fire inspectors increased powers, establishing a division of Fire Prevention, and forcing changes in rules regarding fire prevention, drills, alarm systems, sprinklers and fire escapes.[26] And even in Boston, three years after the Cocoanut Grove fire it could be written: "Under the impetus given by the worst fire in the city's history, the State is on its way to a system of building and inspection regulations that may become a model." [27] The extent to which the normative changes implied in these examples were implemented and the question as to how much they actually touched on the structural flaws in the involved systems, are of course matters that would have to be more fully researched. Yet the new norms certainly suggest that punishment of "guilty individuals" *per se* does not automatically prevent some structural changes.

OTHER SIMILAR PHENOMENA

The general phenomena that we have discussed is not peculiar to disaster situations. Something akin to it has been observed in everything from the content of American movies dealing with social problems to the assumptions being made in the present day "war on poverty." Thus Gans has noted of certain kinds of contemporary films: "psychological explanations have replaced moral ones, but the possibility that delinquency, corruption and even mental illness reside in the social system is not considered, and the resolution of the problem is still left to a hero assisted by the everpresent *deus ex machina*." [28]

And it has been said of the poverty program initiated in 1964: "The guiding assumption is that social pathology is caused less by basic defects

[26] Douglas Newton, ed., *Disaster, Disaster, Disaster; Catastrophes Which Changed Laws*, New York: Franklin Watts, 1961, pp. 133–134. As the subtitle indicates, this book contains a series of examples of normative changes occasioned by disasters.

[27] Quoted in *ibid.*, p. 195.

[28] Herbert Gans, "The Rise of the Problem Film," *Social Problems*, 11 (Spring, 1964), p. 328.

in the social system than by defects in particular individuals and groups which prevent their adjusting to the system. The prescription is therefore to change the deviants, not the system." [29]

Or as Weinstock has said of the approach to the poverty problem: "The underlying assumption here again is that poverty, social and economic deprivation, results from an inadequcy of the personality rather than an inadequacy in the socio-economic system. . . . Only measures aiming at individual rehabilitation . . . are encouraged, while measures designed to modify the structure of the economy . . . are rejected." [30]

As in the instance of blame assignment after disasters, the process of fault finding in these other situations, seems rooted in the very institutional fabric of American society and likewise serves to distract attention away from structural flaws. If the individual is the source of difficulties, there is no need to raise questions about the societal context. Clearly it is not only in the Soviet Union that a process akin to the "cult of personality" serves to protect the existing structure from rapidly changing to meet certain cultural values and goals, however malfunctioning the system may be along particular lines.[31]

[29] *The New York Review of Books*, October 14, 1965, p. 39 in a review article by Christopher Jencks on the Moynihan Reports.

[30] S. Alexander Weinstock, "Ideology and the Locus of Blame" (unpublished paper presented at the 1965 annual meeting of the American Sociological Association, Chicago, Illinois).

[31] Lieberson and Silverman in discussing race riots in American society make a somewhat similar observation. They note: "We have encountered a number of accounts in the popular literature attributing riots to communist influence, hoodlums, or rabble-rousers. Although lower-class youths and young adults are undoubtedly active during riots, potential participants of this type are probably available in almost any community. What interests us is the community failure to see the riot in terms of institutional malfunctioning or a racial difficulty which is not—and perhaps cannot—be met by existing social institutions." See Stanley Lieberson and Arnold Silverman, "Precipitants and conditions of race riots," *American Sociological Review*, 30 (1965), pp. 887–898.

For Further Reading

BOOKS

Baker, G. W., and Chapman, D. W., *Man and society in disaster*. New York: Basic Books, 1962.

A collection of papers covering the history of disaster research.

Beach, H. D., and Lucas, R. A. *Individual and group behavior in a coal mine disaster*. Washington, D.C.: National Academy of Sciences, 1960. (National Research Council, Disaster Study 13).

One of ὰ series of publications on disaster.

Disaster Research Group, *Field Studies of Disaster Behavior* (Washington, D.C.: National Academy of Sciences, 1961). (National Research Council, Disaster Study 14.)

An inventory of 114 field studies of human behavior in different disaster situations.

Lang, K. and G. E. *Collective dynamics*. New York: Crowell, 1961.

A text with special emphasis on disruption in social processes, leadership, conformity, public opinion, mass movements, and fashion.

McPhee, W. N. *Formal theories of mass behavior*. New York: Free Press, 1963.

For the advanced student; an attempt to develop mathematical models for mass behavior.

Smelser, N. J. *Theory of collective behavior*. New York: Free Press, 1963.

A pioneering attempt to provide a comprehensive theory of collective behavior.

Turner, R., and Killian, L. M. *Collective behavior*. Englewood Cliffs, New Jersey: Prentice-Hall, 1957.

An excellent text which integrates research and theory; raises intriguing suggestions concerning the distortion of events by the mass media (such as MacArthur's march in Chicago).

ARTICLES

Buckner, H. T. A theory of rumor transmission. *Publ. Opinion Quart.*, 1965, 29 (1), 54–70. SA 14, B8521.

Reconciles the Allport-Postman and the Caplow theory of rumor by noting segmental observations. Both are correct when seen in a particular situation: (1) whether the individual has a critical transmission set for the rumor and (2) whether the individual engages in a single interaction or in multiple interactions in discussing the rumor.

Crawford, F. R., and Moore, H. T. Relocation of disaster-displaced families. *Sociol. soc. Res.*, 1957, 41 (4), 264–269. SA 7, 6087.

The outstanding finding is the apparent reluctance of people to leave the area of the city in which they had been living, their insistence on returning to a location where they had suffered greatly.

Deutsch, M. The 1960 swastika-smearings: analysis of the apprehended youth, *Merrill-Palmer Quart.*, 1962, 99–120. SA 11, A4606.

The majority of the youths came from broken or disturbed homes; did not do well in school.

Deutscher, I., and Kong-ming, P. Functional analysis of collective behavior in a disaster. *Sociol. Quart.*, 1961, 2 (1), 21–36, SA 9, A0601.

Latent functions (based on Kansas City tornado in 1957) include: (1) boost to certain segments of the economy; (2) release from monotony; (3) renewed sense of unity in the larger community; (4) gratification to those persons and agencies who prepare for disasters; (5) opportunity to publicize the work of certain agencies; (6) a rationale for reuniting kinship groups; (7) opportunity for increased criminal behavior.

Fogleman, C. W., and Parenton, V. J. Disaster and aftermath: selected aspects of individual and group behavior in critical situations. *Social Forces*, 1959, 38 (3), 129–135. SA 10, A2457.

Participant observation of effects of Hurricane Audrey in Louisiana in 1957. Most behavior was family-oriented.

Forman, R. E. Resignation as a collective behavior response. *Amer. J. Sociol.*, 1963, 69 (3), 285–290. PA 38, 8264.

Panic and rational behavior in crises have been documented; in this study, failure to respond effectively to an air attack signal seems due to an attitude of resignation.

Hundley, J., and Quarantelli, E. L. A test of some propositions about crowd formation and behavior. Microfiche, 65–17, *Clearing-house for Sociological Literature* (University of Wisconsin-Milwaukee), SA 14, C2194.

A partial report of a test of the six conditions that Smelser states are necessary for the appearance of a hostile outburst; four were consistent with the data gathered on a college riot, but two were not substantiated.

Kelley, H., *et al.* Collective behavior in a simulated panic situation. *J. exp. soc. Psychol.*, 1965, 1 (1), 19–54. PA 39, 9999.

The percentage of persons who escape declines as the severity of the penalty for failure increases, and as size of the group increases. If members of the group take cues from each other, as compared to making decisions independently, effect upon escape may be either deleterious (when there is little optimism) or salutary (when there is optimism).

Kerckhoff, A. C., Back, K. W., and Miller, N. Sociometric patterns in hysterical contagion. *Sociometry*, 1965, 28 (1), 2–15. SA 14, B9422.

A theoretical synthesis is offered which calls for an overrepresentation of isolates at the beginning of an epidemic, a rapid spread through sociometric channels later, and finally a crowd reaction throughout the population involved. Compared to the diffusion of an innovation.

Palmer, G. J., Jr., and Sells, S. B. Behavioral factors in disaster situations. *J. soc. Psychol.*, 1965, 66 (1), 65–71. PA 39, 13172.

Data from diverse sources such as strategic bombing surveys, displaced persons and prisoners of war, surgical and cancer patients, mothers of children with leukemia, flood tornado or hurricane victims, lead to recommendation of preparation and warning.

Schultz, D. P. Theories of panic behavior: a review. *J. soc. Psychol.*, 1965, 66 (1), 31–40. PA 39, 15060.

Several theories of panic behavior (McDougall, LaPiere, Cantril, Mintz, Foreman and Freud) are reviewed and discussed.

Turner, R. H. Collective behavior. In R. E. L. Faris (Ed.), *Handbook of modern sociology*. Chicago: Rand-McNally, 1964. Pp. 382–425.

A very comprehensive and analytic review.

Index